ROMAN STATE &

CHRISTIAN CHURCH

ROMAN STATE
&
CHRISTIAN CHURCH

A Collection of Legal Documents
to A.D. 535

P. R. COLEMAN-NORTON

VOLUME TWO

WIPF & STOCK · Eugene, Oregon

Wipf and Stock Publishers
199 W 8th Ave, Suite 3
Eugene, OR 97401

Roman State & Christian Church Volume 2
A Collection of Legal Documents to A.D. 535
By Coleman-Norton, P. R.
Copyright©1966 SPCK
ISBN 13: 978-1-5326-6616-2
Publication date 8/23/2018
Previously published by SPCK, 1966

AD MAIOREM DEI GLORIAM

PER QVEM REGES REGNANT ET LEGVM CONDITORES

IVSTA DECERNVNT

ATQVE

IN MEMORIAM

IMPERATORVM CAESARVM

CONSTANTINI THEODOSII IVSTINIANI

AVGVSTORVM NOMINATORVM MAGNORVM

QVI PROVIDENTIA DEI FIDEI DEFENSORES

ECCLESIAM CHRISTIANAM ENIXISSIME CONFIRMAVERVNT

CONTENTS

VOLUME ONE

Preface	vii
Abbreviations	ix
Table of Documents	xi
Introduction	xxxvii
Names and Dates of Emperors	lxxiii
Documents Nos. 1–177	1

VOLUME TWO

Documents Nos. 178–486	371

VOLUME THREE

Documents Nos. 487–652	845
Appendix on Persecutions	1179
Titles of Address	1197
Glossary	1199

INDEXES

Sources	1249
Persons	1254
Places	1279
Subjects	1288
Biblical Quotations and Allusions	1344
Classical Quotations and Allusions	1348
Legal Quotations and Allusions	1350
Patristic Quotations and Allusions	1355

178. EDICT OF THEODOSIUS I ON EXEMPTION OF BISHOPS AS WITNESSES IN LAWSUITS, 381

(*CT* 11. 39. 8)

By this ordinance, which Justinian preserves (*CI* 1. 3. 7), relief of bishops from giving evidence in lawsuits is ordained.

Part of the proceedings transacted in the [1] consistory before Emperors Gratian, Valentinian,[2] and Theodosius [3] in the consulate of Syagrius and Eucherius [4] on 29 June [5] in Constantinople.

In the consistory [6] Emperor Theodosius Augustus said:
"A bishop is not required for testimony either because of his honour or by the laws."

The same person said:[7]
"It is not becoming for a bishop to be admitted to speak his testimony, for both his person is dishonoured [8] and a bishop's [9] privileged position is confounded."

1. *CI* inserts "sacred", the usual adjective (*sacer*) here.
2. The second of this name.
3. That all three emperors were present is doubtful, for at this time only Theodosius governed the East, whence the edict emanated.
4. *CI* characterizes them as "most distinguished men".
5. A day earlier according to *CI*.
6. *CI* omits this phrase.
7. *CI* reads "He also said".
8. Justinian alters *dehonoratur* to *oneratur* (burdened), probably because upon a busy bishop devolved heavy duties, for some of which see no. 28, n. 1 *ad fin*.
9. The word is *sacerdos*, on which see no. 16, n. 4.

179. MANDATE OF GRATIAN, VALENTINIAN II, AND THEODOSIUS I ON HERETICS' INCAPACITY TO BUILD CHURCHES, 381

(*CT* 16. 5. 8)

This order forbids Eunomians and Arians and Aetians to erect churches.

The same Augusti to Clicherius,[1] count of the East.
We command that none of the Eunomians and of the Arians or of the dogma of Aetius [2] should have the opportunity of constructing

churches in a municipality or in the rural districts. But if this should be presumed rashly by anyone, the said building, where what is forbidden to be constructed shall have been constructed, also the estate or the private possession straightway should be appropriated to our fisc's resources, and all places which shall have accepted either the abode or the ministers of this sacrilegious dogma shall become immediately fiscal property.

Given on 19 July at Constantinople, Eucherius and Syagrius being consuls.

1. Mommsen emends this name to Glycerius.
2. On him see nos. 103, n. 5, and 112.

180. MANDATE OF GRATIAN, VALENTINIAN II, AND THEODOSIUS I ON AMNESTY FOR PRISONERS AT EASTERTIDE, 381

(CT 9. 38. 6)

This directive differs chiefly from earlier enactments on the same subject (nos. 135, 145, 171) in so far as it excludes counterfeiters and those guilty of incest (two hitherto unmentioned classes of criminals) as well as recidivists from persons entitled to release from prison because of Easter.

Justinian uses this ordinance's last paragraph and no. 201 to construct his constitution in CI 1. 4. 3.

Emperors Gratian, Valentinian, and Theodosius Augusti to the most distinguished Antidius, vicar.[1]

The day of paschal joy permits not even those persons [2] who have committed crimes to groan; now at last let the horrid prison be opened to the unwonted light.

But we propose that foreign from indulgence should be a person who haughtily shall have animated his nefarious knowledge of crimes toward treason; who, seized by parricidal frenzy, has stained his hand by his own blood; who, moreover, has been defiled by the murder of any person; who has been an invader of another's bed and couch; who has been a ravisher of virginal modesty; who, morally blind, has violated the venerated bond of cognate blood by profane incest; or who has composed for mind and body poisons which have been sought from noxious herbs and have been murmured over in dread secrecies;[3] or who, as a copyist of the sacred face and a seeker of the divine features, with sacrilegious skill has engraved their images.[4]

181. INTERMENT IN CONSTANTINOPLE, 381

Therefore to those persons who have been condemned even under such a kind of absolution we confine our Serenity's indulgence by this limit of our ordinance:[5] that crimes, unless once committed, may not have remission of pardon, lest the imperial Liberality's kindliness should be renewed for those persons who have reckoned impunity for an old crime not for correction rather than for custom.[6]

Recited on 21 July at Rome, Syagrius and Eucherius being consuls.

1. His diocese is unknown.
2. The Latin has an abstract noun (*ingenium* [character]) in the neuter plural for this word.
3. An (ancient) traditional accompaniment of preparation of poisons.
4. For *sacred* and *divine* applied to emperors and for a counterfeiter therefore being *sacrilegious* see no. 168, n. 1.
5. The thought seems to be that persons who have committed crimes (subject to pardon) other than those just mentioned may be freed at Easter on the condition that they are not recidivists (about to be mentioned).
6. This is what the relative clause says, but the meaning may be that, if they should be released, recidivists would regard their release not for reforming their ways but for continuing their habitual criminal activity, for they could reckon on being released, if caught, at the next announcement of amnesty. On the other hand, the emperors may mean that old offenders, if pardoned, would consider not that they had been freed to mend their ways, but that such release was merely an imperial custom.

181. MANDATE OF GRATIAN, VALENTINIAN II, AND THEODOSIUS I ON INTERMENT IN CONSTANTINOPLE, 381

(*CT* 9. 17. 6)

In an effort to stop the practice of burial within Constantinople, where the custom seems to have started after churches began to enshrine within their precincts the relics of saints, the emperors direct that urban interment must cease.

Justinian adopts this statute's last sentence, which he condenses (*CI* 1. 2. 2).

Emperors Gratian, Valentinian, and Theodosius Augusti to Pancratius, urban prefect.[1]

All bodies which, enclosed in urns or in sarcophagi, are kept above ground should be removed and placed outside the city,[2] that they both may exhibit an appearance of humanity and may leave sanctity to the domicile of the inhabitants.

Moreover whoever shall have been neglectful of this command and shall have dared to attempt any such thing after this command's threat should be fined in the future by a third part of his patrimony.

Also the office staff which obeys you shall lament, when affected by the fine of fifty pounds of gold.[3]

And [4] lest anyone's deceitful and cunning shrewdness may lead him away from this command's intention and may calculate that the abode of apostles [5] or of martyrs [6] has been conceded for burying bodies,[7] they should know and should perceive that they themselves have been withheld also from these places, just as from the rest of the city.[1]

Given on 30 July at Heraclea, Eucherius and Syagrius being consuls.

1. Of Constantinople.
2. Constantinople.
3. Obviously a threat to the prefect's apparitors, lest they should connive at violation of the ordinance.
4. Justinian condenses this sentence to represent only so much of the law as he wishes to retain: "None should think that the abode of apostles or of martyrs has been conceded for burying bodies."
5. Of the five patriarchates of the ancient Church (see no. 53, n. 3) only that of Constantinople appears to have been without apostolic association, unless one accepts the late (fifth-century) tradition that St Andrew, the first-called (πρωτόκλητος) apostle (John 1. 40–1), as a missionary to the Balkans, arrived in Byzantium (see no. 62, n. 2 *ad init.*), organized that see before St Peter, his younger brother, became bishop of Rome, and then appointed St Paul's "beloved Stachys" (Rom. 16. 9) to be its next bishop. Thus St Andrew's three primacies over St Peter—call, age, possession—confirmed Constantinople in its rivalry with Rome. At any rate, the sovereigns can speak of apostles here, because—to mention only one out of many—St Andrew's relics were translated from Patras, Greece, where he had been martyred, to Constantinople about 25 years before this constitution's date and were deposited in the Church of the Holy Twelve Apostles (on which see no. 463, n. 5). F. Dvornik, *The Idea of Apostolicity in Byzantium and the Legend of the Apostle Andrew* (Cambridge, Mass., 1958), treats this tradition.

Since 1208 most of St Andrew's relics have reposed in the crypt of his cathedral at Amalfi, Italy, whither the Latin Christians conveyed these, after they, incited by Venetian venality, had interrupted the Fourth Crusade to capture Constantinople in 1204. The relics secrete an oleaginous substance (*manna di Sant' Andrea*), whose virtue attracts many of the faithful to assist at his annual festival on 30 November.

The importation of corpses of many saints into Constantinople flourished during the fourth century, doubtless "that the new Rome might have a celestial population equal to that of the old" (E. W. Kemp, *Canonization and Authority in the Western Church* [Oxford, 1948], 26), but especially to enhance that capital's claim in its rivalry with Rome (on which see no. 375, n. 7).

6. From evidence assembled by P. E. D. Riant and F. de Mély in their monumental *Exuviae Sacrae Constantinopolitanae* (3 vols., Genève, 1877–1904) it appears that during the Latin occupation of Constantinople (1204–61) scarcely any considerable community in the West was omitted from sharing the sacred memorials of martyrs with which the capital was crammed. The three-day sack of 13–15 April 1204, amid scenes of carnage, was succeeded by several months of thorough search for such relics (with or without their reliquaries) as had been concealed from the first ravishers. Pope Innocent III (1198–1216) acquiesced in this act of pious plunder, since he saw in the capital's capture and in the conversion of the Byzantine Empire into a Frankish feudal state both the subjection of a schismatical people and the union of Eastern and Western Christendom under the Papacy. And the intermittent pillage persisted until the Greek government in exile across the Sea of Marmara at Nicaea re-established itself in Constantinople.

7. It is not clear whether corpses had been buried in the very tombs of the saints or simply in churches containing such tombs. If the former, the practice was violation of sepulchre (on which see no. 641, n. 17); if the latter, churches were crowded with works of dubious workmanship. In any event, the emperors explicitly interdict urban interment, which had been outlawed eight centuries earlier (see no. 641, n. 14).

182. MANDATE OF GRATIAN, VALENTINIAN II, AND THEODOSIUS I ON TRANSFER OF CHURCHES TO ORTHODOX BISHOPS, 381

(*CT* 16. 1. 3)

The enforcement of this command, addressed to the governor of the province of Asia and requiring heretics and schismatics to surrender possession of their churches to orthodox bishops, created great disturbances in the East. The bishops named in the mandate were all Easterners—for the obvious reasons that most heresies and schisms originated and flourished in the East and that Theodosius, who issued this directive, then presided over the eastern part of the Empire.

The same Augusti to Auxonius, proconsul of Asia.

We order all churches to be surrendered presently to bishops who, since they produce no disagreement by profane division[1] but the orderly relation of the Trinity by assertion of the Persons and by the unity of the Divinity, confess that the Father and the Son and the Holy Spirit are of one majesty and virtue, of the same glory, of one splendour; who, it shall be established, have been associated in the communion of Nectarius, bishop of the Constantinopolitan Church, and of Timothy, bishop of the Alexandrian city in Egypt; who also, it shall have been established, are in communion in regions of the East with Pelagius, bishop of Laodicea,[2] and with Diodore, bishop of Tarsus; in the province of Asia and in the diocese of Asia, with Amphilochius, bishop of Iconium, and with Optimus, bishop of Antioch;[3] in the diocese of Pontus, with Helladius, bishop of Caesarea,[4] and with Otreius of Melitene and with Gregory, bishop of Nyssa; with Terennius, bishop of Scythia,[5] with Marmarius, bishop of Marcianopolis.

It shall be necessary that those in communion and fellowship of acceptable bishops [6] should be allowed to occupy Catholic churches, but that all who dissent from the communion of the faith of these, whom this specific mention has expressed, should be expelled from the churches as manifest heretics and that henceforth to them should be not allowed at all the episcopal authority [7] and the power of obtaining churches, that the priesthood [8] of the true and the Nicene faith [9] may continue pure and that after our command's plain formulary an opportunity for malignant subtlety may not be given.

Given on 30 July at Heraclea, Eucherius and Syagrius being consuls.

1. The division is that of the divine substance, a matter which, when not conceived correctly according to orthodox standards, begot heresies.
2. This Laodicea was in Syria.
3. This Antioch was in Pisidia.
4. This Caesarea was in Cappadocia.
5. More properly bishop of Tomi in Scythia.
6. The word is *sacerdotes,* on which see no. 16, n. 4.
7. The phrase represents *pontificium.*
8. The word is pluralized: *sacerdotia,* on which see no. 158, n. 1.
9. As defined at the Church's First General Council at Nicaea in 325.

183. MANDATE OF GRATIAN, VALENTINIAN II, AND THEODOSIUS I ON EXEMPTION OF CHRISTIAN ACTRESSES FROM THE THEATRE, 381

(CT 15. 7. 9)

This order, addressed to an African administrator, repeats almost verbatim a previous directive sent to the prefect of Rome (no. 170).

The same Augusti to Herasius, proconsul of Africa.

Whatsoever women, born from such dregs, shall have shunned their theatrical duties should be assigned to dramatic services, if not yet, however, reverence for the most holy religion and for the secrets of the Christian law,[1] which must be preserved forever, has claimed them for its faith.

We also command that those women, who have deserved by our Gentleness' favour to be free from a rather base public service, should remain free from the association [2] of prejudice connected with the theatre.

Posted at Carthage on 28 August, Syagrius and Eucherius being consuls.

1. Religion.
2. See no. 170, n. 3.

184. MANDATE OF GRATIAN, VALENTINIAN II, AND THEODOSIUS I ON TRUE WORSHIP OF GOD, 381

(CT 16. 10. 7)

By this statute penalty is set for persons who sacrifice to pagan deities and who do not worship God with pure prayers.[1]

Emperors Gratian, Valentinian, and Theodosius Augusti to Florus, praetorian prefect.[2]

If any madman, so to speak, and sacrilegious person shall have immersed himself, as a consulter of uncertain events, in prohibited diurnal and nocturnal sacrifices and shall have believed that a shrine or a temple for commission of such a crime must be used by him or shall have supposed one must be approached by him, he shall know that he must be subjugated by proscription,³ since by just instruction we warn that God must be worshipped by pure prayers, but must not be profaned by dire incantations.

Given on 21 December at Constantinople, Eucherius and Syagrius being consuls.

1. See introd. to no. 242.
2. Of the East.
3. Probably of property instead of citizenship.

185. MANDATE OF GRATIAN, VALENTINIAN II, AND THEODOSIUS I ON SPECIAL COURTS FOR PROSECUTION OF HERETICS, 382

(CT 16. 5. 9)

Besides establishing penalties for Manichaeans this constitution authorizes—for the first time, so far as is known—the prosecution of heretics in a special tribunal, before which informants may bring information about heretics. No evidence, however, exists that this innovation in procedure was put into practice.

The same Augusti to Florus, praetorian prefect.[1]

Whoever of the Manichaeans flees the company of good persons by the deception of the solitary life and chooses the secret crowds of the worst persons [2] should be subjected thus to the law as a profaner and a corrupter of Catholic discipline, which we all respect; should live as incapable of making a will; while living, should expend nothing on outlawed persons; while dying, should leave nothing to unworthy persons; should restore [3] all his property to persons who are his own folk not by character, but by nature, or to his nearest relatives should release it to be managed better, if lawful succession shall be lacking;[4] should understand that it has been obligated to the fisc's ownership, if agnation is lacking, without fraudulent contrivance. Thus far concerning solitaries[5].

But those whom they denominate with a monstrous appellation Encratitans, along with Saccoforians or Hydroparastatans, when convicted in court, when betrayed by crime, or when discovered in a slight trace of this wickedness, we order to be afflicted with the supreme penalty and with implacable punishment—that condition, which we have imposed on all this workshop from the inception of the law passed long ago,[6] remaining concerning their property.

Your Sublimity, therefore, should provide inquisitors,[7] should open court, should accept informers and denunciators without the odium of delation. None should make void the establishment of this accusation by the usual prescription.[8]

None should convoke secret and hidden assemblies of this character:[9] it should be forbidden in the countryside; it should be prohibited within city walls; it should be condemned in public and private dwellings.

And it should be investigated with utmost examination, so that whosoever shall not have assembled on the day of Easter in obedience to religion should be considered undoubtedly such persons as we have condemned by this law.

Given on 31 March at Constantinople, Antony and Syagrius being consuls.

1. Of the East.
2. The idea seems to be that no Manichaean can circumvent the law's penalties (as hereinafter recounted) by retiring from public life to seek a solitary life among Manichaeans in secret communities.
3. The choice of this word (*restituere*) is reminiscent of the primitive notion that an owner of property acted as a steward of his family's estate even at his death, for by his will he was supposed to provide that his lawful heirs should receive all the property of which he had been—so to speak—the manager in their interests.
4. That is, to his agnates, if he has no lawful heirs of his own body.
5. Hermits.
6. No. 176 seems to be the law intended, although it was enacted less than a year before the present law.

The *workshop* (*officina*), in the imperial opinion, is the factory of false doctrines.

7. The word is *inquisitores* (a very early instance of its use in religious persecution), destined to become so dreaded in the later history of Christendom.
8. By *usual prescription* is meant the ordinary statute of limitations for instituting actions. But what limitation for actions of the type described in the text applied at this time (382) is unknown (see no. 65, n. 6 *ad fin.*).
9. Heretical gatherings are meant.

186. MANDATE OF GRATIAN, VALENTINIAN II, AND THEODOSIUS I ON ECCLESIASTICAL EXEMPTION FROM PUBLIC DUTIES, 382
(*CT* 11. 16. 15)

Gratian in this constitution recognizes that by ancient custom (no. 32) the Church is exempt from public duties of a menial character. Later emperors, however, with few exceptions apparently (nos. 226, 262, 265, 327), see in such immunity a serious loss to the State's revenues and finally (no. 435) rescind all exemptions from public burdens.

Justinian preserves most of this law (*CI* 10. 48. 12).

The same Augusti to Hypatius, praetorian prefect.[1]
Eminences [2] of high ranks, also consistorial counts, also our notaries and all chamberlains and ex-chamberlains should be freed from all menial public services. Moreover a similar privilege should extend to all others protected by palatine [3] or governmental [4] prerogative within the palace, only if they shall have shown that by earlier statutes they have the right to an exception of this sort, to the effect that benefits of this sort can be shown to have been given not to individual persons but to have been granted in common to a high rank or to a corporation —with the ancient custom remaining in regard to churches,[5] rhetoricians,[6] and grammarians [6] of each learning [7]. . . .

Given on 9 December, Antony and Syagrius being consuls.

1. Of Italy.
2. Abstract (*culmina*) for concrete, i.e. "eminent persons".
3. These are the *palatini*, who, though field troops, in the Dominate succeeded the praetorian guards of the Principate. Most of them were concentrated either near Constantinople, where detachments were assigned to duty with the imperial palace as the emperor's bodyguards, or in Italy, for in the peninsula the western capital was shifted from Rome in 303 to Milan and thence in 404 to Ravenna. They were organized in a large corps (*schola*).

But *palatini* included also civilians connected with the palace as functionaries in the financial administration of the Empire, which they served in the bureaux of the fisc, of the largesses, of the private estates, and were notorious for their venality and extortion. In view of the civil character of the others whom this constitution exempts, perhaps the civil, not the military, palatines are meant here.

4. The adjective is *militaris*, for the verb *militare* and the noun *militia*, of which all three refer originally to military service, by the time of Septimius Severus (193–211) were applied to governmental service of a civilian character, because that emperor "militarized" the imperial bureaucracy. The corres-

ponding Greek equivalents are στρατιωτικός, στρατεύεσθαι, στρατεία. See nos. 46, n. 17; 320, n. 3; 476, n. 39.

But signs of society's enslavement in the State's service appeared already in the age of the Antonines (138–93), when the whole of life began to become bureaucratic. And after bureaucratization of life had brought decay in all orders of society, the State under the Severi (193–235) forced further bureaucratization of humanity to serve its own needs. This additional bureaucratization was seen especially in the militarization of the civil service.

5. In Justinian's copy of this law *churches* is omitted—rightly, according to the editors, for it seems that not until 411 (no. 327) were the churches relieved of contribution to the menial public services, when the law has the tone that this immunity was awarded for the first time to churches as corporations (as here) as distinct from the clergy serving the churches.

Since the rest of the law (after the numeral 7 in the translation) is concerned with the persons excepted—*churches*, as corporations (though, of course, a corporation is a juristic person, as opposed to a natural person, in Roman law), seem to have been inserted here in the manuscriptal tradition—and since most of what remains in the law is a minute and long catalogue of what such services consist, it is proposed to summarize these, that the reader may be spared their detailed recital: making flour, baking bread, working in a mill, providing horses or vehicles for public transportation (save for occasional use on the Rhaetian frontier and for the Illyrian expeditionary force), performing personal services, supplying workmen, burning lime, furnishing lumber (of specified kinds) and charcoal (save for the mint and the arsenals), constructing or repairing public or sacred edifices, billeting officials and soldiers, maintaining roads and bridges, finding recruits, contributing to expenses of delegations on special public services, such as collection of taxes.

The rest of the law declares that for those exempted the exemptions, while effective even after their release from governmental service, cease at their death.

6. As early as 74 Vespasian granted immunity to rhetoricians and grammarians (*FIRA* I. 420–2), thus, in effect, creating State subsidy for education. Of the Christian emperors Constantine I was the first to continue the exemption in either 321 or 324 (*CT* 13. 3. 1).

7. That is, of Greek and of Latin.

Cf. *supra* n. 5 for the lacuna.

187. MANDATE OF GRATIAN, VALENTINIAN II, AND THEODOSIUS I ON DISPOSITION OF REMARRIED PERSONS' PROPERTY, 382
(CT 3. 8. 2)

To their law (repeated in CI 5. 9. 3) on disposition of property by a remarrying woman the emperors append a final clause addressed to men who remarry and in it apply the same provisions, but in their case reinforce the observance of these by the restraint of religion, which can mean only Christianity in view of the fact that these sovereigns (particularly Gratian and Theodosius) are the first Roman rulers who show what may be called an active Catholic conscience—due chiefly to the influence of St Ambrose, bishop of Milan, upon them.

A remarried widow must leave to any or all children of her first marriage any property received in any way by virtue of her prior marriage and may not alienate any of it to any extraneous person or any successor born from a subsequent marriage; but if no children from a previous marriage exist or if on their death she has inherited property from them, she has free power to will it to whomever she wishes. A remarried widower must do likewise in disposing of property acquired from his late wife and their children.

Since the above accurately summarizes the statute's provisions, which inherently have no Christian significance, only the section (§3) of Christian interest and that of the corresponding part of the interpretation are translated.

The same Augusti to Florus, praetorian prefect.[1]
... We [2] wish husbands also to be admonished by a similar example of both piety and law. And though we do not constrain them by the bond—as it were—of a sanction rather severely imposed, nevertheless we restrain them by the law of religion, that they may know that that which is commanded to mothers by the necessity of the proposed observance is expected more readily from themselves in consideration of justice; lest, if necessity shall have persuaded thus, in regard to their person must be exacted from them by the aid of a sanction what meanwhile may be proper to be desired and to be expected.

Given on 17 December at Constantinople, Antony and Syagrius being consuls.

Interpretation: ... In this law also he [3] has wished fathers, after their wives have died, if they shall have come to other marriages, to observe also a similar condition: that if from a former wife shall have been sons or daughters, of whom some should die and should make a place for their father in succession to their own portion, after his death the bequeathed portion should benefit the brothers or the sisters who will survive from that very marriage,[4] and it should not be able to pass through paternal power to other persons.[5]

1. Of the East.
2. Justinian's version stops where this section starts.
3. The emperor.
4. That is, the first marriage. See no. 570, n. 1.
5. The stepbrothers and the stepsisters of the children from the prior union.

188. MANDATE OF GRATIAN, VALENTINIAN II, AND THEODOSIUS I ON CLERGYMEN'S PRIOR DISCHARGE OF PUBLIC DUTIES, 383

(*CT* 12. 1. 99)

Although this command concerns primarily Jews attempting to avoid public services as municipal senators, yet it pertains also to Christians, who are prohibited from entering the clergy ere they have performed similar services.

Justinian copies part of this law in *CI* 1. 9. 5.

The same Augusti to Hypatius, praetorian prefect.[1]
After other matters.

The order [2]—whereby persons of the Jewish law [3] flatter themselves—by which immunity from curials' public services is [4] given to them should be rescinded,[5] since not even to clergymen is it free to deliver themselves to the divine services before they should pay completely all the duties due to their native community.

Therefore whosoever has been dedicated truly to God should establish another person, provided with his property, to complete for him the public services.

Given on 18 April at Milan, Merobaudes for the second time and Saturnine being consuls.

1. Of Italy.
2. It is uncertain what order is meant, but perhaps *CT* 16. 8. 2 (dated 330) or 16. 8. 3 (dated 321) is intended.
3. Religion.
4. Justinian reads "was".
5. Here ends Justinian's excerpt.

189. MANDATE OF GRATIAN, VALENTINIAN II, AND THEODOSIUS I ON APOSTATE CHRISTIANS' WILLS, 383

(CT 16. 7. 2)

When these emperors' earlier ordinance by depriving apostate Christians of the right to make wills (no. 175) had created confusion in the inheritance of property, they modified its unconditional terms.

The same Augusti to Postumian, praetorian prefect.[1]

To Christian believers [2] who have turned to pagan rites and cults we forbid all power of making a will in favour of any person whatsoever, that they may be without Roman law.

But only from those Christian catechumens,[2] who by having neglected the venerable religion shall have passed over to altars and temples, if they shall have children or brothers-german, that is, their own or statutory succession, should be taken the right of making a will according to their own inclination in favour of any other persons whatsoever.[3]

And likewise the rule must be observed in respect to their persons in taking property under a will, that they may not claim for themselves any rights at all in taking the inheritance of a will, except for their own and statutory successions, which could come to the said persons from the property of parents or of brothers-german, even by the disposition of an executed will, if the circumstances shall be thus, and that undoubtedly they may be bound to be excluded from all power not only of making but also of enjoying wills under the right of acquiring an inheritance.

Given on 20 May at Constantinople, Merobaudes for the second time and Saturnine being consuls.

1. Of the East.
2. The contrast is between *Christiani fideles* and *Christiani catechumeni*, a literal distinction as old as Tertullian (*De Praes. Haer.* 41 = CSEL 70. 53; written *c.* 200), though the word catechumen (κατηχούμενος) occurs in Gal. 6. 6. The period of persecution necessitated the catechumenate, which flourished in full form during the third century and then after the Church's triumph in the fourth century began its gradual decline.

The most famous institution connected with the catechumenate was the celebrated Catechetical School (τὸ τῆς κατηχήσεως διδασκαλεῖον: Eusebius, *HE* 6. 3. 3) at Alexandria, which Sozomen (*HE* 3. 15 *ad init.*) called "the sacred school of sacred studies" (τὸ ἱερὸν διδασκαλεῖον τῶν ἱερῶν μαθημάτων) and of which Clement and Origen and St Dionysius the Great were the leading lights. Its institution may be ascribed also to other reasons than apparently its primary purpose of instructing persons in the principles of Christian belief before their baptism into the Church. The school served to combat the Egyptian Church's heretical propensities and to champion the Christian cause against pagan philosophers' polemics in the cosmopolis wherein East and West met. It also was an academy which aimed to afford a higher education which—its expositors hoped—was comparable with that obtained in the older and more celebrated Museum, which was founded probably by Ptolemy I Soter *c.* 290 B.C. See no. 98, nn. 4 and 5.

3. That is, such apostates may devise their property only to their children and blood-brothers. Though this law is silent about apostate catechumens who have no lawful successors, yet they probably were penalized by not being permitted to make a will (as were the apostate believers mentioned in the second paragraph), with the result that they died intestate. In this case, since they were without lawful successors, their property passed to the fisc (as in nos. 185, 575, 599).

190. MANDATE OF GRATIAN, VALENTINIAN II, AND THEODOSIUS I ON APOSTATE CHRISTIANS' WILLS AND ON PENALTIES FOR MANICHAEANS, 383

(*CT* 16. 7. 3)

This ordinance, of which a brief part was retained by Justinian (*CI* 1. 7. 2), besides prohibiting apostate Christians from making wills, restricts to a five-year period (*post mortem*) contests of wills made by such persons ere their lapse and debars an apostate from impugning the will of another apostate. It also penalizes Manichaeans.

The same Augusti to Hypatius, praetorian prefect.[1]
By denial of liberty of making a will we avenge the crime of Christians who turn to altars and temples.[2]
Also should be punished the shameful acts of those who by disregard for the dignity of the Christian religion and name have polluted themselves with Jewish contagions.
But that penalty, which both our predecessor Valentinian[3] of divine authority has assigned and our decrees no less often have ordered,[4] should follow continually and perpetually those who have preferred at any time to attend the Manichaeans' nefarious retreats and wicked recesses. Moreover the same penalty should follow the authors

of this persuasion, who have deflected unsteady minds to their own fellowship, as those guilty of such error; nay, we ordain that even weightier punishments—according to the governors' impulses and to the crime's character—should be imposed generally and extraordinarily upon the nefarious artificers of this wickedness.

But lest either perpetual outrage of accusation should harass the dead or questions of inheritance wholly outdated by the difference of long periods of time should be agitated always into revived conflicts, we assign a limit of time to questions of this character: that, if [5] anyone [6] accuses the deceased of having violated and deserted the Christian religion and contends that the said person went over to the sacrileges of temples or to Jewish rites or to Manichaeans' infamy [7] and affirms that on this account a will not at all could be made, within a continuous quinquennium, which has been established for actions of voidance,[8] he may make use of this action and may obtain the beginning of a future trial of this sort:[9] to the effect that, when the said person whose transgression[10] is to be accused is living and is shown to have been a participant of this shameful act [10]and wicked deed,[10] he, having testified under public attestation, may prove his indictment;[11] for he who through his silence is proved to have shown perfidy to the Supernal Name, thus acquiescing in such wicked acts,[10] may not make henceforth an accusation about a transgression,[10] as though ignorant of it.

Given on 21 May at Padua, Merobaudes for the second time and Saturnine being consuls.

1. Of Italy.
2. Of the pagans.
3. The first emperor of that name. Probably the reference is to his legislation in no. 156.
4. Such as nos. 176 and 185.
5. Justinian's quotation starts here.
6. Most likely such a one would be an heir.
7. Justinian omits the phrase about the Manichaeans.
8. So Gratian, seven days later, if each date is correct, prescribed such a period for those desirous of declaring a will void (*CT* 2. 19. 5). The difference in the dates may be resolved by supposing that the latter ordinance, whose content must have been known by 21 May, due to some delay in drafting was promulgated a week later than the present law.

A period of five years was applied not only for actions of voidance, as here, but also was used in outlawing actions, e.g. for adultery (*CI* 9. 9. 5; dated 223) as well as for inquiries concerning the status of deceased persons (*CI* 7. 21. 1-8 [dated *ante* 215—c. 229]; cf. *D* 40. 15).

9. Here ends Justinian's excerpt.

10. That is, apostasy.
11. The Latin after this word is corrupt. No attempt to emend it seems satisfactory, but the translation here given, it is hoped, is not too far from what was intended by the legislator.

191. MANDATE OF GRATIAN, VALENTINIAN II, AND THEODOSIUS I ON HERETICS' USE OF CHURCHES, 383

(*CT* 16. 5. 10)

This constitution, while it forbids eviction of the heretical Tascodrogitans from their homes, denies them the use of a church for their religious meetings.

The same Augusti to Constantian, vicar of the Pontic diocese.
The Tascodrogitans indeed should not at all be expelled from their houses; nevertheless a crowd of heretical superstition should not meet at any church or, if perchance it shall have met, it should be repelled without any delay from its meeting-places.
Given on 20 June at Constantinople, Merobaudes for the second time and Saturnine being consuls.

192. MANDATE OF GRATIAN, VALENTINIAN II, AND THEODOSIUS I ON SUPPRESSION OF HERETICS, 383

(*CT* 16. 5. 11)

This document is another in the series of directives issued by Theodosius the Great against heretics.

The same Augusti to Postumian, praetorian prefect.[1]
Absolutely all persons whomsoever the error of diverse heresies excites, that is, Eunomians, Arians, Macedonians, Pneumatomachians, Manichaeans, Encratitans, Apotactitans, Saccoforians, Hydroparastatans, should not assemble in any gatherings, should not collect any multitude, should not draw any people to themselves and should not show walls of private houses after the likeness of churches, should

practise either publicly or privately nothing which can be detrimental to Catholic sanctity.

And if there shall have been anyone who may transgress what so evidently has been prohibited, by all good persons' common agreement he should be expelled, because such opportunity has been allowed to all whom the veneration and the excellence of correct religious observance delight.

Given on 25 July at Constantinople, Merobaudes for the second time and Saturnine being consuls.

1. Of the East.

193. MANDATE OF GRATIAN, VALENTINIAN II, AND THEODOSIUS I ON CURIALS' SURRENDER OF PROPERTY BEFORE ADMISSION TO THE CLERICATE, 383

(*CT* 12. 1. 104)

By this statute municipal senators who enter ecclesiastical service must surrender their estates.

The same Augusti [1] to Postumian, praetorian prefect.[2]

Curials who prefer to serve churches rather than municipal senates, if they wish to be what they pretend, should disdain those goods which they stealthily withdraw. For we do not free them [3] otherwise, unless their patrimonies have been disdained. This is indeed not proper, for spirits bound by divine worship to be possessed by desires for patrimonies.

Given on 7 November at Constantinople, Merobaudes for the second time and Saturnine being consuls.

1. Occasionally the name of a deceased emperor—in this case Gratian, who died on 25 August 383—is implied in the superscription (as here) of constitutions issued by his colleagues for some time after his death. This practice is reminiscent of the old rhetorical parallel of oxymoron, where Gratian, "being dead, yet speaketh" (Heb. 11. 4; cf. 2 Cor. 6. 9 and Cicero, *Lael.* 7. 23).
2. Of the East.
3. From municipal senates (*curiae*).

194. MANDATE OF GRATIAN, VALENTINIAN II, AND THEODOSIUS I ON HERETICAL ASSEMBLIES, 383

(CT 16. 5. 12)

Another constitution in the Theodosian series of statutes against heretics.

The same Augusti[1] to Postumian, praetorian prefect.[2]

The instruction—odious to God and to man—of errors, namely Eunomian, Arian, Macedonian, Apollinarian, and of all other sects which the pure faith of Catholic observance by its venerable reverence for the true religion condemns, should not assume, by either public or private attempts, the right either of collecting congregations or of establishing churches within the localities of cities and fields and villas and should not practise the celebration of their perfidy or the solemnization of their detestable communion and should not usurp and have any regulations for creating priests.[3]

The said houses, also, whether in cities or in whatever places throngs of such teachers and ministers shall be gathered for Easter,[4] should be subjected to our fisc's ownership and legal right,[5] so that those who have been wont to practise either the teaching or the mysteries[6] of such assemblies, when hunted from all cities and places and constrained by the published law's vigour, may be expelled from gatherings and may be ordered to return to their own lands, whence they have proceeded,[7] lest any of the said persons may have the power either of going to any other places whatsoever or of straying into the cities.

But if these regulations which our Serenity has established should be executed rather carelessly, the office staffs of the provincial governors and the chief magistrates of cities in which a gathering of a prohibited congregation shall be shown to have been found should be subjected to a sentence of condemnation.[8]

Given on 3 December at Constantinople, Merobaudes for the second time and Saturnine being consuls.

1. See no. 193, n. 1.
2. Of the East.
3. The word is *sacerdos*, which frequently means "bishop" and possibly may be translated thus here. See no. 16, n. 4.
4. Easter, of course, then was and is now the chief feast in the Christian calendar.
5. Perhaps a hendiadys: "legal ownership".
6. See no. 75, n. 42.

7. This seems to take no note of heretics born, say, in Antioch who assemble in Antioch, but to be aimed at heretics absent from their native localities for one or another reason. It appears to be an authorization for local police to expel heretical strangers.

8. A hendiadys; literally "to sentence and to condemnation".

195. RESCRIPT OF VALENTINIAN II, THEODOSIUS I, AND ARCADIUS ON LUCIFERIANS, 383 or 384

(CSEL 35. 45-6)

The Luciferians, whose schism seems not to have endured beyond the first generation of their adherents, took their name from Lucifer, bishop of Cagliari in Sardinia, whose eloquent orthodoxy and obstinate espousal of St Athanasius, patriarch of Alexandria, led them to adopt the extreme position that all priests who had participated in Arianism, even after these had renounced that heresy, should be debarred from the priesthood and that bishops who through compulsion had temporized with heretics and who had recognized even repentant heretics should be excommunicated. When their persistence provoked persecution, these sectaries, who never numbered many, through two priests, Marcelline and Faustinus, after Lucifer's death in 371 addressed to the emperors a petition (known briefly as the *Libellus Precum*[1]), wherein they explained their grievances and implored imperial protection.

This rescript, called in the manuscripts a *Lex Augusta*, is the reply of Theodosius, who in it directs Cynegius Maternus, praetorian prefect of the Orient, to take measures against the further pursuit of these over-zealous orthodox.

To these prayers the Augustan Law thus replies.
Greeting, Cynegius, most dear to us.
Although for human hearts there ought to be no greater reverence than for the divine law [2] nor can there be added anything to this law,[2] whose encompassing eminence, as the controller of the universe and of the earth, when propitiated, protects everything which the favour of Almighty God has wished to be under us, nevertheless because by Faustinus and Marcelline, priests very abounding in faith, our Clemency has been petitioned, we have feared that if by us there would have been no response to the petitioners, we should appear to give assent to these persons[3] who against our design have added something to the divine law,[2] to which we are subject, and therefore we rule on each point as follows: that we respect the petition which has

been offered, but that in accordance with our judgement we wish or order that nothing should be added to the faith. For no one ever has been of so profane a mind that, since he ought to follow Catholic teachers, he himself should decide for teachers what ought to be followed.

And it is a very acceptable and just praise of the petition, which has compassed almost the whole rank and file of heretical superstition (which is contrary to the Catholic faith), for it has revealed both whence it had arisen and under what sponsor it had advanced, since indeed, when the antiquity of the whole age [4] has been altered at the persuasion of certain persons, the innocent, driven into exile for the faith, have laid down their life with the highest praise.[5]

But vengeance has not been postponed in respect to them who, having plotted against good morals and celestial ordinances, for a little while, as a result of their controversy in respect not to faith but to faction, were perverting the minds of many persons by detestable ingratiation; for the patience of Almighty God has been moved to so great an extent that the punishment, which is due to guilty persons after death, they should suffer before death in an example for all. But not even by this circumstance they have been able to be converted and to be turned to God's commandment: by secret contrivances they beset, they pursue, they assail Catholics; so great is the perseverance of error that they prefer to sin daily with other adherents of opposite observance than to concur with Catholics in right opinions.

And in this matter must be praised the presentation of the petitioners, who, communicating with Gregory of Spain and Heraclidas of the East,[6] obviously holy and praiseworthy bishops, wish to live in the Catholic faith without assault and annoyance to anyone and to be disturbed by no plots and proceedings of attackers, and to whom in fact it is pleasing to preserve with all religious scrupulousness for all time the faith once received.

Accordingly let whatever has deserved to be eternal be inviolate; let not proceedings, let not attack, let not another's deceit make any assault; let them enjoy their own way of life wherever they shall wish; let them enjoy divine love in respect to the Catholic faith, dearest and fondest cousin Cynegius.

Your Sublimity should order our Serenity's command, whereby we reverence with all favour the Catholic faith (without which we cannot be saved) to be observed in such a way that it may protect and may defend from the injuries of base persons and heretics Gregory and Heraclidas, the bishops of the sacred law,[2] and all other priests like them, who have given themselves to an equal observance, and let all know that this abides in our heart: that we believe that the worshippers of Almighty God are none other unless Catholics.

1. Its full title seems to be *Confessio Verae Fidei et Ostentatio Sacrae Communionis et Persecutio Adversantium Veritati*. It is a very long document, consisting of some forty pages.

2. Christianity, as often.

3. *These persons* are the Arian persecutors of the Luciferians and they—the emperors think—will persist in their persecution if they shall have learned that the petition has not been answered. So in the rest of the sentence the sovereigns announce their favourable acceptance of the petition, but at the same time admonish petitioners as well as persecutors *that nothing should be added to the faith*—an admonition explicit in the case of the Arians, but implicit in the case of the Luciferians, who, unless they should abandon their attitude against ex-Arians, could be considered to import an innovation into the faith. This latter point is perhaps made clearer in the next and final sentence of the paragraph, which advises the petitioning priests not to usurp the teaching function of bishops, especially since a council at Alexandria, over which St Athanasius himself had presided in 363, had decreed pardon for repentant Arians (whether priests or bishops)—a decision which led to the formation of the Luciferians.

4. By *the antiquity of the whole age* probably is meant the orthodox Christian faith, "which was once delivered unto the saints" (Jude 3) in the first age of Christendom.

5. Lucifer himself had endured exile—not to mention St Athanasius, who had experienced exile five times.

6. The one was bishop of Elvira in Spain and the other was bishop of Oxyrhynchus in Egypt. After Lucifer's death they were leaders of the Luciferians at opposite ends of the Inner Sea.

196. MANDATE OF GRATIAN, VALENTINIAN II, AND THEODOSIUS I ON EXPULSION OF HERETICAL CLERGYMEN FROM CONSTANTINOPLE, 384

(CT 16. 5. 13)

Another directive, issued by Theodosius the Great in his attempt to outlaw heretics, bars heretical clergy from the capital.

The same Augusti [1] to Cynegius, praetorian prefect.[2]

The Eunomians, the Macedonians, the Arians, and the Apollinarians are names notorious for their errors among the obligatory services of the sacred religion.

All persons, accordingly, who claim for themselves either the pontificate or the ministry of these professions, who assert that they are priests ³ of a banned name and who impose on themselves the name of ministers of a criminal religion, who say that they teach what is proper either not to know or to unlearn,⁴ should be expelled, without any intervention of favour, from all hiding-places, explored with rather diligent search, of this city;⁵ let them live in other places and let them be separated entirely from good persons' gatherings.

Given on 21 January at Constantinople, Richomer and Clearchus being consuls.

1. See no. 193, n. 1.
2. Of the East.
3. The word is *sacerdotes*, on which see no. 16, n. 4.
4. From the emperor's viewpoint, of course.
5. Constantinople.

197. LETTER OF VALENTINIAN II, THEODOSIUS I, AND ARCADIUS ON CLERICAL IMMUNITY FROM SECULAR COURTS, (?)384

(CS 3)

This law, designed especially for Egypt, where previous laws providing clerical immunity from secular courts have been perverted, renews episcopal jurisdiction over clergymen by forbidding clergymen to be haled into lay courts and concentrates it in the person of the patriarch of Alexandria.

Emperors Valentinian, Theodosius, and Arcadius Augusti to Optatus, Augustal prefect.¹

Our Clemency has been moved very gravely that certain things have been perpetrated and have been committed with wicked temerity against the laws (no less divine than human) by those who claim for themselves the names of bishops, also that some clergymen of the orthodox, whose age and sacerdotal office were incompatible with this outrage, have been harassed, have been fatigued by journeys, have been delivered to torturers, and that all these things have been committed by those who were wearing the titles of the name of the sacerdotal office for protection for effrontery.²

Finally, when in the consistory had been read petitions by which episcopal piety, requesting something, is resisted,³ in this⁴ ... and therefore by a perpetual law we ordain that the name of bishops or of those who serve the Church's needs should not be dragged into the courts of either ordinary or extraordinary judges.[5] They have their own judges and to them is nothing in common with public laws—in so far, however, as pertains to ecclesiastical cases, which, it is proper, are decided by episcopal authority.

Therefore for whomsoever shall have been occasioned a judicial inquiry which pertains to Christian holiness, it shall be proper for them to litigate under such judge [5] as should be that head of all the bishops—but in his own districts, that is, throughout the diocese of Egypt, dearest and most agreeable Optatus.

Wherefore your laudable Authority with tempered judgement should interrupt and should terminate anything of such matters—Bishop Timothy,[6] whom all have preferred for themselves even to their own court, continuing to have episcopal authority over a sacred trial. For he is a man not only venerated by the respect of all bishops, but also already approved by our judgement.

Given on 4 February at Constantinople.

1. On this title see no. 489, n. 12.
2. Literally "coverings of the forehead" (*tegumenta frontis*), which in the tropical sense seems to be what appears in the text.
3. Editors suppose that the reference is to bishops being blamed because in cases pertaining to religion they have sought secular aid.
4. Editorial conjecture fills in translation the lacuna thus: "matter we see that a remedy is found".
5. See no. 161, n. 3.
6. Patriarch of Alexandria.

198. MANDATE OF GRATIAN, VALENTINIAN II, AND THEODOSIUS I ON AMNESTY FOR PRISONERS AT EASTERTIDE, 384

(*CT* 9. 38. 7)

Again the emperors release persons accused of minor crimes from prison or from punishment, excepting, however, those charged with certain major crimes (see nos. 135, 145, 171, 180).

The same Augusti [1] to Marcian, vicar.[2]
Religious respect for the annual public prayer [3] urges that we should order all persons who have been accused as guilty of minor

crime to be freed entirely from the danger of prison and from the dread of punishments.

Whence it appears that those whom atrocious cupidity has compelled to more violent enormities are excepted. And among these is first and greatest the crime of treason, then those of homicide and poison [4] and magic, sexual debauchery [5] and adultery and (of equal enormity) sacrilege and violation of sepulchres, robbery and falsified [6] fashioning of money.

Given on 22 March at Milan, Ricomer [7] and Clearchus being consuls.

1. See no. 193, n. 1.
2. Of a diocese unknown.
3. The phrase is *anniversaria obsecratio*, which, commentators believe, refers to Easter.
4. Or "sorcery", on which see no. 135, n. 4.
5. *Stuprum* always implies infliction of dishonour on the subject and covers a wide field of sexual offences, though it is not used of commerce with prostitutes.
6. Obviously a transferred epithet (hypallage): the money is counterfeited.
7. Richomer is the commoner form, as appears in the subscription of no. 196.

199. MANDATE OF GRATIAN, VALENTINIAN II, AND THEODOSIUS I ON JEWISH OWNERSHIP OF CHRISTIAN SLAVES, 384

(*CT* 3. 1. 5)

This constitution forbids Jews to buy Christian slaves and orders such slaves already owned by Jews to be sold to Christians.

The same Augusti [1] to Cynegius, praetorian prefect.[2]

None of the Jews at all should buy a Christian slave or should contaminate an ex-Christian by Jewish sacraments.

But if a public investigation shall have discovered that this has happened, both the slaves ought to be taken away and such masters should be subject to a penalty suitable and appropriate to the crime—with this addition: that if any slaves either still Christian or ex-Christian Jews shall have been found among the Jews, they should be redeemed from an undeserving slavery when a proper price has been paid by Christians.

Accepted on 22 September at Reggio, Ricomer [3] and Clearchus being consuls.

Interpretation: It is proper that before all things it should be observed that to no Jew it should be permitted to have a Christian slave; certainly by no means he should dare that, if he should have a Christian, he should presume to transfer him to his own law.[4] But if he shall have done this, he should know that, after the slaves have been taken away, he shall undergo a punishment worthy of so great a crime.

For before this law's issuance it had been ordained that he should know that the price which he had given for a Christian slave, if he had been befouled by Jewish pollution, would be paid to him by Christians,[5] that the slave might continue in the Christian law.[4]

1. See no. 193, n. 1.
2. Of the East.
3. See no. 198, n. 7.
4. *Lex* in the sense of religious belief or observance, which is a common meaning in late Latin.
5. Of the previous laws prohibiting Jews from owning Christian slaves (nos. 76 and 79) none contains the provision that Christians will reimburse Jews on release of such slaves.

200. LETTER OF VALENTINIAN II, THEODOSIUS I, AND ARCADIUS ON PAPAL ELECTION, 385

(CSEL 35. 47-8)

In December 384 Siricius, who had been first a lector and then a deacon of the Roman Church, was elected bishop of Rome [1] in succession to Pope St Damasus I. Although the anti-pope Ursinus, a rival to Pope Damasus in 366, continued his claim to the Papacy, the emperors consent to the selection of Siricius, who later was canonized, and praise his piety in this letter to Pinian, who probably was vicar of Rome.

This document is important because it shows the first imperial confirmation of a papal election.

Congratulatory letter on Pope Siricius' ordination.

Hail, Pinian, most dear to us.

That the people of the eternal city [2] should rejoice in harmony and should choose an excellent bishop we see belongs to the tradition of the Roman people and we are glad that this occurs in our times.

Accordingly, inasmuch as they have wished that the religious

Siricius as a bishop of holiness should preside over the bishopric so much that they rejected ³ the base Ursinus by acclamation, the aforesaid bishop should remain with our congratulation, most dear and most agreeable Pinian, if indeed in one acclamation both for him to be chosen and for the rest to be rejected is a great proof of integrity and of honesty.

Given on 24 February at Milan.

1. In his pontificate Theodosius I reconstructed over St Paul's grave on the Ostian Road the basilica (see no. 211, n. 1), in which St Siricius' name is still seen on one of the columns (*ILCV* 1. 1857) surviving the conflagration of that church in 1823.
2. See no. 140, n. 1.
3. Literally "dishonoured" or "outraged".

201. MANDATE OF GRATIAN, VALENTINIAN II, AND THEODOSIUS I ON AMNESTY FOR PRISONERS AT EASTERTIDE, 385

(*CT* 9. 38. 8)

By this statute, which Justinian repeats (*CI* 1. 4. 3), the emperors continue their custom of freeing prisoners because of Easter, but specify, as hitherto (nos. 135, 145, 171, 180, 198), those to whom is denied this boon.

The same Augusti [1] to Neoterius, praetorian prefect.[2]

Hereafter none should await our Perpetuity's proclamations, which perhaps may be rather late:[3] governors should execute that indulgence which we have been wont to confer.

As soon as the paschal day shall have appeared, let prison hold none confined, let the bonds of all be loosed.

But from these we separate those by whom we have observed that the joys and the common rejoicing are contaminated especially, if they should be released. For who should be indulgent during holy days to a committer of sacrilege? Who should pardon in a time of chastity an adulterer or a person guilty of incest?[4] Who should not prosecute more vigorously amid the greatest peace and the common joy a rapist?[5]

He who by some enormity of wickedness has not allowed the buried to rest should receive no respite from bonds. A poisoner,[6] a magician, a counterfeiter of money [7] should suffer tortures. A homicide [8] should expect what he always has done.⁹ Also a person guilty of treason ought not to hope for pardon from his lord, against whom he has undertaken such things.¹⁰

Given on 25 February at Milan, Arcadius Augustus for the first time and the most distinguished Bauto being consuls.

Interpretation: A committer of sacrilege, an adulterer, an incestuous person (when guilty),¹¹ a rapist, a violator of sepulchres, a poisoner, a magician, a counterfeiter of money, a homicide by no means should be absolved during the days of Easter.

All the rest, whom guilt of minor cases constrains, should be absolved specifically during the venerable ¹² days of Easter.

1. See no. 193, n. 1. But in repeating this statute Justinian adds the name of Arcadius.
2. Of Italy.
3. That is, after Eastertide. Previous laws on release of persons from prison because of imperial interest in Easter are dated after that day. The present law seems designed to create a standing operating procedure.
4. Justinian adds "or of sexual debauchery".
5. Justinian adds "of a virgin".
6. Or "sorcerer", on whom see no. 135, n. 4.
7. Justinian adds "and a violator".
8. Justinian adds "and a parricide".
9. That is, death.
10. In repeating this law in *CI* 1. 4. 3 Justinian adds here the last paragraph of no. 180.
11. One manuscript omits the parenthesized words.
12. This adjective in Latin is a transferred epithet, but in English is translated in agreement not with *Easter* but with *days*.

202. MANDATE OF VALENTINIAN II, THEODOSIUS I, AND ARCADIUS ON CLERICAL EXEMPTION FROM THE PUBLIC POST, 385

(*CT* 8. 5. 46)

The emperors command that the public post shall appropriate the property of clergymen when the superintendence of post cannot secure their services.

The constitution's preamble is omitted, because it does not pertain to clerics.

Emperors Valentinian, Theodosius, and Arcadius Augusti to Cynegius, praetorian prefect.¹

... But in the case of those persons who have acquired not earthly, but heavenly, privileges, we ordain that this must be observed: that if the sacrosanct religion already holds anyone from the class of persons of this sort and the supervisorship of the public post cannot accept his service, the public post should acquire the aforesaid person's property.

Given on 9 April at Milan, Arcadius Augustus for the first time and the most distinguished Bauto being consuls.

1. Of the East.

203. RESCRIPT OF MAXIMUS ON SUPPORT OF ORTHODOXY, 385

(CSEL 35. 90-1)

This letter from Maximus, the imperial usurper in the West, to Pope St Siricius is in part the emperor's defence against the pope's protest about the former's execution of some Priscillians [1] and partly the emperor's authorization for a Gallic synod to try the case of a certain Agroecius, who was ordained unduly to the priesthood.

The document has additional significance in that it was evoked by what seems to have been the earliest execution of Christian clergy by the Christian civil—and that the highest—authority.

Maximus, Great, Victor, Perpetual Triumpher, Ever-August to cousin Siricius.

We have received your Sanctity's letters, which were most acceptable to us and which clearly suited both the title of bishop and the most splendid city's [2] dignity. Moreover for the Catholic faith, about which you have wished to consult our Clemency, I avow that I have a greater concern on this account, because I experience a greater and a special decision of the Divinity in respect to me, who, of course, have risen to power straight from the baptism of salvation [3] and to whom always in all endeavours and events God has been a patron and of whom today he is and, as I hope, forever may deign to be a protector and a guardian, dearest father.

Moreover about Agroecius, who, you relate, has risen unduly to the rank of priest, what can I offer to our Catholic religion more reverently than that about this very person, of what character soever he may appear, Catholic bishops should judge? And in accordance with the convenience of all these, whether those who dwell within the Gauls [4] or those who dwell within the five provinces,[4] I shall ordain an assembly in whatever city they shall have selected, that, with the said bishops judging and investigating, it may be decided what the customary right accepts and what is the law. For they themselves, who know these matters, which must be maintained by books [5] and by our ancestors' most religiously scrupulous ordinances, can better declare these.

Moreover we profess that we have this intention and will: that the Catholic faith, with all bishops agreeing by the distant removal of all dissension and unanimously serving God, may continue steadfastly unimpaired and inviolable. For our accession has detected and has discovered some matters so defiled and polluted by the stain of impious persons, that unless our precaution and cure, which came from fear of Supreme God, speedily had carried assistance against these matters, mighty schism and destruction surely would have arisen, so that these diseases, with difficulty able to be healed, later would have hardened.[6]

Moreover I prefer that your Sanctity may know neither by arguments nor by dubious or uncertain suspicions, but from their very deeds revealed by their own confession in the trials, rather than from our mouth,[7] what wickedness moreover most recently [8] it has been disclosed that the Manichaeans [9] commit; because without a blush [10] we can not mention such crimes, not only shameful in action but also scandalous in description.

And in the emperor's hand: May the Divinity preserve you for many years.

1. Their heresy, derived partly from Manichaeanism, originated in Spain *c.* 370 and took its name from its leading exponent, Priscillian, bishop of Avila, who, excommunicated by a synod at Zaragoza in 380 and deposed in 384 by a synod at Bordeaux, appealed to Maximus at Trèves in 385, when he was convicted of *maleficium* (magic) and was executed with six adherents. His literary remains (*CSEL* 18) cast little light on the charge that he was a sorcerer, though Sulpicius Severus, his contemporary, states that Priscillian was believed to have practised magical arts from his youth (*Chron.* 2. 46. 5 = *CSEL* 1. 99).

Maximus appear to have been eager in his suppression of Priscillianism, because he hoped thus both to conciliate the Gallic episcopate to his imperial claims and to collect money for his soldiers from the confiscated estates of the wealthy sectaries. But both his severe punishment and his subsequent persecution of Priscillians produced protests principally from St Ambrose, bishop of Milan, and St Martin, bishop of Tours, as well as Pope St Siricius.

It seems that St Optatus of Milevis in Africa, Priscillian's contemporary, in his treatise *De Schismate Donatistarum*, 3. 6 (= *CSEL* 26. 86), was the first bishop to champion the State's infliction of capital punishment on heretics and schismatics: a liberal exegesis of the Pauline precept in 1 Cor. 5. 5 was enough to establish the doctrine of the delivery of such persons "for the destruction of the flesh, that the spirit may be saved". And it is interesting to note that two generations later Pope St Leo I the Great (440-61), in whose correspondence first clearly appears the medieval Papacy, approved Priscillian's execution by the secular authorities on the ground that "they saw . . . that both divine and human law would be subverted, if ever it should have been licit for such men to live with such doctrine" (*Ep.* 15 *ad init.* = *PL* 54. 679-80). Consult H. C. Lea, *A History of the Inquisition of the Middle Ages* (New York, 1922 [first published 1887]), 1. 212-5.

Priscillianism flourished during the fifth century, produced martyrs venerated as saints in Spain, commenced its decline in the sixth century, and died soon after its last condemnation by a synod at Braga in 563.

2. Rome.

3. Maximus was baptized before his departure from Britain for Gaul to wrest the western part of the Empire from Gratian.

4. The geographical division of Gaul ascends, of course, into republican times, for at least by the date of Caesar's *De Bello Gallico* (51 B.C.) we learn from its famous initial sentence that all Gaul was divided into three parts. But this Gaul was Farther Gaul (Gallia Ulterior), i.e. Transalpine Gaul, and sometimes was called Hairy Gaul (Gallia Comata), because the Gauls let their hair grow long, although the southern section along the Mediterranean Sea was termed sometimes Breeched Gaul (Gallia Bracata), because the natives there wore breeches (*bracae*). This coastal region became Gallia Narbonensis officially after its subjugation by the Romans (118-106 B.C.) and took its name from their colony of Narbo Marcius (mod. Narbonne) established therein. It also was called simply the Province (Provincia), for it was the first transalpine province. Caesar's other three parts of Gaul became under Augustan organization Gallia Aquitanica, Gallia Lugdunensis (formerly Gallia Celtica), Gallia Belgica.

There was also a Hither Gaul (Gallia Citerior), i.e. Cisalpine Gaul (usually called Gallia Cisalpina), which was northern Italy and took its name from the fact that Gallic invaders had settled there permanently in the fifth century B.C. Eventually it was known also as Gallia Togata, when the Roman settlers, wearing the toga as their national garment, had outnumbered the Gallic population. The district later acquired three other names, each chosen with respect to the proximity of a part to the river Po (Padus): Gallia Transpadana, Gallia Circumpadana, Gallia Cispadana.

West of the Rhine and the Alps and north of the Pyrenees by 305 Diocletian had divided Gallia Ulterior (or simply Galliae, as it often was termed) into two dioceses: Galliae and Viennensis. The latter contained five provinces, to which Maximus alludes: Novempopuli, Aquitanica, Narbonensis, Viennensis, Alpes Maritimae. Although later this number was increased to seven by the subdivision of the second and the third, the diocese of Vienne still was known as Quinque Provinciae (Five Provinces).

5. That is, the Christian writings generally received beside the Sacred Scriptures: conciliar canons and patristic works touching on ecclesiastical order and discipline.

6. The choice of this meaning for *concrescere*, which also can mean "increase", continues the medical metaphor.

7. This statement seems to mean that Maximus is forwarding to Siricius the *acta* of the trial at Trèves.

8. This phrase (*adhuc proxime*) appears to indicate some new crimes admitted at Treves in addition to those confessed at Bordeaux.

9. The Priscillians still are called Manichaeans, because probably no distinction between them yet was drawn.

10. Such modesty in the military mind is marvellous and merely means that Maximus masks his predatory persecution of the Priscillians with pious phrases to placate the pope.

204. MANDATE OF GRATIAN, VALENTINIAN II, AND THEODOSIUS I ON EXEMPTION OF PRIESTS FROM TORTURE, (?)385

(CT 11. 39. 10)

This constitution, repeated by Justinian (*CI* 1. 3. 8), permits priests to testify in lawsuits without being subjected to torture, which apparently it still requires in certain cases for clergy of inferior grade.

The same Augusti [1] to Paulinus, Augustal prefect.[2]

Priests should speak their testimony without the outrage of torture,[3] so that, however, they should not make false pretences. But all other clergymen, who follow their grade or order,[4] if they shall have been summoned to speak their testimony, should be heard just as the laws command.

Nevertheless for litigants should be reserved an action for falsehood,[5] if peradventure priests, who have been commanded to speak their testimony on account of a superior position without any corporal outrage, shall have suppressed the truth for the very reason that they have nought to fear. For by much more are they deserving of punishment, if they, on whom by our order very much [6] has been conferred, are found in secret crime.

Given on 25 July, Arcadius Augustus for the first time and Bauto being consuls.

204. EXEMPTION OF PRIESTS FROM TORTURE, (?)385

Interpretation: Priests can speak their testimony without the outrage of torture,[3] that is, without corporal punishment. But other clergymen, who follow after their order,[4] if they shall have been used for speaking testimony, should be heard just as the laws command, in such a way that an action for falsehood [5] should be reserved against priests, if in some way they shall be shown to have lied; because more deserving of punishment are they, if they, to whom the law exhibits reverence, when unmindful of their profession, are detected in the crime of untruth.

1. See no. 193, n. 1.
2. On this title see no. 489, n. 12.
3. Literally "question" (*quaestio*), an execrable euphemism now linguistically rare except in historical novels and in studies on ancient and medieval trials, but practically current among modern police in certain countries.

In Roman criminal procedure torture to elicit testimony (as distinct from torture as a penalty for conviction) applied only to slaves in the Republic, but in the second century of the Empire was extended to citizens as witnesses (*D* 48. 18. 10. 1, 12, 15, 18. 3). However, in most cases only lower-class citizens (*humiliores*) were "put to the question" and then ordinarily as a last resort. Upper-class citizens (*honestiores*), whose wealth, magisterial and/or senatorial rank (whether in the capital or in the provinces), and birth made them (and their children) privileged persons not reported, were exempted except in certain cases, such as treason. The earliest extant evidence of torture of freeborn witnesses in civil procedure appears to have been in 316 (*CT* 9. 19. 1), when such examination was sanctioned. For the Empire the evidence is collected in *D* 48. 18 and *CI* 9. 41, wherein jurisconsults' responses and imperial constitutions still observed at Justinian I's codification of the law are contained.

4. That is, come next in order as inferior. See no. 325, n. 6.
5. This *falsi actio*—we should expect either *actio falsi* or *actio de falso*—appears to be unillustrated in modern manuals on Roman private law, for it pertains to public law, but it probably proceeded from the fundamental statute on forgery, the Cornelian Law on Forgeries (*Lex Cornelia de falsis*) of 81 B.C., which still was enforced in Justinian's reign (*II* 4. 18. 7; *D* 48. 10; *CI* 9. 22-4). Since Cicero calls it the [*Lex*] *Cornelia testamentaria nummaria* (*In Verr.* 2. 1. 42. 108) and others give as an alternative title simply *Lex Cornelia testamentaria* (*Coll.* 8. 2 and 7; *II* 4. 18. 7), the law touched not only general forgery (*falsum*), but also forgery pertaining to wills (*testamenta*) and counterfeiting coins (*nummi*). Senatusconsults and imperial constitutions later widened the statute's scope to include many offences cognate with forgery, such as a testifier's false testimony treated here. Penalties (cf. references *supra*) varied with the period, with the enormity of the crime, with the criminal's status: for slaves usually death, but deportation ordinarily for freemen.
6. Justinian inserts "of honour".

205. MANDATE OF VALENTINIAN II, THEODOSIUS I, AND ARCADIUS ON INDULGENCE TO ARIANS, 386
(CT 16. 1. 4)

The campaign of Theodosius I against heretics in the East resulted in transference of their hopes to the West, where the Arians discovered an *amica curiae* in the person of Justina, widow of Valentinian I and mother of Valentinian II, whose influence over her son after Gratian's death in 383 had become so great that Arian officials infiltrated themselves into the imperial service. When St Ambrose, bishop of Milan, refused to relinquish the Basilica Portiana (now San Vittore al Corpo) to the Arians for the paschal celebration in 385, the orthodox Christians demonstrated so effectively that the imperial support was withdrawn; but Justina returned to the attack by persuading Valentinian to issue the following statute, which made it a capital offence to attempt anything against assemblies of Christians who subscribed to the Council of Rimini (359).[1]

Part of this statute is repeated in CT 16. 4. 1 with the same date. There is no evidence that either was enforced and it appears that the law was abrogated by nos. 215 and 217. Perhaps the Code's compilers overlooked this ordinance when they excluded pro-Arian legislation of Constantius II and Valens and pagan legislation of Julian II, for the orthodoxy of Theodosius II, who ordered the compilation, was opposed to such inclusion.

Emperors Valentinian, Theodosius, and Arcadius Augusti to Eusignius, praetorian prefect.[2]

We give the facility of assembling to those [3] who believe according to those matters which have been voted to endure forever in the times of Constantius [4] of deified [5] memory, when bishops [6] had been convened from all the Roman world [7] and the faith had been declared by those very persons (who now are known to dissent) [8] at the Council of Rimini [1] and also had been confirmed by the Council of Constantinople.[9] The authority of assembly also should extend to the persons [3] for whom we have so ordered, but with those [8] who think that facility of assembling has been granted only to themselves knowing that, if they shall have tried to do any turbulent act contrary to our Tranquillity's command, they shall pay penalties of treason even by their head and blood as authors of sedition and of the disturbed peace of the Church,[10] with punishment no less awaiting those who shall have tried to supplicate us surreptitiously or secretly contrary to this our order.

Given on 23 January at Milan, the most noble boy [11] Honorius and Evodius being consuls.

1. Although the Athanasians were in the majority at this council, the semi-Arian minority won the day after the council's conclusion, for the latter repulsed an anathema against Arianism and extracted from the former by threats some concessions, on which, as the event proved, were based again and again in the West their claims. Constantius II, who had convoked the council, later circulated an imperial formulary of an Arianizing creed and exiled non-subscribing bishops. See nos. 104 and 105.

2. Of Italy.

3. The semi-Arians are meant.

4. The second of that name. The date is 359.

5. See no. 127, n. 7.

6. See no. 16, n. 4.

7. The members were almost entirely Westerners, for the Easterners met at Seleucia in Pisidia later in the same year (359).

8. The orthodox bishops who by coercion or by guile had subscribed at Rimini to the semi-Arian creed, but later denounced it.

9. Canon 7 of this council (the Second General Council in 381) implicitly recognizes the Council of Rimini in setting conditions for the reception of Arians and of other heretics into the Church, but only after they have abjured formally their several heresies.

10. *CT* 16. 4. 1 is the part of this ordinance beginning in the translation at *those* (second n. 8 in text), omitting *knowing that,* ending with *Church.*

11. See no. 146, n. 5.

206. MANDATE OF GRATIAN, VALENTINIAN II, AND THEODOSIUS I ON VENERATION FOR MARTYRS, 386

(*CT* 9. 17. 7)

This ordinance, which Justinian copies differently twice (*CI* 1. 2. 3 and 3. 44. 14), forbids sale of martyrs' relics and authorizes construction of shrines to their memory.

The same Augusti [1] to Cynegius, praetorian prefect.[2]
None should transfer a buried body to another place.[3]
None should sell,[4] none should buy,[5] a martyr.[6]
But if anyone of the saints has been buried in any place whatsoever, persons should have it in their power that they may add whatever building they shall have desired in veneration of that place, which must be called a martyry.[7]

Given on 26 February at Constantinople, the most noble boy [8] Honorius and Evodius being consuls.

1. See no. 193, n. 1.
2. Of the East.
3. *CI* 3. 44. 14 contains only this sentence, to which is added "without the emperor's words".
4. The verb is *distrahere*, which from its fundamental meaning of "to tear in pieces", "to separate forcibly" is used also in mercantile language "to sell separately", "to retail".
5. The verb is *mercari*, which may mean "to traffic".
6. Justinian uses this sentence for his law in *CI* 1. 2. 3, where *martyr* is pluralized.

The entire sentence seems to mean that none should traffic in separated relics of a martyr.

On relics consult R. Peyrefitte, *The Keys of St Peter* (New York, 1957), 21, 28–33, 66–7, 139–45, 232–4, 263–83, 323–6, for their use and abuse.

If the bodies (Acts 19. 12) and even the shadows (Acts 5. 15) of the apostles, while alive, could heal the sick, it was no wonder that there arose the belief that the sacred bones and other relics of the saints, especially of martyrs, had no less virtue. This belief found its immediate instance in the curative powers exercised by Jesus and doubtless in his well-known encounter with the woman who "said within herself, 'If I may but touch his garment, I shall be whole'" (Matt. 9. 21; cf. 14. 36). Despite the Hebrews' ceremonial laws against defilement (Num. 19. 11–22), there is evidence that veneration or, at least, respect was accorded to the bones of Joseph (Ex. 13. 19; Josh. 24. 32) by the Israelites and that the prophet Elisha's bones restored to life a dead man (2 Kings 13. 21; cf. Ecclus. 48. 13–14). See also next note.

The superiority of martyrs, whose intercessions before "the throne of grace" (Heb. 4. 16) became one of the Christians' highest hopes, over other saints, even those whose death "is precious in the sight of the Lord" (Ps. 116. 15), is quite understandable, for no other religion, as has Christianity, has so glorified its individual witnesses, who "resisted unto blood, striving against sin" (Heb. 12. 4) and "of whom the world was not worthy" (Heb. 11. 38).

7. It is interesting to note that the earliest extant account of a Christian martyrdom, the Smyrnan Church's epistle generally entitled—the manuscripts are not in agreement—*The Martyrdom of St Polycarp*, suggests that after 22 February 156 (the date of St Polycarp's martyrdom) his bones were put where it was meet, obviously in a place where, as the letter continues, "the Lord will let us assemble in gladness and joy to celebrate his martyrdom's birthday for both the commemoration of those who already have contested and the training and the preparation of those who will [contest hereafter]" (18. 2–3). These relics then were preserved, probably in a small tomb and under an altar (cf. Rev. 6. 9–11)—for the Roman catacombs show such structures whereat early

Christians celebrated Holy Communion—and possibly in a shrine which later Christians called a martyry. See also no. 577, n. 13 *ad fin.*

The divine worship in martyries naturally had overtones of the martyr to whose memory such an edifice had been erected. St Augustine seems to have spoken for the ancient Church (whether Western or Eastern), when he distinguished such a shrine from a pagan temple by writing (*De Civ. Dei*, 22. 10): "To such deities of theirs they both built temples and placed altars and established priests and made sacrifices; but to our martyrs we build not temples as if to deities, but memorials as if to dead persons, whose spirits live with God; nor there we erect altars wherein we may sacrifice to the martyrs, but to the one God both of the martyrs and of us." On how this distinction disappeared consult J. Pelikan, *The Riddle of Roman Catholicism* (Nashville, 1959), 135–6, where he shows how the separation between veneration (*dulia*) and adoration (*latria*) gradually became blurred.

8. See no. 146, n. 5.

207. LETTER OF VALENTINIAN II, THEODOSIUS I, AND ARCADIUS ON AMNESTY FOR PRISONERS AT EASTERTIDE, 386

(CS 8)

This last and most elaborate law in a series of several statutes on pardon for criminals at Eastertide (nos. 135, 145, 171, 180, 198, 201) orders the release of persons not charged with certain specified crimes entailing capital punishment.[1]

Emperors Valentinian, Theodosius, and Arcadius.

For our Serenity's endeavours, by which we always are animated through natural kindness—even beyond the practice of established and annual clemency—to increase indulgences according to custom, the season desired by good minds has arrived. For not at any other time is it more proper for the imperial Piety to equal such benefits than when throughout the whole world a sacred day is renewed with festal celebration. And indeed beyond that clemency, proclaimed—as it were—and transmitted by our ancestors for the observance of religion, we reveal the aid of our sacred mind with utterly profuse humanity for liberating almost all whom the laws' severity shall have constrained.

Moreover throughout all this intervening time, which flows between the venerated and the celebrated days,[2] we relieve them from chains, we release them from exile, we withdraw them from mines, we free them from deportation, since it is quite certain that there is almost no day on which we do not order something clement and holy, because we consider that we even suffer a certain loss of hours, if there shall not have appeared some person who may be liberated.[3]

And from this haste it appears that we always seize with eagerness [4] this necessary occasion [5] for relaxing the laws for guilty persons [4]— in so far, however, as just humanity allows—and we continue this voluntary sanctity [6] through all periods of seasons. For it is not proper that amid festive ceremonies and venerable rites of a sacred season dissonant voices of unfortunate persons should sound, that guilty persons with unkempt hair in deathly dishevelment [7] should be dragged to common pity,[8] that groans, drawn from the heart's depth, should be heard; since assuredly well-suited to each other are sacred and gladsome occasions and it is not seemly to feel, to hear, to see anything sad amid serene words of prayers and pious voices dedicated to the Eternal Divinity.

Wherefore we do not suppress the leniency known by our benefits; rather we open also the prison, we remove the chains, we fittingly banish uncombed hair in prison dark with filth. We snatch all persons from deadly punishments except those for whom aid is not proper in view of the magnitude of their crimes. Let those crimes excepted from the general indulgences have their own fate and let the appropriate outcome hold those guilty of the greater crimes.[1] We shall not do injury to the shade [9] of any dead person by absolving homicides. We shall not leave unavenged the bed [9] of any person by having remitted the punishment of adultery [9] and of such crimes. We preserve intact the case of treason, which extends widely. We join to the happiness of persons to be absolved neither any persons sinning against stars [10] nor poisoners [11] nor magicians nor persons guilty of counterfeiting: therefore not deserving of the enjoyment of the festive light are they by whom are committed crimes greater than a prudent clemency is wont to absolve.

And lest our rather joyous speech should be engaged longer in this series of crimes, with the excepting of the usual and the well-known crimes, we free the others,[12] dearest and most agreeable Antiochine.[13]

Wherefore your Excellency shall order that our Gentleness' ordinances should be fulfilled as swiftly as possible, in order that the joyous orders may be extended rather rapidly, and that whosoever should deserve to be absolved in the common celebration of all persons should be released.

Given on 22 April at Constantinople, the most noble boy [14] Honorius and Evodius being consuls.

1. See no. 171, n. 1.

2. These seem to be the holy paschal days, of which seven precede and seven succeed Easter (nos. 220 and 238).

3. Perhaps a reminiscence of what Suetonius calls the memorable and praiseworthy remark of Emperor Titus (79–81), who, remembering at suppertime that he had done nothing for anyone all that day, said "Friends, I have lost a day" (*Tit.* 8. 1). The Suetonian phrase with slight change reappears in *LNT* 5. 1 *ad init.* (dated 9 May 438), 52 years after its reminiscence here.

4. Editors supply this phrase in Latin.

5. This or some such word is necessary to complete the sense. Editors note the omission.

6. The significance of this word (*sanctimonia*) is not clear: pardoning criminals does not necessarily confer sanctity upon pardoners. But it may refer to what follows.

7. Literally, "bristling hair fatally dishevelled"—as a sign of mourning for their imminent fate.

8. The sense seems to be that the wretched state of the accused being dragged by police to prison arouses all persons' pity—a situation to be shunned at Eastertide.

9. The Latin word is plural.

10. That is, astrologers, elsewhere called *Chaldaei* (because from pre-classical times Chaldaeans had been known for their knowledge of astronomy and astrology) or *genethliaci* (because they cast a horoscope dependent upon a client's natal hour) or, quite frequently, *mathematici* (because they employed numerical calculations). See no. 313, n. 1.

11. Or "sorcerers", on whom see no. 135, n. 4.

12. That is, criminals.

13. His office is unknown.

14. See no. 146, n. 5.

208. MANDATE OF GRATIAN, VALENTINIAN II, AND THEODOSIUS I ON PROHIBITION OF CHRISTIANS AS CHIEF PRIESTS, 386

(*CT* 12. 1. 112)

Evidence of the survival of paganism appears in this directive sent to Egypt, for the order forbids Christians to serve as chief priests in pagan cults.

The same Augusti [1] to Florentius, Augustal prefect.[2]

In attaining the high priesthood [3] should be preferred that person who shall have performed more for his native community and, however, shall not have withdrawn from the cult of the temples through observance of Christianity. Indeed it is indecorous, nay rather—that we may speak more truly—unlawful, for temples and temples' customary ceremonies to belong to the care of those persons whose conscience the divine religion's [4] true account has imbued and for whom themselves it was obligatory to avoid such public service, even if they were not prohibited.

Issued on 16 June at Constantinople, the most noble boy [5] Honorius and Evodius being consuls.

1. See no. 193, n. 1.
2. On this title see no. 489, n. 12.
3. The pagan *archierosyne* (transliterated from ἀρχιερωσύνη) must not be confused with the Christian priesthood. This priesthood was regarded sometimes—as the text shows—as a liturgy or public service, at other times as an office with an honorary title (*CT* 12. 1. 75). Entrance upon this office, whose tenure might be for one year or for a prescribed period or for life, varied in the Empire: appointment by local magistrate(s) or by municipal senate, co-optation by other priests, hereditary incumbency, sale to highest bidder, election.

While ordinarily the officiant was not exposed to an ethical examination, yet some priesthoods imposed on their incumbents external propriety, for which may be consulted Julian the Apostate's celebrated epistles on priestly conduct (*Ep.* 429C–32A, 452A–4B, 288A–305D), sent in 362 and 363 to high priests. Civil priests also produced games and other public spectacles at their own expense.

Since a civil priest enjoyed certain prerogatives, perhaps the emperors by this statute also sought to rebuke Christians who coveted this office to obtain its privileges.

A generation later (see no. 337, n. 3) the civil priesthood could be held by Christian laymen without performing any religiously sacerdotal service, for the ancient title was retained, although the religious duties disappeared progressively as the Christianization of the Empire proceeded.

4. Christianity in contrast to paganism, which still survived.
5. See no. 146, n. 5.

209. MANDATE OF GRATIAN, VALENTINIAN II, AND THEODOSIUS I ON SUSPENSION OF LITIGATION ON SUNDAY, 386
(*CT* 2. 8. 18)

This statute directs the suspension of all judicial procedure and of claims for payment of debts on Sundays. It is repeated in *CT* 8. 8. 3 and 11. 7. 13, which therefore are not translated.

210. SUBSTITUTES FOR DECURIONS, 386

Emperors Gratian,[1] Valentinian, and Theodosius Augusti to Principius, praetorian prefect.[2]

On the Sun's day,[3] which our ancestors properly called the Lord's,[3] the contention of all lawsuits, legal matters, court actions[4] should cease entirely.

No one should demand a public or a private debt to be paid.

And there should not be any cognizance of controversies even before arbiters themselves, either demanded in law courts or selected voluntarily.

And who shall have deviated from the holy religion's inspiration or ritual should be judged not only infamous but also sacrilegious.

Posted[5] on 3 November at Aquileia. Accepted on 24 November at Rome,[6] the most noble boy[7] Honorius and[8] Evodius being consuls.[9]

1. See no. 193, n. 1.
2. Of Italy.
3. See no. 34, n. 5.
4. In *CT* 11. 7. 13 *court actions* is omitted.
5. *CT* 8. 8. 3 reads "Given" for this word.
6. In *CT* 11. 7. 13 the information about acceptance is missing.
7. See no. 146, n. 5.
8. *CT* 8. 8. 3 inserts "the most distinguished" here.
9. To *CT* 8. 8. 3 is the following appendix:

"Interpretation: On the Sun's day, which deservedly is called the Lord's, all persons' action at law should cease, so that neither private nor public debt should be exacted and neither public nor private trials should occur. And who shall not have observed this should be held accused of sacrilege."

210. MANDATE OF GRATIAN, VALENTINIAN II, AND THEODOSIUS I ON SUBSTITUTES FOR DECURIONS BEFORE ADMISSION TO THE CLERICATE, 386

(*CT* 12. 1. 115)

This law commands municipal senators desiring to become clergymen to provide substitutes (to whom, if necessary, they must surrender their property) to perform the public services to which they have been subject.

The same Augusti[1] to Cynegius, praetorian prefect.[2]

Clergymen belonging to a municipal senate should know that if they themselves desire to remain exempt,³ other persons, who in undergoing public services should replace the presence and the person of the withdrawers, must be made adequate from their own patrimony.

Given on 31 December at Constantinople, the most noble boy⁴ Honorius and Evodius being consuls.

1. See no. 193, n. 1.
2. Of the East.
3. From public duties, to which their rank and their estate had subjected them as laymen.
4. See no. 146, n. 5.

211. RESCRIPT OF VALENTINIAN II, THEODOSIUS I, AND ARCADIUS ON CONSTRUCTION OF ST PAUL'S BASILICA, 386

(CSEL 35. 46–7)

Though this rescript carries the names of three joint-emperors, it usually is believed to have originated with Theodosius, who ordered the Basilica of St Paul-without-the-Walls (San Paolo fuori le Mura)¹ to be built on the site of a small church constructed by Constantine I in Rome. The instructions are addressed to Sallust, who, as urban prefect of Rome, reported on the situation.

On the construction of the Basilica of Saint Paul the Apostle.

Valentinian, Theodosius, and Arcadius Augusti to Sallust, urban prefect.

To us, upon consideration of the veneration already sacred from ancient times,² desiring to adorn the Basilica of Paul the Apostle for the sake of sanctity of religion, to enlarge it in proportion to the number of the assemblage, to exalt it on account of zeal for devotion, has been pleasing your Sublimity's dutifulness, which you have allotted to surveying all matters, as the occasion demanded, and because you have made known to our Serenity's ears by carefulness of suitable language the entire site and aspect of the place, for it has been proper that we, better informed, order what must be ordered.

Wherefore, after consultation with the venerable priest ³ has been shared and after all—both the most distinguished order ⁴ and the Christian people—have been informed as to what we order, your Sublimity should investigate the matter with more careful consideration and with full examination of the circumstances. And if it shall have pleased the people as well as the Senate to renew the old road, which passes behind the basilica and which is adjacent to the bank of the Tiber River,[5] so that the present road may be added to the space for the future work, so far by the architects you [6] shall arrange the plan of the future basilica as the level surface favourable for the structure shall have presented itself, lest any unevenness may obscure the splendour of the more enlarged edifice, if indeed in every aspect of the walls it is the finest beauty which the plan shows ought to be observed at once by the chief façade of great buildings.

Now the project itself demands the following: that after a sincere investigation a schedule of the work to be constructed should be tendered and a preliminary estimate of all expenses according to the prices of materials which obtain in the most sacred city [7] should be arranged rather fully and should be sent to our Clemency with due expedition, that our Serenity's assent may approve the common consent of all, whereby may be arranged more easily in view of the merits of so great a religion that which our devoted intention has decided.

And by another hand, that of the emperor: May the Divinity preserve you for many years, dearest and fondest cousin.

1. Restored by many popes, notably by St Leo III (795-816), it became one of the seven patriarchal basilicas of Rome. After it had been almost entirely destroyed by fire in 1823, Pope Leo XII (1823-9) ordered the work of reconstruction, which, completed in 1854, perhaps has recaptured the magnificence of the structure, formerly considered by many to have been the finest and most interesting church in Rome. The sarcophagus of the Apostle Paul is in the basilica, whose Theodosian reconstruction is witnessed by the inscription in *ILCV* I. 1761.

See the admirable article by G. Belvederi, "L'origine della basilica ostiense", in *Rivista di archeologia cristiana*, 22 (1946) 103-318.

2. The adverb—*antiquitus*—is somewhat exaggerated. Although St Paul had been executed about two miles distant from the basilica in 64 or 67, it seems that no church had been erected on the present site much before 200.

3. St Siricius, bishop of Rome, if *sacerdos* (as often) stands for *episcopus* (see no. 16, n. 4).

4. The Roman Senate. See no. 325, n. 6.

5. The present Via Ostiense runs along the eastern end of the basilica and is behind it, for the main entrance of the church is at its western end (where is the chief façade, turned toward the Tiber), and about 550 yards north of the edifice passes along the eastern bank of the river, which makes a curve there.

6. The Latin shows no subject and the verb is in the third person singular number: either Sallust's Sublimity should be understood—which is more

likely, for to Sallust his sovereign writes—or the Senate and the People collectively (*Senatus Populusque Romanus* = SPQR) are meant (see the text *supra* at n. 4)—which is less likely, for it is simpler that one person should be in over-all charge of construction.

7. Rome.

212. MANDATE OF VALENTINIAN II, THEODOSIUS I, AND ARCADIUS ON ILLEGAL DETENTION OF ECCLESIASTICAL LAND, 387

(*CI* 7. 38. 2)

The fact that Catholic Christianity was made the State's religion (no. 167) seven years before the present constitution and that Justinian, the *imperator theologicissimus*, re-enacted this directive when pagan shrines in the Eastern Empire no longer served their pristine purpose, conspires to cast a Christian colour upon the phrase *ius templorum* (legal right of temples[1]) in it.

The mandate orders, then, the restoration of illegally held ecclesiastical lands to the Church, both without any compensation to the detainers and apart from any statute of limitations.

Emperors Valentinian, Theodosius, and Arcadius Augusti to Dexter, count of the private estates.

We order all lands which of the legal right of the State or of the legal right of the temples in any province whatever have been sold or in any other way have been alienated by imperial tenant-farmers to be restored by those persons who wrongly and contrary to the laws occupy these—no prescription of long time [2] hindering, so that it may not be permitted for the unjust purchasers to exact even the price.

Given on 3 July at Constantinople, Valentinian Augustus for the third time and Eutropius being consuls.

1. Long ere 387 Christians were familiar with ναός = *templum* as a synonym for ἐκκλησία = *ecclesia* (2 Cor. 6. 16, *et al.*) referring to the Church of God.

It is generally held that before persecution of the Christians ended in 311 Christians had stated meeting-places for worship, although such places were usually unostentatious and were unmarked by architectural elegance—doubtless to avoid attention of their enemies. Wherever in ante-Nicene patristic literature the words ναός or *templum* occur with Christian connotation, these words almost always carry the metaphorical meaning that God's temple is in the Christian's heart. Apart from a few debatable passages, the earliest definite use of *templum* as a place of Christian worship appears to be by Lactantius, *Inst. Div.* 5. 2. 2 (= *CSEL* 19. 403), where he writes that, when he was called to Bithynia to teach oratory, God's temple was overthrown (*dei templum everteretur*). By "God's temple" Lactantius must mean the *ecclesia* in Nicodemia, the capital of Bithynia, whose desecration and destruction in 303 he described (*De Mort Pers.* 12. 2–5 = *CSEL* 27. 186–7).

On the existence of Christian churches before 311 and for the various names given to them consult J. Bingham, *Origines Ecclesiasticae: or, The Antiquities of the Christian Church*[2] (London, 1711), 97–137.

2. See no. 65, n. 6 *ad fin*.

In *CT* 15. 1. 22 = *CI* 8. 11. 6 (dated 383) it is ordained that prescription of time shall not prejudice a public right (*ius publicum*), which there is equivalent to the legal right of the State (*ius rei publicae*) here near the beginning of this paragraph.

213. MANDATE OF GRATIAN, VALENTINIAN II, AND THEODOSIUS I ON SUPPRESSION OF APOLLINARIANS, 388

(CT 16. 5. 14)

This constitution announces various disabilities to be enforced particularly against the Apollinarian sectaries.

The same Augusti [1] to Cynegius, praetorian prefect.[2]

Apollinarians and all other followers of diverse heresies we order to be barred from all localities, from cities' walls, from the society of honourable persons, from the fellowship of holy persons.

They should not have the ability of ordaining clergymen.

They should lack the capability of convening congregations either in public or in private churches.

No authority for appointing bishops should be given to them; the bishops themselves also, after they have been deprived of the name, should lose the appellation of this office.

They should go to places which can seclude the said persons most of all, as if by a kind of wall, from human fellowship.

Also to these conditions we add the following: that to all the aforesaid persons should be denied avenues of approaching and of addressing our Serenity.

Given on 10 March at Thessalonica, Theodosius Augustus for the second time and Cynegius being consuls.

1. See no. 193, n. 1.
2. Of the East.

214. MANDATE OF VALENTINIAN II, THEODOSIUS I, AND ARCADIUS ON PROHIBITION OF JEWISH–CHRISTIAN MARRIAGE, 388

(*CT* 3. 7. 2)

This celebrated constitution, which Theodosius repeats (*CT* 9. 7. 5) and Justinian confirms (*CI* 1. 9. 6), forbids Jews and Christians to intermarry and regards such intermarriage as adultery.

Emperors Valentinian, Theodosius, and Arcadius Augusti to Cynegius, praetorian prefect.[1]

Let not any Jew take a Christian woman in marriage and let not a Christian man choose wedlock with a Jewess.[2]

For if anyone shall have committed any act of this kind, the crime of this transgression shall acquire the condition of adultery—with the liberty to make an accusation opened also to public voice.[3]

Given on 14 March at Thessalonica, Theodosius Augustus for the second time and the most distinguished [4] Cynegius being consuls.

Interpretation: By this law's severity it is prohibited that either a Jew should make a marriage with a Christian woman or a Christian man should take a Jewish wife.[2]

But if any persons shall have involved themselves in such union contrary to the prohibition, they should know that they must be punished by the penalty with which adulterers are condemned [5] and that the accusation of this crime has been permitted not only to relatives but also to all persons for the purpose of prosecution.[6]

1. Of the East.
2. This prohibition of religious intermarriage found precedents in both Jewish and Christian antiquity, probably for fear lest such unions would induce either a Jew or a Christian to worship other gods. Thus Jews were forbidden to wed Gentiles, e.g. in Ex. 34. 16; Deut. 7. 3–4; 1 Kings 11. 2; Ezra 9. 12; Neh. 10. 29–30, 13. 23–9; Tobit 4. 12–13. When Israelites disregarded this ban, idolatry resulted, as is recorded, e.g. in Judges 3. 5–7; 1 Kings 11. 1–8, 16. 31.

And St Paul preached against mixed marriages between Christians and infidels in 2 Cor. 6. 14-18 (but cf. 1 Cor. 7. 12-16, on which Tertullian comments *in extenso* [*Ad Ux.* 2. 2-8 = *CSEL* 70. 111-24]).

3. By *CT* 9. 7. 2 (dated 326) Constantine I restricted the right of initiating accusations of adultery to the nearest of kin, such as the guilty woman's father, husband, brother, paternal uncle, and male first cousins on either side. Theodosius I here removes the restriction.

4. *CT* 9. 7. 5 omits the superlative adjective.

5. By the *Lex Iulia de adulteriis coercendis* of 18 B.C. the penalty was death by the sword (*II* 4. 18. 4), but Tacitus remarks that Augustus evaded his own laws when he punished adulterers by death or by exile (*Ann.* 3. 24. 2-3). In 326 Constantine I commanded death by the sword (*CI* 9. 9. 29 [30]. 4), but in 339 Constantius II and Constans I ordained that the culprit should be sewn alive into a sack or should be burned (*CT* 11. 36. 4). While the burning apparently was complete cremation, the punishment by the sack, which was used also for parricides, to whom this law likens adulterers, involved also insertion of a dog, a rooster, a viper, an ape (a symbolical selection of animals), then the sack was cast into the sea (*D* 48. 9. 9. pr.), for the reason that the adulterer neither should pollute the air while alive nor should contaminate the earth when dead, and because the ancients considered that lustration by sea-water expiated guilt (e.g. Euripides, *Iph. Taur.* 1193).

6. The interpretation of *CT* 9. 7. 5 is briefer: "Neither a Jew should take a Christian woman nor a Christian man a Jewess as a wife. If one shall have done this, by anyone's accusation one should be punished just as in the case of adulterers."

The constitution or at least the interpretation might have saved space for the jurisconsult Modestin's famous definition: "Marriage is a union of male and female, a sharing of all life, a participation in divine and human law" (*D* 23. 2. 1), since it might have been explained that the last clause would be impossible of fulfilment if Christians and Jews should have intermarried, for "participation in divine law" must have meant the wife's right to share in the sacred rites (*sacra privata*) of her husband's family. By 388 it was quite possible for a legal sophist to have interpreted this text *more Christiano* and to have held that no Jewess could have assisted with her Christian husband in the Church's worship and *more Iudaico* that no Christian husband could have worshipped in a synagogue with his Jewish wife. Therefore no true marriage could have existed in either case.

Pitra prints (2. 603) a late Greek paraphrase, which he links to this law: "Christians should not unite [with Jews] for marriage, being thence suspected in respect to a public accusation about adultery."

215. MANDATE OF GRATIAN, VALENTINIAN II, AND THEODOSIUS I ON OPPRESSION OF HERETICS, 388
(CT 16. 5. 15)

Part of the price for succouring Valentinian, who had fled from Italy to Greece at the invasion of the usurper Maximus, apparently was the demand by Theodosius, before he took the field against their rival, that Valentinian should rescind the privileges bestowed by him on heretics. At any rate this constitution annuls the heretics' privilege of assembly and of worship (see no. 205), granted two years earlier.

The same Augusti[1] to Trifolius, praetorian prefect.[2]

All persons of diverse and perfidious sects, whom madness of miserable conspiracy against God engages, should not be allowed to have anywhere an assembly, to enter into discussions, to conduct secret meetings, to build impudently by the offices of an impious hand altars of nefarious transgression and to apply the simulation of mysteries[3] to the true religion's injury.

And that this may obtain a fitting result, you should constitute as observers[4] certain very faithful persons, that they can both restrain them and bring them, when arrested, to the courts for the purpose of paying, according to previous ordinances, the severest penalty both to God and to the laws.

Given on 14 June at Stobi, our Lord Theodosius Augustus for the second time and the most distinguished Cynegius being consuls.

1. See no. 193, n. 1.
2. Of the East.
3. See no. 75, n. 42.
4. Literally "for looking-glasses" (*in specula*).

216. MANDATE OF VALENTINIAN II, THEODOSIUS I, AND ARCADIUS ON PUBLIC DISCUSSION OF RELIGION, 388

(CT 16. 4. 2)

This ordinance bans public meetings to discuss religious topics, for it seems that in the East several heretical sects had held such gatherings to disseminate their theological tenets.

The same Augusti to Tatian, praetorian prefect.[1]
No opportunity either of debating about religion or of discussing it or of offering any advice about it should be extended to anyone [2] who has gone into public to do this.
And if anyone hereafter with offensive and damnable attempt shall have believed that it is possible to contravene a law of this type or shall dare to persevere in the performance of pestiferous persistence, he should be restrained by appropriate penalty and proper punishment.
Given on 16 June at Stobi, Theodosius Augustus for the second time and Cynegius being consuls.

1. Of the East.
2. Probably any clergyman is meant.

217. MANDATE OF GRATIAN, VALENTINIAN II, AND THEODOSIUS I ON ARIAN PRETENSIONS, (?)388

(CT 16. 5. 16)

This directive, issued by Theodosius the Great, assails Arians who plead imperial permission to indulge in their religious practices.

The same Augusti [1] to Cynegius,[2] praetorian prefect.[3]
We have learned that some of the Arians [4] quote a formulary of our ordinances to the effect that it is lawful for them to practise what appears to them to suit their advantage.[5]
But, since this law has been annulled,[6] they should know that no ordinance of this character has issued from our [7] sacred office.
Whatever, therefore, shall have been quoted by these persons for

their own benefit, whoever shall have circulated hereafter the said formularies should be held as guilty of forgery.

Given on 9 August at Constantinople,⁸ Theodosius Augustus for the second time and the most distinguished Cynegius being consuls.

1. See no. 193, n. 1.
2. The editors report that Cynegius was buried on 19 March 388.
3. Of the East.
4. Probably the Homoeans, moderate Arians, are meant.
5. Theodosius may have had in mind Valentinian's permission allowing Arians to assemble (no. 205).
6. Or "by this law's annulment"; see no. 215, introd.
7. The reference is to Theodosius.
8. The editors note that on 9 August Theodosius was not in Constantinople, but was en route from Thessalonica into Italy.

218. RESCRIPT OF VALENTINIAN II, THEODOSIUS I, AND ARCADIUS ON TESTAMENTARY RESTRICTIONS FOR EUNOMIANS, 389

(CT 16. 5. 17)

The denial of the capability of bequeathing and accepting property, first applied to Manichaeans (no. 176), is extended by this ordinance to Eunomians and is made retroactive. This law was abrogated five years later (no. 246).

Emperors Valentinian, Theodosius, and Arcadius Augusti to Tatian, praetorian prefect.¹

Eunomian eunuchs should not have the liberty either of making or of taking a will.²

We wish this to be observed in the case of all persons whom the law shall have found living and none to be protected by the privilege of any past will, since, whether wills are shown to have been made previously ³ or to have been uncompleted,⁴ after this statute of our response ⁵ they may not have the liberty of possessing property or of petitioning for it—even of leaving an heir in the first category ⁶— by being a fideicommissary,⁷ by being a legatee, by being a secret fideicommissary ⁸ or by whatever naming of an heir the arrangement of the law has fixed in matters of this kind;⁹ but all property which shall have been proved to belong to or to be about to belong to such persons should be claimed as vacant property ¹⁰ for our fisc's resources.

In sum, they should have nothing in common with all other persons. Given on 4 May at Milan, Timasius and Promotus being consuls.[11]

1. Of the East.
2. The Latin is quite compressed. We should say "of making a will or of taking property bequeathed in a will".
3. Another example of retroactive legislation, on which see no. 176, n. 8.
4. When a will had been proved to be incomplete, e.g. if its maker had not complied with any of several sets of conditions (such as observance of certain formalities in regard to signature and attestation, disinheritance of certain persons by name if not nominated as heirs, bequest of a definite portion of property to certain persons, institution of heir in proper form, legal capacity of testator and witnesses and heir to perform their parts), the will was invalid *stricto sensu* and succession to the estate proceeded according to the rules of intestacy. However, the praetor could and often did apply the principle of equity to probate and thus would protect as heir the person named in the will, for the essence of the Roman will was the nomination of a universal successor to a deceased testator.
5. Literally "oracle" (*oraculum*), a term sometimes applied in late Latin to an imperial rescript (*rescriptum*), though the one implies speech and the other implies writing. But, so far as we know, this document was not a reply—did ancient oracles customarily offer advice unasked?—to any request.
6. Literally "by the first name" (*principali nomine*). A Roman had the privilege of naming several heirs in order, in the event that the first heir might refuse the estate (especially if it should be insolvent) or might predecease the testator or might be disqualified, for the grand goal of testation was to avoid intestacy. In this case, however, it appears that a Eunomian cannot name any heir at all.
7. A *fideicommissarius* is the beneficiary (A) of a trust, which is charged by the testator (B) upon the legal heir (C) to pay from the inheritance. Trusts (*fideicommissa*) entered Roman law in the principate of Augustus, though in the free Republic their existence had only moral recognition and their fulfilment depended on the honour of the heir.
8. Another instance of abstract for concrete: literally "by a secret bequest given for the benefit of a third person" (*tacito fideicommisso*). Such an arrangement presumably was oral.
9. Roman heirs are divisible into three classes: (1) his own (i.e. the testator's) and necessary heirs (*sui et necessarii heredes*)—those under the deceased's paternal power (*patria potestas*); (2) necessary heirs (*necessarii heredes*)—slaves who, as a last resort, could be named in the will (and freed) to prevent their masters' inheritance, if they should have died insolvent, from being sold in their masters' name, and thus would preserve them from posthumous disgrace; (3) extraneous heirs (*extranei heredes*)—all other persons not in the preceding categories.
10. On the meaning of this see no. 176, n. 7.

11. Perhaps it is to this law that Gibbon refers, when he attributes to Theodosius an entirely imaginary sense of irony in decreeing "that, as the Eunomians distinguished the nature of the Son from that of the Father, they should be incapable of making their wills or of receiving any advantage from testamentary donations" (3. 152).

219. MANDATE OF VALENTINIAN II, THEODOSIUS I, AND ARCADIUS ON PENALTIES FOR MANICHAEANS, 389
(CT 16. 5. 18)

Various disabilities are announced in this statute against Manichaeans.

The same Augusti to Albinus, urban prefect.[1]

Whosoever under the name of the Manichaeans disturb the world [2] should be expelled, under threat of judgement, indeed from the whole world,[3] but especially from this city.[4]

Moreover the said persons' wills, nay rather even their property, when confiscated to the people, should not keep the force of wills nor should it be lawful for property to be left through them or to the said persons.

In sum, they should have nothing in common with the world.[2]

Given on 17 June at Rome, Timasius and Promotus being consuls.

1. Of Rome.
2. The word is *mundus*, which means "the universe", "mankind"—a concept larger than *orbis terrarum* (cf. *infra* n. 3), which means "the circle of the earth", "the earth", especially the world of men wherein the Roman Empire's laws could be enforced.
3. The phrase is *ex omni orbe terrarum*. For *orbis terrarum* cf. *supra* n. 2.
4. Rome.

220. MANDATE OF VALENTINIAN II, THEODOSIUS I, AND ARCADIUS ON PASCHAL DAYS AND SUNDAYS AS LEGAL HOLIDAYS, 389

(CT 2. 8. 19)

Among other calendar regulations these emperors declare the paschal season and Sundays as holidays. The interpretation to this law adds Christmas and Epiphany to this list.

Justinian preserves this statute (CI 3. 12. 6).

Emperors Valentinian, Theodosius, and Arcadius Augusti to Albinus, urban prefect.[1]

We order all days to be judiciary. It shall be lawful for only those days to remain holidays which a rather indulgent year has accepted throughout doubled months for a respite from labour: for mitigating aestival heats and for gathering autumnal crops.[2]

We also assign, as usual, 1 January for rest.[3]

To these we add the natal days of the greatest cities, Rome and Constantinople,[4] by which the laws ought to be published, because these have been born also from them.[5]

We number in the same observance Easter's sacred days, which either precede or succeed (in each case seven in number),[6] and also the Sun's days,[7] which are revolved upon themselves by repeated reckoning.

It is necessary to have equal reverence [8] also for our days, which have produced either the origins of light or the beginnings of sovereignty.[9]

Given on 7 August at Rome, Timasius and Promotus being consuls.

Interpretation: We command that cases should be heard according to the laws on all days throughout the year's course.

And although the law has granted four months for collecting fruits, yet we have believed that it must be done so conformably with the nature of the provinces and conformably with the presence of the proprietors, that from 24 June until 1 August harvest holidays should be conceded and from 1 August until 23 August permission for pleading cases should be bestowed. But from 23 August until 15 October vintage holidays should be conceded.[2]

Also the Lord's days,[7] which are kept as holidays, we remove from hearing legal matters or from exacting debts; also the holy days of Easter, that is, the seven which precede and the seven which succeed.

We also desire the natal day of our Lord [10] and the day of the Epiphany [11] to be celebrated without judicial din.

Also it is appropriate for the birthday of the emperor or the beginning of his reign to be observed with equal reverence.

1. Of Rome.
2. Since summer and autumn technically comprise six months, the interpretation (q.v.) of the law properly clarifies the statute's vagueness and specifies part of June and all of July for the first period and part of August and all of September and part of October for the second period.

So in Minucius Felix, *Oct.* 2. 3, the vintage holidays brought relief from judicial duties. Earlier, however, in republican Rome during the Ciceronian age the last four months of the year were so crowded with spectacles and festivals that there was scarcely any work for a lawyer to do in court (Cicero, *Ad Att.* 1. 1. 2) and after August no criminal case (except trials for *vis* [violence] —usually interpreted as violence accompanied by armed bands to provoke riot—sedition, disturbances of various kinds, major breaches of official duty) could be initiated until January (see A. H. J. Greenidge, *The Legal Procedure of Cicero's Time* [Oxford, 1901], 456–7).

3. Caesar's reform of the Roman calendar in 46 B.C. (Suetonius, *Iul.* 40. 2) changed the year's initial month from March to January.
4. The traditional birthdays of Rome and Constantinople are respectively 21 April (753 B.C.) and 11 May (A.D. 330). The *Natale di Roma* is still a popular festival in Rome, marked by public receptions and by nocturnal illuminations. The celebration in Constantinople seems to have been ended by the Turkish capture of that city in 1453.

That Rome's birthday was 21 April is clear from Cicero (*De Div.* 2. 47. 98), who records it and equates it to the feast of Pales (the Italic tutelary god of shepherds), called the Parilia or Palilia, as well as from Plutarch (*Rom.* 12. 1), who remarks that the Romans annually celebrated it and called that day their fatherland's birthday. As for Constantinople: Hesychius (*Patria Cplis.* 1. 55) gives its day of dedication and annual celebration as 11 May (ed. T. Preger, *Scriptores Originum Constantinopolitanarum* [Leipzig, 1907], 2. 143).

In one Ciceronian passage (*Ad Att.* 4. 1. 4) is a triple reference to birthdays: the commemoration day of Brundisium (Brindisi, Italy), of the Temple of Safety (*Salus*) on the Quirinal Hill in Rome (cf. Nepos, *Att.* 13. 2), of Cicero's daughter Tullia—all three on the same day (5 August 57 B.C.). So it appears that the day whereon even a colony was founded also was celebrated.

5. True in each case by 389 (the year of this statute): although Rome was no longer the western capital (Milan, which had succeeded Rome in 285, was to yield in 395 to Ravenna), yet Roman law began there; when Constantinople became the eastern capital (330), imperial law was issued ordinarily thence.
6. Justinian inserts probably from no. 385 "also Christ's natal day and day of Epiphany and at what time the commemoration of the apostolic Passion, the teacher of all Christianity, is celebrated rightly by all persons; and also on the aforesaid most holy days we do not open the opportunity for spectacles",

220. PASCHAL DAYS AND SUNDAYS AS HOLIDAYS, 389   425

7. Justinian inserts "which our ancestors properly called the Lord's" from either *CT* 2. 8. 18 or 8. 8. 3 or 11. 7. 13 (these constitute no. 209). See also no. 34, n. 5.

8. Justinian inserts from no. 209 "that there should not be any cognizance of controversies before arbiters themselves, either demanded in law courts or selected voluntarily".

9. A periphrasis for their birthdays and their accessions.

In the case of these three emperors, who inaugurate legally this observance of their anniversaries, it is not known on what day any of them was born. Valentinian was acclaimed Augustus by the army on 23 November 375; Theodosius was raised to the purple by Gratian on 19 January 379; Arcadius received the imperial title from Theodosius on 19 January 383.

Justinian concludes his version thus: "Moreover in the fifteen paschal days should be deferred both compulsory collection of the grain-supply tax and exaction of all public and private debts."

10. Early in the fourth century (before 354) the Roman Church seems to have selected the feast of Christmas to offset the great pagan festival of the Unconquered Sun (*Sol Invictus*) and from Rome the celebration spread eastward. Thus devotion to Christ, "the Sun of Righteousness" (Mal. 4. 2), supplanted the commemoration of the cult of the Unconquered Sun.

11. As the name suggests, the feast of the Epiphany is of eastern (Greek) origin. The earliest references to the celebration of the manifestation of Jesus in the world point to the early third century in Egypt, where the event was commemorated on 6 January. But the evidence is interpreted variously: some suppose that this festival was introduced to supplant the manifestation of Osiris (Serapis, *al.* Sarapis), the Egyptian saviour-god (on whom see no. 111, n. 4); others opine that the feast celebrated Jesus' birth and/or baptism—particularly the latter. The association of the three Magi with the appearance of Jesus appears to be an African addition of the early fifth century.

Consult E. Stauffer's chapters on "Myth and Epiphany" and "Art Thou He That Should Come?" in his *Christ and the Caesars* (London, 1955), 15–41.

221. MANDATE OF VALENTINIAN II, THEODOSIUS I, AND ARCADIUS ON PROHIBITION OF CORPORAL PUNISHMENT DURING LENT, 389
(CT 9. 35. 5)

The title explains the law.

Emperors Valentinian, Theodosius, and Arcadius Augusti to Tatian, praetorian prefect.[1]

During the sacred days of Quadragesima,[2] during which absolution of souls is awaited, there should be no punishments of the body.

Given on 6 September at Forum Flaminii, Timasius and Promotus being consuls.

1. Of the East.
2. On the meaning of this word see no. 169, n. 3.

222. MANDATE OF VALENTINIAN II, THEODOSIUS I, AND ARCADIUS ON EXPULSION OF CLERICAL HERETICS FROM THEIR RELIGIOUS ASSEMBLIES, 389
(CT 16. 5. 19)

By this directive clerical leaders of heretical sects must be ejected from their meeting-places in or near Constantinople.

The same Augusti to Tatian, praetorian prefect.[1]

Those who retain the leadership of perverse dogma, that is, bishops, priests, deacons, and lectors, and any persons who under the veil of clerical office try to impose a blot upon religion, when established under the name of any heresy or error whatever, by all means should be expelled from their deadly meeting-places, whether they appear to be within the city[2] or in suburban places.

Given on 26 November at Milan, Timasius and Promotus being consuls.

1. Of the East.
2. Since the addressee was praetorian prefect of the East, it is likely that Constantinople is meant.

223. MANDATE OF VALENTINIAN II, THEODOSIUS I, AND ARCADIUS ON TREASURE-TROVE, 390
(CT 10. 18. 3)

In this constitution the emperors consider that divine inspiration may induce discovery of buried treasure.

Emperors Valentinian, Theodosius, and Arcadius Augusti to Neoterius, praetorian prefect.¹
Those persons who have found treasures by the inspiration of Divine Power ² or by Fortune's leadership we permit to enjoy the things found without any fear.³
Given on 2 March at Constantinople, Valentinian Augustus for the fourth time and Neoterius being consuls.

1. Perhaps of Illyricum.
2. From this document's date it seems that *by the inspiration of the Divine Power* (*suadente numine*) the Christian God is meant. But the discovery of treasure-trove through divine assistance ascends into pagan antiquity. From Hermes (Mercury), who was *par excellence* the divine inventor, comes the Greek common noun ἕρμαιον, which *inter alia* signifies treasure-trove. Persons probably prayed to Hermes to help them to find hidden treasure, just as Roman Catholics ask the aid of St Anthony of Padua (1195–1235) to lead them to their lost property.
Perhaps the best-known ancient case of divine inspiration causing discovery of treasure-trove is in Plautus' *Aulularia*. There the Lar Familiaris (on whom see no. 242, n. 6) or household god reveals to Euclio a hoard of gold buried by Euclio's grandfather. The Lar's action arises from the devotion of Phaedria, Euclio's daughter, who daily prays to him and supplicates him with garlands, incense, wine, or some other gift and who needs a dowry, which otherwise Euclio cannot provide (2–27). Even if the Latin play by Plautus (254–184 B.C.) may not have been adapted from a Greek comedy by Menander (?343–?291 B.C.), it doubtless descends from some Greek drama of the fourth century B.C. and thus testifies to belief in divine intervention in mortal interests.
Moreover, if Greeks believed that "a dream is from Zeus" (Homer, *Il.* 1. 63; cf. 2. 1–34), if Romans thought that Jupiter ordered dreams (e.g. Livy, *Ab Urbe Cond.* 21. 22. 6–9; Cicero, *De Div.* 1. 24. 49), if the Hebrew God expressly declared that he sometimes would reveal himself in dreams (Num. 12. 6; Joel 2. 28) and thus appeared to Abimelech (Gen. 20. 3), Laban (Gen. 31. 24), Solomon (1 Kings 3. 5), if in primitive Christian antiquity persons, such as the Magi and Joseph, were "warned of God in a dream" (Matt. 2. 12, 22) and if it was said of the latter that to him "an angel of the Lord appeareth in a dream" (Matt. 2. 19; cf. 2. 13), then Cicero's (106–43 B.C.) tale, taken from the Stoic

Chrysippus' (?280–?207 B.C.) treatise on dreams, is not malapropos, for in it a man had a dream, consulted a diviner, was told that a treasure was buried beneath his bed, dug there, and discovered a quantity of gold and silver. But Cicero comments that there must be many poor persons, deserving of the god's help, who never are warned by a dream how to find treasure (*De Div.* 2. 65. 134).

Completing Cicero's complaint, Boethius (?480–?524), the last pagan philosopher of prominence, who was conversant with Christian professions, believes that it is only chance which occurs when one digs the ground for the sake of cultivating a field and finds therein a hidden treasure (*De Cons. Phil.* 5. 1 *ad fin.*). He bases his belief on Aristotle, whom he quotes and who asserts that what commonly is ascribed to chance really results from an unexpected coincidence of causes (*Phys.* 2. 4–6 = 195B–8A).

3. From the edict (*CT* 10. 18. 2) preserved just before the present constitution, which is ten years later, it appears that the finder, if in Constantinople at least, might have had two causes for fear: (1) that he must offer a fourth part of the find to the owner of the property whereon he found it; (2) that he was subject to an unspecified penalty, if he prospected on another's property either on his own initiative or because of common report that there treasure was concealed. The earlier edict removed two other reasons for fear: (1) chicanery due to information lodged by anyone in the name of either the fisc or private citizens; (2) danger of torture on account of either the quality of the metal or the amount of the find. Still earlier (*CT* 10. 18. 1; dated 315) the finder had another fear to face: that of torture if he failed to report to the fisc his find and then to give one half of it to the fisc. The fisc's interest in finds ascends to Hadrian's reign (117–38), wherein that emperor ruled that the State should share equally with the finder who found treasure-trove on land belonging to the fisc or to the people or to the emperor (*II* 2. 1. 39).

224. MANDATE OF VALENTINIAN II, THEODOSIUS I, AND ARCADIUS ON EXEMPTION OF CLERICAL PROPERTY FROM MUNICIPAL LEVY, 390

(*CT* 12. 1. 121)

It seems that Theodosius the Great, whose capital was at Milan, whence this ordinance was issued, was the author of this constitution to free from levy for the municipal senates the estates of such senators as had become either priests or deacons or exorcists before his second consulate (388).

The same Augusti to Tatian, praetorian prefect.[1]
Whoever from the curial order [2] has undertaken either the rank of

priest or the ministry of deacon or the office of exorcist before my Gentleness' second consulate,³ all his patrimony should be held exempt and free from curial bonds.

But he who under any title whatever shall have devoted himself after the aforesaid consulate's prescribed period to religious duties of divine worship should know that all his patrimony must be surrendered.

Given on 17 June at Milan, Valentinian Augustus for the fourth time and Neoterius being consuls.

1. Of the East.
2. See no. 325, n. 6.
3. Before 388.

225. MANDATE OF VALENTINIAN II, THEODOSIUS I, AND ARCADIUS ON DEACONESSES' LEGACIES, 390

(CT 16. 2. 27)

By this constitution, which was repealed both in the same year of its issuance (no. 227) and also 65 years later (no. 488), deaconesses, some of whom were widows, are forbidden to bequeath their property to churches or to clergymen or to paupers. Sozomen (*HE* 7. 16 *ad fin.*) says that Theodosius enacted this statute as the result of a scandal in the Constantinopolitan Church.

Some scholars see in this law an important restriction of the right recognized by Constantine I as belonging to the Church, which he allowed to accept legacies (no. 36); others believe that the law again attacks legacy-hunting clerics, who were still active despite previous prohibition (no. 150); still others consider the law only as a means of protecting, against the abuse of maternal power, the children's rights to their parents' succession.

This law also fixes the minimum age for admission of women into the diaconate—the only section of it adopted by Justinian (*CI* 1. 3. 9)—and forbids Christian women to cut their hair.

Emperors Valentinian, Theodosius, and Arcadius Augusti to Tatian, praetorian prefect.[1]

According to the apostle's precept [2] no woman should be transferred to the society of deaconesses, unless sixty years have elapsed and she has the desired progeny at home.[3]

Then, after a guardian has been requested for her children, if their age demands it, she should entrust to suitable persons her property to be managed by careful conscientiousness, but she herself should obtain of her estates only the revenues, over which she should have complete power of keeping, of alienating, of giving, of selling, of bequeathing, either as long as she lives or when she dies,[4] and her will is unrestrained. She should spend nothing on jewels and adornment, nothing on gold, silver, and all other decorations of a distinguished house under the claim of religion;[5] but she should transfer all her property intact to her children or to nearest relatives or to any other persons whomsoever by the judgement of her own free will and, whenever she shall have died,[6] she should appoint as heirs no church, no clergyman, no pauper. For it [7] necessarily should lack validity, if it [7] shall have been made by the dying woman contrary to the prohibition concerning the persons specifically described.

By all means, if anything shall have been extorted from the dying woman by these persons, nothing should be conferred upon clergymen for the evasion of this venerable sanction by a secret trust through cunning device or through anyone's shameful connivance; they should be deprived of all property which they had coveted.[8] And if by chance anything is discovered to have been transferred through letter, codicil, donation, will, finally by any way at all, to those persons whom we have debarred by this sanction, this should not be fetched into court,[9] but he who understands that he is qualified should receive the succession from an intestate person according to this statute's definition, if anyone recognizes him as a son, if anyone proves him a relative; finally, if anyone either by chance or by will is discovered an heir, a legatee, a fideicommissary,[10] for the entire estate or for part of it, by open codicils,[11] he should enjoy the gift of fortune, the fruit of his knowledge, and, after these persons have been debarred and deprived, he should exercise an heir's control over the inherited substance.

Women who shall have shorn their hair contrary to divine and human laws[12] at the prompting of a profession, of which they have been persuaded,[13] should be debarred from the doors of a church. It should not be right for them to approach the consecrated mysteries [14] nor by any supplications they should be entitled to frequent the altars venerated by all—to the end that even a bishop himself, if he shall have permitted a woman with shorn head to enter, when he has been removed from his position, should be debarred with companions of this ilk [15] and should know that nothing will aid him,[16] not only if he shall have recommended that this[17] is to be done, but also if he shall have discovered that this[17] is demanded by any persons, and, finally, that this[17] has been done in any way at all.[18]

Without doubt this shall be as a law for persons needing punishment and as a customary practice for persons already punished, that the latter may have evidence [19] and the former may begin to fear judgement.

Given on 21 June at Milan, Valentinian Augustus for the fourth time and the most distinguished Neoterius being consuls.

1. Of the East.
2. So St Paul (1 Tim. 5. 9) commanded that a widow under sixty years of age should not be accepted into the order of widows, on which see no. 92, n. 1.
3. This is Justinian's excerpt, which, however, excises the clause concerning children. Pitra (2. 477) has a late Greek version of it.
4. The Latin is euphemistic: "when she yields to the fates".
5. That is, as if for religious purposes.
6. Another euphemism: "whenever she shall have gone to meet the day".
7. Her last will is meant.
8. Literally "at which they eagerly had gazed".
9. That is, this information must not be cited in court as proof of the citer's claim.
10. On him see no. 218, n. 7.
11. Clandestine documents thus are excluded.
12. What human law may have existed on this subject probably was derived from what St Paul wrote in 1 Cor. 11. 3–15.
13. For a woman to be shaven or shorn against her will was considered a disgrace among certain ancient peoples. Among the Greeks it was the sign of a slave (Aristophanes, *Aves*, 911) or of infamy (id., *Thesm.* 838). Among the Germans a husband could punish his adulterous wife by shearing her hair (Tacitus, *Ger.* 19. 1)—a modern analogue is the partisans' treatment of women who had carnal connection with German soldiers in German-occupied territories in World War II. But shaving the head was also a mark of mourning among the Jews: when an Israelite had captured a Gentile woman in war and wanted to wed her, she shaved her head in mourning for her parents (Deut. 21. 10–13), but also probably if parentless, to signify her purification from pagan defilement, if unmarried, or possibly, if married, to show her lamentation for her previous husband. And likewise among the Greeks it was customary for women voluntarily to shave their hair when mourning, according to Plutarch (*Quaest. Rom.* 14D), St Paul's late contemporary.

The *prompting of a profession of which they have been persuaded* apparently ascends to the Pauline context (n. 12 *supra*). St Paul, it is supposed, points to some of the Christian women in Corinth who claimed for themselves equality with men, an equality doubtless engendered by his doctrine of Christian freedom with its removal of distinction of sex (Gal. 3. 28). The privilege to cut their hair then came from this *profession*. The claim to this right persisted among Christian women elsewhere. To take only one instance, almost mid-way between St Paul and Valentinian: Tertullian denounces Christian women in

Africa who shave their head or shear their hair (*De Virg. Vel.* 7. 2 = *CSEL* 76. 89).

14. See no. 75, n. 42.

15. Either the bishop's clergy who concurred with his practice or the women whom he thus admitted.

16. To regain his office or to make a successful defence of his act.

17. The admission of such a woman.

18. Either with or without his knowledge.

19. That this is why they have been punished.

226. MANDATE OF VALENTINIAN II, THEODOSIUS I, AND ARCADIUS ON ECCLESIASTICAL EXEMPTION FROM PUBLIC DUTIES, 390

(*CT* 11. 16. 18)

This law repeats much of an earlier statute (no. 186) on the same subject, especially in respect to what public services of a menial character are not required from the Church as a corporation.

Emperors Valentinian, Theodosius, and Arcadius Augusti to Tatian, praetorian prefect.[1]

We order that by all means none should obtain the benefits of [2] extraordinary public services,[3] but whatever the common performance of such service shall have demanded from all peoples, this we order should be fulfilled by all persons without distinction as to merits and to persons.

To be sure, occasion is not lacking when we free the privileges either of merits or of ranks [4] from participation, if indeed we should forbid persons excepted by law to undertake those public services which are called menial,[5] obviously lest to the services of these should be summoned also the titles [6] of the most distinguished ranks of the governmental [7] highest dignity or the consistorial counts. And these rights by a similar privilege we bestow upon churches,[8] rhetoricians,[9] and grammarians [9] of each instruction.[10]

And lest in secret should lie hidden what it is, the enumeration of menial public services,[5] indicated by their own names, follows [5]. . . .

The men thus enumerated shall know that all these rights pertain to their own privilege, that they may understand that these have not been granted to their wives' properties and have been limited to their own patrimonies by the period of their life. For an heir shall not be able to claim securely these rights, which have been conferred upon individual persons in consideration of their labours.

Given on 5 July at Milan, Valentinian Augustus for the fourth time and Neoterius being consuls.

1. Of the East.
2. To fill the sense "exemption from" in English should be added.
3. Extraordinary public services included payment of extraordinary taxes and of superindictions (additional taxes assessed when normal taxes were insufficient) and liability for conscripted labour and for extra transport provision.
4. Abstract for concrete: "deserving persons . . . high-ranking persons" are meant.
5. See no. 186, n. 5, where is explained the omission in that document, because there and here is a long list of the menial services without ecclesiastical interest.
6. Again abstraction to *dignity*: "men whose titles indicate the most distinguished posts in the loftiest echelon of governmental service". See no. 586, n. 2.
7. On this adjective see no. 186, n. 4.
8. As in no. 186 (cf. n. 5 *ad init.*), so here the editors think that *churches* has been interpolated.
9. See no. 186, n. 6, for the same concession.
10. That is, of Greek and of Latin.

227. MANDATE OF VALENTINIAN II, THEODOSIUS I, AND ARCADIUS ON RESCISSION OF LAW ON DEACONESSES' LEGACIES, 390

(*CT* 16. 2. 28)

Apparently the clerical interest at the imperial court had been sufficiently strong to compel the cancellation of the two-months-old law (no. 225) forbidding deaconesses to bequeath property to the Church, for its annulment was announced by the following constitution.

The same Augusti to Tatian, praetorian prefect.[1]

Lest anyone, namely, a clergyman, or lest anyone in the Church's name should seize slaves, household furnishings, property,[2] as a despoiler of the weaker[3] sex, and, in the absence of relatives by marriage and by blood, should conduct himself under pretext of Catholic discipline as an heir of a living person, he should notice that

434   228. SEQUESTRATION OF MONKS, 390

the law [4] which recently has been promulgated about deaconesses or widows has been revoked to that extent that it should be withdrawn from the records of all persons, if it has been registered already, and that anyone should know that either, as a litigant, it must not be used for his benefit or, as a governor, it must not be executed.

Given on 23 August at Verona, Valentinian Augustus for the fourth time and Neoterius being consuls.

1. Of the East.
2. Literally "booty" (*praeda*), but perhaps "estates" (*praedia*) should be read.
3. Literally "infirm", i.e. female.
4. No. 225.

228. MANDATE OF VALENTINIAN II, THEODOSIUS I, AND ARCADIUS ON SEQUESTRATION OF MONKS, 390
(CT 16. 3. 1)

During the latter part of the fourth century and until the Council of Chalcedon in 451, when the hierarchy finally gained firm control over the ascetical clergy, the communities of the Empire, especially in the East, frequently were cast into confusion by intermittent invasion of itinerant monks, who not only participated egregiously in ecclesiastical politics, particularly in Alexandria [1] and Constantinople,[2] but also recruited the ranks of the pauperized portion of the populace and, as religious fanatics and as opponents of political and social injustice, often were ringleaders of riots.

Monastic interference with execution of verdicts in criminal cases (see no. 237) seems to have inspired this order, which commands monks to live in solitary places distant from municipalities, but which was repealed (no. 237) two years later.

Emperors Valentinian, Theodosius, and Arcadius Augusti to Tatian, praetorian prefect.[3]

Whosoever are found in the profession of monks should be ordered to go to and to dwell in desert places and waste solitudes.

Given on 2 September at Verona, Valentinian Augustus for the fourth time and Neoterius being consuls.

1. Palladius, in his *Historia Lausiaca*, which is devoted almost entirely to Egyptian monasticism as he observed it in the fourth century's last decade (see no. 284, n. 2), and in his *Dialogus de Vita Sancti Joannis Chrysostomi*, 17 [PG 47.

58–60], which is our primary source for St Chrysostom's life (see no. 284, n. 1), paints a rather favourable picture of the ascetic in the Alexandrian patriarchate. But against this must be set the stories of Egyptian monks, who often swarmed from the desert into Alexandria, led tumults, attacked soldiers, defended usually or occasionally opposed the patriarchal policy against Constantinople (see no. 284, n. 4), and—most notoriously—induced the death of Hypatia, on whom see no. 98, n. 14.

2. Although monasticism is said to have been introduced into Constantinople as early as Constantine I's reign, it appears that "the true beginnings of Byzantine monasticism coincide with the reign of Theodosius" (H. Delehaye in N. H. Baynes and H. St L. B. Moss, eds., *Byzantium* [Oxford, 1948], 144–5). Just one year after the period of this sylloge ends, 108 monasteries are known to have existed in Constantinople and in Chalcedon across the Sea of Marmara from the capital. Of these how many were centres of indolence and how many were centres of industry is unknown.

3. Of the East.

229. MANDATE OF VALENTINIAN II, THEODOSIUS I, AND ARCADIUS ON RELIGIOUS SIGNIFICANCE OF THE DECURIONATE, 390

(CT 12. 1. 122)

In this law the emperors invest the decurionate with religion's sanctity and insist that it is sinful to desert it.

The same Augusti to Tatian, praetorian prefect.[1]
Those persons to whom we have granted splendid magistracies and whom we also have adorned with the insignia of dignities, if they have not a municipal senate to which they are bound either by the tie of kinship or by the bond of blood, should be co-opted into the most splendid senatorial order and that most noble senate.

But the arrangement should be different for those who began to be curials immediately when they were born. For these persons indeed should employ the prerogative of the conferred dignity and the splendour of the bestowed honour should adorn them, but they should abide in the bosom of their native community and, just as if dedicated to the fillets,[2] should guard the perennial mystery.[3] For them to depart should be a sin. But concerning their sons it has been provided sufficiently that they must remain in their ancestral municipal senates, since licence of departure has been taken from their fathers.

Given on 2 September at Verona, Valentinian Augustus for the fourth time and Neoterius being consuls.

1. Of the Orient.
2. On these see no. 520, n. 6.
3. Christianity must be meant in view of the document's date. The same attempt to surround the office with a religious air occurred seven years later (no. 263). On *mystery* see no. 75, n. 42.

230. MANDATE OF VALENTINIAN II, THEODOSIUS I, AND ARCADIUS ON PROFANERS OF BAPTISM, 391

(*CT* 16. 7. 4)

Since Christian apostasy involves ecclesiastically the profanation of Christian baptism, imperial legislation inveighs against such pollution of Christian birthright. While this law is in the title "On Apostates", it may have been aimed at those who either repeat baptism or deviate from the orthodox formula of baptism.

Justinian also has this constitution (*CI* 1. 7. 3), of which the initial part is found also in *CT* 11. 39. 11.

Emperors Valentinian, Theodosius, and Arcadius Augusti to Flavian, praetorian prefect.[1]

Those who shall have betrayed the holy faith and shall have profaned holy [2] baptism [3] should be segregated from all persons' association, should be debarred from testifying,[4] should not have—as we previously have ordained [5]—the making of a will, should succeed to no one in an inheritance, should be written by no one as heirs.

And these also we should have commanded to be banished to a distance and to be removed rather far away, if it had not seemed to be a greater penalty for them to dwell among men and to lack men's approbation.

But they never shall return to their previous status, the shame of their conduct shall not be obliterated by penitence [6] and shall not be concealed by any shade of elaborate defence or protection, since things which are fabricated and fashioned cannot protect indeed those who have polluted the faith which they had vowed to God and who, betraying the divine mystery,[7] have turned to profanations. And indeed for the lapsed and the errant there is help, but for the lost—

that is, the profaners of holy baptism—there is no aid through any remedy of penitence, which is wont to be available for other crimes.

Given on 11 May at Concordia, Tatian and Symmachus being consuls.

1. Of Italy. See also no. 231, n. 1.
2. *CT*. 11. 39. 11 has "sacred" (*sacrum*) for *holy* (*sanctum*).
3. Justinian adds "by heretical superstition".
4. Here *CT* 11. 39. 11 stops, adds "and the rest", and appends the subscription.
5. Possibly no. 218, where Eunomians, who held inadequate views on baptism, thus are penalized.
6. Pitra prints (2. 577) a late Greek paraphrase as far as this point: "They who have betrayed the holy faith and have profaned the holy baptism should not be associated with any person or should not be witnesses in others' wills, should not have the making of a will, and, written by none as heirs, should not inherit as heirs.

"And these we were about both to banish and to punish rather vindictively, if we had not considered it to be a greater penalty for them not to be allowed to dwell among men and to be esteemed among men.

"They should not return to their previous status, for their very sin is not carried into forgetfulness as a result of penitence."

The "not" in the second sentence seems to be misplaced and is not found in either of the Latin documents. If it should be inserted, it should be read rather before "to be esteemed".
7. See no. 164, n. 18.

231. MANDATE OF VALENTINIAN II, THEODOSIUS I, AND ARCADIUS ON DISHONOUR FOR APOSTATE NOBLES, 391

(*CT* 16. 7. 5)

This directive degrades and brands with infamy noblemen who have forsaken Christianity.

The same Augusti to Flavian,[1] praetorian prefect.

If any splendour of rank has been conferred upon or has been inborn in those persons who, turned from faith and blinded in mind, had departed from the sacrosanct religion's revered cult [2] and had delivered themselves to sacrifices, let it be lost, that they, when degraded from their position and status, may be branded with infamy and not even in the lowest portion of the ignoble crowd may be numbered.

For what can be for these in common with men, if they, detesting by abominable and dangerous minds the grace of communion, have withdrawn from men?

Given on 11 May at Concordia, Tatian and Symmachus being consuls.

1. Virius Nicomachus Flavianus, a learned pagan philosopher and a master of augural lore, on whose career consult S. Dill, *Roman Society in the Last Century of the Western Empire* [2] (London, 1899), 19-21, 35-6. As a past proponent of reactionary paganism and the future restorer of the pagan Altar of Victory to its former place in the Roman Senate, Flavian probably did not over-exert himself to secure obedience to this statute, issued when he was praetorian prefect of Italy.

2. Literally "cult and reverence", but probably a hendiadys.

232. LETTER OF VALENTINIAN II, THEODOSIUS I, AND ARCADIUS ON EXPULSION OF HERETICS FROM COMMUNITIES, 391

(*CT* 16. 5. 20)

This constitution is a general order for extrusion of heretics from cities and villages and a ban against their assemblies.

Copy of a sacred letter.

We order the heretics' polluted contagions to be driven from cities, to be ejected from villages, and the communities [1] not at all to be available for any meetings, lest in any place a sacrilegious company of such persons should be collected. Neither public meeting-places to their perversity nor more hidden retreats to their errors should be granted.

Given on 19 May at Rome, the most distinguished Tatian and the most distinguished Symmachus being consuls.

1. Some such expression should be understood here.

233. MANDATE OF VALENTINIAN II, THEODOSIUS I, AND ARCADIUS ON ADMISSION OF CURIALS TO THE CLERICATE, 391

(CT 12. 1. 123)

The emperors establish certain regulations for such municipal senators as have entered the Church to serve as clergymen.

The same Augusti to Tatian, praetorian prefect.[1]

Our sanctions' clear authority [2] has proceeded previously concerning those persons who, after having deserted a municipal senate, either have acquired senatorial rank or by the pretext of Christianity have separated themselves from the association of curials, to the effect that, if either position or religion defended the said persons, whatever from their curial property [3] they themselves either retained or had transferred to others should be held as obligated to public assessments.

By our command [2] also has been expressed a clear time—from what consulate they should know that to the municipal senate must be surrendered all their patrimony, if they had fled for refuge from the curialate [4] to the Church.

Whatever from curials' property shall have come to anyone soever on separate occasions of bestowal should be held as obligated to the denarism or ounce in that part in which it had been retained in the originator's name.[5]

Moreover we obligate those persons who, having obtained any honours, have changed their natural title [6] for the new rank, after the honour to those public services for which they shall be shown to be debtors to their native community.

Moreover concerning the sons of such persons there is the definition of a clear sanction,[7] which, since it does not allow fathers to withdraw from their native communities, cannot liberate sons from the municipal senate's public services.

Moreover, if any persons, engaged in divine worship and serving the sacrosanct mysteries,[8] rely on their sons' statutory succession, if their sons hitherto hold no place in the Church or are not protected by those offices which have been embraced by the laws, we decree that these persons should serve the municipal senate with their fathers' properties.

Moreover a municipal senate shall claim for itself estates unoccupied and vacant without natural succession—as we clearly have expressed [9]—for the purpose of having the solace of the properties for which is lacking the number of persons in respect to performances of services.

Given on 28 July at Constantinople, Tatian and Symmachus being consuls.

1. Of the East.
2. No. 224 and probably no. 229.
3. That is, the property which as municipal senators they owned.
4. The Latin concrete is translated better here by the English abstract.
5. This sentence is clarified somewhat by *CT* 12. 1. 107, the only other *locus* (apparently) where *denarismus* occurs in Latin. There it seems that a tax of a denarius or of an ounce (? of gold) is collected ordinarily in the name of a previous owner from a recipient of property inherited from or donated by the previous owner, who had been a member of a municipal senate.
6. This means not a change in the name received at birth (*naturale nomen*), but rather the social class into which they have been born and which they now leave on promotion to a higher class by becoming recipients of some honours conferred by the State, which then expects such persons to perform such public services as devolve upon such honoured persons.
7. The oldest legislation on this point seems to ascend to Constantine I's reign (*CT* 12. 1. 7, 12. 1. 12). Later emperors confirmed and elaborated Constantine's regulations. Especially applicable are *CT* 12. 1. 86 (dated 381) and no. 229 (dated 390).
8. See no. 75, n. 42.
9. *CT* 5. 2. 1 (dated 319, but editorially postponed to 352).

234. MANDATE OF VALENTINIAN II, THEODOSIUS I, AND ARCADIUS ON CLERICAL INTERFERENCE IN CRIMINAL CASES, 392

(*CT* 9. 40. 15)

Ecclesiastical efforts to save condemned criminals from satisfying their sentences, whether by appeal or by abduction, are prohibited by this law.

The same Augusti to Tatian, praetorian prefect.[1]
If anyone shall have been convicted as a defendant of a very great crime and shall have been subjected to sentence, the competent judgement should be fulfilled and clever artifice should not be furnished with stratagems of this sort: that he is declared to have been snatched by clergymen or is pretended to have appealed.
But if anyone after the judgement shall have offered assent to this licence by vendible connivance, he shall sustain pena'ties not at all light. For proconsuls, counts of the East, Augustal prefects, also vicars, having been afflicted with the disgraceful mark,[2] shall pay to the fisc's assets thirty pounds of gold apiece, but ordinary judges,[3] having

been disgraced similarly, shall be compelled to pay fifteen apiece. Moreover office staffs of the aforesaid persons shall be subject to the same costs as their own governors, if they shall have defaulted in suggestion and shall not have applied the law's command and shall not have thwarted by imposition of force the convicted persons from being removed and if they shall not have carried into effect and execution that which shall have been determined.

Given on 13 March at Constantinople, Arcadius Augustus for the second time and Rufinus being consuls.

1. Of the East.
2. That is, made infamous. The metaphor descends from the censorial *nota* made on the civic registers by the censors, whenever they believed that a citizen should be degraded for cause. See no. 173, n. 10.
3. The five officials listed here were civil governors: proconsul for the provinces of Achaea, Africa, Asia; count of the East for the diocese of the East; Augustal prefect for the diocese of Egypt (see no. 489, n. 12); vicar for other dioceses; ordinary judge (usually called simply judge, sometimes archon, assistant, cognitor, consular, corrector, dicast, eparch, hegemon, moderator, ordinary cognitor, prefect, president, proconsul, propraetor, prostates, rector, strategus) for other provinces.

This great variety of titles—not to include various circumlocutions—arises from historical origins and is connected also with a governorship's importance and with a province's size.

235. MANDATE OF THEODOSIUS I, ARCADIUS, AND HONORIUS ON CLERICAL INTEREST IN APPEALS, 392

(*CT* 11. 36. 31)

In a futile effort to discourage appeals to higher courts this directive penalizes a governor's (or a judge's) aides, when appeals have been taken from a judge's verdict, and allows no excuse that any of the clergy has encouraged a litigant to appeal.

Emperors Theodosius, Arcadius, and Honorius Augusti to Hypatius, Augustal prefect.[1]

An office staff which has reported that convicted persons appeal or persons after confession appeal should pay thirty pounds of gold to the fisc, and not any person of the bishops or of the clergy or of the people should be reported to intervene or to have intervened. For it is not right that from due severity should be deprived those persons, who have disturbed by rebellious contumacy the public peace, already confused by the disorder of their acts—the judge himself also not being ignorant that he must be punished by the same fine as the office staff, unless he shall have fulfilled his duty after pronouncement of sentence.

Given on 9 April at Constantinople, Arcadius Augustus for the second time and Rufinus being consuls.

1. On this title see no. 489, n. 12.

236. MANDATE OF VALENTINIAN II, THEODOSIUS I, AND ARCADIUS ON SUPPRESSION OF CIRCENSIAN CONTESTS ON SUNDAY, 392

(CT 2. 8. 20)

The emperors ban by this enactment games in the circus on Sundays, save when their birthdays fall on such days.

The same Augusti to Proculus, urban prefect.[1]
On the Sun's festal days [2] contests of the circuses must be prevented, that no uproar from the spectacles [3] may avert the Christian law's [4] venerated mysteries,[5] except on our Clemencies' birthdays.

Given on 17 April at Constantinople, Arcadius Augustus for the second time and Rufinus being consuls.

1. Of Constantinople.
2. See no. 34, n. 5.
3. It is possible that *concursus spectaculorum* may mean "running together [of the populace] to the spectacles". Whether the crowded condition of the streets adjacent to the arenas or the racket rising from the spectators is meant, in any event either would have the effect of distracting persons' minds from the celebration of religious worship. Probably the latter circumstance is meant (see no. 243, n. 6), at least so far as was the case at Constantinople, where the citizens were divided into factions and "fought with throats in the Hippodrome and occasionally with knives in the streets".

The most famous factional riot in this sylloge's period occurred in 532 at Constantinople—the notorious Nika sedition, so called from the factional slogan of νίκα (conquer), shouted by the rioters, who rioted for a week, burned many public buildings (including the Theodosian Church of the Holy

236. CIRCENSIAN CONTESTS ON SUNDAY, 392

Wisdom, on which see no. 505, n. 1), and were pacified only after myriads (between 30,000 and 50,000) of Constantinopolitans had been massacred by a promiscuous carnage in the Hippodrome (consult J. B. Bury, "The Nika Riot" in *Journal of Hellenic Studies*, 17 [1897] 92–119; H. Lamb, *Constantinople: Birth of an Empire* [New York, 1957], 84–105).

Although by 70 in Rome in the Circus Maximus, whence any contests celebrated there were called the Circensian Games (*ludi circenses*), there were four factions (*factiones*) or companies of contractors who provided horses, riders, drivers, chariots, and all other requisites for the races, yet long ere the Nika riot the favourite factions in Constantinople were only two: the Blues and the Greens. To the traditional white (*albata*) and red (*russata*) had been added green (*prasina*) and blue (*veneta*)—so Tertullian, *De Spect.* 9 *ad fin.*; Suetonius, *Gaius*, 55. 2, *Vit.* 7. 1—purple (*purpurea*) and gold (*aurata*) under Domitian (Suetonius, *Dom.* 7. 1) being only temporary additions c. 83. The factions took their names from the jockeys' and the charioteers' coloured tunics, whose colours popularly were held to symbolize seasonal hues: white for winter's snow, green for spring's verdure, red for summer's heat, blue for autumn's haze (Tertullian, loc. cit.). Perhaps the Constantinopolitan predominance of Greens and Blues was interpreted as indicative of the age-old contest between the blue sea (or sky) and the green earth (Cassiodorus, *Var.* 3. 51).

Though οἱ πολλοί were in both major parties in Constantinople, the Blues generally recruited their leaders from the senatorial and land-owning aristocracy and usually supported orthodoxy, but the Greens normally found their chiefs among industry and the civil service and frequently favoured heterodoxy (see F. Dvornik, "The Circus Parties in Byzantium" in *Byzantina-Metabyzantina*, 1. 1 [1946] 119–33).

The most eloquent Christian diatribe against spectacles of any kind probably is Tertullian's treatise *De Spectaculis* (*CSEL* 20. 1–29). About a century earlier Pliny the Younger in an eloquent epistle (9. 6) inveighed against those citizens whose interest was excited by the colours of the charioteers' tunics. On spectacles consult L. Friedländer, *Roman Life and Manners in the Early Empire* (London, 1913), 2. 1–130, esp. 19–40 for races in the circus with his notes thereon in 4. 499–510 and with his appendices on charioteers and racing in 4. 148–66.

4. Religion.
5. See no. 75, n. 42.

237. MANDATE OF VALENTINIAN II, THEODOSIUS I, AND ARCADIUS ON RESTORATION OF MONKS, 392
(CT 16. 3. 2)

This law repeals one issued two years previously (no. 228), when monks were banned from municipalities for intervention into the processes of justice.

The same Augusti to Tatian, praetorian prefect.[1]
We order monks, to whom municipalities have been forbidden, while they are nourished [2] by judicial injustices, to be in their original status by the withdrawal of this law.[3]
Since, therefore, our Clemency's order [3] has been abolished, we grant to them free entrances into towns.
Given on 17 April at Constantinople, Arcadius Augustus for the second time and Rufinus being consuls.

1. Of the East.
2. If this reading is correct (for others have been proposed), the idea may be that the monks thrived, when they had the opportunity (now restored), on their attempt to save convicted criminals from execution of their sentences, but that when they had been compelled by the previous law to live in desert solitudes they languished and received few recruits.
3. No. 228.

238. MANDATE OF VALENTINIAN II, THEODOSIUS I, AND ARCADIUS ON SUSPENSION OF LITIGATION AT EASTERTIDE, 392
(CT 2. 8. 21)

Within three years of similar legislation on this subject (no. 220) Theodosius found it necessary to repeat briefly that litigation should be suspended during the seven days before and after Easter.
Justinian preserves this statute in *CI* 3. 12. 7.

The same Augusti [1] to Tatian, praetorian prefect.[2]
All legal actions, whether public or private, should be excluded from [3] the fifteen paschal days.

Given on 27 May at Constantinople, Arcadius Augustus for the second time and Rufinus being consuls.

1. It has been noted (no. 193, n. 1) that an emperor's death did not necessarily erase immediately his name from constitutions issued later by his colleagues. In any event it is unlikely that news of Valentinian II's murder on 15 May 392 at Vienne, France, reached Constantinople by this mandate's date.
2. Of the East.
3. Justinian reads "should stop during" and adds with slight modification a clause from no. 37.

239. MANDATE OF VALENTINIAN II, THEODOSIUS I, AND ARCADIUS ON HERETICAL ORDINATION AND WORSHIP, 392

(*CT* 16. 5. 21)

By this constitution penalties are enacted against heretics who ordain and are ordained clergymen and against persons permitting heretics to conduct religious services on their premises.

This statute seems to be the first of several directed against either owners or rentiers of large estates on which Christians lived, but which were not within the municipal magistrates' jurisdiction. The owner or the possessor—as the case might have been—was practically supreme in his control of the serfs and of the slaves who farmed his plantation and apparently he appointed ecclesiastical ministers as he appointed his stewards. Therefore in the interests of orthodoxy a limitation of such owners' or rentiers' rights was considered necessary by the emperors, who repeat such legislation for almost a generation.

The same Augusti [1] to Tatian, praetorian prefect.[2]

In the case of heretical errors we decree that whosoever shall have been proved either to have ordained clergymen or to have undertaken the office of clergymen must be fined ten pounds of gold each and that, forsooth, the place in which prohibited practices are attempted, if the owner's connivance shall have been obvious, shall be attached to our fisc's resources.

But if it shall have been proved that the rentier had not known this, because it had been done secretly, we order the leaseholder of this estate, if he is free-born, to pay ten pounds [3] to our fisc; if, descended from servile dregs, he scorns the penalty of the fine because of his poverty and low degree, after having been beaten with cudgels he shall be condemned to deportation.

Furthermore we especially provide the following: that if the villa shall have been imperial or subject to any public right at all and if the leaseholder or [4] the manager shall have granted the privilege of assembling, they shall be fined ten pounds of gold by this published condemnation.

But if it shall have been revealed that any persons have been found to perform such mysteries [5] and to usurp even now for themselves the titles of clergymen, we order ten pounds of gold apiece to be exacted and them to pay these.

Given on 15 June at Constantinople, Arcadius Augustus for the second time and Rufinus being consuls.

1. See no. 238, n. 1.
2. Of the East.
3. The quality of the coin is not named, but it undoubtedly is gold, as elsewhere in this ordinance.
4. The conjectural *vel* for the textual *et* is translated.
5. See no. 75, n. 42.

240. MANDATE OF VALENTINIAN II, THEODOSIUS I, AND ARCADIUS ON DISTURBERS OF RELIGION, 392
(CT 16. 4. 3)

Even if this police measure may not have been directed against heretics primarily, it still protects orthodox believers.

The same Augusti [1] to Potamius, Augustal prefect.[2]

Whoever, neither warned by the general law nor corrected by a suitable sentence, should disturb the Catholic faith and people is deserving of deportation.

Given on 18 July at Constantinople, Arcadius Augustus for the second time and the most distinguished Rufinus being consuls.

1. See no. 238, n. 1.
2. On this title see no. 489, n. 12.

241. MANDATE OF THEODOSIUS I, ARCADIUS, AND HONORIUS ON SANCTUARY, 392
(CT 9. 45. 1)

The age-old flight to sacred buildings for protection from just or unjust pursuers was not unknown in the pre-Christianized Empire.[1] So it was not at all a novelty that, after the State had recognized Christianity and as the Christian clergy's influence in public affairs became prominent, persons seeking sanctuary should not neglect to consider Christian churches as affording superior asylum.[2] As the custom continued, legislation to control it became necessary.

The first authentic attempt on the State's part to regulate the privilege of sanctuary [3] for persons fleeing to churches appears to be the subsequent constitution, which commands the surrender of debtors to the fisc.[1]

Emperors Theodosius, Arcadius, and Honorius Augusti to Romulus, count of the sacred largesses.

It shall be necessary either for debtors to the State,[4] if they shall have believed that flight to the churches for refuge can be made, to be dragged thence from their hiding-places or for demands concerning these to be made on bishops themselves who are proved to conceal them.

Therefore your eminent Authority should know that hereafter none of the debtors ought to be defended by clergymen or that the debt of him, whom they shall have believed ought to be defended, ought to be paid by them.

Given on 18 October at Constantinople, Arcadius Augustus for the second time and Rufinus being consuls.

1. But Tiberius, the second emperor, abolished the customary right of asylum throughout the Empire (Suetonius, *Tib.* 37. 3), probably because in Greek communities the temples were crowded with the most profligate slaves seeking sanctuary from their masters, with debtors desiring protection from their creditors, and with persons pursued for capital crimes (Tacitus, *Ann.* 3. 60. 2). But the practice persisted, for some six years later in his reign the emperor's daughter-in-law (and niece) and grandson (and grandnephew) were warned to embrace the deified Augustus' statue in the Roman Forum and there to implore the aid of the Senate and the People against Tiberius' persecution of them (Tacitus, op. cit., 4. 67. 6).

2. The churches were, in fact, like the "cities of refuge" instituted among the ancient Jews (Num. 35. 6, 9–34; Josh. 20). However, the Christian right of sanctuary possibly did not descend from the Hebrew practice, but probably was derived from the pagan investment of sacred places and objects with inviolability.

In this aspect the Church appears as a patron (*patronus*) conferring protection or patronage (*patrocinium*). Consult F. de Zulueta, "Patronage in the Later Empire" in *Oxford Studies in Social and Legal History* (Oxford, 1909), 1. 2. 12. For another type of patronage see introd. to no. 345.

3. A law of Constantine granting rights of asylum to the Church in 324 is considered by modern scholars to be a forgery.

4. These were probably delinquent in payment of taxes.

242. MANDATE OF THEODOSIUS I, ARCADIUS, AND HONORIUS ON PAGAN RITES OFFENSIVE TO CHRISTIANITY, 392

(*CT* 16. 10. 12)

Of the 25 laws in the title "On Pagans, Sacrifices, and Temples" in *CT* 16. 10 this is chronologically the first which assigns violation of religion, that is, Christianity, as the reason why pagan rites should not be performed. Although there is little doubt that most of the ordinances which suppress various aspects of pagan religion and cover the period 320-435 (both anterior and posterior to the present statute in this series) have been inspired by Christian interest, yet only six (this and nos. 184, 263, 340, 382, 424) explicitly refer to Christianity and therefore alone are translated.

Of these 25 constitutions[1] the first six belong to 320-56, the next twelve fall within 381-99, the last seven date from 407-35. The greatest activity in the shortest space, then, is revealed by the middle group, which reflects the interest of Theodosius I and his sons Arcadius and Honorius, though it is true that the legislation of the latter—whether of both or of one—continues to the penultimate constitution (*CT* 16. 10. 24; dated 423). In this middle period the influence of St Ambrose, bishop of Milan, upon Theodosius probably accounts for this drastic legislation to extirpate idolatry. But these ordinances were not enough to eradicate the outlawed observances, for, as the event proved, new laws to enforce the execution of the old enactments or to supplement the old statutes emanated from the emperors in the next period.[2]

Emperors Theodosius, Arcadius, and Honorius Augusti to Rufinus, praetorian prefect.[3]

Absolutely no person from any class or order of men or of dignities or placed in power or retired from office,[4] whether powerful by lot of birth or humble in class, condition, fortune—in absolutely no place or in no city—either should sacrifice an innocent victim to images

242. PAGAN RITES OFFENSIVE TO CHRISTIANITY, 392

lacking sense or by a more secret expiation [5] in having worshipped his Lar [6] with fire, his Genius [7] with wine, his Penates [6] with incense,[8] should kindle lights, should place [9] incense,[8] should hang garlands.

But if anyone for the purpose of sacrificing shall dare to immolate a victim or to consult the quivering entrails,[10] he, as guilty according to the example of treason, when reported by an accusation allowed to all persons, should receive appropriate sentence, even if he shall have inquired nought contrary to the emperors' welfare or concerning their welfare. For it suffices for the enormity of the crime to wish to rend the laws of Nature herself, to examine forbidden things, to disclose hidden matters, to attempt prohibited things, to seek the end of another's welfare, to promise the hope of another's death.

But if anyone by having placed [9] incense shall worship images, made by mortal work and about to last for a lifetime, and if in a ridiculous manner, when fearing suddenly what he himself has fashioned, either after a tree has been bound with fillets or after an altar has been built by excavated sods, shall have attempted to honour vain images with the reward of a gift (though humble, still a complete injury to religion), this person, as guilty of violation of religion, shall be punished in respect to that house or estate [11] wherein—it shall have been established—he has served a heathen superstition. For all places which—it shall have been established—have fumed with vapour of incense, if, however, these places shall be proved to have been in the ownership of burners of incense, we decree must be joined to our fisc.

But if anyone shall have attempted to practise such kind of sacrifice in public temples or shrines or in others' buildings or fields, if it shall have been established that these have been usurped in the owner's ignorance, he should be forced to pay 25 pounds of gold in the category of a fine, but an equal punishment shall repress the conniver with this wickedness as well as the sacrificer.

And we desire indeed this to be observed by the governors and the defenders and the curials of each and every city, so what has been discovered by the defenders and the curials should be reported instantly to a court and what has been reported should be punished by the governors.

Moreover, if the defenders and the curials shall have believed that anything should be hidden through partiality or should be disregarded through negligence, they shall be subject to judicial censure; but if the governors, when told, shall have postponed punishment through carelessness, they shall be punished by a cost of thirty pounds of gold—their office staffs also being subject to an equal penalty.

Given on 8 November at Constantinople, Arcadius Augustus for the second time and Rufinus being consuls.

242. PAGAN RITES OFFENSIVE TO CHRISTIANITY, 392

1. That the reader may have a convenient synopsis of these constitutions, a short summary of the several subjects is given here: Soothsaying and Divination: 1, 9, 12; Sacrifices: 1, 2, 4–13, 15, 17–20, 23, 25; Temples: 3, 4, 7, 8, 10–13, 15, 16, 18, 19, 25; Priests: 14, 20; Pagans: 21–5.

2. In 423 Theodosius II supposed that no pagans survived (*CT* 16. 10. 22), but this opinion, if he seriously professed it, was both optimistic and premature, because two months later in the same year he inveighed against pagan sacrifices (*CT* 16. 10. 23) and in 438 he renewed his prohibition of such sacrifices in another law (no. 429), which practically closes a long series of anti-pagan legislation, though even as late as 529 appeared legislation against polytheistic pagans, who must be excluded from the pedagogical profession (no. 600).

For the tenacity of paganism in the West see S. Dill, *Roman Society in the Last Century of the Western Empire* [2] (London, 1899), 3–112. See also Huttman and Introd., n. 49.

3. Of the East.

4. The connotation is fulfilment of official duties entitling one to honourable discharge.

5. As the rest of the sentence shows, such worship would be private, because it was devoted to personal and familial deities.

6. The Lares and Penates commonly were the household gods, whose images stood in a Roman house on the hearth or in a little shrine or in a small chapel. The Lares were of Etruscan provenience, while the Penates were Latin in origin. The Lar as a tutelary divinity was worshipped by the Romans as the protector of a particular locality. The word by metonymy means "hearth" and by synecdoche signifies "home" in Roman usage. See *D* 25. 3. 1. 2.

7. The Genius was the divine nature innate in everything, whether animate or inanimate (the phrases *Genius Augusti* and *genius loci* illustrate each), but in contrast to the Lar and Penates was considered rather the tutelary deity of a person (somewhat like our Holy Guardian Angel, commemorated on 2 October by Roman Catholics—at least in the United States).

8. For *incense* the first word is *odour*, really the fragrance emitted by the incense itself, for which the second word is *tus* (here pluralized into *tura*).

9. On altars.

10. The phrase is Vergilian (*Aen.* 4. 64). The entrails are said to be "breathing" (*spirantia*), because, freshly extracted from the slaughtered animal, they show to the consultant some signs of life. The practice was called *extispicium*.

11. That is, confiscation is the penalty.

243. MANDATE OF GRATIAN, VALENTINIAN II, AND THEODOSIUS I ON PROHIBITION OF SPECTACLES ON SUNDAY, 392-5
(CT 15. 5. 2)

The editors, believing that the subscription to this law is incorrect, assign to 392-5 (not 386) this regulation about public entertainment, of which the ban on presentation on Sundays is repeated.

Emperors Gratian, Valentinian, and Theodosius Augusti to Rufinus, praetorian prefect.[1]

None at all of the governors should have time for either theatrical plays or contests in the circus or chases of wild beasts,[2] except on only those days on which we were born[3] or we obtained the sceptre of sovereignty—and on these days they should appear at the celebration only before noon, but should cease to return to the spectacle after the banquet.[4]

And moreover all persons, whether governors or private persons, should know that at the spectacle no gold at all ought to be given for a prize, which is permitted to consuls alone, to whom we have committed the control of this expenditure because of the merits of their lives.

We also forewarn the following: that none should offend against our law, which we issued some time ago,[5] that one should not provide a spectacle for the people on the Sun's day[6] and should not disturb divine worship by having caused such a celebration.[7]

Given on 20 May at Heraclea, the most noble boy[8] Honorius and the most distinguished Evodius being consuls.

1. Of the East.
2. This chase of wild beasts (*ferarum cursus*) appears to be confined to the chase performed in the amphitheatre where hunters pursued and slaughtered feral animals for the spectators' amusement. CT 15. 11. 1 (dated 414) puts no restriction on anyone in the provinces killing lions at any time, pertains to the provincials' safety from such animals' attack, but prohibits anyone without permission to hunt and then to sell wild beasts.
3. Literally "were brought into the light". See no. 236.
4. A banquet or a feast (*epulae*) customarily was given on a public festival.
5. No. 236.
6. See no. 34, n. 5.
7. See no. 236, n. 3.
The Church generally eschewed the State's traditional entertainments (as

heathenish or obscene or sanguinary) and gradually evolved an elaborate ceremonial of worship, wherein laymen enjoyed some share and which served to some extent as an emotional substitute for the more exciting spectacles. See no. 236, n. 3 *ad fin*.

8. See no. 146, n. 5.

244. MANDATE OF THEODOSIUS I, ARCADIUS, AND HONORIUS ON CHRISTIAN ACTS OF ANTI-SEMITISM, 393

(*CT* 16. 8. 9)

The sovereigns by this statute forbid Christians to harass Jews.

The same Augusti to Addeus, count and master of each soldiery throughout the East.[1]

It sufficiently is established that the Jews' sect has been forbidden by no law.

Wherefore we are disturbed gravely that their assemblies have been banned in certain places.

Therefore your sublime Grandeur, after this command has been received, shall restrain with appropriate severity the excess of those who under the name of the Christian religion venture upon all illicit acts and try to destroy and to despoil synagogues.

Given on 29 September at Constantinople, Theodosius Augustus for the third time and Abundantius being consuls.

1. *Magister utriusque militiae per Orientem*, on which see no. 106, n. 4.

245. MANDATE OF THEODOSIUS I, ARCADIUS, AND HONORIUS ON HERETICAL CONSECRATION OF BISHOPS, 394

(*CT* 16. 5. 22)

This brief order needs no comment.

Emperors Theodosius, Arcadius, and Honorius Augusti to Victor, proconsul of Asia.

Heretics should have neither authority for creating bishops nor lawful confirmation of bishops.

Given on 15 April at Constantinople, Arcadius Augustus for the third time and Honorius Augustus for the second time being consuls.

246. MANDATE OF THEODOSIUS I, ARCADIUS, AND HONORIUS ON TESTAMENTARY RIGHTS OF EUNOMIANS, 394

(CT 16. 5. 23)

This statute is a rare instance of repeal of an earlier statute (no. 218), which denies to Eunomians the right to make a will and to inherit property left by a will. It is believed that this repeal resulted from the insidious influence over Arcadius exerted by Eutropius, his castrated counsellor,[1] who was friendly to the Eunomians.

Later the prohibition was restored (no. 249), only to be rescinded again (nos. 252 and 277) and again to be restored (no. 321). Such shifts in imperial legislation within the space of 21 years are eloquent.

The same Augusti to Rufinus, praetorian prefect.[2]

Some time ago we believed that a law [3] ought to be promulgated to the Eunomians that they should not take or leave anything by will, but this law [3] now, indeed, on fuller consideration we revoke.

They should live under the common law; they should designate and likewise should be designated heirs.

Given on 20 June at Adrianople, Arcadius Augustus for the third time and Honorius Augustus for the second time being consuls.

1. No ancient or modern historian has a good word for this character, who, as chief chamberlain (see no. 448, n. 2) to Arcadius, dominated disastrously his emperor from 395 till his fall from grace in 399, for which year he held the eastern consulship—the first eunuch in Roman history so honoured and thus castigated by Claudian in the line *Omnia cesserunt eunucho consule monstra* (*In Eut.* 1. 8). It would almost exhaust the vocabulary of vituperation to expose Eutropius' viciousness, for even vice had not enough varieties to extinguish this eunuch's energies. Perhaps his only merit is that Eutropius manoeuvred the appointment of St John Chrysostom to the Constantinopolitan patriarchate in 398. When Gainas the Goth, who had become master of the soldiers (on whom see no. 106, n. 4) in the Eastern Empire, demanded Eutropius' dismissal, Eutropius sought sanctuary in Hagia Sophia (on which see no. 285, n. 2),

though he himself had only recently procured the passage of a law abolishing the right of asylum in churches (Socrates, *HE* 6. 5; Sozomen, *HE* 8. 7). Chrysostom refused to surrender Eutropius to the pursuing soldiers and preached two sermons in the crowded cathedral on the vanity of human affairs, while the consul clung to one of the altar's columns (*PG* 52. 391–414). The ordinance ordering the eunuch's exile is a masterpiece of imperial invective (*CT* 9. 40. 17), which followed him to Cyprus, whence soon he was recalled to be beheaded at Chalcedon.

2. Of the East.
3. No. 218.

247. MANDATE OF THEODOSIUS I, ARCADIUS, AND HONORIUS ON ASSOCIATION OF CHRISTIANS WITH PLAYERS, 394

(*CT* 15. 7. 12)

The preamble of this constitution is omitted as not pertinent to Christianity, because it bans the posting of mimes' and charioteers' and actors' pictures in public porticoes or places where also are installed imperial images. The translated section (partly used in *CI* 1. 4. 4) forbids Christians to consort with actors and actresses to wear nuns' habits.

The same Augusti to Rufinus, praetorian prefect.[1]

... To these measures we add the following: that female mimes [2] and women who acquire gain by the wantonness of their body should not wear publicly the dress of those virgins who have been consecrated [3] to God and that no woman and no child, if such a one is known to be of the Christian religion, should be contaminated by association with an actor.[4]

Given on 29 June at Heraclea, Arcadius Augustus for the third time and Honorius Augustus for the second time being consuls.

1. Of the East.
2. *CI* 1. 4. 4 starts with *female mimes* and ends with *God*.
3. Pitra prints (2. 598) a late Greek and defective paraphrase of *CI*'s excerpt: "Female mimes and actresses [the feminized form of the word in the next note], whoever in the theatre from their own body acquire gain ... publicly the dress ... consecrated ..."

Tertullian thinks that in his time—two centuries earlier—between matrons and prostitutes no distinction in dress has remained (*Apol.* 6. 3). And in *CT* 15. 7. 11 (dated 393) no actresses of mimes are allowed to wear gems, figure-adorned silks, gilded textiles, purple-dyed garments, but may appear in checkered and varicoloured silks and may adorn themselves with gold without gems on their necks and arms and girdles.

4. The word is *thymelicus* (transliterated from θυμελικός), which meant originally a theatrical musician as opposed to a stage player (see no. 651, n. 8 *ad fin.*).

248. MANDATE OF THEODOSIUS I, ARCADIUS AND HONORIUS ON HERETICAL INSTRUCTION, 394

(*CT* 16. 5. 24)

This constitution (repeated in *CI* 1. 5. 2) forbids heretics to give instruction in their doctrines.

The same Augusti to Rufinus, praetorian prefect.[1]
Heretics' madness should not attempt any longer either to perpetrate what matters it shall have invented or to hold unlawful councils or to teach or to learn anywhere profane precepts.[2]
Bishops of the said persons should not dare to commend their faith, which they have not, and to create ministers, because they are not.[3]
Such audacity should not be neglected and increase through the connivance of judges and of all persons to whom through our paternal[4] constitutions attention to this matter has been commanded.[5]
Given on 9 July at Constantinople, Arcadius Augustus for the third time and Honorius Augustus for the second time being consuls.

1. Of the East.
2. Justinian's opening sentence (*CI* 1. 5. 2) combines this with the similarly situated sentence in no. 166: "All heresies, prohibited by both divine laws and imperial constitutions, should cease forever and none should attempt any longer either to teach or to learn what profane precepts he shall have invented."
In *CT* 9. 16. 8 = *CI* 9. 18. 8 (dated 365 or 370 or 373) it is stated that the guilt of learning and of teaching prohibited matters is similar.
3. The parenthetical clauses, of course, present the orthodox position, for obviously heretics had some faith in which they believed and some clergy who shepherded their souls.
4. The reference is to Valentinian I, as no. 166 shows.
5. *CI* 1. 5. 2 after this thus concludes: "Moreover those who shall have been detected even by light evidence to deviate from the adjudged course of the

Catholic religion are comprehended in the designation of heretics and must submit to statutes passed against them."

Its superscription and subscription are those of no. 166, save that for "Auxonius" in the latter it reads "Ausonius".

249. MANDATE OF ARCADIUS AND HONORIUS ON CONFIRMATION OF THEODOSIUS I'S LEGISLATION ON HERESY, 395

(*CT* 16. 5. 25)

Within two months after the death of Theodosius the Great, the last sole sovereign of the undivided Empire,[1] his sons confirmed and re-enacted his statutes against heretics.

Emperors Arcadius and Honorius Augusti to Rufinus, praetorian prefect.[2]

We ordain, renewing also by our ordinance,[3] all penalties and all punishments, which by the statutes [4] of our father [5] of divine memory have been established against heretics' stubborn spirit, and that whatever has been conceded to them by any special statute [6] contrary to the delinquents' merit, in the hope of correction, is to be invalid.

Moreover with special mention we condemn the Eunomians' perfidious mind and most worthless sect and we establish that all things which have been ordained against their insanity [7] are to be maintained inviolate, adding the following: that none of the said sect should have the right of entering the governmental service [8] or of making a will or of taking property in accordance with a will—in order that all, who have also a common religion's insanity, may have a common penalty—voiding, of course, whatever by our father [5] had been conceded to the said persons by special benefit in the matter of the right of making a will.[9]

Given on 13 March at Constantinople, Olybrius and Probinus being consuls.

1. He also was a good Christian as well as a devout Catholic, though he was noted for his hot temper—a trait traceable doubtless to his Spanish origin.
2. Of the East.
3. The etymological figure is retained: *decreto . . . decernimus.*
4. Such as nos. 166, 167, 173, 176, 179, 185, 190–2, 194, 196, 205, 213, 215, 217–9, 222, 232, 239, 245, 248.

5. Theodosius I.
6. Such as nos. 215, 217, 246.
7. Such as nos. 173, 179, 192, 194, 196, 218.
8. See no. 186, n. 4.
9. No. 246.

250. MANDATE OF ARCADIUS AND HONORIUS ON CONFIRMATION OF ECCLESIASTICAL PRIVILEGES, 395

(CT 16. 2. 29)

Previous imperial laws favouring the Church are confirmed by this constitution.

Emperors Arcadius and Honorius Augusti to Hierius, vicar of Africa.

Whatsoever matters have been ordained by our ancestors at various times we command should remain inviolate and unimpaired concerning the sacrosanct churches.

Therefore nothing should be changed from their privileges and on all persons who serve the churches protection [1] should be conferred, because we desire that in our times should be an increase of reverence rather than should be a change from those things which formerly have been offered.

Given on 23 March at Milan, Olybrius and Probinus being consuls.

1. Since the text is corrupt, the editors suggest that "of all [privileges]" perhaps should be inserted here.

251. MANDATE OF ARCADIUS AND HONORIUS ON HERETICAL ASSEMBLIES, 395

(CT 16. 5. 26)

Besides being a ban on meetings of heretics this statute prohibits heretics from becoming clergymen.

The same Augusti to Rufinus, praetorian prefect.[1]
None of the heretics, whom our deified [2] father's [3] innumerable

laws⁴ already restrain, should dare to assemble illicit gatherings and with profane mind to contaminate Almighty God's mysteries [5]— either publicly or privately or in secret or openly.

None should dare to arrogate to himself the name of bishop or with polluted mind to assume unlawfully ecclesiastical rank and their most holy names.

Given on 30 March at Constantinople, Olybrius and Probinus being consuls.

1. Of the East.
2. See no. 127, n. 7.
3. Theodosius I the Great.
4. See no. 249, n. 4.
5. Singular in Latin for the more usual plural; see no. 75, n. 42.

252. MANDATE OF ARCADIUS AND HONORIUS TESTAMENTARY RIGHTS OF EUNOMIANS, 395

(*CT* 16. 5. 27)

This directive rescinds so much of no. 249 as pertains to Eunomians and repeats the grant of no. 246, which authorizes Eunomians to take and to leave property by will, previously forbidden by no. 218.

The same Augusti to Caesarius, praetorian prefect.[1]

We order that the power of making wills should be given to Eunomians and that there should be conceded to them that which the recently given order of our deified [2] father contained.[3]

Given on 24 June at Constantinople, Olybrius and Probinus being consuls.

1. Of the East.
2. See no. 127, n. 7.
3. The reference is to no. 246, for which Arcadius is believed to have the responsibility, but here he hides behind the name of his deceased father, Theodosius I, who was living at the time of no. 246, in view of the fact that he and his brother only three months earlier have withheld testamentary rights from all heretics (no. 249).

253. MANDATE OF ARCADIUS AND HONORIUS ON PENALTIES FOR DEVIATION FROM CHRISTIANITY, 395

(CT 16. 10. 13)

Notwithstanding the comprehensiveness of Theodosius I's constitution against paganism as a violation of Christianity (no. 242) and the severity of its sanctions, his sons consider it necessary within a triennium to re-enact it in the subsequent statute. The reason for this repetition is not obscure: lax enforcement of the law by provincial officials, who condoned offences against previous constitutions.

Emperors Arcadius and Honorius Augusti to Rufinus, praetorian prefect.[1]

We ordain that none may have the liberty of approaching any shrine or temple whatever or of performing abominable sacrifices at any place or time whatever.

Let all persons, therefore, who strive to deviate from the Catholic religion's dogma, hasten to observe those statutes which recently we have decreed[2] and not dare to neglect those statutes which formerly have been ordained either about heretics or about pagans, knowing that whatever either of punishment or of cost[3] has been ordained against them by our deified[4] father's[5] laws[6] now must be executed more zealously.

Moreover governors of our provinces and apparitors[7] obedient to them, also chief men of cities, defenders as well as curials, managers of our estates—in which we learn that illicit heretical meetings assemble without fear of cost for this reason, because these cannot be assigned to the fisc, since, to be sure, they already belong to its control—should know that if anything attempted contrary to our ordinances[2] shall not have been avenged and punished instantly, they themselves must be subjected to all losses and punishments which have been set by the old statutes.[6]

But specifically by this law we ordain and decree severer punishments against the governors: for if these measures have not been observed with all diligence and caution, not only the fine which has been established against them,[8] but also the fine which has been pre-determined against those who appear to be the authors of the crime,[8] are to be effective and, however, the fine is not to be remitted for those on whom it has been imposed justly because of their contumacy.

Besides we judge that the office staffs which shall have neglected the statutes must be corrected by punishment.

Given on 7 August at Constantinople, Olybrius and Probinus being consuls.

1. Of the East.
2. Nos. 248, 249, 251.
3. That is, through payment of a fine.
4. See no. 127, n. 7.
5. Theodosius the Great.
6. See nos. 242, 249, n. 4, and *CT* 16. 10. 10 and 11 (both dated 391).
7. The Latin has the abstract (*apparitio*) for the concrete (*apparitores*) in antimeria.
8. See no. 242.

254. MANDATE OF ARCADIUS AND HONORIUS ON DEFINITION OF HERETICS, 395
(*CT* 16. 5. 28)

Since laws against heretics were executed by public tribunals generally [1] and because laic judges ordinarily were not too versed in doctrinal matters, doubtless certain guilty persons occasionally eluded punishment by their ability to quibble with ecclesiastical terms. This condition perhaps caused the issuance of this order, which deals with those who deviate only slightly from orthodox criteria.

Justinian appends the first sentence of this constitution to earlier orders (*CI* 1. 5. 2) of 379 and of 394 (see nos. 166 and 248).

The same Augusti to Aurelian, proconsul of Asia.

Whoever shall have been discovered to deviate even by a slight token from the Catholic religion's opinion and path are comprehended by the term of heretics and are bound to submit to the sanctions promulgated against them.

And therefore your Experience should recognize that Heuresius [2] ought to be considered a heretic and not in the numbers of the most holy bishops.

Given on 3 September at Constantinople, Olybrius and Probinus being consuls.

1. But see no. 185 for an apparent exception.
2. Though obviously a bishop in Asia, Heuresius (*al.* Euresius) is otherwise unknown, despite the attempt to identify him with the Luciferian bishop Ephesius.

255. MANDATE OF ARCADIUS AND HONORIUS ON DIVINE OATHS IN PACTS AND IN TRANSACTIONS, 395

(CT 2. 9. 3)

By this directive, repeated in CI 2. 4. 41 without the interpretation, the emperors ordain punishment for persons who, after they have concluded pacts or transactions, refuse to fulfil such promises as they have made by invocation of God's name.

Emperors Arcadius and Honorius Augusti to Rufinus, praetorian prefect.[1]

If anyone who has attained his majority [2] shall have thought that it is possible to contravene pacts or transactions made by no command of a compeller, but by free judgement and by will, either by addressing a judge or by supplicating the emperors or by not fulfilling those promises which he shall have strengthened by the name of Almighty God invoked as his guarantor, not only he should be branded with infamy, but also, when deprived of right of action, after the penalty which is proved to have been inserted in the pact has been repaid, he should be without the ownership of the property in question and of the gain which he would have acquired from that pact or transaction. And all these shall be awarded at once to the advantage of those persons who shall have preserved unviolated the pact's rights.

We also order to be worthy of either the loss of this lawsuit or the performance of the pact those persons who by inserting our names into the agreements shall have sworn that the emperors' safety [3] is the confirmation of the pacts which have been entered.

Given on 11 October at Constantinople, Olybrius and Probinus being consuls.

Interpretation: If anyone after the twenty-fifth year of his age [2] shall have presumed against his own pact or decision, which he, when constrained by no power, has produced, but is known to have made by his own will, either to address judges or to approach with prayers the minds of powerful persons against that which he has done or shall have neglected to fulfil the things which under the interposition of an oath he witnesses by the writing of his own decision, not only as a result of this fact he should be pronounced infamous, but also he should not be permitted to plead the case itself and he should be compelled to pay the penalty which he has placed in the pact; and whatever had been awarded to his side by the said writing should be granted straightway to those persons who shall have preserved the produced pact's decision without any opposition.

We also command to be constrained by stipulation of a similar penalty those persons who conjure the names of the lords [4] by inserting these into the agreements, but shall have neglected to fulfil the decisions; and for the performance of a preserved pact this [5] should accrue to those persons who shall have preserved the oaths and the decisions.

1. Of the East.

2. In legal language such a person is *maior annis* (greater in years), which means that he has passed his twenty-fifth year, when curatorship of normal minors (*curatio minorum*) ceased (*II* 1. 23. pr.).

3. Literally "a being safe and sound", then by extension "safety", "welfare", "salvation" (*salus*). One swore *per salutem Caesaris* or *Caesarum* (so Tertullian, *Apol.* 32. 2) or ὑπὲρ σωτηρίας . . . Καίσαρος (so an inscription from Egypt in W. Dittenberger, *Orientis Graeci Inscriptiones Selectae* [Leipzig, 1905], 2. 678. 1), an oath permissible for Christians—despite Matt. 5. 34-7. Christians, however, condemned (*Mart. Pol.* 9. 2, 10. 1 = Eusebius, *HE* 4. 15. 18, 21) swearing "by Caesar's fortune" (τὴν Καίσαρος τύχην), which pagans used (e.g. Arrian, *Epict. Diat.* 4. 1. 14; cf. Dio Cassius, *Hist. Rom.* 44. 6. 1, 57. 8. 3), since they construed it an extension of the oath "by Caesar's Genius" (*per Caesaris genium*) or "by the emperor's Genius" (*per principis genium*)—the Genius, on whom see no. 242, n. 7, being a mortal man's tutelary divinity— (e.g. *Lex Salpensana*, 25 = *FIRA* 1. 205 [dated 82-4]; Tertullian, *Apol.* 28. 3, 32. 2, 35. 10, *Ad Scap.* 2 *ad med.* = *PL* 1. 778, *Ad Nat.* 1. 17 = *CSEL* 20. 89; *D* 12. 2. 13. 6; cf. Suetonius, *Gaius*, 27. 3). Another form, apparently innocuous, "by respect for the emperor" (*per principis venerationem*) is attested by *CI* 4. 1. 2 (dated 223). See also no. 1, n. 4 *ad init.*

On the other hand, there were in the early days Christians who refused to take any oath at all, probably because of the divine command in the Sermon on the Mount (Matt. 5. 33-6; cf. Jas. 5. 12). Such a one was a certain Basilides, a Roman soldier from Alexandria in the third century, who steadfastly affirmed that his profession of Christianity prohibited swearing and whose confession of his faith carried him to prison and thence to decapitation (Eusebius, *HE* 6. 5. 5-6).

4. The emperors (*domini*).

5. Probably the penalty, whereof at least part would be paid to the observers of the pacts.

256. MANDATE OF ARCADIUS AND HONORIUS ON HERETICS IN GOVERNMENTAL SERVICE, 395

(CT 16. 5. 29)

This directive authorizes the master of the offices to discharge any heretic in the imperial bureaux and to forbid him residence in the capital.

The same Augusti to Marcellus, master of the offices.

We order your Sublimity to investigate whether any of the heretics dare to perform governmental service [1]—an insult to our laws—either in the secretarial bureaux [2] or among the secret service agents [3] or among the palatines,[4] to whom all opportunity of governmental service,[1] after our deified [5] father's [6] example,[7] also is denied by us.

Moreover, whomsoever you shall have detached as sharing in this offence, together with the persons to whom they have offered connivance for subversion both of our laws and of religion, you shall order not only to be removed from governmental service,[1] but also to be kept outside this city's [8] walls.

Given on 24 November at Constantinople, Olybrius and Probinus being consuls.

1. See no. 186, n. 4.
2. Collectively called *scrinia*, which means "book boxes", "letter cases", "files". Among these bureaux are counted: (1) *a censibus*, which investigated the financial position of persons who aspired to senatorial or equestrian status; (2) *a cognitionibus*, which collected information on and concocted opinions for judicial questions submitted to the emperor for settlement; (3) *a commentariis*, which recorded official activities of higher magistrates; (4) and (5) *a consiliis* and *a studiis*, which perhaps were synonymous and probably were associated with the sovereign's judicial activity considered administratively or provided special advice on complicated governmental affairs or on extraordinary legal matters; (6) *a diplomatibus*, which issued written permission to travel by the imperial post; (7) *a dispositionibus*, which compiled the programme for the emperor's movements and prepared the corresponding arrangements; (8) *ab epistulis*, which, divided into Greek and Latin departments at least in Constantinople, dealt with the emperor's private and official correspondence; (9) *a libellis*, which received petitions to the emperor and prepared imperial replies thereto; (10) *a memoria*, which drafted imperial constitutions of edictal or mandatory character; (11) *a rationibus*, which treated the emperor's financial affairs as well as controlled the empire's fiscal administration.

Of their heads most were masters (*magistri*), but one (*comes dispositionum*) at least was a count.

3. The *agentes in rebus* composed the large corps (*schola*) of the State's secret service numbering 1,174 (exclusive of supernumeraries) in 430 (according to *CT* 6. 27. 23), whose administrative duty was nominally the efficient operation of the imperial postal service, but this was combined with the political duty of espionage.

The characteristic service of couriers as spies ascended to the "New Empire" of Egypt (*c.* 1580 B.C.) and was perfected under the Persian Empire (*c.* 550-330 B.C.), whence Augustus, who instituted the Roman imperial post, appears to have adopted it.

4. See no. 186, n. 3.
5. See no. 127, n. 7.
6. Theodosius I.
7. No. 249.
8. Constantinople.

257. MANDATE OF ARCADIUS AND HONORIUS ON CHRISTIAN OFFICIALS IN EGYPT, 396

(*CI* 1. 4. 5)

This directive appears earlier in *CT* 14. 27. 1, but without application to Christians, when it directs that councillors [1] and treasurers [2] in Egypt should be selected from artisans.[3]

Emperors Arcadius and Honorius Augusti to Gennadius, Augustal prefect.[4]

Chief elders [1] and financial officials [2] should not be established from artisans [3] unless Christians.[5]

And this your office staff diligently should maintain with vigilance.

Given on 5 February at Constantinople. Posted at Alexandria in the Eutycheum,[6] Arcadius Augustus for the fourth time and Honorius Augustus for the third time being consuls.

1. These seem to have been the chiefs (*archigerontes*—transliterated from Greek) of a sort of senate (γερουσία) in Egyptian towns. Elsewhere they appear to be comprehended under the term "primates of the Alexandrian populace" (*primates Alexandrinae plebis*), the title whereunder *CT* sets this law (14. 27), and to be called "Alexandrian leaders" (*principales Alexandrini*) in *CT* 12. 1. 189 = *CI* 10. 32. 56 (dated 436) and "leaders of the Alexandrian municipal senate" (*primates ordinis Alexandrini*) in *CT* 12. 1. 190 = *CI* 10. 32. 57 (dated 436), though the latter law changes *primates* to *summates* without appreciable difference of meaning.

2. The word is *dioecetes* (transliterated from διοικητής), which has several meanings, of which all relate to administration, particularly to that of finance. In Egypt a *dioecetes* was a financial official.

3. The word *ergasiotanus* is reported apparently only here.

4. On this title see no. 489, n. 12.

5. *CT* has "selected from the number of", which is better Latin, and is silent about the necessity of choosing only Christians.

6. Apparently a temple dedicated to Good Success. Its site is not known.

258. MANDATE OF ARCADIUS AND HONORIUS ON EXPULSION OF HERETICS FROM CONSTANTINOPLE, 396

(*CT* 16. 5. 30)

With slight modification—to make it of wider application—this directive against heretical assemblies Justinian retained in the law (*CI* 1. 5. 3).

Emperors Arcadius and Honorius Augusti to Clearchus, urban prefect.[1]

All heretics should know beyond doubt that from them must be taken all places of this city,[2] whether these are held under the name of churches or what are called deaconries[3] or even deaneries,[4] if in private houses or places of this kind they appear to provide opportunity for meetings—these houses or private places being necessarily incorporated into our fisc.[5]

Moreover all clergymen of the heretics should be driven from the most sacred city[1] and it should not be permitted for them to assemble within these limits.[6]

Furthermore to all these it should be forbidden to meet in profane assemblies to perform a litany within the city[2] by night or by day—a penalty of a hundred pounds of gold having been fixed against your Sublimity's office staff,[7] if anything of this kind is permitted to occur either publicly or in private houses.[8]

Given on 3 March at Constantinople, Arcadius Augustus for the fourth time and Honorius Augustus for the third time being consuls.

1. Of Constantinople.
2. *CI* omits this phrase, thus extending the area beyond Constantinople.
3. The word is *diaconicum*, transliterated from Greek, of which four uses are reported: the deacon's place in a church (Sophocles and Souter); the chapel,

usually a sacristy, the southern of three parallel apses of a church in Eastern Christendom, where necessary supplies for the service of the altar were kept and preparations for the Holy Sacrifice were made (Du Cange and Maere); the liturgical book specifying the deacon's functions (Maere); the bidding prayer offered by the deacon (Sophocles and Maere). But it must mean something else here: probably from the context a place where a church's deacons live.

4. For *decanicum*, transliterated from the Greek, two meanings are recorded: a prison attached to a prelate's establishment (Du Cange and Sophocles) and a place where a group of ten monks dwells (Souter).

5. For *incorporated into our fisc CI* reads "appropriated to the Catholic Church", thus renouncing some 130 years later the State's claim.

6. *CI* omits this paragraph.

7. *CI* adds the Latin for "or the governor's [office staff] fifty [pounds of gold]", just in case the lower echelon fails to enforce the law.

8. Pitra prints (2. 602) a late Greek paraphrase of this law: "Heretics should be expelled from every place, whether they call this their church or something else. But if it is a private place, the Church also should claim this.

"But they should not conduct litanies by night or by day or other meetings—the office staff of the city's prefect paying a hundred pounds of gold, but that of the governors in the provinces paying fifty pounds of gold, if they should have permitted anything contrary to the measures ordered."

259. MANDATE OF ARCADIUS AND HONORIUS ON APOSTATE CHRISTIANS' WILLS, 396

(*CT* 16. 7. 6)

This directive is another in a series of constitutions (nos. 175 and 189) concerning will-making privileges denied to Christians lapsed into paganism.

Emperors Arcadius and Honorius Augusti to Caesarius, praetorian prefect.[1]

This penalty pursues those persons who, when they were Christians, have defiled themselves with the impious superstition of idols, namely that they should not have the power of making a will in favour of strangers,[2] but that to these persons should succeed the specific stock of their own family, that is, father and mother, brother and sister, son and daughter, grandson and granddaughter, and that none should claim for himself the power of proceeding farther.

Given on 23 March at Constantinople, Arcadius Augustus for the fourth time and Honorius Augustus for the third time being consuls.

1. Of the East.
2. That is, as the sequel shows, not close relatives by blood.

260. MANDATE OF ARCADIUS AND HONORIUS ON EXPULSION OF EUNOMIANS FROM MUNICIPALITIES, 396
(CT 16. 5. 32)

This constitution survives apparently in two versions, of which the longer is translated, and enjoins the extrusion of Eunomian heretics from municipalities.

The same Augusti to Caesarius, praetorian prefect.[1]
Lest the Eunomians' so great madness should persist, your sublime Magnificence should hasten with all zeal to search for the Eunomians' authors and teachers;[2] and particularly their clergymen, whose frenzy has prompted so great error, should be expelled as exiles from municipalities[3] and should be segregated from human assemblies.
Given on 22 April[4] at Constantinople, Arcadius Augustus for the fourth time and Honorius Augustus for the third time being consuls.

1. Of the Orient.
2. The untranslated version (CT 16. 5. 31) condenses the foregoing into "Authors and teachers of the Eunomians' crime, when searched for".
3. The rest is omitted by the shorter version.
4. The date of the briefer law is 21 April.

261. MANDATE OF ARCADIUS AND HONORIUS ON CONFIRMATION OF ECCLESIASTICAL PRIVILEGES, 397
(CT 16. 2. 30)

By this constitution are confirmed privileges earlier conferred upon the Church.

The same Augusti to Theodore, praetorian prefect.[1]
After other matters.
By the present sanction we ordain not anything new other than we

confirm those things which appear to have been bestowed previously.

Therefore the privileges, which previously reverence for religion has obtained, we forbid even under threat of punishment to be curtailed, so that those who obey the Church also may enjoy fully those benefits [2] which the Church enjoys.[3]

Given on 31 January at Milan, Caesarius and Atticus being consuls.

1. Of Italy.
2. These consisted chiefly of the immunity from public services.
3. The last paragraph of this law shows a close resemblance to no. 265, issued almost six months later.

262. MANDATE OF ARCADIUS AND HONORIUS ON CONFIRMATION OF PAPAL PRIVILEGES, 397

(CT 11. 16. 21)

In confirming privileges conferred upon the pope the emperors exempt the Church of Rome from performance of certain public services.

The same Augusti to Theodore, praetorian prefect.[1]

The venerable Church's privileges, which deified [2] emperors have bestowed, ought not to be violated.[3]

Accordingly also duteous observance shall guard inviolate what they have bestowed with regard to the bishop of the city of Rome, so that the Church should recognize [4] nothing of an extraordinary public service [5] or of a menial performance.[6]

And the rest.

Given on 31 January at Milan, Caesarius and Atticus being consuls.

1. Of Italy.
2. See no. 127, n. 7.
3. For a close verbal resemblance see the first paragraph of no. 265.
4. That is, recognize as its responsibility to discharge.
5. See no. 226, n. 3.
6. Cf. *supra* n. 3 and see no. 186, n. 5, for kinds of menial performances.

263. MANDATE OF ARCADIUS AND HONORIUS ON RELIGIOUS SIGNIFICANCE OF THE DECURIONATE, 397

(*CT* 12. 5. 3)

This statute (repeated in *CI* 10. 32. 52) again surrounds the duties of the decurionate with religious sanction, after an earlier attempt (no. 229) apparently had little effect.

Emperors Arcadius and Honorius Augusti to Probinus, proconsul of Africa.

What governor [1] can be found so unjust that in cities endowed with magnificent status and rich in the desired numerousness of curials he would impel [2] anyone to repetition of a completed burden, so that, though some have not yet been quite initiated into the municipal senate's sacred rites,[3] continuance of oft-repeated duties [4] would afflict others?

Given on 17 March at Milan, Caesarius and Atticus being consuls.

1. Literally "arbiter of affairs" (*arbiter rerum*).
2. *CI* reads "compel" (*compellat*) for *CT*'s impel (*inpellat*).
3. A reference to some sort of Christian ceremony—in view of the document's date—connected either with entrance into the local senate or with the senate's sessions or with both.
4. A hendiadys.

264. MANDATE OF ARCADIUS AND HONORIUS ON EXPULSION OF APOLLINARIANS FROM CONSTANTINOPLE, 397

(*CT* 16. 5. 33)

By this directive Apollinarian heretics are ordered to depart from Constantinople and persons harbouring them in the capital forfeit their estates to the fisc.

The same Augusti to Eutychian, praetorian prefect.[1]

We order teachers of Apollinarians to depart with all promptitude from the dwellings of the city [2] dear to us, so that if they, concealed in hiding-places for the purpose of holding (as they think) secret meetings, shall have neglected to leave, those places or houses wherein they shall have assembled the aforesaid meetings should be annexed to the fisc's account.

Given on 1 April [3] at Constantinople, Caesarius and Atticus being consuls.

1. Of the East.
2. Constantinople.
3. The month is suspected by the editors, since Eutychian entered office early in September of this year.

265. MANDATE OF ARCADIUS AND HONORIUS ON CONFIRMATION OF ECCLESIASTICAL PRIVILEGES, 397
(CT 11. 16. 22)

This constitution seems compounded from nos. 261 and 262.

The same Augusti to Theodore, praetorian prefect.[1]
The venerable Church's privileges we do not permit to be violated, so that the churches should recognize nothing of an extraordinary public service or of a menial performance.[2]
Therefore whatever reverence for religion has obtained by ancient ordinances we forbid even by threat of punishment to be curtailed, so that they who obey the Church also may enjoy fully those benefits [3] for which provision has been made.[4]
Given on 12 June at Milan, Caesarius and Atticus being consuls.

1. Of Italy.
2. This sentence is almost word for word with the opening sentence and the consecutive clause of the last sentence of no. 262. For extraordinary services see no. 226, n. 3; for menial services see no. 186, n. 5.
3. See no. 261, n. 2.
4. This sentence repeats almost exactly the last sentence of no. 261.

266. MANDATE OF ARCADIUS AND HONORIUS ON SANCTUARY, 397

(*CT* 9. 45. 2)

This constitution treats the situation where Jews, embarrassed by debt or harassed by other charges, pretend to wish to become Christians, that they may seek sanctuary in churches.

Justinian also has this law (*CI* 1. 12. 1).

Emperors Arcadius and Honorius Augusti to Archelaus, Augustal prefect.[1]

Jews who, when harassed by some accusation or by debts, pretend that they wish to be united with the Christian law,[2] that they by fleeing to churches for refuge can avoid accusations or burdens of debts, should be prevented and should not be received before they shall have paid their entire debts or shall have been cleared by proved innocence.

Given on 17 June at Constantinople, Caesarius and Atticus being consuls.

1. On this title see no. 489, n. 12.
2. Religion.

267. MANDATE OF ARCADIUS AND HONORIUS ON CLERICAL PRIVILEGES, 397

(*CT* 16. 8. 13)

In this statute the sovereigns confirm earlier emperors' enactments exempting Jewish religious leaders from compulsory senatorial duties and announce that such privileges also have been conferred upon Christian clerics.

The same Augusti to Caesarius, praetorian prefect.[1]

Jews should be bound by their own ceremonies.

Meanwhile in preserving their privileges let us imitate the ancients, by whose sanctions it has been determined that those sacred privileges which are conferred upon the venerable Christian law's [2] first [3] clergymen should continue by our Divinity's consent for those persons who are subjected to the control of illustrious patriarchs,[4] for rulers of synagogues [5] and patriarchs [6] and all others who are engaged in that religion's rite. For this also the deified [7] Emperors Constantine [8] and Constantius,[9] Valentinian [9] and Valens [9] by divine [10] decision have decreed.

Therefore they should be free also from senatorial services and should obey their own laws.

Given on 1 July, Caesarius and Atticus being consuls.

1. Of the East.
2. Religion, as usual.
3. Either high-ranking or first in time when Christianity was recognized as a lawful religion by the Edict of Milan (no. 12) in 313.
4. See no. 23, n. 3.
5. See no. 23, n. 2 *ad fin.*
6. Mommsen suggests either deletion of this word or Seeck's substitution of "fathers" (see no. 23, n. 2 *ad fin.*) for it.
7. See no. 127, n. 7.
8. In *CT* 16. 8. 2 (dated 330) and 4 (dated 330 or 331).
9. This emperor's statutes on this subject are not extant.
10. That is, imperial, for divinity even then hedged a king (cf. Shakespeare, *Hamlet*, 4. 5. 122), and *Divinity*, as in this law, was a title assumed by Roman emperors.

268. MANDATE OF ARCADIUS AND HONORIUS ON PENALTIES FOR EUNOMIANS AND MONTANISTS, 398

(*CT* 16. 5. 34)

This law assigns various penalties for Eunomian and Montanist clergy and for persons permitting them to hold meetings. It also orders their heretical books to be burned and assigns capital punishment for persons failing to surrender such writings.

The same Augusti to Eutychian, praetorian prefect.[1]

Clergymen of the Eunomian or of the Montanist superstition should be expelled from the society and the intercourse of all communities and cities.

If perchance any living in the country shall be proved either to assemble the people or to engage in any meetings, they should be deported forever—the manager of an estate having been punished by the final penalty [2] and the owner being deprived of an estate whereon unpropitious and condemned meetings shall be proved to have been held with them knowing it and keeping silence.

But if, after the order has been published formally, they shall be proved to have been caught in any city whatsoever or to have entered any house for the purpose of celebrating their superstition, both they themselves should be smitten with the final penalty,[2] after their goods have been confiscated, and the house, in which they shall have entered (in this way as has been said) and from which they immediately shall not have been ejected and reported by the owner—male or female— of the house, without delay should be annexed to the fisc.

We order the books containing the teaching and the matter of all their crimes to be sought by all means at once with the greatest keenness and to be produced by strict authority to be burned by fire at once under governors' supervision.[3] And if perchance anyone is proved to have secreted or not to have produced any one of these by any pretext or fraud whatsoever, he should know that he must suffer capital punishment as a retainer of injurious books and writings on a charge of sorcery.

Given on 4 March at Constantinople, Honorius Augustus for the fourth time and Eutychian being consuls.

1. Of the East.
2. Death.
3. See no. 382, n. 1.

269. MANDATE OF ARCADIUS AND HONORIUS ON ORDINATION OF MONKS IN A SHORTAGE OF SECULAR CLERGYMEN, 398

(*CT* 16. 2. 32)

To prevent the withdrawal of laymen available for secular duties the emperors direct that, when there is a shortage of clergymen to serve churches, bishops shall select monks for parochial duties.

This statute is repeated partly in no. 272.

The same Augusti to Caesarius,[1] praetorian prefect.[2]

If perchance bishops think that they need any clergymen, they shall ordain them more properly from the number of monks.[3]

They should not insist with ill will on those obligated by public and private accounts, but they should have those already approved.

Given on 26 July,[4] Honorius Augustus for the fourth time and Eutychian being consuls.

1. In no. 272 the prefect is Eutychian.
2. Of the East.
3. This sentence is very similar to the last sentence of no. 272.
4. No. 272 is dated on the next day and is issued at Mnizus.

270. MANDATE OF ARCADIUS AND HONORIUS ON RECRUITMENT OF CLERGYMEN FROM LOCAL DISTRICTS, 398

(*CT* 16. 2. 33)

In pursuance of the late imperial policy of restriction of movement of individuals from place to place the emperors order ordinands for the priesthood especially in rural communities to be drawn from their own districts as an economic measure.

Justinian repeats this constitution (*CI* 1. 3. 11).

The same Augusti to Eutychian, praetorian prefect.[1]

For churches which have been established on the landed estates of various persons (as is usual), also in villages or in any places at all, clergymen should be ordained not for another landed estate or village, but from that where it shall have been proved that the church is, so[2] that they should recognize the load and the burden of their own capitation tax.[3]

Also a definite number of clergymen according to the bishop's judgement should be ordained for the churches in proportion to each individual village's size or population.[4]

Given on 27 July at Mnizus, Honorius Augustus for the fourth time and Eutychian being consuls.

1. Of the East.
2. Justinian omits the adverb.
3. Thus their own districts would not lose income by losing ordinands to other communities. See no. 67, n. 37.

The *Constitutiones Apostolorum* (8. 47. 13-16, 32-4) contain rules on migration of clergymen in major orders with or without commendatory letters. The custom of carrying such "letters of commendation" (2 Cor. 3. 1) arose in the apostolic age (see Acts 15. 22-31 for the decision to send such a letter and its contents and reception) and was an institution inherited from Judaism (cf. Acts 9. 1-2, 22. 5, 28. 21).

4. Pitra (2. 480) has a late Greek paraphrase of this law: "For rural churches clergymen should not be ordained, unless from the same village wherein the church is situated, that they also should contribute taxes according to the capitation tax and from these villages, lest they should be ordained immoderately, but should be ordained in proportion to the village's productive power [δύναμις] and great number [πολυπλήθεια (of inhabitants)] and by the bishop's judgement."

271. MANDATE OF ARCADIUS AND HONORIUS ON RESTRICTION OF EPISCOPAL URISDICTION, 398

(CI 1. 4. 7)

By this law a bishop's jurisdiction is restricted to suits in which both litigants have agreed to accept episcopal arbitration.[1] Thus litigation before a bishop is placed on the same basis as the older civil procedure, wherein both parties concur in the choice of a judge offered to them by the magistrate.[2]

The same Augusti to Eutychian, praetorian prefect.[3]
If any persons in accordance with an agreement shall have wished to litigate before a bishop of the sacred law,[4] they shall not be forbidden, but they shall experience the judgement of him (only in a civil affair) sitting voluntarily in the fashion of an arbiter.

And this [5] shall not be able and shall not be bound to injure them in whose case it shall have been established that they, when summoned to the aforesaid judge's inquiry, have been absent rather than have come voluntarily.[6]

Given on 27 July at Milan,[7] Honorius Augustus for the fourth time and Eutychian being consuls.

1. Hitherto either litigant could bring suit before a bishop (no. 28), even if his opponent should have objected (no. 65); but, because most magistrates by this century's close were Christian and would not discriminate against Christian disputants, it perhaps appeared appropriate that both parties to a suit should agree to arbitration in the event that they desired the more expeditious decision available in an episcopal audience (*episcopalis audientia*).

2. Editors suggest that this law belongs to no. 272 at either its beginning or its end.

3. Of the East.
4. The Christian religion.
5. The fact that such a judgement is possible.
6. Pitra prints (2. 537) a late Greek version, which varies only in the last sentence: "And this shall not be able and is not bound to be averse from them, that a law-court has been provided on the aforesaid matters to be judged and has been established from choice and assent."
7. Editors think that Mnizus should be the place.

272. MANDATE OF ARCADIUS AND HONORIUS ON CLERICAL INTERFERENCE IN CRIMINAL CASES, 398
(CT 9. 40. 16)

Six years after earlier legislation forbidding ecclesiastical intervention on behalf of convicted criminals had been enacted (nos. 234 and 235), the law on this subject was modified to allow the clergy to appeal for such persons in cases where a sense of humanity or a miscarriage of justice could be demonstrated.

Justinian has portions of this ordinance [1] (parts of which are repeated in CT 11. 30. 57 and no. 269)[2] in CI 1. 4. 6 and 7. 62. 29.

Emperors Arcadius and Honorius Augusti to Eutychian, praetorian prefect.[3]

After other matters.

To none of clergymen or monks, also those whom they call fellow-travellers,[4] should it be permitted to claim and to hold by force and by illegal seizure persons sentenced to punishment and convicted for the enormity of their crimes.[5] But to them we do not deny the opportunity of interposing an appeal in a criminal case through consideration of humanity, if the times support it,[6] that there should be a rather careful investigation in a case wherein justice is thought to have been crushed contrary to a person's welfare either through error or by a judge's partiality: on this condition, that whether a proconsul, a count of the East, an Augustal prefect, vicars [7] shall have been judges, they should know that there must be reference not so much to our Clemency as to the most honourable powers.[8] For we desire their judgement to be complete over these cases, that they more justly can punish convicted persons, if the matter is such and the crime shall have required it.[9]

Also, after the time of appeal has been passed, none either should hold or should defend convicted persons going to the place of punishment under armed guard, but the judge should know that he must be penalized by a fine of thirty pounds of gold and the chiefs of the office staff by a capital sentence, unless either this illegal seizure is punished immediately or, if the boldness of clergymen and of monks is so great that it should be thought that a war [10] rather than trial will result, the crimes are referred to our Clemency, that a severer punishment soon may proceed by our judgement.

To the blame of the bishops, of course, as in all other such circumstances, it shall redound, if they shall have known and shall not have punished any of those acts which we forbid by this law to be done, perpetrated by monks perchance in that part of a district in which they themselves [11] direct the people by the instruction of the doctrine of the Christian religion.[12]

And from the number of these they shall ordain clergymen more properly, if perchance they think that they need any.[13]

And the rest.

Given on 27 July [14] at Mnizus, Honorius Augustus for the fourth time and Eutychian being consuls.

1. See no. 271, n. 2.
2. Since all of *CT* 11. 30. 57 is included in this law, it is not translated.
3. Of the East.
4. That is, in the Christian life. The word is *synodites* (transliterated from Greek) and meant originally a member of any assembly, but came to denote an orthodox Christian.
5. With this sentence the excerpts in *CI* begin. That in *CI* 1. 4. 6 suspends temporarily at its end. See no. 399, n. 11.
6. That is, if made within the legally prescribed limits of time for an appeal to be made. See no. 65, n. 6 *ad med.*
7. *CI* 7. 62. 29 reads "proconsuls" and "Augustal" for two of these officials, whose position is described in no. 234, n. 3. See also no. 489, n. 12.
8. This is an abstract characterization of the praetorian prefects.
9. Here both *CT* 11. 30. 57 and *CI* 7. 62. 29 stop, while *CI* 1. 4. 6 resumes, substituting, however, "but" for the first nine words.
10. A rather strong word (*bellum*) for street-fighting.
11. The bishops are meant.
12. *CI* 1. 4. 6 ends here. See no. 269, n. 3.
13. For this paragraph *CI* 1. 4. 6 has as its concluding sentence: "And in a criminal case, through consideration of humanity, if circumstances are favourable, we deny not to them an opportunity of interposing an appeal."
14. The editors think that the copy of this law in *CT* 11. 30. 57 should be dated 7 January or June 399.

273. MANDATE OF ARCADIUS AND HONORIUS ON SANCTUARY, 398

(CT 9. 45. 3)

The emperors establish conditions in this constitution (adapted by *CI* 1. 3. 12) to prevent certain classes of persons from seeking sanctuary in a church and to compel the clerical stewards to pay the debts of such persons as temporarily have achieved asylum.

The same Augusti to Eutychian, praetorian prefect.[1]

If in the future any male slave, female slave, curial, public debtor, procurator, fisher for murices,[2] finally anyone whosoever involved in public or private accounts, fleeing to the Church for refuge, either shall have been ordained a cleric or shall have been defended by clerics in any way at all and should not be returned immediately, when a charge has been preferred, to his original status,[3] decurions indeed and all persons whom a customary function calls to due public service should be recalled to their original lot by the judges' skilful vigour,[4] just as by immediate arrest.[5] And we no longer allow the law [6]—which did not forbid decurions to be clerics, after surrender of their estate had ensued—to benefit them.[7]

But also those whom they call stewards, that is, persons who have been wont to handle ecclesiastical accounts, should be compelled—deferment having been removed—to that repayment of a debt, either public or private, in which it shall have been proved that those persons whom clerics shall have received to be defended and shall not have believed ought to be produced immediately are obligated.

And the rest.

Given on 27 July at Mnizus, Honorius Augustus for the fourth time and Eutychian being consuls.

1. Of the East.
2. From the murex, a mollusc, one of the marine gastropods, having a rough shell, was extracted a purple dye. The catching of such animals and the manufacture of dye from their secretive juices was a well-known industry of Tyre. In so far as the celebrated Tyrian purple was made from the murex it was a monopoly, although purple dyes from vegetables were prepared in Arabia and Egypt and Greece. At any rate, in the Empire the Tyrians possessed the exclusive privilege of processing the imperial purple. Thus the inclusion of murex-gatherers (*murileguli*) here may be ascribed to imperial anxiety for the maintenance of the supply of dye.

Several constitutions in *CT* show imperial concern for the personnel of this industry, for the purity of the product, for the restriction of the right of

274. CLERICAL EXEMPTION FOR GUILDSMEN, 399   479

possessing purple-dyed clothing. Some of these statutes are re-enacted in *CI*, confirming the State's century-continued interest in the subject. (1) personnel: *CT* 10. 20. 5 (371), *CT* 13. 1. 9 (372), *CT* 10. 20. 12 (385) and *CI* 11. 8. 9, *CT* 10. 20. 14 (424) and *CI* 11. 8. 11, *CT* 10. 20. 15 (425) and *CI* 11. 8. 12, *CT* 10. 20. 16 (426) and *CI* 11. 8. 13, *CT* 10. 20. 17 (427) and *CI* 11. 8. 15; (2) purity: *CT* 1. 32. 1 (333) and *CI* 11. 8. 2; (3) restriction: *CT* 10. 21. 3 (424) and *CI* 11. 9. 4, *CT* 10. 20. 18 (436) and *CI* 11. 9. 5.

3. There seems to be an omission here, for the apodosis concludes about municipal senators only.

4. Or "vigorous skill", apparently a hendiadys.

5. Literally "by the hand immediately imposed".

6. No. 224.

7. Here ends Justinian's shortened version, which reads: "If any curial shall have been ordained a cleric and should not be returned immediately, when a charge has been preferred, to his original status, this person should be recalled to his original lot by the judges' skilful vigour, just as by immediate arrest. For we no longer allow the law—which did not forbid decurions to be clerics, after surrender of their estate had ensued—to benefit clerics."

Pitra prints (2. 464) a late Greek version of Justinian's adaptation.

274. MANDATE OF ARCADIUS AND HONORIUS ON CLERICAL EXEMPTION FOR GUILDSMEN, 399

(*CT* 13. 1. 16)

The emperors here take a poor view of clergymen engaged in business and of members of commercial guilds enjoying clerical exemption and they ordain that suits against such persons should be tried speedily.

Emperors Arcadius and Honorius Augusti to Clearchus, urban prefect.[1]

We order all guildsmen about whom a complaint has arisen to be sued as speedily as possible, that either, pursuing tradesmen's profits, they may forsake the exemption of clergymen or, serving the Most Sacred Divinity, they may abstain from crafty gains under your Sincerity's oversight. For the services of religion and of shrewdness are distinct.

Given on 8 May at Constantinople, the most distinguished Theodore being consul.

1. Of Constantinople.

275. MANDATE OF ARCADIUS AND HONORIUS ON PUNISHMENT OF MANICHAEANS, 399

(CT 16. 5. 35)

By this order, of which Justinian utilizes the last sentence (*CI* 1. 5. 4), persecution of Manichaeans is renewed.

The same Augusti to Dominator, vicar of Africa.

We decree that obnoxious Manichaeans and their detestable assemblies, previously condemned[1] by just punishment, should be repressed also by special order.

Wherefore, when they have been sought, they should be brought to a magistrate and should be checked by appropriate and very severe correction of their detested guilt.

The stings of authority should be aimed also against those persons who with damnable provision shall protect these in their own houses.

Given on 17 May at Milan, the most distinguished Theodore being consul.

1. As in nos. 156, 176, 185, 192, 219.

276. MANDATE OF ARCADIUS AND HONORIUS ON PENALTIES FOR IMPAIRMENT OF ECCLESIASTICAL PRIVILEGES, 399

(CT 16. 2. 34)

By this constitution persons attacking or neglecting the Church's privileges are fined for their attack or neglect.

Justinian uses part of the first sentence of this statute (*CI* 1. 3. 13), which part Pitra prints also in a late Greek version (2. 460).

The same Augusti to Sapidian, vicar of Africa.

If the venerable Church's privileges shall have been either violated by anyone's rashness or neglected by anyone's carelessness, the offence should be punished by a condemnation of five pounds of gold,[1] just as also has been established previously.[2]

Therefore, if anything contrary to the laws shall have been obtained[3] by surreptitious action against churches or clergymen either by heretics or by persons of this character,[4] we nullify it by this sanction's authority.

277. RESCISSION OF DISABILITIES, 399 481

Given on 25 June at Brescia, the most distinguished Theodore being consul.

1. Justinian omits the rest from his version.
2. This law is not extant.
3. By a petition to an official or even to the emperor.
4. Since this statute was aimed at conditions in Africa, probably the Donatists, rather schismatics than heretics, were meant by this addition. The reference to *rashness* (*temeritas*), which can be interpreted as rash criminality, in the preceding paragraph then could point to the Circumcellions, who, constituting the militant and fanatic faction of the Donatist movement, were notorious for their malicious (and sometimes murderous) outrages upon orthodox Christians.

277. MANDATE OF ARCADIUS AND HONORIUS ON RESCISSION OF DISABILITIES FOR EUNOMIANS, 399

(*CT* 16. 5. 36)

This constitution illustrates the vacillation in the policy of Arcadius, who cancels some and continues other repressions for Eunomians (see introd. to no. 246). Conjecture, but not certainty, may explain whose interest to relieve the Eunomians influenced the imperial enactment.

The same Augusti to Eutychian, praetorian prefect.[1]

We remit for Eunomians the penalty of being deprived of making a will [2] and of changing their status of aliens.

We allow them to have unrestricted power both of making donations from their own property, as they may wish, and of receiving property in turn from others as a donation.

But they should refrain from councils, they should abandon illicit meetings, and they should know that for them assemblies have been forbidden or penalties have been prepared, so that the manager of an estate or the steward of an urban house, in which profane mysteries [3] shall have been celebrated, should be smitten with final punishment [4] and the estate and the house themselves should be claimed for the fisc, if there shall have been resistance to our order with the owner knowing it and not prohibiting it.

Moreover the ministers of the wickedness, whom they call bishops by their own false nomenclature, if they shall have been arrested in any assembly, should be deported, after all their property has been taken from them.

Given on 6 July at Constantinople, the most distinguished Theodore being consul.

1. Of the East.
2. The privilege of testation, announced in no. 249, was rescinded also by no. 252.
3. See no. 75, n. 42.
4. Death.

278. MANDATE OF ARCADIUS AND HONORIUS ON EPISCOPAL JURISDICTION IN ECCLESIASTICAL INTERESTS, 399
(CT 16. 11. 1)

Honorius here repeats briefly Gratian's apparently ineffective legislation (no. 161) on the distinction between ecclesiastical and secular lawsuits.

Emperors Arcadius and Honorius Augusti to Apollodore, proconsul of Africa.

As often as there is an action about religion, it is proper for bishops to deliberate on it; but it is necessary for all other cases, which pertain to ordinary [1] judges or to the usage of the public law, to be heard in accordance with the laws.

Given on 20 August at Padua, the most distinguished Theodore being consul.

This law does not need interpretation.

1. That is, laic as opposed to ecclesiastical. Provincial governors are meant.

279. MANDATE OF ARCADIUS AND HONORIUS ON SUPPRESSION OF SHOWS ON SUNDAY, 399

(CT 2. 8. 23)

This ordinance bans theatrical plays, chariot races, and other spectacles on Sundays not imperial birthdays.

The same Augusti to Aurelian, praetorian prefect.[1]
On the Lord's day,[2] to which the name has been given from very reverence, neither theatrical plays nor horses' contests nor any spectacle which has been found to enervate souls [3] should be celebrated in any community. But the emperor's birthday, even if it shall have fallen on the Lord's day,[2] should be celebrated.
Given on 27 August at Constantinople, the most distinguished Theodore being consul.

1. Of the East.
2. See no. 34, n. 5.
3. The phrase is as old as Cicero (*Tusc. Disp.* 2. 11. 27).

280. MANDATE OF ARCADIUS AND HONORIUS ON CLERICAL EXEMPTION FROM SENATORIAL SERVICE, 399

(CT 12. 1. 163)

By this ordinance municipal senators who have attained holy orders after 388 either must find substitutes for themselves in the senates or must cede their property to their senates, while all other clergy of lower grades must be recalled to public service in their native municipalities.

The same Augusti to Eutychian, praetorian prefect.[1]
If after our deified [2] father's second consulate [3] any persons, leaving the municipal senate, have transferred themselves to the society of clergymen, if already they have become bishops or priests or deacons, they should continue, indeed, in God's sacred and more secret mysteries,[4] but they either should be compelled to offer to the municipal senate substitutes for themselves or according to the law

formerly enacted [5] should deliver their property to the municipal senate.

All the rest—lectors, subdeacons, or those clergymen to whom clergymen's privileges are not due—should be brought directly to the public services of their native municipality.

Given on 11 December,[6] Theodore being consul.

1. Of the East.
2. See no. 127, n. 7.
3. Theodosius I was consul for the second time in 388.
4. See no. 75, n. 42.
5. No. 224.
6. The date may be incorrect, for Eutychian seems to have demitted his prefecture by 27 August.

281. MANDATE OF ARCADIUS AND HONORIUS ON SUPPRESSION OF SPECTACLES ON CERTAIN HOLY DAYS, 400
(*CT* 2. 8. 24)

This statute forbids presentation of spectacles in the first week of Lent, in Easter week, on Christmas, and on Epiphany.

The same Augusti to Hadrian, praetorian prefect.[1]

Because of consideration for religion we order and decree that on the seven days of Quadragesima,[2] on the seven paschal days, by whose observances and fasts sins are purged, also on the day of the Birth [3] and of the Epiphany,[4] spectacles should not be produced.

Given on 4 February at Ravenna, Stilicho and Aurelian being consuls.

1. Of Italy.
2. See no. 169, n. 3.
3. See no. 220, n. 10.
4. See no. 220, n. 11.

282. MANDATE OF ARCADIUS AND HONORIUS ON CLERICAL EXEMPTION FROM TAXATION AND PUBLIC LABOUR, 401

(CT 16. 2. 36)

The emperors herein exempt from taxation as well as from public labour such clergymen as trade commercially in foodstuffs.

The same Augusti to Pompeian, proconsul of Africa.

All clergymen of the Catholic religion within that limit[1] whereby they engage in the practice (predetermined by law) of buying and of selling victuals should be considered immune from the tax in gold.

We also order relief to be given to these whom both the rank of clerical office and—what is not less—a holier life protects from performance of public labour.[2] For we would not permit any of them who shall be proved exempt by laws to be subject to injustice.

And the rest.

Given on 14 July at Milan after the consulate of the most distinguished Stilicho and the most distinguished Aurelian.

1. The *limit* (*modus*) is either the "limit" established of tax-exempt profits permitted in no. 165 or the restriction to "very small commercial activities" authorized in no. 107. The privilege of engaging trade enjoyed by the clergy was cancelled by no. 478.

2. The performance of public labour likely was of a compulsory character and probably was associated with public service. While grammatically *from performance of public labour* stands in the relative clause, yet it belongs logically with the notion of the granting of relief.

283. MANDATE OF ARCADIUS, HONORIUS, AND THEODOSIUS II ON TUMULTUOUS ASSEMBLIES, 404

(CT 16. 4. 4)

While there is nothing in this constitution *prima facie* to indicate that the Church is involved in any way, yet because it appears in the section of the Theodosian Code concerning those who contend about religion and since its date and provenience coincide with the commotion centring about St John Chrysostom, patriarch of Constantinople,[1] it appears that it refers to the Church.

Emperors Arcadius, Honorius, and Theodosius Augusti to Anthemius, master of the offices.

All office staffs should be warned to abstain from tumultuous meetings; and whoever shall have dared with sacrilegious mind to combat our Divinity's authority, after they have been deprived of their belt [2] should be punished by proscription of their property.

Given on 29 January at Constantinople, Honorius Augustus for the sixth time and Aristaenetus being consuls.

1. See nos. 284–6, 297
2. See no. 476, n. 39.

284. EDICT OF ARCADIUS ON CHRYSOSTOM'S ADHERENTS, 404
(PG 47. 13)

In his *Dialogus de Vita Sancti Joannis Chrysostomi* [1] Palladius, bishop of Helenopolis first and then of Aspona,[2] records four [3] imperial statutes directed against the adherents of St John Chrysostom, patriarch of Constantinople, who was expelled from his see, partly because he had angered Empress Eudoxia and the courtiers through his plain preaching against moral laxity and luxury, partly because he had introduced too many thoroughgoing reforms into the capital's ecclesiastical life and institutions, partly because he had incurred the enmity of Theophilus, patriarch of Alexandria, who personally directed the opposition against the most celebrated orator in the history of Greek-speaking Christendom.[4]

If anyone is not in communion with Theophilus and Arsacius and Porphyry,[5] let such a one be excluded from the episcopate and let him lose besides whatever property of money or of goods he appears to have.

1. The most recent edition of this primary source for St John Chrysostom's life is by P. R. Coleman-Norton (Cambridge, 1928). See no. 297, n. 3.
2. Between the tenure of his two bishoprics Palladius, who had been extruded from Helenopolis as one of Chrysostom's supporting suffragans, spent six years as an exile in Egypt amid the monks, with whom he also had sojourned for a little over a decade before his consecration and of whose conversation he has left a lively record in his remarkable *Historia Lausiaca* (the *locus classicus* for Egyptian monachism of the fourth century).
3. Palladius reports in indirect discourse two rescripts: (1) that whoever

conceals or receives in his house a bishop or a priest in communion with John [Chrysostom] is to have his house confiscated (*PG* 47. 13; dated 404); (2) that those in positions of honour are to be expelled from their position in office, that governmental officials are to lose their belts [see no. 476, n. 39], that the rest of the people and the artisans, after having been fined heavily in gold, are to be subjected to exile (*PG* 47. 37; dated 406). The fourth statute is no. 297.

To illustrate these laws Palladius lists by name over thirty persons of varying clerical rank who were banished, in some cases with torture and maltreatment en route (*PG* 47. 71–2).

4. So Palladius presents him (*PG* 47. 8–9, 19–20, 26–7, 30).

The proud position of the Alexandrian patriarchate—its apostolic foundation in the Hellenistic East's most memorable megalopolis until the conversion of Byzantium into Constantinople (see no. 62, n. 2), its complete control over the entire Egyptian Church exceeding that of any prelatial prerogative elsewhere (not excluding even the territorially wider papal power over western churches), its steady glory gained from its seat in a former (332–30 B.C.) capital city of world-wide fame in education (see no. 98, n. 5) and science (see nos. 52, n. 4 *ad med.*, and 98, n. 3) and theology (see no. 189, n. 2 *ad fin.*) as well as from its distinguished doctor of the Church and chiefest champion of orthodoxy, St Athanasius, who had endured exile five times for his attitude toward emperors' authority—appears to have been the basis for its patriarchs' bitter animus against the Constantinopolitan patriarchate (see no. 375, n. 7), which, although of no apostolic association (see no. 181, n. 5), engaged the imperial interest for its enhancement as the supreme see in the Christian East.

So Theophilus in 403–4 against St Chrysostom in Constantinople (see also no. 297), so St Cyril in 431 against Nestorius at Ephesus (see nos. 397, 398, 401–12, 425), so Dioscore in 449 against St Flavian at Ephesus (see nos. 449, 455, 458, 459), on these three occasions in the first half of the fifth century defeated their patriarchal colleagues of Constantinople and procured their depositions. But the third triumph declined into disaster, when in 451 at Chalcedon (see nos. 463, 470 [I, II, IV], 479, 481) the combination of Roman pope and Constantinopolitan emperor carried the day against the Alexandrian patriarch, whose extra-territorial influence thereafter was impaired (see no. 495 and introd. to no. 527). Add now N. H. Baynes, "Alexandria and Constantinople: A Study in Ecclesiastical Diplomacy" in his *Byzantine Studies and Other Essays* (London, 1955), 97–116.

5. These three prelates presided over the then three eastern patriarchates (see no. 53, n. 3): Theophilus at Alexandria, Arsacius (Chrysostom's successor) at Constantinople, Porphyry at Antioch.

285. MANDATE OF ARCADIUS AND HONORIUS ON EXPULSION OF FOREIGN CLERGYMEN FROM CONSTANTINOPLE, 404
(CT 16. 2. 37)

As a result of the tumults in Constantinople over St John Chrysostom's retention of its patriarchal see, Arcadius orders all bishops and clerics, who came to the capital either to support or to oppose Chrysostom, to depart from the city.

Justinian adapts this directive for general purposes (CI 1. 3. 15).

The same Augusti to Studius, urban prefect.[1]

Since the persons cannot be discovered on investigation of the perpetrated conflagration,[2] as your Eminence's report has revealed, we loose from custody of jail the clergymen, so that they, when placed on ships, may return to their own homes.[3]

Nor the houses, which shall be proved to have accepted foreign [4] bishops or clergymen after publication of the edicts and our Serenity's proclamations, should be free from the peril of confiscation—the same regulation being observed, if any house shall have accepted the city's [5] clergymen conducting novel and riotous meetings outside the Church.[6]

Therefore to bar approaches of sedition it is settled by our decision that all foreign bishops and clergymen should be driven from this most sacred city.[7]

Given on 29 August at Constantinople, Honorius Augustus for the sixth time and Aristaenetus being consuls.

1. Of Constantinople.
2. Soon after Pentecost 404, probably on 20 June, when Chrysostom entered into his second and final exile, Hagia Sophia (begun perhaps by Constantine I and by Constantius II dedicated in 360) caught fire and was destroyed totally along with the Senate House, whither flames spread. Palladius, Chrysostom's biographer, was an eyewitness of the conflagration, of which he gives a graphic description in his *Dialogus* (PG 47. 35-6). For the later Hagia Sophia see no. 505, n. 1.
3. Since the urban prefect's investigation, while serving as a pretext for severe prosecution of Chrysostom's adherents, produced no proof that the Johnnites had set the fire (Palladius, loc. cit.), Arcadius ordered the release of such clergy as had been imprisoned.

Socrates (HE 6. 18 *ad fin.*), however, says that certain of Chrysostom's adherents caused the conflagration and also names the urban prefect Optatus and calls him a pagan and a persecutor of the Johnnites because of this fire. It seems that Studius, whose favourable feelings toward Chrysostom unfitted him to prosecute the designs of Chrysostom's enemies, was succeeded sometime after the catastrophe by Optatus, who then organized punitive measures (Palladius, op. cit., in *PG* 47. 14). So far as *CT* is concerned, no. 286 (dated 11 September 404) is the last law addressed to Studius and 2. 33. 4 (dated 12 June 405) is the first statute sent to Optatus in his second prefecture—for he or another of the same name had been urban prefect on 24 November 398 (*CT* 12. 1. 160).

On the word for *homes* see no. 242, n. 6.

4. That is, not resident in Constantinople.

5. Constantinople.

6. This paragraph is the only part of the law's text preserved by Justinian, whose version reads: "We forbid illicit meetings outside the Church to be conducted in private dwellings—peril of confiscation of the house being imminent, if its owner shall have accepted in it clergymen conducting novel and riotous meetings outside the Church."

Palladius himself, being a "foreign" bishop in his character as bishop of Helenopolis (a suffragan see of the patriarchate), carried to Rome a copy of the constitution, which he gives in *oratio obliqua* (*PG* 47. 13): "The house concealing a bishop or a clergyman or, in short, accepting in the household a communicant of John is to be confiscated." This reproduces the first part of the paragraph.

From Chrysostom's letter to Pope St Innocent I, which Palladius has inserted in his *Dialogus* (*PG* 47. 11), it appears that the soldiery's barbarous profanation of Chrysostom's cathedral on Easter Eve of 404 caused at least those Christians faithful to him (Palladius claims the capital's entire citizenry) to celebrate the Easter feast amid trees and thickets of the environs. See P. R. Coleman-Norton, "The Correspondence of S. John Chrysostom (with Special Reference to His Epistles to Pope S. Innocent I)" in *Classical Philology*, 24 (1929) 280-3.

7. Cf. *supra* n. 5 and see no. 284, n. 3 *ad fin*.

286. MANDATE OF ARCADIUS, HONORIUS, AND THEODOSIUS II ON TUMULTUOUS ASSEMBLIES, 404

(*CT* 16. 4. 5)

This law is similar to an earlier law of this year (no. 283) and differs from it chiefly in the penalties and in the class of persons forbidden to attend tumultuous assemblies.

The same Augusti to Studius, urban prefect.[1]

If anyone should possess slaves in this most sacred city,[2] he should make them to forbear from tumultuous meetings, knowing that for each and every slave, who shall have been discovered to be present at forbidden assemblies, he must be smitten by a loss of three pounds of gold—the slaves, of course, being punished.

And we wish that this rule should be maintained in respect to money-changers and all other guilds of this genial city under a rather severe penalty, so that each and every guild should be bound in the category of a fine to the payment of fifty pounds of gold on behalf of those who from its members shall be revealed to engage in illicit assemblies.

Given on 11 September at Constantinople, Honorius Augustus for the sixth time and Aristaenetus being consuls.

1. Of Constantinople.
2. Constantinople.

287. MANDATE OF ARCADIUS, HONORIUS, AND THEODOSIUS II ON ILLICIT ASSEMBLIES, 404
(CT 16. 4. 6)

Like the two earlier laws of this year (nos. 283 and 286), this constitution is aimed at persons meeting in State-forbidden religious assemblies, but is widened by extension from Constantinople to the provinces and decrees excommunication for persons not in communion with the patriarchs of Constantinople and Alexandria and Antioch. In the latter respect it combines parts of two other constitutions (nos. 284 and 297) assigned to 404 and 406.

The same Augusti to Eutychian, praetorian prefect.[1]

Governors of provinces should be warned that illicit assemblies of those who, having relied on the religion of the orthodox churches, after the sacrosanct churches have been spurned, attempt to assemble elsewhere should be prevented—those who dissent from the communion of Arsacius, Theophilus, Porphyry,[2] the sacred law's [3] most reverend bishops, being driven without doubt from the Church.

Given on 18 November at Constantinople, Honorius Augustus for the sixth time and the most distinguished Aristaenetus being consuls.

1. Of the East.
2. On these prelates see no. 284, n. 5.
3. That is, as usual, the Christian religion.

288. LETTER OF ARCADIUS, HONORIUS, AND THEODOSIUS II ON EPISCOPAL DEPOSITION OF BISHOPS, 405

(CS 2)

This constitution, which Theodosius (*CT* 16. 2. 35) and Justinian (*CI* 1. 3. 14) abridge, is directed against bishops (probably Priscillians) who are deposed by fellow-bishops sitting in council and are condemned to live at least a hundred miles from their former sees.

Emperors Arcadius, Honorius, and Theodosius Augusti to Hadrian, praetorian prefect.[1]

As veneration is due to innocent bishops, so also punishment should be regulated for restless and deposed bishops.

For as those serving God and shining by the integrity of the divine episcopacy offer their own life not only for their own distinction but also for an example to the people subjected to them and obeying them, so those whose sins are rather unworthily beneath the profession of integrity and who have revealed contrary to statutes their careless spirits, if they should be proved to have been excluded and degraded from bishoprics, ought to be separated from the cities which they have stained [2] by their own error, and to be disclosed to themselves and to others as an object of dread by the establishment of banishment. For veneration for the best bishops and disgracing censure for the worst produce the most good persons.

From reports of bishops we have learned that certain bishops of the Christian law,[3] whose delicts both have been detected by an episcopal assembly and have been punished by their verdict, remain in the midst of those cities in which such crimes have been committed and seek disturbances among the people, gather disturbers of the peace, are authors of tumult among the people, call themselves innocent after a trial, collect the populace and are greeted as if still bishops, petition the sacred court,[4] gain by lies responses [5] and furtive rescripts.

Accordingly by this law we ordain that whosoever [6] shall have been deposed from episcopal rank and title by bishops in session, if he shall have been discovered to be undertaking something either against the verdict [7] or against the peace and to seek again the episcopal office, from which he appears to have been excluded,[8] he should spend his life—according to the law of Gratian of divine memory [9]—a hundred miles distant from that city which he unworthily has corrupted.[10] He should be separated from the assemblages of those from whose association he has been parted;[11] he should stay aloof from the city which he has held; he should be segregated from the people whom as a deceitful teacher of life he has corrupted.

According to this law's [12] tenor it should be illegal for persons of this sort to approach our sacred offices [4] and to obtain rescripts by petition.[13] All things which have been obtained by petition on the part of persons degraded from the episcopal office by their own fault, or which shall have been obtained by petition,[14] should remain ineffective, because those persons on whose defence they rely [15] shall know that it will not be without reprimand for themselves, if they shall promise support to them, who appear not to have merited divine [16] approbation,[17] Hadrian, dearest and fondest cousin.[18]

Therefore your sublime Magnificence shall publish this law by edicts throughout all dioceses entrusted to you, that this which has been procured for peace has been established for confirmation of episcopal judgement, has been invented for reprimanding faults, should be honoured by all and should be disclosed to bishops.[19]

Given on 4 February at Ravenna, Stilicho being consul for the second time.[20]

This law does not need interpretation.[21]

1. Of Italy.
2. An editorial conjecture is translated.
3. Religion.
4. That is, the emperor's.
5. See no. 218, n. 5.
6. Here begin the excerpts in *CT* and *CI*.
7. *CT* and *CI* have "security" for this word and introduce "public" into the next phrase.
8. *CT* and *CI* read "expelled".
9. *CI* omits the words between dashes.

According to Sulpicius Severus (*Chron.* 2. 47. 6) the emperor debarred Priscillians from their churches and sent them into exile.

10. *CI* has "has disturbed" and with *CT* omits *unworthily*.
11. Theodosius omits the rest of the sentence and Justinian omits all of it.
12. *CT* omits *this law's* and starts the sentence with "and".
13. That is, with a view to reinstatement.
14. *CT* omits the second relative clause.

Sulpicius Severus (op. cit., 2. 48. 5) says that the Priscillians procured from Gratian a rescript annulling his earlier enactment against them.

15. Such as Macedonius, master of the offices, and Volventius, governor of an unidentified Spanish province, who had been fautors of Priscillianism in Gratian's reign (Sulpicius Severus, op. cit., 2. 48. 5, 49. 1. 3).

16. Probably alluding not to God, but to the emperor, for *divinus* in late Latin often stands for "imperial".

17. Literally "judgement", with which word Theodosius ends his excerpt.
18. For this sentence Justinian has as the conclusion of his version: "He neither should approach our sacred offices nor should hope to obtain by petition rescripts, but also should be deprived of things obtained by petition—their defenders also incurring indignation."
19. The words *and . . . bishops* translate an editorial conjecture.
20. Justinian reads "Stilicho and Aurelian being consuls".
21. This sentence is added to the Theodosian version.

289. MANDATE OF ARCADIUS, HONORIUS, AND THEODOSIUS II ON REBAPTISM, 405
(CT 16. 6. 4)

This law seems to have been the harshest as well as the lengthiest yet enacted against rebaptizers. In it are assailed especially Donatists.

The same Augusti to Hadrian, praetorian prefect.[1]

By this decree's authority we have made provision to extirpate the Catholic faith's adversaries. Accordingly by this new constitution we have ordained especially that that sect, which, lest it be called a heresy, preferred the appellation of schism, must be destroyed.

For those whom they call Donatists are said to have progressed so far in crime that with noxious temerity they have repeated sacrosanct baptism, thus trampling upon the mysteries,[2] and with contagion of a profane repetition they have infected persons once cleansed by the Divinity's gift, as has been the tradition. Thus it has happened that heresy was born from schism. Thence enticing error attracts erroneously credulous minds to the hope of a second pardon, for it is easy to persuade sinners that forgiveness formerly offered can be offered again—but, if this can be given twice in the same way, we do not understand why it should be denied thrice. Moreover these persons pollute with the sacrilege of repeated baptism both slaves and persons subject to their legal authority.

Wherefore by this law we ordain that whoever hereafter shall have been discovered to have rebaptized should be brought before the governor who presides over a province, in order that he, when punished by confiscation of all his property, should pay the penalty of poverty, with which he should be afflicted in perpetuity—on this condition: that for the children of those persons, if they dissent from the depravity of the paternal association, what shall have been their parental property should not be lost and that, if perchance the perversity of the paternal depravity has implicated them and they prefer to revert to the Catholic religion, the opportunity of acquiring the property should not be denied to these persons.

Moreover those places or estates, which hereafter shall have been proved to have provided a retreat for deadly sacrileges, should be added to the fisc's resources, if only the owner—male or female—shall be reported either to have been present perchance or to have given consent—and these, indeed, infamy shall mark justly by a sentence. But if without these persons' knowledge a crime of this kind is proved to have been committed in their house by a leaseholder or a manager, when the preceding judgement of confiscation of the estate has been suspended, the authors of the crime wherein they [3] have been implicated, after having been corrected with a leaden scourge, shall receive exile, with which they should be afflicted for all their lifetime.

And lest perhaps it may be allowable to hide in silence the guilty knowledge of a sinful shame perpetuated within domestic walls, to slaves, if perhaps they should be forced to rebaptism, should be the opportunity of fleeing for refuge to a Catholic church, that by its protection against the authors of this crime and of this group [4] they may be defended by the protection of freedom given to them and that to them it may be permitted under this condition to guard the faith, which their masters have tried to wrest from them when unwilling. And it is not proper for the Catholic dogma's defenders to be constrained to wickedness by that law, with which all other persons who have been placed under power are constrained and it is particularly suitable for all persons without any distinction of condition or of status to be guardians of a heavenly bestowed sanctity.[5]

Moreover those who of the aforesaid sects shall not have feared to repeat baptism or who shall have not [6] condemned this crime by consenting in their own mingling with this group should know that in perpetuity has been denied the power not only of making a will, but also of acquiring anything under pretext of a donation or of engaging in contracts, unless by emendation of their intention they shall have corrected the error of a depraved mind by reverting to the true faith.

Also let the same punishment no less constrain those persons, if any shall have provided connivance at the meetings or the ministries of the persons mentioned; so that the governors of provinces, if they shall have thought in contempt of this sanction that their consent ought to be given, should know that they must be fined twenty pounds of gold and that their office staffs also must be subjected to a similar condemnation. The chief magistrates and the defenders of municipalities should know that, if they shall not have executed that which we command or if⁷ violence shall have been inflicted upon a Catholic church in their presence,⁸ they also must be restrained by the same fine.

Given on 12 February at Ravenna, Stilicho for the second time and Anthemius being consuls.

1. Of Italy.
2. See no. 75, n. 42.
3. It is not clear from the Latin whether by *they* the owners or the non-owners are meant, but the punishment in this case, at any rate, falls only on the non-owners.
4. That is, of rebaptizers.
5. In clearer and briefer words the sense of this paragraph seems to be (1) that slaves, when about to be forced by their masters to submit to rebaptism, may seek sanctuary in a church, and (2) that they then, as defenders of Catholic doctrine against rebaptism, are not bound by the law of persons (touching the obedience of slaves to masters) to be passive parties to such a sin as rebaptism.
6. Either the previous verb's negative must be understood or one must be supplied here.
7. The conditional conjunction must be supplied from the previous one.
8. Presumably violence would come from rebaptizing masters trying to regain possession of their orthodox slaves, who have found refuge in a church, and perhaps organizing fellow-sectarians to assist them. Since such attempts easily could be converted into riots, municipal authorities assisting (in the French sense) at such proceedings were subjected to fines.

290. MANDATE OF ARCADIUS, HONORIUS, AND THEODOSIUS II ON REBAPTISM, 405
(CT 16. 6. 5)

This second order against rebaptism was published on the same day as no. 289 and adds Montanists¹ to Donatists in its prohibition.

The same Augusti to Hadrian, praetorian prefect.²

Lest the polluted sect of Donatists or of Montanists should violate divine grace by repeated baptism, we abolish by the severity of this command the opportunity for deception, when we ordain that certain punishment should pursue persons of this sort and that they who by perverse dogma had contested against the Catholic religion should experience the law's vengeful judgement.

Therefore we order that if anyone hereafter shall have been discovered to rebaptize, he should be brought before the governor who

presides over a province, in order that he, when punished by confiscation of all his property, should pay the penalty of poverty.[3]
And the rest.
Given on 12 February at Ravenna, Stilicho for the second time and Anthemius being consuls.

1. Since the Donatists in Rome were known as *Montenses* (Hill Folk) or *Rupitae* (Rock Dwellers) from their practice of meeting in a catacomb constructed in a suburban hill (see no. 301, n. 4) and because the present law apparently concerns the West, whereas the Montanists were strongest in the East and were not notorious for insistence on rebaptism, probably *Montanists* should be emended to "Montenses", i.e. *Montensium* for *Montanistarum*.
2. Of Italy.
3. Most of this sentence appears in no. 289, par. 4.

291. EDICT OF ARCADIUS, HONORIUS, AND THEODOSIUS II ON REBAPTISM, 405

(*CT* 16. 6. 3)

This third order, of which only one sentence survives, against rebaptism was published on the same day as nos. 289 and 290.

Emperors Arcadius, Honorius, and Theodosius Augusti.
An edict.
We do not tolerate rebaptizers' devious errors.
And the rest.
Given on 12 February at Ravenna, Stilicho for the second time and Anthemius being consuls.

292. EDICT OF ARCADIUS, HONORIUS, AND THEODOSIUS II ON MANICHAEANS AND DONATISTS, 405

(*CT* 16. 5. 38)

Renewed efforts to suppress Manichaeanism and Donatism are evident in this document.[1]

The same Augusti and Theodosius Augustus.
An edict.
None should recall to memory a Manichaean, none a Donatist, who especially, we have learned, cease not to be mad.

There should be one Catholic worship, there should be one salvation, the Trinity's sanctity, equal and harmonious within itself, should be sought.

But if anyone should dare to associate himself with forbidden and illicit practices, he should not escape the toils of innumerable previous constitutions and of the law recently published by our Gentleness[2] and, if by chance seditious mobs shall have assembled, he should not doubt that the quickened goads of sharper irritation must be bared.[3]

Given on 12 February at Ravenna, Stilicho for the second time and Anthemius being consuls.

1. Wider publication for this law was authorized later in this year (no. 294).
2. If not no. 289 of the same date, this law is not extant.
3. The last clause is a rather elaborate exercise in words to assure a violator that he will deserve a severer punishment.

293. MANDATE OF ARCADIUS AND HONORIUS ON RESCISSION OF JULIAN II'S RESCRIPT ON BEHALF OF DONATISTS, 405

(CT 16. 5. 37)

After the suicide (398) of Gildo, a Moorish chieftain, who, as count of Africa, had oppressed Rome's African subjects for a dozen years and had favoured the Donatist faction, the Catholics there at last secured from Honorius the repeal of Julian the Apostate's rescript granting to Donatists the privilege of assembly (no. 120).

The same Augusti to Hadrian, praetorian prefect.[1]

We will that the rescript which the Donatists are said to have procured from Julian, then emperor, should be prefixed to an edict,[2] posted in the most frequented places, and that the records into which an allegation of this kind has been inserted[3] should be subjoined, whereby both the Catholic belief's steadfast constancy and the Donatists' desperation, falsified by perfidy, may become known to all.[4]

Given on 25 February at Ravenna, Stilicho and Aurelian[5] being consuls.

1. Of Italy.

2. The word is *programma* (transliterated from Greek), often applied to a proclamation of a praetorian prefect.

The standard operating procedure was for the official who published the law to place his proclamation beneath it.

3. The *rescript* (no. 120) was placed in the records of the governors (*iudicum gesta*) of the province of Africa, so asserts St Augustine (*Cont. Ep. Par.* 1. 12. 19 Æ *CSEL* 51. 41). Despite the strong word *allegation*, which seems to suggest that the rescript was forged, the document's authenticity was accepted by Augustine, in whose mention of it (loc. cit. in introd. to no. 120) appears the phrase *allegationis gesta* (records of the allegation).

4. It is of interest to know that Julian's anti-Christian legislation was still on record over forty years after his death, despite its rescission by his successors in that interval. The failure to include such statutes in the Theodosian Code cannot be charged to Theodosius II, who for the sake of scholarship commanded its compilers not to omit obsolete ordinances (*CT* 1. 1. 5).

5. A scribal error; Anthemius was consul in 405, when Stilicho was consul for the second time.

294. MANDATE OF ARCADIUS, HONORIUS, AND THEODOSIUS II ON CHRISTIAN UNITY, 405

(*CT* 16. 11. 2)

This directive orders that an edict on unity, sent originally throughout Africa (no. 292),[1] should be circulated more widely in Africa.[2]

Emperors Arcadius, Honorius, and Theodosius Augusti to Diotimus, proconsul of Africa.

The edict[1] on unity which our Clemency has sent through African regions we desire to be published throughout various places, that to all persons it may become known that the one and the true Catholic faith in Almighty God, which right belief confesses, must be retained.

Given on 5 March at Ravenna, Stilicho for the second time and Anthemius being consuls.

1. Nothing in the edict (no. 292) indicates that it was sent to Africa except the mention of Donatists, whose chief stronghold was there.

2. Apparently only in the province, whose governor was a proconsul, and not throughout the diocese, whose governor was a vicar.

295. LETTER OF HONORIUS ON CONVOCATION OF A THESSALONICAN COUNCIL, 405

(PG 47. 14-15)

Palladius, bishop of Helenopolis, in his dialogue on the life of St John Chrysostom,[1] patriarch of Constantinople, preserves the last of a series of three letters [2] from Honorius to Arcadius about the scandalous treatment of the Eastern Church's golden-mouthed orator, who was sent into exile. Importuned by Pope St Innocent I, to whom Chrysostom had appealed, Honorius summoned a synod of Italian bishops, who petitioned the emperor to request Arcadius, his older, but feeble, brother and joint-emperor, to convoke a synod in Thessalonica which should solve the matters at issue.[3] But Arcadius did not comply.

This epistle, rather peremptory in tone, reveals imperial impatience and is virtually a mandate.

For the third time I write to your Clemency, requesting that you devise correction concerning the plot against John, the bishop of the Constantinopolitans; and, as it appears, nothing has been done. As a result, again I have written through bishops and priests,[4] since I am very concerned for ecclesiastical peace, because of which also our Empire lives peaceably, that you should deign to command the bishops of the East to convene in Thessalonica. Also the bishops of our West, having selected men steadfast against evil and falsehood, have dispatched five bishops, two priests, one deacon[5] of the greatest Church of the Romans. And deign to regard them with all honours,[6] that either, convinced that Bishop John has been expelled justly, they may instruct me to withdraw from communion with him or, having proved that the bishops of the East are acting with malice prepense, they may dissuade you from communion with them.

As to what the Westerners think about Bishop John, of all the letters written to me I have appended two, equivalent to all in import, the letters of the bishop of Rome and of the bishop of Aquileia.[7]

But above all, I bid your Clemency, demand that Theophilus of Alexandria,[8] even though unwilling, should be present, through whom especially it is said that all these evils have arisen, that the synod of the assembled bishops, hindered in no respect, may arbitrate a peace proper to our times.

1. See nos. 284, n. 1, and 297, n. 3.
2. The first is in M 3. 1123-4. The second is in *CSEL* 35. 85-8. Neither is legislative in tone.
3. So Palladius professes (*PG* 47. 14), but this synod is unrecorded by the ecclesiastical historians of the fifth century. Toward the close of the seventh

century Theodore of Trimuthus quotes in full a decree promulgated by the pope in an Italian synod (*PG* 47. 59–60), whose decision accords generally with Palladius' statements (*PG* 47. 15, 78), but is silent about a synod to be held in Thessalonica. Dom Chrysostom Baur believes (*S. Jean Chrysostome et ses oeuvres dans l'histoire littéraire* [Louvain, 1907], 45) that most of the documents quoted by Theodore were composed *dans l'intérêt littéraire de son écrit*.

4. These carried his letter.

5. These, already mentioned, are named by Palladius, after he has quoted the letter, but he names only three bishops and two priests, none of whom is known outside his *Dialogus*.

6. On the contrary they were imprisoned in Constantinople and then were reconveyed to Rome.

7. Neither letter is extant.

8. The crafty patriarch who persecuted Chrysostom.

296. LETTER OF ARCADIUS, HONORIUS, AND THEODOSIUS II ON SWIFT JUSTICE FOR DONATISTS, 405
(*CT* 16. 5. 39)

This statute demands speedy settlement of cases in which Donatists have been convicted.

The same Augusti to their Diotimus,[1] greeting.

We agree that heretics of the Donatist superstition at whatever place,[2] when either confessing or convicted, with the tenor of the law observed, should pay fully the due penalty without delay.

Given on 8 December at Ravenna, Stilicho for the second time and Anthemius being consuls.

1. Proconsul of Africa, where Donatism was rampant.
2. That is, no matter in what court; possibly, of whatever rank.

297. RESCRIPT OF ARCADIUS ON CHRYSOSTOM'S ADHERENTS, 406
(PG 47. 37)

This constitution is another in the series [1] aimed against St Chrysostom's adherents, after that Constantinopolitan patriarch was extruded from his see principally through the ambition of Theophilus, patriarch of Alexandria.[2]

Palladius, who wrote Chrysostom's biography in dialogistic form,[3] asserts that Atticus, the next successor but one to the exiled saint, procured this directive, when he had noted that none of the eastern bishops or even of the Constantinopolitan laity would communicate with him after his accession.

If anyone of the bishops is not in communion with Theophilus and Porphyry [4] and Atticus, let him be expelled from the Church and let him be separated from the personal property of his possessions.

1. See no. 284, n. 3.
2. See no. 284, n. 4.
3. Apparently the only other ancient biographies of saints extant in the unusual form of a dialogue are those by Sulpicius Severus (*PL* 20. 183–222), who devotes most of his dialogue to the virtues of St Martin of Tours, and by Pope St Gregory I, who relates the lives of various Italian saints and especially at length the life of St Benedict of Nursia, the founder of Benedictinism (*PL* 77. 149–430 and 66. 125–204, in which *locus* there also is a Greek version by Pope St Zacharias).
See P. R. Coleman-Norton, "The Use of Dialogue in the *Vitae Sanctorum*" in *JTS* 27 (1926) 388–95.
4. Porphyry was patriarch of Antioch.

298. MANDATE OF ARCADIUS, HONORIUS, AND THEODOSIUS II ON JURISTIC RESTRICTIONS FOR MANICHAEANS, PHRYGIANS, AND PRISCILLIANS, 407
(CT 16. 5. 40)

This ordinance (repeated largely in *CI* 1. 5. 4), while it mentions a few other restrictions, concerns itself chiefly with forbidding Manichaeans again (see nos. 176, 185, 219), Phrygians, and Priscillians testamentary rights and privileges.

The same Augusti to Senator, urban prefect.[1]

Recently we have declared what we thought about Donatists.[2] Especially, however, we prosecute with most merited severity Manichaeans and Phrygians and Priscillians.[3] Accordingly to this class of persons let there be in common with all others nothing of customs and nothing of laws.

And first, indeed, we wish it[4] to be a public crime,[5] because what is committed against divine religion is effected to the injury of all persons.

And also we prosecute these persons by confiscation of their property, which, however, we command them to cede to all nearest kinfolk, in such a way that the order, just as in successions, of ascendants and of descendants and of collateral blood-relatives—even to the second degree—may be maintained.[6] And so, finally, we allow these relatives to have the right to take the property, if they themselves are not polluted also by an equally guilty conscience.

We also wish the heretics themselves to be withdrawn from every gift and inheritance coming under any title whatsoever.

Furthermore we do not leave to anyone so convicted the capacity of donating, of buying, of selling, finally of contracting.

Also the legal inquisition extends[7] beyond death. For, if in crimes of treason it is allowed to accuse a deceased person's memory, not undeservedly the said person also ought to undergo judgement in this case. Therefore the last will of that person, who is convicted of having been either a Manichaean or a Phrygian or a Priscillian,[8] should be void, whether he left property by testament or by codicil or by letter or by any kind of will whatsoever—that same condition concerning the above described degrees having been kept also in this case; but we do not permit children to be heirs or to enter, unless they shall have departed from the paternal depravity. To be sure, we grant pardon to those repenting their transgression.[9]

We also wish slaves to be without guilt, if, abandoning[10] their masters' sacrilege, they shall have crossed with more faithful service to the Catholic Church.[11]

To our patrimony should be added the estate on which a meeting of persons of this character has assembled itself, when the owner, although not implicated by participation in the crime, nevertheless knows of it and does not forbid it; and if the owner has been ignorant of it, the overseer or the manager of the estate, after he has been chastised with a lead-tipped scourge, should be consigned to the perpetual labour of the mines, but the leaseholder, if he is of sufficient social status, shall be deported.

The governor of the province, if by dissimulation or by partiality he shall have deferred these crimes when reported or shall have neg-

298. JURISTIC RESTRICTIONS, 407

lected these when clearly proved,[12] should know that he must be penalized by a fine of twenty pounds of gold. Also the penalty of ten pounds of gold shall constrain both the defenders and the chief magistrates of each and every city and also the provincial office staffs, unless in executing those commands, which have been made by the governors in this matter, they shall have bestowed the most sagacious attention and the most skilled service.[13]

Given on 22 February at Rome, Honorius Augustus for the seventh time and Theodosius Augustus for the second time being consuls.

1. Of Rome. In *CI* Senator appears as praetorian prefect.
2. For this recent legislation see nos. 289-94, 296.
3. *CI* omits what the Augusti thought about Donatists and starts the statute thus: "We prosecute with most merited severity Manichaeans—whether male or female—and Donatists." *CI* does not mention Phrygians or Priscillians in this ordinance.
4. No subject is expressed in Latin, but "heresy" probably is meant.
5. That is, it is open to any person to make accusation.
6. Apparently the order of intestate succession is meant. The second degree ends with (1) grandfather and grandmother as ascendants, (2) grandson and granddaughter as descendants, (3) brother and sister as collateral blood-relatives.
7. *CI* has the subjunctive mood here: "let extend" or "should extend".
8. *CI* reads only *a Manichaean* (cf. *supra* n. 3 *ad fin.*).
9. *CI* inserts from no. 275 the following sentence here: "The stings of authority should be aimed also against those persons who with damnable provision shall protect these in their own houses."
10. *CI* shows that some such reading should be substituted for whatever was the word originally used, which Justinian's commissioners rejected as meaningless, if not inappropriate.
11. Here *CI* ends its adaptation of this statute.
12. The idea is "deferred trial of . . . neglected punishment of".
13. Pitra prints (2. 517 and 602) two late Greek summaries of this law with slight variations in the last sentence: "We permit Manichaeans or Donatists to have nothing in common from law or custom with all other persons, but they should be constrained also by public accusation and their property should be confiscated and they neither should take anything from donation or last will nor should donate anything nor should make any contract at all.

"And charges against them should be sought after death.

"And their children should not succeed [as heirs] them, when the parental error has not been avoided, the same penalty being imposed on him who receives these persons, but their slaves should be guiltless, if they have crossed to the orthodox religion."

299. MANDATE OF ARCADIUS, HONORIUS, AND THEODOSIUS II ON CONFESSION OF CATHOLICISM AS A TEST OF ORTHODOXY, 407
(CT 16. 5. 41)

This constitution enacts that a simple confession of the Catholic faith is sufficient to quash a prosecution for heresy.

The same Augusti to Porphyry, proconsul of Africa.

Though it is usual to expiate crimes by punishment, nevertheless we wish to amend men's depraved desires by admonition to penitence.

Therefore whatever heretics, whether they are Donatists or Manichaeans or of any other depraved belief and sect, who have assembled for profane rites, shall have accepted by a simple confession the Catholic faith and rite, which we wish to be observed by all men, although they shall have nourished by long and long-lasting meditation a deep-seated evil to such an extent that they also appear subject to previously issued laws,[1] yet, as soon as they shall have confessed God by a simple religious ceremony, we ordain that these persons should be absolved from all guilt, so that for every guilty act, whether it has been committed previously or it is committed afterward (a situation which we do not wish to be), although punishment seems especially to press upon the guilty, it should suffice for withdrawal of the accusation that they have condemned their error by their own decision and have embraced the name of Almighty God, which even amid their dangers [2] has been sought, because nowhere ought to be lacking religion's aid, when invoked in afflictions.

Therefore, as we command the previous laws,[1] which we have established for the destruction of sacrilegious minds, to be applied with every effect of execution, so we ordain that those persons who shall have preferred the faith of simple religion, though by a late confession, should not be bound by laws [1] which have been issued.

And accordingly we have made these sanctions, that all may know that punishment for men's profane desires is not lacking and that it redounds to the true religion and that there is support of the laws.

Given on 15 November at Rome, Honorius Augustus for the seventh time and Theodosius Augustus for the second time being consuls.

1. Such as nos. 40, 56, 66, 67, 103, 156, 159, 160, 163, 166, 167, 173, 176, 179, 185, 190–2, 194, 196, 205, 213, 215, 217–19, 222, 232, 239, 245, 248, 249, 251, 253, 254, 256, 258, 260, 264, 268, 275, 277, 287, 289–94, 296, 298.

2. These probably would be the tortures and the subsequent danger of death resulting from torture or imposed as a sentence in their trial.

300. MANDATE OF ARCADIUS, HONORIUS, AND THEODOSIUS II ON ADVOCATES AS REPRESENTATIVES OF THE CHURCH, 407
(CT 16. 2. 38)

Besides confirming past privileges for the Church and its clergy, this law allows advocates or lay representatives to represent the Church in obtaining privileges for the Church from the emperors, thus extending to the Christian Church the similar privilege formerly conceded to pagan corporations.

Emperors Arcadius, Honorius, and Theodosius Augusti to Porfyry,[1] proconsul of Africa.

After other matters.

Also by this order we decree that the privileges which the laws' authority has decreed for churches and for clergymen [2] should continue holy and inviolate.

And to them we grant this special and particular privilege: that whatever rights pertaining only to the Church shall have been procured from us—not through crown officials,[3] but by advocates [4]—at their [5] decision both should become known to governors and should obtain effect.

Moreover bishops [6] of the province [7] shall be very careful, lest under this excuse, namely, of privilege, also anything disadvantageous should be imposed on them contrary to their interest.

Given on 15 November at Rome, Honorius Augustus for the seventh time and Theodosius Augustus for the second time being consuls.

1. Usually spelled Porphyry.
2. While much of such legislation covered the entire Empire, yet, so far as the African province is concerned, among such statutes are nos. 11, 15, 16, 106, 148, 183, 250, 276, 278, 282, 292, 294.
3. It is not quite clear who these (*coronati*) are. While it is known that *coronati* had some kind of jurisdiction in religious matters as heads of the imperial cult in the provinces, yet at this late date in the Christianized Empire, if crown officials are meant, they probably were concerned only with Christian affairs. On the other hand, they may have been clergymen whose tonsure (*corona*) gave them this name.
4. Lawyers of professional training.
5. It is uncertain whether *their* represents clergymen's or lawyers'.
6. The word is *sacerdotes*, which can include priests (see no. 16, n. 4).
7. Africa.

301. LETTER OF HONORIUS AND THEODOSIUS II ON SUPPRESSION OF HERETICS AND PAGANS, 407-8

(CS 12)

Sections of this constitution appear also in CT 16. 5. 43 and 16. 10. 19. It not only reaffirms the validity of earlier statutes against pagans, heretics, schismatics, but also apparently adds new strictures against those persons who persist in their deviation from orthodox Christianity.

Emperors Honorius and Theodosius Augusti to Curtius, praetorian prefect.[1]

Assuredly, indeed, the sole care of bishops, religious men of God, in noticing crimes, their sedulity in admonishing, their authority in teaching ought to have corrected heretics' profane spirits and pagans' superstition. Nor, however, have the statutes of our laws ceased to be valid, that these may restore, even through proposed fear of punishment, the deviators to Almighty God's worship and also may mould the ignorant to divine services. But doubtless the very potency of evil, confounding human as well as divine matters, drives many persons, deceived by depraved persuasions, both to present and to future destruction and destroys in God's as well as our sight the lives of hapless persons, whom both here it surrenders to the laws and there forces to undergo sentence.

Therefore, compelled by Donatists' pertinacity, by pagans' madness, which, indeed, the governors' mischievous sloth, their office staffs' connivance, the municipal senates'[2] contempt inflame, we think it necessary to renew what we have ordered. Wherefore all[3] statutes which have been made by us through the authority of general laws against the Donatists, who also are called Montenses,[4] the Manichaeans or the Priscillians or against the pagans,[5] we decree not only are to continue but are to be brought to fullest execution and effect, so that the buildings of both the said persons and the Caelicolans, who have congregations of some new dogma, also may be appropriated by the churches.

Moreover the punishment proposed by law will be bound to regard as convicted those who shall have confessed that they are Donatists or shall have fled the Catholic bishops' communion by a perverse religion's pretext, although they pretend that they are Christians.[6]

Moreover the temples' allowances for provisions should be withdrawn and these, for the purpose of benefiting the expenses of the very devoted soldiers, should aid the account pertaining to provisions.[7]

Images, if any even now stand in temples and shrines and if any

301. SUPPRESSION OF HERETICS AND PAGANS, 407–8

either have received or receive any worship of pagans, should be removed from their positions, since we know that this has been decreed by a rather oft repeated ordinance.[8]

The temples' buildings themselves, which are in communities or towns or outside towns, should be appropriated to public use.

Altars in all places should be destroyed and all temples on our estates should be transferred to suitable uses; the proprietors should be compelled to destroy the altars.

It should not be allowed at all to engage in banquets in honour of a sacrilegious rite in these rather deadly[9] places or to celebrate any ceremony.

Also to bishops of the localities[10] we grant the faculty of ecclesiastical power to prohibit the said practices.[11]

For we also have given the management of Maximus, Julian, Eutychus, the secret service agents,[12] to this matter, that the statutes which have been enacted by general laws against Donatists, Manichaeans, and against heretics of this type and pagans may be fulfilled. And, however, they shall know that in all matters the statutes' procedure must be maintained, that to the governors they should report crimes, which appear to have been committed contrary to prohibition, to be punished according to the power of the laws.

And indeed, Curtius, dearest and fondest cousin, the penalty of a fine (long ago established) of twenty pounds of gold, shall constrain the governors—a like fine having been set for their office staffs and the municipal senates,[1] if these things which we have ordained shall have been neglected by their carelessness.[13]

And this provision for restraining men's morals and religion your sublime Magnificence both shall cause to be sent to the provinces' governors and shall order to be observed with due vigour by all persons.

Given on 25 November at Rome. Posted at Carthage in the Forum under [14] the edict of Porphyry, the proconsul, on 5 June,[15] the most distinguished Bassus and the most distinguished Philip being consuls.

1. Of Italy.
2. The word is *ordines*, on which see no. 325, n. 6.
3. Here begins *CT* 16. 5. 43.
4. This was a local name for Donatists in Rome: "Hill Folk" (no. 290, n. 1).
5. To take only the laws issued by Honorius and Theodosius II, who strictly speak only of such statutes which carry their names, against the aforesaid heretics and schismatics as well as pagans in general, among such legislation are nos. 239, 253, 275, 287–94, 296, 298, 299 and *CT* 16. 10. 14–19 (dated from 396 to 407–8).
6. Here ends *CT* 16. 5. 43 and *CT* 16. 10. 19 begins.

7. The *res annonaria* was the quartermaster's account, from which soldiers received (since the mid-third century, when scarcity of metal and depreciation of currency were marked) their wages in provisions.

All the different meanings of *annona* are connected with the supply of provisions. In general and in the widest sense, it is the yearly produce or the annual income of natural produce. Especially it is the means of subsistence and, in this meaning, for the most part, grain. By metonymy it is the market price of grain or the grain stored in the State's granaries or the gratuitous grain-supply (on which last see no. 141, n. 3). In the late Principate the *annona* was enlarged to include such items as beasts of burden, bread, cloth, fodder for cattle, lard, meat, oil, salt, vessels, vinegar, wine, wood.

In the early Dominate the *annona* became an annual tax in kind and was imposed on all landowners—whether corporate or individual—throughout the Empire and was varied according to governmental needs and provincial conditions. Sometimes (as here) exemptions were granted by emperors. In this period also the *annona*, after it had been collected, was issued to officials as salaries, to soldiers as rations, to the people as doles. (Hence we find the appropriate phrases of *annona civilis, annona militaris, annona publica*.) The prefect had as his assistants procurators, who were stationed throughout the Empire, and professional persons, who were organized in guilds (see no. 584, n. 7) for procuring and transporting provisions. It is believed also that of such surpluses as existed some were sold under the State's auspices to contractors for resale and others were granted to the Church for use in its charitable institutions (see nos. 510, 537, 584). But losses under this system of taxation in kind were large: theft, embezzlement, wastage in transport, spoilage in storage were known evils which struck at the system's efficacy.

8. This statement is exaggerated, so far as extant legislation is concerned. Only no. 63 (not included in *CT* or *CI*) and *CT* 16. 10. 18 (in 399) and 19 (in 407-8) support the authors' assertion that the ordinance often was repeated. Although there are prohibitions against worship of images (e.g. *CT* 16. 10. 6 [dated 356]), yet one constitution considers images as works of art and is content simply to interdict idolatry (*CT* 16. 10. 8 [dated 382]) and other laws accept their existence but punish sacrifices before them (e.g. no. 242).

9. That is, deadly from the Christian viewpoint.

10. Where existed pagan temples.

11. *CT* 16. 10. 19 resumes after the next two sentences.

12. The *agentes in rebus*, on whom see no. 256, n. 3.

13. For this sentence *CT* 16. 10. 19 reads (and then ends): "Moreover we constrain the governors by a penalty of twenty pounds of gold and by a like regulation their office staffs, if these things shall have been neglected by their carelessness."

14. The preposition may be construed literally, for the publisher of an imperial constitution often posted his own explanatory edict with it, sometimes above it, but here apparently below it.

15. It is tempting to ascribe the long delay of more than six months between the law's issuance in Rome and its publication in Carthage to the proconsul's reluctance to disturb the Donatists, whose headquarters were there. On the other hand, the delay may have been due to negligence in distribution or to vicissitude of transportation or to another circumstance now not known.

302. MANDATE OF HONORIUS AND THEODOSIUS II ON TRIAL OF BANDITS DURING LENT OR AT EASTERTIDE, 408
(CT 9. 35. 7)

By this directive (repeated and extended in *CI* 3. 12. 8) the emperors suspend the earlier law (no. 169) which forbade trial of criminal cases during Lent.

Emperors Honorius and Theodosius Augusti to Anthemius, praetorian prefect.[1]

Governors of provinces should be advised that in the trials of Isaurian bandits [2] they should consider no venerable day of Quadragesima [3] or of Eastertide to be excepted, lest there may be postponed the exposure of their wicked plans, which must be investigated by tortures [4] of the bandits, since the Highest Divinity's pardon is expected very easily in this action, by which the safety and the preservation of many persons are provided.

Given on 27 April at Constantinople, Bassus and Philip being consuls.

1. Of the Orient.
2. Contemporary non-legal sources, of which the correspondence of St John Chrysostom paints a competent picture, relate these predators' savage raids into the south-eastern section of Asia Minor since 401 (see no. 523, n. 5).

Justinian reads "of bandits and especially of Isaurians", for he seems to have been confronted with the same situation over a century later.

3. On the meaning of this word see no. 169, n. 3.
4. See no. 204, n. 3.

303. MANDATE OF HONORIUS AND THEODOSIUS II ON JEWISH SACRILEGE OFFENSIVE TO CHRISTIANS, 408
(CT 16. 8. 18)

This constitution, which Justinian repeats (*CI* 1. 9. 11), forbids Jews to burn a cross in connection with Aman,[1] their religious feast.

Emperors Honorius and Theodosius Augusti to Anthemius, praetorian prefect.[2]

Governors of provinces should forbid Jews, in a certain ceremony of their festival Aman[1] for remembrance of a former punishment, to ignite and to burn for contempt of the Christian faith with sacrilegious mind a simulated appearance of the Holy Cross,[3] lest they should connect our faith's sign with their sports;[4] but they should retain their rites without contempt of the Christian law,[5] because without doubt they shall lose privileges previously permitted to them, unless they shall have abstained from illicit acts.

Given on 29 May at Constantinople, Bassus and Philip being consuls.

1. This is now known as Purim, which commemorates the deliverance of the Persian Jews from the machinations of Haman, the minister of Ahasuerus (erroneously identified with Xerxes I, king of Persia [485-465 B.C.]). The festival, traditionally instituted on 14-15 Adar 473 B.C. (Esther 3. 7, 13; 8. 9, 12; 9. 17-32), is still observed by Jews in either February or March.

J. G. Frazer, *The Scapegoat*[3] (London, 1913), 354-68, 392-407, 412-23 (in Part 6 of *The Golden Bough*), convincingly shows that the Jewish festival of Purim descends from the ancient Babylonian festival of the Sacaea.

2. Of the Orient.

3. Since Haman was hung on a gallows (Esther 7. 10), which apparently resembled a cross, it seemed appropriate to burn him in effigy as part of the licence connected with the celebration of Purim (see next note).

While this practice may have appealed to Jews, it was abhorred by Christians, who, according to St Cyril, bishop of Jerusalem, as early as 348 (some twenty years after St Helena, mother of Emperor Constantine I the Great, had discovered the Cross in Jerusalem, on which invention see no. 54, n. 6) accorded marks of adoration to the Cross (*Catecheses*, 4. 10, 4. 14, 13. 4, 16. 4, *et al.* = *PG* 33. 468, 472, 776, 924). See also no. 393, n. 1.

4. This translates a brilliant editorial conjecture (*iocis*) for the unanimously reported reading (*locis*): *sports* for "places".

Some of the licence (mummery, songs, dances, games, pranks, plays) associated with the observance of Purim in the Middle Ages has been traced into Talmudic times (see *The Jewish Encyclopedia*, s.v. Purim). On this gayest of Jewish holidays, during the synagogue service the Book of Esther is read and the children in the congregation twirl their gragers (noisemakers) every time that Haman's name is mentioned—to drown the mention of his name.

5. Religion.

304. MANDATE OF HONORIUS AND THEODOSIUS II ON EMPLOYMENT OF CHRISTIANS AT COURT, 408
(CT 16. 5. 42)

This directive, while aimed ostensibly at pagans, may be extended to include heretics and schismatics. It apparently was applied only temporarily, for in 527 it still was necessary to exclude by law non-Christians from governmental service (no. 567).

Emperors Honorius and Theodosius Augusti to Olympius, master of the offices, and to Valens, count of the domestics.

Those persons who are hostile to the Catholic sect we forbid to perform governmental service [1] within the palace, that none who differs from us in faith and in religion may be associated with us in any way.

Given on 14 November at Ravenna, Bassus and Philip being consuls.

1. See no. 186, n. 4.

305. LETTER OF HONORIUS AND THEODOSIUS II ON DISTURBANCE OF SACRAMENTS, 408
(CT 16. 5. 44)

From this statute it appears that certain specified groups were disturbing—how, we are not told—Catholic sacraments and that this directive was designed to stop such interference.

The same Augusti.

Hail, Donatus,[1] most dear to us.

Donatists', heretics', Jews' new and unusual audacity has disclosed practices wherewith [2] they wish to disturb the Catholic faith's sacraments.

Beware lest this pestilence may spread and may proceed more widely with its contagion.[2]

Therefore we command the punishment of just chastisement [3] to be exhibited against those persons who shall have attempted anything which is contrary and opposed to the Catholic sect.

Given on 24 November at Ravenna, Bassus and Philip being consuls.

1. Proconsul of Africa.
2. An editorial conjecture gives this translation.
3. Doubtless death.

306. MANDATE OF HONORIUS AND THEODOSIUS II ON SCHISMATICAL ASSEMBLIES, 408
(CT 16. 5. 45)

This constitution forbids illicit meetings of Christian dissidents and orders confiscation of their churches and exile for heretics.

The same Augusti to Theodore, praetorian prefect [1] for the second time.

The watchfulness [2] of defenders,[3] of curials, and of all office staffs should guard lest anyone who dissents from the Catholic Church's bishop [4] should have opportunity for illegal assembly within any community or in any remote part of its territory.

We decree also that the places themselves should be added to public legal control—every excuse barred—and that those persons who dare to dispute and to assert the things which divine instruction condemns, after they have been proscribed, should be driven into exile.

Given on 27 November at Ravenna, Bassus and Philip being consuls.

1. Of Italy.
2. The Latin has the concrete *specula* (watchtower, lookout).
3. Of municipalities.
4. A case of antimeria: "episcopate" is meant. The word is *sacerdos*, on which see no. 16, n. 4.

307. LETTER OF ARCADIUS AND HONORIUS ON RETURN OF EX-CLERGYMEN TO CIVIL DUTIES, 408

(CS 9)

The emperors rule that all former clergymen must return to service either with their municipal senates or with their municipal guilds and that the leading municipal senators must be fined, if they shall have been guilty of collusion with ex-clergymen seeking to shun such service.

An epitome of this constitution is preserved in CT 16. 2. 39.

Emperors Arcadius [1] and Honorius Augusti to Theodore, praetorian prefect [2] for the second time.

Would indeed that only those persons whose life cannot relapse into an inferior state might assume the name of clergymen! [3] There would be common rejoicing and human veneration easily would attend pious rites and divine worship. But vices easily creep along, so that error also creeps in thither where there can be nothing unless pure. And if the censure of an episcopal court should provide watchfully that among good persons there should not be those who cannot be good persons, nevertheless, lest crimes, when detected, should flourish and unrestricted pertinacity should be in sinning persons, it pleases us that whatever [4] clergyman a bishop shall have judged unworthy of his office and shall have separated from the Church's ministry, or whoever shall have abandoned voluntarily the sacred religion's professed service,[5] the municipal senate at once should claim him for itself; that for him no longer can be a free return to the Church and that he should join,[6] according to the status of the persons or [7] the amount of his patrimony, either his municipal senate or a guild of his municipality, provided that they should be obligated to whatever public services they shall be suited and so that there also should not be opportunity for collusion; that [8] from the ten principal curials individually should be exacted two pounds of gold apiece to be paid to our treasury, if they shall have shown illicit connivance and foul collusion with any person,[9] and to all [10] the most reprobate persons should be prevented entrance to all offices of governmental service.[11] For nowhere can be faithful they whom the Church shall have rejected as unfaithful to the Highest God, Theodore, dearest and fondest cousin.

And your illustrious Magnificence shall cause this to come to the notice of all persons by letters given to the governors of each and every province, that formally posted edicts may declare this to all persons.

Given on 27 November at Ravenna, the most distinguished [12] Bassus and the most distinguished [12] Philip being consuls.

Interpretation:[13] Whatsoever clergyman his own bishop shall have proved to be of evil life and shall have removed from his rank because of baseness of character, or if a clergyman himself by his own will shall have left the profession of the clericate, straightway by the governor he should be joined to the curials, that, if he thus is suitable because of his lineage and his property, he can compel him to fulfil his duty among the curials themselves.

However, if he is a person of the lowest class, this law has determined that he should stay among the guildsmen or he should serve in the public service for which he shall have been suited, so that persons of this sort should be excused in no wise by the curials through any collusion whatever. But if this shall have been done, the curials should know that for each and every person two pounds of gold apiece must be paid by them to the fisc.

1. Arcadius died on 1 May 408; but see nos. 193, n. 1, and 238, n. 1.
2. Of Italy.
3. The sequence of tenses follows the Latin system. In the optative subjunctive mode the imperfect tense expresses a wish that something were so now—hence *might assume*.
4. Here begins the Theodosian excerpt.
5. *CT* reads more simply "the sacred religion's profession".
6. In *CT* the verb is passive.
7. *CT* reads "and" for *or*.
8. *CT* has "therefore".
9. This word is pluralized in *CT*.
10. *CT* omits the adjective.
11. Here *CT* ends. See no. 186, n. 4.
12. *CT* omits the superlative adjective.
13. This is appended to the Theodosian version.

308. LETTER OF HONORIUS ON CHRISTIAN SUPERVISION OF RESTORATION OF CAPTIVES, 408

(*CS* 16)

This constitution, partly preserved with many abbreviated words by Theodosius (*CT* 5. 7. 2) and extremely shortened by Justinian (*CI* i. 4. 11), who, however, repeats the entire Theodosian version in a later title (*CI* 8. 50. 20), regulates postliminial assistance for returned prisoners of war and particularly directs that Christians should be active in such succour.

Doubtless this law was drafted to offset some of the recent results of "the wide course of barbarian savagery" (to which its text alludes at n. 4 *infra*) occasioned by the increasing waves of barbarian incursion in the West: Visigoths had invaded Italy in 401–3, 405–6, 408; Ostrogoths had sacked Switzerland in 401; Vandals, Alans, Sueves had fallen upon France in 406; Visigoths had assailed Austria in 408—all prior to the promulgation of this statute.

Emperor Honorius to Theodore, praetorian prefect for the second time.[1]

By having punished the authors of public calamity we indeed have given chastisement for the tribulation of injuries,[2] but with haste for restoring liberty to our provincials we think that at one and the same time counsel must be taken by arms and by laws.

Hence finally reason, when applied to the cares of wars, and a salutary constitution have advised that it must happen that [3] none should detain unwillingly persons of different provinces, of whatever sex, status, age, whom the wide course of barbarian savagery [4] had led away by captive constraint, but that there should be a free opportunity for those desiring to return to their own places.

And if for these persons anything of garments or of sustenance is claimed to have been expended for the use of men worthy of being restored,[5] it should be furnished for humanity and a greedy recovery of expenditure for food should not stain the glory of a good deed,[6] when perhaps compensation of services shall have repaid the costs of that sustenance. And we do not permit this to come into examination,[7] lest the persons desiring to return to their own places should be retarded by unseemly disputes [8]—those persons excepted, whom anyone shall be shown to have purchased from barbarian vendors and by whom it is equitable because of public interest for the price of their status to be refunded to the purchasers, lest consideration of an enormous [9] loss should cause the purchase to be denied to persons placed in such exigency [10] and we should be found rather to have thwarted the deliverance of those for whose freedom we have wished to have regard. It is proper for these persons [11] either to restore to their purchasers the price given for themselves or to make return for the benefit by labour, service, or work for a quinquennium, for the purpose of having their freedom, if they have been born in it, unimpaired.[12] Nor should honour [13] groan that the brief time of a quinquennium has been given to the purchasers for compensation of perhaps a larger cost, because the frailty of human life perhaps can fail within the established time's limits and not attain to the law's benefit. At all events, they should believe that what they have conferred on the ground of humanity has been lost by chance, though in God's judgement what human compassion has given to another person it bestows upon itself.

Wherefore after observance of the regulation of the law, whose moderateness—it is not doubtful—is pleasing, they should be restored to their own abodes and for them all things have been preserved unimpaired by the right of postliminium [14] and by the responses [15] of the old jurisprudents.[16]

And this sanction we wish to be so kept that if anyone, who is discovered to be an overseer and a leaseholder and a manager safeguarding the estate of an absent owner, shall have tried to withstand its commands by sacrilegious temerity, he should not doubt that he shall be delivered to the mines or shall incur the penalty of deportation.[17] But if the owner of an estate shall have attempted to contravene [18] our Gentleness' salutary ordinance, he should know that his property must be claimed by the fisc and that he must be deported by the sentence of the province's governor.[19]

And that an easy execution may proceed for these orders, it has pleased us that priests [20] of the Christian religion (who hold the churches of the neighbouring and the nearest places [21] and whose character the performance of such commands befits) and also curials of the nearest communities [21] should be admonished that they should approach the governors for the purpose of asking our law's assistance for cases of such needs when these emerge.[22]

And lest anyone should defend the guilt of his contumacy by ignorance of the command, Theodore, dearest and fondest cousin, your illustrious Magnificence shall cause the tenor of the law to come by your letters and edicts to the notice of all governors and provincials,[23] so that all governors should know that ten pounds of gold must be exacted from them and as much in weight [24] from their apparitors, if what has been commanded should be shown to have been neglected in anyone's favour,[25] since we order the most salutary sanction's execution to be required from all indeed, but especially by the governors' and their office staffs' care and obedience.

Given on 3 December [26] at Ravenna, the most distinguished Bassus and the most distinguished Philip being consuls. Accepted on 17 December.

Interpretation:[27] When those persons who have been led off by enemies at the time of their captivity, if they have accepted from any persons anything either for food or for clothing, shall have wished to return to their own places, not anything at all should be demanded in return for their expenses.

However, if a plunderer [28] shall have accepted a price for his prisoner, without doubt a purchaser should receive what he shall have proved that he had given. But if he shall not have had the price, the prisoner should serve the purchaser for a quinquennium and after the quinquennium without price he should be restored to his free-born condition; and when he shall have returned to his own place, he should receive all his own property unimpaired and safe.

And if anyone shall have tried to resist this so just an ordinance, he should know that he must be deported in exile; moreover, if he shall have been a rentier,[29] he should know that his property must be added to the fisc's resources.

To be sure, we wish Christians, who are bound to be eager for redemption, to be solicitous for prisoners.

This care also should pertain to curials; also all governors should know that they shall give ten pounds of gold to the fisc, if they shall have neglected this law's commands.

1. *CT* and *CI* have "Emperors Honorius and Theodosius Augusti to Theodore, praetorian prefect", whose prefecture was of Italy.

2. It is uncertain whether the reference is to the recent defeat of Constans, the emissary of Alaric's puppet-emperor Attalus, in Africa or to a slightly earlier victory of Sarus over an army of the usurper Constantine III in Gaul, for the chronology of the period is confused.

3. Here begins the Theodosian version, which Justinian follows in his longer copy.

4. Theodosius reads simply *barbarian savagery* as the subject.

5. Theodosius condenses the protasis to ". . . sustenance has been expended for use". The restoration is recovery of health after rigours of captivity.

6. After *humanity* Theodosius temporarily stops by reading "and a recovery of expenditure for food should not remain."

Doubtless many such captives were Christians in this generation after orthodox Christianity had been proclaimed to be the Empire's official religion (no. 167) and they would profit from the Church's practice of collecting funds for ransom of prisoners of war (*CA* 4. 9). See also nos. 127, n. 5, and 515, n. 3.

7. That is, such cases must not be taken to court.

8. Here Theodosius resumes.

9. Theodosius omits this adjective and starts the clause with "for whenever".

10. Theodosius omits from here to the end of the sentence.

The idea in *lest consideration . . . such exigency* is that possibility of no repayment of the ransom to the purchaser might decide a possible purchaser to deny to a prisoner the opportunity of regaining his freedom.

11. Theodosius clarifies this by substituting "ransomed".

12. Again Theodosius begins an omission here.

13. That is, an honourable person (abstract for concrete).

14. By the *ius postliminii* returning Roman citizens, who had been prisoners

of war, recovered as far as possible all their former civil rights, which during their captivity had been in abeyance (usually) without prejudice. Two exceptions to automatic recovery occur: captivity dissolved permanently his marriage and temporarily his right of possession of property. In the latter case he had to recommence his assertion of this right. Statutes on the right are in *CT* 5. 7 and *CI* 8. 50.

15. The juriconsults' *responsa* (replied opinions on legal questions addressed to them) had an incalculable influence in the evolution of Roman law. Justinian's *Digesta* or *Pandectae*, enacted into law on 30 December 533 (the best part of his *Corpus Iuris Civilis*), is their *monumentum aere perennius* (Horace, *Carm*. 3. 30. 1).

16. For this sentence Theodosius has "Therefore they should be restored to their own abodes under the regulation by which we have ordered for those persons, and for them all things have been preserved unimpaired by the right of postliminium and also by the ancients' responses."

For *have been preserved* Justinian writes "must be preserved".

17. Theodosius more simply gives "Accordingly, if any overseer, leaseholder, and manager shall have tried to withstand this command, he should not doubt that he shall be delivered to the mines along with the penalty of deportation."

18. A good case of tmesis in Latin—the compound verb being separated by four words.

19. Theodosius links this sentence with the previous sentence, reading "but if the owner of an estate, he should know that his property must be claimed by the fisc and that he must be deported".

20. Or bishops (*sacerdotes*, which can mean either priests or bishops and on which in its abstract form see no. 158, n. 1).

21. That is, to where the redeemed prisoners are found.

22. Theodosius, who ends temporarily his version here, exhibits this variation: "And that an easy execution may proceed, we wish Christians of the nearest places to administer the care of this matter. It also has pleased us that curials of the nearest communities should be admonished that they should know that our law's assistance must be brought to such cases as they emerge."

Justinian's shorter version (*CI* 1. 4. 11) of this entire law shows simply the subsequent sentence: "We wish Christians of the nearest places to administer care that none should detain Roman prisoners who shall have returned, that none should inflict them with outrages or with injuries."

23. Theodosius resumes after this word.

24. This phrase Theodosius omits.

25. For the clause Theodosius reads "if they shall have neglected the command", and thus ends his version.

26. Theodosius dates this 10 December and gives "Honorius Augustus for the eighth time and Theodosius Augustus for the third time being consuls" and then omits the notice of acceptance.

Justinian in both citations follows Theodosius except for adherence to the date of *CS*.

27. This is appended to the Theodosian version.

28. That is, some Roman raider who has bought a prisoner from a barbarian must be reimbursed by his prisoner.

29. The word is *possessor*, which should not mean the same as the *dominus* of the law.

309. MANDATE OF ARCADIUS, HONORIUS, AND THEODOSIUS II ON CONFIRMATION OF EPISCOPAL JURISDICTION, 408

(*CT* 1. 27. 2)

This constitution (repeated with modification in *CI* 1. 4. 8) strengthens the first legislation given by Constantine the Great on this subject (no. 28) in that it rules that a bishop's decision in a suit of private law is not appealable and authorizes secular execution of his verdict.

Emperors Arcadius,[1] Honorius, Theodosius Augusti to Theodore, praetorian prefect.[2]

Episcopal judgement should be valid for all who shall have chosen [3] to be heard by bishops.[4] For since private persons can conduct a hearing between those who consent, even when the judge does not know this, we permit that this should be allowed to these men whom we necessarily venerate[5] and that to their adjudication must be rendered that reverence which needs must be paid to your powers, from which it is not allowed to appeal.[6]

Also, lest the [7] investigation should be futile, execution should be given to the decision by the public [8] office staff.[9]

Given on 13 December, Bassus and Philip being consuls.

1. Arcadius' name should be deleted, for he had died more than seven months before the issuance of this order. See no. 307, n. 1.
2. Of Italy.
3. *CI* reads "assented".
4. The word is *sacerdotes*, on which see no. 16, n. 4.
5. *CI* omits this much of this sentence.
6. Ordinarily appeal from judicial decrees of the praetorian prefects was not entertained by the emperors (*CT* 11. 30. 16 [dated 331] and 58 [dated 399]), but eventually was permitted (*LNT* 13 [dated 439]) in a modified process, which was confirmed by Justinian (*CI* 7. 42 [dated 439]) in 534.

7. *CI* inserts "episcopal".
8. *CI* reads "governors' ".
9. Pitra prints (2. 537) a late Greek paraphrase: "The bishop's judgement should be acceptable to all, whosoever should have chosen to be heard by bishops. And [we order that] the judgement by him should be reverenced, through which it is necessary to refer to your powers, against which it is not allowed to appeal from the magistrates controlling the office staffs, lest the bishop's judgement and whatever decision is given to the matters judged should be invalid."

310. LETTER OF HONORIUS AND THEODOSIUS II ON SACRILEGE AND ON ENFORCEMENT OF LAWS ON HERETICS, SCHISMATICS, AND NON-CHRISTIANS, 409

(*CS* 14)

Here the emperors establish for African provinces the administrative procedure to be pursued (1) in cases of forcible entry into churches and of subsequent disturbance of divine worship and of outrages upon the clergy, (2) in enforcing existing enactments against heretics, schismatics, Jews, pagans, (3) in assessing penalties for disobedience to the law.

This statute, which is epitomized in *CT* 16. 2. 31 (copied with omissions in *CI* 1. 3. 10)[1] and in *CT* 16. 5. 46, has a long preamble of complaint about the laxity of African magistrates and municipal senates in executing the laws.

Emperors Honorius and Theodosius to the illustrious Theodore, praetorian prefect.[2]

It is not doubtful that there happened by the connivance of governors and by their culpable dissimulation there remained unpunished a deed [3]—which we learn under public attestation has been committed and likewise has not been punished—for disturbing the public peace in contempt of the Christian religion, which with due worship we venerate. Dissimulation is near to transgression in a governor, whom ignorance of the committed crime does not defend.[4]

We have ascertained that throughout the province of Africa so much had been allowed to certain persons' temerity that with various tortures they afflicted the Christian law's [5] bishops, who had been wrested from their own homes or—what is more atrocious—had been dragged from the Catholic Church's sanctuaries; that moreover to the outrage alone of divine worship they exhibited, to the observation of persons rushing together in crowds, other bishops defiled by part of their hair pulled off or disfigured by another kind of outrage—with the result that pardon would be more difficult in the case of those whose safety contempt had forgiven.[6]

Neither the African governors' authority prosecutes by the right of the power entrusted to them a crime of such great wickedness and a monstrous disgrace never found hitherto, nor their due care for reference has caused the case to come to our notice. We do not believe that by them could have been unknown what is said to have been committed in the municipalities and what the constant care of both magistrates and municipal senates [7] and the duty of apparitors, namely policeman,[8] who carry messages and give information,[9] reveal to the absence of the authorities.[10] For is it allowable to make known trivial matters, but to keep secret more serious matters? They would not have kept silent what they dreaded to become known to their own governors through another person, unless they knew that the governor was unwilling to punish it. Was it to be waited for accusations instituted contrary to their profession's sanctity, so that bishops would prosecute their own injuries and would demand vengeance by the death of criminals, on whom it is fitting for them, though unwillingly, to be avenged? The persuader of pardon for another, the teacher of forgiveness, is led into this necessity: that either he himself should seem to have managed for himself what another person would not deny to him, if he asked him, or he, if about to comply with the precepts of his episcopal office, should be subject to the violence of unpunished guilty persons. Unless either the authorities' vigour or the governors' conscientiousness with praiseworthy authority should protect the Catholic Church's bishops and other ministers, they will be delivered to the audacity of the worst persons.

Wherefore we command that the authority of the various governors throughout Africa, without harm to guiltless persons, should search for those persons who are said to have committed such things and either should consign them to the mines or should force them to undergo the penalty of deportation, after they have been produced for a proper examination, if it shall have been learned that they (of whatever dignity and honour the accused ones have been proved to be) are convicted by manifest proof—their property having been united to our fisc, that they may have their life conceded to them by our Clemency's custom, which shall not be granted in future time to similar crimes.

Therefore we have established that the matters of the present law must be observed by all persons forever,[11] Theodore, dearest and fondest cousin, and we desire this, when prefixed to your illustrious Magnificence's letters and when published by edicts, to come to the notice of all: that if [12] anyone shall have burst into this type of sacrilege, that, rushing into Catholic churches, he should bring any outrage upon bishops and ministers [13] or the worship itself and the place, whatever occurs should be [14] brought to the authorities' notice by letters of the municipal senates,[7] the magistrates, and the curators [15] and by denunciations of the apparitors, whom they call policemen,[8] so that may be declared the names of those who shall have been able to be recognized. And if it shall be said that the crime was committed by a multitude, if not all, at least some can be recognized and by their confession the names of their associates may be made known.

And thus the province's governor shall know that outrage to the Catholic Church's bishops and ministers,[13] also to the place itself and to the divine worship, must be punished by a capital sentence against convicted or confessed culprits, and he should not expect that the bishop would demand vengeance for his own injury, for to him the sanctity of the episcopal office [16] has left only [17] the glory of forgiving.

And for all persons it should be not only free but also praiseworthy [18] to prosecute as a public crime atrocious outrages inflicted on bishops and ministers [13] and to obtain vengeance in the case of such culprits,[19] that in this way at least wicked persons' audacity, because it is confident that action cannot be brought against them by a bishop, should dread because of the others' accusations.

And [20] if a violent multitude shall not have been able to be brought into court by the performance of the civilian apparitors [21] and by the assistance of municipal senates or of rentiers, because it defends[22] itself by arms or by the difficulty of places, the[23] African governors, when this law's tenor has been prefixed to letters sent to the excellent count of Africa,[24] should demand the aid of armed service, that culprits of such crimes may not escape.

And lest [25] Donatists or the vanity of all other heretics and of those others [26] whom the cult of the Catholic communion cannot convince, namely Jews and Gentiles, whom commonly they call pagans,[27] should think that the ordinance of the laws previously promulgated against themselves have decreased in vigour, all governors should know that they must obey with faithful devotion the commands of these laws and among the chief matters of their duties they must [28] execute whatever we have decreed against these persons.

But [29] if any of the governors by the sin of connivance, a trick of dissimulation,[30] should neglect the execution of the present law, he should know that, when he has lost his office, he will suffer a severer action of our Clemency and that his office staff also, if it shall have neglected its own safety by despising the hint,[31] must be subjected to [32] a condemnatory judgement of twenty pounds of gold, its three chief men also being punished.

Also, if the men of a municipal senate [7] shall have been silent—for regard for the guilty persons—about any such offence committed in their own municipalities or its territories, they should know that they will undergo the penalty of deportation and the loss of their own properties.

Given on 15 January at Ravenna, our Lords Honorius Augustus for the ninth time and Theodosius Augustus for the fifth time being consuls.[33]

1. This law is assigned to Arcadius and Honorius and is dated 398 (25 April by *CT*, 26 April by *CI*), but editors believe that it belongs to 409.
2. Of Italy.
3. It is not known to what precise act the emperors refer, but from the rest of the introductory matter it appears to have been some physical outrage upon the African clergy.
4. Cf. the modern maxim *ignorantia legis neminem excusat* (descended through the medieval axiom *ignorantia iuris non excusat*, which is based on *D* 22. 6. 9. pr.: *regula est iuris ignorantiam cuique nocere*), which is sufficiently wide to cover this case, and *CT* 1. 1. 2, where the emperors in 391 assert that they do not permit anyone either to be ignorant of or to pretend ignorance of their constitutions.
5. Religion.
6. The idea seems to be that, though the maltreated bishops might deem it beneath their dignity to prosecute their assailants, the emperors could not forgive easily such assaulters whose immunity otherwise would be secured.
7. The word is *ordines*, on which see no. 325, n. 6.
8. The Latin has the singular number, probably used collectively. The *stationarii* (policemen), who were stationed as a kind of rural constabulary at fixed posts throughout the Empire, here are associated with the apparitors.
9. This seems to be the sense of this relative clause, which literally is "which [duty] is the servant of messages and of informers".
10. This is a mixture of enallage and paradox. Reversing the enallage, one cannot reveal anything to absent authorities. The result is paradoxical. What is meant is that the outrage was reported, but that the governors either took care not to receive the report in person or, if received, took no cognizance of it.
11. Literally "through eternity", which seems over-strained.
12. Here begin *CT* 16. 2. 31 and *CI* 1. 3. 10.
13. The words are *sacerdotes et ministri*, of which the first may be widened to include priests and the second may be extended to embrace minor clergymen in addition to deacons (as opposed to bishops and priests). See nos. 15, n. 3, and 16, n. 4.
14. For the rest of this sentence Justinian reads "noticed [with a view to punishment] by the province's governors". He also omits the next sentence.
15. The plural from *CT* is preferred to the singular of *CS*. These were municipal officers.

16. Theodosius and Justinian omit this phrase.
17. Justinian omits this word.
18. Justinian omits *not . . . also*.
19. Here *CT* and *CI* stop temporarily.
20. *CT* and *CI* resume here, reading "but" for *and*.
21. Abstract in Latin for concrete in English, as in no. 253, n. 7.
22. Plural in *CS*, but singular in *CT* and *CI*.
23. From here to the paragraph's end Justinian's version reads "the provinces' governors also, when military aid has been sought earnestly by official letters, should not delay to impose an appropriate punishment upon such excess". With this *CI* ends.
24. The commander of the armed forces in North Africa.
25. Here begins *CT* 16. 5. 46.
26. An instance of enallage. The emperors mean "all other vain heretics and those others", but they substitute a noun for an adjective.
27. See no. 148, n. 4.
28. *CT* reads "they should not hesitate to execute".
29. *CT* omits the conjunction.
30. *CT* omits the appositive words.
31. That is, by not taking their cue from what may happen to their superior, the governor, they neglect their part in enforcing the law and so will be punished.
32. *CT* has "punished by".
33. This consulship was in 412, but the editors refer this law to 409, the date for *CT* 16. 5. 46. Variant dates for the day also exist: 14th and 16th.

311. MANDATE OF HONORIUS AND THEODOSIUS II ON SELECTION OF CHRISTIANS AS CIVIC DEFENDERS, 409

(*CI* 1. 55. 8)

This directive allows only Christians to be appointed to the post of defender of a city and orders episcopal and sacerdotal sanction for selection to such office.

Emperors Honorius and Theodosius Augusti to Caecilian, praetorian prefect.[1]

We command defenders to be appointed thus, that they, imbued with the orthodox religion's sacred mysteries,[2] should be created by decree of the most reverend bishops and clergymen and distinguished men and rentiers and curials;[3] and report concerning their appointment must be made to the most illustrious praetorian power,[4] that by the said magnificent office's [5] letters their authority may be confirmed.

But if the defenders shall have known that anything contrary to public discipline by any person whatsoever has been done toward the injuring of rentiers, they should have the power of reporting this to the illustrious and magnificent praetorian prefects and the illustrious masters of the cavalry and of the infantry, also the masters of the offices and the counts of the sacred largesses as well as of the private estates.

Given on 21 January at Ravenna, Honorius Augustus for the eighth time and Theodosius Augustus for the third time being consuls.

1. Of Italy.
2. See no. 75, n. 42.
3. These words reappear in no. 541.
4. That is, to the praetorian prefect of the prefecture in which the defender of the city dwells.
5. The word is *sedes* (seat), but it denotes the office which the occupant has and now is restricted usually to its ecclesiastical significance of "see" from the chair whereon a bishop sits.

312. MANDATE OF HONORIUS AND THEODOSIUS II ON EPISCOPAL INTEREST IN PRISONERS, 409

(*CT* 9. 3. 7)

This constitution (repeated in *CI* 1. 4. 9) commands provincial governors to interrogate prisoners on Sundays about their needs and bishops to exhort governors not to neglect this duty.

Emperors Honorius and Theodosius Augusti to Caecilian, praetorian prefect.[1]

After other matters.

On all Lord's days [2] governors should see and should question prisoners led from custody in prison, lest humane treatment should be denied to these confined persons by corrupt custodians of prisons. They should cause food to be furnished to those not having it, since there have been decreed two or three farthings [3] daily or as much as the registrars,[4] to whose expenses the alimonies for paupers contribute. shall have estimated.

And these prisoners must be led to the bath under trusty custody.

Fines of twenty pounds of gold have been established for the governors and of the same weight for their office staffs and fines of three pounds of gold have been set for the municipal senates,[5] if they shall have scorned these very salutary statutes.

Nor on the part of the Christian religion's bishops shall be lacking laudable care, which should press this admonition upon an appointed governor's observation.

Given on 25 January at Ravenna, Honorius Augustus for the eighth time and Theodosius Augustus for the third time being consuls.

Interpretation: On all Lord's days [2] governors should lead prisoners from prison under trusty custody, that sustenance may be supplied to them by Christians or by priests and that they may be led to the bath on the aforesaid days under custody in consideration of religion. If any governors shall have neglected to fulfil this, they should be forced to fulfil the penalty, which the law itself has established.

1. Of Italy.
2. See no. 34, n. 5.
3. A *libella* was a small silver coin, the tenth part of a denarius, and was used proverbially for a very small sum of money.
4. These were the *commentarienses*, who compiled lists of prisoners.
5. See no. 325, n. 6.

313. MANDATE OF HONORIUS AND THEODOSIUS II ON CONVERSION OF ASTROLOGERS, 409
(*CT* 9. 16. 12)

This statute, repeated by Justinian (*CI* 1. 4. 10), seems to be the first law offering to astrologers a choice of exile or conversion to Christianity and authorizing bishops to assist at bonfires of books on astrology.[1]

Emperors Honorius and Theodosius Augusti to Caecilian, praetorian prefect.[2]

We decree that astrologers should be driven not only from the city of Rome, but also from all municipalities, unless they, never returning in the future to their former error, have been prepared, after the books of their error have been burned by a fire under bishops' eyes,[3] to transfer their faith to the Catholic religion's cult. But if they shall not have done this and shall have been caught in municipalities contrary

313. CONVERSION OF ASTROLOGERS, 409

to our Clemency's salutary constitution and shall have insinuated the secrets of their error and profession, they should receive the punishment of deportation.[4]

Given on 1 February at Ravenna, Honorius Augustus for the eighth time and Theodosius Augustus for the third time being consuls.

1. Although ancient astronomy, which had entered the Mediterranean area from Mesopotamia via Egypt, by prolonged research eventually could predict the recurrence of celestial phenomena, yet ancient astrology, its younger sister and of the same provenance, professed to be a science capable of forecasting terrestrial events and human happenings which are based, by a sort of sympathy, upon the motions of the heavenly bodies. Many of the acutest minds in antiquity (e.g. Aristotle, *Metaph.* 12. 8 = 1073A–4B) accepted astrology, which affected almost every part of ancient culture, particularly philosophy and medicine. Although application to astrologers was made by the early emperors, notably by Tiberius, the second sovereign, who in his household had Thrasyllus, an astrologer, as an adept in the art (Tacitus, *Ann.* 6. 20. 3—21. 5; Suetonius, *Tib.* 14. 4, 62. 3; Cassius Dio, *Hist. Rom.* 55. 11, 57. 15. 7, 58. 27. 1–3), nevertheless certain later rulers, particularly Diocletian, whose law against astrologers (*CI* 9. 18. 2; dated 294) is the earliest extant, regarded this so-called science with suspicion as subversive to the State's welfare as well as to the sovereign's safety. But it was left to the Christian emperors to legislate extensively against the art (*CT* 9. 16 and *CI* 9. 18), despite the common Christian acceptance of astrology and the long prayer to the planets and the Supreme God for the continuance of the dynasty of Constantine I (the first Christian emperor), composed by Julius Firmicus Maternus, a Christian astrologer, in his *Mathesis* (1. 10. 14), written during 334–7.

Although many ecclesiastical writers, especially Origen among the Greeks (see Thorndike, op. cit., 1. 455–9) and St Augustine among the Latins (see Thorndike, op. cit., 1. 513–21) attacked astrology, yet as late as the thirteenth century St Albert the Great (1193?–1280), the chief savant in that century and surnamed the "Universal Doctor", who of medieval scholastics did most to adapt Aristotle's natural philosophy to Christian use, accepted the art of astrology as compatible with Christianity (*De Gen. et Cor.* 2. 3. 5, ed. by Borgnet, *Beati Alberti Magni Opera Omnia* [Paris, 1890], 4. 451).

For an excellent account of astrology in Roman antiquity consult F. H. Cramer, *Astrology in Roman Law and Politics* (Philadelphia, 1954). Cramer concludes his essay at the end of the early Empire, but promises that the second part of his survey will examine the evidence in the late Empire.

2. Of Italy.

3. See no. 382, n. 1.

4. Pitra has a late Greek paraphrase (2. 502) reading "Astrologers should burn their own books in the bishops' eyes and thus should surrender themselves to the orthodox religion, preserving hope of no return to their own error. But

the refusers should be banished from Rome itself and from each city, if, employing their teaching, they should appear either in the city or in the cities."

314. MANDATE OF HONORIUS AND THEODOSIUS II ON CAPITATION FOR RURAL CLERGYMEN, 409

(CI 1. 3. 16)

This directive allows an aspirant for clerical office to enter the priesthood, though the owner of the rural property on which the candidate lives and works is unwilling to forgo his services, provided that the aspirant pays the poll tax[1] and secures a substitute for his services.

Emperors Honorius and Theodosius Augusti to Anthemius, praetorian prefect.[2]

Whoever shall have been rated for taxes[3] should abstain from all clerical office, when the owner of the land is unwilling, so that even if he shall have been a clergyman in that village wherein he is known to dwell, under this condition he should assume the religious priesthood: that he both may be compelled to[4] acknowledge the burden of the capitation tax[1] by the owner himself and may perform the rural services by what substitution he shall have preferred—this immunity, of course, having been granted, that the fixed capitation tax[1] is remitted for the venerable churches[5]—no rescript against this law being valid in the future.

Given on 28 February, Honorius Augustus for the eighth time and Theodosius Augustus for the third time being consuls.

1. See no. 67, n. 37.
2. Of the Orient.
3. Pitra's late Greek version (2. 480) reads "If anyone has been rated for taxes among registered farmers, he".
4. Pitra omits *be compelled to*, later substitutes "senatorial" for *rural*, and finally omits the last phrase *in the future*.
5. The landowner must pay the tax and presumably the aspirant must reimburse the landowner, but the church, which the cleric now serves in place of the landowner, is relieved from the tax.

315. MANDATE OF HONORIUS AND THEODOSIUS II ON PENALTIES FOR CAELICOLANS AND CHRISTIAN CONVERTS TO JUDAISM, 409

(CT 16. 8. 19)

This constitution allows Caelicolans one year within which they may return to Catholicism with impunity and ascribes high treason to persons who compel Christians to apostatize to Judaism.[1]

Justinian quotes different parts of this law in CI 1. 9. 12 and 1. 12. 2.

The same Augusti to Jovius, praetorian prefect.[2]

The unusual name of Caelicolans in some way has indicated [3] a new crime of superstition.

Unless these persons shall have returned to God's worship and Christian reverence within a year's limits,[4] let them know that they too must be restrained by those laws by which we have ordered heretics to be circumscribed.[5] For it is certain that whatever differs from Christians' faith is contrary to Christian law.[6]

And certain persons, unmindful of their life and also of the law, still dare to treat [7] this [8] in such a way that they compel certain ones of the Christians to assume the foul and loathsome name of Jews. And although they who have done this have been condemned rightly by previous emperors' laws,[9] nevertheless it is not displeasing to admonish them rather often, lest persons trained by Christian mysteries [10] should be compelled to accept perversity both Jewish and alien to the Roman Empire after adoption of Christianity.[11]

And if anyone shall have believed that this ought to be attempted, we order the authors of the deed with their participants to be bound to the penalty provided by previous laws,[9] since indeed it is more grievous than death [12] and more savage than murder, if anyone of Christian faith should be polluted by Jewish disbelief. And therefore we command that none, guilty or innocent, fleeing to the churches for refuge, should be dragged from the churches and particularly that no Jew should be allowed to remove anyone's slave [13] and by[14] a faithful and God-devoted order we ordain [15] under this regulation, namely that if anyone shall have attempted to contravene this law, he should know that he himself must be held for the crime of treason.

Given on 1 April at Ravenna, Honorius Augustus for the eighth time and Theodosius Augustus for the third time being consuls.

1. Though it is tempting to think that, because this constitution combines Caelicolans and Jews in its penalties, Juvenal earlier knew the Caelicolans as a Christian heretical sect in satirizing (Sat. 5. 14. 97) the Jews as worshipping

nothing except clouds and a divinity of heaven (*caeli numen*)—for the avoidance of the divine name in later Hebrew literature led to such substitutes as this, which the Romans often misunderstood to indicate worship of the sky (*caelicola*: "a worshipper of the sky")—yet it appears that as early as *c.* 130, when Juvenal wrote that part of his *Satires* and when, of course, formal Christianity had completed its first century, Caelicolans as a sect of Christians were unknown. Moreover, though they combined Christian and Jewish ceremonies and doctrines, Caelicolans appeared first about the commencement of the fifth century, as this constitution claims, and then in North Africa among Donatists, as St Augustine apparently asserts (*Ep.* 44. 13 = *CSEL* 34. 120–1).

2. Of Italy.

3. This verb translates the recorded conjecture *indicavit*, perhaps better than the received reading *vindicavit* (has claimed), which editors have emended to *vindicabit* (will claim).

4. Justinian omits the phrase in *CI* 1. 9. 12.

5. Here Justinian in *CI* 1. 9. 12 interpolates a sentence concocted from no. 301, par. 3 *ad fin.* (the consecutive clause).

If *we* is taken *stricto sensu* by applying the pronoun only to this constitution's authors, their statutes on this subject—so far—are nos. 287–94, 296, 298, 299, 301, 304–6, 310.

6. Justinian ends here his first selection for his law in *CI* 1. 9. 12. The thought is reminiscent of Matt. 12. 30 = Luke 11.23; cf. Mark 9. 40 = Luke 9. 50.

7. The word (*attrectare*) frequently implies handling in an unlawful manner.

8. That is, the Christian law or religion, as in text at numeral 6 *supra*.

9. Such are nos. 23, 80, 91, 190.

10. See no. 75, n. 42.

11. The Latin is briefer (*post Christianitatem*), but an expansion of the phrase seems desirable.

12. The phrase is reminiscent of that in Eccles. 7. 26.

13. This sentence is corrupt to this point and the translation is the best editorial conjecture.

14. Here Justinian begins his second selection for his law in *CI* 1. 12. 2, in which he reads "devoted" for the second adjective.

15. Justinian inserts "that to none is it permitted to remove persons fleeing for refuge to the sacrosanct churches".

316. MANDATE OF HONORIUS AND THEODOSIUS II ON SUPPRESSION OF AMUSEMENTS ON SUNDAY, 409

(CT 2. 8. 25)

This constitution exceeds all previous statutes on the subject of public entertainment on Sundays (nos. 236, 243, 279, 281), since it no longer exempts imperial anniversaries happening to coincide with the Lord's day.

Emperors Honorius and Theodosius Augusti to Jovius, praetorian prefect.[1]

After other matters.

On the Lord's day,[2] which they commonly call that of the Sun,[2] we allow absolutely no amusements to be produced, even if perchance, as the years' ends return upon themselves, on this day either the beginning of our sovereignty shall have shone or the solemnities due to the birthday[3] are allotted.

Given on 1 April at Ravenna, Honorius Augustus for the eighth time and Theodosius Augustus for the third time being consuls.

1. Of Italy.
2. See no. 34, n. 5.
3. Probably each emperor's birthday is meant.

317. MANDATE OF HONORIUS AND THEODOSIUS II ON PETITIONS FROM HERETICS OR PRO-HERETICAL PERSONS, 409

(CT 16. 5. 47)

Legislation against heretics descends into minute details, when it is enacted that a successful petitioner for an imperial decision should find his granted request inoperative, if it can be proved that he has disobeyed laws against heretics.

The same Augusti to Jovius, praetorian prefect.[1]

If anyone shall have attempted to contravene those statutes, which many times have been established for the common salvation, that is, for the sacrosanct Catholic Church's interests, against heretics and followers of a different dogma, he should lose his granted requests—even with the benefit of our annotation.[2]

And the rest.

Given on 26 June at Ravenna, Honorius Augustus for the eighth time and Theodosius Augustus for the third time being consuls.

1. Of Italy.
2. An *annotatio* is the emperor's note on the margin of a petition.

318. MANDATE OF HONORIUS AND THEODOSIUS II ON SPEEDY TRIAL OF LAWSUITS INVOLVING THE CHURCH, 409
(*CT* 2. 4. 7)

This constitution commands rapid disposition of legal cases in which the Church is involved.

Emperors Honorius and Theodosius Augusti to Jovius, praetorian prefect.[1]

After other matters.

Whatever cases perchance pertain to or shall be able to pertain to the venerable Church, their actions should be terminated by the judges' swift trial, but with the preservation of the methodical order of the laws. For it is not fitting that when the defence of a venerable place and name has been undertaken, the inner chambers of public courts [2] should be kept waiting for a long time.

Given on 26 June at Ravenna, Honorius Augustus for the eighth time and Theodosius Augustus for the third time being consuls.

Interpretation: In view of reverence for sanctity and faith the churches' cases, when these shall have been brought to the public court, ought to be terminated without any delay and the defenders of a venerable place ought not to be kept in suspense by any tardiness.

1. Of Italy.
2. The brief phrase is *publica secretaria*.

319. MANDATE OF HONORIUS AND THEODOSIUS II ON LIMITATION OF CORPSE-CARRIERS IN CONSTANTINOPLE, 409

(CI 1. 2. 4)

By this directive Theodosius sets the number of corpse-carriers serving the Church in the capital at a maximum of 950 and directs that normal attrition of their guild should not lead to replacement. Apparently, when the number of these servitors should have declined to an operationally impracticable level, further imperial legislation would be made to recruit members of this corporation.

Emperors Honorius and Theodosius Augusti to Aetius, urban prefect.[1]

Not more than 950 corpse-carriers for the sacrosanct Church of this most glorious city [2] should be assigned and to none should be available an opportunity of adding to these or of changing these or of substituting one into a deceased person's place, since immunity has been granted to none other of guildsmen beyond the aforesaid number through patronages [3] and all authority of renewal has been denied for claiming things similar to those which have been conferred for the honour or the necessary services of the sacrosanct Church.

Given on 21 August at Eudoxiopolis,[4] Honorius Augustus for the eighth time and Theodosius Augustus for the third time being consuls.

1. Of Constantinople.
2. Constantinople.
3. That is, no influential person's plea avails in this case.
4. Selymbria, a Thracian town on the Propontis, about 45 miles distant from Constantinople, was renamed in honour of Eudoxia, wife of Emperor Arcadius.

320. MANDATE OF HONORIUS AND THEODOSIUS II ON HERETICS IN GOVERNMENTAL SERVICE, 410

(CT 16. 5. 48)

This constitution, while it bans recruitment of heretics for governmental service, yet retains such as already are bound to serve therein. Evidently persons so bound were employing the excuse of heresy to avoid such service.

The same Augusti to Anthemius, praetorian prefect.[1]
We decree that Montanists and Priscillians and other breeds of such

sort of nefarious superstition, scorning the varied punishments of vengeance established through manifold sacred ordinances,[2] are not at all to be admitted to the enlistment oaths of the governmental service [3] which obeys our commands. But if the curial origin or the obligation of the municipal senates [4] or of the cohortaline governmental service [5] should tie any of these persons to services and to functions, we order that they should be bound to these, lest under the colour of a condemned religion they may elicit for themselves supports for a desired exemption. For it is not pleasing that these persons should be freed from the needs of the cohortaline governmental service [5] or of the municipal senates [4] as a result of the law [6] which, promulgated in the western territories, so censured the aforesaid cults that it removed these persons from all entrance into contracts and almost from the Roman way of life.

Given on 21 February at Constantinople, the most distinguished Varanes being consul.

1. Of the East.
2. Such as nos. 268, 290, 298, 301 for the sects named.
3. See no. 186, n. 4, and *infra* n. 5.
4. The word is *ordines*, on which see no. 325, n. 6.
5. These are the *cohortalini* (sometimes called *cohortales*), a word which confirms the military character of the civil service (cf. *supra* n. 3), since it comes from *cohors* (cohort). They were members of less important office staffs.
6. Theodosius probably means the constitution published at Rome and translated as no. 298.

321. MANDATES OF HONORIUS AND THEODOSIUS II ON DISABILITIES FOR EUNOMIANS, 410

(*CT* 16. 5. 49, 50)

These two constitutions, of which the second statedly supplements the first and is dated at the same time, revoke the concessions granted to Eunomians by Arcadius eleven years previously (no. 277) and restore the disabilities enacted against them by the same emperor fifteen years earlier (no. 249).

I

The same Augusti to Anthemius, praetorian prefect.[1]
With those provisions, which the law [2] of our Clemency's deified [3]

321. DISABILITIES FOR EUNOMIANS, 410

father[4] long ago has established against the Eunomians, remaining, we decree that henceforth they neither should give to each other nor should acquire anything from each other by gift, likewise that they neither should leave nor should take anything by will. They should be without the emoluments which they were wont to take from gifts or the will of decedents by reciprocal inducements through fraud and circumvention, in order that they totally should be deprived of participation in each right and that only by intestacy they should succeed to those persons whom the order (published by the old laws) has prescribed for the right of succession; so that, if from these persons there shall have been no survivor who legally may be called to an inheritance by intestacy, then the property of a person deceased in this superstition should belong to our fisc.

Also gifts prohibited in the aforesaid manner should come to the increments of our treasury, so that, however, it should be allowed to none of these persons to request anything from our Munificence and to none to take anything, even if we shall have been willing perchance to bestow anything voluntarily,[5] but the gifts should stay always in the fisc's legal power, unless a reason of public utility shall have subjected these things to sale.

Given on 1 March, the most distinguished Varanes being consul.

II

The same Augusti to Strategius, count of the private estates.

Concerning the same matter let it be added:

Thus, that the office staff of the private estates should know clearly that it redounds to their own peril, if from the aforesaid property anything at anytime to anyone shall have been allowed to be delivered through their own dissimulation, since in no way and on no account this law's authority ought to be circumvented.

Given on 1 March, the most distinguished Varanes being consul.

1. Of the East.
2. No. 249.
3. See no. 127, n. 7.
4. Arcadius, father of Theodosius II.
5. Since he was only ten years old, Theodosius made this provision against heretical influence upon himself.

322. MANDATE OF HONORIUS AND THEODOSIUS II ON RETURN OF CLERGYMEN TO CIVIC STATUS, 410

(*CT* 12. 1. 172)

The emperors ordain that clergymen have the option of performing municipal duties or of surrendering their patrimony to their municipal senates.

The same Augusti to Herculius, praetorian prefect of Illyricum.

The decisions which, previously published to the prejudice of the municipal senates in past times during the investigation of your magnificent office [1] and contrary to the reasonableness of truth, have absolved through favour persons obligated to the municipal senates, should be inactive, and all persons whom the lot of birth has obligated to municipal public services should be compelled to sustain their own status.

Moreover we command that those persons who under the patronage of the clerical office have defrauded their native municipality of the public services due should be restored under this condition: that, in consideration of the time and in view of the rank which they hold in the churches, either they should return to their former status and should comply with the municipal services or their patrimonies should be assigned to the municipal senates.

Also those persons who voluntarily have introduced themselves into the companies of the municipal senates should abide in that status which they have chosen, but the laws' authority should be maintained concerning their children.[2]

Given on 24 May [3] at Constantinople, the most distinguished Varanes being consul.

1. See no. 311, n. 5. Herculius was in office from 408.

2. This paragraph belongs syntactically to the preceding paragraph, but, since it discusses a separate situation, it is separated in translation.

It is difficult to understand why persons of their own accord should have sought service as municipal senators and should have incurred public burdens avoided by most of their fellow-subjects qualified to be such senators and to perform such services, unless they had been activated by the highest patriotism or by a *nouveau riche*'s ambition or by familial instigation.

3. An alternative date is 25 June.

323. MANDATE OF HONORIUS AND THEODOSIUS II ON HERETICAL ASSEMBLIES, 410

(*CT* 16. 5. 51)

It is believed that this renewed effort to suppress heretical meetings resulted from the victory over the army of Priscus Attalus,[1] a puppet emperor established by Alaric I, the Visigothic king, for this statute, which closely resembles no. 339, rescinds a rescript favouring the Donatists in the attempt to keep them loyal to the Empire during the crisis.

The same Augusti to Heraclian, count of Africa.

By the entire rescission of the response,[2] whereby persons had crept secretly to their own rites of heretical superstition, all enemies of the sacred law[3] should know that they must be punished by the penalty both of proscription and of life,[4] if they shall have attempted further to assemble in public through the cursed temerity of their wickedness.[5]

Given on 25 August, the most distinguished Varanes being consul.

1. He had been urban prefect of Rome in 409 and his expedition toward Ravenna proved abortive.
2. Not extant. See no. 218, n. 5.
3. Religion.
4. Literally "blood".
5. The crime of heresy.

Mommsen suggests that "lest in any way true and divine worship should be defiled by contagion" should be added from no. 339.

324. LETTER OF HONORIUS AND THEODOSIUS II ON THE CARTHAGINIAN CONFERENCE BETWEEN CATHOLICS AND DONATISTS, 410

(*PL* 11. 1260-1, 1367-8; 43. 816-17)

The century-old Donatist controversy in Africa (see e.g. no. 17) drew toward its close at the Conference of Carthage in 411, for which the following epistle was sent to Marcelline, a tribune and notary, who presided as high commissioner in the imperial interest and at whose order it was read twice during the conference: on both the first and the third day, in the proceedings (*gesta*) of which it is preserved.

The appointment of a secular official to judge between the rival claims perhaps indicated not so much that the civil power claimed to decide doctrinal questions as that the imperial government's concern was directed toward the settlement of serious disturbances which force had failed to stop, for a Catholic delegation had requested in 410 Honorius to send a commissioner to arrange for a conference with Donatists in Africa.

Emperors Caesars Flavius Honorius and Theodosius, Pious, Fortunate, Victors and Triumphers, Ever-August to their own Flavius Marcelline, greeting.

Amid the greatest cares of our Empire reverence for the Catholic law [1] is either ever the first or the sole, for neither we do anything in the labours of war nor we ordain anything in the counsels of peace, except that the pious populace of our world may maintain the true worship of God, considering that it also had been appropriate to fill formerly with either terror or admonition the Donatists, who by vain error and superfluous dissension taint Africa, that is, the largest part of our Empire and one loyally obedient to secular officials. Nevertheless, it does not grieve us to repeat rather often the same measures, which the God-devoted authority of all previous sovereigns has determined, lest, if in our times perchance anything shall have been concocted to the Catholic law's [1] injury, by a just judgement posterity can impute this to us. Nor, to be sure, to our Conscience is unknown the word of the celestial oracle,[2] which the Donatists' harsh interpretation professes to be able to obtain by its own error; and, although this rather gently invites depraved souls to amendment, yet previously also we have ordered it to be abolished, lest any occasion for superstitions may be provided.[3] Now also by similar authority we decide that deception must be prevented and we justly state the following: that willingly we rescind those measures which had been ordained, lest anyone may think that he can sin under our sponsorship against the divine religion.

And although all hold that there is one manifest opinion that the full truth of the Catholic law [1] is approved by the right worship of men and by celestial decision, by a desire for peace and for favour we willingly have received a delegation of venerable bishops,[4] which desires that the Donatist bishops should foregather to a conference at a very famous city,[5] in order that, after bishops whom each side shall have delegated have been chosen, clear reasoning, when discussions have been held, may suppress the superstition. And this matter we order to be settled within four months,[6] that also our Clemency, as it desires, rather quickly can recognize the converted minds of the peoples. And if within this prescribed period the Donatists' bishops studiously shall have declined to assemble, by the proclamation of a triple edict [7] let the period for the stubborn persons be closed; and when this period has been passed and completed, if, when called, they shall have dis-

324. CATHOLIC-DONATIST CONFERENCE, 410

dained to attend, let the people, who will have recognized that their own teachers by their silence have been defeated, yield with the churches [8] and let them rejoice at last that they have been worsted and let them know that there must be obedience, if not to our ordinances, at least to the Catholic law's [1] true commands.

And indeed for this disputation we wish you to sit as judge in the chief place—you remember quite fully whatever you previously have received in our mandates—and we wish you to undertake every care either in convening the bishops or in summoning them, if they shall have disdained to attend, that you with approved skill can execute both these measures which previously have been ordered and those which you know now have been ordained, for the purpose of preserving above all the following condition: that,[9] with the new deception [10] abolished, you should maintain [11] unimpaired and inviolate those regulations which in regard to the Catholic law [1] either ancient usage formerly has ordained or the religious authority of our ancestors has established or our Serenity has confirmed.

Of course, that suitable supports should not be able to be lacking for your acts, our Serenity has impressed upon the admirable men, the proconsul and the vicar,[12] that, if they desire to retain the position of their offices, if they desire their own apparitors [13] to avoid extreme punishments, they should make abundant provision that the necessary persons should be assigned both from their own office staffs and from the apparitors [13] of all the judges. Moreover it shall pertain to your Diligence, if you shall have detected any delay by any artifice, to indicate it in submitted reports, that proper correction may punish the negligent.

Of course it shall be appropriate that you report everything which either the completed conference, after the bishops have assembled, will have declared or the sentence passed upon the stubborn will have determined against those perchance who absent themselves, that we can know rather quickly what our imperial injunction has contributed toward confirming the Catholic faith.

And by the divine hand: Farewell, Marcelline, most dear to us.

Given on 14 October at Ravenna, the most distinguished Varanes being consul.

1. Religion.
2. A synonym for an imperial constitution (see no. 218, n. 5). It is not certain with which of the several constitutions concerning heretics and schismatics this constitution should be identified. Constantine I, so the Donatists claimed, sent a letter to Verinus, vicar of Africa, granting them freedom of movement (PL 11. 1257, nos. 544 and 549), but this has not survived. St Augustine dates it 5 May 321. However, it may refer to a more recent law.

3. On 25 August 410 Honorius issued a constitution (no. 323) repealing whatever previous constitution it was to which n. 2 *supra* refers.

4. The Fifteenth African Council (410) resolved to send a deputation to Honorius to request rescission of a recent edict of toleration and to attempt again what discussion could do.

5. Carthage.

6. Since the present document was issued on 14 October 410, this period would have ended in February 411. But it seems that Marcelline, who was to preside at the conference, required more time to study the situation and to ensure the success of the meeting, for in February 411 he issued his own edict in explanation of the imperial letter and summoned the bishops for 1 June of that year (see no. 325).

7. This phrase (*trini edicti vocatio*), which seems to mean that the edict should be read publicly at three stated intervals ere the expiration of the time set in it, undoubtedly reflects very ancient Roman tradition of public announcement in legal procedure. As early as 449 B.C. the Twelve Tables provided that a litigant requiring the services of a witness should shout before the doorway of the desired witness's house on three successive days that he requested his aid (*FIRA* I. 31; *TT* 2. 3) and that a creditor should exhibit his judgement-debtor, whom he was holding in bonds for sixty days (while his debt was unpaid), in the Forum on three successive market-days and should declare publicly the amount for which his debtor had been judged liable (*FIRA* I. 33; *TT* 3. 5)—in the obvious hope that some citizen, whether relative or friend, would pay the debt, because on the third occasion the debtor, if the debt were still unsolved, either could suffer capital punishment or could be sold into slavery.

Later the *Lex Caecilia et Didia* of 98 B.C. enacted that a bill must be promulgated on three successive market-days ere the voting-day (Cicero, *De Dom.* 16. 41). This statute may have had some influence on edictal procedure.

For other interesting examples of the significance of the number three in Roman law consult H. Goudy's short essay, *Trichotomy in Roman Law* (Oxford, 1910), esp. 8–17.

8. That is, surrender the Donatist-controlled churches to the Catholics.

9. From here to the sentence's end is the sole section of this constitution preserved in *CT* 16. 11. 3.

10. In *CT* is *superstitione* (superstition) for *subreptitione* (deception or plot). Possibly Pelagianism is meant, for Donatism was too old to be called new.

11. For *custodias* (you should maintain) *CT* reads *custodiri praecipimus* (we order to be maintained).

12. The one was governor of the province of Africa, in which Carthage lay; the other was in charge of the diocese of Africa, of which the province was a part. Contrary to the usual arrangement of the chain of command in the Dominate, the provincial governor of Africa was beyond the jurisdiction of

both the diocesan vicar of Africa and the praetorian prefect of Italy, but was responsible directly to the emperor.

13. In Latin abstract (*apparitio*) for concrete (*apparitores*).

325. EDICT OF MARCELLINE ON THE CARTHAGINIAN CONFERENCE BETWEEN CATHOLICS AND DONATISTS, 411

(PL 11. 1261–3; 43. 817–19)

This edict of the presiding judge of the conference between Catholics and Donatists supplements the imperial instruction to him (no. 324). Its interest lies in the indirect evidence indicating that Marcelline has taken pains to study the situation and to proclaim an impartial attitude in the forthcoming debate. In his edict Marcelline makes not a few concessions to the Donatists in an effort to secure their attendance.

What the most clement prince, our Lord Honorius, has decreed for confirmation of the Catholic faith is shown by the tenor of the afore-issued constitution: therefore, receiving willingly the delegation of venerable bishops,[1] he has not permitted Africa, ever devoted to his rule, to be befouled and to be tainted any longer by a different kind of religion, for through zeal for peace and faith he has desired that so many people's discords, which come from ancient[2] persuasion, should be settled by the manifestation of the truth, that he may recall, after a disputation of both factions has been held, those whom he clearly has seen that he cannot check by imperial ordinances proclaimed by himself and that cannot be drawn to one opinion of belief.

For he has desired all bishops of the Catholic as well as the Donatist party to assemble in one place, that, after rather skilled men have been chosen from each party and after the truth of sure faith has been discussed, clear reason may overcome superstition: to what extent there is anything which anyone soever thinks can be appropriate for his party, let it be brought into the open and thus let the light of real faith, even though late, become visible. Therefore a petition agreeable to each party has challenged the emperor to this decision, for as by the Catholics recently has been requested a conference, so it is not doubtful that a very short time previously the Donatists' bishops in a trial by illustrious magistrates have requested a conference.[3] And since the imperial Clemency willingly has given assent and has decreed that a general council be held in Africa at the request of bishops of each party, it [4] has desired that I sit in the chief place as judge over this dispute.

Wherefore all bishops of the Catholic as well as the Donatist party throughout Africa I remind by the tenor of this edict that within the period prescribed by the law, that is, within four months, which day will be ended without doubt on 1 June, they should not delay to assemble at the splendid Carthaginian city for the purpose of holding a council. Let not that party which, it shall have been established, has failed to be present appear to have judged about the merit of its own belief.[5]

Also of all the provinces I summon with equal admonition all curators, magistrates, and men of the municipal senate,[6] likewise overseers, managers, and elders of each and every community, at pain of losing their own office [7] and at peril of their safety, that they should hasten to summon the bishops of each party, in communities and places wherein they dwell, either by production of public acts or by an extant document of any writing,[8] so that, if within that very time they shall not have been able to be found in the communities, the meaning of the imperial command as well as the tenor of this edict may become known to them even when sought throughout the rural districts, in order that within these four months I may know by report of the men of the municipal senate [6] the intention of each and every individual.

Also I wish the Donatist party's bishops to know this: if any of them shall have replied that he will attend, without any delay presently by men of the municipal senate [6] must be surrendered to him with all his rights his former church, which perchance is held by Catholics pursuant to imperial command.[9]

Moreover, if all or each and everyone, found in their own communities, shall have replied that they will attend, both the churches and those places, which, it shall have been established, had been theirs or had been held by them, must be restored to their right and control by the direction of the aforesaid men of the municipal senate;[6] that, when the original status has been re-established for the said persons, the beginning of the disputation may start.[10]

And since the most august prince has wished to commit to me the entirety of so important a matter, I also admit that I willingly accept the following: that if concerning my person any hesitation should be advanced, I shall not refuse that with me should sit another judge of either higher or equal rank, whom the very persons of the Donatist party and belief shall have selected.

Moreover, whether with another or alone I shall be present to judge in this matter, I promise, by the paradoxical mystery [11] of the Trinity, by the mystical meaning of the Lord's Incarnation, and by the safety of the abovementioned emperors,[12] I shall judge nothing else except what the allegations, when examined, of the parties shall have been able to show and what belief in the truth shall have discovered.

Nor indeed have I been able to pass the following point in silence: that they should know—whether sentence shall have been given for Donatists or for Catholics—in no case shall the Donatists' bishops suffer any molestation, but they, unrestricted and free from every kind of harm, shall return to their own residences; and this I promise that I shall provide—both by the fearful day of judgement and by the abovementioned mysteries.[11]

Moreover let all who had been appointed to each and every province know that in no respect they henceforth ought to summon any of the Donatists in any matter or to create any molestation from a higher administration for the said persons, unless they prefer to come under punishment for contempt of the rather recent command.

Moreover it shall be open to all persons of the Donatist party to make free complaint about the illegal exactions and plunderings on the part of those who have been sent,[13] if perchance they know that any have been committed, in order that, after the nature of the crimes has been proved, deserved vengeance may proceed against them.

And by another hand: Let it be posted.

1. In 410 from the Fifteenth African Council, which sent a deputation to the emperor, who was asked to authorize a Catholic-Donatist conference.
2. This is an exaggerated statement, for the schism was only a century old.
3. Nothing about this Donatist petition or trial seems to be known elsewhere.
4. Honorius is meant.
5. That is, absence of either faction will be interpreted as evidence that such faction's belief in its tenets is too weak to win victory in the conference.
6. It is not clear what is meant by this expression *viri ordinis*, which gave them rank, as the context shows; and, since it is surprising that among the other persons named there is no mention of civic councillors, that is, *men of the municipal senate*, it is suggested that to these the phrase refers. In this sense, then, *ordo* or *ordines* (its plural) appears also in nos. 211, 224, 301, 310, 312, 320, 328, 433, 497, 500.

But *ordo* has wider meanings than those contained in *ordo senatorius* (senatorial order) and similar locutions—as any adequate Latin lexicon shows. It can mean any class, condition, degree, grade, rank, station, status of persons, with the added connotation of some permanency of its members therein, whether bound by common economic or social or vocational interests—as one would surmise in so regimented and stratified a society as that of the Dominate. In this sense *ordo* occurs in nos. 33, 242, 429, and in its Greek equivalent of τάξις in nos. 62, 529 (n. 2), 534, 567 (at n. 9), 651 (at n. 28).

And especially in ecclesiastical Latin *ordo* is used for an order in the Church, that is, an ecclesiastical rank or office. In this sense *ordo* appears in nos. 85 (at n. 12), 204 (at n. 4), 478 (at n. 11), and in its Greek equivalent of τάξις in nos. 614 (at nn. 11 and 16), 629 (at n. 11), 651 (at n. 22).

For τάξις as *officium* (office staff) see nos. 555, n. 8 (where it is military), 567, n. 15, 651, n. 26.

7. Literally "under the guilt of the judging of their own office".

8. These phrases seem to mean that the summoners may rely either on general or on special documents to aid their activity, but it is not absolutely certain wherein the distinction lies.

9. St Augustine justly remarks in his summary of the conference that Marcelline exceeded the emperor's mandate in making this concession to the Donatists (*Brev. Coll.* 1. 2 = CSEL 53. 39). While this act may have been designed as bait to secure their attendance (as Augustine asserts), it also may be interpreted as a sign that the conference would start on fair terms. In his edict announcing his decision after the conference Marcelline admits that this permission was his own and apart from the imperial command, when he orders such churches to be retransferred to the Catholics (no. 328, n. 12).

Some time in 405 Honorius seems to have emitted legislation suppressing the Donatists, banishing their clergy, transferring their churches to the Catholics (*PL* 33. 806).

10. This sentence looks to an earlier commencement of the conference, but, as the event proved, no such universal Donatist consent to attend enabled the conference to begin before June.

11. See no. 75, n. 42.

12. The edict lacks a superscription and only Honorius is named in its text. See also no. 255, n. 3.

13. To administrative posts throughout the diocese of Africa.

326. EDICT OF MARCELLINE ON PROCEDURE AT THE CARTHAGINIAN CONFERENCE BETWEEN CATHOLICS AND DONATISTS, 411

(*PL* 11. 1263–6; 43. 819–21)

Among our documents this edict of the imperial referee of the conference at Carthage between Catholics and Donatists occupies an important position, because it minutely explains the judicial machinery designed to direct the State's investigation of and decision on a controversy dividing the Church in Africa for a century.

Although the importance of this affair, which is undertaken about

326. THE CARTHAGINIAN CONFERENCE, 411

acknowledgement of truth and of religion,[1] might be examined by an investigation of rather little time for it, yet it had been appropriate that it should be considered because of the very gravity and the authority of the disputants. For to none is it ambiguous of how great weight is the case which must be discussed among episcopal personages. But since the august Dignity has entrusted to me the cognizance of this dispute and has given me as a judge for those to whom I am inferior, I act as judge with respect to so important a title [2] and I have taken thought for the faith, the object of my solicitude, by this consideration—that I wish to be judged about my judgement.

Therefore by the authority of this decision I have determined that all bishops of each party must be advised that, before they begin the legal investigation, not more than seven bishops apiece of both parties will make speeches in the mutual debate among themselves and these for the duty of discussion the choice of their own parties shall have furnished; therefore the imperial Authority has ordered a fixed number to be chosen from the parties.

Also shall attend another seven apiece, bishops chosen from each party for the trial, who, since the regulation of silence has been maintained from the beginning through all the conference, should understand that they are present only for this: that, if any from the debating seven apiece on each side shall have wished to take counsel with any one of them, that person may withdraw with the said person to the side and, when the matter for the consultation has been communicated there patiently, he should return to his own place for the purpose of maintaining the fulfilment of his duty; that the one, for whom this is necessary, should commend by silence what ought to be heard, that the other, for whom this is his duty, should strengthen by speech what has been undertaken.[3]

Moreover for the conference the most suitable place will be that of the Baths of Gargilius,[4] whither on 1 June only the said bishops who have been designated ought to convene. Accordingly the following point is quite clear: thither absolutely no assembly of the populace ought to be made, whither it is not permitted for all the bishops themselves to convene. For, when the patience of debate, which is friendly only to silence, shudders at the din of a multitude in troops, it makes no difference whether the congestion of the people or a crowd of bishops impedes it. Therefore only the mentioned bishops should convene at the aforesaid place and time: yet so that all the remaining bishops of each party, before the day which has been preappointed for the investigation, by letters hastening to my Excellence from each party should write that they will hold as valid whatever shall have been done by their seven fellow-bishops apiece from each side. And by these letters, however, let all also add for me the evidence of their own signature. For it is most equitable that their general conference be promised to be held valid by all, who are chosen by all.[5] Therefore let none—either layman or bishop—beyond the prescribed number attempt against this prohibition to approach into that most peaceful place of assembly—nay rather, let them gather their people by pious admonition of quiet and self-discipline, treating this throughout their own churches previously, that from the day and the place of debate all the multitude may restrain itself, that by the religious command for patience they may prepare the people already enticed toward Christian peace. For not only the bishops but also the people, endowed with reason toward this opinion, agree with respect to the aforesaid debaters that, when a rather important employment of minds takes a concentrated stand, nothing disturbing, nothing tumultuous, finally nothing stormy [6] absolutely ought to cause a noise for persons meditating about truth. For that which may advantage the welfare of all may be made public later; one ought to provide beforehand solitude for those discussing the truth; surely by me must be proclaimed by all means the decision in such a way that it, when released to public notice, may be considered by the entire populace of splendid Carthage acting as judge. So, to be sure, to the eyes not only of this city but also of the whole province will be opened the entire order of the completed debate, that the explanations of the debating bishops as well as the attendant succession of my pronouncements [7] may be unfolded in documents publicly distributed. For this in a judge is the security for his fidelity: that he fears not judgement about himself.

Therefore, that into the investigation for eliciting truth calumnious suspicion in any measure may not creep and that by absolutely no clouds the pleading of any party may obscure the very clear light, which absolute confidence in visible proofs will make clear in the minds of the people, such provision also has been made necessarily against deceptions of suspicions and inventions of deceit. Let all know that this not only ought but also is advantageous to be maintained, namely, that, with me first subscribing in all matters in respect to my interpellations, also all the debating bishops, entirely apart from absolutely any excuse, should subscribe to their own explanations on paper. For the merit of trustfulness demands that against him who perchance has tried to withdraw perfidious assent from his own assertions and to deny what he has said, even the authority of his own testimony should take its stand—and this is where victory advantages truth alone.

Moreover those who perform the function of stenography, in addition to those who attend upon my Excellence from the public offices, also four ecclesiastics apiece from each party in turn ought to assist as notaries; and lest confidence in them waver because of any trickery, let four bishops apiece, chosen from each party, be set in supervision over them, that they by very vigilant and careful observation may watch the said scribes and notaries, that, when they have left in turn with the said scribes and notaries,[8] thereupon they may cause to be arranged in a very clear copy what has been said, that, nevertheless, while the aforesaid bishops still are engaged in debate, any part of a completed question may be transferred into clear writings, that these, when subjoined with the subscription from seven bishops apiece, may convey speedy information to public expectation.[9]

Moreover after the conference's first day postponement of the investigation shall provide the opportunity of the next day for the copying and the signing of the proceedings' records, so that, if any point perchance shall have remained from the preceding conference, the inquiry may recur for the third day.[10] Therefore the interval of one day shall separate the entire time for conferring, turn by turn, whereby the proceedings, thereupon to be subscribed, can be copied through the assistance of the aforesaid persons, who are to measure their duty by this limit—not that they should say anything, but that they should preserve what has been said.

Moreover, until the disclosed truth untangles all ambiguities, after the conclusion of the questions has been completed, the impression of my seal and of those of the eight guardians [11] shall seal the sheets thereupon written and also subscribed.

Also this edict's authority shall become known to the Maximians, whereby they should understand that they must be absent from the conference, where the religious command of the clement sovereigns has determined that between Catholics and Donatists is to be distinguished and to be decided every controversy, and that they cannot be aided in any respect because they delude themselves with the name of Donatists, since they are said to be condemned by the Donatists. If anyone of these in any way shall have been unwilling to respect the regulations provided carefully, established honestly, ordained diligently, which the tenor of this statement embraces against all plots of manifold suspicion, not only he confesses what he thinks about his own cause, but also he shows what he devises.

Meanwhile for the judge such a prerogative of justice suffices that he has made the people of the Carthaginian populace, which soon he will have as his judge, for him the witness of this admonition concerning all the bishops.

It remains that before the day of the conference the bishops of each party, with delay absolutely removed and by their letters sent to my Excellence, should promise that they will execute the entire tenor of this ordinance—and this particularly speedily, that the said letters, by which they shall profess that they consent to all the points of this very edict, may be marked by the subscription also of the primate bishops.¹² For it is sufficient to join the universal—that I may speak so—subscription of all bishops to these letters, by which they shall have promised that they will hold as valid the entire series of the debate of the seven conferees apiece.

1. Perhaps a hendiadys: "of the true religion".
2. That is, he feels his humility in presiding as judge over episcopal debaters.
3. The sense of this sentence seems to be that there will be on each side seven bishops to act as private advisers but not to make public addresses, which duty falls to their colleagues already chosen.
4. Of the few Gargilii known none, though one or two seem to have been African in origin, appears to be identified with the person after whom these baths were named.
5. This points to popular election of bishops, of which perhaps the most generally known in our day occurred within the memory of men living in 411, for St Ambrose had been selected unanimously and by acclamation in 374 to be bishop of Milan in Italy, where he presided with such distinction that he was canonized and chosen to be one of the four Doctors of the Western Church—which honours he shares with his more learned friend, St Augustine, bishop of Royal Hippo (Hippo Regius) in Numidia, who was one of the seven prelates delegated to debate at this conference.
6. Conjecturing *intempestus* (stormy) for *intempestivus* (unseasonable).
7. Conjecturing *pronuntiationes* (pronouncements) for *prosecutiones* (explanations), for the former is more characteristic of a judge's rulings.
8. This seems to mean that they shall leave the conference room in some system of shifts to transcribe in another part of the baths their notes into fair copies. This is illustrated several times during the conference (e.g. *PL* 11. 1417): two stenographers fill their notebooks, ask for relief by the next relay (which is granted), depart with episcopal supervision.
9. Our phrase is the reverse: "the expectant public".
10. This, indeed, proved necessary, for the conference's first day, due to Donatist obstruction, was consumed in preliminaries of which the chief was the challenging of all bishops: 545 (for between the issuance of the edict and the conference the Catholics raised no objection to the Donatist plea that the purpose of having only 36 prelates present was to keep their large number from being known and so were willing to admit all, provided that no disturbance should arise), of whom 266 were Catholic and 279 were Donatist (*PL* 11. 1350). Besides, signatures to documents introduced for absentees had to be attested. The final figure for the Catholics was 286 (*PL* 11. 1350, 1508).

At the next meeting—3 June—the time was wasted over other details. On 8 June the third and last session was held and then Marcelline pronounced his decision.

11. The eight bishops who supervise the secretarial work are meant.

12. That is, the metropolitans of the several provinces in the civil diocese of Africa.

327. LETTER OF HONORIUS AND THEODOSIUS II ON ECCLESIASTICAL EXEMPTION FROM PUBLIC DUTIES, (?)411

(CS 11)

Honorius grants to church-owned real estate immunity from public services of a menial character [1] and extends its exemption from taxation for construction and repair of roads as well as for surtaxes.

This statute is epitomized in *CT* 16. 2. 40, which in turn is abbreviated in *CI* 1. 2. 5.

Our Lords the Emperors Honorius and Theodosius Augusti to Melitius, praetorian prefect.[2]

Your Magnificence's religious report has admonished our Clemency, which rightly cares with devoted assiduities for the sacrosanct religion's services, to confirmation of the privileges which antiquity has assigned to the churches, that when attempts of rash men, who have the desire always to attack Christian innocence, have been crushed utterly, we should ordain this rule of our decision, to which henceforth no adversary should exist with impunity.

Therefore, after[3] the tenor of a reasonable plan has been pondered, since what remedy ... the confused affairs leave a way for very wicked attempts,[4] it pleases us to prescribe by stern regulation from what obligatory duties specifically the churches of each and every city should be held immune.

Certainly the first abuse to be dispelled is that of the well-known usurpation: that estates dedicated to uses of the celestial mysteries [5] should not be harassed by the burden of menial public services.[1]

The injustice of road-making [6] should bind no unit of taxable land which enjoys the lot of such privileges;[7] from this should be demanded nothing extraordinary or specially imposed;[8] no restoration of bridges,[9] no duty of transportation [10] should arise. No gold and other such taxes should be requested.[11] Finally, nothing which the sudden burden of adventitious need shall have required beyond the regular impost should be added to its payments.[12]

The churches should be free only for the duties of divine preaching (of which they well are conscious) and should spend all the moments of all the hours in engaging in prayers. Because they are protected, they should rejoice forever in our generosity; and we rejoice in their devotion toward the worship of eternal piety.

Wherefore, after the tenor of the present response,[13] which shall endure for all time with perpetual validity, has been learned, when all things which we prescribe by this sanction's authority in respect to the sacrosanct worship have been confirmed, your sublime Magnificence, along with us becomingly equipped with religious intentions for a matter of this kind, shall admonish the governors of provinces by speedily written orders that they clearly should know that all persons who henceforth perhaps shall have attempted by exertion of rash presumption anything to the injury of the churches and of our command must be smitten with severest menace, so that persons detected in such deeds, in the impetuous contumacy of their sin, after [14] the severity of due punishment, which must be given by law to sacrilegious persons, should accept [15] the exile of perpetual deportation.

Given on 24 June at Ravenna, our Lord Theodosius Augustus for the fourth time being consul.[16]

1. See introd. to no. 186 and n. 5 to that document.
2. Of Italy.
3. *CT* and *CI* begin here.
4. Both *CT* and *CI* omit the causal clause, which is defective. A translated editorial conjecture is "since is sought what remedy may occur and since bishops' confused requests leave" etc.
5. See no. 75, n. 42.
6. The phrase means both building and repairing a road.
7. *CI* omits this much of this paragraph.
8. In the form of taxation. See no. 226, n. 3.
9. The reference to bridges is not in Justinian's law.
10. On this word see no. 107, n. 13.
11. This sentence *CI* omits.
12. Here *CT* and *CI* stop temporarily.
13. See no. 218, n. 5.
14. Here resume *CT* and *CI*.
15. Both *CT* and *CI* have a more picturesque verb *uratur* (should be burned) for *utantur* (should accept), which is pluralized in *CS*.
16. The subscription is defective. Both *CT* and *CI* date the document 25 May 412.

328. EDICT OF MARCELLINE ON DONATISM, 411
(*PL* 11. 1418-20; 43. 840-1)

At the conclusion of the Conference of Carthage on 8 June 411 Marcelline, the imperial referee, composed and read his decree in favour of the Catholics on every count.[1] On 26 June Marcelline, no longer as a judge but as the emperor's executive officer charged with carrying his sentence into effect, emitted the following edict to supplement his decree. Appeal from the edict was made to Honorius, who replied with a mandate on 30 January 412, which gave the death-blow to the Donatists (no. 329).

Flavius Marcelline, most distinguished tribune and notary, said:
I indeed should wish—and now I desire it with all the intensity of prayers—that, as from how great a demonstration of truth and, at length, of revealed error joy has arisen, so from such great conversion of ancient superstition and of opinion changed for the better rejoicing might be born. For who can doubt that there are great delights, when an unhoped cure is procured for an inveterate illness? And in such matters the restoration rather than the constant retention of health produces a greater cause for exultation. But because the obstinacy of abandoned minds, which the chains of likewise depraved persuasion had entwined, either neglects or—what is worse—fears through impudence to return to the road of revealed salvation, now must be exhibited and executed the decision that those whom milder medicines do not recall to good health, after truth has been displayed close at hand, a keener application of cure may restore.

For to whom cannot the latest reason—as the appended series of the proceedings [2] shows and as the examples set in the divine rolls [3] also testify—clearly declare, even if it could be able to be proved, that one person cannot at all be made a defendant because of the offence of another person's crime; and that the state of the whole Church ought not to be subverted on account of the accusation against Caecilian,[4] concerning whom nothing reprehensible has been able to be proved; and that by a sentence passed against him on the part of those who have separated themselves from the body of the Church it has not been valid to prejudge him when absent, just as in recent times the condemnation produced by the Maximians against the absent Primian has not prevailed to harm the said person? [5]

To whom also for the cause of reproof should not suffice entirely the proof—clarified by so many judgements—of the schism begun by Donatus,[6] Caecilian's acquittal and clearance,[7] and the final decree of Constantine, of triumphal memory, wherein rather clearly expressed are shown both Caecilian's [4] innocence and Donatus' [6] and his associates' calumnious accusation,[8] also the clearance of Felix the

Aptungitan, his ordinator,[9] shown by the documents of the proconsular decree?

Wherefore, if these so clear and evident measures are unable to cure an inveterate disease, the sanies of a stinking wound must be checked, that, when freedom to harm another—since this course rather has been chosen—has been blocked, it may begin to harm only itself. For through these means it will happen that at some time it is going to be healed. Therefore detected falsehood should submit its neck to declared truth.

Wherefore by the authority of this edict I impress upon all men of the municipal senate,[10] owners of estates, overseers, leaseholders both of the divine household [11] and of private properties, and the elders of all localities that, mindful of the laws, of their positions, of their reputation, and of their own safety, they should strive to prohibit meetings of Donatists in all communities and districts, so that they may hasten without any delay to transfer to the Catholics the churches, which, it is established, have been granted to them up to the day of this decree by my kindness and apart from the imperial order,[12] unless they prefer to be enmeshed by the snares of so many ordinances. And these churches, indeed, if they shall have wished to join in Catholic unity, it is quite decided, will belong to them.

Moreover it is by all the more reason and by this knowledge, after unity has been revealed in every way and superstition has been refuted, that they ought to be diverted from the application of their own wickedness.

Moreover let those who shall have participated in meetings after the prohibitions of these laws indubitably know that they cannot any longer escape the punishment prescribed by the imperial judgement—and they in the first place who, it is quite clear, have returned to their profane meetings and communion after respect for the acknowledged Catholic law.[13] And that this might not happen previously, so great a punishment I had postponed partly through consideration of patience and with the hope of correction in some degree. Thus far, therefore, let it suffice that the enemies of the Christian faith have insulted the laws. Especially since it is certain that their persons are known, what need is there of so many ordinances for them to be placed under restraints, since no improvement has ensued?

But let the Donatists know that the Catholic bishops' verdict itself endures also after the truth's victory, in order that they may understand that they themselves can be received, since have been completed the conferences, which, it is retained in public knowledge, have been offered to them previously and which, it is quite certain, now are offered without doubt.[14]

Moreover it is certain that the guarantee of the former edict is to be maintained in all cases.¹⁵ Wherefore each and every bishop of the communion of Donatus ⁶ ought to return to his own place without any disquietude and molestation, that, when established in his own place, he either may return to the one and the true Church or without dissimulation may not delay to make satisfaction to the laws.

Moreover those who know that in their own estates they have gangs of Circumcellions should know that, unless they in every way shall have desired eagerly to repress and to restrain insolence of these persons, those places particularly will be confiscated soon by the fisc. Therefore in this point consideration is had for both the Catholic law ¹⁶ and the public peace, that their madness should be stopped.

Moreover a re-perusal of the proceedings,² whereby it is revealed that the abovementioned error of schism by Donatists has existed, will be able to instruct your Sanctities ¹⁷ that both Caecilian ⁴ and the rest, whom wickedly they had believed ought to be accused, have been acquitted.

And in another hand: Let it be posted.

Given at Carthage after the most distinguished Varanes' consulate on 26 June.

1. St Augustine summarizes it (*Brev. Coll.* 3. 25. 43 = *CSEL* 53. 91–2) in a summary of the proceedings, of which 578 of the 883 articles survive (*PL* 11. 1231–1418).

2. That is, the minutes of the conference's proceedings (*gesta*).

3. Although the *codex* of vellum was used for permanent copies of literary works as early as our first century, not until the fourth century did it become a serious rival to the *volumen* of papyrus. By the fifth century the book ousted the roll in most of the Mediterranean area.

Probably not the Bible is meant, but the imperial constitutions are indicated. If the latter, the reference apparently is to *CT* 9. 40. 18 (dated 399). If the former, Marcelline may have had in mind especially Deut. 24. 16 (2 Kings 14. 6; 2 Chron. 25. 4) or Ezek. 18. 19–20.

4. The Catholic bishop of Carthage, about whom the Donatist controversy began (see nos. 10, 15, 17, 27).

5. The Latin represented by *it has not . . . him when absent* varies in the two editions of this document. The translation at this point adopts a conjecture given in *PL* 43. 840.

The Maximians deposed Primian, the Donatist bishop of Carthage, *in absentia* at a council held in 393 at Cabarsussi, but the "orthodox" wing of the Donatists rehabilitated Primian in 394 at Bagai in a council which contained thrice the number of that at Cabarsussi.

6. On Donatus, bishop of Casae Nigrae, who is said to have started the schism, see no. 17, n. 7.

7. Caecilian was acquitted at the Council of Rome in 313 and again at the Council of Arles in 314.

8. See no. 27.

9. Felix, bishop of Aptunga, consecrated Caecilian in 311 bishop of Carthage. The record of his trial is in *CSEL* 26. 197–204.

10. The word is *ordo*, on which see no. 325, n. 6.

11. That is, of imperial leaseholds let by the emperor's agents.

12. On Marcelline's generosity in this respect—pending the outcome of the conference—see no. 325, n. 9.

13. That is, the first to be punished will be future backsliders, who shall have made their submission to Catholicism as a result of Marcelline's decision after the conference and then shall have reverted to Donatism.

14. The conferences to be held were for the purpose of settling any details about the implementation of Marcelline's judgement in favour of the Catholics given at the conference already held.

15. See no. 325 and the following sentence.

16. Religion, as at n. 13 *supra*.

17. Apparently the edict is addressed to bishops.

329. MANDATE OF HONORIUS AND THEODOSIUS II ON PENALTIES FOR DONATISTS, 412

(*CT* 16. 5. 52)

By this famous constitution (*Cassatis quae*), which annuls all laws favouring Donatists and confirms all laws condemning them, Honorius gave the deathblow to the century-old schism of Donatism. It provides an elaborate scale of penalties for clerical and lay Donatists and restores Donatist-controlled churches to Catholics.

The same Augusti to Seleucus, praetorian prefect.[1]

With the provisions, which have been able to be gained by request through pragmatic sanctions or by our hand's annotation,[2] annulled and with those provisions, which long ago have been defined on this matter, remaining and with the former emperors' sanction preserved: unless from the day of the published law all Donatists, bishops[3] as well as clergymen and laymen, shall have returned to the Catholic sect,[4] whence they sacrilegiously have departed, then illustrious persons[5] should be compelled to pay in the category of a penalty to our fisc fifty pounds of gold apiece; admirable persons,[5] forty pounds of gold; senators, thirty pounds of gold; most distinguished persons,[5] twenty pounds of gold; civil priests,[6] thirty pounds of gold; chief

329. PENALTIES FOR DONATISTS, 412

magistrates, twenty pounds of gold; decurions, five pounds of gold; merchants, five pounds of gold; plebeians, five pounds of gold; Circumcellions, ten pounds of silver.

And unless these persons shall have been brought by the leaseholders [7] under whom they live or by the managers [7] to the prosecutor [8] demanding them, they themselves should be held for punishment, so that persons of our household [9] should not be regarded as immune from judgement of this kind.

Their husbands' fines should bind separately also wives.

Confiscation of all their property certainly shall pursue those whom these imposed penalties no wise shall have corrected.

Also owners' [10] admonition or rather frequent flogging shall recall slaves or tenant farmers from the depraved religion, unless they themselves prefer, even if they are Catholics, to be held for the aforesaid costs.

Moreover the clergymen and their ministers [11] and the very pernicious bishops,[3] removed from African soil, which they have polluted by sacrilegious rite, should be sent separately into exile under proper escort to individual regions—with their churches or conventicles and estates, if heretics' wicked largess has contributed anything to their churches, claimed for the Catholic sect's [4] ownership and control, just as we long ago have ordained.[12]

Given on 30 January at Ravenna, Honorius Augustus for the ninth time and Theodosius Augustus for the fifth time being consuls.

1. Of Italy.
2. See no. 317, n. 2.
3. See no. 16, n. 4.
4. Some such noun should be supplied, unless the adjective is used substantively. The MSS. show variant readings here.
5. On these gradations see no. 586, n. 2.
6. The word is *sacerdotales*. See no. 208, n. 3.
7. Of imperial estates (*saltus*), which were common in Africa, where Donatism principally flourished.
8. Perhaps this person was Dulcitius, a tribune and notary, reported to be in Africa at this time as the *executor* (the word here) of imperial orders against Donatists.
9. That is, of the imperial household's estates.
10. That is, masters in respect to slaves and proprietors in relation to tenants. The word is *dominus*.
11. See no. 15, n. 3.
12. See no. 301.

330. MANDATE OF HONORIUS AND THEODOSIUS II ON EXILE OF JOVINIAN, (?)412
(CT 16. 5. 53)

It is tempting to associate this ordinance with that Jovinian who was an outspoken opponent of Christian celibacy and was condemned as a heretic in 390 and in 391. The only objections are the date and the addressee, but editorial conjecture changes the date to 398, which fits into the data of Jovinian's life as well as solves the difficulty about the addressee, Felix, urban prefect of Rome, who from another ordinance (CT 6. 2. 21) is known to have held that office in that year and not in 412, unless the present document is correct.[1]

Our information about Jovinian comes from Saints Ambrose, Augustine, Jerome, Siricius—all contemporaries: the first three being three of the four Doctors of the Western Church [2] and the fourth a pope. Probably through lack of sympathy with Jovinian's protestations against asceticism these saints have ruined his reputation, but at least they have reproduced his arguments [3]— and those in his *ipsissima verba*—though in fragments and only for criticism.

It appears that Jovinian, originally a monk and then converted to a less austere, if not to a luxurious, life, taught that: (1) virginity is not superior to matrimony, (2) abstinence from meat is no better than partaking thereof with thanksgiving,[4] (3) one baptized with the Spirit as well as with water cannot sin, (4) absolute equality exists between virtues and between vices,[5] (5) in the future life there is only one grade of reward and of punishment, (6) the Blessed Virgin Mary was not perpetually a virgin.

The same Augusti [6] to Felix, urban prefect.[7]

The bishops' complaint deplores that Jovinian conducts sacrilegious gatherings outside the most sacred city's [8] walls.

Wherefore we command that the aforesaid person should be arrested and, after having been beaten with a leaden scourge, should be confined by exile with all the rest of his adherents and attendants; moreover that he himself, as the machinator, should be expelled with swift speed to the isle of Bua [9] and that the rest—just as it shall have been pleasing,[10] provided that the band of superstitious conspirators shall be dissolved by the separation of exile itself—should be deported in perpetuity to solitary islands situated at a great distance from one another.

Moreover, if anyone by pertinacious improbity shall have repeated such prohibited and condemned things, he should know that he will suffer a severer sentence.

Given on 6 March at Milan, Honorius Augustus for the ninth time and Theodosius Augustus for the fifth time being consuls.[11]

1. Of course, there is the possibility that Felix survived fourteen years to be

reappointed, despite the fact that we already know two occupants of that office in 412: Palmatus (*CT* 14. 2. 4) and Epifanius (*CT* 6. 18. 1).

2. The fourth is Pope St Gregory I (590–604).

3. Conveniently collected by W. Haller in *Iovinianus* (Leipzig, 1897).

4. Toward the end of the prologue to his *Historia Lausiaca* (our best source for the rise of monachism in Egypt) Palladius, a younger contemporary of Jovinian, in a discussion on food and drink maintains that "to drink wine with reason is better than to drink water with pride".

5. This was a celebrated Stoic paradox, classically presented by Cicero (*Parad. Stoic.* 20–6).

6. If 398 is the date, Arcadius must be substituted for Theodosius.

7. Of Rome.

8. His activities were centred at Rome.

9. An islet (the ancient Bavo or Boa) in the Adriatic Sea off the coast of Yugoslavia. In the Dominate many political offenders and heretics were sent thither. See no. 46, n. 16.

10. That is, Felix should decide whither they would be sent.

11. If 398 is the date, then the subscription should read "Honorius Augustus for the fourth time and Eutychian being consuls".

331. MANDATE OF HONORIUS AND THEODOSIUS II ON RECOVERY OF EXPOSED CHILDREN, 412

(*CT* 5. 9. 2)

This constitution denied to masters or to patrons the right of recovery of children abandoned by them, provided that a bishop attests by his signature immediately after such exposure that the exposer has exposed the child and that the finder has taken it honestly.

Justinian has part of this statute (*CI* 8. 51. 2).

Emperors Honorius and Theodosius Augusti to Melitius, praetorian prefect.[1]

To masters or to patrons we leave no access of recovery, if good will (mercy's friend) shall have acquired children [2] exposed [3] in a measure to death—for one shall not be able to call his own whom he has despised as it perishes [4]—provided that as witness there shall have followed immediately an episcopal signature, concerning which there can be no delay at all for the purpose of security.[5]

Given on 19 March at Ravenna, Honorius Augustus for the ninth time and Theodosius Augustus for the fifth time being consuls.

G

Interpretation: Who for mercy's sake shall have acquired an exposed boy or girl, with the master or the patron knowing it,[6] shall continue in the ownership of the said child, provided that a bishop or clergymen shall have subscribed to a testimony about its acquisition, since afterward anyone shall not be able to call his own whom he is proved to have abandoned to death.

1. Of Italy.
2. The Latin has no nominal object, for which *children* is supplied in translation.
3. Justinian adds "by themselves" i.e. by masters or by patrons.
4. Here Justinian ends his excerpt, which he appends to a constitution ascribed in 374 to Valentinian I, Valens, and Gratian, as follows: "Each and every one should rear his own offspring. But if he shall have thought that it ought to be exposed, he shall be subject to the punishment which has been established".
5. According to an earlier law issued by Constantine I in 331 (*CT* 5. 9. 1) the finder of an exposed child can keep the foundling as a son or as a daughter or as a slave and can maintain successfully his title to it, provided that it can be shown that the abandoners have acted knowingly and voluntarily.
6. That is, the exposers consciously and willingly abandoned the child.

332. MANDATE OF HONORIUS AND THEODOSIUS II ON CHRISTIAN IMMUNITY FROM JEWISH PROSECUTIONS, (?)412
(*CI* 1. 9. 13)

This ordinance, bereft of its Christian aspect, appears in *CT* 2. 8. 26 with an interpretation [1] and without the interpretation reappears in *CT* 8. 8. 8. It both guarantees to Jews freedom from lawsuits on their religious days and demands the same for orthodox Christians if the former should prosecute the latter on Jewish holy days.

The same Augusti to John, praetorian prefect.[2]
We command that on the Sabbath day and on the remaining days [3] at the time when Jews observe their own cult's reverence none ought to do anything [4] or in any way to be sued (so that, however, also to them should not be given permission to sue orthodox Christians on the said day,[5] lest perchance Christians as a result of suit of Jews should sustain any molestation by officials on the aforesaid days),[6]

since it is established that the remaining days [7] can suffice for fiscal advantages and litigations of private persons.

Given on 26 July at Ravenna, Honorius Augustus for the ninth time and Theodosius Augustus for the fifth time being consuls.[8]

1. The interpretation, containing nothing Christian, is not translated.
2. Of Italy.
3. Such as their high holy days.
4. That is, to be forced to perform a public service.
5. This is sound legal doctrine, for Ulpian asks (D 2. 2. 1. pr.) "For who will reject for himself to be pronounced the same law which he himself has pronounced or has caused to be pronounced for others?"
6. Justinian inserts this parenthesis into the Theodosian version.
7. That is, all days exclusive of the Sabbath and holy days, not just the Sabbath.
8. CT gives "eighth" and "third" for *ninth* and *fifth* (which sets the date three years earlier in 409), but editors emend the Theodosian dating to conform with CT 16. 8. 20, of which this law in its Theodosian form may have been a part, for each of the doublets indicates that it is an extract of a longer law.

333. MANDATE OF HONORIUS AND THEODOSIUS II ON JEWISH REVERENCE FOR CHRISTIANITY,

412 or 418

(CT 16. 8. 21)

As this law forbids anyone to molest Jews, so it ordains that Jews should not be disrespectful toward Christianity.

Justinian has this constitution (CI 1. 9. 14).

The same Augusti to Philip, praetorian prefect in Illyricum.[1]

No one, on the ground that he is a Jew, when he is innocent, should be contemned nor any religion whatsoever should cause a person to be exposed to contumely.

Their synagogues or habitations should not be burned indiscriminately or should not be damaged wrongfully without any reason, since, moreover, even if anyone should be implicated in crimes, yet the vigour of the law-courts and the protection of the public law appear to have been established in our midst, lest anyone should have the power to venture on vengeance for himself.

But as we desire this to be provided for the persons of the Jews, so we decree also that the following warning ought to be made: that Jews perchance should not become insolent and, elated by their own security, should not commit anything rash against reverence for the Christian worship.

Given on 6 August at Constantinople, Honorius Augustus for the ninth time and Theodosius Augustus for the fifth time being consuls.

1. *CI* styles Philip simply as praetorian prefect.

334. MANDATE OF HONORIUS AND THEODOSIUS II ON CONFIRMATION OF EPISCOPAL JURISDICTION, 412
(CS 15)

This ordinance, epitomized in *CT* 16. 2. 41, besides confirming to bishops the right to hear cases concerning clergymen, sets standards for proof to be produced for plaintiffs.

Emperors Honorius and Theodosius Augusti to the illustrious Melitius, praetorian prefect.[1]

Not in vain the prudence [2] of the ancients has established that there should be relief for attacked innocence and that there should be found vengeance for exculpated persons, lest a calumniator's [3] unrestricted exertion [4] might afflict the guiltless. Indeed the penalty ordained for criminal accusations terrifies the accused and makes the accuser more cautious by contemplation of the punishment, lest anyone, incited at any time by the goads of personal enmities, should present to judges charges which cannot be proved. This equity of the forum,[5] confirmed by the ancients' responses [6] and by the eternity of our laws,[7] has been brought to all persons and now ought to advantage clergymen, for whom it is proper not to be accused unless before bishops.[8] And it is proper for them to have nothing in common,[9] lest a bishop [10] of the venerable cult and a minister [10] dedicated to the Christian law [11] (to whom greater reverence must be paid than to all other such persons by consideration for religion) because of a calumniator's [3] careless decision may be defiled by the advancement of a yet unproved accusation of any kind [12] and lest to such persons, to whom it is worthy to have paid reverence [13] in accord with merit, we allow wrong to be done unjustly and illicitly without punishment.[14]

Wherefore by the eternity of a law which will please [15] all persons [16] we ordain that if [17] a bishop or a priest, a deacon and everyone who is a minister [10] of an inferior grade of the Christian law [11] shall have been accused by any person soever before bishops, since it is not proper elsewhere, that man—whether of exalted honour or of any other dignity soever—who should seize upon this sort of wretched [18] exertion [3]—that a person polluted by any sins or crimes should present information by falsifying against persons approved by their service, either holding a position in the priesthood [19] or serving the divine mysteries [20]—should know that he ought to introduce matters to be shown by proofs and to be demonstrated by documents.

And if any fault is in him, a minister [10] of religion who ought to be removed because of the pollution of his life cannot engage in the sacred mysteries.[21] But if he [22] is of this madness which appears to have attacked the way of life of such men by a concocted accusation supported by no proofs or [23]... if therefore anyone shall have brought unprovable charges concerning persons of this character, he should understand by this sanction's authority that he subjects himself to loss of his own character, in order that by hurt to his honour and by detriment to his reputation he may learn at least for the future that it is not allowed to attack hereafter with impunity the respect belonging to another person. For, just as it is equitable for bishops, priests, deacons, and all others,[24] when dishonoured, to be removed from the venerable Church, if charges against these shall have been able to be proved, so that they, when contemned afterward and bent under contempt of wretched humiliation, may not have an action for injuries,[25] so it is bound to appear to pertain to similar justice that we have commanded a due punishment to be given to attacked innocence.

And accordingly bishops shall be bound to hear cases of this character only under many persons' attestation and by records.[26]

Given on 11 December at Ravenna, Honorius Augustus for the ninth time and Theodosius Augustus for the fifth time being consuls.

1. Of Italy.

2. Perhaps "jurisprudence", for *prudentia* sometimes equals *iuris prudentia* in late Latin. Cf. *infra* n. 6 for its application here.

3. In Roman law a person was guilty of *calumnia* who in bad faith instituted a false or malicious action at law. In addition to disqualification for various functions (*infamia*) it is supposed that the Lex Remmia (mentioned by Cicero, *Pro Sex. Rosc. Amer.* 19. 55) authorized that a convicted calumniator should be branded on the forehead by the letter K, which signified *kalumnia* (the archaic spelling).

4. The word is *intentio*, which also signifies that part of the praetorian *formula* which instructs the judge as to the plaintiff's allegation of right or of fact.

5. In the Forum Romanum during the Republic and in the various imperial *fora* (e.g. Caesar's) during the Empire justice was administered in Rome. Similarly court was conducted in the market-places of municipalities. Eventually the word *forum* came to mean "tribunal" or "court" and in legal phrases so survives: e.g. *forum ecclesiasticum*. See also no. 62, n. 11.

6. See *D* 48. 2. 7 for a jurisprudent's opinion.
7. *CT* 9. 1 contains examples.
8. An adaptation of this clause begins the summary in *CT*.
9. Perhaps with the secular courts is meant.
10. See no. 310, n. 13.
11. Religion.
12. Unless the Latin is read literally to mean that the advancement of any kind of accusation has not yet been approved, here is an instance of synesis, where the participle belongs grammatically with one noun and logically with another noun.
13. The antecedent *such persons* (*talibus personis*) of this clause and the words *all other such persons* (*ceteris personis*) three lines above this clause probably refer to clergymen of inferior grades, not to ministers of other cults, who already have been included in the *equity of the forum* mentioned in the previous sentence as already *brought to all persons*.
14. An example of inconcinnity even in Latin.
15. Another case of synesis: the Latin construes the English clause with *eternity*.
16. Or "in all respects".
17. Here resumes *CT*, which inserts "therefore" after the conjunction.
18. *CT* has "laudable" ironically and suspends temporarily after the next word.
19. See no. 158, n. 1.
20. See no. 75, n. 42. *CT* has the rest of this paragraph.
21. See no. 75, n. 42.
22. The accuser.
23. The lacuna is editorial and the text is resumed by *CT*.
24. The minor clergy are meant.
25. By *injuries* the Romans meant any wilful disregard of another's personality and thus included trespass to the person in its widest extent: assault and battery, slander and libel, witchcraft, malicious lawsuit, malicious nuisance, public insult, unlawful detention of a free person, insult to the dead, entry of a person's house against his will, attempt against the chastity of boys or of females—any of these was a ground for an *actio iniuriarum*. Three elements chiefly concurred to constitute such a violation: intent, illegality, infliction without consent of injured person. Penalties varied according to public opinion and to circumstances surrounding the commission of the crime.

An injury was considered atrocious (*iniuria atrox*), as in no. 478 at n. 11, (1) from the fact (*ex facto*), as when anyone suffered physical outrage; (2) from the place (*ex loco*), as when the wrong occurred in a public place; (3) from the person (*ex persona*), as when a magistrate or a senator was insulted by someone of inferior rank or a parent by his children or a patron by his freedmen; (4) from the position of the wound (*ex loco vulneris*), as when anyone was struck in the eye (*GI* 3. 225; *II* 4. 4. 9). Any third person, whose reputation might suffer incidentally, could institute action on this delict, which, however, could be prosecuted only at the offended person's request and could not be brought either by the victim's heirs or against the wrongdoer's heirs.

26. Produced in court.

335. MANDATE OF HONORIUS AND THEODOSIUS II ON REBAPTISM AND ON CELEBRATION OF EASTER, 413

(*CT* 16. 6. 6)

Besides hitting at rebaptizers, this constitution assails the Novatians, who persist in celebrating the paschal festival on a day not so observed by the orthodox.

Part of this mandate constitutes *CI* 1. 6. 2.

Emperors Honorius and Arcadius Augusti to Anthemius, praetorian prefect.[1]

No person should engage in the crime of rebaptizing nor should try to pollute with the filth of profane religions and with the squalors of heretics those persons who shall have been initiated by the rite of the orthodox. Although we trust that through fear of the severest threat none at all has committed this crime after it has been forbidden, yet, that persons of depraved mind may refrain from illicit acts, even when compelled, we wish it to be renewed that if [2] anyone shall have been found to have rebaptized, after the law was enacted,[3] anyone from the Catholic sect's mysteries,[4] he should be stricken with the former statute's [5] punishment along with the rebaptized person, because he has committed a sinful crime, provided that, however, he who has been so persuaded is capable of crime because of his age.[6]

Furthermore we do not permit to be unpunished that crime which has been left unheeded by previous emperors and is practised to the injury of the sacred law [7] by accursed persons and particularly by those, who, as deserters and fugitives from the society of Novatians, contend that they rather are to be considered the supporters of the aforesaid sect, whose name comes from the crime, since they desire to be called Protopaschitans.[8] But if the Novatians shall have believed that the day of Easter, commemorated through centuries, ought to be proclaimed and celebrated on another day than that observed by bishops of the orthodox, let deportation as well as proscription pursue the sponsors of that convention.⁹ And against these persons ought to be promulgated an even severer punishment, seeing that in this sin they surpass even the heretics' insanity, since they, by observing the feast of Easter at another time than that of the orthodox,¹⁰ venerate almost another Son of God—not him whom we worship.

Given on 21 March at Constantinople, the most distinguished Lucius being consul.

1. Of the Orient.
2. Here begins Justinian's statute in *CI*.
3. This clause *CI* omits. It is unknown what statute is meant: perhaps one of nos. 158, 163, 289, 290.
4. That is, one who was baptized into the orthodox faith. See nos. 7, n. 13, and 75, n. 42.
5. For *former statute's CI* has "supreme": that is death. Cf. *supra* n. 3 *ad fin*.
6. Here ends Justinian's quotation.

Pitra (2. 513) has a late Greek paraphrase of Justinian's statute, which is read as "If anyone has been found to have rebaptized anyone and to have been rebaptized himself, unless indeed because of his age he, being a child, knew not what was happening, he should submit to the extreme punishment."

7. Religion.
8. Certain dissidents among the Novatians formed a new sect, the Protopaschitans, and claimed that they alone preserved the true tenets of Novatianism.
9. In the sense either of an assembly (such as this splinter-group of Novatians) or of an agreement (such as the decision to celebrate Easter on a day set by their own calculation); perhaps the word (*conventio*) hits both meanings.
10. See no. 52 for the earliest law on the celebration of Easter.

336. MANDATE OF HONORIUS AND THEODOSIUS II ON REBAPTISM, 413

(*CT* 16. 6. 7)

This last document on rebaptism in the Theodosian Code assails also the Eunomians and is incomplete.

The same Augusti to Anthemius, praetorian prefect.¹

We order that the Eunomians' abominable assemblies and calamitous conventicles should be prevented entirely; that those persons, who, when they have usurped the title of bishops or of clergymen or of ministers,² preside over assemblies of this kind or in whose houses or fields the Eunomians' illicit conventicles are held, unless by ignorance the owners are defended against this crime, when they shall have been caught in this crime, should incur the sentence of proscription and should be repressed by loss of their goods; but that those persons, who are discovered in their monstrous madness to rebaptize persons who have been imbued with the faith,³ as has been said, with these persons who are rebaptized, if they are of that age at which a crime can be attributed. . . .

Given on 29 March, the most distinguished Lucius being consul.

1. Of the East.
2. Bishops and priests and deacons are meant (see no. 15, n. 3).
3. That is, orthodox Christians.

337. MANDATE OF HONORIUS AND THEODOSIUS II ON PENALTIES FOR DONATISTS AND HERETICS, 414

(*CT* 16. 5. 54)

This elaborate directive establishes numerous disabilities and penalties for Donatists and heretics, as the Donatist schism drew toward its solution.

The same Augusti to Julian, proconsul of Africa.

We ordain that Donatists and heretics, whom the patience of our Clemency has spared until now, be overthrown by competent authority, in order that by this manifest statute they may realize that they are incapable of making wills and have no power of entering into any kind of contract, but that, branded by perpetual infamy, they must be segregated from honourable gatherings and from public assembly.

Moreover those places in which until now the dire superstition has been preserved should be joined to the venerable Catholic Church, so that bishops, priests, both all their prelates and ministers,¹ when despoiled of all their properties, should be sent for the sake of exile individually to separate islands and provinces.²

Moreover, whoever shall have received these persons for the sake of sheltering them, when fleeing the proposed punishment, should know both that his patrimony must be added to our fisc's assets and that he will suffer the penalty which has been proposed for these persons.

Also we manifestly impose the losses of patrimony and pecuniary penalties on men and women, both private persons and dignitaries—and these must be inflicted according to their status.

Therefore, if anyone shall have been invested with the rank of proconsul or vicar or count of the first order, unless he shall have converted his mind and purpose to Catholic observance, he should be compelled to pay two hundred pounds of silver to be added to our fisc's resources. And let it not be thought that this alone can suffice to restrain their design, but as often as he shall have been convicted of having entered into such communion, so often the fine should be exacted; and if it shall have been established five times that the said person is not recalled from error, then he should be referred to our Clemency, that we may judge more severely about his whole property and about his status.

Moreover we bind also the remaining distinguished persons by conditions of this character: namely that a senator, who is fortified by no extra privilege of rank, when found in the Donatists' herd, should pay a hundred pounds of silver, civil priests [3] should be compelled to pay the same sum, the ten chief curials should be sentenced fifty pounds of silver, the remaining decurions should pay ten pounds of silver—whosoever shall have preferred to persist in heresy.

Moreover leaseholders of our household, if they shall have allowed these practices to be used on the estates of our venerable property, should be compelled to bring by payment—in the category of a penalty—as much as they have been wont to pay in rental. The same authority of the sacred order shall bind also emphyteuticaries.[4]

Moreover, if leaseholders of private persons shall have permitted meetings to be held on the said estates or if by their indulgence the sacred mystery [5] shall have been defiled, report by the governors should be made to the knowledge of the proprietors, whose interest it shall be, if they desire to avoid the sacred command's penalty, either to correct those who err or to replace those who persist and to provide for their estates such directors as observe the divine orders. If they shall have neglected to attend to this, they also should be fined to the amount of the rentals which they have been wont to receive by the authority of the order, as issued, in order that what could have accrued to their profits may be added to the sacred treasury.

Moreover, if the various governors' officials shall have been caught in this error, they should be held to the payment of thirty pounds of silver in the category of a penalty; also, if they, after having been condemned five times, shall have been unwilling to abstain, they, when they have been punished by lashes, should be subjected to exile.

Moreover the severest punishment shall restrain slaves and tenant farmers from bold acts of this kind. And if tenant farmers, after they have been constrained by lashes, shall have continued in their course, then they should be fined by a third part of their peculium.⁶ Moreover all things which have been able to be collected from such classes of persons and places should be directed forthwith to the sacred largesses.

Given on 17 June at Ravenna, Constantius and Constans being consuls.

1. Probably *both . . . ministers* is merely a blanket repetition and clarification of the preceding personages, but see no. 15, n. 3.
2. This seems exaggerated, since the strength of the Donatist clergy was so superior to the number of islands and provinces available that more than one would have had to be sent to any one place.
3. The word is *sacerdotales*. On the civil priesthood see no. 208, n. 3.
4. A synonym for emphyteutes, on whom see no. 537, n. 6.
5. See no. 75, n. 42.
6. Here and in nos. 421 and 510 appears one form of the *peculium* (for another type see no. 624, n. 3).

A tenant farmer (*colonus*, on whom see no. 528, n. 5) could acquire personal property, which was called peculium (probably after the analogy of a slave's peculium—on which see below—because his serf-like status was not far superior to servitude). It seems that, though a tenant farmer's peculium was legally under his own control, yet he could not alienate any of it without his landlord's consent (*CT* 5. 19. 1).

The commonest form of peculium was property given by a master to his slave as the latter's private property, over which the slave retained customary ownership in the absence of legal right to it. The peculium might have been the slave's savings from his exceptional industry or rewards for extraordinary services or capital to engage in business. On manumission the ex-slave, now a freedman, ordinarily became owner of what previously he had possessed, less, of course, any payment from it to his master for his freedom, if his master had placed a price on it—as did the unknown master of the chief captain who told St Paul "With a great sum obtained I this freedom" (Acts 22. 28).

338. MANDATE OF HONORIUS AND THEODOSIUS II ON VALIDITY OF PROCEEDINGS AT THE CARTHAGINIAN CONFERENCE BETWEEN CATHOLICS AND DONATISTS, 414

(*CT* 16. 5. 55)

After Marcelline, the presiding judge at the Conference of Carthage in 411 between Catholics and Donatists, had been killed in 413, the Donatists' hopes revived—only to be repressed by this imperial order confirming the validity of the official minutes of the meeting.

Although many Donatists were reconciled to Catholicism after Honorius had issued in 412 his mandate outlawing Donatism (no. 329), yet later imperial constitutions and patristic evidence show that regions of resistance persisted—particularly in rural districts—and that groups of these schismatics survived the general subversion of African Christendom by Islam in the seventh century.[1]

In a modified form this mandate appears in *CI* 7. 52. 6.[2]

The same Augusti to Julian, proconsul of Africa.

Through the dutiful investigation[3] of Marcelline, a man of admirable memory, have been done against the Donatists those things which, transferred to the public records, we wish to have perpetual validity.

For the State's guaranty must not perish at a judge's death.

Given on 30 August at Rome, Constantius and Constans being consuls.

1. Consult W. H. C. Frend, *The Donatist Church* (Oxford, 1952), 312–14.
2. Justinian omits the reference to Marcelline and the Donatists and thus makes the rule of general application.
3. Reading *notione et sollicitudine* as a hendiadys.

339. MANDATE OF HONORIUS AND THEODOSIUS II ON HERETICAL ASSEMBLIES, 415

(*CT* 16. 5. 56)

Since this order is addressed to Africa, it probably is another statute in the series of constitutions against Donatists. It repeats part of no. 323, issued five years earlier.

The same Augusti to Heraclian, count of Africa.

All persons who had crept secretly to their own rites of heretical superstition should know that they, as enemies of the sacrosanct law,[1] must be punished by the penalty both of proscription and of life,[2] if they shall have attempted further to assemble in public through temerity of practising their wickedness,[3] lest in any way true and divine worship should be defiled by contagion.

Given on 25 August, Honorius Augustus for the tenth time and Theodosius Augustus for the sixth time being consuls.

1. The Catholic religion.
2. Literally "blood".
3. The crime of heresy.

340. EDICT OF HONORIUS AND THEODOSIUS II ON ALLOCATION OF PAGAN RELIGIOUS PROPERTY TO THE CHURCH, 415

(*CT* 16. 10. 20)

Only that part of the second section of this constitution, addressed to the Carthaginians (as we can infer from its initial sentence and as we learn from *CI* 1. 11. 5, which preserves only parts of two of its four sections), concerning the Christians is translated here, for the rest of the edict directs the suppression of pagan superstition and orders the confiscation of property held by pagan sects.

Emperors Honorius and Theodosius Augusti.
... Moreover those properties, which by numerous statutes we have wished to belong to the venerable Church, the Christian religion rightfully shall claim for itself[1]. ...
Given on 30 August at Ravenna, Honorius Augustus for the tenth time and Theodosius Augustus for the sixth time being consuls.

1. Other parts of the edict—as well as of the title wherein it occurs—show that most of the property belonging to the pagan sects was confiscated for the imperial estates. Apparently the Church received only certain selected properties. Also *numerous statutes* seems to be an exaggeration, for only no. 301 permits the Church to claim such pagan property.

341. MANDATE OF HONORIUS AND THEODOSIUS II ON PUNISHMENT OF JEWISH PROSELYTIZERS OF CHRISTIANS, 415

(*CT* 16. 8. 22)

While this constitution begins by considering the particular case of Gamaliel, the Jewish patriarch, whose degradation is ordered for causes now unknown or because he has done what this law forbids him to do in the future, yet it widens into a directive against Jews who proselytize Christians and keep Christian slaves.

Justinian retains a part of this law (*CI* 1. 9. 15).

The same Augusti to Aurelian, praetorian prefect[1] for the second time.

Since Gamaliel[2] has supposed that with impunity he could transgress, all the more because he has been raised to the peak of honours, your illustrious Authority should know that our Serenity has sent orders to the illustrious master of the offices that the diplomas[3] of the honorary prefecture should be taken from him, so that he should be in that honour in which he had been established before his prefecture; and that henceforth he should cause no synagogues to be founded; and that, if there are any in a desert,[4] if they can be destroyed without sedition, he should effect it; and that he should have no opportunity of judging between Christians; and that, if[5] any contention should be between them and Jews, it should be ended by governors of a province.[6]

If either he himself or anyone of the Jews shall have attempted to mar a Christian or a person of any sect whatever—free-born or slave—with the Jewish mark,[7] let him be subjected to the laws' severity.

Also, if he retains in his control any slaves of Christian holiness, according to the Constantinian Law let them be delivered to the Church.[8]

Given on 20 October at Constantinople, Honorius Augustus for the tenth time and Theodosius Augustus for the sixth time being consuls.

1. Of the East.
2. Gamaliel VI was the twelfth and last patriarch, a title given to the religious leader of the Palestinian Jews after 66 or 70. His office and the theologians attached to it after several shifts were transferred *c*. 250 to Tiberias, where it remained until the patriarchate was abolished at Gamaliel's death in 425. Four years later Theodosius permanently diverted (*CT* 16. 8. 29) to the imperial exchequer the annual tax, the so-called apostole (ἀποστολή) or coronary gold (*aurum coronarium*), which Jews voluntarily had contributed to maintain the patriarchal office and to support its resident scholars. Before its permanent payment to the fisc in 429, however, it temporarily and for a quinquennium (399–404) had been allocated to the imperial treasury (*CT* 16. 8. 14 and 17).

The apostole was not new to Jews, since nearly every Jewish embassy sent from Palestine to Rome carried a gold crown as a gift either to the Senate and the Roman People or to a chief magistrate, who then dedicated it in the Capitol (see e.g. Josephus, *Ant. Iud.* 14. 12. 2. 304 and 3. 313, where Mark Antony received it). The custom apparently commenced among conquered peoples, who were required to provide enough gold for transformation into a crown, which was held, usually by a public slave, over a victorious general's head in his triumph celebrated on his return from the wars to Rome (see *FIRA* 1. 244-5, where a senatusconsult of 170 B.C. acknowledges such a gift from Thisbeans). From this practice was developed in the Principate a freewill offering of the so-called coronary gold, whether or not the gold was converted into a crown, by wealthy provincials and dignitaries and municipalities to the emperors on their accessions, on the anniversaries thereof, and on opportune occasions. By the end of the second century this donation was transmuted into a compulsory payment, as an assessed tax (see C. G. Bruns, *Fontes Iuris Romani Antiqui*[7] [Tübingen, 1909], 268–70, where Emperor Severus Alexander's edict in 222 remits to Italians and provincials the monies voted for gold crowns at his accession to the throne). The term also loosely embraces other gold objects presented by foreign or subject peoples to the Roman State and stored in the Capitol in Rome.

3. That is, patents of nobility (*codicilli*), for the patriarchs were saluted as *clarissimi et illustres* in 392 (*CT* 16. 8. 8), as *illustres* in 396 (*CT* 16. 8. 11), as *spectabiles* in 404 (*CT*. 16. 8. 15).

4. Why synagogues in desert places rather than in communities should be destroyed is not clear, though the destruction of pagan temples in rural districts was authorized in 399 (*CT* 16. 10. 16), that the material basis for all superstition might be ended.

5. Justinian's excerpt adapts the rest of this sentence thus: "If any contention should be between Christians and Jews, it should be ended not by elders of the Jews but by ordinary governors."

State-recognized jurisdiction of Jewish courts competent to consider civil causes everywhere (see no. 17, n. 3 *ad med.* for perhaps earlier limitations) dated at least from 398 (*CT* 2. 1. 10).

6. Since there was only one governor of a province at any one time "provinces" seems the better reading.

7. Perhaps circumcision is meant.

8. No. 76.

342. MANDATE OF HONORIUS AND THEODOSIUS II ON PENALTIES FOR MONTANISTS, 415

(*CT* 16. 5. 57)

In this constitution penalties are assessed against Montanists who assemble for worship and ordain clerics.

The same Augusti to Aurelian, praetorian prefect[1] for the second time.

Montanists should understand that from them has been taken every opportunity of assembling or of holding meetings and of creating clergymen, so that, if they shall have held illicit assemblies, their clergymen, whether bishops or priests or deacons, who shall have tried to contrive nefarious conventicles or shall have dared to create clergymen or even shall have acquiesced in being created clergymen, shall receive the sentence of deportation.

Moreover those who shall have received them for holding forbidden gatherings without doubt should understand that they must be deprived of that very property, wherein they shall have permitted this to be done and the cursed mysteries [2] to be celebrated, whether this property shall have been a house or an estate; moreover, if managers shall have received those persons without their owners' knowledge, they shall not doubt that they, after they have been punished severely, must be sent into exile.

Also, if now there are belonging to them any buildings, which ought to be called not churches but deadly caves, these with their dedicated offerings should be adjudged to the venerable churches of the orthodox sect.[3] And this, indeed, must be accomplished in such manner that there should be abstention from private persons' properties, lest under pretence of properties belonging to Montanists' churches pillaging and plundering may be perpetrated against private persons.

Given on 31 October at Constantinople, Honorius Augustus for the tenth time and Theodosius Augustus for the sixth time being consuls.

1. Of the Orient.
2. See no. 75, n. 42.
3. See no. 7, n. 13.

343. MANDATE OF HONORIUS AND THEODOSIUS II ON PENALTIES FOR EUNOMIANS, 415

(CT 16. 5. 58)

A variety of civil disabilities are recorded in this constitution against the Eunomians, who persist in their practice of repeated baptism, ordain their own clergy, and continue to assemble.

The same Augusti to Aurelian, praetorian prefect[1] for the second time.
Let there be adjudged to the fisc's resources the houses belonging to Eunomian clergymen which are occupied in the famous city,[2] in

343. PENALTIES FOR EUNOMIANS, 415

which houses it shall have become clear that nefarious meetings have been held or baptism has been repeated—baptism which is conceded once by God after the manner of man, who has been born once.

And lest this crime may be perpetuated also by all other heretics, we warn other heretical clergymen to expect a similar penalty, if they nefariously shall have believed that divine baptism ought to be repeated.

Also not beyond the penalty of deportation shall be he who of his own accord and voluntarily shall have allowed himself rashly to be tainted with or wrongly to be called away to a second baptism and repeated mysteries [3] of the faith granted once.[4]

The same penalty of deportation—apart from anyone's intercession—shall occur for Eunomian clergymen, if they shall have dared to engage in meetings either in this famous city [1] or in the provinces, municipalities, and territories or to create or to be created clergymen of the pestiferous dogma.

Therefore, after earlier laws which have been promulgated both about forbidden gatherings of Eunomians and also about interdicted last wills [5] or gifts [5] have been confirmed,[6] we add the following: that if any of the Eunomians by a special favour [7] had gained the right that to them was granted the making of a will or was bestowed the permission of giving property or of accepting property from someone's liberality, they should be deprived of this favour and should be equal to the rest to whom they are equal in depravity of dogma. To no Eunomian at all should it be lawful to make a will in favour of a Eunomian; to none of the said perversity should it be lawful to accept anything in accord with a Eunomian's will; no Eunomian should give to or should accept from a Eunomian the gift of an estate or of a house, even if some fraud shall have been contrived against the law through a person of another sect acting as an intermediary or through a title of a fictitious sale. Only those persons who shall have descended in accordance with the laws from an intestate person should succeed to their inheritance and the state of succession should be open only to those persons to whom the rights of blood-relation convey the lawful inheritance of intestate persons.

Also, if there shall have been any meetings in their houses or estates, according to the rule of general sanctions such property without doubt should be added to our treasury, the owner charging this loss to himself, who knowingly has permitted prohibited gatherings to be conducted under his own roof or on a rural estate.

The following should be executed unhesitatingly: that wherever shall have been found Eunomian clergymen who have been sponsors of repeated baptism, they, when arrested, should be sent into perpetual exile under the penalty of deportation.[4]

The following also should be added: that no Eunomian either should be in governmental service [8] or should receive a province to be governed by the administration of any office whatsoever.

And the rest.

Given on 6 November at Constantinople, our Lords Honorius Augustus for the tenth time and Theodosius Augustus for the sixth time being consuls.

1. Of the East.
2. Constantinople, as the subscription shows.
3. See no. 164, n. 18.
4. This and the next paragraph are construed loosely in Latin with the preceding paragraph.
5. Made by Eunomians.
6. Nos. 218, 249, 321.
7. Nos. 246, 252, 277.
8. See no. 186, n. 4.

344. MANDATE OF HONORIUS AND THEODOSIUS II ON JEWISH OWNERSHIP OF CHRISTIAN SLAVES, 415

(*CT* 16. 9. 3)

This law lets Jews own Christian slaves, provided that such slaves are permitted to retain their own religious beliefs.

Emperors Honorius and Theodosius Augusti to Annas, Didascalus, and elders of the Jews.[1]

Apart from chicanery[2] we authorize Jewish masters to have Christian slaves—with only this condition allowed: that they allow them to keep their own religion.

And therefore governors of provinces, after they have inspected the trustworthiness of information,[3] should know that there must be repressed the insolence of those who shall have thought that by timely petitions they [4] can be accused.

And we ordain that all deceptions fraudulently elicited or to be elicited must be annulled.

If anyone shall have done contrary, punishment as if for sacrilege should be produced.

Given on 6 November at Ravenna, Honorius Augustus for the tenth time and Theodosius Augustus for the sixth time being consuls.

1. Annas and Didascalus are not identifiable. Perhaps *Didascalus* is a title, should be translated as "teacher" (for it seems that *didascali* also were connected with synagogues), and should stand in apposition to Annas. For the elders see no. 23, n. 2.

2. That is, either the emperors guarantee no trickery in their application of this law, which reverses previous statutes forbidding Jews to own Christian slaves (nos. 76, 79, 199, 341), or Jews may not be subjected to malicious prosecution (*calumnia*) or Jews may not resort to *chicanery* in acquiring Christian slaves.

3. Which is laid before a governor as a matter of public knowledge. The words *trustworthiness of information* are in Latin *fide publicationis*.

4. Jews.

345. MANDATE OF HONORIUS AND THEODOSIUS II ON ECCLESIASTICAL LIABILITY TO PUBLIC DUTIES, 415
(*CT* 11. 24. 6)

Evasion of performance of public duties, especially of payment of taxes, led in the Dominate to the practice of small communities placing themselves under the protection (patronage)[1] of powerful persons, who through imperial favour sometimes were immune from certain kinds of public services. In this corrective statute, of which Justinian retains only one section (*CI* 11. 59. 14), is translated only the part (§6) wherein the eastern emperor confirms the Constantinopolitan and the Alexandrian patriarchates' possession of real estate acquired in this way, provided that these sees assume the responsibility of meeting the poll-taxes assessed against such properties.

Emperors Honorius and Theodosius Augusti to Aurelian, praetorian prefect.[2]

... Moreover, whatever the venerable churches, that is the Constantinopolitan and the Alexandrian, are disclosed to have possessed until the time of the arrangement made by your Sublimity's illustrious predecessor,[3] this we, because of respect for religion, command should be retained firmly by these, but under this condition, of course, that for the future they should know that without doubt must be undertaken all the payments which the mother villages[4] owe and the public villages[5] owe in view of the declaration of the ancient capitation tax.[6] ...

Given on 3 December, Honorius Augustus for the tenth time and Theodosius Augustus for the sixth time being consuls.

1. For another type of patronage (*patrocinium*) see no. 241, n. 2.
2. Of the Orient.
3. Probably Anthemius, who was praetorian prefect of the East from 405 till early in 415.
4. These *metrocomiae* (transliterated from μητροκωμίαι) were the chief villages and the administrative centres of a district.
5. Perhaps the ordinary villages as distinct from the mother villages.
6. See no. 67, n. 37.

346. MANDATE OF HONORIUS AND THEODOSIUS II ON RETURN OF LUKEWARM JEWISH CHRISTIANS TO JUDAISM, 416

(*CT* 16. 8. 23)

The emperors order provincial governors to authorize Jews half-heartedly interested in Christianity to return to Jewish worship.

The same Augusti to Annas, Didascalus, and elders of the Jews.[1]

By both old and our own sanctions [2] it has been established, since we have learned that persons bound to the Jewish religion have desired to associate themselves with the Church's fellowship because of evasion of crimes and in view of different necessities,[3] that this is done not through devotion to faith but by surreptitious action of pretenders.[4]

Wherefore governors of provinces in which such things are said to have been committed should understand that obedience to our statutes must be offered in such manner that those persons whom they have perceived neither to cling to constancy of religious confession in this said cult nor to have been imbued with the faith and the mysteries [5] of the venerable baptism should be permitted to return to their own law,[6] because regard is had rather for Christianity.

Given on 24 September at Ravenna, Theodosius Augustus for the seventh time and Palladius being consuls.

1. See no. 344, n. 1.
2. Of surviving statutes affecting Jews only no. 266 seems apposite.
3. Perhaps compulsory public services.
4. The text is corrupt.
5. See no. 75, n. 42.
6. Religion.

347. MANDATE OF HONORIUS AND THEODOSIUS II ON ECCLESIASTICAL SICK-NURSES, 416
(CT 16. 2. 42)

As a consequence of the brutal murder of the celebrated Hypatia in March 415 by a band of lay sick-nurses (*parabalani*),[1] who were under the supervision of St Cyril, patriarch of Alexandria, Pulcheria, the empress-regent for her younger brother Theodosius II, instituted an investigation, in which opposite reports were received from Cyril and from Orestes, prefect of Egypt. What a certain Aedesius, an imperial commissioner sent from Constantinople to Alexandria, reported to Pulcheria is unknown, but it seems that the imperial authority recognized the guild of *parabalani* as a dangerous threat to the public peace and issued the following law (preserved partly by Justinian in *CI* 1. 3. 17) to restrict their non-medical activities and privileges.

The same Augusti to Monaxius, praetorian prefect.[2]

Because amid all other useless matters of the Alexandrian legation this also has been written in the decrees:[3] that the most reverend bishop should not permit[4] certain persons not to depart from the Alexandrian city (and this indeed has been inserted in the legation's petition on account of the terror of those who are called sick-nurses), it[5] pleases our Clemency that clerics should have nothing in common with public affairs or matters pertaining to a municipal senate.[6]

Furthermore those who are called sick-nurses[7] we order to be not more than five hundred, so that not the rich and those who buy this office, but the poor from the guildsmen in proportion[8] to the Alexandrian population should be provided, after their names have been made known, of course, to the excellent Augustal prefect[9] and through him necessarily referred to your Grandeur.

And to these[10] we do not allow the liberty of going either to any public spectacle whatever or to a meeting-place of a municipal council or to a court; unless perhaps as individuals they shall have approached a judge on account of their own cases and needs, when in litigation they accuse someone or themselves have been accused by another or one as a syndic has been appointed in a case common to the whole guild—under this regulation: that if any of them shall have violated these conditions, he should be removed from the lists of the sick-nurses[11] and should be subjected to suitable punishment and never should be restored to the same duty.[12]

Moreover to the excellent Augustal prefect[9] we have given the power of substituting to the place of the deceased persons under the condition which is designated above.[13]

347. ECCLESIASTICAL SICK-NURSES, 416

Given on 29 September at Constantinople, Theodosius Augustus for the seventh time and Palladius being consuls.

1. The word (adapted probably from παράβολος) is reported in Latin only here and in no. 349 and in Justinian's copies of these laws. On the word's origin see W. Schubart, "Parabalani" in *The Journal of Egyptian Archaeology*, 40 (1954) 100.

The *parabalani* belonged to a religious guild, whose members recklessly exposed themselves to contagion in attending sick persons. They were associated especially with Alexandria and had, though laymen, certain clerical immunities and, as religious fanatics, often incited riots against rich oppressors of the poor. See no. 349, n. 1.

2. Of the East.

3. A delegation of Alexandrians apparently had petitioned the imperial court against the unrestrained terrorism of the *parabalani*, about whom the Alexandrian senate had inserted its decisions in the petition.

4. There is a gap in the text here and this verb is supplied to complete the sense.

5. Justinian's excerpt starts here.

6. Justinian adds "with which corporation they have not been connected".

7. Justinian stops temporarily. Here and at n. 11 he uses an indeclinable noun (*parabalanin*) for sick-nurses.

8. Our phrase is borrowed from the Latin *pro rata*, but what proportion is meant is unknown.

9. For this title see no. 489, n. 12.

10. Here begins Justinian's second excerpt. The demonstrative pronoun refers to the sick-nurses.

11. Singular number in *CT*, but in *CI* an indeclinable noun, on which see n. 7 *supra*.

12. Here Justinian's version ends.

13. According to Ulpian (*ob.* 228) selection of physicians (within a prescribed number) was forbidden expressly to the provincial governor—not to mention a bishop (see text of no. 349 at n. 7, where the patriarch appoints *parabalani*)—and was enjoined upon municipal senators and rentiers of any community, that they might choose proper and competent physicians, to whom they would commit themselves and their children when sick (*D* 50. 9. 1). Probably the large number of sick-nurses made such selection operationally impracticable by municipal senators and rentiers in a city as populous as was Alexandria and resulted in first the prefect and then the patriarch filling their ranks in Alexandria, whose repuation in medical science—as well as in all other scientific areas (see no. 98, n. 3)—was supreme at that time according to Ammianus (*Res Gestae*, 22. 16. 18), St Cyril's contemporary.

348. MANDATE OF HONORIUS AND THEODOSIUS II ON JEWISH OWNERSHIP OF CHRISTIAN SLAVES, 417

(CT 16. 9. 4)

This constitution, of which Justinian adapts the earlier part (*CI* 1. 10. 1), forbids Jews to purchase or to acquire by gift Christian slaves, but permits them to have such slaves as they have received by inheritance or by trust on condition that no proselytism occurs.

The same Augusti to Monaxius, praetorian prefect.[1]

A Jew must neither buy a Christian slave nor acquire one under title of a gift.[2]

Whoever shall not have observed this should be deprived of ownership wantonly procured for himself—the slave himself being presented with freedom for a reward,[3] if he shall have thought that of his own accord what shall have been done ought to be made known.

But he may possess in his property all others whom, established as participants in the right religion, his abominable superstition appears to have acquired already or hereafter shall have obtained in the category of an inheritance or of a trust—under this stipulation: that he should not join them, either unwillingly or willingly, to the filth of his own sect, so that, if this regulation shall have been violated, the authors of so great a crime should be penalized by capital punishment and by concomitant confiscation.

Given on 10 April at Constantinople, Honorius Augustus for the eleventh time and the most distinguished Constantius for the second time being consuls.

1. Of the East.
2. See no. 79, n. 2.
3. See no. 79, n. 3.

349. MANDATE OF HONORIUS AND THEODOSIUS II ON ECCLESIASTICAL SICK-NURSES, 418

(CT 16. 2. 43)

The influence of St Cyril, patriarch of Alexandria, at the imperial court succeeded in procuring this constitution augmenting the number of lay sick-nurses (*parabalani*) and returning them from the authority of the prefect of Egypt to his own control.¹

Justinian has this mandate (*CI* 1. 3. 18).

The same Augusti to Monaxius, praetorian prefect.²
Previously we have ordered that there should be five hundred sick-nurses,¹ who are allocated for healing sick bodies of infirm persons. But because we have learned that these are not sufficient at present, instead of five hundred we order that six hundred should be established,³ so that according to the judgement of the most reverend bishop of the Alexandrian city six hundred sick-nurses should be selected from those who previously had been sick-nurses ⁴ and who have experience of healing in view of their practice for such duty (dignitaries ⁵ and curials, of course, excepted).

Moreover, if any of these shall have been removed by natural lot,⁶ another should be substituted according to the said bishop's ⁷ will (dignitaries ⁵ and curials excepted), so that these six hundred should obey the most reverend bishop's orders and directions and should be under his care—the remaining matters, which the tenor of the previously issued law ⁸ embraces concerning the said sick-nurses either about spectacles or about courts and all other matters, being observed, just as already has been enacted.

Given on 3 February at Constantinople, Honorius Augustus for the twelfth time and Theodosius Augustus for the eighth time being consuls.

1. The return of these rabble-rousers (see no. 347, n. 1) to Cyril's control is another testimony to the Alexandrian patriarch's power, which—in the fifth century at least—almost paralleled that of the Pharaohs or of the Ptolemies and which increased in proportion to the distance from the imperial court, since of eastern patriarchates Alexandria was the most distant and most of its incumbents were egregiously ambitious and impatient of the emperors' authority.

Here and elsewhere in this document *CI* uses *parabalanin* (an indeclinable noun) for *sick-nurses*.

2. Of the East.

3. Justinian condenses the foregoing thus: "We order that six hundred sick-nurses, who are allocated for healing sick bodies of infirm persons, should be established...."

4. This word is supplied in translation.

5. On this word see no. 495, n. 9.

6. A euphemism for death.

7. The word is *sacerdos*, on which see no. 16, n. 4. See also no. 347, n. 13.

8. No. 347.

350. RESCRIPT OF HONORIUS AND THEODOSIUS II ON CONDEMNATION OF PELAGIUS AND CAELESTIUS, 418

(PL 45. 1726–7; 48. 379–86; 56. 490–2)

This document banishes both the British monk Pelagius and his disciple Caelestius, whose inadequate views on the dogmas of grace and of original sin not only originated the heresy designated by the former's name but also earned for each heresiarch papal as well as conciliar condemnation.

Pelagius appeared *c.* 400 in Rome, where he attracted converts, of whom Caelestius, an advocate, was the chief. Both men apparently met little protest against their preaching until they left Italy in 411 for Africa, where Caelestius remained, while Pelagius went to Palestine. When Caelestius applied for ordination at Carthage, he was accused of heresy by Paulinus, a deacon from Milan, and, after his doctrines had been denounced by a local synod summoned to consider the charges in 411, he departed for Asia Minor, where he became a priest at Ephesus. In 415 Paulus Orosius, an Iberian priest, who had fled from the Arian Visigoths to Africa and thence had passed to Palestine, charged Pelagius with heresy before a local synod in Jerusalem; but Orosius' lack of Greek and his interpreter's inferior linguistic ability were not able to overcome Pelagius' profession of orthodoxy, with the result that the synod, considering that the problem concerned the Latins primarily, resolved to refer the matter to Pope St Innocent I—a reference, however, not implemented then. Later in 415 the Synod of Diospolis (Lydda) in Palestine acquitted Pelagius of charges of heresy brought by Heros of Arles and Lazarus of Aix, two Gallic bishops, who had been extruded from their sees and whose absence from the synod was an advantage for the subtle Pelagius.

This double acquittal of Pelagius in the East, despite the polemics of St Augustine and St Jerome,[1] alarmed the Africans. In 416 councils at Carthage and Milevis condemned Pelagius and Caelestius *in absentia* and asked Pope Innocent to anathematize Pelagianism.[2] In three letters[3] the pope denounced this heretical doctrine so completely that the African prelates supposed that the controversy was settled.[4] But after Pope St Zosimus had succeeded Innocent in 417, the heresiarchs saw new hope. Caelestius now came to Rome to rehabilitate himself and Pelagius, from whom he carried a confession of faith.[5] Caelestius also presented his own profession of belief[6] to Zosimus, who examined him before a domestic synod in September 417, found no fault in him, and so informed the African bishops,[7] to whom he wrote that no doubt of Caelestius' orthodoxy would remain, if they should fail to press personally in Rome their accusations. At a second synod, also in September, Pelagius' profession was reviewed with the result that Zosimus also exonerated him and in another epistle[8] accused the Africans of haste in accepting the accusations aimed in the East against the heresiarch.

In answer to this papal action, more than two hundred African bishops assembled in a council at Carthage in November 417, renewed their condemnation of Pelagianism, and informed Zosimus that Innocent's pronouncements [3] against Pelagius and Caelestius would stand, so far as the Africans were concerned, until the heretics should have recanted their heresy.[9] The pope soon saw that he had proceeded too far and too fast and then tried to retreat by a rescript [10] on 21 March 418 to the Africans, to whom he replied that, though no papal decision could be debated, yet Innocent's position would prevail pending additional deliberation.

At this juncture and in the following rescript of 30 April 418 Emperor Honorius joined the controversy. The sequel is soon told. On 1 May 418 a plenary council of over two hundred prelates from all the African provinces convened at Carthage and in nine canons [11] again condemned Pelagianism. Since both the court and the council had called the turn, Zosimus saw the inadmissibility of his action and issued later in 418 an encyclical epistle condemning Pelagianism.[12]

Sacred rescript against Pelagius and Caelestius.
Emperors Honorius and Theodosius Augusti to Palladius, praetorian prefect.[13]

We are informed by widespread report that a new subtlety with a character of cunning artifice suddenly has emerged to confuse the light of Catholic simplicity ever radiant with pure brilliance. And this, concealed by the lies of pseudo-science, has raged uncontrollably with so much mad controversy that it affects the serene stability of heavenly faith, while it invents fictions of a new crime [14] in thinking that it will be a notable mark of common cheapness [15] to be in accord with all and that it will be a token of singular wisdom to overthrow things generally approved. And of this impious exposition it has been reported that Pelagius and Caelestius are the authors.

These persons ascribe so stern a severity of sinister will to God, the progenitor of all things, and to his ever-excellent Majesty, eternally powerful and passing beyond every beginning, that when he was assuming the creative charge [16] of fashioning the universe and was pondering by profound comprehension of spirit the quality of man to be made, he preferred a foul beginning for the produced work [17] and he predicted death for him about to be born.[18] They maintain [19] that this [20] has not arisen by the snares of forbidden sin, but that the law of an utterly immutable ordinance has caused it: to avoid the onset of fatal oblivion the abstinence from sinning is of no avail, whose [21] power was considered so assigned that it cannot be terminated in the future. They maintain [19] that the error of the first-born man, upon whom had seized the reasonless blindness of a seduced mind,[22] has not descended to posterity;[23] and that to such an extent in him,[24] whom an unhappy allurement of seductive grace had seized, the transgression of a forbidden danger appeared, since the manifest authority of the Catholic law [25] everywhere witnesses that that person [24] was the beginning [26] of the ruin of all,[27] who,[24] it is clear, violated the careful commandment of the divine injunction; and they maintain [19] very many other things which discussion rejects, which the law refutes, which it would be very wearisome to recollect even under the ordering of punishing.[28]

And those things ought to be excised by an accelerated remedy and by a speedy celerity, lest by strengthened exercise of wickedness young persons scarcely can be able to be restrained. For indeed recent report has deafened the ears of our Gentleness that within our most sacred city [29] and other places the pestiferous virus has been implanted in certain persons' hearts in such a way that, after the path of simple belief had been sundered and after men had been divided into zealous and asseverative factions,[30] material for unquiet discord has been introduced and that, after new tinder for offence had been kindled, the attacked peace of the most blessed Church totters, when with wavering interpretation some follow this and others that, and that the absolute perspicuity of holy priests, explaining clearly what all persons ought to follow, causes disorder in view of the mental comprehension of subtle ingenuity, because certain novel instigators agitate profane investigation, duteous Palladius, dearest and most beloved.

Wherefore your illustrious Authority—long life to it [31]—should know that we by law have ordained that after Caelestius and Pelagius,[32] originally the heads of the detestable dogma, have been expelled from the city,[29] if, besides, any adherents of this sacrilege in any places can be found or emit any utterance relative to [33] damned depravity, they, after they have been seized by anyone, should be haled before a competent judge. And let anyone,[34] whether he shall be cleric or laic, have the power of indicting these persons and without any notice of pressing the suit—the persons whom he shall have detected introducing, after having abandoned the light of common knowledge, the darkness of new disputation, to wit, against apostolic teaching and evangelical and clear and errorless thought, by fighting with the crafty cunning of an ignorant sect and by covering the brilliant faith by circumlocutions of the truth in their discussion. Therefore these persons, when anywhere found conferring about this so nefarious crime, we command to be seized by anyone whatsoever and, when led before a public hearing, to be accused by all indiscriminately, so that a public decision may follow upon proof of the convicted crime—the persons themselves having been condemned to the deportation of inexorable exile. For it is proper that the source of crime be separated from public society and that in common intercourse those persons do not take their place, who not only ought to be detested because of an unspeakable deed but also ought to be avoided because of the example of a poisoned character.

Moreover it is our pleasure that throughout all our Empire, where the world is extended,[35] such promulgations should be diffused, lest perchance pretended ignorance may furnish food for error and anyone may think that with impunity he may dare to maintain what he has feigned that he does not know has been condemned by public activity.

Given on 30 April at Ravenna, our Lords the Augusti being consuls, Honorius for the twelfth time and Theodosius for the eighth time.

1. Augustine's four early treatises against Pelagianism are dated 412–15 and are in *CSEL* 42. 1–48; 60. 1–151, 153–229, 231–99. Jerome's dialogue on Pelagianism, his last controversial work, dated 415, is in *PL* 23. 517–618.

2. The conciliar letters are in *PL* 45. 1711–12.

3. Dated 27 January 417, these are in *PL* 20. 582–97; 45. 1714–15; 56. 458–64, 467–71, 482–5.

4. Augustine said in a sermon at Carthage on 23 September 417 that the case was closed. His words *causa finita est* (*Serm.* 131. 10 = *PL* 38. 734) apparently fathered the famous phrase *Roma locuta est; causa finita est* (Rome has spoken; the case has been closed). On this consult Kidd, 3. 102.

5. It is in *PL* 45. 1716–18.

6. Partly preserved in *PL* 45. 1718–19.

7. The papal letter is in *CSEL* 35. 99–103.

8. The papal letter is in *CSEL* 35. 103–8.

9. The synodal letter is summarized in *PL* 45. 1723–4; 51. 227.

10. *CSEL* 35. 115–17.

11. In *PL* 45. 1728–30.

12. Only fragments of it are found in *PL* 45. 1730–1.

13. Of Italy.

14. We should reverse the parts of speech perhaps and say "of criminal novelty".

15. Again perhaps we should prefer a reversal and say "of cheap popularity".

16. A hendiadys probably; literally "the artisan and the care".

17. We should say "the work of production".

18. A variant reading gives: "he anticipated an end of the work produced for the beginning and prepared death for him about to be born". This variation accords more closely with the Pelagian insistence on the final death of the body (adopted from Stoicism) in defiance of the last two clauses in the Apostles' Creed.

19. The translator has supplied the subject and the predicate to govern what otherwise appear to be independent infinitives with subjects in the accusative case.

20. This demonstrative word apparently refers to *death*.

21. The relative must refer to *oblivion*, unless Honorius and Theodosius are accusing Pelagius and Caelestius of believing that sinlessness cannot prevail eventually over sinfulness.

22. Ordinarily *mens capta* means "a crazed mind", but none ever has suggested that Adam was demented.

23. A reference to the Pelagian denial of original sin.

24. That is Adam, whose transgression is narrated in Gen. 3. 1–6 (cf. 2. 15–7).

25. Religion, as often.

26. Tropical translation for *vestibulum*.

27. This doctrine first appears in Rom. 5. 12—6. 23. Cf. also 1 Cor. 15. 22.

28. That is, even in the administration of punishment it would be very tedious to rehearse all their heretical opinions, for which punishment is ordered.

29. Probably Rome, though the document was drafted at Ravenna, as the subscription shows.

30. Literally "after zeals of asserting had been divided into factions".

31. Literally "about to live to all age".

32. Pelagius at this time still was in the East, where he seems to have died without returning to Rome.

33. Or possibly "proceeding from".

34. The subject in Latin is unexpressed, but some such subject is meant.

35. A variant reading is "throughout almost all the world, where our Empire is extended".

351. EDICT OF PALLADIUS, MONAXIUS, AND AGRICOLA ON CONDEMNATION OF PELAGIANISM, 418

(PL 45. 1727–8; 48. 392–4; 56. 492–3)

This edict implements the imperial order exiling Pelagius and Caelestius (no. 350).

Copy of the edict of Junius Quartus Palladius.

Junius Quartus Palladius, Monaxius, and Agricola, praetorian prefects for the second time,[1] proclaimed:

Against Pelagius and Caelestius, who by perverse discussions destroy the faith of Catholic dogma, the imperial will has grown hot, that they should be punished in having been banned from the venerable city [2] and the association of good people.

Therefore all ought to be warned of this edict, lest anyone should offer credulous assent to errors of a perverse persuasion. And if that person [3] should be a layman [4] or a clergyman who shall have relapsed into the impurities of this mental mist, when haled by anyone whomsoever before a judge without distinction of an accusing person [5] and when stripped by confiscation of his property, he shall undergo irrevocable exile. For the Supernal Majesty [6] acquires not only reverence as a result of ignorance of a recondite matter,[7] but also injury as a result of adoption of a vain disputation.

1. Palladius was prefect of Italy, Monaxius was prefect of the East, Agricola was prefect of the Gauls. It is not clear whether Agricola or all three were in their second tour of duty as praetorian prefects, but probably only Agricola is meant.
2 Rome.
3. That is, one who has subscribed to Pelagianism.
4. Literally "a plebeian".
5. That is, it matters not who shall be the accuser.
6. It is unclear whether is meant God or the emperors.
7. Or, if *secretum* be taken more literally in a separative sense, the meaning is that reverence is shown by not knowing anything about a matter which has been outlawed. But see no. 75, n. 42.

352. RESCRIPT OF HONORIUS ON PAPAL ELECTION, 419

(CSEL 35. 60-1)

This is the first of several imperial constitutions (nos. 352-67, 371) concerning the schism which ensued at the death of Pope St Zosimus in 418 and which resulted from a double papal election, wherein one faction elected Eulalius, an archdeacon, and another faction selected Boniface, a priest.

When both clerics had been consecrated and each proceeded to act as pope, Rome was rent by tumults from the rival parties' clashes, which Symmachus, urban prefect, reported to Emperor Honorius at Ravenna.

The emperor replies to his prefect, who has asked for guidance, that he confirms the election of Eulalius, whose selection preceded Boniface's by one day, forbids Boniface to remain in Rome, commands appropriate punishment for the ring-leaders of the riots.

Eventually, after examination, Honorius chose Boniface as the legitimate bishop (no. 365).

It is difficult to discover the cause of the controversy, which appears to have arisen primarily from factional rivalry, because no evidence that the rivals were previously enemies exists and since mostly presbyters preferred Boniface and mostly deacons demanded Eulalius. The importance of the schism is that the State intervened to settle the issue.

Copy of the sacred letter.

When all the events had been examined, it has been quite clear from your Sublimity's praiseworthy report that in the ordination to the venerable bishopric the insolence of a few persons has desired to assail the old-time peacefulness. For, when, after the departure [1] of the venerable Zosimus, the multitude had given utterance harmoniously in common judgement about the worthiness of Eulalius to be chosen in succession and when the confirmation of his successor was guarding fully for itself all matters which the rule of Catholic teaching was demanding, we exceedingly are amazed that there have been some persons who through contempt for the customary procedure were hastening to the ordination of another person. And to punish their deed our Gentleness rightly would be obliged to rouse itself, except that, however, in this case we decided that they should be subject to pardon, because they, after considering attentively and speedily their own lapse, have returned to the choice of pleading an excuse, begging that they may be pardoned on this account in that they have complained that they had to endure force.[2]

Therefore your Sublimity should know by our Clemency's present authority that our wish and interest are agreed in respect to Eulalius as bishop of the sacred law,[3] on whom a competent number of ordainers, the customary procedure of a legitimate time and place, the character of a rightly venerated name have conferred the highest honour. Moreover, since it is agreed that all things have been lacking to Boniface,[4] we deem that our decision has been awaited unnecessarily, because those who had presumed seem to have condemned their own ordained bishops by presentation of their prayers.[5]

Accordingly by an absolute command we ordain that, when the extraordinary audacity has been dispelled and interdicted,[6] Boniface forthwith should be debarred from the city.[7] It will be a display of modesty on his part for him, accommodating himself to heavenly institutions, to depart voluntarily; but we order him to be expelled, if too stubbornly resisting and unwilling. Of course, your Sublimity, dearest and fondest cousin Symmachus, shall order that the authors of the people's sedition with their associates should be detained and that they should be punished appropriately, that an affair rashly undertaken should not pass unpunished. And in this matter it has pleased us that the most distinguished Afrodisius, the tribune and notary, should be directed by our Gentleness that, with him present, there should be fulfilled quickly what we have ordained, that the peace of the people may not be disquieted by any disturbance and that the community in peace may respect him [8] whom pursuant to old-time custom the respected rites of the sacred law [3] have acknowledged.

Given on 3 January at Ravenna.

1. Euphemistic for "death".
2. A petition of priests of the Bonifacian party professed that the higher clergy and the better elements among the laity were excluded from election when they tried to enter the Basilica of San Giovanni in Laterano (see no. 364, n. 12), which the Eulalian faction had seized and where Eulalius was selected. Thus their choice of Boniface they excused by the fact that they had not participated in the canvass which chose Eulalius.
3. Christianity.
4. That is, such factors as have been recited in the case of Eulalius.
5. Honorius takes the view that the Bonifacian party's attempt to exculpate its act necessarily proves its illegality.
6. The sense seems to be that the ordination should be annulled.
7. Rome.
8. Eulalius.

353. RESCRIPT OF HONORIUS ON A PRIESTLY PETITION, 419

(CSEL 35. 65–6)

The second imperial constitution on the controversy between Eulalius and Boniface (see introd. to no. 352) was evoked by a petition from priests of the latter's party, who had attracted the emperor's attention to the possibility that Symmachus, urban prefect of Rome, had not submitted impartial reports of the disturbance.

Honorius orders the rescission of earlier orders in the case and commands the presence of the rival claimants at his court, where bishops summoned from several provinces will canvass the situation.

To a petition of priests the emperor sent a sacred rescript of this kind to Symmachus, urban prefect.[1]

After the delivery of your Sublimity's report to our Gentleness' ears a document of the priests produced in us a cause for not unnecessary deliberation. Therefore it is fitting that, with uncertainty removed, the trustworthiness of the events should be examined at close quarters and that in the presence of many giving their opinions there should be established what part the omitted exposition of events charges and what part the inspected exposition of events supports,[2] in order that, after the character of the action of each side has been weighed carefully and simultaneously, that which has been determined properly in respect to the one may endure and that which has been adopted inconsiderately in respect to the other may not abide, Symmachus, dearest and fondest cousin.

Wherefore your illustrious and exalted Grandeur, after all previous decrees have been suspended and with no interim prejudgement arranged, by the authority of the present rescript, shall summon with suitable urgency both most religious men, that is, Boniface and Eulalius, that before 8 February they should not delay to expedite their presence at the city of the Ravennates [3]—with all, who are the performers of each ordination, equally warned that, with excuse withdrawn, they should not be absent, that each one may appear as the defender of his own act against the other, after precedents of ecclesiastical induction have been produced, and by having exculpated himself may prove that the other rather has been delinquent against the Catholic law [4] in having ventured upon the election of an undeserving person: each one being due to obtain a judgement about his own status, if he shall have neglected to be present, thus giving it obviously to be understood that he himself has done improvidently, nay illegally, what he should not dare to defend publicly.[5]

By our Serenity's writings we are summoning also from different provinces a suitable number of bishops, that the discussion of very many persons in our presence may put an end to the matter which has been brought into doubt.

Moreover, since all points should be reserved unimpaired for future decision, it is fitting that none should delude oneself about past matters, for the transcript of the present decision will inform what ought to be observed for the future in affairs of this kind.

Given on 15 January by Aphthonius.[6]

1. Of Rome.
2. It is believed generally that Symmachus, who was biased against Boniface, suppressed in his reports to Honorius evidence unfavourable to Eulalius—at any rate this the petition from the Bonifacian party alleged. The emperor, until the petition had supplied him with what the urban prefect had omitted, presumably knew only what an inspection of his official's report had revealed.
3. From 404, when Honorius selected Ravenna for his residence, until 476, when the Western Empire fell, Ravenna was the permanent imperial seat in the West.
4. Religion.
5. That is, in the presence (*coram*) both of the emperor and of the rival claimant.

6. In another letter (*CSEL* 35. 66–7) this man is described as a decurion of the imperial court (*decurio sacri palatii*). Since decurions as such are not listed in the *Notitia Dignitatum* (the official register of all the more important offices in the Empire about this time), they probably served in some secretarial capacity among the several bureaus (*scrinia*) charged with correspondence. See no. 481, n. 1.

354. LETTER OF HONORIUS ON THE EULALIAN-BONIFACIAN SCHISM, 419
(*CSEL* 35. 67–8)

In this third imperial document about the dispute between Boniface and Eulalius (see introd. to no. 352) the emperor instructs a synod convoked at Ravenna (see no. 353) how to judge the case and assures its members that the rescission (no. 353) of his previous decision (no. 352) leaves to them a free field for their findings.

The synod, however, was unable to solve the situation and was content to ban both claimants from Rome under penalty of condemnation, pending a settlement by a larger council, which, as the event proved, was unnecessary.

Copy of the sacred letter to the synod.

Our Clemency indeed has ordered all matters in the present command appropriate to your Beatitudes, that you may determine by your decision what is fitting to be observed for the people's peace. We also remember that by us has been ordered especially this, which fairness demands, that those bishops who, it is established, have been present at or later have subscribed to the ordinations of the said persons,[1] without harm to themselves and with their authority continuing, may not sit as judges or may not be able to offer any testimony, lest they should appear not so much to proffer a new decision as to protect a past act. These, therefore, as we have said above, shall be bound to absent themselves from this discussion.

Your Beatitudes should know also that the following point likewise must be maintained: that for neither faction has been established the previously arranged decision which earlier had been shown by us.[2] For since the swiftly determined orders for the people's peace have been withdrawn by our Piety's ensuing authority,[3] as a result neither faction can claim or fear anything.

Therefore, heeding God's judgement, which in such a cause obviously resides at the same time in you, it is fitting that you, after all matters have been investigated, should maintain that which can hold unimpaired the reverence for the Christian law [4] by the infusion of the heavenly spirit.

1. Eulalius and Boniface.
2. Honorius refers to his first decision, based on a biased report, in favour of Eulalius (see no. 352).
3. The emperor cancelled his decision against Boniface, after he had perused the priests' petition alleging partiality in the urban prefect's report (see no. 353).
4. Religion.

355. MANDATE OF HONORIUS ON ROMAN CELEBRATION OF EASTER, 419
(CSEL 35. 69)

This imperial command empowers Achilleus, bishop of Spoleto, to conduct the paschal services in Rome during the vacancy of the Roman see due to the dispute between Eulalius and Boniface, its rival claimants (see introd. to nos. 352 and 354).

Copy of the sacred letter to Achilleus, the Spoletan bishop.

Since it is agreed that a verdict about the Roman bishopric is to be postponed because of the shortness of time which the celebration of the days [1] has caused, a celebration which did not permit the bishops to be absent from their own churches,[2] our Serenity rightly has believed that it ought to be arranged that your Beatitude with appropriate respect should hasten to the venerable city,[3] in order that you may celebrate for the people with wonted solemnity the days of holy Easter with that peacefulness which is suitable and that it may not hinder the customary procedure because manifold necessity has caused the synod to be postponed.

We impress upon you especially and foremost, of course, the following caution: that no mention of those persons [4] about whom it is agreed that they have been suspended by sentence should be made at all.

1. Of Eastertide.
2. The prelates were in conclave at Ravenna. But no explanation about a substitute for Achilleus at Spoleto is made.
3. Rome.
4. Eulalius and Boniface.

356. LETTER OF HONORIUS ON ROMAN CELEBRATION OF EASTER, 419

(CSEL 35. 68–9)

Since the synod called at Ravenna to compose the schism between Boniface and Eulalius (see introd. to no. 353) made little progress during Lent and because Easter was approaching, Honorius in this document to Symmachus, urban prefect of Rome, decrees that Rome shall not be without episcopal celebration of the paschal holy days and therefore notifies the urban prefect that Achilleus, bishop of Spoleto, will function as bishop at the festival and that the prefect shall hold the principal persons of the city's several quarters responsible for any riot in connection with the celebration.

This synod because of its internal dissension could not end the present case. Whereupon Honorius, the venerable emperor, believed that this matter ought to be postponed for a larger council and meanwhile ordered both, namely Boniface and Eulalius, to depart from the city [1] because of the days of holy Easter, which were approaching, and ordered the Spoletan bishop, Achilleus by name, to celebrate the sacred mysteries,[2] making this same matter known by his writing to Symmachus, urban prefect.[3]

Of weighty deliberations there ought not to be a speedy decision and principles which are authorized to be maintained in perpetuity must not be produced rashly.

Concerning the eternal [4] city's bishops the investigation under the bishops' scrutiny often was shattered by the factions' altercation, but, lest anything hasty should be produced by the speed of judgement, the following point is settled in our Clemency's opinion: that, since the nearness of the holy days was demanding a bishop's presence and since in the most sacred city [1] it would not be right to celebrate presently the days of Eastertide without a bishop, therefore, Symmachus, dearest and fondest cousin, your illustrious Magnificence should know that we have chosen Achilleus, who, it was agreed, is alien from the factions' partiality, that he may perform the mysteries [2] of the sacred observance. But, after the festal days have been fulfilled, from the bishops' judgement we shall discuss with riper counsel what ought to be maintained.

By all means we admonish that, after the chief men [5] of the districts [5] have been summoned, you should see to the public discipline and peace and to them you should order our decrees' precepts to be disclosed, lest anyone, of course, should dare to provoke any tumult or sedition. And if any shall have excited any movement through mad persuasion, they should know that there must be punishment not only for those who shall have been caught in the disturbance, but also for the chief men ⁵ of the districts.⁵ For we know that the public peace is preserved easily, if inciters' passions and excitements shall have ceased.

1. Rome.
2. See no. 75, n. 42.
3. Of Rome. This long and introductory caption is of medieval origin.
4. See no. 140, n. 1.
5. Rome was divided under and after Augustus into fourteen districts (*regiones*), subdivided into wards (*vici*), which varied from seven to 78 in number to a district. These were governed by locally selected magistrates (*magistri*, who are called here *primates* first and then *priores*, but *primores* in no. 153).

During the fourth century developed an ecclesiastical division of Rome into seven districts, which eventually displaced the civil division. The heads of these regions then were called *regionarii* and were deacons, whose full title was *diaconi regionarii* and who had seven assistants entitled *subdiaconi regionarii*. Notaries (*notarii*), defenders (*defensores*), and acolytes (*acolyti*) assigned to these regions also had the adjective *regionarius* attached to their titles. The general functions of a *diaconus regionarius* included care of the poor and maintenance of the churches in his district.

357. ORATION OF HONORIUS ON ROMAN CELEBRATION OF EASTER, 419

(*CSEL* 35. 69–70)

By this document in the series of imperial enactments about the contest between Eulalius and Boniface (see introd. to no. 352) the emperor excuses to the Roman Senate the delay in decision about these rivals by the Synod of Ravenna and also instructs the Senate to exert an influence for peace in Rome.

There is no hint that Honorius spoke this speech in proper person. Like many presidential messages to the United States Congress, it may have been read to the Senate by an official.

Oration of the emperor to the Senate.

Conscript fathers, we know that our delay cannot be blamed by you, to whom always in every affair is acceptable the ripeness of counsels and of judgement. Of course, about matters of highest importance there ought not and there cannot be a speedy decision, which, it is fitting, should be both everlasting and acceptable as well as perfect in every part.

Between the bishops,[1] whom in the most sacred city [2] the will of persons favouring interests or of factions had chosen, we had ordered that there should be a hearing by all the bishops who were present and the trial has been renewed at different times.[3] But since the investigation of a fair trial introduced longer delays, and a careful inquiry of judges discovered more matters for which a speedy conclusion could not be imposed, and the celebration of the festal days [4] demanded swiftness of decision, we have believed that the entire business ought to be postponed, lest we should incur something imprudent.

Accordingly there has been sent the religious Achilleus, bishop of the city of Spoleto, by whom the celebration of the holy days [4] may be conducted. It is the duty of your Honours by wholesomeness of counsel to restrain toward peace the feelings of the common people, since you are unable to doubt that our adjournment is commendable and necessary.

Given on 15 March.

1. Eulalius and Boniface.
2. Rome.
3. From this statement it seems that the synod's sessions were intermittent.
4. Of Eastertide.

358. EDICT OF HONORIUS ON ROMAN CELEBRATION OF EASTER, 419

(*CSEL* 35. 70–1)

In this edict to the Roman populace Honorius informs the citizens that the contention between Boniface and Eulalius, rivals for the Roman bishopric (see introd. to no. 352), still is unsolved, that in the meantime the Romans should observe the paschal days peacefully, that punishment will be dealt to disturbers of the peace.

Edict of the same emperor to the people.

Judging it the greatest solicitude for the faith, excellent citizens,[1] we have believed that nothing hasty or immature ought to be produced. For in the cause of religion we think that there should be decided those matters which without error and fault-finding of verdict should be approved by all.

358. ROMAN CELEBRATION OF EASTER, 419

Accordingly, since in the inquiry about the bishops [2] who had been created in the city [3] was clinging in the bishops' [4] judgement an uncertainty of intention and since, when the process was increasing as a result, an end could not be put to the rivalling interests and since our deliberation was long dependent on varied matters, we have ordained that the entire business should be postponed for future investigation to a new council of bishops with fuller number,[5] in order that the case, when pondered from every part, may achieve the end which fairness or religion was demanding, after the days of Easter have been completed. At the same time, because nothing about a bishop can be decided, temporarily we have chosen one [6] who should celebrate the revered mysteries [7] during the holy days,[8] that for you, citizens,[1] the customary celebration by a bishop may be at your service for the sacred city's [4] honour.

Wherefore, having imitated our patience, with calm spirits accept what we urge on behalf of public peace: let the worship of the holy days [8] pass with due tranquillity, let no riot disturb public peace, let special partiality not appear in respect to anyone who may be censured.[9] For it is fitting that with suspended minds you should reserve all matters unimpaired for our judgement and that you without any frenzy but with due modesty should await rather than demand a bishop. But if, following wicked instigators, you shall have chosen riots and tumults rather than peace and self-restraint, you will show what you favour and not only over you, but also over your leaders, to whose counsels you adhere, shall impend the destruction of your welfare, to which you drive us. For not deserving of pardon is he who will not be able to be restrained from wickedness by our Humanity's warnings.

Given on 15 March.

1. The emperor employs the old word *Quirites*, which denotes the Romans in their civil capacity and ascends—so tradition tells—to the regal period.
2. Boniface and Eulalius.
3. Rome.
4. Those meeting at Ravenna (see no. 354).
5. This plan proved needless, for events in Rome soon settled the case (see no. 364).
6. Achilleus, bishop of Spoleto (see nos. 355-7).
7. See no. 75, n. 42.
8. Of Eastertide.
9. Since the controversy has not been composed, Honorius is anxious that no demonstration *pro* or *con* may be made, for one of the two rival bishops will be found at fault eventually and in the emperor's opinion it is pointless to prejudge the issue.

359. LETTER OF HONORIUS ON CONVOCATION OF THE SPOLETAN COUNCIL, 419

(CSEL 35. 71–2)

The next step by the emperor to solve the schism caused by the rival claims of Eulalius and Boniface to be bishop of Rome (see introd. to no. 352), after the Synod of Ravenna had failed to reach a conclusion shortly before Easter of 419, was to summon a larger council to convene at Spoleto. On this subject are extant at least four imperial letters (nos. 359–62), of which the present letter summons St Paulinus, bishop of Nola, to Spoleto.

As the event proved, the council never met and the order for its convocation was rescinded (no. 366), because the unauthorized return of Eulalius to Rome and the subsequent riot, when he attempted to preside at the paschal ceremonies, caused Honorius to support Boniface, whom he recognized as the legitimate incumbent of the papal see (no. 365).

Letter of the same emperor to the holy Paulinus, the Nolan bishop.
To the holy and venerable father Paulinus, bishop.

Already, then, there was a definite opinion on our part that nothing could be concluded by those bishops who had assembled for the synod,[1] since your Beatitude, having made excuse about your body's indisposition, could not endure the harm of the journey. And through a holy man's [2] absence not the things indeed which were about to be upheld, but the vices meanwhile are objects of joy, since wicked and old ambition long has wished to have a contest with a blessed man and one of holy life [3] and thinks that it has confidence for venturing upon the walls by force against these good things of apostolic institution.[4] O truly worthy cause, which only the blessed life of your crown [5] can decide!

Accordingly we announce a postponed judgement, that the divine precepts may be expressed from your Veneration's mouth, for you, having followed these, have been filled with these.[6] Nor can exist another producer of these precepts than you, who are specially approved as the apostle's worthy disciple.[7]

Accordingly, holy lord, deservedly venerable father, just servant of God,[8] after the labour has been despised, for the purpose of conferring a divine service, indulge us this boon of your visitation, if so it ought to be called, that when all matters have been postponed, since the tranquillity of the temperate air is favourable,[9] you may deign, for the purpose of being present at the synod, to show yourself without interruption also to our desires and benediction, which we wish.

1. At Ravenna.

2. That is, Paulinus himself, to whom Honorius ascribes much influence.
3. Thus Boniface is characterized.
4. The latter part of the causal clause seems to mean that Eulalius is confident that he can become pope, even if he must storm the walls to occupy the papal throne. In *apostolic institution* lies a reference to St Peter and St Paul as founders of the Roman Church.
5. The poetic metaphor suggests that the victories which Paulinus has won, and for which he has been crowned—so to speak—as a winner in the contest for perfection, alone can solve the situation wherein the Roman Church finds itself.
6. The tortuous Latin yields this sense.
7. Perhaps a play upon the name of Paulinus as derived from that of St Paul.
8. So, continuing the inference, St Paul calls himself, albeit without the adjective (Titus 1. 1).
9. As is learned from no. 360, the synod was set for 13 June.

360. LETTER OF HONORIUS ON CONVOCATION OF THE SPOLETAN COUNCIL, 419

(*CSEL* 35. 72)

This letter, treating the same subject as nos. 359, 361, 362, summons unnamed African bishops to a synod at Spoleto.

Also of the same emperor to African bishops.

Our Serenity not only in all cases but particularly in these which pertain to the venerable religion desires to have a considered decision.

We believe that the dispute arisen about the eternal [1] city's bishopric already has been reported even overseas. And this has not been able to be ended by a few persons and, therefore, it is agreed that the judgement of many persons is needed.

Wherefore your Sanctities, whom goodness of life and learning in law [2] commend, with excuses removed should deign to hasten before 13 June to the Spoletan city, that that which truth or the rule of religion shall have dictated, with God equally assisting the minds of all, may be decided by a verdict, lest any longer the apostolic see's bishopric may be disquieted.[3]

1. See no. 140, n. 1.
2. Religion, as often.
3. Or possibly by expansion "lest any longer the vacancy in the apostolic see's bishopric may be protracted".

361. LETTER OF PLACIDIA ON CONVOCATION OF THE SPOLETAN COUNCIL, 419

(*CSEL* 35. 73)

This letter, treating the same subject as nos. 359, 360, 362, summons Aurelius, bishop of Carthage, to a synod at Spoleto.

Letter of the same emperor [1] to the holy Aurelius, the Carthaginian bishop.

Indeed we had wished that another reason for seeing your Veneration had occurred, that we might enjoy your Benediction's desired aspect.

But because in regard to the pope of the city of Rome a reprehensible ambition has inflicted a contest and does not think that a holy life must be sought in a bishop, a smaller number of bishops than the custom of a synod demands has protracted a judgement, begun on this discussion,[2] for more and most learned men, of whom your Sanctity is the chief. For when the vices which the divine religion's sacrosanct commandment rejects [3] have been removed, the rewards of purity and of merit ought not to be revealed by others than such men.

And although the letter [4] of the Lord Augustus, my blood-brother the emperor,[5] could have sufficed, yet I also have added mine, whereby I might entreat your Sanctity's arrival.

Accordingly I ask, holy lord, deservedly venerable father, that you, for the purpose of conferring a twofold favour (both of your benediction desired by us and of proffering a judgement necessary in view of your Beatitude), should deign to show yourself, with all matters laid aside, looking upon God, concerning the establishment of whose bishop the labour of coming ought not to be refused.

1. Though the document's superscription contains the words *eiusdem principis* (of the same emperor) referring to Honorius, it is obvious from the later reference to him that the writer was not Honorius but rather was Galla Placidia, his half-sister, whom he made Augusta in 421 when he was compelled to accept as his colleague Flavius Constantius, her second husband, who then took the style of Constantius III. She acted as regent for her son Valentinian III during his minority (425–*c.* 437) and continued to exercise political influence till her death in 450.

2. At Ravenna.

3. The allusion probably is to St Paul's precepts about the virtues to be exercised and the vices to be eschewed by a bishop (1 Tim. 3. 2–7; Titus 1. 7–9).

4. The letter is no. 360.

5. Honorius.

362. LETTER OF PLACIDIA ON CONVOCATION OF THE SPOLETAN COUNCIL, 419

(CSEL 35. 73-4)

This letter, treating the same subject as nos. 359-61, summons African bishops to a synod at Spoleto.

Circular letter of the same [1] to Augustine,[2] Alypius,[3] Euhodius,[4] Donatian,[4] Silvanus,[4] Novatus,[4] and Deuterius,[4] bishops.

Our Piety is certain that to your Venerations [5] has come the news that in regard to the pope of the city of Rome vices fight with purity and that the conflict of this matter has been so lengthy that among so many bishops, who had assembled for a synod,[6] because certain ones were dissenting, not yet has been able to be preferred a life based on apostolic commandment.[7]

However, since that faction, which disagrees, agrees in the meantime that it knows well your life, they have admitted without doubt that it would be quite obvious for your Sanctities' [5] judgement to be awaited, for whose presence a verdict to be expressed should be postponed and for which you, excelling in merit of life, also rightly are sought from the transmarine regions, in order that you may be able to judge.

But although the sacred authority of the Lord Augustus, my blood-brother the emperor,[8] summoning you to a synod in Italy, has come to you and must not be neglected,[9] we judge that also specially should be added our Serenity's letter, whereby I entreat that you, granting your Benedictions' [5] desirable aspect without excuse, may judge this letter pleasing to Almighty God, because, for the purpose of producing a verdict both on behalf of a distinguished bishop and on behalf of a holy life's merits,[10] you perceive that the remuneration of this vexation has been fixed in a divine reward.

Given on 20 March at Ravenna.

1. See no. 361, n. 1.
2. Bishop of Hippo Regius, later canonized and considered one of the four Doctors of the Western Church in the patristic period.
3. Bishop of Thagaste.
4. An African bishop of an unknown see.
5. Singular in Latin, as if addressed to each bishop individually.
6. At Ravenna.
7. See no. 361, n. 3.
8. Honorius.
9. See no. 361, n. 4.
10. Thus Placidia characterizes Boniface.

363. LETTER OF CONSTANTIUS ON EXECUTION OF IMPERIAL ORDERS ABOUT EULALIANS, 419

(CSEL 35. 76)

When Symmachus, urban prefect of Rome, reported to Count Flavius Constantius, Emperor Honorius' brother-in-law,[1] that Eulalius, who was bickering with Pope St Boniface I for the possession of the Papacy, had re-entered Rome contrary to imperial commands (see introd. to nos. 352-4) and that rioting had occurred, in the same report he requested the count to send from the imperial court a speedy reply of instructions.[2] In response Constantius cautions Symmachus that Honorius' orders, contained in a missive carried by the count's messenger (no. 364), about the settlement of the contest between the contenders must be obeyed.

Letter of the illustrious Count Constantius to Symmachus, urban prefect.

That we can know that all things are settled and that the authors of factions may not escape the notice of a loyal messenger and examiner, we have directed Vitulus, our clerk, that with swift haste he should carry to your Excellency and to the people the address[3] and the decision of our Lord, the most unconquered prince, and we warn as follows: that whatever is contained in the sacred commands should not be violated with any temerity and that what measures[4] have been ordered should be put into effect with swift urgency, lest the august Clemency, because it now is known that there has been delay, when aroused, should not delay to make reform by its Majesty's vigour.

1. Constantius also was the father of Valentinian III and for a short time in 421 was joint-emperor with Honorius in the West (no. 373, n. 1).
2. Symmachus' report is in CSEL 35. 74-6.
3. Probably Honorius' oration to the Senate (no. 357).
4. See no. 364 for these.

364. LETTER OF HONORIUS ON PENALTIES FOR EULALIANS, 419

(CSEL 35. 76-8)

When Honorius discovered that Eulalius, the rival contestant for the papal see (see introd. to no. 352), had returned to Rome without authorization for the

364. PENALTIES FOR EULALIANS, 419

purpose of presiding at the paschal ceremonies, in this document the emperor informs Symmachus, the urban prefect, what measures should be taken against Eulalius, his clerical and lay adherents, the chief men of the city's wards, if they could not control the urban mob, and the prefect's staff, if they should be slow in effecting the imperial instructions.

Copy of the sacred letter to Symmachus, urban prefect.[1]

When our Clemency, desirous of restoring peace, had found for correcting the error of the first disturbances [2] this kind of plan, that until a clear verdict about the establishment of the urban bishopric should proceed,[3] each of the persons on whose account tumult previously had appeared, debarred from dwelling in the most sacred city,[4] should wait in expectation of the future decision at a distance, where he should be restricted, clearly described for each,[5] we cannot conceal with equanimity that against our Clemency's orders has been declared almost open war, by which they were trodden under foot, and that the head of this movement has been Eulalius, who has transgressed the orders, since he has not been patient to be absent for a little while according to the schedule of the orders, dearest cousin Symmachus.

Hence your Sublimity should know that we have decided this: that both the earlier schedule of the salutary order and the moderate ordinance of the synod [6] ought to be maintained—which we judge cannot be done otherwise, unless Eulalius in every way should be hard pressed so that he, departing with all speed from the city,[4] should not offer by his presence incitements to the arrogant populace and for innocent persons should not be the cause of death. And to him, who shall have no excuse from this in asserting that he against his will is being detained by the populace, it ought not to be doubtful, if he shall have continued in this persistency of presumption, that a verdict already postponed must be published not only about his status but even about the hazard to his life,[7] for guilt now merits no grace, which, when it is proclaimed, is not needed.

Moreover, if any of the number of the clerics shall have decided that he ought to communicate [8] with Eulalius while the trial is in abeyance, he should know that he must be convicted by a like verdict, but the laics, who shall have thought that after our Gentleness' prohibition communion with Eulalius can be desirable, should know indeed that they shall suffer death, if slaves, and that, if masters, they cannot be freed from this danger.

Moreover, unless the chief men [9] of the districts [9] shall have tamed and bridled the spirit of the uncouth populace, they should know that they must be arrested and subjected to the last judgement.[10]

Moreover the Spoletan bishop,[11] according as it previously had been determined, shall fulfil during the holy days of Easter the schedule of the festal celebration. And we ordain that the Lateran Church [12] should be opened for him alone to celebrate the mysteries,[13] with the rest, who may have wished to anticipate this, repelled. Of course, if the aforesaid bishop of the city of Spoleto shall have been hindered, we warn that none other ought to be accepted to fulfil the schedule of the holy mysteries [13] in his stead.[14]

Moreover on all billboards [15] or in the places which are frequented by crowded assembly these things, which we have decided, should be published, that to all it may be clear both that we have been unwilling that anything tumultuous should be perpetrated and that they still should expect that the disturbed circumstances are bound to be settled.

Of course, your Sublimity should know that the chief clerk and the rest of the office staff who follow your direction not only must be ruined by the expenses of a most burdensome fine, but also shall receive the punishment of death, unless with strenuous attention applied to our Clemency's statutes they shall have hastened to give effect to them.

Given on 26 March at Ravenna.

1. Of Rome.
2. That is, the controversial election of two popes.
3. The emperor means the confirmation of either Boniface or Eulalius as the legitimate bishop of Rome.
4. Rome.
5. Eulalius was sent to Antium (Anzio) about 36 miles south of Rome on the sea-coast, but Boniface was sent to the cemetery of St Felicitas: that is, he lived in the group of buildings at her cemetery, which originally was the Catacomb of Maximus (discovered in 1884), on the Via Salaria, not far from the city's wall. It is interesting to note that two basilicas were built over the cemetery: the one dedicated by Boniface to the saint, who with her seven sons was martyred in 162; the other dedicated to Boniface himself, probably in memory of his enforced sojourn there.
6. The Synod of Ravenna, convoked to compose the controversy between the two claimants, had proposed that each should withdraw from Rome pending its decision as to who was the legitimate pope (see introd. to no. 354).
7. Whether eternal or temporal is not clear, for Honorius may be hinting at more than mere excommunication in his use of *salus* (life).
8. In the ecclesiastical sense, that is, partake of Holy Communion with Eulalius.
9. Of Rome; see no. 356, n. 5.
10. Apparently a euphemism for the death sentence.
11. Achilleus of Spoleto.
12. St John Lateran (San Giovanni in Laterano), the cathedral church of Rome and one of its seven patriarchal basilicas. Its façade parades the proud

title of "Mother and Head of All Churches of the City and of the World" (OMNIVM VRBIS ET ORBIS ECCLESIARVM MATER ET CAPVT). The phrase doubtless was derived from the so-called Donation of Constantine (*Edictum Constantini ad Silvestrum Papam*), the early medieval forgery and the hoary hoax of history, wherein Emperor Constantine I the Great informs (*PL* 8. 575) Pope St Silvester I in 315 that he has sanctioned on his Lateran estate the construction of a church, which is to be called, cherished, venerated, and proclaimed as "Head and Vertex of All Churches in the Entire Circle of the Earth" (*caput et vertex omnium ecclesiarum in universo orbe terrarum*).

13. See no. 75, n. 42.
14. The text is defective, but the best conjecture has been translated.
15. In late Latin a *titulus* may mean—in addition to its classical meanings—a pillar whereon notices are affixed or a church. The latter significance starts at the beginning of this century and may be what the emperor means. The meaning continues into modern usage, especially in connection with the titular churches in Rome assigned to members of the College of Cardinals; e.g. the oldest cardinal priest in point of seniority (1951), Alessio Ascalesi, archbishop of Naples, is characterized in the *Annuario Pontificio* thus: "del Titolo di San Callisto".

365. RESCRIPT OF HONORIUS ON CONFIRMATION OF PAPAL ELECTION, 419

(*CSEL* 35. 79–80)

In this constitution Honorius announces to Symmachus, urban prefect of Rome, his decision to acknowledge the claim of Boniface to be the lawful bishop of Rome over that of his rival Eulalius (see introd. to no. 352).

Copy of the sacred letter to Symmachus, urban prefect.

With especial moderation our Serenity has acted, lest presumption should be able to find a foothold. Therefore in the judgement of the venerable bishops [1] the trial was postponed, that apart from any disturbance a calm discussion might determine whatever religion and truth demanded.

But the text of your report has shown that by the usurpation of Eulalius contrary to the venerable synod's decision many things have been done unlawfully, since he, supplying to the people by his presence a cause for raging, has desired to destroy everything which our Guidance preserves.[2] For, when by our command and by the decision of the bishops, in whose synod a rather large number had been gathered, it had been determined also by the rivals'[3] consent and declaration that this should happen, namely, that whoever would have entered the city[4] to arouse the populace should know that he was to be condemned specifically, he,[5] forgetful of himself, has proved by his present deed what kind of commencement[6] he seems to have had.

Therefore, since it is agreed that after so many crimes this man rightly has been expelled from the city,[7] to which the judgement both of our Clemency and of the bishops seems to have decided that the said person ought not to have access, dearest and fondest cousin Symmachus, your Sublimity should know that we have decided that the venerable Bishop Boniface, to whose governance we have thought that our authority rightly should be joined, ought to enter the city,[4] that under his direction respect for the religious law[8] may be fulfilled with wonted regularity.

Given on 3 April. Accepted on 8 April.

1. Assembled at Ravenna to decide between Eulalius and Boniface, but dissolved in late Lent without having settled the issue.
2. The Synod of Ravenna had voted that each claimant should withdraw himself from Rome until a final decision would have been reached. While both obeyed this order initially, Eulalius returned to Rome in time, as he hoped, to preside over the ceremonies celebrated during Eastertide.
3. Boniface and Eulalius.
4. Rome.
5. Eulalius.
6. That is, his attitude which led to the start of the schism.
7. Eulalius is believed to have been relegated to an Italian bishopric, either in Etruria or in Campania according to a conflicting tradition. By *city* is meant Rome.
8. Christianity.

366. MANDATE OF HONORIUS ON CANCELLATION OF A CONCILIAR CONVOCATION, 419

(*CSEL* 35. 81–2)

The penultimate imperial document in the controversy between Eulalius and Boniface (see introd. to no. 352) informs Largus, proconsul of Africa, that Honorius has acknowledged the claim of Boniface to the papal see and that the proconsul should notify the African bishops that the council designed to decide

366. CANCELLATION OF A CONVOCATION, 419

between the claimants to the Roman see will not be held. Doubtless similar instructions were sent elsewhere, but this order seems to be the only one extant.

Copy of the sacred letter to the proconsul of Africa.

Honorius, Victor, Renowned, Triumpher, Ever-August to Largus, proconsul.

Amid all cares those which we judge pertinent to the episcopate [1] do not trouble us less. For when was being investigated the dispute about confirming the bishop of the eternal [2] city and when those bishops, who had been placed together,[3] considered that for so important a matter they were too few for announcing a verdict, it had been our pleasure, as the sacred letters have urged, that from the African or the Gallic provinces more bishops should come, for this reason, obviously, lest in the intervening time something should be ventured against that which our decision had ordained or which the synod's decision seemed to have decided.

But having scorned all these matters, Eulalius by his sole usurpation believed that the delay should be seized.[4] And it is well known that this man, as was fitting, has been expelled by our authority and the holy Boniface has been confirmed as bishop.

And since the matter has been concluded, our Clemency had judged it unsuitable that the bishops should be exposed to the ill effect of travel by sea or by land. Hence your Excellency should know that the synod has been cancelled. Therefore by the previously sent sacred utterances and by your authority advise the individual bishops, that they should know that there must be obeyed this order which stops them, in order that each may be free for prayers in his own church,[5] as is suitable, because the case now appears to have been concluded by an excellent decision.

Given on 7 April.

1. See no. 158, n. 1.
2. See no. 140, n. 1.
3. In a synod at Ravenna (see introd. to no. 354).
4. That is, unwilling to await the final settlement, Eulalius, so to speak, took possession of the postponement of the dispute from the Synod of Ravenna to a larger council by entering Rome and seizing the papal power—in contrast to Boniface, who was content to expect the decision in his absence.

One conjecture, though none is needed, suggests that *moram* (delay) should be *Romam* (Rome). Such transposition of letters is not unknown.

5. That is, he may devote his time to religious services in his cathedral and not undertake a useless journey.

367. LETTER OF LARGUS ON CANCELLATION OF A CONCILIAR CONVOCATION, 419
(CSEL 35. 82)

This document implements the imperial instructions (no. 366) sent to Largus, proconsul of Africa, who transmits these to St Aurelius, bishop of Carthage, who with other African bishops had been summoned to an Italian council convoked to decide the dispute between Boniface and Eulalius (see introd. to no. 352) and then cancelled. Doubtless provision for additional distribution was made.

Letter of Largus, proconsul, to Aurelius, bishop of Carthage.
Largus to the lord, honourable father, Aurelius, bishop.
The contest concerning the worthiness of the bishop, whom God has approved as suitable for his own people, has ceased.
Therefore the imperial Clemency has confirmed the holy and venerable Boniface as bishop of the city of Rome, for whose selection he ordered some time ago your Sanctity to be summoned, as his sacred utterances, published with respect, testify.
Therefore you, for whom the necessity for sailing has been removed, ought to visit speedily [1] your own people and churches.
And by another hand: May the divine favour keep you safe for very many years, lord and deservedly honourable father.

1. It is not clear why Largus ordered Aurelius to be speedy in episcopal visitation, unless he had believed that in preparation for the voyage the bishop cancelled his episcopal schedule, which this letter directs him to resume.

368. LETTER OF HONORIUS AND THEODOSIUS II ON CONDEMNATION OF PELAGIANISM, 419
(CSEL 57. 296-9)

This additional document in the dossier of Pelagianism (see nos. 350 and 351), although addressed primarily to St Aurelius, bishop of Carthage, shows by its subscription that it authorizes St Augustine, bishop of Hippo Regius, to admonish his clergy of the penalties which they will incur, if they shall have transgressed the imperial instructions against participating in Pelagianism.
Augustine preserves the letter (*Ep.* 201).

Emperors Honorius and Theodosius Augusti to Aurelius, bishop, greeting.

368. CONDEMNATION OF PELAGIANISM, 419

A short time ago it had been ordained that Pelagius and Caelestius, the devisers of an abominable dogma, should be expelled from the city of Rome just as if some contaminations of Catholic unity, lest they might pervert the minds of ignorant persons by perverse persuasion.[1] And in this matter our Clemency has followed your Sanctity's judgement, with which it is agreed by all persons that these men have been condemned by a just consideration of the sentence. But because the pertinacious evil of a stubborn crime has required that the imperial order should be repeated, we also by a recent ordinance [2] have decreed that if anyone, not ignorant that the said persons are lying hidden in any part soever of the provinces, had delayed either to eject them or to surrender them, he should be subject to the prescribed penalty just as if a participant.

However, especially for correcting the stubbornness of certain bishops, who either by tacit consent add to or do not, by public opposition, subtract from the wicked arguments of these persons, it will be fitting that your Sanctity's authority continue, most dear and most benevolent father, in so far as the Christian devotion of all persons concurs in the abolition of an absurd heresy. Accordingly your Worship by competent [3] writings shall cause that all about to know by the decree of your Holiness that this decree has been prescribed for them should be warned that whosoever shall have neglected through impious obstinacy to subscribe to the condemnation of the aforesaid persons, whereby a pure mind may be disclosed, after they have been punished by the loss of their episcopal office and after they have been expelled forever from the cities, should be deprived of communion, which is forbidden them.[4] For since we ourselves, pursuant to the Nicene Council,[5] with sincere confession adore God, the creator of all things and the guardian of our sovereignty, your Sanctity will not permit persons of a detestable sect, designing novel and unusual things to the harm of religion, to hide by secret parleys a sacrilege once condemned by public authority. For one and the same guilt is theirs, who either by concealing connivance or by not condemning the heresy [6] show culpable favour.

And by another hand: May God preserve you, most dear and most benevolent father, safe for many years.

Given on 9 June at Ravenna.[7]

Given in the same tenor also to the holy Augustine, bishop.

1. No. 350.
2. Not extant.
3. That is, competent in the legal sense, for bishops before Augustine's time had jurisdiction in certain matters recognized by the State (no. 28).
4. The text is uncertain and the thought is condensed. The meaning seems

608   369. INTERCESSION FOR SHIPWRIGHTS, 419

to be that (1) they shall be demoted from episcopal rank, (2) they shall be exiled in perpetuity, (3) they shall be deprived of communion.

5. The First Ecumenical Council of the Christian Church, held at Nicaea in 325, officially defined the Christian faith.

6. The translator has supplied an object for the participle, although *connivance* perhaps may be construed also as the object of the second participle.

7. One manuscript adds the Latin for "Monaxius and Plinta being consuls".

369. MANDATE OF HONORIUS AND THEODOSIUS II ON EPISCOPAL INTERCESSION FOR SHIPWRIGHTS, 419

(*CT* 9. 40. 24)

This directive, which Justinian adapts (*CI* 9. 47. 25), is of a peculiar character. At a bishop's petition it pardons persons who have shown barbarians how to build ships, but it provides that for the future such persons shall suffer capital punishment. It also testifies to the treacherous tendency of technicians to foster their private interests by flouting the public interest, which demanded that the Empire's enemies should not be taught technical arts to assist them in their raids against the Romans.

The same Augusti to Monaxius, praetorian prefect.[1]

After those persons who have transmitted to barbarians the previously unknown [2] practical knowledge of building ships have been liberated from imminent punishment and imprisonment because of the petition of the most reverend Asclepiades, bishop of the Chersonese city,[3] we decree capital punishment to be designed both for themselves and for all others, if anything similar shall have been perpetrated in the future.[4]

Given on 24 September at Constantinople, Monaxius and Plinta being consuls.

1. Of the East.

2. The reference must be to seaworthy ships, for even landlocked barbarians already knew how to construct vessels for use on lakes and rivers.

3. Of the several ancient cities and peninsulas of this name that in the Tauric Chersonesus (Crimean Peninsula), near the modern Sevastopol, probably is meant. If so, the barbarians were Scythians, whose maritime raids would be dreaded.

But the law perhaps looked to wider application than in the East, for it was just as much the concern of the West (already in these troubled times experiencing persistent barbarian invasions) that the hungry Germans should not harry Africa (see no. 646, n. 1 *ad init.*), which, as the granary of Europe, served both halves of the Empire. But the law came too late, for ten years later the Vandals, who had been in Spain since 409, sailed against the African provinces, most of which they controlled for over a century and whence they preyed on southern Europe until Justinian destroyed their power in 533 (see no. 646, n. 1 *ad fin.*).

4. Justinian's version is quite short: "For those who have transmitted to barbarians the previously unknown practical knowledge of building ships we decree capital punishment to be designed."

By rescinding reference to episcopal intercession Justinian probably—of course, Asclepiades had died ere Justinian's age, but the emperor could have made an exception for any maritime bishop's intervention—took a more serious view of such interference than had Theodosius a century earlier, unless the latter's concession simply showed how compelling was the prelate's petition on this one occasion and could not be cited as a precedent in the future.

For examples of barbarians' exploitation of their civilized neighbours' weapons see Toynbee, 8. 16–19.

370. EDICT OF HONORIUS AND THEODOSIUS II ON SANCTUARY AND ON EPISCOPAL VISITATION OF PRISONS, 419

(CS 13)

This ordinance extends the area of ecclesiastical sanctuary to fifty paces beyond the doors of a church and allows bishops not only to visit prisoners on errands of mercy but also to intervene in certain miscarriages of justice.[1]

Emperors Honorius and Theodosius, Pious, Augusti.

It is proper that humanity, known previously to our times, should modulate justice.

For when very many persons have fled from cruel fortune's violence and have chosen the enclosure of ecclesiastical defence, they, when confined therein, suffer no less imprisonment than that which they have avoided, for at no times an egress is opened for them in the light of the vestibule.

And therefore the sanctity of ecclesiastical reverence shall adhere to fifty paces beyond a basilica's doors. And whoever shall have held a person going forth from this place should incur the crime of sacrilege.

For nothing of compassion is devoted to persons fleeing for refuge, if the freer air is denied to the afflicted.

We concede also to a bishop [2] this power: that he may enter the courts of a prison with the aid of compassion, may heal the ill, may feed the poor, may comfort the guiltless, and, when he, after having investigated thoroughly, has learned the case of each and every person, in accordance with the law may conduct his interventions before the competent judge. For we know—and this has been made an object of petition in numerous audiences—that often very many persons are cast into prison so that they may be deprived of the freedom of approaching a judge and, when a rather humble person once has begun to suffer custody before his case is known, he is compelled to endure the penalty of outrage.

A contumacious office staff should pay immediately to our fisc two pounds of gold, if a feral [3] janitor shall have debarred a bishop [2] caring for such holy matters.

Given on 21 November at Ravenna, the most distinguished Monaxius and the most distinguished Plinta being consuls.

1. While as early as 392 the emperors had forbidden clerical intervention in criminal cases (nos. 234 and 235), in 398 was made some modification (no. 272), which was broadened in 419 by the present law. Episcopal intercession for criminals can be traced to its perhaps first mention in canon 7 of the Council of Sardica (c. 343), before the State definitely allowed by law this right. Pretermitting such well-known episcopal interventions as those of St Martin of Tours with the usurper Maximus on behalf of the Spanish heresiarch Priscillian in 385 (Sulpicius Severus, *Chron.* 2. 50. 5–6 [= *CSEL* 1. 103]) and of Leontius, the Roman leader of the schismatic Novatians, with Theodosius I in 387 for Quintus Aurelius Symmachus, the pagan senator, who had supported Maximus against Theodosius and who subsequently was accused of treason (Socrates, *HE* 5. 14 *ad fin.*), we find that St Augustine asserted episcopal intercession early in the fifth century, anterior to the present statute, in *Epp.* 133, 139, 152, 153 (= *CSEL* 44. 80–4, 148–54, 393–5, 395–427). Scriptural warrant for such interference doubtless was derived from the Saviour's words in Matt. 25. 36.

2. The word is *sacerdos*, on which see no. 16, n. 4.

3. The adjective relating to death (*feralis*) is not too unusual when applied to a janitor of a jail, since mortality of prisoners in antiquity was doubtless high. Of course, if *feralis* is understood in its later sense of "bestial", prison guards' savagery was probably as prevalent then as now and some of them perhaps considered those in custody as caged beasts.

371. RESCRIPT OF HONORIUS ON PAPAL ELECTION, 420

(*CSEL* 35. 83–4)

The last imperial constitution in the controversy between Pope St Boniface I and Anti-pope Eulalius (see introd. to no. 352) was occasioned by Boniface's request that the emperor should provide against possible renewal of schism in the event of the decease of the pope, whose illness had encouraged Eulalius' adherents to make another attempt at extruding the pope.

Honorius, whose well-known indolence had not impaired his interest in the ecclesiastical establishment, in this document, addressed to the pope, enacts that in contested papal elections neither claimant shall be recognized and that a new election shall be conducted.

Letter of Emperor Honorius to Boniface, the Roman bishop, in which he has ordained that if again two bishops shall have been ordained, both should be expelled from the city.[1]

Victor Honorius, Renowned, Triumpher, Ever-August to the holy and venerable Boniface, pope of the eternal [2] city.

We have received the writing of your Beatitude with rejoicing due to your Reverence, giving greatest thanks to Almighty God, because we have learned that your Holiness after long indisposition has been restored to desired health, and, therefore, since your venerable messengers are returning, we show our joy by the testimony of our sacred letters and we ask that in daily prayers your Apostolicity may deign to apply its interest and devotion in respect to our health and rule.

Moreover know that our Piety has quite determined the following matter, because your Holiness has been anxious about the disorder among the churches or the people, that nothing of this kind in any way can happen; our Clemency has believed that satisfactory provision has been made about this.

Finally we will this by proclamation of your Beatitude to come to the knowledge of all clergymen: that, if anything perchance shall have happened by human eventuality to your Worship, which we do not desire, they all should know that they must desist from electoral solicitations and that, if perchance contrary to what is right two by the rashness of rivals shall have been ordained, none of them absolutely will become bishop, but that in the apostolic see will remain only that one whom from the number of clergymen divine judgement and the approval of all shall have selected by a new ordination.

Wherefore this must be heeded: that pursuant to our Serenity's admonition all should maintain quiet mind and calm spirits and

1. Rome.
2. See no. 140, n. 1.

372. LETTER OF HONORIUS AND THEODOSIUS II ON CLERICAL COHABITATION AND ON DELATION ABOUT RAPISTS OF CONSECRATED VIRGINS,

420

(CS 10)

This ordinance, epitomized by CT 16. 2. 44 (copied in CI 1. 3. 19 save for its interpretation) and by CT 9. 25. 3, prohibits the practice of celibate clergy to have in their houses women ostensibly as housekeepers, whom they called sisters,[1] but who were their concubines,[2] despite the Nicene Council's prohibition [3] almost a century earlier (325). But at the same time the emperors in this statute forbid that clerics married prior to ordination should separate from their wives.[4]

The law's concluding paragraph frees from odium delators about rapists of consecrated virgins.

Emperors Honorius and Theodosius Augusti to Palladius, praetorian prefect.[5]

The faithful suggestion [6] of a religious priest [7] demands a discipline commendable to the world. For it follows good morals [8] that clergymen serving the sacred ministries should not be joined to extraneous women, whom they excuse by the stained association of the appellation of "sister".[9] We indeed believe that in devoted minds is this reverence for God that the consciousness of depraved persuasion does not know the habitation of this lodging. But, although it does not penetrate into this association and friendship,[10] rumour contaminates and the addition of the other sex affords occasion for evil morals, because the example of obscene suspicion draws to the allurement of crime persons placed outside [11] and living under public law.

Since these things are so, your illustrious and exalted Eminence should publish by edicts posted everywhere the sanction of the present response,[12] that all persons may know that [13] whoever are supported by the priesthood [14] of any rank whatever [15] or are distinguished by the honour of the clericate should realize that associations with extraneous women are prohibited to them, with only this faculty conceded to them: that they may keep within the precincts of their homes mothers, daughters, and blood-sisters, for in respect to these the natural bond permits no perverse crime to be considered.

Moreover the affection of pure morality urges that those women who acquire lawfully [16] wedlock before their husbands' priesthood [14] should not be deserted.[17] For not unsuitably have been joined to clergymen those women who have made their husbands worthy of the priesthood [14] by their association.[18]

Moreover the ordinances of the foregoing laws also confirm the following part of the request,[19] that [20] whatever rapist, careless of himself,[21] shall have solicited a virgin dedicated to God, after his property has been confiscated, should be punished by deportation—freedom to bring this accusation having been granted to all persons without fear of delation.[22] Nor is it proper that an informer whom a humane motive urges on behalf of the purity of religion should be prosecuted.[23]

Given on 8 May [24] at Ravenna, our Lord Theodosius Augustus for the ninth time and the most distinguished Constantius for the third time being consuls.[25]

1. Other names beside "sister" (*soror*) occur. Pious pretence—perhaps based on St Paul's question about his having "power to lead about a sister, a wife, as well as other apostles, and as the brethren of the Lord, and Cephas [St Peter]" (1 Cor. 9. 5)—called such a woman "mother" (*mater*) or "daughter" (*filia*) or "beloved" (*agapeta*); but "sister" was quite common, since it continued classical and pagan nomenclature—as appears in Tibullus (*Eleg*. 3. 1. 23–8), Seneca (*Hipp. sive Phaed*. 611), Martial (*Epig*. 2. 4. 3–8, 10. 65. 14–15, 12. 20. 1–2). Names on a lower level include "adopted woman" (*adscititia*), "sent-in woman" (*intromissa*), "secretly introduced woman" (*subintroducta*), and "brought-over woman" (*superinducta*); of these the third term seems the commonest and today is the scholarly word used to stigmatize such a woman.

2. One of the contributing causes to St Chrysostom's exile from his patriarchate of Constantinople (404) was the anger aroused among the capital's clergy by his effort to extirpate this evil (Palladius, *Dial. de Vita Chrys*. 5 = PG 47. 20). We have two of his sermons against such women (PG 47. 495–532). On concubinage see no. 525.

3. Its canon 3 expresses the same thought found in this statute.

4. In Spain (c. 300) the Council of Elvira (Illiberis) by its canon 33 produced the oldest conciliar ordinance concerning clerical celibacy, when it ordained that all altar-serving clerics must abstain from their wives and must not beget children. It was in that same country and at the close of that same century, when the Papacy under Pope St Siricius (384–99) started its campaign to secure sacerdotal celibacy, that the First Council of Toledo (400) by its canon 1

went so far as to require married clergymen to separate from their wives and to refuse promotion to clerics who were parents.

5. Of Italy.

6. It is not clear whether such a recommendation (*suggestio*), ordinarily official, was made at stated intervals to the emperor or was caused by priestly pricks of conscience in this case.

7. See no. 16, n. 4.

8. The unexpressed subject may be personal. If so, it may be read thus: "For he insists in accord with good morals" etc.

9. *CT* 16. 2. 44 and *CI* for these two sentences read "It is not becoming for a man who follows a discipline commendable to the world to be stained by the association of the appellation of 'sister'."

At this point these epitomes temporarily end.

10. The text probably is corrupt and editors make various suggestions. By *it* is meant likely "depraved persuasion".

11. That is, the laity.

12. See no. 218, n. 5.

13. Here *CT* 16. 2. 44 and *CI* resume, reading "therefore" for *that*.

14. See no. 158, n. 1.

15. We should say "whoever rely on any rank whatever in the priesthood" to give themselves some prestige.

16. *CT* and *CI* convert the adverb into an adjective.

17. So St Paul preached (1 Cor. 7. 10, 27, 39).

18. Here *CT* 16. 2. 44 and *CI* end finally.

Perhaps here is an allusion to 1 Cor. 7. 14 and 16.

19. The term is *desiderium* and refers to part of the *suggestio* (n. 6 *supra*).

20. Here begins *CT* 9. 25. 3.

21. That is, careless of his welfare or of his life.

22. This means that an informer shall not suffer from the stigma affecting those who professionally lay information before magistrates. Moreover severe penalties against delators occur in *CT* 10. 10.

23. Or "examined" in a court, because he has brought information.

24. The date of *CT* 9. 25. 3 is 8 March.

25. *CT* 16. 2. 44 adds this Interpretation: "Whoever enjoy the clericate's office are forbidden to have intimacy with extraneous women. They shall know that within their homes only the solaces of mothers, sisters, or daughters have been granted to them, because Nature's law permits nothing base to be done or to be conceived in respect to such persons. Moreover those women who have been in wedlock before the clericate's office must be kept as a solace."

373. LETTER OF CONSTANTIUS III ON EXPULSION OF PELAGIANS FROM ROME, 421

(PL 45. 1750; 48. 404-7; 56. 499-500)

This document is a renewed order, addressed to the urban prefect of Rome, to expel the Pelagians, particularly Caelestius, the chief disciple of the heresiarch Pelagius (see no. 350).

Decree of Emperor Constantius, father of Valentinian Augustus III, to Volusian, urban prefect, given in the Year of Christ 421.

Emperor Flavius Constantius, Pious, Fortunate, Augustus, Victor to Volusian, urban prefect.

The aspects not only of past superstition but also of recent falsehood, which long ago [1] we had ordered to be corrected, by daily reports are announced to become greater. And since discord disturbs people's minds, we command to be repeated the measures [2] which long ago we had ordered.

Wherefore, when this has been read, your Excellence should seek diligently for all who hate God's piety and should cause them to be expelled immediately from the city's [3] walls, in such a way, however, that they may not have permission of abiding, indeed, within the hundredth milestone.

Caelestius also more and more we order [4] to be driven from the city.[3] For it is certain that after these persons have been removed from the midst grateful concord [5] will maintain its old stability.

Of course, then, if any such thing shall have been announced,[6] know that your Superiority's office staff must be subject to a capital sentence. For we do not permit it to be unpunished that our commands are delayed by the negligence of performance.

Farewell, dearest and fondest cousin.

And an added subscription: Let what we have ordered be executed, because this is advantageous to your reputation.

1. An exaggeration: Constantius shared with Honorius the rule of the West for only seven months (8 February-11 September).
2. He probably refers to no. 350, which was promulgated almost three years before Constantius became co-emperor.
3. Rome.
4. Either the earlier order was not enforced or it was disobeyed.
5. Literally "gratefulness and concord": taken as a hendiadys.
6. From the rest of the sentence it seems that Constantius does not want to have a report of negligence on his prefect's part.

374. EDICT OF VOLUSIAN ON EXPULSION OF PELAGIANS FROM ROME, 421

(PL 45. 1751; 48. 408-9; 56. 500)

This magisterial edict of the urban prefect of Rome implements the preceding imperial injunction (no. 373).

Edict posted by Volusian, urban prefect.[1]

Volusian, urban prefect, proclaimed:

Hitherto coverts favourable to culprits have withdrawn from the courts Caelestius, the disturber of divine faith and of public peace. Now the laws and now the edicts shall pursue him in his absence.[2] And to him, as before, residence in the eternal[3] city is denied, that, if he shall have been tarrying even in the vicinity, he may not escape due ruin.

By the caution of this edict we warn in advance also all in respect to the punishment of their rashness and boldness, lest any inimical person[4] may suppose that a lurking-place ought to be provided for a guilty person, that whoever shall have supposed that a person accused by divine and human laws ought to be hidden at his house needs must incur[5] punishment and the verdict[6] of proscription, because a penalty of this kind has been set.

1. *PL* 56. 500 commences the caption with "Copy of an" and omits *urban* in the next line.
2. That is, from his hiding-place.
3. See no. 140, n. 1.
4. Perhaps inimical to the administration or, more simply, a person who is a wrongdoer.
5. *PL* 56. 500 reads "incur the verdict of proscription, because a penalty of horrid punishment has been set for anyone whoever" etc.
6. Literally "pen" (*stilus*); that is, the shelterer's name would be entered on a roll of those proscribed.

375. MANDATE, LETTER, RESCRIPT OF HONORIUS AND THEODOSIUS II ON ECCLESIASTICAL JURISDICTION IN ILLYRICUM, 421-3

(*CT* 16. 2. 45; *PL* 20. 679 [*leg*. 769]-771)

Three documents, of which the first is preserved in *CT* and is repeated in *Cl* 1. 2. 6 and 11. 21. 1, discuss ecclesiastical jurisdiction over the prefecture of Illyricum.[1] In 379 Gratian assigned Illyricum to his new colleague in the East, Theodosius I, but to prevent the ecclesiastical loss of Illyricum to the patriarchate of Constantinople Pope St Damasus I improvised the device of exercising his patriarchal jurisdiction, which until then had been acknowledged without question, over the prefecture by appointing the bishop of Thessalonica as his vicar. This expedient, though contested occasionally by the Constantinopolitan patriarchs, who professed the eastern principle that ecclesiastical and civil divisions must conform, lasted until 421, when our first document transferred ecclesiastical jurisdiction from Rome to Constantinople, perhaps due to the influence exerted by Atticus, patriarch of Constantinople, over Theodosius II, who seems to have been the primary author of the constitution. Apparently, however, immediate representations made by Pope St Boniface I to Honorius inspired the second document, which requested Theodosius II to restore the papal jurisdiction over Illyricum and which was followed by the third document consenting to such restoration.[2]

But Theodosius must have changed his mind, for otherwise his rescissory constitution would have been in his Code and because the mandate of 14 July 421 (our first document) still stands in both his and Justinian's Code. However, despite this the popes seem to have succeeded in maintaining their jurisdiction over the prefecture of Illyricum till the Acacian schism started in 484, when the bishop of Thessalonica adopted the same attitude as the patriarch of Constantinople and consequently his delegated power ceased along with his communion with Rome.[3]

Strictly speaking, as will be seen, the second and the third documents are not legislative texts, but they show the background of such preparation, even if they are not genuine. There is the possibility, of course, that Theodosius fulfilled his word and then after Honorius' death, feeling safer and again yielding to eastern pressure, rescinded the edict which, he wrote, he had sent.

I

The same Augusti[4] to Philip, praetorian prefect of Illyricum.

We order, all innovation ceasing, the ancient custom and the pristine ecclesiastical canons, which until now have prevailed, to be observed throughout all the provinces of Illyricum.[5] Then, if any doubt shall have emerged, it should be fitting that this should be reserved for a sacerdotal council and a holy court, not apart from the knowledge of the most reverend man of the sacrosanct law,[6] the bishop of the Constantinopolitan city, which enjoys the prerogative of Old Rome.[7]

Given on 14 July, Eustathius and Agricola being consuls.[8]

II

Copy of the letter of the most pious Emperor Honorius to Theodosius Augustus.

In all cases, indeed, in which our aid is asked, we cannot refuse an intercession to your Clemency's ears; but we owe necessarily greater care and interest to those matters whereby the holy apostolic see's wishes are supported. For since our Empire is governed always by divine favour, without any doubt ought to be respected by us with special veneration the church of that city,[9] from which both we have received the Roman principate and the sacred ministry [10] has received its beginning, if, indeed, a delegation sent to us shall have asked from our Piety nothing else except what may concord with the discipline of the Catholic faith and with equity. For it seeks that the privileges which, long ago established by the fathers,[11] have been preserved until our times may continue undisturbed. And in this regard your Serenity considers that nothing at all ought to be detracted from the ancient ordinances, if any such have been composed in the rules of the canons [12] and that, lord, the reverence of so many centuries ought not to be impaired by new-fangled prejudices.

Whence, after our Piety's address has been reviewed, your Majesty, mindful of Christianity, which celestial compassion instils in our breasts, should ordain that the ancient arrangement should be maintained, after there have been removed all things which are said to be procured by the plottings of hostile bishops [13] throughout Illyricum, lest under Christian sovereigns the Roman Church may lose that which it has not lost under other [14] emperors.

III

Rescript of Theodosius Augustus to Honorius Augustus.

He deserves a worthy hearing, whoever appears to carry to our Clemency the addresses of a perpetual sovereign, holy lord, august, venerable father,[15] then especially in consideration of the Christian religion, which so has been instilled in your Majesty's respected mind that it, having spread itself more widely, is preserved in our heart. For God our author so has fashioned the later rulers among Christian sovereigns that, after all plotting has been frustrated, that which has been ordained by our ancestors may be preserved. And yet not only in

375. JURISDICTION IN ILLYRICUM, 421-3

those matters which divine aid has preserved uncorrupted your Perpetuity's addresses are heeded by us with swift goodwill and all acknowledged respect, but especially in this matter, because the name of that famous city [9] hitherto preserves the safety of our generation and our whole Empire.

Whence, with all plotting of beseeching bishops throughout Illyricum removed, we have determined that there should be observed what the pristine apostolic discipline and the old canons declare. And on this matter, pursuant to the decision of your Perpetuity's divine response,[16] we have sent written directions to the illustrious praetorian prefects of our Illyricum [17] that, the bishops' plottings ceasing, they particularly may provide that the ancient arrangement should be maintained, lest the most holy church of the venerable city,[9] which for us has hallowed the perpetual empire of its own name, may lose the privileges established by the men of old.

1. Great care must be used to distinguish the civil prefecture from the civil diocese of Illyricum. The prefecture of Illyricum was the smallest of the four prefectures into which the Empire had been divided finally by 395 at the death of Theodosius I, and it contained two dioceses, Macedonia and Dacia, each divided into provinces, which numbered twelve, though the former had six and the latter had five, for one was split between both. Its territory lay roughly between 36° and 42° east longitude. To the prefecture of Italy belonged the diocese of Illyricum, which comprised six provinces and lay roughly between 30° and 36° east longitude.

Diocese of Macedonia: Provinces of Achaea, Macedonia, Creta, Thessalia, Epirus Vetus, Epirus Nova with part of Macedonia Salutaris.

Diocese of Dacia: Provinces of Dacia Mediterranea, Dacia Ripensis, Moesia Prima, Dardania, Praevalitana with part of Macedonia Salutaris.

Diocese of Illyricum: Provinces of Dalmatia, Pannonia Prima, Pannonia Secunda, Savia, Noricum Mediterraneum, Noricum Ripense.

2. Since Honorius died on 27 August 423, the last document, addressed to him, cannot be dated later.

3. E.g. Pope St Boniface I after the date of our first document sent three letters to bishops in Illyricum in assertion of his jurisdiction (*Epp.* 13-15 [dated 3 and 11 March 422] in *PL* 20. 774-84).

On ecclesiastical Illyricum see L. Duchesne, *The Churches Separated from Rome* (New York, 1907), 154-79. On the position of the Thessalonican bishops see Denny, 630-1, and Jalland, 272-8. On the tragic consequences of the western cession of the prefecture of Illyricum to the eastern emperor see J. B. Bury, *The Invasion of Europe by the Barbarians* (London, 1928), 68-71, 78-80.

4. Honorius and Theodosius II, who were uncle and nephew.

5. That is, that the ecclesiastical jurisdiction should coincide with the civil jurisdiction, boundary for boundary—a principle derived from canon 2 of the

Second Council at Constantinople in 381, which canon in turn developed from canon 6 of the First General Council at Nicaea in 325, when territorial limitations of episcopal action were decreed for the patriarchal sees of Alexandria and Antioch and Rome. The *innovation* looks to the papal vicariate at Thessalonica instituted by Pope St Damasus I. Consult S. L. Greenslade, "The Illyrian Churches and the Vicariate of Thessalonica" in *JTS* 46 (1945) 17-29.

6. The Christian religion.

7. The Second General Council (Constantinople I) in 381 conferred upon the bishop of Constantinople (canon 3) the primacy of honour next after the bishop of Rome, because Constantinople was New Rome (see no. 442, n. 7 *ad init.*), and the Fourth General Council in 451 at Chalcedon confirmed (canon 28) the Constantinopolitan canon (see no. 470, n. 70).

CI 11. 21. 1 (dated 421) uses (without reference to the patriarch of Constantinople) only the last part of this mandate, which it transforms thus: "The Constantinopolitan city should enjoy the prerogative not only of Italic right(s) [already granted in 365 or 370 or 373 by *CT* 14. 13. 1], but also of Old Rome itself."

Justinian reinforces this position (*CI* 1. 17. 1. 10; dated 530) by referring to the writing (*D* 1. 3. 32. pr.) of Julian (*c.* 100–*c.* 169), the reviser of the praetorian edict (*FIRA* 1. 335–89), who wrote that "all communities ought to follow the custom of Rome, which is the capital of the world, but itself not other communities". Taking this statement as his text, the emperor employs this exegesis: "But it must be understood that is meant not only Old Rome, but also our royal [city, viz. Constantinople], which, God being propitious, was founded with better auguries" (see nos. 62, n. 2 *ad init.* and 617, n. 10).

C. Dawson in *The Making of Europe* (New York, 1945), 112–13, acutely observes: "Thus the primacy of the new Patriarchate was explicitly based on its connection with the imperial government, as against the principle of apostolic tradition, on which the three great Sees of Rome, Antioch and Alexandria founded their authority. And its subsequent evolution was conditioned by the same principles. It developed as the state church and the instrument of imperial ecclesiastical policy. While Rome and Alexandria each possessed a distinct and continuous theological tradition, the teaching of Constantinople fluctuated with the vicissitudes of imperial politics. Its tradition was in fact diplomatic rather than theological, since in every dogmatic crisis the primary interest of the government was to preserve the religious unity of the Empire, and the Patriarchate became the instrument of its compromises."

The *Decretum Gelasianum* (ed. by F. von Dobschütz in *Texte und Untersuchungen zur Geschichte der altchristlichen Literatur* [Leipzig, 1912], 38. 4)—so-called because it is believed that this document dates from Pope St Gelasius I's pontificate (492–6), but perhaps renamable as the *Decretum Damasinum*, if it can be pre-dated to the pontificate (366–84) of Pope St Damasus I (so Jalland, 255–7)—makes much of the Petrine association with Rome (see no. 167, n. 2), Antioch (ibid.), and Alexandria (see no. 53, n. 2), the three patriarchates in existence ere the promotion of Constantinople (see no. 470, n. 70) and of Jerusalem (see no. 470, n. 44) to such position. The obvious claim of Rome, coupled with the Lord's promise to St Peter (see no. 442, n. 7), to outrank all other patriarchates may be considered to depend upon this document, which perhaps was proposed primarily to contest the claim of Constantinople, where the eastern sovereign of the Empire still sat, after his western colleague had removed his capital from Rome to other Italian cities—first Milan (303) and then Ravenna (404).

But whereas in 381 the Constantinopolitan canon 3 accepts Constantinople's inferiority to Rome, in 421 this mandate asserts Constantinople's equality with Rome.

Consult F. Dvornik, "Pope Gelasius and Emperor Anastasius I" in *Byzantinische Zeitschrift*, 44 (1951) 111–16.

8. Pitra (2. 462) gives a late Greek paraphrase for this document without superscription and subscription, as follows: "We order, all innovation ceasing, the old and ancient ecclesiastical canons, whichever until now have prevailed, to be observed even throughout all the province of Illyricum, so that, if any doubt grows, it is fitting that this should be brought for decision to an episcopal synod and to a holy court and to the divine law, not apart from the knowledge of the most reverend man and archpriest [ἀρχιερεύς, i.e. archbishop] of Constantinople, who enjoys the prerogative of Elder Rome."

9. Rome.

10. The word is *sacerdotium*, on which see no. 158, n. 1.

11. Since the closing words of the letter support this statement, it seems that the papal jurisdiction over the prefecture antedated Damasus' device to assert it at the time of the prefecture's transfer to the eastern emperor's care.

12. This retorts neatly to the first sentence of the preceding constitution.

13. Either those who resented the previous arrangement whereby the bishop of Thessalonica represented the pope and were jealous of this preference or those who upheld the claim of Constantinople, or those who favoured both.

14. That is, pagan princes before Constantine I's time.

15. Cf. *supra* n. 4; but *pater* (here) or *parens* (as e.g. in no. 65) often was used as a polite mode of address. See no. 426, n. 4.

16. See no. 218, n. 5.

17. The plural is strange, unless Theodosius means that the order which he has sent—but which, if sent, has not survived or was rescinded—is to be binding upon successive prefects.

376. MANDATE OF HONORIUS AND THEODOSIUS II ON CHRISTIAN RESTITUTION TO JEWS, 423

(CT 16. 8. 25)

By this constitution (renewed four months later, CT 16. 8. 27)[1] compensation for Jewish synagogues and votive offerings acquired by the Church is directed. According to Evagrius (HE 1. 13), however, St Simeon Stylites,[2] the celebrated pillar saint, persuaded Theodosius to rescind a law that the Antiochian synagogues seized by Christians should be restored to Jews.

The same Augusti to Asclepiodotus, praetorian prefect.[3]

It is pleasing that for the future absolutely no synagogues of the Jews either should be taken by force indiscriminately or should be consumed by flames and that if after the law[4] by a recent attempt any synagogues have been seized or have been claimed for the churches or at least have been consecrated to the venerable mysteries,[5] in return for these should be provided for them places in which they can build according to the measure,[6] obviously, of those lost.[7]

But if any votive offerings have been taken, they also should be returned to the said persons, if they not yet have been dedicated to the sacred mysteries;[5] but if venerable consecration does not allow the restoration, a price of the same amount should be given in return for these.

As for the rest: no synagogues should be built henceforth; old ones should continue in their form.[8]

Given on 15 February at Constantinople, Asclepiodotus and Marinian being consuls.

1. This statute, as reissued, is silent about Christianity and is not translated.
2. On him see no. 411, n. 3.
3. Of the East.
4. No. 244.
5. See no. 75, n. 42.
6. That is, commensurate with the ones usurped or burned.
7. The word (*tollere*) can mean here either "taken" or "destroyed"; in any event the synagogues were *lost* (whether by seizure or by fire) to the Jews.
8. That is, in their present condition.

377. MANDATE OF HONORIUS AND THEODOSIUS II ON ECCLESIASTICAL EXEMPTION FROM PUBLIC DUTIES, 423

(*CT* 15. 3. 6)

By this constitution the emperors impose upon churches a share in the performance of some public services which formerly have been considered menial.

Of this law Justinian repeats part in *CI* 11. 75. 4 and paraphrases part in *CI* 1. 2. 7.

The same Augusti to Asclepiodotus, praetorian prefect.[1]

May it be far from us that we should count among menial public services [2] the construction of a public road and the care [3] of bridges and paved roads dedicated [3] with the titles of great emperors.

Therefore no class of men by the merits of any rank or respect ought to be remiss in regard to constructions and repairs of roads and bridges.

We gladly assign the divine dwellings [4] and the venerable churches [5] to so laudable a list.

It shall be appropriate for this law to be published to all provinces' governors, that they may know that what [6] antiquity has decreed must be given to public roads must be furnished without the exception of either any reverence or rank.[7]

Given on 15 March at Constantinople, Asclepiodotus and Marinian being consuls.

1. Of the East.
2. On these see no. 186, n. 5.
3. In *CI* 11. 75. 4 Justinian pluralizes this word.
4. That is, the imperial houses.
5. Justinian omits *and the venerable churches* and ends his law in *CI* 11. 75. 4 at the end of this paragraph.
6. That is, what services on the part of the subjects.
7. In *CI* 1. 2. 7 Justinian paraphrases this law thus: "To the constructions of roads and bridges we gladly assign also the divine dwellings and the venerable churches to so laudable a list, because these are not counted among menial public services."

378. MANDATE OF HONORIUS AND THEODOSIUS II ON JEWISH CIRCUMCISION OF CHRISTIANS, 423
(*CT* 16. 8. 26)

This constitution (renewed two months later, *CT* 16. 8. 27)[1] not only re-endorses previous laws against Jews and pagans and heretics, but also forbids Christians to molest Jews and to seize or to burn synagogues and punishes Jews who assist or commit circumcision on Christians.

Justinian quotes part of the last sentence (*CI* 1. 9. 16).

The same Augusti to Asclepiodotus, praetorian prefect.[2]

Known and published to all are our and our ancestors' ordinances, by which we have restrained abominable pagans', Jews', and also heretics' spirit and audacity.[3]

Yet, having embraced willingly the occasion of repeating the law,[4] we wish the Jews to know that in reply to their wretched requests we have ordained nought other than that those persons who inconsiderately do very many things under the pretext of venerable Christianity should forbear from injury to and persecution of them and that now and hereafter none should seize and none should burn their synagogues.

Yet the Jews themselves shall be condemned by proscription of goods and by perpetual exile, if it shall have been established that they have circumcised a man of our faith or have delivered one to be circumcised.[5]

And the rest.

Given on 9 April at Constantinople, Asclepiodotus and Marinian being consuls.

1. See no. 376, n. 1.
2. Of the East.
3. Perhaps a hendiadys is meant: "spirited audacity" or "audacious spirit".
4. No. 244.
5. Justinian, omitting *yet* and *themselves*, keeps only this sentence.

379. MANDATE OF HONORIUS AND THEODOSIUS II ON JEWISH OWNERSHIP OF CHRISTIAN SLAVES, 423

(CT 16. 9. 5)

This law prohibits Jews from purchasing Christian slaves and thus reverses a previous and conditional permission (no. 344).

The same Augusti to Asclepiodotus, praetorian prefect.[1]
After other matters.
None of the Jews should dare to buy Christian slaves. For we consider it execrable for very religious slaves to be defiled by very impious purchasers' ownership.
But if anyone shall have done this, he shall be subject to statutory punishment without all delay.
And the rest.
Given on 9 April at Constantinople, Asclepiodotus and Marinian being consuls.

1. Of the East.

380. MANDATE OF HONORIUS AND THEODOSIUS II ON CONFIRMATION OF LAWS ON HERETICS, 423

(CT 16. 5. 59)

This law confirms earlier laws' withdrawal of privileges against all heretics, including those named in it.

The same Augusti to Asclepiodotus, praetorian prefect.[1]
After other matters.
Manichaeans and Phrygians, whom they call Pepyzites or Priscillians or by another more secret name, likewise Arians and Macedonians and Eunomians, Novatians and Sabbatians, and all other heretics should know that also by this constitution are denied to them all things which the authority of general sanctions has forbidden to them—those persons who shall have tried to contravene the interdicts of the general constitutions being worthy of punishment.
Given on 9 April at Constantinople, Asclepiodotus and Marinian being consuls.

1. Of the East.

381. MANDATE OF HONORIUS AND THEODOSIUS II ON ENFORCEMENT OF LAWS ON HERETICS, 423
(CT 16. 5. 60)

By this law Theodosius I's and Arcadius' legislation against heretics is signalized by Theodosius II for enforcement.

The same Augusti to Asclepiodotus, praetorian prefect.[1]
Concerning all heretics, whose error and name we execrate, that is, concerning Eunomians, Arians, Macedonians, and all others, whose sects it is disgusting to insert in a most pious sanction (to all of whom the names are different but the perfidy is the same), we order that there must be maintained those enactments [2] which our Clemency's deified [3] grandfather [4] and father [5] have made—all persons knowing that if they shall have continued in the said madness they shall be subject to the threatened punishment.

And the rest.[6]

Given on 8 June at Constantinople,[7] Asclepiodotus and Marinian being consuls.

1. Of the East.
2. Among such statutes are nos. 166, 167, 173, 176, 179, 182, 185, 191, 192, 194–6, 205, 213, 215, 217–19, 222, 232, 239, 245, 248, 249, 251, 254, 256, 258, 260, 264, 268, 275, 277, 289–94, 296, 298, 299.
3. See no. 127, n. 7.
4. Theodosius I.
5. Arcadius.
6. This statute may be the first part of no. 382.
7. Since this city was Theodosius II's seat, it was this emperor who issued this law and therefore his grandfather and his father (nn. 4 and 5 *supra*) are meant.

382. MANDATE OF HONORIUS AND THEODOSIUS II ON PENALTIES FOR HERETICS AND FOR CHRISTIAN PLUNDERERS OF NON-CHRISTIANS, 423

(*CT* 16. 10. 24)

This document (partly reproduced in *CI* 1. 11. 6) prescribes penalties for Christians who do not celebrate Easter at the orthodox time and who participate in attacks on Jews and on pagans when these persons live peaceably and attempt nothing disorderly or illicitly. The latter injunction shows that, contrary to later practice of ecclesiastical persecution in Europe, only acts are prohibited and that Jewish or pagan opinion as such is tolerated.[1]

The same Augusti to Asclepiodotus, praetorian prefect.[2]
After other matters.[3]

Manichaeans and those whom they call Pepyzites and also those who are worse than all heretics in this one opinion, that they dissent from all about the venerable day of Easter, if they persist in the said madness, we punish with the same penalty: confiscation of goods and exile.

But to [4] Christians, who either really are or are said to be, we commend specially this: that they, having abused the authority of religion, should not dare to lay hands on Jews and pagans, who are living quietly and are attempting nothing disorderly and contrary to the laws. For if they shall have been violent against quiet persons and shall have ravished their goods, they should be compelled to restore not only those goods which they shall have snatched, but, when summoned to court, three or four times [5] the value of what they shall have seized.

Also governors of provinces and their office staffs and the provincials [6] should know that if they shall have permitted this to be done,[7] they, who shall have done this,[8] must be punished.

Given on 8 June at Constantinople, Asclepiodotus and Marinian being consuls.

1. Probably the only exceptions to this attitude among the laws affecting the Church apart from intolerance of heretical doctrines (on which see—for book-burning—nos. 66, 268, 422, 459) were Honorius' order of 409 to burn astrologers' books (no. 313) and Theodosius II's ordinances of 448-50 (nos. 445 and 459) to burn Porphyry's books (perhaps anticipated by Constantine I's reference c. 333 to these [no. 66, n. 3]), since apparently such anti-Christian treatises aroused the imperial animus.

Although unofficial book-burning of non-Christian works by Christians ascended into the apostolic age (Acts 19. 19), yet Augustus, the first Roman emperor, was the earliest emperor to order offensive books to be fed to the flames. Acting apparently on the *Lex Iulia de maiestate* (Tacitus, *Ann.* 1. 72. 3-4) and adopting the Sullan adaptation of *maiestas* (Cicero, *Ad Fam.* 3. 11. 2; cf. also *De Inv.* 2. 17. 53), but omitting the harsh penalty for libel proposed in 449 B.C. by the Twelve Tables (*FIRA* 1. 52; *TT* 8. 1), according to Suetonius (*Aug.* 55), Augustus had for his first victim Titus Labienus, a celebrated orator, who seized every opportunity to attack Augustus. In 7 the emperor had his writings without exception burned (Seneca Rhetor, *Controv.* 10. pr. 5). The last recorded bonfire of books in the reign was in 12, when aediles in the capital and magistrates in the peninsula and in the provinces were charged with superintending the cremation of vituperative treatises (Dio Cassius, *Hist. Rom.* 56. 27. 1).

So far as divine positive law is concerned, Christian emperors in commanding consignment of unorthodox writings to bonfires doubtless depended on the divine caution against "false prophets" (Matt. 7. 15; cf. Matt. 24. 11, 24; Mark 13. 22) and on the apostolic admonitions against heretical doctrine (e.g. Gal. 1. 7-9, Col. 2. 8; cf. 1 Cor. 5. 11, 2 Thess. 3. 6, Acts 20. 28-31, 1 Tim. 6. 20, 2 Tim. 2. 15-17, Titus 1. 9, Jude 3; add also *CA* 1. 6, where the faithful are forbidden to read heathen literature). See also J. M. Pernicone, *The Ecclesiastical Prohibition of Books* (Washington, 1932), 26-31, for a review of evidence about book-banning in this sylloge's period. Add now C. A. Forbes, "Books for the Burning" in *TPAPA* 67 (1936) 114-25; F. H. Cramer, "Bookburning and Censorship in Ancient Rome" in *Journal of the History of Ideas*, 6 (1945) 157-96; A. S. Pease, "Notes on Book-Burning" in M. H. Shepherd, Jr., and S. E. Johnson, eds., *Munera Studiosa* (Cambridge, Mass., 1946), 145-60.

2. Of the East.

3. This statute may be the conclusion of no. 381.

4. Hence to the end is in *CI* 1. 11. 6.

5. *CI* reads "but, when convicted, twice". While Justinian's penalty is quite precise, the alternative assessment allowed by Theodosius leaves to the judge leeway between triple and quadruple fines.

6. *CI* reads "chief magistrates" (*principales*) for provincials (*provinciales*).

7. *CI* has "if they themselves should not avenge such acts, but should have permitted this to be done by the common people".

8. That is, not the actual rapinists, but the lax officials.

383. MANDATE OF HONORIUS AND THEODOSIUS II ON HERETICS IN GOVERNMENTAL SERVICE, 423

(*CT* 16. 5. 61)

By this directive Theodosius clarifies the law of 415 (no. 343), which forbids any Eunomian to belong to the imperial service or to be associated with provincial administration.

The same Augusti to Asclepiodotus, praetorian prefect.[1]

By removing all ambiguities of dubious interpretation by this decision, we command it to be published that the law [2] which is known to have been promulgated about Eunomians and all others of execrable religions forbidden to be in governmental service [3] and about the rites of their professions pertains not at all to those who are cohortalines.[4] For they are obligated to those apparitorships in which veterans, after their terms of military service [5] have been completed, are compelled to sustain the duty of commissary.[6]

Given on 8 August at Eudoxiopolis, Asclepiodotus and Marinian being consuls.

1. Of the East.
2. No. 343.
3. See no. 186, n. 4.
4. See no. 320, n. 5.
5. Here *militia* (the same word as at n. 3 *supra*) apparently is used in its original meaning of military service, which is reinforced by the reference to the commissariat.
6. So ordained by *CT* 8. 4. 16 (dated 389). See nos. 110, n. 5, and 502, n. 3.

384. RESCRIPT OF THEODOSIUS II ON ECCLESIASTICAL EXEMPTION FROM CAPITATION, 424

(*CT* 11. 1. 33)

Evidently in reply to a request for decision forwarded by the praetorian prefect of Illyricum, to whom a delegation of provincials from Macedonia and from Achaea had come for relief from taxation, the emperor grants partial relief in the earlier part of his rescript and then especially exempts the Church in Thessalonica from payment of poll-taxes on its members.

The section granting this exemption, repeated by Justinian (*CI* 1. 2. 8, 10. 16. 12), is translated.

Emperor Theodosius Augustus to Isidore, praetorian prefect of Illyricum.
. . . The sacrosanct Church of the Thessalonican city shall be excepted, to such an extent, however, that it[1] should know that by my Divinity's favour only the amount of its own capitation tax[2] must be alleviated and that the State must not be harmed by the burden of extraneous taxes through the abuse of the ecclesiastical name.[3]

Given on 10 October at Constantinople, the most distinguished Victor being consul.

1. *CI* 1. 2. 8 omits *shall . . . it*.
2. See no. 67, n. 37.
3. This is a very compressed way of stating that the imperial revenues must not be impaired by persons who do not enjoy official standing in the local church and who try to claim immunity from the poll-tax on the ground that they are connected officially with it.

385. MANDATE OF THEODOSIUS II AND VALENTINIAN III ON PROHIBITION OF AMUSEMENTS ON CERTAIN HOLY DAYS, 425

(*CT* 15. 5. 5)

This law is another enactment against public spectacles on certain religious festivals. It adds Pentecost to the list of holy days announced in no. 220.

The same Augustus and Valentinian Caesar[1] to Asclepiodotus, praetorian prefect.[2]
On the Lord's day,[3] which is the first day of the whole week, and on Christ's natal day[4] and day of Epiphany,[5] also on the days Easter and of Pentecost: (inasmuch as the garments, expressing the light of the celestial baptism, attest the new light of holy baptism),[7] and also at what time the commemoration of the apostolic Passion, the teacher of all Christianity, is celebrated rightly by all persons,[8] since all entertainment of theatres and of circuses has been denied throughout all cities to the peoples thereof, the minds of faithful Christians[9] should be occupied wholly with God's worship.

If any persons even now are engaged either by the madness of Jewish impiety or by the error and by the insanity of obtuse paganism, they should know that there is one time for prayers and another for pleasures.¹⁰

And lest anyone should think that he is constrained, as if by some greater necessity of duty to the emperor, to our Divinity's honour and that, unless by neglect of the divine religion he should give attention to the spectacles, perhaps our Serenity's enmity would be incurred by him, if he shall have shown less devotion toward us than he was wont: none should doubt that then particularly respect is rendered to our Gentleness by human kind, when the whole world's obedience is paid to Almighty God's virtues and merits.

Given on 1 February at Constantinople, Theodosius Augustus for the eleventh time and Valentinian Caesar ¹ for the first time being consuls.

1. See no. 28, n. 7.
2. Of the East.
3. See no. 34, n. 5.
4. See no. 220, nn. 6 and 10.
5. See no. 220, nn. 6 and 11.
6. The Latin has *quinquagesima* (fiftieth), which may mean either Quinquagesima (the Sunday before Lent) or Pentecost (the seventh Sunday after Easter), for each is fifty days before or after Easter. However, because the order places the word after that for Easter and the succeeding reference to the white vestments of the newly baptized, who were received into the Church on the vigil of Pentecost (or Whitsunday, so called from such clothing), points to the termination of Eastertide, it seems that Pentecost, which is of equal rank with Easter (whereas Quinquagesima is not), is meant.
7. On the garments cf. *supra* n. 6.
8. Justinian seems to have copied parts of this sentence so far in *CI* 3. 12. 6.
9. Literally "of the Christians and of the faithful": taken as a hendiadys.
10. Perhaps a reminiscence of Eccles. 3. 1–8.

386. MANDATE OF THEODOSIUS II AND VALENTINIAN III ON RESTRAINT OF REVERENCE TO IMPERIAL IMAGES, 425

(*CT* 15. 4. 1)

The emperors forbid that their statues or images should be honoured with excessive adoration, which they desire to be paid only to God.

Justinian preserves only the first sentence of this law (*CI* 1. 24. 2).

Emperor Theodosius Augustus and Valentinian Caesar [1] to Aetius, praetorian prefect.[2]

If ever our statues or images are erected either on festal days, as is customary, or on ordinary days, the governor should be present without a vainglorious exaltation of adulation, that he may show that his presence has been added as a distinction to the day or to the place and to our Memory.

Our likenesses, when exhibited at games, also should demonstrate that our Divinity and praises flourish only in the hearts and in the secret places of the minds of the persons assembling; but worship exceeding men's dignity should be reserved for the Supernal Divinity.[3]

Given on 5 May, Theodosius Augustus for the eleventh time and Valentinian Caesar [1] being consuls.

1. See no. 28, n. 7.
2. Of the East.
3. Suetonius says (*Tib.* 26. 1) that Emperor Tiberius forbade his statues and images to be placed without his permission and he permitted this only on the condition that they should be placed not among the gods' likenesses, but among the temples' adornments. Evidently Tiberius took a dim view of emperor-worship, whereon see no. 127, n. 7.

387. MANDATE OF THEODOSIUS II AND VALENTINIAN III ON CONFIRMATION OF EPISCOPAL JURISDICTION, ON HERESY, AND ON CHRISTIAN SLAVES, 425

(CS 6)

This constitution, which appears in abbreviated form in *CT* 16. 2. 47 and 16. 5. 64 and possibly 16. 5. 62, where are indications that these laws are

387. JURISDICTION AND HERESY, 425

excerpts of a longer law, considers several subjects, all of which, it seems, concern conditions in Gaul. It restores to ecclesiastical cases episcopal jurisdiction, which evidently the usurper John [1] cancelled, it provides penalties for various heretics and schismatics, it decrees disabilities for Jews and pagans, who also are forbidden to have Christian slaves or servants.

Emperors Theodosius Augustus and Valentinian Caesar [2] to the illustrious Amatius, praetorian prefect of the Gauls.[3]

The privileges of all churches or of clergymen,[4] which the tyrant [1] had begrudged to our age, we restore with ready devotion: namely, that whatever each and every bishop has obtained from the deified [5] emperors should be preserved as established through continual eternity [6] and that no one's presumption should dare to meddle in a matter wherein we ourselves profess that it has been rather fully warranted by us.

Also clergymen who the ill-starred usurper [1] had proclaimed ought to be brought indiscriminately before secular judges, we reserve for episcopal hearing [7]—with those privileges remaining which antiquity has sanctioned in their cases. For it is not right that ministers of divine service should be subjected to judgement of temporal powers.[8]

Accordingly your illustrious Authority shall command that even under the penalty of sacrilege should be observed those rules which, destined to endure for all time, we have ordered to be sent to the notice of the provinces, especially comprehending this in your illustrious commands: that in all matters concerning ecclesiastical privileges the old emperors' statutes should be preserved.

Moreover we command that the various bishops following the nefarious error of the Pelagian and the Caelestian teaching should be assembled by Patroclus,[9] bishop of the sacrosanct law,[10] and that they, because we trust that they can be corrected, unless within twenty days from the time of assembly—within which we have granted the opportunity of deliberating—they shall have corrected their errors and shall have returned themselves to the Catholic faith, should be expelled from the Gallic districts and that in their place should be substituted a more faithful episcopate, in order that the stain of the present error may be wiped from the people's souls and the blessing of a future and more upright teaching may be instituted.

Indeed, because it is not seemly for religious people to be depraved by any superstitions, we [11] command that Manichaeans and all [12] heretics or schismatics or astrologers [13] and every sect hostile to Catholics ought to be barred from the very sight of the various cities, in order that these may not be befouled by the contagion of even [12] the presence of criminals.[14]

Also to Jews or to pagans we deny the liberty of pleading cases or of serving the government [15] and we do not wish that persons of the Christian law [10] should be in service to them, lest by the occasion of mastership they may change the sect of the venerable religion.[16]

Therefore we order all persons of ill-starred error to be banished, unless an early correction shall have come to their aid.

Given on 9 July [17] at Aquileia, our Lord Theodosius Augustus for the eleventh time and Valentinian Caesar [2] being consuls.

1. For eighteen months in 423-4 a certain John, who had been a bureaucratic clerk at Ravenna, ruled the government in the West after the death of Honorius, until he was deposed by Theodosius II's generals, who led an expeditionary force from the East.

2. See no. 28, n. 7.

3. In *CT* 16. 2. 47 and 16. 5. 64 this law is addressed to Bassus, count of the private estates. See also no. 203, n. 4.

4. *CT* 16. 2. 47 omits this alternative.

5. See no. 127, n. 7.

6. *CT* 16. 2. 47 reads for this clause "namely, that whatever has been ordained by the deified emperors or what each and every bishop has obtained for ecclesiastical purposes should be preserved under penalty for sacrilege as established through continual eternity" and omits the rest of the sentence.

7. After *hearing CT* 16. 2. 47 omits the rest of the sentence.

8. *CT* 16. 2. 47 ends here.

9. Patroclus (*al.* Patrocles), archbishop of Arles, was patronized both by Constantius III, brother-in-law of Honorius, and by Pope St Zosimus. The latter elevated the see of Arles into an archbishopric and gave Patroclus metropolitan authority over four provinces in southern Gaul and also made him papal vicar of all Gaul.

10. Religion.

11. *CT* 16. 5. 64 starts here.

12. *CT* 16. 5. 64 omits this word.

13. Literally "mathematicians", but in post-Augustan Latin *mathematicus* (transliterated from μαθηματικός) is a not uncommon description of an astrologer, who, of course, dabbles in arithmetic.

14. *CT* 16. 5. 64 ends here.

15. See no. 186, n. 4.

16. That is, not to cause a change in Christian doctrine, but to exchange Christianity for Judaism or paganism and thus to cease to be Christians.

17. *CT* 16. 2. 47 has 8 October, *CT* 16. 5. 62 has 17 July, *CT* 16. 5. 64 has 6 August. Of these three dates the editors believe the last to be correct.

388. MANDATE OF THEODOSIUS II AND VALENTINIAN III ON EXPULSION OF HERETICS FROM ROME, 425

(CT 16. 5. 62)

This constitution, which may be the original draft of part of no. 387, concerns only the city of Rome, whereas the other law covers a wider area. It orders the departure of various heretics and other undesirable persons from Rome, unless they shall return within twenty days to communion with the pope.

Emperor Theodosius Augustus and Valentinian Caesar [1] to Faustus, urban prefect.[2]

We command Manichaeans, heretics, schismatics, or astrologers and every sect hostile to Catholics to be banned from the very sight of the city of Rome, that it may not be befouled by the contagion of the presence of criminals.

Moreover commonition must be administered particularly concerning these persons, who by depraved persuasions withdraw themselves from the venerable pope's [3] communion and by whose schism [4] the rest of the populace also is infected.

By previous arrangement we have granted to these persons a truce of twenty days, and unless within these they shall have returned to the unity of communion, they, when expelled as far as the hundredth milestone, should be tormented by the solitude which they select.

Given on 17 July [5] at Aquileia, Theodosius Augustus for the eleventh time and Valentinian Caesar [1] being consuls.

1. See no. 28, n. 7.
2. Of Rome.
3. St Celestine I.
4. Probably the Novatian.
5. An alternative date is 6 August.

389. MANDATE OF THEODOSIUS II AND VALENTINIAN III ON PUNISHMENT OF HERESY, PERFIDY, SCHISM, PAGAN SUPERSTITION, AND RELIGIOUS ERROR, 425

(CT 16. 5. 63)

Confiscation of property is set by this law as the penalty for persons convicted of heresy, perfidy, schism, pagan superstition, error hostile to the Catholic faith.

The same Augusti to George, proconsul of Africa.

We censure all heresies and all perfidies, all schisms and pagans' superstitions, all errors inimical to Catholic law.[1]

But if . . . any persons,[2] let this our Clemency's established punishment also attend them and let them know that they must be punished by proscription as sacrilegious superstition's authors and guilty participants, in order that from perfidy's error, if they cannot be retracted by reason, at least they should be recalled by terror and that—with all access of petitions denied forever—they should be punished with the severity due to their crimes.

And the rest.

Given on 4 August[3] at Aquileia, our Lord Theodosius Augustus for the eleventh time and Valentinian Caesar[4] being consuls.

1. Religion.
2. There is an editorial hiatus here.
3. An alternative date is 6 July.
4. See no. 28, n. 7.

390. MANDATE OF THEODOSIUS II AND VALENTINIAN III ON CONFIRMATION OF ECCLESIASTICAL PRIVILEGES, 425

(CT 16. 2. 46)

This short extract of an apparently larger law confirms existing privileges for the Church and for the clergy.

Emperors Theodosius Augustus and Valentinian Caesar[1] to George, proconsul of Africa.

After other matters.

Privileges of previous laws conferred on the Church or on clerics should be preserved.

And the rest.

Given on 6 July [2] at Aquileia, our Lord Theodosius Augustus for the eleventh time and Valentinian Caesar [1] being consuls.

1. See no. 28, n. 7.
2. 4 August is an alternative date.

391. MANDATE OF THEODOSIUS II AND VALENTINIAN III ON APOSTATE CHRISTIANS' WILLS, 426
(CT 16. 7. 7)

The statute of limitations for starting a lawsuit to void an apostate Christian's will (no. 190) is abolished by this ordinance, which Justinian also accepts (CI 1. 7. 4).

Emperors Theodosius and Valentinian Augusti to Bassus, praetorian prefect.[1]

After other matters.

The voice of continuous accusation shall assail the sacrilegious name of each and every apostate and the investigation of a crime of this character should not be prevented by being limited by any periods of time.[2]

And although previous interdicts [3] against these persons suffice, nevertheless we repeat also this: that after they shall have deviated from the faith, they should have no power of making a will or of giving any gift, but that they should not be allowed to cause a fraud to the law by a fictitious sale [4] and that all the property from an intestate person should be conferred upon kinsfolk, preferably upon persons following Christianity.

Moreover we wish the right of action against sacrileges of this sort to be perpetuated to such an extent, that to all persons coming into an inheritance from an intestate person we do not deny the unrestricted voice of suitable accusation even after a sinner's death. Nor shall we permit this obstruction, if it should be said that no charge was preferred in litigation while the profane person was living.

But lest the interpretation of this crime should range too widely through indefinite uncertainty, by this present response [5] we pursue those persons who, when they have assumed the name of Christianity, either have made sacrifices or have ordered these to be made. And their perfidy, when proved, even after death must be punished in this way: that after their gifts and wills have been rescinded, those on whom statutory succession confers an estate may obtain the inheritance of such persons.

Given on 7 April at Ravenna, Theodosius Augustus for the twelfth time and Valentinian Augustus for the second time being consuls.

1. Of Italy.
2. See no. 65, n. 6.
3. Such as nos. 175, 189, 190, 230, 231, 259.
4. Literally "by [false] appearance of selling" (*venditionis specie*). On the Roman law of sale consult J. B. Moyle, *The Contract of Sale in the Civil Law* (Oxford, 1892).
5. See no. 218, n. 5.

392. MANDATE OF THEODOSIUS II AND VALENTINIAN III ON TESTAMENTARY BENEFITS FOR CHRISTIAN CONVERTS, 426

(*CT* 16. 8. 28)

The emperors extend various testamentary privileges for Jews and Samaritans who have been converted to Christianity.

Emperors Theodosius and Valentinian Augusti to Bassus, praetorian prefect.[1]

If a Jew's or a Samaritan's son or daughter or grandchild—one or more—with better counsel shall have departed from his own superstition's darkness to the Christian religion's light, it should not be permitted for their parents—that is, father or mother, grandfather or grandmother—to disinherit them or to pass by them silently in a will or to leave to them anything less than they could acquire, if they were called by intestacy to the inheritance.[2]

But if it perchance shall have happened thus, we order that, when the will has been rescinded, the person should succeed by intestacy—liberations which shall have been given in the said will, if they are within the legitimate number,[3] holding their validity.

392. TESTAMENTARY BENEFITS FOR CONVERTS, 426

If it shall have been proved clearly that such children or grandchildren have committed any very great crime against their mother or father or grandfather or grandmother—the legitimate punishment remaining against them, if meanwhile an accusation shall have proceeded legally—yet under such a charge, for which credible and clear proofs shall be supplied, the parents should leave to them only the Falcidian portion of the due succession,[4] that they may appear to have merited at least this in honour of the selected religion—punishment for the crimes remaining (as we have said), if these shall have been proved.

And the rest.

Given on 8 April at Ravenna, Theodosius Augustus for the twelfth time and Valentinian Augustus for the second time being consuls.

1. Of Italy.
2. This phrase the translator supplies to complete the sense.
3. Although in the Republic no limitation upon the number of slaves to be freed at any time is known, early in the Empire (2 B.C.) the *Lex Fufia et Caninia* regulated the testamentary liberation of slaves in an effort to end reckless manumission, by which, it seems, testators desired to glorify themselves. Justinian annulled (528) the law (*CI* 7. 3).

From Gaius, who expressly says that this statute had no applicability to manumission other than by will, we learn its provisions (*GI* 1. 42–6): a testator having only one or two slaves can manumit either or both; if he has from three to ten, he can free only one-half; if he has from eleven to thirty, he can liberate only one-third; if he has 31 to 100, he can release only one-fourth; if he has 101 to 500, he can enfranchise only one-fifth; in no case more than 100 can be given their freedom; if a testator manumitted more than the permitted number, none of such slaves could be freed.

4. The Falcidian fourth (*quarta Falcidia*), as the jurists call it, was established by the *Lex Falcidia* (40 B.C.) to provide that in every case the heir to an estate should have one-fourth of the clear proceeds of the estate (*GI* 2. 227). For the terms of the law's principal clause see *D* 35. 2. 1. pr.

The Falcidian law was the third and last attempt in the Republic to induce an heir to accept an inheritance (*II* 2. 22. pr.), since by the Twelve Tables a testator could bequeath, after his debts had been paid, the rest of his estate to legatees (*GI* 2. 224; *FIRA* 1. 37; *TT* 5. 3). Consequently an heir, who stood to inherit only the name of heir in the case of a testator who had willed his entire property in legacies and manumissions, often refused to enter and thus nullified the testament. Partial remedies, effected by the *Lex Furia* (c. 183 B.C.) and by the *Lex Voconia* (169 B.C.) and explained by Gaius (*GI* 2. 225–6), resulted in evasion and it remained for the *Lex Falcidia* to furnish the final relief until Justinian's reforms in the conception of heirship, whereby the heir became the executor—retaining, however, the Falcidian fourth, unless the testator had forbidden it expressly.

393. MANDATE OF THEODOSIUS II AND VALENTINIAN III ON THE SIGN OF THE CROSS, 427 or 447

(*CI* 1. 8. 1)

The emperors forbid anyone (probably without authorization) to carve or to paint the sign of the Cross [1] on specified objects and order punishment for such violation.

Emperors Theodosius and Valentinian Augusti to Eudoxius, praetorian prefect.[2]

Since to us is diligent care that by all means the religion of the Supernal Divinity should be protected, to none it is permitted [3] to carve or to paint the Saviour Christ's sign either on the ground or on a flint-stone or on marbles placed on the ground,[4] but whatever is found should be removed.[3]

If anyone shall have attempted the contrary to our statutes, we specially order him to be punished [5] with a most grievous penalty.[6]

Given on 21 May, Hierius and Ardaburius being consuls.[7]

1. As early as late in the second century Christians commonly made the sign of the Cross upon their foreheads; for its extensive employment see the oft-cited passage in Tertullian, *De Cor.* 3 *ad fin.* St Cyril of Alexandria, who was alive when this law was issued, if its earlier date is correct, asserts in his treatise *Contra Iulianum,* 6 *post med.,* that Emperor Julian the Apostate chided the Christians for adoring the wood of the Cross (see no. 303, n. 3 *ad fin.*), for signing the Cross on their foreheads, and for carving the Cross on the entrances to their houses. The patriarch produced this work in ten books between 429 and 441 and reproduced in it—only to refute—passages from the emperor's diatribe *Adversus Galilaeos,* written in 363. Julian's charge and Cyril's counter-charge on this point are in *PG* 76. 796–801. (Scholars have reconstructed the emperor's anti-Christian attack from the archbishop's quotations and have assigned to this animadversion the *locus* of 194C.)

2. Of the East.

3. This verb is an infinitive in Latin and depends upon an understood verb of ordering.

4. In the plural (as here) *marmor* often means "pavements".

5. This is the sense, but the Latin is ungrammatical.

6. Pitra prints (2. 638) a late Greek paraphrase: "None should carve or should draw the Cross on the ground or on a millstone or on marble placed on the ground, but one should remove it, knowing that he who transgresses this submits to a most grievous penalty."

7. Since some manuscripts and editions omit, perhaps correctly, the first consul's name, editors conjecture a date twenty years later, when the second consul was in office.

394. MANDATE OF THEODOSIUS II AND VALENTINIAN III ON EPISCOPAL INTEREST IN FREEDOM OF PROSTITUTES, 428

(*CT* 15. 8. 2)

By this constitution, which Justinian repeats (*CI* 1. 4. 12 and 11. 41. 6), the emperors free daughters and female slaves from fathers' and masters' legal control, when the latter have compelled the former to a life of prostitution, and ordain commitment to the mines as punishment for such procurers. Bishops are authorized to intercede for such women.

Emperors Theodosius and Valentinian Augusti to Florentius, praetorian prefect.[1]

We permit fathers and masters, who as procurers impose upon daughters or on female slaves the necessity of sinning, neither to enjoy the right of control nor to rejoice in freedom from so great a crime.[2] Therefore it is our pleasure that these men should be removed by such indignation, lest they should have power to enjoy the right of power over them or what can be acquired thus from them.

But let it be permitted to female slaves and to daughters, if they wish, or to persons whom a rather lowly lot has condemned, hired out because of poverty, when the assistance of bishops and of governors [3] and of defenders [4] has been implored, to be released from all necessity of miseries;[5] so that, if the procurers shall have believed that they ought to insist or should inflict upon these unwilling women the necessity of sinning, they not only should lose that power which they had had over them, but also, when proscribed, should be delivered to the punishment of assignment in exile to the public mines, which is a punishment less than if anyone should be forced at a procurer's command to endure the sordidness of coition which she does not wish.

Given on 21 April, Felix and Taurus being consuls.

1. Of the East.
2. The full thought requires "from punishment" or "from consequences" to be inserted after *freedom*.
3. Or perhaps "judges"; the word is *iudices*.

4. The full phrase probably is "defenders of municipalities", the officials whose duty was to protect the people's interests from upper-class or official encroachment.

5. Justinian's second copy of the law repeats the entire Theodosian version, but his first copy is abbreviated and ends here: "If procurers, who are fathers or masters, shall have imposed on daughters or on female slaves the necessity of sinning, it should be permitted to daughters or to female slaves, when the assistance of bishops has been implored, to be released from all necessity of miseries."

But according to the Roman conception of injuries, on which see no. 334, n. 25, and which seemed wide enough to embrace enforced prostitution, no person in another's power could institute an action of injuries against a parent, even if the injury was atrocious (*D* 47. 10. 3). So it seems that an exception to this doctrine is allowed.

395. MANDATE OF THEODOSIUS II AND VALENTINIAN III ON PENALTIES AND DISABILITIES FOR HERETICS AND SCHISMATICS, 428
(*CT* 16. 5. 65)

This lengthy constitution (divided by *CI* between 1. 5. 5 and 1. 6. 3) ordains sundry penalties as well as civil disabilities for membership in most of the heretical and the schismatical sects then prominent.

Emperors Theodosius and Valentinian Augusti to Florentius, praetorian prefect.[1]

Heretics' insanity ought to be repressed in such a way that before all things they cannot doubt that the churches which, taken from the orthodox, they hold anywhere immediately must be surrendered to the Catholic Church, because it cannot be tolerated that whoever ought not to have had their own churches should detain still the churches once possessed or founded by the orthodox and seized by their own temerity.

Next,[2] that if they should join to themselves other clergymen or priests[3] (as they themselves consider them), a fine of ten pounds of gold for each and every such person, exacted from him who has appointed or who has let himself be appointed such, or, if they should pretend poverty, from the common corporation of clergymen of the said superstition or even from their funds,[4] should be paid to our treasury.[5]

395. PENALTIES FOR HERETICS AND SCHISMATICS, 428

After this, since not all must be punished with the same severity, to Arians,[6] indeed, Macedonians, and Apollinarians, whose villainy is this, that deceived by noxious meditation they believe falsehoods about the fount of truth,[7] it should not be permitted to have a church within any municipality; moreover from Novatians and Sabbatians should be withdrawn the privilege of all innovation,[8] if peradventure they shall have attempted any; but Eunomians, Valentinians, Montanists, or Priscillians, Phrygians, Marcionites, Borborians, Messalians, Euchitans or Enthusiasts, Donatists, Audians, Hydroparastatans, Tascodrogitans, Photinians, Paulianists, Marcellians, and Manichaeans, who have attained to the lowest villainy of crimes, nowhere on Roman soil should have the right of assembly and of prayer [9]—the Manichaeans also being deserving of expulsion from municipalities,[10] since to all [11] these must be left no place wherein even on the very elements may be made an injury.

To these persons may be allowed absolutely no governmental service [12] save cohortaline [13] in the provinces and military, with no right of making reciprocal donations and a testament or a last will at all conceded [14] and with all laws, which formerly have been issued and have been promulgated at different times against these persons and all others who resist our faith ever being valid by vigorous [15] observance — whether concerning donations made to heretics' churches [16] or concerning property left in whatsoever way in accordance with a last will or concerning private buildings in which they shall have met with the owner permitting it or conniving at it, and which must be claimed by us for the venerable Catholic Church, or concerning a manager, who shall have allowed it, with the owner not knowing it, and who shall submit to a fine of ten pounds of gold or exile, if he is free-born, but shall go to a mine after lashes, if he is of servile status;[17] so that they may be in condition neither to assemble in a public place nor to build churches [18] for themselves nor to plan anything for circumvention of the laws, for they must be forbidden by all civil and military aid and also by that of senates [19] and defenders [19] and governors under menace of twenty pounds of gold.[20]

Also continuing in their own firmness are all those laws which have been promulgated concerning governmental service [21] and [22] the right of donation and the making of a will, either utterly denied or barely conceded to certain persons,[22] and various punishments regarding different heretics, so that not even a special favour gained against the laws can avail.

To none of the heretics must be given permission of bringing again to their own baptism either free-born persons or their own slaves, who have been initiated into the mysteries [23] of the orthodox, or of forbidding those persons, whom, not yet joined to their own superstition, they shall have purchased or shall have possessed in whatsoever way, to follow the Catholic Church's religion. And if any person shall have done this or, when he is free-born,[24] shall have permitted it to be done to him or shall not have reported the deed, he shall be condemned by exile and by a fine of ten pounds of gold and to each [25] shall be denied permission of making a will and a donation.

And we determine that all these regulations should be maintained in such a way that to none of the governors it may be permitted to command for a crime reported to him a minor or no punishment, unless he himself wishes to suffer that which he shall have conceded to others by his dissimulation.[26]

Given on 30 May at Constantinople, Felix and Taurus being consuls.

1. Of the East.
2. There is no principal verb to govern the following consecutive clause.
3. The word is *sacerdos*, often meaning bishop and perhaps so here. See no. 16, n. 4.
4. The word is *donarium*, which can mean either the place in a religious edifice where offerings are kept or the offering itself.
5. The word is *aerarium*, not *fiscus*. In the Empire usually the former signifies the public treasury, the latter denotes the imperial privy purse; but the former occasionally is used indifferently for the latter.
6. *CI* 1. 5. 5 begins here with a longer list of sects than is in *CT* and, omitting the characterizations about the first five sects, simply lists the sectarians sect by sect and adds the following to the roster: Pneumatomachians, Tetraditans or Tessarescaedecatitans, Papians, Pepyzites, Batrachitans, Hermeiecians, Ophitans, Encratitans, Apotactitans, Saccophorians.
7. Probably Christ.
8. This includes construction of new churches.
9. Perhaps a hendiadys: "of assembling for prayer".
10. *CI* adds "and of surrender to final punishment", viz. death. It seems that Manichaeans were the *only* heretics liable to the penalty. This attitude of the earlier emperors is in strong contrast to that shown by Christian sovereigns of later centuries, when the latter pursued their policies in the suppression of heresy.

The exception against the Manichaeans may be explained on the assumption that they were almost beyond the pale of humanity. Legislation against them ascends as high as the reign of Diocletian, who *c.* 302 characterized them as infecting the whole world with poison and condemned their leaders (with their writings) to be burned to death (see no. 156, n. 1).

11. By omitting *all CI* implies that only Manichaeans are meant.
12. See no. 186, n. 4.
13. See no. 320, n. 5.
14. *CI* omits this much of this paragraph and now resumes.

15. Literally "green" (cf. Vergil, *Aen.* 6. 304, for the famous characterization of Charon, the infernal ferryman, whose old age is green—*viridis senectus*), but English has the same figure.

16. For the simple *churches CI* reads "conventicles, which these very persons try boldly to call churches".

17. Since these disabilities and penalties occur previously in nos. 176, 218, 298, where they are aimed at certain sects, here the net is cast more widely.

18. *CI* has before this word *quasi*, which has the same significance in English.

19. These are in communities (see no. 394, n. 4).

20. As a fine, though the noun is not expressed.

21. Such are nos. 256, 304, 320. Cf. *supra* n. 12.

22. Such are nos. 176 and 219. Words between the numbers are omitted by CI 1. 5. 5, which ends at the paragraph's end, where *CI* 1. 6. 3 begins and includes the rest.

23. See no. 75, n. 42.

24. Apparently a slave could not protest, but had to obey his master.

25. Both the administrator and the recipient of rebaptism.

26. This may mean either his connivance or his carelessness in assigning a light or no penalty.

Pitra prints (2. 517 and 602) two late Greek digests (probably parts of an interpretation) of this law with minor variations in the penultimate sentence: "All heretics mentioned in the enunciation should have no place for prayer or for meeting—the Manichaeans especially also being expelled from every city.

"And the laws variously introduced against them should prevail and nothing either of donations or of bequests should be valid for the places which they dare to call churches, but the orthodox Church should claim these, unless the manager contrary to the owner's judgement has acquiesced. For then, if the manager is well-born, he is exiled and shall pay ten pounds of gold, but if a slave, is whipped and is exiled.

"And the heretic should cease to be of the governmental service—no rescript against the measures commanded prevailing."

396. LAW OF THEODOSIUS II AND VALENTINIAN III ON SEDUCTION FROM ORTHODOXY, c. 429

(Pitra, 2. 556)

From a larger law survives a short clause prescribing confiscation of property and capital punishment for a person who by perverted teaching seduces a Christian from the orthodox religion.

Moreover one should know that whoever tries to drag a Christian from the right faith through his perverted teaching both shall suffer confiscation of property and shall undergo punishment through blood.

397. LETTER OF THEODOSIUS II AND VALENTINIAN III ON CONVOCATION OF THE EPHESIAN COUNCIL, 430

(M 4. 1112–6)

Both orthodox Catholics and heretical Nestorians succeeded in persuading Emperor Theodosius II to summon what proved to be the Third General Council in an attempt to define the person of Christ as well as his Mother's maternity [1] by the common sentence of all.

The circular letter addressed to both St Cyril, patriarch of Alexandria, and all metropolitans, commands their appearance with suffragans at Ephesus by Pentecost 431 and enjoins that no interim innovation into the faith may be introduced ere the synod should meet. The encyclical is a statesmanlike specimen of Christian Caesarism, in that Theodosius emphasizes the connection of the Empire's welfare with God's worship.

The translation is from Greek, for Mansi has two variant Latin versions here and in 5. 531–2.

Sacred letter sent to Cyril, bishop in Alexandria, and to bishops throughout the territory of metropolitans.

Emperors, Caesars Theodosius and Valentinian, Victors, Triumphers, Greatest, Ever-August, Augusti to Bishop Cyril.

Our State's condition depends upon piety toward God and this natural connection [2] exists to a great degree. For it is a reciprocal relation and each is enhanced by the advancement of each, so that both the true religion by righteous act and the State assisted by both [3] are distinguished. Therefore, since by God we have been appointed to reign [4] as well as happen to be the bonds both of piety and of welfare for our subjects, we maintain the connections of these ever unbroken by mediating between Providence and men. And we perform that service for the State's enhancement, but we, extending ourselves—so to speak—through all our subjects, that is, that they act piously and live according to what is proper for pious persons, make provision by taking needful care for each,[5] for it is impossible for him who lays claim to the one not to take thought likewise for the other.

397. CONVOCATION OF THE EPHESIAN COUNCIL, 430

Before all other matters we devote zeal that the ecclesiastical situation should continue agreeable to God and profitable for our times and from all persons' concord should have tranquillity and quietness because of peace in ecclesiastical affairs, and that blamelessness should be attached to pious religion and that those who both are called to the clergy and fulfil the great priesthood [6] should be free from all blame in life.

Considering that these aims are strengthened by love for God and by mutually kind opinion of pious persons, often previously, because of matters which then had happened, we have judged necessary a God-beloved synod of most holy bishops from all quarters. However, we have been rather hesitant with regard to the vexation to their Godlinesses, but now the controversy over ecclesiastical necessities and public needs which are associated with these has shown this [7] to be most necessary and indispensable.

Wherefore, lest the circumstances of the proposed inquiry upon such useful matters, if neglected, should take a turn for the worse (and this is alien from the piety of our times), your Godliness shall give heed that after the ensuing holy Easter—let it be said with God! [8]—you come to the city of the Ephesians of Asia on the very day of the holy Pentecost, after having provided that a few very holy bishops—as many as you should approve—from the province assigned to you should come with you to the said city, so that in no wise there should be a deficiency both in those available for the most holy churches in the said province and in those suitable for the synod.

For by our Serenity [9] the same things concerning the aforesaid most holy synod have been written to the God-beloved bishops of the metropolises everywhere,[10] so that by this means the commotion which has occurred from disputed matters should be ended according to ecclesiastical canons and that correction should be given to matters which have happened not decently and that certainty should exist both for piety toward God and for utility of the State.

Of course, prior to the most holy synod and the resulting formula in all matters to be given by it with a common vote, no innovation shall be made privately by any persons.

And we have been persuaded that each of the most God-beloved bishops,[11] knowing that the most holy synod has been urged by this our ordinance for the sake of both ecclesiastical and ecumenical circumstances, will assemble eagerly for the purpose of contributing what he possibly can to matters appearing so necessary and for God's pleasure. And we, making such provision for these matters, shall permit equally none to be absent and he who has not come straightway in the aforesaid time to the ordained place shall have no defence either toward God or toward us.[12] For indeed he who has been summoned to the sacerdotal synod and does not come readily is shown to be not of a right conscience.

May God preserve you for many years,[13] most holy and most pious father.

Given on 19 November at Constantinople in the consulate of our Lords, Lifelong Augusti, Theodosius for the thirteenth time and Valentinian for the third time.

And, when it had been read, the acts recorded in Ephesus by the holy and ecumenical synod on account of the impious Nestorius are matters of record.

1. On Nestorius consult J. F. Bethune-Baker, *Nestorius and His Teaching* (Cambridge, 1908), and F. Loofs, *Nestorius and His Place in the History of Christian Doctrine* (Cambridge, 1914).

2. A hendiadytic phrase traceable in reverse to Plato, *Ep.* 7. 344A.

3. This refers both to religion and to righteousness, which sheds lustre upon religion.

4. The Latin translator has a picturesque phrase: *imperii habenas nobis tradiderit* (has delivered to us the reins of empire).

5. That is, both religion and welfare.

6. These are bishops. See no. 158, n. 1.

7. Synod.

8. A pious formula.

9. "Divinity" is a variant lection.

10. But the council's complexion was almost entirely eastern: the Church of Rome sent three legates and the African Church was represented by a Carthaginian deacon.

11. See no. 16, n. 4.

12. Some forty bishops later gave adherence to what the 158 bishops present had decided. No record of divine or imperial punishment for non-attendance survives.

13. Literally "times".

398. LETTER OF THEODOSIUS II AND VALENTINIAN III ON CONCILIAR ATTENDANCE, 430

(M 4. 1109–12)

This document is an accompanying letter to the circular call for the Council of Ephesus (no. 397) and is addressed to St Cyril, patriarch of Alexandria, who was to preside at the synod's sessions. In it the emperor accuses the patriarch of being the instigator of all the controversy which necessitated the council's convocation and of being hypocritical in his letters to various members of the imperial family, but Theodosius pardons Cyril on the condition that the prelate hastens to the council and strives there for restoration of peace to the Church.

The translation is from Greek, for Mansi has two variant Latin versions here and in 5. 527–8.

Copy of the sacred letter sent by the most pious Emperor Theodosius to Cyril, bishop of Alexandria.

Emperors, Caesars Theodosius and Valentinian, Victors, Triumphers, Greatest, Ever-August, Augusti to Bishop Cyril.

To us is the greatest concern for godliness, on account of which offenders are considered worthy of pardon. But the need for pardon is not assuredly praiseworthy in the case of persons who ought to be praised by us and to be honoured particularly because of the holy religion. But it is proper that priests should be admired both from their morals' uprightness and from their exactness concerning the faith and should show frankness throughout their whole life and also should know that inquiry rather than presumption discovers the nature of each circumstance and particularly the doctrine concerning piety. For from the beginning not the threatening of any potentate or of one thinking that he is a potentate, but the counsel of holy fathers and of a sacred synod [1] has established this for us ourselves. And yet it is clear to everyone that religion should have its certainty not from command more than from intelligence.

Now, therefore, let your Godliness instruct us how possibly you, despising us, whose so great concern for piety you know, and the priests everywhere, for whom, when congregated, it is better to settle a controversy, have cast, at least so far as you could, disturbance and division into the churches, as if, moreover, a rather audacious attack befits the doctrine concerning piety rather than exactness, and harmony has no greater influence in our own view than audacity, and subtlety pleases us rather than simplicity. And assuredly we supposed that so much honour for us would not be accepted by your Piety or that all things would be cast into confusion,[2] when also we know that it is displeasing! But now our concern is for holy tranquillity. Know that you have excited everything—as was not proper. Nor is it astonishing at all that he who has overstepped the mean has not checked his attempt in these matters as far as the churches and the priests are concerned, but even has believed about us ourselves something unworthy of our Piety. Or what reason had you to write some things to us and to the most pious Augusta Eudocia, my consort, but other things to the most pious Augusta Pulcheria, my sister, unless you have supposed that we differ in opinion as a result of your Godliness' letters?[3] And it would be absolutely blameworthy for a person who is thus far removed from us to know from curiosity that this has existed, if indeed it was so, and to wish to produce this which has not existed is rather anyone's concern than a priest's.[4] At any rate, it is the part of one and the same eagerness and purpose[5] for you to be about to wish to separate the concerns of the churches and the concerns of the emperors, as if for you no other occasion for good repute exists.

Therefore, that you may know what our situation is, know that both the churches and the Empire have been united and, yet more, that through our commands and with the providence of God [6] our Saviour they shall be united,[7] and that pardon has been granted to your Godliness, lest there may be a pretext or lest you can say that you have been censured because of your doctrine about piety.[8] For we desire that this matter [9] should be investigated [10] in the presence of the sacred synod [11] and that what should seem to be well should prevail, whether those who have been defeated should claim pardon from the fathers or not. But assuredly we shall not allow the cities and the churches to be cast into confusion nor indeed to be unexamined the doctrines, of which it is proper that the presidents of the priesthood [12] everywhere should sit as judges—through whom we both are and shall be rather much in control of the true opinion.[13] At all events, none[14] to whom there is even a little share in the State is worthy to speak freely, if he shall choose to shun such a verdict according to his own boldness, since it shall not be permitted to him, even if he should wish, because our Divinity necessarily praises those who with eagerness come to such an investigation, but will not allow that anyone should wish to order rather than to advise or to be advised about such matters.

Wherefore it is necessary for your Devoutness to come at the time which the other letters, sent to all the bishops of the metropolises, signify,[15] and not to expect to regain for yourself your relation with us, unless you should cease all vexation and commotion and should come willingly to the inquiry of the matters to be examined. For thus you, neither smitten by private grief nor bearing ill will against anyone contrary to what is proper, can seem to have done what had been done roughly and unreasonably, but still in defence of your opinion,[16] and thereafter to come rightfully. For we shall not allow persons to come otherwise.

1. Perhaps a hendiadys: "a synod of holy fathers".
2. This sentence is somewhat obscure in its irony. Perhaps Theodosius means that he wonders how Cyril can honour him by writing to him in opposition to Nestorius, if Cyril thinks that Theodosius' theological tenets are determined by Nestorius and if Cyril thereby causes ecclesiastical confusion, which displeases Theodosius.
3. As we now have these letters (really treatises) addressed in 430 to members of the imperial family in an effort to wean them from sympathy with Nestorius, patriarch of Constantinople, and to win their interest for orthodoxy, the first is directed to Theodosius (PG 76. 1133–1200), the second is addressed to Arcadia and Marina, the emperor's younger sisters (PG 76. 1201–1336), the third is sent to Pulcheria and Eudocia, the sovereign's eldest sister and wife (PG 76. 1336–1420).

While Theodosius' attitude to Cyril's attempts seems somewhat egotistical on the assumption that a princess-sister could not differ in opinion from an emperor-brother, it perhaps is ascribable to his jealousy of his sister's superiority, which was demonstrated throughout his long reign.

4. This is the emperor's opinion, but we should think it proper for an orthodox priest to have been concerned about the imperial household's disunity in theological doctrine, when a monarch, who was also a legislator, showed sympathy with a heresiarch's opinion. That the priest was the patriarch of Alexandria and that the heresiarch was the patriarch of Constantinople (the eastern capital) makes the desire of the former to discredit the latter all the more significant.
5. Perhaps a hendiadys: "eager purpose".
6. "Christ" is a variant reading.
7. Theodosius proved himself not a poor prophet in his claim concerning the unity of Church and State—so far as the Byzantine Empire was concerned—since not seldom the Constantinopolitan patriarch was little more than the court chaplain in the millennium of life left to the Eastern Empire.
8. An adopted variant εὐσέβεια for ἐκκλησία (Church).
9. Nestorianism.
10. An earlier meaning of this word is "to be trained naked".
11. To be convened at Ephesus in the coming year.
12. That is, the bishops.
13. Another instance, if implemented, of imperial dominance over doctrine.
14. That is, any bishop. Bishops in the Christianized Empire increasingly participated in the civil administration (see Index of Subjects, s.v. bishop, as civil administrator).
15. See no. 397 for the imperial encyclical.
16. A reference to Cyril's campaign against Nestorianism.

399. MANDATE OF THEODOSIUS II AND VALENTINIAN III ON PROCEDURE IN LAWSUITS AGAINST CLERGYMEN AND ON SANCTUARY, 430

(H 241)

This constitution concerns procedure in preferring charges against bishops or priests or deacons, in so far as are established penalties suffered by rich accusers and by poor plaintiffs, if they lose such a suit. It also guarantees a sort of ambulatory sanctuary for criminals, who may not be seized when walking with clergymen.

About accusation of a bishop, a priest, or a deacon and that it should not be lawful to restrain persons subject to punishment walking with them.

Emperors Theodosius and Valentinian Augusti to Virus,[1] prefect of the East.

We, indeed, seized with more than usual respect, dare to speak [2] about holy and venerable priests and subordinate priests and even Levites [3] and to name with all respect those persons to whom the whole earth bows its head.

For we have heard that disloyalty toward the living God and our Empire exists in the city.[4]

But if anyone, emboldened or rash in respect to the law, shall have wished to be bold against the Church or a clergyman, through whom our Empire prevails, if a wealthier person shall have preferred the accusation, he should be forced to pay to our fisc by a penalty reserved,[5] that is, a hundred pounds of gold and a hundred pounds of silver, and thus should plead a case with the administrators of the Church;[6] but if he shall have been a poorer person, he should consider first in his own disloyal mind and thus should accuse and should plead a case of crime.

To the hurt of our treasury [7] none ever should dare by any disloyalty to assail those serving in Christ's palace;[8] but we have commanded that he should be brought hence to the senate of the earth [9] and that his hands should be fastened with lead. But if he shall have wished to live a free life, let the cares of the Catholic Church be nought to that one.[10]

Moreover concerning persons who are subject to punishment, if any shall have walked with a bishop or with a priest or even with a deacon, whether in a street or in the countryside or in any place whatever, we command that these persons in no way should be restrained or should be brought to judgement, since the Church abides in its priests.[11]

Given on 18 December at Ravenna, Theodosius Augustus for the thirteenth time and Valentinian Augustus for the third time being consuls.

1. Haenel emends this name to Albinus, who was praetorian prefect of the East.
2. Literally, "to make a conversation" (*sermonem facere*).
3. Ever since Moses under God's mandate had separated the male members of the family and later of the tribe of Levi, the third son of the patriarch Jacob (Gen. 29. 34), for the sanctuary's service, which included care of the Tabernacle and its sacred apparatus (Num. 1. 47–54), with but few exceptions (as in Judges 17. 7–13, 18. 3–6, 14–22) priests and the mass of the Levites, who are mentioned together about 25 times in the Bible, had separate functions, whereby the latter assisted the former and anticipated the diaconal duties in the Christian dispensation. So here Levites appear to be deacons, an equation often made in patristic writings.
4. Either Rome, because the constitution came from Ravenna, or Constantinople, because the mandate was sent to the prefect of the East.
5. The penalty is the stake which a wealthy plaintiff posts to support the righteousness of his case and then forfeits to the fisc if he loses his suit.
6. That is, the clerical defendant whom the plaintiff has sued.
7. Literally "our patrimony having been taken by surprise". Possibly the idea is that the imperial fisc would lose some of its revenues (cf. *supra* n. 5), if none should prosecute a clergyman.
8. The Church.
9. Perhaps by this curious expression is meant, if not the Roman or Constantinopolitan Senate (cf. *supra* n. 4), a competent secular court.
10. The notion perhaps is that a person who rashly prosecutes either the Church or its clergy runs the risk of not only losing his lawsuit but also his previously carefree life, which now must be burdened with cares through the payment of the penalty prescribed in the previous paragraph. The moral, in other words, is: if one wishes to live freely and untroubledly, one should not resort to legal action against the Church.
11. Perhaps this rescue of criminals descends from King Numa's reign (716–693 B.C. is the traditional time), for he, who is said to have instituted the Vestal virgins, sanctioned that if in their walk through the Roman streets they had chanced to meet a criminal en route to his execution, such an encounter saved his life (Plutarch, *Numa*, 10. 3). It also is reported about the flamen Dialis that if a person being conducted to flogging had fallen at his feet as a suppliant, it was a sin for him to be whipped on that day, and that if a man in bonds had been brought into this priest's house, it was necessary to release him (Gellius, *Noct. Att.* 10. 15. 8, 10). See also no. 272 *ad init.*

400. MANDATE OF THEODOSIUS II AND VALENTINIAN III ON SANCTUARY, 431

(M 5. 437-45)

This directive establishes careful regulations for the reception and the conduct of persons seeking sanctuary in churches. It takes a particularly stern view of those who refuse to surrender their weapons on attaining asylum and provides for the removal of such recalcitrants.

The integral constitution appears to have been composed in Greek, but shorter versions occur in both *CT* 9. 45. 4 and *CI* 1. 12. 3, where in each it is found in Greek and Latin, thus affording an excellent example of how the commissioners chosen to compile these codes exercised their power of excision.

Royal statute about persons fleeing for refuge to a church.[1]

A certain ancient custom from the times of error [2] and a certain disposition of natural [3] law because of piety have prevailed always to such an extent that divine ceremonies have been distinct in every period and people from public administrations and human functions, and that these have been arranged not only in the highest posture of affairs, but as if in a certain heaven on earth, and whither it is lawfully right for only pure and holy persons to approach.[4] Hence the following, which naturally is implanted in all persons' thoughts, also results: that in no way the things hallowed to God can be polluted and men's insolence can advance against divine power. For how can be defiled whatever is always necessarily pure? Or how can be befouled whatever, when once sanctified, ceases not to be such?

Wherefore, although we have been persuaded by acts which lately [5] have been dared nefariously against the divine altar as a result of barbaric insanity that neither the pure is defiled nor what is naturally holy has been soiled, nevertheless, since it has happened (which it has been hoped in no way would happen), the audacity of abominable persons has extended as far as piety, so that neither to unholy persons even may appear to be profane these things which are divine nor in sanctified and hallowed places may it be possible for these things to exist, which not even in other places indiscriminately is it tolerable that these occur irrationally,[6] we, in respect to the preservation of pure religion by the watchfulness of piety, exclude every insolence, which arises from persons acting either boldly or involuntarily, from Almighty God's Church. And indeed, if the erroneous religion of heathen antiquity—God being what was anyone's opinion—so practised the observance of its own superstition that it entrusted altars not so all persons but to certain priests and it dedicated temples (just as if alto elevated by the earth) in the acropolises and the securer districts of cities and it worshipped idols, which were fabricated, and it held with very great and august vanity fabricated idols, by how much more is it proper for us to guard religion with all observance—us to whom God with true religion, not deserting heaven, has descended and (just as if by a certain exchange made between God and men) man has received God upon earth and God has raised man to heaven?

Moreover before other things, in this matter also especially they [7] placate God, when they have laid hold upon the highest control over affairs in providing for men's safety and life and security, in which matters (according to the nature implanted in us) we unite by no means one to another without harm to another, so that on no ecclesiastical edifices or on holy altars from excessive exhaustion of those fleeing for refuge and fearlessness and rashness and presumption and audacity and even insanity may befall some outrage (beyond what is proper) and so that at least a single and a final haven for wretched and helpless persons with bosom made wider may receive them. It is not fitting that the earth's serenity should be taken from him who retreats from the sea's billow and crags; war lays aside its menace toward him against whom the battle-line has been engaged, when he flees for refuge. Formerly sanctuary, repulsing the laws' authority perforce,[8] shielded persons accused of various charges, and so that humane feeling might not be taken from persons in fear, antiquity dedicated an altar of safety even in our statues [9] and they who lay hold upon even the traces of our images [10] rejoice in being both freed and secure from the menaces of adverse fortune. Therefore, if so much as a touch of the image because of imperial majesty has given aid to persons in need, how much succour ought to exist for persons fleeing for refuge to the holiest altars?

Therefore [11] let the temples of the Great God be open to persons who fear [12] and let the common altar receive the suppliants fleeing for refuge and let no superior—as it were—menace repulse the divine aid, conveyed commonly to all persons, from its [13] homes. For what sort of compassion for misfortunes will be left in the case of shipwrecked persons, if you shall close the seashore and shall muddy the fountain for thirsty persons? Or what sort of cure will remain for human misfortunes, if God has been denied to them? For in our times we [14] not only ordain that the divine altars and the people's [15] oratory, fenced by a circuit of quadrate walls, should contribute to the safety of persons fleeing for refuge, but we order whatever happens to be beyond this as far as the church's outside doors,[16] through which it happens that persons, desiring to pray, enter first,[17] should be an [18] altar of mercy [19] for persons fleeing for refuge, so that the places encompassed between the temple, which we have described in the aforesaid space [20] as a refuge,[21] and the holy [22] church's first doors behind the public places (whether they are in buildings or in gardens or in courtyards or in baths or in porticoes) should protect the entering refugees after the likeness of the innermost [23] temple.[24] And although indeed by reason of religion and of devotion the places separated from each other by a little space have been divided by no little space [25] of observation, yet with regard to broadening security for persons fleeing for refuge and to extending air to devout persons we order that all the aforeshown circuit without distinction should be a haven of safety and [26] that none should lay sacrilegious [27] hands upon them to drag forth these persons, lest he who dares this, when seeing himself in misfortune, himself also should flee for refuge to seek aid.

And this extent of space we grant humanely in time of fear to live in security rather than to wander,[28] lest it should be permitted to anyone of those fleeing for refuge to stay or to eat or to sleep or to pass the night in God's temple or at the holy altars—the clergymen forbidding this for religion's sake and the persons fleeing for refuge observing it on piety's account,[29] lest either persons fleeing for refuge should seem to flee for refuge with profane intent by mixing their own needs with religion or persons able to exclude such shameful acts from the divine edifice should seem to violate the piety of which they happen to be the interpreters.[30]

But if it is proposed that one should quarrel at all with another,[31] it is preferable that the clergymen, when repelling human and natural outrages from the holy altars, should be considered bold rather than impious and should sin in regard to man than in regard to God, since, when this law has been ordained, any suspicion of inhumanity cannot extend justly to clergymen, because much provision for the fear and for the security of persons fleeing for refuge has been made. For we, though not desiring that God's temple should be befouled by human [32] nature and necessity, that the divine mystery should be mixed with wanton weakness, that divine things should be stained by profane things, that holy things should be defiled by unsound things, have not excluded from persons fleeing for refuge the ability to ask for aid; but we have resolved that these persons should be safeguarded also by wider intervals and by greater spaces—by preserving what befits both divinity and humanity.

We [33] order that persons fleeing for refuge should have not at all or introduce within a holy [34] church weapons in iron or defensive in another form,[35] since we ban these not only from the divine temples and altars, but also, as for the rest, from rooms and dwellings and gardens [36] and baths [36] and courtyards and porticoes [37]—whatever according to the aforesaid account we have shown shield persons fleeing for refuge. For it is not lawful to introduce into the most holy temples or ecclesiastical places through over-elaboration materials for discord or for wars. Let suffice the aid of God, to whom weapons and laws and majesty [38] are subject, for persons fleeing for refuge. For we, whom always rightly the weapons of military authority surround and whom it is not proper to be without bodyguards,[39] when entering God's temple, abandon our weapons outside, doffing our diadem, and by the appearance of lesser majesty [40] is promised the more to us the awe of majesty. Only because of the presentation of offerings we approach to the most holy altar and together with our entrance into the precinct surrounding the divine circles we depart and we arrogate to ourselves nothing from the near Divinity.[41]

Wherefore [42] it is fitting that persons fleeing for refuge without weapons to God's holy house and to the most sacred [43] altar, in any province whatever or throughout this city,[44] should be prevented by the clergymen from sleeping and from partaking of food for themselves in the temple or even at the altar apart from any outrage.[45] And thus it is necessary that this regulation should be made for them,[46] so that it may appear that no outrage exists on the part of the person preventing this action, but that the reason of religion demands it. Let them remind reverent persons of the site's sanctity and purity and let them explain that to religious rites there is nothing common with human needs. Let [47] them show successively [48] the intervals which within the ecclesiastical precincts have been determined for their [49] safety and peace, and let them explain that capital punishment has been determined against persons entering these rashly. Let them know that religion ought not to be polluted by human befoulments or that he who wishes because of the same religion to be free from outrage ought not to defile it by the outrage of physical need.[50] If anyone [51] should not assent and should not consent to all [52] these things, let religion be preferred to gentleness and let recklessness be routed [53] from the divine places to the aforesaid places.[54] For he who has feared greatly shall be [55] without danger and religion shall not be defiled by the admixture of human needs.

But persons begging aid from the Greatest God and entering with weapons into the most holy temples or with equipment which by natural and national law is excluded from religion, and trying not only to introduce these into its holiness but also to engage in strife—a thing which is tolerable, because they are aided or are heard or see cruelty[56]— you [57] shall advise by most plenary command of austerity and by fearful threats not to do this particularly, for what sort of hope does one put in religion who, girt with weapons,[58] enters for its outrage?

But [59] if any person, blinded by inciting insanity to disregard any of our constitutions,[60] happens to be in any place of the church whatsoever or within the temple or around the temple or even outside it, we order that straightway this person should be compelled to lay aside his weapons by the clergymen alone on the bishop's authority and rather sternly for their own welfare,[61] after hope and assurance [62] have been given to them that they will be defended by religion better than by protection of weapons. But if, when warned by our law's authority and by the ecclesiastical voice, they should continue in their own ignorance's course and should not abandon their weapons, which contrary to legality and not for safety's sake but because of audacity for sedition and for sacrilege they have accepted, let them know that, through so many and such declarations—when religion has been propitiated, since defence has been given to God by our Serenity and by the bishops—according to their own error and by entering armed men they shall be extracted and shall be subjected to all calamities.[63] And these things shall occur piously, which ought to occur because they have committed errors which are serious and worthy of tragedy. For is it not fitting that we should beware of and should suspect the things dared lately against religion and the Divinity by very wretched persons and on this account should remove every road and starting-point [64] of insanity, lest whatever tragic [65] insanity first has committed erroneously as an example, this same act immediately—and may it not happen!—should be dared in the fashion of sacrilege?

But,[66] not without the decision or the order of the bishop or also of you [67] judges living in this [68] city or anywhere else, an armed person ought to be delivered from the churches, lest, if this should be permitted [69] to many and various persons against wretched persons, confusion [70] may be created from this.[71] For we desire that persons fleeing with weapons for refuge should fear in regard to correction and that weapons, but not safety, in summary,[72] should be taken from them.

And this rather chiefly we legislate through this law: that such lawless and sacrilegious disturbances either in their inception should be settled, when weapons have been laid aside in the very first stages, by the fairest admonition or, if persisting by basest intensity, should be ended by the aforesaid measures with regard for very splendid authority through most orderly [73] justice and strict piety.

And these very things—which concerning religion we have ordered to be observed reverently and with all maintenance,[74] circumspection, honour, purity, sanctity, reverence, piety, and particularly by persons fleeing for refuge, when neither humane feeling is prevented by religion nor religion is contemned by humane feeling, since what is proper has been ordained both for divinity and humanity—you [75] shall contrive by applied edicts to come to the whole world and the knowledge of all persons, so that also persons fleeing for refuge may be secure through the benevolence of what has been determined and that by no person's rashness measures fashioned for religion's honour may be maintained.[76]

The law was posted on Indiction 14,[77] Pharmouthi 12.[78]

Interpretation:[79] Churches and places dedicated to God should protect accused persons who, compelled by fear, shall have taken refuge therein, in such a way that none should presume to offer violence and force to holy places for seizure of accused persons.

But we order that whatever space either in porticoes or in halls or in houses or in courtyards adjacent to a church belongs to it should be guarded, just as the inner parts of a temple, so that compulsion of fear should not constrain accused persons to stay around altars and to defile places worthy of veneration.

Of course, if any persons shall have fled for refuge to holy places, they should lay aside immediately whatever weapons they shall have borne with them and they should not suppose that they are defended rather by protection of weapons than by veneration for holy places. But if they shall have been unwilling to lay aside weapons and if they shall not have trusted the bishop or the clergymen, they should know that they must be dragged away by the forces of armed men.

But if anyone shall have tried for any reason at all to drag away any accused person whatsoever from holy places, he should know that he must be condemned to capital punishment.

1. For this *CT* and *CI* read in their Greek versions "Emperors Theodosius and Valentinian Augusti to Antiochus, most magnificent prefect and consul". Antiochus was praetorian prefect of the East.
2. That is, paganism.
3. Editorial emendation shifts this word from *disposition* to *law*.
4. A variant adds "by statutes".
5. The allusion probably is to Nestorian activity.
6. Or "unjustly" or "with impunity".
7. The emperors.
8. This adverb is added by a manuscriptal variant.
9. By *CT* 9. 44. 1 was confirmed in 386 the ancient right of sanctuary granted to persons fleeing to the imperial statues. This right of asylum arose in the early days of the Principate (Tacitus, *Ann.* 3. 36. 1, 4. 67. 6), though the general right of refuge was far older in Mediterranean lands (e.g. the six cities of refuge appointed by Moses in Num. 35. 6, 11-15, 25-9, 32, and Zeus' altar in Homer, *Od.* 22. 334-6).
10. See no. 1, n. 4 *ad med.*
11. Here begin *CT* and *CI*, each of which omits the conjunction.
12. Here *CT* and *CI* temporarily end.
13. The reference probably is to any city.
14. *CT* and *CI* resume here.

15. A variant gives "temple's", which *CT* and *CI* adopt.
16. That is, the area or precinct.
17. The Latin of *CT* attests this Greek clause, which *CT* omits from its Greek version and *CI* omits entirely.
18. A Greek variant inserts "propitious".
19. *CT* turns this word into "safety" in Latin.
20. *CT* and *CI* read "manner" by the insertion of one letter.
21. For *as a refuge CT* and *CI* read "as fenced around".
22. Omitted by *CT* and *CI*.
23. The Latin of *CT* attests this adjective (but in the comparative degree), omitted by the Greek of *CT* and *CI*.
24. Here *CT* and *CI* suspend for a space.
25. A variant reads "manner" (cf. *supra* n. 20).
26. Here *CT* and *CI* resume.
27. A variant transforms the adjective into a noun.
28. For *humanely . . . wander CT* and *CI* abbreviate to "for this purpose".
29. Again *CT* and *CI* stop temporarily.
30. It is observed that these classes are arranged chiastically in respect to their previous order (preceding n. 29 in text).
31. Strife between refugees in sanctuary is meant.
32. A variant reading inserts "need and".
33. Here *CT* and *CI* resume.
34. Omitted by *CT* and *CI*.
35. Considerable manuscriptal and editorial variation exists here: (1) the word for *form* is not elevated to the Greek text of *CT*; (2) the adjective *defensive* is taken by *CT* as agreeing with *form* understood and by the Greek of *CI* as meaning "weapon" (which is possible), depending upon *form* ("in another form of weapon"). Perhaps the solution is "defensive weapons in iron or in another form".
36. In the singular here, but in the plural in *CT* and *CI*.
37. *CT* and *CI* again suspend their versions here.
38. Or "the Empire".
39. Literally "spear-bearers".
40. In doffing the diadem.
41. The idea seems to be that a speedy departure is effected, once the presentation has been made, and that the emperors do not abuse their privilege of being seated in the sanctuary nearer to God's altar than other worshippers.
42. Here *CT* and *CI* resume.
43. *CT* and *CI* use the positive degree.
44. Constantinople, as the subscription shows, to which the Latin of *CT* prefixes "genial" (*alma*).
45. Here *CT* and *CI* again cease.
46. The clergy are meant.

47. *CT* and *CI* resume here and change the two principal verbs of the sentence into participles.
48. Omitted by *CT* and *CI*.
49. For the pronoun *CT* and *CI* read "persons fleeing for refuge".
50. *CT* and *CI* omit this sentence.
51. *CT* and *CI* substitute "a person fleeing for refuge".
52. Omitted by *CT* and *CI*.
53. A variant reading, preferred by *CT* and *CI*, is read here.
54. *CT* and *CI* again suspend.
55. An editorial conjecture is translated.
56. Both Mansi's Greek and Latin yield this translation, which is obscure.
57. The addressee, Antiochus (n. 1).
58. This phrase *CT* has only in Latin and transfers it to the subsequent sentence.
59. *CT* and *CI* resume here, after condensing the previous sentence as follows: "But we warn persons seizing with weapons the holy churches not to do this particularly."
60. The words *any . . . constitutions* are not in *CT* and *CI*. The Greek seems to be corrupt, yet gives this sense.
61. *CT* and *CI* omit this phrase.
62. For this word *CT* and *CI* have "oath".
63. For this sentence *CT* and *CI* read "But if, when warned by the ecclesiastical voice, after so many and such declarations, they should not abandon their weapons, when religion has been propitiated, since defence has been given to God by our Serenity and by the bishops, by introduced armed men they shall be extracted and shall be subjected to all calamities", and then suspend.
64. An instance of hysteron proteron.
65. A rejected marginal reading is "military"!
The words *tragedy* (above) and *tragic* (here) may refer to the conventions of Greek tragic drama, but probably mean no more than the modern English connotations of these words—a meaning found also in Greek.
66. *CT* and *CI* resume here.
67. *CT* and *CI* read "us and of the judges".
68. The Greek of *CI* inserts "certain" (δεῖνα)—an odd word in this context—and the Latin of *CT* inserts "kindly" (cf. *supra* n. 44).
69. *CT* and *CI* insert "by such authority granted indifferently".
70. *CT* and *CI* add "and disturbance".
71. Here *CT* and *CI* permanently end except for their subscriptions and the former's interpretation (noted later).
72. The text is uncertain.
73. An editorial conjecture is translated here.
74. Inconcinnity in Greek reproduced in English.
75. Cf. *supra* n. 57.
76. That is, the right of sanctuary, which redounds to the honour of religion,

will be restricted through anyone's rash attempt to retain his weapons after he has been received in sanctuary. Such an attempt then will result in the rejection of the refugee who has abused the right of sanctuary by refusing to surrender his weapons. In this sense, then, the mentioned maintenance will be possible only if no one shall have refused rashly to respect the regulation.

CT has this subscription: "Given on 23 March at Constantinople, the most distinguished Antiochus being consul and he who shall be announced." *CI* in its subscription omits "the most distinguished" and supplies Bassus as the other consul.

77. See no. 435, n. 9.
78. Pharmouthi was an Egyptian month corresponding to April.
79. Translated from the Latin appendix to *CT*, for it appears only there.

401. LETTER OF THEODOSIUS II AND VALENTINIAN III ON CONCILIAR PROCEDURE, 431

(M 4. 1117–20)

This epistle to the Council of Ephesus accounts for the presence of the imperial representative, Candidian, count of the domestics, whose duty—the letter declares—is not to participate in debate on doctrine, but to preserve order in the sessions and to hold the bishops to the prescribed agenda.

Sacred letter sent to the holy synod through Candidian, count of the domestics, who took upon himself the synod's good order.

Emperors, Caesars Theodosius and Valentinian, Victors, Triumphers, Greatest, Ever-August, Augusti to the holy synod.

We make much provision for all matters contributing [1] to the State, particularly for matters pertaining to piety, through which the abundance of all other blessings accrues to men. Wherefore, indeed, recently we have written reasonable words about your Godlinesses' assembling at the Ephesians' metropolis. But because it is necessary to provide properly for your most sacred synod's suitable discipline and quiet by supervision,[2] we have not disregarded this, so that by this means calm may be guarded [3] from every quarter. And we have been persuaded that your Godlinesses need no external aid to provide peace for this and other matters. But not to overlook this also pertains to our harmonious [4] provision concerning piety.

Therefore Candidian, the most magnificent count of the devoted domestics, has been commanded to go from us even to the sacred [5] synod, but not to participate in the inquiries to be made about dogmas (for it is not lawful for a person not in the catalogue of most holy bishops to mingle in ecclesiastical problems), but by every means to remove from the said city the laics and the monks, both those who already have foregathered on this account and those who are about to assemble (since indeed it is not right that persons who in no way are necessary for the coming investigation of dogma should excite uproars and on this account should hinder persons who are obligated by your Holinesses to make regulations peacefully), and to provide that no discord from antipathy should be extended further,[6] lest as a result of this your most sacred synod's investigation should be obstructed and the accurate examination of the truth should be hindered as a result of the disorderly echoing perchance arising, but [7] with forbearance each of the aforesaid [8] should propose or should oppose what issues as the best opinion [9] and thus, according to proposal and counter-proposal, the search concerning the true dogma should be solved[10] apart from any commotion and by your Sanctities' common vote should attain a formula both free from faction and agreeable to all.

Moreover the said most magnificent Candidian has been commanded in the first instance by our Divinity to watch narrowly by every way that none of your most sacred synod should return homeward or wish to go to our sacred court or prefer to journey somewhere else or to leave the place [11] appointed for the investigation;[12] nor [7] should be proposed other ecclesiastical examination at all, when any persons demand it, or a proposition which has arisen in any way whatever from anything, when not directed toward the proposed investigation of the holy dogma, before every controversy of the matter to be examined has been settled and the matters profitable for the search for the truth [13] have achieved a conclusion, when examined with accuracy, corresponding with the orthodox religion.

Your Godlinesses shall know that it has seemed best to our Serenity that either before your sacred synod or in a public court there [14] no accusation involving money or crime should be started against anyone, but that if perchance it should happen that this involves anyone, the entire investigation about these matters should be brought to the great-named city.[15]

The most magnificent Irenaeus [16] only for friendship's sake has travelled with Nestorius, the most God-beloved bishop of this great-named city,[15] and on no account will participate either in your most sacred synod's problems or in the matters entrusted to the most distinguished Candidian, who has been sent by us.[17]

1. A variant reading is "profitable".
2. Perhaps a hendiadys: "disciplined quiet". See no. 73, n. 17.

3. A variant reading is "may exist".
4. A variant adjective is "complete".
5. The superlative degree is recorded as a variant.
6. What seems to be meant is that differences disclosed in the heat of discussion should not be developed into discord because of any debater's dislike of another disputant's decision.
7. The sense seems to shift here from what has been commanded to Candidian to how the council should confer.
8. The accredited conferees.
9. The Greek is obscure at this point and this translation represents what seems to be the situation.
10. A variant reading is "decided".
11. A variant reading "formula", if adopted, would alter *to leave* to "to abandon"—the sense then being to depart from the agenda by discoursing on matters alien to it.
12. Of these instructions at least the second and the fourth were violated despite Candidian's efforts.

John, patriarch of Antioch, held a minority council of forty-odd bishops in his own lodging on 26 June 431 and he with his party abstained from the synodal sessions beginning with the fourth.

Communications between the council and the capital was established by documents as well as by deputations sent by the rival factions (see no. 407).

13. Literally, "for the true search".
14. Ephesus.
15. Constantinople.
16. A count friendly to Nestorius and later bishop of Tyre.
17. This sentence lacks a principal verb in Greek.

402. EDICT OF CANDIDIAN ON CONCILIAR PROCEDURE, 431

(PG 84. 595-6)

When Candidian, count of the domestics, sent in 431 as the imperial commissioner to the Third General Council of the Church at Ephesus, which had been convoked to settle the Nestorian controversy, could not prevail upon the already assembled prelates to await the delayed arrival of the Antiochene delegates, whose votes St Cyril, patriarch of Alexandria and chief organizer of the council, had reason to fear would be cast in favour of Nestorius, patriarch of Constantinople, he issued in the following edict, which was ineffectual, his protest against the premature opening of the council on 22 June 431.

402. CONCILIAR PROCEDURE, 431

Testimony of Count Candidian, which he, hearing that the synod was to convene in the morning, published publicly in Ephesus.

Flavius Candidian, the most eminent count of the most devoted domestics, to Cyril, the most holy bishop of the church of the metropolis,[1] and to the most reverend bishops, who have assembled with him.

Your Religiosities know that, from the time when I came to the Ephesian city, I have besought your general and holy synod nothing else except that with peace and concord should be expounded the matters which pertain to right faith and our confession, just as our lord and most pious emperor has ordered.[2] And the evidence, which the truth itself shows, satisfies me that we have done nothing else except this. Moreover, since and while I realized that you were about to assemble in a very holy church [3] contrary to the wish of other bishops, because John, the most holy bishop of the Antiochene metropolis, and those who are with him[4] are not yet arrived, I have not ceased from asking that that which I have said above should happen, and I have warned each and every person on account of this, lest perchance a particular synod [5] may seem to be held.

But finally, nevertheless, since you have congregated in the most holy church, I have hastened to oppose this and to do the things which have seemed best to our lord and most pious prince,[2] though I may seem to do so unnecessarily, as long as you knew once for all these same things from his Divinity's letter sent to you. However, I have shown that this is the arrangement of our said lord and most pious prince.[2] For I have said that he wished our faith to be strengthened without any discord by all wise persons and does not wish any particular synods [5] to be held, because he especially knows that these transform our religion and the orthodox faith into heresies and schisms. Moreover, as long as your Reverences were demanding the letter of our lord and most pious prince,[2] which has been sent to the holy synod, I read it—previously indeed I did not assent to do this— and indeed I shall not object to say so for this reason, because all who had been ordered to assemble for the most holy synod were not present.[6] But because your Religiosities say that they do not know what has been commanded by our lord and excellent prince,[2] to me it has seemed to appear necessary that the divine and adorable letter should be read, though all the other most reverend bishops were not present.

But nevertheless, even after I have shown to you what has been decreed divinely,[7] I have continued in this same entreaty, begging your Reverences and asking that nothing new should be done before all the most holy fathers and bishops should come together to the synod, but that you should delay for only four days for the most holy bishop of the Antiochenes' metropolis,⁴ along with the others who are with him,⁸ and also those who are with the most holy bishop Nestorius;⁹ that, when your Religiosities equally have assembled and all the holy synod has been gathered, with you all together being present, at the same time in unity should be decided what matters—to which we are foreign, perchance, if any exist—may come into doubt; and that then with the consensus of you all should be shown who seems to believe wrongly and contrary to ecclesiastical rules or at least that all equally profess rightly, as the holy fathers' religion obliges. Though making these admonitions and requests in suppliance, therefore, not once but even rather often, I have accomplished nought.

But because nothing of these things, which have been said by me, has been observed, but by you I have been ejected insultingly and forcefully, I have considered it necessary by my evidence to establish this plainly for you and by this edict to say clearly that none of you should do anything new, but should await the presence of all the holy bishops and thus in a general council should decide what pertains to the Catholic and the holy faith. But if anyone, led by his own wish, shall have wished to disturb those things which have been ordered by the immortal and excellent head,² let him know that he shall charge to himself whatever shall have resulted, but he should not impute the prejudice to another. And indeed it shall not irk me to repeat again these same things.

Moreover, since, as your Sanctities know, this has pleased our lord and most pious prince ² that during the presence simultaneously of all the holy bishops, who have been summoned by his Divinity, may be dissolved those matters which come into citation, I have prefixed to this edict also the letters which have been sent to your most holy synod and which have been written to me myself by their Divinities,¹⁰ that you, knowing through all these what things have been commanded by our lord and excellent emperor,² may cease from such presumption.

Therefore know that a copy of this ordinance also has been transmitted to our lord, the most pious emperor.²

Posted on 22 June in the Ephesian city.

1. Alexandria.
2. Theodosius II.
3. The council met in St Mary's Church.
4. John of Antioch, attended by some forty bishops, had been en route for a month. About 21 June Cyril was notified of the delay and of the hope that they would arrive within a week, but this notification, it appears, simply accelerated his plan to start the synod's sessions in their absence, especially after John's messengers had given him John's message: "If I delay, do what you will do" (M 4. 1232). Cyril reports this announcement and adds that John's delay was

because he knew that Nestorius would be condemned (loc. cit.)—a not unnatural reason, since Nestorius was John's friend. Another reason for Cyril's speed was that sickness had fallen upon the fathers, of whom several had died.

5. As opposed to universal, not necessarily one-sided, for there were fautors of Nestorianism already there, though in a minority.

6. When Candidian had tried in person to postpone the first session of the synod, he was pressed for his authority to delay it. Whereupon he read his instructions, which were scorned by the Cyrillian faction. Then he published this edict as a protest. Cf. *supra* n. 4.

7. That is, imperially.

8. Or "in the same situation" (*pariter*), but it probably means those in John's company. See no. 404, n. 6.

9. But Nestorius and his adherents already were in Ephesus. Perhaps Candidian means their protest against Cyril's haste.

10. Theodosius II and Valentinian III.

403. LETTER OF CANDIDIAN ON CONCILIAR PROCEDURE, 431

(PG 84. 596–7)

Despite the edict of Candidian, Theodosius II's commissioner to the Council of Ephesus in 431, the anti-Nestorian faction in that synod continued to meet in the absence of some forty delayed delegates. Their impatient action provoked the following letter from the imperial representative.

Also another testimony of the most eminent Candidian after the synod.[1]

Since I have learned from many most reverend bishops that some of them, after the first session of the particular synod [2] has been held, have been induced by compulsion to that point that some of them are said even to have subscribed to the acts which have been done by those persons who on the first day had assembled,[3] on this account I write by letter to all who on the said day have not convened,[4] conjuring them by Almighty God and by his Christ and by the Holy Spirit and the preservation of the lords of the world,[5] that you should do nothing beyond those things which have been commanded by our lords, the most pious emperors,[5] but that you should wait for a universal synod and the presence of the most holy bishops and likewise the decision of our lords and the most pious princes.[5]

Therefore your Religiosities should know that a report about all matters has been made to them.[5]

1. Not after the sessions stopped, but after the sessions started.
2. So characterized because the absence of some two score members prevented it from being called a general council.
3. The first session sat on 22 June.
4. He means those who, though in Ephesus, have abstained from the first session, because they have been awaiting the arrival of those still en route to the council.
5. Theodosius II and Valentinian III.

404. EDICT OF CANDIDIAN ON CONCILIAR PROCEDURE, 431

(PG 84. 597)

This is another edict of Candidian, imperial representative at the Council of Ephesus in 431, to the effect that the members already present should withhold deliberations until the arrival of absentees known to be en route and shortly expected. Apparently this ordinance, unlike the first edict, was obeyed, for the synod's second session convened on 10 July, after the Antiochene and the Roman delegates had arrived.

Also an edict of the most eminent count to the synod.

Flavius Candidian, the eminent and the most glorious count of the most devoted domestics, paying attention to the confusion and the disturbance of the entire city.[1]

I have been possessed by no mediocre wonder. For it is too contrary to reason for anyone's mind not to be moved deeply by those acts which occurred yesterday.[2] For my Devotion thinks that not anyone of the most reverend bishops does not know that not once nor only twice, but even rather often, I have made obvious to all persons—according to those things which have been commanded by the divine and inviolable head[3]—that, with all the most reverend bishops assembling simultaneously on an equal basis, the question about the pious and orthodox faith's accuracy ought to be discussed.

Wherefore also I have declared by writing and without writings to them, to whom it was my duty to declare, that none should hold a particular synod[4] and, moreover, that no one should meet with it, if anyone should presume to do anything irrationally. For it is clear that whatever things have been done by one party will be deemed contrary to the decision which has been given by the lords of the world[5] and neither stable nor legitimate.

And on this account and now I admonish each and every one that he should wait the arrival of John, the Antiochene bishop, most pleasing to God in all respects, and of those who have been announced to be coming in like manner,[6] and besides of those who, it is said, will be present from the West.[7]

It is impossible that anything of the things which are done in part [8] and in any way whatever should be considered worthy of any consideration for this reason, because it has been done contrary to the commands of the lords of the world.[5]

1. The superscription stops abruptly. See no. 73, n. 17.
2. 22 June, the synod's first session.
3. Theodosius II.
4. As opposed to a general council with all accredited members attending.
5. Theodosius II and Valentinian III.
6. That is, late; or, perhaps, with him (*pariter*). John's party arrived on 26 June. See no. 402, nn. 4 and 8.
7. These were three papal legates, who reached Ephesus on 10 July.
8. That is, by one faction (*ex parte*).

405. LETTER OF THEODOSIUS II AND VALENTINIAN III ON CONCILIAR PROCEDURE, 431

(M 4. 1377-80)

Since Candidian, imperial commissioner at the Council of Ephesus, could not effect a reconciliation between the Alexandrian opponents and the Antiochene supporters of Nestorius, patriarch of Constantinople, Theodosius, who had received reports [1] from his representative, wrote to the assembled fathers, forbidding any prelate to leave Ephesus, announcing the dispatch of another commissioner, and commanding the conferees both to revoke such decisions as had been reached and to rediscuss the matters at issue.

The translation is from Greek, for Mansi has two variant Latin versions here and in 5. 567-8.

Copy of the royal letter sent to the sacred synod at Ephesus by Palladius, magistrian,[2] which overthrows what has been done by them by reason of the disputation being bound to begin anew.

Emperors, Caesars Theodosius and Valentinian, Victors, Triumphers, Greatest, Ever-August to the most sacred synod at Ephesus.

Since the most magnificent Candidian, count of the devoted domestics, had informed us, our Piety has learned that certain things have been done in confusion and contrary to decorum in the Ephesians' metropolis,[3] because neither all—as had been decreed—the most godly bishops have assembled (since the bishop of the megalopolis of Antioch with other metropolitans is now about to approach) nor the persons already present have consulted or have agreed with one another nor they have examined the matters concerning the faith according to the necessary objective or as it was contained in our sacred letter, which had been sent, but so that the enmity of some is evident toward others on account of much partisanship concerning matters decreed in any way whatever, since they are unable to make use of a veil.[4]

Wherefore anyone could recognize that what had happened has been done with calculation. Accordingly it has seemed best to our Divinity that such authority [5] should come to have no place at all: that since the things done inconsistently are fruitless, the doctrine concerning piety—as has been decreed—should be examined first and that what seems best according to the entire synod in common should prevail for the future time [6]—for our Piety does not accept purposeful prejudices, but is so displeased with what has happened that until the dogmas about piety have been examined by the entire synod and someone from our sacred palace has been sent with [7] the most magnificent Candidian, the count, for the purpose of examining [8] (pursuant to our command) what has been transacted and of preventing the inconsistencies, we [9] command anyone of the congregated bishops neither to depart from the Ephesians' city nor to come to our sacred court nor to return to his native community.

So that this should be permitted to none or so that none should hope to prosper in this with impunity, this letter suffices to command to your Godlinesses that nothing more beyond our command should be added to what has happened.

Your Holinesses shall know that letters have been sent to the most distinguished governors of the provinces: that they should permit absolutely none returning to his native community or city to be admitted without our command.

For it is necessary for all things, examined without contention and with truth and according to that which pleases God, thus to be confirmed by your [10] Godliness, since our Divinity makes provisions not for men now or even for the most holy and the most godly bishop Nestorius or for anyone else, but for dogma itself and for truth itself.

Given on 29 June,[11] Flavius Antiochus being consul and he [12] who shall be announced.

1. In the margin of his edition of this epistle Mansi occasionally notes that these were falsified.

405. CONCILIAR PROCEDURE, 431

2. See no. 67, n. 43.

3. Mansi notes in Latin that Candidian's false narration has deceived the emperors. But on the whole, there seems to have been little tumult during the first day's prolonged session (22 June), despite Candidian's claim in his edict (no. 404 *ad init.*). Four days later (26 June) the arrival of the Antiochene contingent (hostile to St Cyril, patriarch of Alexandria, who presided at the council, but friendly to Nestorius, patriarch of Constantinople, who had been educated at Antioch and had served as an abbot of a monastery there ere his elevation) led to verbal clashes.

4. That is, to cloak their disagreement.

Mansi notes in Latin that "All these things have been reported falsely to the emperors, as is clear from preceding accounts." But there is no reason to suspect that Candidian had suppressed in his last report news of the arrival of the Antiochenes on 26 June (no. 404, n. 6), for it is unlikely that, if he had written to Theodosius after their appearance on that day, his message could have reached Constantinople (about 225 miles from Ephesus *by air*) in time to have enlightened the emperor by the 29th, when Theodosius dated his letter to the council.

5. A variant is "consequence". The idea is that such a procedure to reach the decision reported by Candidian should be unauthoritative because of the enmity evinced and on account of the absence of the Antiochenes.

6. Mansi's final comment in Latin notes that "Pursuant to the secret report the emperors rescind the council's acts."

7. Since Candidian already was at Ephesus, the preposition (ἅμα, which the old Latin translator equates with *cum*) must be understood to imply assistance in dealing with the situation. In August arrived Count John as the new commissioner (not so much to support as to supersede Count Candidian), who carried another imperial letter (no. 406).

8. Literally "going into".

9. The pronoun is really "it", referring to *Piety*.

10. A variant reading is "our".

11. An alternative date is 19 June, which is absurd, because the first session of the synod sat on 22 June.

12. Later a certain Bassus.

406. LETTER OF THEODOSIUS II AND VALENTINIAN III ON CONCILIAR DEPOSITIONS, 431

(M 4. 1396-7)

This letter, addressed by Theodosius to 51 bishops assembled at Ephesus [1] in the Church's Third General Council, was brought thither by John, count of the sacred largesses, who succeeded Candidian as the commissioner in the imperial interest. In it the emperor accepts the depositions of Nestorius, patriarch of Constantinople, St Cyril, patriarch of Alexandria, Memnon, metropolitan of Ephesus and exarch of Asia—which shows simply imperial ignorance of the situation in the synod, for the pro-Cyrillian faction deposed Nestorius and the pro-Nestorian party deposed Cyril and Memnon. Eventually orthodoxy won the day, however, and of the three only Nestorius lost his see. Theodosius also congratulates the councillors on their preservation of the faith and suggests that they prepare to plan their departure in peace.

The translation is from Greek, for Mansi has two variant Latin versions here and in 5. 593-5.

Copy of the sacred letter sent through John, count of the sacred largesses,[2] by the most pious emperors to the holy and great synod.

To [3] Celestine, Rufus, Augustine, Alexander, Acacius, Tranquilline, Valentine, Iconius, John, Acacius,[4] Ursus, Firmus, Himerius, Dexian, Berinian, Palladius, Asterius, Juvenal, Flavian, Helladius, Rambulus, the other Alexander, Maximus, Phritilas, Perigenes, Cyrus, the other John, Eutherius, Hellanicus, Bosporius, the other Cyrus, Vinatius, Peter, Dynatus,[5] Dorotheus, Antiochus, Dalmatius, Eusebius, Seleucus, Eleusius, Eulogius, Sappius,[6] Timothy, Pius, Troilus, Irenian,[7] Monimus, Olympius, Theophilus, Julian, Basil, and the remaining most godly bishops.

We consider that how much zeal for piety and the ancestral faith we continue to have has been shown distinctly from many previous circumstances and not least we have believed that to all persons throughout the world this has become clear recently in respect to the convocation of your synod. For since we are not patient of any controversy emergent even for a moment, we have summoned your Sanctities to assemble earnestly about attending to its speedier settlement, because we consider that labour about piety will be in no wise burdensome to your Godlinesses. Nevertheless through imperial foresight we have relieved the annoyance of this by the convenience of both time and place. For we have appointed the Ephesians' city, easy of access from land and sea and bountifully furnishing to its residents the necessaries of all domestic and imported produce, so that our [8]

406. CONCILIAR DEPOSITIONS, 431   673

Serenity's and your Holinesses' synod's pious objective should concur easily and should be brought into action.

Wherefore also now we have accepted the deposition of Nestorius and of Cyril and of Memnon, which has been made known by your Pieties.[9]

As for the other things done by you: we have perceived that concerning Christianity you guard the faith and the correctness, which from our fathers and ancestors we have received and which the most sacred synod held in the presence of Constantine of divine lot harmoniously confirmed.[10]

Therefore each one of your most sacred assembly shall take thought, after all controversy has been dissolved and offences have been excised, with peace and concord to return to his native land.

And not only that your Sanctities, exhorted by our Piety's letter, may look both to concord and to the universal peace of pious dogma, we also have sent, after having read it, the letter of Acacius, bishop of Beroea, counselling this also.[11] Since he has been unable to join your most sacred assembly because of his great age,[12] he has presented, through what he has written, matters befitting his godliness and contributing to the orthodox religion. A perusal of the said letter will show of what sort these are.

However, your Sanctities shall know that the most magnificent and the most distinguished John, count of the sacred largesses,[2] has been dispatched for this purpose, so that he, who knows our Divinity's objective about the faith, should effect whatever matters he may regard as profitable.

1. Of these prelates at least nine apparently never attended the council, since their names are not in Mansi's several rosters of bishops present and subscribing to the conciliar acts (4. 1123-8, 1211-26, 1235-6, 1269-70, 1363-8). The most egregious errors are those naming Pope St Celestine I, who was represented by three legates; Rufus, bishop of Thessalonica, who sent Flavian, bishop of Philippi, in his place; St Augustine, bishop of Hippo Regius (Royal Hippo), who died (430) before the council had convened!

2. In no. 408 John is called master of the divine offices.

3. The sees of the bishops, save for the absentees, are in one or more of Mansi's lists (cf. *supra* n. 1).

4. Pursuant to the cases of Alexander and John and Cyrus (*infra*), one would expect this Acacius to be characterized as "the other".

5. An alternative spelling is Donatus.

6. Spelled Sapricius in a variant reading.

7. Given in Mansi's Latin column as Herennian.

8. The text has "your" (ὑμετέρας) for *our* (ἡμετέρας) without note of variation, but the former undoubtedly is a misprint.

9. Mansi marginally notes in Latin that "The emperor, deceived by the Orientals' false report, approves Cyril's and Memnon's deposition as lawfully made."
10. The First Ecumenical Council at Nicaea in 325, convoked by Constantine I.
11. This letter has not survived.
12. At this time he was about 109 years old.

407. COLLOQUY BETWEEN THEODOSIUS II AND BISHOP THEODORET ON CONCILIAR DECISIONS, 431
(PG 83. 1473-6)

In a letter (preserved only in Latin) of Theodoret, bishop of Cyrus, addressed to Alexander, bishop of Hierapolis, the Greek ecclesiastical historian, who was of the pro-Nestorian party, preserves the *ipsissima verba* of the emperor and himself when the latter was one of eight delegates sent by the pro-Nestorians from the Council of Ephesus to present their case to Theodosius, who received the delegation at Chalcedon.

While the whole letter is of interest, only the part giving the dialogue, in which is revealed the informal way wherein can be expressed a sovereign's will, is translated.

Letter of Theodoret, bishop of Cyrus, written from Chalcedon to Alexander the Hierapolitan.

... Moreover the most pious emperor[1] knew that the throng was assembling against us[2] and, accosting us alone, said: "I know that you are assembling improperly."

But I said to him: "Because you have given to me confidence in speaking,[3] hear me with favour. Is it just that even excommunicated heretics work[4] in the churches, but that we, who fight for the faith[5] and because of this by others have been deprived of communion, do not enter into a church?"

And he replied: "And what should I do?"

I therefore replied to him: "What your count of largesses[6] has done at Ephesus. For when he found that some were assembling, but that we were not assembling, he checked them by saying: 'If you shall not be peaceful, I shall not permit either party to assemble.' And your Piety also ought to have ordered the bishops here not to allow either those[7] or us to assemble until we should meet, that your just decision might become known to all persons."

408. DISSOLUTION OF THE EPHESIAN COUNCIL, 431   675

To this he said: "I myself cannot give orders to a bishop." [8]

Accordingly I replied: "Therefore you shall not give orders to us: and we shall take a church and we shall assemble. And your Piety will learn that many more are with us than with those."

Besides this we said to him that our assembly had neither reading of the Sacred Scriptures nor oblation, but only "prayers for the faith and your Majesty and religious conversations".

He therefore has approved and has not prohibited further this to be done. . . .[9]

1. The Greek βασιλεύς is represented by the Latin *rex* (king), but the Romans preferred *imperator* for the title of their emperors.

2. While awaiting the outcome of the audience with the emperor, Theodoret preached occasionally to the people, who heard him with too much interest to please the anti-Nestorians. After the fourth occasion, at which Theodosius seems to have been in the congregation, the anti-Nestorians began to throw stones at Theodoret and his companions.

3. Probably Theodoret inferred this from the emperor's presence at his sermon.

4. The word is *agere*, which has many meanings. The idea is to perform ecclesiastical functions.

5. In defending Nestorianism Theodoret obviously believes that he is supporting orthodox opinions.

6. John, the commissioner sent to supersede Candidian.

7. The anti-Nestorians.

8. Contrast his attitude with that of Constantius II (no. 94).

9. On this scene Mansi has a marginal note: "It is not probable that these things occurred between Theodoret and the emperor."

408. LETTER OF THEODOSIUS II AND VALENTINIAN III ON DISSOLUTION OF THE EPHESIAN COUNCIL, 431

(PG 84. 625-6)

On 11 September 431 Theodosius II received at Chalcedon two rival delegations from the Third General Council of Ephesus, which had been convoked to settle the Nestorian controversy, and then, agreeing with the acts of the majority, though refraining from condemnation of the minority's position, dissolved the synod in the following letter.

408. DISSOLUTION OF THE EPHESIAN COUNCIL, 431

Letter of Theodosius.

Emperors, Caesars Theodosius[1] and Valentinian, Victors, Triumphers, Greatest, Ever-Adored to the holy synod which has met in the Ephesian city.

You indeed knew from many other persons our intention, even if we were not to write it now, and what great zeal we have for the correct faith and for the churches' unity, since we have been taught this by our fathers and by our grandfathers and since we continually hitherto prefer nothing to the sound faith, on account of which we also a little while ago hastened to assemble your Sanctities to Ephesus. And, while you were assembled, we wrote everything to this effect that because of it the true faith might result without contention and that what formerly it held might remain unshakably, while you were united for friendship.

But since, because of the intention of impiety, among you occurred often certain contentions and several acts which undoubtedly followed the dissensions, we, wishing that the discord among you all should be ended, dispatched John,[2] the most eminent and the most revered master of the divine offices,[3] that the contentions which had been created among you might be dissolved. But while this also seemed necessary, that several of you should come hither (in order that our Piety also present might hear in your presence that union, which we desire, came to pass with pious assent), we also accomplished this, since we are very eager that all matters should be arranged agreeably.

But because dissension, already commenced, still continues, we, considering that your Religiosities suffer hardship from the very compulsion of a council,[4] have granted that you all should return from Ephesus to your own places and should again occupy your own churches. Each and every one should do this with the bishops who have come from his province. But only Cyril, who once was the Alexandrian bishop, and Memnon, who was the Ephesian bishop, we do not number with you and we know that they are separated from the episcopate,[5] just as it has been written by us to your Sanctities. Returning to your own churches, exercise forethought for the peace of the cities by embracing a kindliness in all respects worthy of the priesthood.[6]

If indeed there is to be any satisfaction of the things which you have done here in any way whatsoever, it is fitting that it will come to pass through those things which afterward shall ensue.[7] Moreover it will be so, if you shall have preserved ecclesiastical decency with public suitability.[8]

1. This name is wanting in the superscription.
2. He succeeded Candidian in August as high commissioner.

3. In no. 406 John is called the count of the sacred largesses.

4. The majority faction had written to the Constantinopolitan clergy and laity that they might be permitted either to lay their case before the emperor or to return to their sees, for the heat was intolerable, funerals were occurring daily, episcopal finances were low.

5. Count John had arrested these prelates, whose deposition (along with that of Nestorius) the oriental opposition in the synod had voted. S on afterward, however, both Cyril and Memnon regained their respective sees.

6. See no. 158, n. 1.

7. This sentence in the Latin is defective.

8. The idea seems to be that if the bishops shall maintain ecclesiastical peace, the public will enjoy the consequent result or at least such peace will result in the public interest.

409. LETTER OF THEODOSIUS II ON DISSOLUTION OF THE EPHESIAN COUNCIL, 431

(PG 84. 631-2)

Shortly after a previous letter (no. 408), in which Theodosius, when dismissing the Third Ecumenical Council from Ephesus, had excepted St Cyril of Alexandria and Memnon of Ephesus from the prelates allowed to return to their sees, the emperor repeated his directive for dissolution and exempted these two archbishops from his earlier ban.

Letter of Theodosius.

After the testimony of John [1] and of the other bishops, who were detained in Chalcedon while the emperor was going into Constantinople with the opposing faction, this letter was directed to Ephesus to the bishops who had assembled with the Alexandrian bishop,[2] after whose preface the text is as follows.[3]

In honourably preferring the Church's peace to all other occupations, we desired to convoke you not only by our governors but also by ourselves,[4] since we believe that it is impious and unworthy of our Sovereignty if the churches should be divided through our being disdainful and not doing everything which is possible.

But since neither it has become possible that you should be united nor your Venerabilities have wished to come to render a judgement about those matters concerning which there is doubt, we have decided that the eastern bishops [5] should return to their own cities and churches and that the Ephesian Synod should be dissolved—in such manner, of course, that Cyril should enter Alexandria, while Memnon remains in Ephesus.

We make known to your Religiosities also only this: that, while we live, we cannot judge the Easterners. For in our eyes they have been convicted in no respect.

If, therefore, any intention of peace has remained,[6] choosing this preferably write in return to us without contention. Otherwise think about your departure and then on those matters which we have written. For we are not evilly disposed in anyone's interest.[7] If there are any such persons, God knows them.

The last letter of all sent. It was directed when already the blessed Cyril, patriarch of Alexandria, had returned to his own city.[8]

1. Patriarch of Antioch and leader of the opposition to Cyril.
2. Cyril.
3. This sentence is an old interpretation. The last phrase apparently looks to an ancient editor, who derived the material for the sentence from a preface which Cyril prefixed to his copy of this letter.
4. He may mean that he took his provincial governors' advice, because they had primary knowledge of the disturbed state of the Empire through breaches of ecclesiastical and then civil peace, as well as that his decision to summon a synod was *motu proprio*.
5. There were only, it seems, four legates from the West: three from Rome and one from Carthage.
6. That is, if they still can reach agreement on disputed points.
7. Or "For we are not the cause of any evil".
8. Probably an ancient commentator's note.

410. LETTER OF ISIDORE ON COMMITMENT OF NESTORIUS TO A MONASTERY, 431
(PG 84. 618-19)

After the Third General Council of Ephesus had condemned on 22 June 431 Nestorius, patriarch of Constantinople, toward the end of its sessions Theodosius II accepted its conciliar condemnation and in September authorized the confinement of Nestorius in the Syrian monastery over which he had presided before his translation to Constantinople. This imperial order was transmitted by a letter from the praetorian prefect.

Letter of the praetorian prefect[1] to Nestorius, that with honour he should return to his monastery,[2] whence he had been called to the episcopate.

For a long time we have postponed those things which seemed best by the synod's decision to be done, although many persons were blaming us vehemently and were uncivil.

But since there has come to us your Sanctity's letter, making it clear that to you it is disagreeable that you remain in Ephesus and that to your Religiosity it is desirable in the future that you take the road,[3] we have arranged for those persons who ought to serve you throughout the entire journey (whether it shall have pleased you to sail or to proceed by the Asian,[4] that is, the Pontic, road), so that they may serve you even to the monastery. And we have dispatched to you transport [5] and provisions,[6] asking clemency from the Lord, that your Sanctity may journey safely and may fare so as it desires.

For we do not believe that you need consolation, when we consider your soul, which is wise, and the many thousand good characteristics in which you are conspicuous above other persons.

1. The superscription begins "Letter of the prefects", which editors, while they have let it stand, note should be altered to *Letter of the praetorian prefect*, who appears to have been Isidore, praetorian prefect of the East (no. 425).

2. This was Euprepianum (named in honour of St Euprepius), situated near Antioch. Nestorius left it in 428 for consecration in Constantinople.

3. A euphemism for his deposition from his see.

4. The text has *asinam* (she-ass), but *Asianam* (Asian) has been suggested quite plausibly (despite the fact that by this time had been created the custom that clergymen—at least bishops—should ride on asses and not on horses) because of the explanatory phrase *per Ponticam viam*. To go by road from Ephesus to Antioch, the direct route would be through the civil dioceses of Asia and Pontus and thence into Syria.

5. Probably animals, for the word *angaria* (which can mean either wagon or animal in the post service) is plural. See no. 434, n. 2.

6. See no. 301, n. 7.

411. LETTERS OF THEODOSIUS II ON ECCLESIASTICAL PEACE AND UNITY, 432

(PG 77. 1448; 84. 656–8)

After the Third General Council of the Church at Ephesus in 431, where Nestorianism was anathematized, earnest efforts were made by Theodosius

II in Nicomedia to effect a reconciliation between Alexandria and Antioch and thus to provide peace in the East by inducing St Cyril, patriarch of Alexandria, to withdraw his so-called Twelve Chapters[1] (to which Nestorius, deposed patriarch of Constantinople, refused his assent) and John, patriarch of Antioch, to abandon his Nestorian sympathies, which stemmed partly from his antagonism toward Cyril.

The emperor's letters were sent to the centenarian Acacius, bishop of Beroea,[2] and to the celebrated St Simeon Stylites, that accomplished athlete of asceticism and the first and the most notorious of the pillar saints (*stylitae*),[3] each of whom had influence with John. The plea of Theodosius was successful.

Separate versions of the first letter written to each ecclesiastic are found to have such little verbal correspondence with it (described as dispatched to them), that it seems that the second and third letters here given represent another attempt to enlist these correspondents' aid in healing the breach caused by Nestorianism in Eastern Christendom.

Mansi has Greek and Latin variant versions in 5. 281–4 and 828–9.

I

Copy of the sacred letter written to Acacius, bishop of the Church of the Beroeans,[4] and Simeon, anchorite of Antioch, and to other provinces, each individually.

Absolutely none of the things which ought to receive attention about our religion has been neglected by us. And your Sanctity, having learned it from the most devout bishop of the Antiochenes and the remaining holy bishops with him, will know this accurately.

Moreover about this matter[5] have arisen certain controversies and difficulties, which we, though we have tried, have been prevented from obliterating hitherto by many matters. Assuredly we shall not choose to depart from this earnestness before the good God graciously shall grant the unity of the holy churches through your prayers; so that it befits your Holiness to ask with all earnestness these things[6] from God, who has made known the approved priests of the Roman religion.

II

Emperor Theodosius' memorandum to Acacius, bishop of Beroea.

From the beginning[7] there has been a need for your Reverence in this respect: that orthodoxy may continue and besides may be increased. For already and before this by your labour and effort[8] the divine members of the Catholic and the true faith have been joined well.[9] And now, because through the wickedness of a certain devil and through neither a sincere nor a regular[10] teaching the seeds of separation have been sown among persons once united and at one and the same time among wise persons. I exhort you to resume that famous virtue (which is known to all), that you hasten, by prayer to God and at the same time to bishops, both to assemble by advices what have been severed and to join all things which are in conflict neither justly nor holily.

Moreover this will be, as we think, easy for your Sanctity, if you shall have exhorted the most reverend John, bishop of the Antiochenes, neither to exert himself for nor to persist in human wilfulness or error; but you should press the more that he should retreat from it. All persons fight against his inventions and novelty of doctrine, for it is fitting that in this your old age your Religiosity should win also this struggle. And as long as you shall have laboured thoroughly, you shall be proclaimed as a victor even over those things which formerly you accomplished bravely.[11]

III

Memorandum to the holy Simeon Stylites by the same Aristolaus.[12]

Perceiving that your Reverence's entire life has been turned toward God and lives in such a way that it can have confidence that it can win his favour even for us, we necessarily have been urged to resort now to this letter, that you may hasten especially in this crisis to pursue a project which truly pertains to Divine Providence. We mean, in truth, that peace, which had been well rooted, should be established; you surely should aim to remove the strife introduced by the contrivance of some devilish malignity. Moreover we, having confidence in your Sanctity's prayers, know well that this will occur by pressure on and exhortation to those persons who will be able to produce this peace and to make it, now sundered, whole again.

For if the most reverend John, the Antiochene bishop, shall have wished to subscribe to the deposition of him [13] who has cast the seeds of contention and shall have made clear that he does not assent to that very dogma adopted by novelty and folly of words,[14] the union of the severed members again will ensue, when all persons concur together in this. For if he shall have done this and shall have agreed with the most reverend Cyril, bishop of Alexandria, with whom both those who are in the West [15] and those who are here [16] and those who are everywhere concur, those members, which by Divine Clemency formerly cohered, also now will be joined. For that superfluous and useless, rather indeed even noxious, doctrine has generated this trouble and disturbance; and by your prayers, just as we trust in God's aid, its repulsion from our souls and its distant flight will be able to restore peace to us and to renew us. For disunion so disturbs us that we think that this is even the primary cause of those things which unfavourably befall. And we trust that according to the Divine Clemency's will all things may benefit our Empire, if the members of the Church and of the right faith shall have been joined and united.

For this accomplishment fight also the best fight, that you may overcome the demons' attempts. For to you this also will be accredited for the greatest war and the bravest victory. And by this attainment you will be a follower of yourself—in doing the things which you have professed. And concerning these things be also confident, having prayed that you may commend to God by your unceasingly accustomed intercessions us and our Empire and all persons who are under our sovereignty, that especially to us, who display a fitting concern for his peace, may be given bountiful blessings by virtue of our worship of him.

1. These later were ratified by the Robber Council of Ephesus in 449, were ignored by the Fourth Ecumenical Council at Chalcedon in 451, were recognized by Emperor Zeno's *Henoticon* (no. 527) in 482. These articles had an Apollinarian aura—to say the least.
2. He is said to have reached the age of 110 years.
3. Simeon (388–459), becoming a monk c. 404, was so avid for self-imposed austerities that he wore a spiked belt which drew blood, then dug a hole and buried his body up to his chin, then immured himself in a cave and later in a cell, then chained himself to a rock on the top of a hill. At long last, after twenty years of such mortification, in meditation of a new move, he finally in 423 ensconced himself, for 36 years until his death in 459, on a column, which eventually was raised to a height of sixty feet in three drums (in honour of the Trinity) and of which the base still may be seen at the so-called Castle of Simeon (Kalat-Sem'an) between Aleppo and Antioch in Syria. This ultimate idea was not new, for he was preceded in the second century of our era by a pagan priest, who twice annually for a week lived on a pillar 180 feet high at the entrance of the Temple of Hera at Hierapolis in Syria (Lucian, *De Dea Syria*, 28). Simeon's "name and genius"—writes the judicious Gibbon—"have been immortalized by the singular invention of an aerial penance", whereby he lived "a life of death" as "an example to mankind"—as Tennyson in his *St Simeon Stylites* asserts about this exhibitionist's extraordinary method of acquiring merit through "pillar-punishment" on his pious perch. But his popularity was profound; his advice was asked by pilgrims and by prelates; his exalted piety excited imitators, who infested Christianity for centuries.

Some may suppose that such anchorites and stylites were anti-social in their personal pursuit of holiness, but Toynbee thinks that they fostered "a form of social action that moved their fellow-men more powerfully than any secular social service on the military or the political plane" and that in their contemporaries' eyes they were "pursuing the highest social aim on behalf of all Mankind" (7. 389). Certainly St Daniel Stylites (409–93), St Simeon's disciple, showed his zeal for social justice in the Constantinopolitan crisis engendered by a usurping emperor's (Basiliscus, 475–6) Monophysitic proclivities (see no. 524) and descended from his pillar to defend orthodoxy in the imperial capital (E. Dawes and N. H. Baynes, *Three Byzantine Saints* [Oxford, 1948], 49–59).

If, as some suppose, Jesus' words "If thou wilt be perfect" (Matt. 19. 21) pointed the path to martyrdom during the period of persecution, they also showed the avenue to asceticism after persecution had stopped, for the old martyr became the new ascetic in the pursuit of perfection.

4. The Greek is compressed (*bishop* and *Church* being represented merely by the articles), but the meaning is not doubtful.

5. The disunity caused by Nestorianism is meant.

6. That is, reunion of the dissonant elements in the Church.

7. From the inception of the Nestorian controversy (428).

8. Perhaps a hendiadys: "by the effort of your labour".

9. Acacius had acquired a reputation for ardent advocacy of orthodoxy more than a half century before this letter was written, and in the interim by his activities in councils and on missions had added to it.

10. The adjective *regularis* means more than our ordinary significance of "regular", which seldom carries the connotation of something being in accordance with a rule or a regulation. Here it is the teaching in accord with ecclesiastical law or canon.

11. The text is defective, but the full idea seems to be that Acacius by his work in restoring unity will win a greater victory than he ever had won in the matters which he formerly and with courage had carried to a successful conclusion.

12. From no. 412 we learn that this man also delivered an imperial letter to John, patriarch of Antioch.

13. Nestorius, ex-patriarch of Constantinople and John's friend of long standing.

14. The very life of heresies depended on new and subtle twists of expression: cf. the difference between Homoousianism and Homoiousianism, where the insertion of "i" (*iota*) is important.

15. St Cyril, who spearheaded the opposition to Nestorius, was in close contact with Pope St Celestine I, who had commissioned him to act as his proxy in 430 to reclaim Nestorius.

16. Not in the East by way of contrast to the West just mentioned, since most of the Antiochene patriarchate supported Nestorius, but those in and near Constantinople.

412. LETTER OF THEODOSIUS II AND VALENTINIAN III ON ECCLESIASTICAL PEACE AND UNITY, 432

(PG 77. 1457-61)

Besides writing to Bishop Acacius of Beroea and to St Simeon Stylites (no. 411), who were advisers of John, patriarch of Antioch, about composing the Antiochene and the Alexandrian differences over Nestorianism, Emperor Theodosius addresses directly the following letter to John in a personal plea to promote the Church's peace by abandoning his advocacy of Nestorius, deposed patriarch of Constantinople.

While this letter summons John to the imperial court for a conference with St Cyril, patriarch of Alexandria, and threatens punishment for non-compliance, yet no evidence exists that such a meeting occurred in Nicomedia, but rather it is believed that the emperor altered his plan and entrusted to the bearer of this letter the mission of reconciling John and Cyril in their respective sees. At any rate, such a mission succeeded.

This translation is from Greek, for Mansi has three variant Latin versions in 5. 278-82 and 663-6.

Copy of the sacred letter sent by Aristolaus, tribune and notary, to John, bishop of Antioch, concerning the holy churches' peace and unity.

Emperors, Caesars, Victors, Triumphers, Greatest, and Augusti, Theodosius and Valentinian to John, bishop of Antioch.

Our aim is the achievement of peace, which you, following the habit of your life, unceasingly profess to fulfil and you, proposed as priests because of this, cease not to teach all other persons. Therefore, since it has happened to us that this is slackening (which is not proper), it is the right time to urge you to this, to which we, persuading all other persons, think that they will come eagerly.

For a situation to be avoided and unexpected has happened in our times: the discord of the true religion's priests, which has surpassed even all power of narration. For when it had been hoped that every kind of controversy, even as far as suspicion, would be removed and that the conclusion of perfect unity would ensue, then pretexts of dissension and of very great turbulence have been kindled. Accordingly in this situation there is great distress and occasion of much despondency in that the teachers of ecclesiastical peace, even the fount of harmony, have turned to so great a degree of discord that they are in need of persons persuading them to be mindful of those things which they have been ordained to profess.

Therefore, hoping to find the solution of so great an evil from the source where it had its origin and carefully taking thought that this can be accomplished successfully, lest the creeping defect of the controversy should spread further, we have this as our object: that, all meeting with us, both the most holy bishop of this glorious city [1] and all the most God-beloved bishops found here and all their clergy, to join the members of the orthodox faith, which recently had been in fair union and have been sundered by an unfortunate calamity intruding, you, we say both you and Cyril, the most holy bishop of Alexandria, having met with each other,[2] should discard the difficulty and the dispute between you, since the most devout men (whom we mentioned) have professed that if you shall subscribe to the deposition of Nestorius and shall anathematize his doctrine, no occasion of controversy will remain; but straightway Cyril, the most holy bishop, and those with him and Celestine, the most saintly bishop of glorious Rome, and all the priests of the orthodox faith everywhere will communicate with your Godliness, while the other matters, if indeed there are any needing to be corrected, will receive easily a proper solution, which you yourself shall effect by acting upon these necessarily and by persuading yourself privately and all persons publicly.

Therefore, because you know that this is our desire and that this is our will, you should wish to take thought for nothing other than by banishing all strife and rivalry to establish carefully and firmly this peace for the most holy churches of the orthodox faith everywhere—and through these for all persons under you [3] by the Almighty's aid—and to come with all speed to the Nicomedians' city,[4] bringing with you none at all of the bishops,[5] except a few clergymen serving your Holiness. And hasten without any delay, knowing that by our sacred letter [6] we have ordered also Cyril, the most holy bishop, likewise to bring himself thither and to hurry with the same eagerness, pledging our word also to him that he should not come into our presence otherwise before you, having met with each other and having discarded the enmity toward each other, would have agreed with the intention of all persons that peace through proper harmony should be established. And we announce also to your Devoutness that this shall be, for men, be they so great, whom the blessings of peace do not captivate and the evils of discord do not cease to escape, shall not be seen by us before and until will have been corrected whatever matters have made us to be disheartened not a little.[7]

But meanwhile, until is established the desired welding of peace and of your [8] harmony and of friendship for each other, even from this meeting by a journey prepared by us,[9] no introduction of episcopal consecrations or depositions or even ordination of whatever kind should precede. But if anything even has happened to have been done in the interim, this alone, undisturbed in peace, should wait for the settlement of the Catholic Church, when most devout clergymen can suffice for the execution of divine services until perfect union has resulted.

You have these commands from us. And we do not doubt that if you have perceived our design, which is sincere and unalterable and worthy of Christian earnestness, you yourself will co-operate with all strength and with all power and will refuse to undergo no labour or trouble, no contempt of insult, no forgiveness of anger in the matter of bringing to a conclusion the things ordained by our Piety for the interest of the orthodox faith and the most holy churches' unity. But if—and this we do not believe—you should attempt by some personal aim or by opposition of human passion to devise measures opposing this our intention and our so just will and if you should slight the other things commanded by us, you shall charge it to yourself, if your Sanctity, having scorned the zeal for the union of God's churches, should have paid deserved penalties.

1. Maximian, who succeeded Nestorius in the Constantinopolitan see.
2. Apparently two meetings are intended: (1) John and Cyril are to meet privately (repeated in next paragraph) and (2) after their reconciliation they are to meet publicly with other bishops and clergy in Constantinople (proposed in this paragraph) and are to announce there their agreement.
3. Perhaps "us" (ἡμᾶς) rather than *you* (ὑμᾶς) should be read.
4. Where Theodosius then was in residence.
5. The idea seems to be that reconciliation would result more rapidly if none of the hierarchy as counsellors should accompany John.
6. This letter has not survived.
7. Editors have suggested several emendations for the Greek, which seems rather tortuous here.
8. Reading the editorial conjecture of *your* (ὑμέτερας) for "our" (ἡμετέρας).
9. Theodosius refers to the journey which each patriarch has been ordered to make to his court.

413. MANDATE OF THEODOSIUS II AND VALENTINIAN III ON SANCTUARY, 432

(*CT* 9. 45. 5)

This constitution concerns slaves taking refuge in churches. It directs that slaves should not enjoy such sanctuary for more than one day, that the clergy should notify the slave's master, that the master should refrain from punishing the slave, that an armed slave should be removed at once, that a master should be guiltless if, in removing his armed and resistant slave, the slave should be slain.

Justinian abbreviates this directive (*CI* 1. 12. 4).

The same Augusti to Hierius, praetorian prefect.[1]

We have believed that a sanction (to be valid forever) should be promulgated concerning persons fleeing for refuge to the holy religion's altars, to the effect that if anyone's slave, having relied only on the veneration for the place, shall have sought a church or altars without any weapon, he should be dismissed from the said place after one day; indeed, notice should be given by the clergymen, whom it concerns, to his master or to him through fear of whom he has seemed to have avoided imminent punishment. And he,[2] with indulgence for the transgressions, with no remaining wrath residing in his heart, should remove him in honour of the place and by respect for him [3] to whose aid he has flown.

But if, armed, when no persons suspect this, he shall have rushed in suddenly,[4] thence straightway he should be dragged away or at least information should be given immediately to his master or to the person from whom such frantic fear has hurried him forward, and to him [5] should not be denied the opportunity of dragging him away at once. But if through reliance upon weapons and by the impulse of frenzy he shall have conceived the intention of resisting, permission for snatching him away and dragging him away (by whatever means he can effect this) should be granted to the master.[6] But if it shall have happened that he [7] even is slain in the struggle of the fight,[8] there shall be no crime on his[9] part and there shall not remain an occasion for kindling an accusation, if he, who has passed from a servile status to the condition of an enemy and of a homicide,[10] has been killed.[11]

But if any of these regulations, which have been established so usefully, shall have been perverted either by negligence or by connivance of those persons who are set in authority over this matter in respect to their office or by any reason, just punishment will not be lacking, that, when removed under the verdict of an episcopal trial from that rank which they have not been able to protect and degraded into the class of plebeians, they should receive the force of judicial activity.

Given on 28 March at Constantinople, Valerius being consul and he who shall be announced.[12]

1. Of the East.
2. The master.
3. The demonstrative pronoun, which may be of any gender in this form (*eius*), refers either to God or to the Church.
4. For all the preceding Justinian reads simply "If anyone's armed slave,

when no persons suspect this, suddenly shall have rushed into a church or to the altars" and begins his excerpt thus.

5. The master or the other person.
6. Perhaps this doctrine is evolved from what is declared in *D* 9. 2. 29. 7, where a magistrate acting somewhat violently against a resistant slave was not liable under the *Lex Aquilia* (? 287 B.C.).
7. The slave.
8. Literally "in the struggle and the fight": taken as a hendiadys.
9. The master's.
10. If the master slays the slave, the latter is not a *homicide*, but in fighting his master the slave is considered a potential *homicide*.
11. Justinian's excerpt ends here.
12. Justinian's subscription names Aetius as the other consul.

414. LETTER OF DOMITIAN ON ECCLESIASTICAL PEACE AND UNITY, *c*. 434

(*PG* 84. 740–1)

In the aftermath of the reunion of churches subsequent to the condemnation of Nestorianism by the Third General Council of Ephesus in 431, imperial attention was attracted toward the submission of such recalcitrant prelates as had not followed the lead of John, patriarch of Antioch, who had been the chief supporter of Nestorius, in making peace with his opponents. One of the documents illustrating Emperor Theodosius II's effort to achieve adherence to the council's acts is the following letter, addressed by Domitian,[1] quaestor of the sacred palace, to Helladius, bishop of Tarsus, who earlier had written to Pope St Sixtus III a request for papal co-operation against reunion!

Letter or memorandum of the most eminent quaestor to Helladius, bishop of Tarsus, urging him to be united with the Antiochene.[2]

Since I know that for your Sanctity has been perfected unimpairedly the bounty of all blessings, I am disheartened not lightly when I, a lover of the churches' peace and by prayers and by action preserving it most holy and unshattered, consider the events which now are happening. In what way you have not embraced recently this peace appears to me very amazing. But even if anyone should concede that, if one person should not enjoy the things which are just, what is useful for one person should be neglected in view of the greater utility of the many, a compensation of this kind may be tolerable; but when no harm is done to him who thinks that he is harmed, nay, on the contrary, who himself harms others, in what way is your Sanctity persuaded to devise that which is not useful to many? For your Sanctity knows what he,[3] though speaking well about other matters, has done in this particular instance, which is of primary importance, and you ought to reckon to yourself that he has been deposed from power.[4]

And your Sanctity knows these things better from me.[5] Therefore I ask that, as I have said, we do not harm in many ways by instilling, indeed, confusion into the multitude and insubordination into the cities, and that you should not be proved purveyors of the worst things, which are not to be desired by many persons; that your Sanctity should speed straightway to enter a conference with Bishop John, most dear to God and most holy, and that you should hasten along with the rest of the bishops of the first and the second provinces of the Cilicians[6] to embrace his peace and communion. For the Divine Virtue[7] should know—because I, for the sake of this thing,[8] in the interim have withheld the divine decree, completed and signed, even promulgated —that I have declared repeatedly to my own self the sweet hope that to my urgings, nay rather to the truth itself, your Sanctity would assent and would correct what things sadden us.[9]

Therefore I beseech your Religiosity that you quickly order this to be done, lest, when the divine letter shall have been published, restitution should be hopeless. And indeed it is certain that in no respect harm can come to your Sanctity, which now particularly is being harmed very much on this account, because it reckons the interests of many persons its own and likewise makes the injuries of very many persons its own. But the Divinity also is wont to exact accountings from those persons to whom it has committed the correction of things.

1. From another letter about this time we are able to identify this official (PG 84. 739).

2. That is, the patriarch John.

3. Nestorius is meant.

4. The hint is that Helladius too may be deprived of his see, unless he abandons Nestorianism.

5. This sentence may seem awkward, but it appears to be true. For in this paragraph Domitian, the emperor's chief legal minister, explains to Helladius that he is doing the bishop a favour by withholding the execution of an imperial decree touching this situation of reunion, until the bishop has been admonished again by him to submit. In this sense it is better for Helladius to know from Domitian than from Theodosius II what he must do.

6. The real organization of the Greek district of Cilicia, which had fluid frontiers, into a Roman province occurred in 64 B.C. under Pompey the Great. In the Diocletianic subdivision of provinces (284-305) the province was divided into three provinces: Cilicia Prima, Cilicia Secunda, Isaurica.

690   415. ECCLESIASTICAL PEACE AND UNITY, C. 434

The see of Helladius was Tarsus, St Paul's "no mean city" (Acts 21. 39) and the chief city of Cilicia Prima.

7. That is, God, whom he thus calls to witness.

8. He means the speedy submission to the oft-expressed imperial will for ecclesiastical peace, which Helladius can help to effect by communion with the patriarch of Antioch.

9. Cf. *supra* n. 5. This withholding action on the part of an imperial official seems unprecedented, but perhaps Domitian counted the cost of such procedure.

415. LETTERS OF DIONYSIUS ON ECCLESIASTICAL PEACE AND UNITY, c. 434

(PG 84. 758-9)

Two letters of Dionysius, master of the soldiery [1] in the Orient, one to Count Titus, his deputy, and one to each bishop named in his first letter, implement the imperial attempt to achieve reunion of recalcitrant and Nestorian-sympathizing prelates with John, patriarch of Antioch, who had submitted to Theodosius II's desire that the solution of the Nestorian controversy by the Third Ecumenical Council at Ephesus in 431 should be accepted.

Since the first is obviously a covering letter for the second, both are joined here.

I

Rescript published as the *terminus* [2] of those which have been written to Titus, the most eminent count and vicar, by Dionysius, the most glorious master of the soldiery.[1]

What the imperial Clemency has decided should be determined about Helladius [3] and Maximin [4] and Alexander [5] and Theodoret,[6] most reverend bishops, the very fulgent divine letter itself shall be able to instruct your Grandeur. Moreover the subjoined letter [7] shows in what way the said persons have been admonished also by us.

Wherefore your Diligence, supporting our command, should exert itself that by every artifice and by very subtle shrewdness what the imperial Authority has decreed should attain to effect. For your Grandeur will enjoy no small glory if you shall have been vigorous to apply speed to so important a case. It pertains to our souls' religion. The nature of the present case pertains—that I should say so—to the Celestial Divinity's [8] concern.

Wherefore both the divine letter and our Authority prepare your Eminence; moreover you shall give suitable obedience to the commands of divine origin that the most reverend cult of the orthodox

415. ECCLESIASTICAL PEACE AND UNITY, C. 434

piety should be reminded day and night that entire tranquillity must be preserved in the cities without any uproar and disturbance.[9]

II

Letter of the most eminent Dionysius, master of the soldiers,[10] which he wrote to each one of the bishops [11] who are named in the imperial letter, that either they should agree with those things which have been done by the Antiochene [12] and should communicate with him or should depart from the churches and the cities.

The unconquered lord [13] is not ignorant how much the devotion to the sincere cult benefits his Sovereignty and how much security and enlightenment the loyal pursuit of the orthodox cult prepares for the provinces. Hence also he is shown to be assuredly worthy to obtain whatever he has believed ought to be besought from a propitious Deity. For it is necessary that all things should befall prosperously, if obedience shall have been given to God in respect to that truth which has been defined by him.

Therefore, influenced by suitable sanctity, because he knew that your Beatitude is not associated with John, bishop of the Antiochene city, in holy things nor communicates with him in adoring the mysteries,[14] he deigns to give a celestial decree, which shines among those decrees which are earlier, that either you communicate with the aforesaid person and with the rest who agree with him in the Celestial Divinity's cult or you depart from the city and the holy church over which you have been known to preside.

Therefore, after the divine letter has been studied, you shall do one of two things. For it is necessary that either you should communicate with John, a bishop of the Catholic Church, in order that, when contentions have been removed, the holy Church may enjoy quiet and peace, which it has created, or, if you contest the divinely given ordinance, you should be compelled to submit; for you shall be debarred from the city and you shall be debarred from the church, if perchance you shall have been unwilling to obey and to agree with a better man.[15]

Therefore let it pertain to your Deliberation that you receive the divine and adorable commands, if you desire to avoid the imperial ire.

1. Here the title (*magister militiae*) varies from the form *infra* at n. 10. See no. 106, n. 4.

2. While this word, of course, indicates a boundary or a limit or an end, it seems to be used in a lexically unillustrated technical sense and so is left untranslated. From the context of the letter it may be collected that *terminus* approximates to definition rather than to conclusion, that is, while it may be Dionysius' "last word" on the subject, it looks more to the instruction of Titus

692   416. ECCLESIASTICAL PEACE AND UNITY, C. 434

by showing him to what limit he should go in applying the imperial command.

3. Bishop of Tarsus. See also no. 414.

4. Bishop of Anazarbus.

5. Bishop of Hierapolis.

6. Bishop of Cyrus and ecclesiastical historian, whose continuation of the *Historia Ecclesiastica* of Eusebius is particularly valuable for events associated with Antioch.

7. The second letter next to be translated.

8. Probably God, not Theodosius, is meant in view of the previous sentence and because by this point in the letter Titus should have understood that Dionysius has been transmitting the imperial will.

9. This sentence is very loose in Latin, but the translation, it is hoped, interprets the sense.

10. Here the title (*magister militum*) varies from the form *supra* at n. 1. See no. 106, n. 4.

11. Including at least those mentioned in the previous letter.

12. John, patriarch of Antioch.

13. Theodosius II.

14. The Latin is so loose that the meaning may be "is not associated with nor communicates with . . . in adoring the sacred mysteries" or "is not associated with . . . in adoring the saints nor communicates with him in adoring the mysteries". See no. 75, n. 42.

15. If the word is personal, John is meant.

416. LETTER OF TITUS ON ECCLESIASTICAL PEACE AND UNITY, *c.* 434

(PG 84. 788)

A certain Titus, probably the deputy of Dionysius, master of the soldiers, continues the Theodosian endeavour to effect the union of eastern prelates with John, patriarch of Antioch, by an admonitory letter to Meletius, bishop of Mopsuestia, who, originally the latter's supporter in the Nestorian controversy, refused to follow his leader's submission to the imperial will. Meletius is taken to task for his recalcitrance by Titus, who threatens punishment for nonconformity. But Meletius persisted in his attitude and, when expelled from his see, induced others to secede from the Church and to form separate congregations, whose care he supervised; and his continued exercise of the episcopal office resulted in the exile of Meletius to Melitene in Armenia Minor (no. 417), where he died, a zealot for Nestorius till the last.

Titus to my lord Meletius, bishop, most dear to God in all respects and most holy.

416. ECCLESIASTICAL PEACE AND UNITY, C. 434

About your Sanctity are broadcast here [1] repeatedly many and various things, in respect to which the result is agreed: [2] that until the present your Sanctity (perhaps dissuaded by some persons, who cannot comprehend what is expedient) is unwilling to communicate with both the Catholic and the orthodox assembly of the whole world.

Now, therefore, though late, desire to take renewed guard against the enemy's wiles [3] and regain the affection of all holy bishops and do not exert yourself toward anticipations and much speech, which can aid no whit, nay rather also harm in the future life. For it is clear that God's Providence wishes all persons to be saved. In what way, therefore, is it credible that it has ordered only your Sanctity to be bound by your own judgements?

Therefore your Angel [4] should know that the divine letter has come, sanctioning certain definite measures against those persons who do not obey and against those persons who do not communicate with the holy and the universal council.[5] For we, who ever pray that the Devil's mischiefs nowise may prevail, have asked John,[6] the archbishop, most dear to God, to wait until this letter is delivered.[7] Therefore it should be your Religiosity's desire to discard indeed evil thoughts and to proceed and to come to Antioch.[8] For it is expedient in many ways that this should be done.

But if after this letter your holy Angel [4] shall not have wished to appear, no one shall have any further occasion whereby he can blame in anything either the said John, the bishop, most holy and most dear to God, or us ourselves, when with all speed we shall begin to execute those very things which have been commanded by the divine head.[9] For if the persons disobedient to the divine letter shall have been arrested in those cities wherein they appear to dwell, the severity shall be intolerable for them.

May you be unharmed.

1. Probably at Antioch.
2. That is, many and varied rumours all agree in the same net result.
3. Probably Satan's subtleties are meant.
4. See no. 551, n. 1.
5. A reference to the Third General Council of Ephesus, to whose condemnation of Nestorianism in 431 all bishops were desired to subscribe.
6. Patriarch of Antioch.
7. It was John who procured at last from Theodosius the order for Meletius' banishment.
8. Mopsuestia in Cilicia was about 65 miles distant from Antioch in Syria, whence this letter probably emanated.
9. Theodosius II.

417. INTERPRETATION OF MANDATE ON EXILE OF MELETIUS, c. 434
(PG 84. 796)

When Meletius, deposed bishop of Mopsuestia, refused to cease his organization of congregations out of communion with the Antiochene patriarchate, which generally had accepted the condemnation of Nestorianism by the Third General Council of Ephesus in 431, Dionysius, master of the soldiers, orders the execution of the imperial mandate of exile for this stubborn prelate (see introd. to nos. 415 and 416).

Interpretation of the order of Dionysius, master of the soldiers,[1] which he wrote to the most distinguished governor of Cilicia Secunda.[2]

The divine Authority by a respectable annotation [3] has ordered Meletius, formerly bishop of the Mopsuestian city, to live at Melitene, a city of the province of Armenia.

Therefore, when our order has been received and after has been read the divine response,[4] which shines among those already sent,[5] you are bound to observe what has been sanctioned by the immortal head,[6] using military aid for the said journey, if you shall have ascertained perchance that such aid will be necessary, by cautioning especially our vicar,[7] to whom we have written about this part, that suitable aid should be allotted, although we think that civilian companies [8] should suffice suitably.

1. See no. 106, n. 4.
2. For the gubernatorial divisions of Cilicia see no. 414, n. 6. The governor has not been identified.
3. In this case the petition requesting the removal of Meletius was presented by John, patriarch of Antioch, with whom Meletius refused to communicate ecclesiastically in his persistent espousal of Nestorianism. On annotation see no. 317, n. 2.
4. See no. 218, n. 5.
5. A complimentary clause to testify to the importance of this subscription to the petition.
6. Theodosius II.
7. Probably Count Titus, as elsewhere.
8. *Civiles ordines* in contrast to professional soldiers' aid (*militare solatium*) seems to mean that, if possible, regular troops should not be requisitioned for this episcopal escort, but that the governor's civil servants, provided with weapons, should be utilized.

418. LETTER OF TITUS ON ECCLESIASTICAL PEACE AND UNITY, c. 434

(PG 84. 796-7)

Count Titus, vicar of the master of the soldiers, writes to Alexander, bishop of Hierapolis, who with other bishops withdrew from communion with Cyril and John, patriarchs of Alexandria and of Antioch respectively, after the Third General Council at Ephesus in 431 had anathematized Nestorianism, and threatens exile for him if he shall continue in his contumacious attitude. This letter apparently had no effect on Alexander, because it is recorded that in 435 he was exiled to the Egyptian mines.

Titus to my lord, father Alexander, bishop, most dear to God and most holy.

How we ever have esteemed your Sanctity with a peculiar love and have busied ourselves to humour it particularly we think that it has known clearly from events themselves.

Therefore, because even now we are restrained as a result of the said good will and because in following Christ we desire that your eminent Religiosity should live, deign, most holy lord, even now, when you shall have received our letter, to communicate with the holy and the Catholic council [1] according to the divine and the adorable letter.[2] For both the most holy Theodoret and the most holy Helladius [3] and others who for a brief time wished to separate themselves from this holy council, recognizing what is irresistible and what is impossible and what is pleasing to God, and that obedience is due to the universal synod and to the imperial sanctions, indeed have withdrawn from discord; moreover they have communicated with the holy and the Catholic synod. Moreover it was fitting for your Sanctity, which clearly knew the situation and has been carried farther temporarily, to do[4] this before all things.

We ask therefore that you do not despise our present pleading letter and that you do not give place to the Devil,[5] who wishes to introduce discords against the Holy and Consubstantial Trinity, but that you scorn his stings and accept the holy synod's concord. For if your Sanctity shall have persisted in delay after this my letter and shall have been unwilling to communicate with these persons, it should be clear what has been made known by the divine letter to be necessary for the future.[6] Assuredly it openly orders that those persons who shall have been unwilling to communicate with the holy synod should be driven from the holy churches into exile.

1. A reference to the Third General Council of Ephesus in 431.

2. Of Theodosius II, who endeavoured to effect the reunion of Eastern Christendom, which had been divided by Nestorianism.
3. On these bishops see no. 415, nn. 3 and 6.
4. That is, has exceeded the limits of orthodoxy.
5. Quoted from Eph. 4. 27.
6. An editorial conjecture for an obscure reading has been adopted.

419. LETTER OF DIONYSIUS ON ECCLESIASTICAL PEACE AND UNITY, c. 434

(PG 84. 797–8)

Another admonitory letter to Alexander, bishop of Hierapolis, who has refused to re-enter into communion with John, patriarch of Antioch, is sent by Dionysius, master of the soldiers. Like that from his subordinate Titus (no. 418), this epistle evoked no submission from Alexander, who eventually was transported into exile.

Dionysius to my lord, father Alexander, bishop, most holy and most dear to God.

The divine and the immortal head[1] desires peace; moreover it applies very much care—and that befitting its Piety—to the cult of the right faith.

Knowing therefore our pious prince's[1] intention, we have thought that first by this our letter your Religiosity ought to be greeted and admonished that it should do the things which are befitting. Moreover among these is also this: that your Sanctity should communicate with John,[2] the bishop most dear to God. For this cause of peace will belong to all the holy churches. For we do not desire the churches to be disturbed any longer and the souls of the inexperienced, not knowing what they do, to be perverted, while confusion engrosses you, who pretend peace for all persons.

Therefore, only mindful both of our friendship and of exhortation, deign to discard all moroseness and likewise to agree with the most religious man, lest we should be compelled to order into execution the divine and imperial ordinances.

May the God of all preserve safely your Religiosity, even praying for us, my lord, most holy father. Your Religiosity will pardon me, if I am compelled to do anything in following the divine ordinance, if you shall have been unwilling to assent to this epistle.

1. Reading *vertex* for *veritas* (truth), as the editors suggest. The reference is to Theodosius II.
2. Patriarch of Antioch.

420. LETTER OF TITUS ON EXILE OF ALEXANDER, *c.* 434

(PG 84. 798–9)

This communication from Titus, count of the domestics and vicar of the master of the soldiers, to Libanius, governor of Euphratesia, of which the capital was Hierapolis, orders the exile of Bishop Alexander, whose see was in the capital, because he persisted in thwarting the imperial attempt to achieve ecclesiastical union in the East after the condemnation of Nestorianism by the Third Ecumenical Council of Ephesus in 431.

Order of the most glorious Titus, keeper of the place,[1] to the most distinguished Libanius, governor of Euphratesia.[2]

Flavius Titus, most glorious count of the most devoted domestics, filling the place of the authority of the master of the soldiery,[3] to Flavius Libanius, most distinguished governor of the province of Euphratesia.

Since those persons who do not agree with John,[4] the bishop, most dear to God, are moreover disturbing the holy churches, while they reject the peace of the world, our most divine princes[5] by their own law have commanded them to be removed from their own places, just as also the venerableness of the adorable and very fulgent letter rather clearly will show.

Therefore, because Alexander, the Hierapolitan bishop, has made his own self a stranger from the lot[6] of the most reverend bishops (for he does not endure to communicate with the aforesaid archbishop in the divine mysteries[7]), your Charity should take care that, on the receipt of this authority, the said Alexander, if he shall have persisted in his purpose, should be removed from his own place and that in his place you should receive him whom the synod of holy bishops shall have approved worthy of ordination. But if this exceeds your power (which we do not think), as long as very loyal soldiers have been stationed in that city,[8] you shall use their aid. For also we have sent directions to them as to what ought to be done, that with co-operative deliberation you may hasten to fulfil our commands. But if there is need even for a greater band or if this matter shall have demanded even our presence, it shall be sufficient for you to indicate this immediately. For, as this clearly has been established, we, executing the divine commands, shall come immediately with sufficient aid.

Moreover, that you may go soon to the aforesaid city [8] and may hasten to fulfil our commands, we have commanded Hypatius [9] to be delegated especially, to whom we also have given orders, that not only he should compel you to obey our commands, but also he should make us to know about your presumption, if so it shall have happened. For suitable punishment opposed to your neglect shall follow.

1. An odd expression for a deputy (*loci servator*), equivalent somewhat to our *locum tenens*.
2. Originally called Commagene.
3. See no. 415, n. 1.
4. Patriarch of Antioch.
5. Theodosius II and Valentinian III.
6. In the sense of number or group (*sors*).
7. See no. 75, n. 42.
8. Hierapolis.
9. From Libanius' reply Hypatius appears to have been on the staff of the master of the soldiers (*PG* 84. 799).

421. MANDATE OF THEODOSIUS II AND VALENTINIAN III ON CLERICS' AND MONKS' INHERITANCES, 434

(*CT* 5. 3. 1)

This legislation enacts that property of clerics and of monks dying intestate and heirless should pass to their churches or monasteries, certain conditions excepted.

Justinian repeats this statute with slight modifications (*CI* 1. 3. 20).

Emperors Theodosius and Valentinian Augusti to Taurus, praetorian prefect [1] and patrician.

If any bishop or [2] priest or deacon or deaconess or subdeacon or cleric of any other rank or monk or woman who has been dedicated to a solitary life [3] shall have died without having made a will and if for that person parents of either sex or children or persons who are related by the laws of agnation or of cognation [4] or wife shall not have survived, the properties which have belonged to that person should be joined in every way to the sacrosanct church or monastery

421. CLERICS' AND MONKS' INHERITANCES, 434

to which he had been appointed—with the exception of those properties which are left by clerics or by monks of each sex who perchance are registered in the census [5] or are subjected to the right of patronage [6] or are subject to the curial status.[7] For it is not just that by the churches [8] should be detained property or peculia,[9] which either are due by the laws to a patron or to an owner of a landed estate [10] to which any of the said persons had been bound or are known to belong to the municipal senates under a certain provision pursuant to the tenor of a constitution long ago issued [11]—action-at-law, of course, having been reserved properly for the sacrosanct churches,[8] if perchance anyone subject to the aforesaid classes shall have died while obligated either from business transactions or from any other ecclesiastical acts:[12] so that, if any lawsuits from claims of this character [13] are pending in courts, they should be settled absolutely,[14] and after this law's publication it should not be permitted to a claimant to enter into court or to inflict annoyance upon stewards [15] or monks or managers,[15] because the claim itself has been abolished and because the property which has been left has been consecrated to the very religious churches or monasteries to which the decedent had been dedicated.

Given on 15 December, Ariovind and Aspar being consuls.

Interpretation: If any bishop or those whom this law mentions or any male or female religious shall have died intestate without children, relatives, or wife, who, however, shall have owed nothing to either a municipal senate or a patron, whatever they shall have left shall belong to the churches or to the monasteries to which they have submitted. And if they shall have wished to make a will, they shall have free power to do so.

1. Of the East.
2. Justinian omits *bishop or*.
3. The words for "nun" (μοναχή; *monacha*) are reported ere this constitution's date, but the authors or their lawyers prefer apparently a relative clause to describe such a woman.
4. On agnation and cognation see no. 599, n. 5.
5. As subject to the poll-tax levied on tenant farmers, who farmed the land on large private and imperial estates generally on five-year contracts. By the time of Constantine the Great (*CT* 5. 17. 1; dated 322) it was illegal for such tenants to leave their farms, and so they became bound to the soil. Such heirless persons' property passed at their death to their landlords. See no. 528, nn. 2 and 5.
6. Heirless freedmen's property passed at their death to their patrons, who had been their masters when the freedmen had been slaves.
7. Heirless curials' property passed at their death to their municipal senates (*curiae*).

8. Justinian adds "or monasteries".

9. On the peculium see nos. 337, n. 6, and 624, n. 3.

10. Cf. *supra* nn. 5–7.

11. Perhaps *CT* 5. 2. 1 (dated 319) is meant.

12. Justinian omits the rest after this point.

13. That is, for estates of deceased clerics, as being vacant.

14. The verb (*sopire*) means literally "to lull to sleep"; the idea is that such a suit should be quashed.

15. Ecclesiastical officials, not necessarily ordained, are meant.

422. GENERAL LAW OF THEODOSIUS II AND VALENTINIAN III ON NESTORIANISM, 435

(M 5. 413)

This constitution [1] outlaws Nestorianism, directs the burning of books containing Nestorian doctrines, prohibits the assembling of Nestorians, and confiscates the property of violators of this law.

Mansi gives it in Greek here and in three variant Latin versions (5. 414, 5. 660–1, 9. 249–50). In abbreviated form it appears in *CT* 16. 5. 66 and *CI* 1. 5. 6. The Greek archetype, as it is believed, is translated.

Copy of the sacred law against Nestorius.

The reverence due from us to the most pious religion demands that persons conducting themselves impiously toward the Divinity should be chastised by deserved punishments and should be addressed by a name suitable to their depravity, so that they, denounced by this disgrace, may endure eternal punishment for their sins and neither, while alive, may be without punishment nor, when dead, may be without dishonour.

Therefore, since [2] Nestorius,[3] the author of a monstrous doctrine,[4] has been condemned,[5] it remains for us to encompass the persons who are likeminded with him and the companions of his impiety with a condemnatory name, lest, abusing the appellation of Christians, they should be adorned by this name, from whose dogma in their impiety they have withdrawn.[6]

Therefore we legislate that persons everywhere sharing Nestorius' nefarious opinion should be called Simonians,[7] for it is proper that those who imitate that one's [8] impiety in aversion from the Divinity should obtain with that one [8] the same appellation. And similarly by a law of Constantine of divine lot [9] Arians on account of the similarity

422. NESTORIANISM, 435

of their impiety are called Porphyrians from Porphyry, for this person, having attempted to struggle against the true religion by the power of his word, has left books of ill-repute [10] rather than treatises of erudition.[11]

And none should dare to have or to read or to copy the impious books of the nefarious and the sacrilegious Nestorius concerning the pure religion [12] of orthodox persons and against the dogmas of the holy synod of the bishops [13] in Ephesus,[5] which, when sought [14] with all [15] zeal, it is necessary to burn publicly.[16] For by this way, when all impiety has been excised from the root, the simple and the easily deceived multitude will be able at any time to find no seed of error.[17]

And no mention of so abandoned persons should be made in any discussion of religion by a name other than that of Simon,[7] or none should furnish for them secretly or openly a house or a field or a suburb or any other place whatsoever for an assembly.[18] For we determine that such persons should be deprived of every licence of assembly—it being clear to all persons that he who both transgresses this law and imitates Nestorius shall be punished by confiscation of property.[19]

Therefore your very great and conspicuous Authority shall provide that this our constitution should come by edicts in the usual way to the knowledge of all persons inhabiting the provinces.

This law we have put in the tongue of both Romans and Greeks, that to all persons it may be clear and known.

1. Theodosius later calls this document a general law (no. 459).
2. Here begin *CT* and *CI*, where this ordinance is addressed by the same Augusti to Leontius, urban prefect of Constantinople.
3. Late patriarch of Constantinople.
4. *CT* and *CI* translate διδασκαλία (teaching) by *superstitio* (superstition).
5. At the Third General Council at Ephesus in 431.
6. *CT* and *CI* say more simply after the causal clause: "a mark of a suitable name should be branded upon his companions, lest they may abuse the appellation of Christians".

With the thought of heretics abusing and being adorned by the name of Christians one may compare St Augustine's complaint in his *De Fide Rerum Quae non Videntur*, 7 *ad med.* (=*PL* 40. 180), where he says that there has arisen no kind of error which is found to so oppose Christian truth that it does not seek and strive to boast in the name of Christ.

7. The reference is to the protoheresiarch Simon Magus of Samaria, whose opposition to St Peter (Acts 8. 9-24) is so overladen with later legend that it is difficult to describe with confidence his doctrine, which seems to have been the last representation of pre-Christian Gnosticism. His profession that he was God the Father among the Samaritans, God the Son among the Jews, God the Holy

Spirit among the Gentiles—if such language is contemporary with its speaker—is both an early and an excellent testimony to Trinitarianism.

For a convenient résumé of the early romancings about Simon consult J. T. Shotwell and L. R. Loomis, *The See of Peter* (New York, 1927), 122–207, where these authors collect and comment on the chief strata of the story.

8. Simon.

9. No. 66.

10. This phrase has been suggested by editors from Constantine's law (no. 66) to give balance here, where the Greek seems defective.

11. In *CT* and *CI* this paragraph reads thus: "But just as by a law of Constantine of divine memory Arians on account of the similarity of their impiety are called Porphyrians from Porphyry, so everywhere sharers of Nestorius' nefarious sect should be called Simonians, that they may seem justly to have obtained the name of that one whose wickedness in abandoning God they have imitated."

Tertullian earlier had noted that it was no novelty for some way of life to give its followers a name taken from their teacher and he instances Platonists, Epicureans, Pythagoreans (*Apol.* 3. 6).

12. *CT* and *CI* read "against the venerable sect".

13. *CT* and *CI* read "decrees of the most holy assembly of bishops held".

14. *CT* and *CI* substitute the infinitival for the participial form.

15. *CT* and *CI* read "diligent".

16. The Greek lacks a principal verb for this sentence, but *CT* and *CI* change the infinitive τολμᾶν (to dare) into *audeat* (should dare). The verb in the relative clause in Greek, δεῖ (it is necessary) they turn into the verb *decernimus* (we decree), which becomes in Latin the sentence's second principal verb. See no. 382, n. 1.

17. *CT* and *CI* omit this sentence.

18. *CT* and *CI* for this sentence, which in Greek again is without a principal verb, read "Moreover none in a discussion of religion should dare to make mention by another name than the aforesaid or should furnish for any of them secretly or openly a meeting-place in his house or villa or suburban estate or any other place whatsoever for holding an assembly."

19. *CT* and *CI* condense this sentence thus: "And we determine that these persons should be deprived of all licence of holding an assembly—all persons knowing that a violator of this law must be punished by confiscation of property."

Herewith *CT* and *CI* end except for the ensuing subscription:

"Given on 3 August at Constantinople, our Lord Theodosius Augustus for the fifteenth time and he who shall be announced being consuls."

The later consul was Valentinian Augustus for the fourth time.

423. EDICT OF ISIDORE, BASSUS, AND REGINUS ON DESTRUCTION OF NESTORIUS' WRITINGS, 435

(M 5. 416-17)

This edict, issued by three praetorian prefects, implements the imperial constitution (no. 422) commanding the destruction of Nestorian writings.

The translation is from Greek, for Mansi has two variant Latin versions here and in 5. 661-2.

Edict of the prefects that the writings of Nestorius should not be read.

Flavius Anthemius Isidore,[1] Flavius Bassus,[2] and Flavius Simplicius Reginus,[3] prefects, proclaim:

Nothing is so dear to the masters [4] as to live piously in all respects. If they do not shrink—so to speak—from alacrity in continuously attending to affairs daily by applying both nights and days upon their thoughts, how much more in the case of piety itself and religion have they not known how to guard these narrowly with all earnestness?

Therefore, when some religion, both unreasonable and insane and full of audacity, is in the process of growth (rather not in the process, but already has claimed a certain deceit of authority), by their own zeal, without any commotion, with all serenity, which indeed is ever innate in them and in all respects is habitual, they have ordered such correction to occur, since they have chastised the leaders of the transgression with due penalties, but have made provision for the rest that they, not harmed, but persuaded for the better by admonition alone, when reformed, may lose none of their belongings; but that they, if they have discovered it straightway, may guard firmly the possession of piety, which is perfect (because it is the chief cause) and eternal (because it exists after this life).[5]

But since mankind, once caught and netted both by deceitful words and by inferior reasonings, is self-willed and, besides, needs both much fear and very grievous punishments,[6] they command that persons who debase the dogmas of the faith both should be quiet henceforth and should change their minds for the better and neither should foregather into any place nor should represent to others any of the places belonging to themselves as a stadium of impiety—whether it is in a city or is set in a remote place or is near to a city—and that absolutely all the earth should be inviolate from such an assembly.

And they, pitying rather than punishing the persons who are devoted to Nestorius' insanities and compositions and who have his books as their source of error, declare that they should give these to the fire and should destroy these, lest reminders of such great error, if circulated in the commonwealth, should become obstructive to the true faith, and also that they should not write others (to light upon which has been illegal from the beginning), lest persons should read such books, the harm from which causes the destruction of everything. For what are more precious than the soul and the faith? And such readings harm these and, while blinding the soul's vital part, prepare to lead it to a worse state.

And lest these persons, if there are any, should escape notice or, if they have a certain appropriate epithet, should suggest the author of this very drama by bringing to remembrance things which it would be better to consign to oblivion, they have ordained for them to be called Simonians,[7] because they will chastise them with very severe punishments, if they should transgress.

And that you may know the serenity and the piety of what has been ordained and the forethought, through which on all occasions they have consideration for their subjects, of our most pious emperors,[4] who alone render to the Almighty through faith the recompense worthy of the benefits bestowed on both themselves and all the world, we have ordained by our edict—according to custom—that the law, full of divine light, should shine forth. And you, if you have obeyed it, shall make yourselves free from punishment and you, if you have learned to be pious for all future space of time, shall cling to immortal benefits, since you are bound to receive as many benefits as both the emperor, who makes the law, and God, who is worshipped piously, are naturally bound to bestow.

1. Of the East.
2. The Greek has Flesbassus or Flesbasius, but the Latin translator rightly has emended by expansion to Flavius Bassus, whose prefecture is unknown, but probably was that of Italy.
3. Of Illyricum.
4. That is, the emperors, Theodosius II and Valentinian III.
5. The Greek is somewhat obscure and the Latin is paraphrased.
6. Perhaps a hendiadys: "needs to fear greatly very weighty penalties".
7. See no. 422, n. 7, for the explanation.

424. MANDATE OF THEODOSIUS II AND VALENTINIAN III ON ERECTION OF THE CROSS ON SITES OF HEATHEN SHRINES, 435

(CT 16. 10. 25)

Besides banning pagan sacrifices, the emperors order that all remaining pagan temples should be razed, that the Cross should be set on such sites, and that death should be the penalty for any violators of their statute.

Emperors Theodosius and Valentinian Augusti to Isidore, praetorian prefect.[1]

All persons of criminal pagan mind we interdict from accursed immolations of sacrificial victims and from damnable sacrifices and from all other practices prohibited by the authority of the more ancient ordinances,[2] and we order that all their shrines, temples, sanctuaries, if any even now remain intact, should be destroyed[3] by the magistrates' command and that these should be purified by the placing of the venerable Christian religion's sign[4]—all persons knowing that if it shall have been established by suitable proofs before a competent judge that anyone has mocked this law, the said person must be punished with death.

Given on 14 November at Constantinople, Theodosius Augustus for the fifteenth time and Valentinian Augustus for the fourth time being consuls.

1. Of the East.
2. See introd. to no. 242.
3. The imperial policy concerning pagan temples vacillated until this time. Thus laws of 342 (CT 16. 10. 3), 382 (CT 16. 10. 8), 399 (CT 16. 10. 15 and 18) legislated preservation of such buildings for various reasons, such as places for public assembly, appreciation of art and architecture, conversion into Christian churches. But a law of 346 or 354 or 356 (CT 16. 10. 4) demanded the immediate closing of pagan temples; laws of 381 (CT 16. 10. 7), 391 (CT 16. 10. 10 and 11), 392 (no. 242), 395 (CT 16. 10. 13), 399 (CT 16. 10. 18), 407 or 408 (CT 16. 10. 19) forbade resort to pagan shrines; laws of 399 (CT 16. 10. 18) and 407 or 408 (CT 16. 10. 19) ordered removal of altars and idols from pagan sanctuaries; laws of 395 (CT 16. 10. 13), 407 or 408 (CT 16. 10. 19), 415 (CT 16. 10. 20) confiscated pagan religious property to the public use or to the imperial treasury or to the Christian religion; and laws of 399 (CT 16. 10. 16) and 435 (no. 424) commanded the complete destruction of pagan temples.
4. The Cross, which in this connection confirms the veracity of the verse "towering o'er the wrecks of time".

425. INTERPRETATION OF MANDATE ON EXILE OF NESTORIUS, 436

(M 5. 256)

Of the constitution exiling Nestorius, deposed patriarch of Constantinople, there remains only the interpretation, whence we learn that Petra (the ancient capital of Edom in Transjordan) was assigned as his—the first, as it seems—abode of banishment.

The translation is from the Greek, for Mansi has two variant Latin versions here and in 5. 660.

Copy of the interpretation of the royal constitution, written to Isidore, praetorian prefect [1] and consul, concerning Nestorius' exile.

Although our zeal for provision for public affairs is conspicuous, nevertheless the most sacred religion's security is no less in our regard. And because this indeed is fostered by us, we believe that we are aided also in public affairs.

And therefore, since Nestorius, late a priest of the Catholic Church, but now a betrayer of the faith, appears to have been entangled in such great magnitudes of abominations, it also is necessary that he, having been subject to our Serenity's sentence, should be crushed by a misery suited to his character—as should be any person who, when the Church's august laws have been abandoned, has appeared to be the author of a lawless heresy and who in corrupting the faith of persons, whom he has attached to participation in his own betrayal, has received upon his own person the accusation of another's betrayal.

Wherefore your honoured Authority, by this pragmatic constitution or by your own revealed authority, should move the aforesaid Nestorius into exile to Petra forever [2] because of the impieties traced to him, in such wise that all his property should be assigned to the Church of Constantinople for the augmentation of the resources of that most august place, whose sacrament he lately has betrayed. For thus devotion toward the most sacred faith will be unharmed in men's souls and our realm's felicity, fortified by religion, will flourish.

1. Of the East.
2. It is known that Nestorius later was transferred to at least three different places in Egypt.

426. LETTER OF THEODOSIUS II ON EXILE OF IRENAEUS AND PHOTIUS, 436
(PG 84. 802–3)

Coincidental with the exile of Nestorius, late patriarch of Constantinople, seems to have been that of Count Irenaeus, his lay friend and adherent, who had travelled with him to the Third General Council at Ephesus a quinquennium earlier and had pleaded his case in Constantinople, whither he went from Ephesus.

This document's interest is enhanced by the later career of its chief subject, for Irenaeus survived his exile both to become, though twice married, bishop of Tyre, whence he was deposed (no. 445), and to compile in Greek a well-documented dossier of the Nestorian controversy, which exists only in a large series of extracts made in Latin after Justinian I's death and is known as the *Synodicon adversus Tragoediam Irenaei* (PG 84. 565–864).

Included in this order is a certain Photius, whom editors suppose to have been a propagandist of Nestorianism in Lydia.

Letter of the emperor.
Interpretation of the letter which has been promulgated to the most eminent and the most glorious prefects [1] concerning the exile of the most eminent Count Irenaeus to Petra.[2]

Since Nestorius, the chief of a revolting rite, has been condemned, it is just that the sharers of his impious rite should experience a very vigorous punishment.

On this account we have decreed that Irenaeus, who not only has followed Nestorius' cursed cult, but also has organized it and has striven to overturn many provinces with him (for this purpose, that he himself might preside over such a rite), when stripped of all dignities and, moreover, of his own property, and, besides, Photius, implicated in the said impieties, when equally stripped of his property, which also shall advantage the public accounts,[3] should be exiled in Petra, that they may be tortured by perpetual poverty and by the loneliness of the localities, most honoured cousin [4] Isidore.[5]

Therefore your glorious and eminent Authority shall obey becomingly this our pragmatic decree,[6] with sufficient support allotted, that the aforesaid violators of our religion should be driven into the path of the aforesaid exile.

Interpretation of the aforesaid command: The divine letter's shining tenor shows what are the measures which about Irenaeus and Photius have been sanctioned by the divine and the immortal head.[7]

Therefore your Magnificence, without delay obeying these measures, which divinely have been decreed, should prepare for the places, to which they have been ordered to be led, with suitable support two post-horses with two extra horses [8] for Orestes and Stephen [9] (who individually have been directed to execute what measures divinely have been decreed and what measures are contained in our commands)—with persons from Syria joining in helping them: both governors of districts and municipal senates of any provinces and, besides, defenders and (as a remaining support or auxiliary) decurions or curials.

1. That is, the praetorian prefects, probably those named in no. 423.
2. Nestorius also was exiled to Petra (no. 425).
3. That is, the imperial treasury.
4. The Latin is *pater* (father), but the usual Latin term is *parens* (cousin), when applied to a layman. See no. 375, n. 15.
5. Praetorian prefect of the East.
6. In late juridical Latin this type of imperial constitution referred ordinarily to a community's affairs.
7. Theodosius II.
8. To transport the baggage allowed to travellers by the public post. Such a pack animal was called a *parhippus* (πάριππος) or a *paraveredus*, which latter is supposed by an astonishing line of alteration to be the linguistic ancestor of the German *Pferd*.
9. If the Latin is correct, it seems that the four horses were allocated to these men, who were the exiles' escorts, and that the exiles and the minor attendants, if any, of the convoy were to walk the distance.

427. LETTER OF THEODOSIUS II AND VALENTINIAN III ON ECCLESIASTICAL PEACE AND UNITY, 436

(PG 65. 880–2)

Certain envoys of St Proclus, patriarch of Constantinople, after having carried to Antioch his *Tome* (a celebrated doctrinal epistle),[1] wherein were condemned certain teachings of Theodore, bishop of Mopsuestia in Cilicia, tried to persuade John, patriarch of Antioch, and his domestic synod to condemn both the tenets and the name of Theodore, who, some justly asserted, was the real author of the heresy associated with the name of Nestorius (a recent predecessor of Proclus in the Constantinopolitan patriarchate), but who had died in the Church's communion.[2] Their failure might have been foreseen, for the Antiochenes, who long had acclaimed Theodore as their greatest teacher, both refused the request and resorted to rioting (so typical of theological opposition in the

427. ECCLESIASTICAL PEACE AND UNITY, 436

Orient). Thereupon Theodosius wrote to John in the interest of ecclesiastical harmony, desiring that "the dead which die in the Lord" [3] should rest in peace, and thus succeeded in soothing the Antiochenes' turbulent temperament.

Facundus also has this letter in his *Defensio Trium Capitulorum*, 8. 3 (= PL 67. 717–18) and it appears also in the *Synodicon* of Irenaeus, 219 (= PG 84. 849–50).

Emperors, Caesars Theodosius and Valentinian, Victors, Triumphers, Most Pious, Ever-August to John, archbishop, the lover of God,[4] and to the [5] synod assembled with him.[6]

Through Proclus, our most religious and most holy [7] father and bishop, our Sovereignty has learned about the turmoil and the tumult which occur [8] in the Orient.

Therefore, since we provide for all persons' quiet and peace, but particularly for the Catholic [9] faith, which protects also [10] our Empire, we write [11] to your Sanctity that you should preserve peace and you should attend to no word of those persons [12] who contrary to their own salvation [13] desire to disturb the holy [14] religion. For our Divinity's [15] intention is this: that all persons, but particularly God's holy churches, through which both we are saved and our Empire prevails, should live in quiet.

Accordingly, providing for the Church's quiet by this word,[16] from you something beneficial we expect.[17] Moreover is anything more beneficial than this, except that you also with the whole Church should decide this: that, as for the rest,[18] no one should venture any such thing [19] against those persons who have died in her peace?[20]

1. In *PG* 65. 855–74.
2. It was not until 553 at the Fifth Ecumenical Council (Constantinople II) that Theodore's doctrines were anathematized.
3. Rev. 14. 13.
4. Irenaeus reads "the most beloved of God and the most blessed".
5. Irenaeus prefixes "holy".
6. Facundus adds "in Antioch".
7. Irenaeus omits *and most holy*.
8. Irenaeus reads "has occurred".
9. Irenaeus has "right" for *Catholic*.
10. For *also* Irenaeus reads "us and".
11. Irenaeus has "have written by this letter".
12. This clause Irenaeus condenses to "and you should consider of no account those persons".
13. Or perhaps "safety", for they, as disturbers, might fall foul of the law.
14. Facundus uses the superlative form and Irenaeus substitutes "most salutary".

15. "Worthiness's" in Irenaeus.
16. That is, ordinance.
17. Irenaeus expands this sentence into two by changing the participle into an imperative. He and Facundus change *beneficial* into "rather beneficial". Irenaeus omits the next sentence, while Facundus omits *we expect . . . than this*.
18. Or perhaps "henceforth".
19. He means anathematization (*damnatio memoriae*).
20. Irenaeus adds "May God preserve you, most venerated fathers, for many years."

428. MANDATE OF THEODOSIUS II AND VALENTINIAN III ON EPISCOPAL EXEMPTION FROM TAXATION, 436
(*CT* 11. 1. 37)

This constitution exempts Cyrus, bishop of Aphrodisias in Caria, Asia Minor, from paying taxes in gold on the basis of the average yield of agricultural products taken over a five-year period. Why such exemption was made and on what basis Cyrus had paid taxes, if at all, are unknown.

The same Augusti to Darius, praetorian prefect.[1]

Though past grants,[2] however they have been procured, remain in their own state, since it is impious for the imperial munificence to be revoked, yet for the future—with the exception of the most reverend Cyrus, bishop of the Aphrodisians' city, whose[3] merits are so great that, even contrary to this kind of general sanction, he shall not be forbidden to enjoy fully a special benefit—whoever by our annotation[4] shall have wished to pay their tributes in gold, after an estimate for a quinquennium has been averaged, with a reckoning of sterility and of fecundity made in accord with the market of things sold, from the said sum, which is calculated by carefully computing the said quinquennium's fruits, should be compelled to pay for each single year a fifth part.

Given on 28 August at Apamea, Isidore and Senator being consuls.

1. Of the East.
2. Some such noun, which is wanting in Latin, must be understood.
3. Cyrus.
4. See no. 317, n. 2.

429. LETTER OF THEODOSIUS II AND VALENTINIAN III ON DISABILITIES FOR JEWS, SAMARITANS, HERETICS, AND PAGANS, 438

(*LNT* 3)

Only so much of this lengthy law, whence Justinian borrows material for three laws (*CI* 1. 5. 7, 1. 7. 5, 1. 9. 18), as affects Christians is translated, since some of it pertains to other persons, on whom it lays various civil disabilities. The law prohibits Jews and Samaritans from having jurisdiction over Christians and penal custody of Christians, anyone from seducing Christians from orthodox worship, construction of new synagogues (which must be confiscated for the Church's profit), pagan sacrifices to the disparagement of Christianity, ten specified heresies.

Emperors Theodosius and Valentinian Augusti to Florentius, praetorian prefect.[1]

Among all other anxieties, which love for the State has enjoined upon us with very vigilant consideration, we perceive our imperial Majesty's especial care to be the pursuit of the true religion. And if we shall have been able to maintain its worship, we open the way of prosperity to human undertakings. And having learned this by the experience of long life,[2] by the decision of a pious mind we have decided to establish the ceremonies of holiness by a law of perpetual duration even to posterity....[3]

And we learn that persons blinded in their senses—Jews, Samaritans, pagans, and all other breeds of heretical monsters—dare this.[4] And if by a curative law we should try to recall them to the sanity of an excellent mind, they themselves will take upon themselves blame for severity, since they do not leave place for pardon by the stubborn sin of an obstinate boldness.

Wherefore, since according to the old maxim [5] no cure must be applied for hopeless diseases, finally, lest deadly sects, unmindful of our age, should spread rather unrestrainedly into our life just as an undistinguishable confusion, we [6] ordain this by law (which shall live for all time): that no Jew, no Samaritan, relying on either law,[7] should enter upon honours and dignities—to none should be available the administration of a civic service—and should not perform even a defender's duty.[8] Indeed, we believe it a sin that persons inimical to the Supernal Majesty [9] and to the Roman laws should be considered also avengers of our laws by possession of a surreptitious jurisdiction [10] and that they, protected by the authority of an acquired dignity, should have the power of judging or of pronouncing what they wish [11] against Christians and very often the bishops themselves of the sacred religion, just as if insulting our faith. . . .[12]

To these rules we add: whoever shall have transferred a slave or a free-born person, unwillingly or by punishable persuasion, from the Christian religion's cult to an abominable sect or rite must be punished capitally along with the loss of his property;[13] that therefore [14] whoever shall have accepted the insignia of office should not possess the acquired dignities,[15] and whoever shall have constructed a synagogue should know that he has laboured for the Catholic Church's profit. Indeed whoever shall have crept into honours [16] should be considered, as previously, of lowest status, even if he shall have gained [17] an honorary dignity. . . .[18]

Moreover let him perceive that his goods have been proscribed and that thereupon to the penalty of blood [19] must be destined he who by perverse teaching has overcome another's faith.[20]

And since it is proper for the imperial Majesty to embrace all matters in this provision that the public interest may be injured in no way, we [21] decide that curials of all communities and cohortalines,[22] of whatsoever sect they may be, when bound to onerous duties, even those of the governmental service,[23] or to various services of their resources and of their personal public services, should adhere to their own orders,[24] lest we should appear to offer because of contumelious solicitation the benefit of immunity to execrable persons, whom we wish to be condemned by this constitution's authority,[25] with this exception observed: that apparitors of the mentioned sects should execute a judge's sentence only in private matters and should not superintend the custody of prisons, lest Christians (as is wont to happen), when sometimes imprisoned by their guards' hatreds, should suffer another incarceration,[26] when it is uncertain whether they seem to have been confined rightfully.

Hence our Clemency perceives that we ought to allot vigilance also over pagan and heathen heinousness, since they, by natural madness and pertinacious licence departing from true religion's path, scorn to practise in any way the nefarious rites of sacrifices and the errors of deadly superstition in hidden solitudes, unless their crimes are publicized by the character of their profession to the outrage of the Supernal Majesty and to the contempt of our time. And a thousand terrors of the promulgated laws and the penalty of threatened exile do not check them, that, if they cannot be corrected, at least they may learn to abstain from the mass of crimes and from the filth of sacrifices. But straightway they sin with this audacity of madness and our patience is attacked by these attempts of vile persons, that, if one should desire to forget them, one cannot disregard them. Therefore, although the love of religion never can be secure [27] and although the pagan madness

429. JEWS, SAMARITANS, HERETICS, AND PAGANS, 438

demands the severities of all punishments, nevertheless we, mindful of leniency innate in us, have decreed by a firm [28] command that whoever with polluted and contaminated thoughts shall have been caught in sacrificing in any place whatsoever, our anger should swell against his property and not [29] against his blood. For we ought to give this better victim [30]—the altar of Christianity having been kept inviolate. Shall we endure longer that the succession of the seasons should be altered, when the temper of the sky has been enraged, since the pagans' embittered perfidy knows not how to maintain Nature's balance? For why has spring forsworn its wonted charm? Why has summer, barren of harvest, forsaken the toiling farmer in his hope of grain harvests? Why has winter's intemperate ferocity with penetrating cold doomed the fertility of the lands with sterility's injury?—unless because Nature transgresses the decree of its own law for the punishment of impiety.[31] And lest we should be forced hereafter to endure this, by peaceful punishment (as we have said) must be appeased the Supernal Divinity's venerable majesty.[32]

It remains, Florentius, dearest and fondest cousin, that what rules have been enacted in countless constitutions against Manichaeans (ever odious to God), against Eunomians (authors of heretical fatuity), against Montanists, Phrygians, Photinians, Priscillians, Ascodrogitans,[33] Hydroparastatans, Borborians, Ophitans, with cessation of inactivity should be entrusted to speedy execution.

Therefore your illustrious and eminent Authority, to whose heart it is dear to devote obedience to divine as well as imperial commands, by your Excellency's duly posted edicts should cause to come to all persons' notice and should order to be announced also to the provinces' governors what we have decreed in the Catholic religion's insatiable honour, that also by their like care they may notify to all communities and provinces what we necessarily have ordained.

Given on 31 January at Constantinople, our Lord Theodosius Augustus for the sixteenth time being consul and he who shall be announced.

Interpretation: This law specifically orders that no Jew and no Samaritan can attain to any honour of governmental service [23] or of administration, neither undertake in any way a defender's duty nor be guards of a prison, lest perchance under the pretext of any duty whatsoever they may dare to vex with outrages on any occasion whatever Christians or even their bishops, lest the abovementioned persons, who are enemies of our law,[34] may presume by our laws either to condemn or to judge [35] any persons.

They should not dare to construct any synagogue anew. For if they shall have done this, they should know that this structure will profit the Catholic Church and that the originators of the structure must be fined fifty pounds of gold. But they should know that this has been conceded to them: that they must repair the ruins of their synagogues.³⁶

This also has been included specifically in this law: that no Jew should dare to transfer to his own law by any persuasion at all a Christian, slave or free-born. And if he shall have done this, after his property has been forfeited he should be punished capitally.

But concerning the rest: this law condemns the sects which, inserted by name, are contained in this law.

1. Of the East.
2. Theodosius, the senior emperor, who enacted this law, was only 37 years of age in 438; Valentinian was about 22 years old.
3. Here is omitted a long question asking, in effect, who is so mad or so savage that, when he sees the works of God in nature, he does not seek their author.
4. The reference is to their failure to seek God, as suggested in the preceding note.
5. Editors laud two *loci* in Hippocrates' *De Arte* (§§ 3 and 14, pp. 192 and 216 in vol. 2 of W. H. S. Jones' edition and translation of Hippocrates' work [London, 1923]) as the source of this *sententia*.
6. Here begins *CI* 1. 9. 18.
7. By this expression is meant either the law of the Eastern Empire or of the Western Empire or the law of the Romans or of the Jews.
8. Justinian omits *no Samaritan . . . law*, though "no Samaritan" seems to have fallen from the text, for he next reads "to whom [plural number] all administrations and dignities have been forbidden", and he omits also *to . . . service*, but after *duty* he adds "and we do not allow him [a Jew] to appropriate a father's honour".
9. Apparently the reference is to the orthodox Christian Deity: thus the four types of persons mentioned in the title are meant.
10. *CI* omits this much of the sentence and joins to the preceding sentence by "lest" what follows.
11. For *what they wish CI* has "any" prefixed to *power*.
12. A short section prohibiting construction of synagogues is omitted as not relevant to Christians.
13. *CI* 1. 7. 5 consists of this clause, which begins thus: "We ordain that he, whoever" etc.
14. Here resumes *CI* 1. 9. 18.
15. At this point *CI* interjects "or if he shall have sneaked into forbidden offices, he should be driven from these entirely".
16. *CI* adds "and dignities".
17. *CI* interposes "illegally".
18. After this is omitted a sentence on penalty for erecting a synagogue.
19. That is, death.

20. With this sentence, which, it is supposed, applies primarily to Jewish seducers of Christians from Christianity, CI 1. 9. 18 ends.

21. Here begins CI 1. 5. 7.

22. CI omits *and cohortalines*, on whom see no. 320, n. 5.

23. See no. 186, n. 4.

24. Their classes in the State's system of regimentation. See no. 325, n. 6.

25. Here ends Justinian's third and last quotation from this law.

26. Possibly the idea is that the guards' cruelty toward their prisoners doubles the bitterness of imprisonment.

27. The idea may be completed by the addition of such a clause as "while these beliefs and practices exist".

28. The adjective is poetic and means "of or belonging to a beam", i.e. "beam-like", "stout as a beam".

29. The negative is suggested by editors, who justly suspect that otherwise the conclusion contradicts the preceding promise of clemency.

30. Perhaps a reminiscence of Vergil, *Aen.* 5. 483-4, where Entellus dedicates a bull as "this better life" for Dares' death.

The sentence with the mention of sacrifice and of blood in the previous sentence presents a confused picture: on the one hand the sanguinary sacrifice of pagans, on the other hand the absence of blood from the Christians' altar; if any sacrificing is to be done in the Christian dispensation, it is the confiscating of pagans' property which will act as a deterrent from continuation of pagan practices.

31. Conversely the pagans considered that the poor performance of the soil came from the governmental support given to Christianity. Thus, when Quintus Aurelius Symmachus, the head of a senatorial delegation to Theodosius I, two generations earlier (384) vainly was requesting the restoration of the Altar of Victory (removed by Gratian in 382 to propitiate Christians) to the Roman Senate, among other things he attributed failure of crops and public famine to this sacrilege (*Rel. de Ara Vict.* 3. 15-17).

32. See no. 242, n. 2.

33. Apparently a by-form for Tascodrogitans.

34. Christianity.

35. An instance of hysteron proteron.

36. This paragraph interprets a paragraph omitted in the translation of the law (see *supra* n. 12), since in the law the paragraph has no specific pertinency to the Church. The interpretation here, however, provides such pertinency and therefore is translated.

Such repair would obviate the need for building new edifices, since even the replacement of a demolished building by another building of similar form and character was regarded simply as the same building, though in somewhat strict interpretation it is another building which is built (*D* 8. 2. 20. 2).

430. MANDATE OF THEODOSIUS II AND VALENTINIAN III ON CORPSE-CARRIERS' SERVICE TO THE CHURCH, 439

(*CI* 1. 2. 9)

This constitution, repeated with extra-Christian additions (*CI* 11. 18. 1), attempts to solve the situation whereby multiple membership in guilds leads to guildsmen claiming immunity from service in one guild on the ground that they serve in another guild. The mandate is aimed at persons who, apparently and originally silversmiths or coinmakers, prefer the less onerous and the more occasional duties of corpse-carriers, but whose service in that guild is merely nominal. In effect it returns such delinquents to duty in their former guild and prohibits substitutes selected in their stead as corpse-carriers from excusing themselves, since the churches need their services.

Emperors Theodosius and Valentinian Augusti to Cyrus, urban prefect.[1]

When persons under the pretext of being corpse-carriers or guildsmen do not fulfil this public service, but try to withdraw themselves from other public services, we believe that there must be resistance to their deceits, lest anyone under the appearance of a public service which he does not pursue should be relieved from the burdens of another public service, lest the public services of silversmiths or of coinmakers[2] should be shunned by those persons who hasten to be called only guildsmen or corpse-carriers.

And so, if anyone of these calls himself a guildsman or a corpse-carrier under the cover of the mere name, he should know that in his place another, who is approved competent for the aforesaid public service, must be substituted, but with a court trial permitted for him who is substituted in the matter of substitution, obviously, for the aforesaid persons or for those chief men[3] who die[4]—from this arrangement none excusing himself because of respect for the sacrosanct churches.[5]

Given on 23 March, Theodosius for the seventeenth time and Festus being consuls.

1. Of Constantinople.
2. Or "of money-changers or of money-brokers". No matter which version is accepted, it appears that at this time there was a shortage of members of these guilds.
3. These are *primates*, in this case officials of the guild.
4. Here *CI*'s later version inserts an extraneous sentence.
The version in the text may be replaced by the following: "but at the

decision of him who is substituted permitted in the matter of substitution" etc. Various emendations—none satisfactory—have been proposed. But it seems clear that the person about to be substituted either has a right to a judicial decision on the matter or may make his own decision about performing service in this guild.

5. This conclusion is adapted from the following sentence in *CI*'s later version: "We command that this should be maintained among all persons impartially, with none excusing himself because of the divine household's [the imperial palace's] patronage, because of respect for the sacrosanct churches, or because of any power whatever of any person whatever."

431. LETTER OF THEODOSIUS II AND VALENTINIAN III ON RETENTION OF CERTAIN SHIPS FOR PUBLIC SERVICE, 439

(*LNT* 8)

This directive orders that ships with capacity beyond 2,000 measures[1] must not be withdrawn from public services for various reasons, which include respect for religion (Christianity) as a pretext.

Justinian repeats most of this law twice (*CI* 1. 2. 10 and 11. 4. 2).

Emperors Theodosius and Valentinian Augusti to Florentius, praetorian prefect.[2]

The human race's frailty furnishes occasions[3] for proposing laws, but the repetition of laws is an indication of our humanity, because, indeed, although the stings of previous laws sufficed for correcting their violators, nevertheless we wish delinquents to be admonished by the law's repetition rather than penalties for delicts to be exacted.

Therefore, having been apprised by your Sublimity's report that the law which formerly had been promulgated about non-exemption of ships[4] has been trodden underfoot, we are compelled by humane feelings to repeat the very salutary ordinances and we[5] command that no ship beyond 2,000 measures'[1] capacity before its fruitful loading or its transport of public goods can be exempted and removed from public uses either by privilege of a person in high office or by respect for religion or by prerogative of a person. And if there should be advanced in opposition a celestial response,[6] whether it be an annotation[7] or a divine pragmatic sanction, it must not assail the most prudent law's regulations.

And this we desire to be observed also in all cases, that generally, if anything of this sort contrary to law or contrary to public utility should be advanced in any suit whatever, it should not be valid,[8] since undoubtedly it proves the petitioner's surreptitiousness.

But lest contempt for the present law should seem to be unpunished, if [9] anything in any way whatever shall have been attempted to the fraud of this statute, we correct this by the confiscation of the ship which is exempted,[10] Florentius, dearest and fondest cousin.

Therefore your illustrious and magnificent Authority by posted edicts should order the law, which shall be valid perpetually, to be brought to all persons' knowledge.

Given on 7 April [11] at Constantinople, Theodosius Augustus for the seventeenth time being consul.[12]

1. The word is *modius*, the largest standard unit in the Roman system of dry measure, usually translated "peck", to which it was approximately equal. The total amount here, then, is five hundred bushels. Conversion into pounds is hazardous, for we know not what commodity must be measured and the United States government varies the weight of a bushel with the foodstuff to be measured—the variation ranging from sixty pounds for wheat to 32 pounds for oats. Moreover in various states of the Union corn and barley differ from federal standards. If the likeliest probability is that wheat is meant, the weight would be 30,000 pounds, which equals fifteen (short) tons.

2. Of the East.

3. As in all languages, the word *semen* (*semina* here) passes tropically from "seed" to "origin", "occasion", "cause".

4. Probably of 406 recorded in *CT* 13. 7. 2 = *CI* 11. 4. 1.

5. Here Justinian's versions start.

6. See no. 218, n. 5.

7. See no. 317, n. 2.

8. This counteracts any special exception which may have been granted. Justinian suspends his quotation here.

9. Here *CI* resumes.

10. Here *CI* ends.

11. In *CI* 1. 2. 10 the date is a day earlier.

12. Each of Justinian's versions adds Festus as the emperor's colleague.

432. MANDATE OF THEODOSIUS II AND VALENTINIAN III ON CLERICAL MISUSE OF IMPERIAL INSIGNIA, 439
(CI 2. 15. 2)

In this directive the emperors forbid the clergymen (among others) to hang imperial cloths or to place the imperial title on other persons' property and impose penalties for violation of the statute.

Such adornment may be made, as the document suggests, by either a lawful or an unlawful possessor of another person's property. On the one hand, the motive may have been to ensure for the possessor some sort of favour from collectors of taxes or immunity from billeting transient officials or members of the armed forces. On the other hand, the motive may have risen from the possessor's malicious desire to subject the owner of the property to the penalties provided by the law, in the hope that the possessor in the interim would profit from favour or immunity and that the owner eventually would be penalized, since normally the owner was responsible for the possessor's conduct relative to the possession.

Emperors Theodosius and Valentinian Augusti to Florentius, praetorian prefect.[1]

None should dare to suspend royal cloths[2] or to place an inscription[3] without a competent governor's command on other persons' properties, which in any way whatever any person whatsoever may possess, although he who possesses it may be shown to be not the owner but an unlawful possessor and a rash intruder.

Moreover we decide that he who shall have dared to do this, if he is a plebeian, shall be subjected to the last punishment,[4] but if a very distinguished person or a curial or a soldier or a clergyman, not only must be punished with confiscation of his property and must be deported from the Roman State, but also should be deprived of liberty,[5] and that all governors ought to be executors of this law.

Moreover we supply permission for lowering or breaking the inscriptions and also for tearing to pieces the cloths not only to persons to whose prejudice any such thing against justice and against the laws is committed, but also to all freemen as well as slaves without fear of false accusation[6] or without charge of crime, since we decree that governors and their office staffs should be fined each thirty pounds of gold, if they either admit such an accusation or allow it, when deposed, to be registered.

Given on 17 June at Constantinople, Theodosius Augustus for the seventeenth time and Festus being consuls.

1. Of the East.
2. The word is *velum*: "cloth", "curtain", "awning", "veil", "sail". Probably a *velum regium* was of purple colour.
3. Probably the force of the adjective extends to this noun.
4. Death.
5. A Greek version adds a clause which may have stood in the original law: "although some should be persons caring for the most pious emperor's private property".
6. See nos. 334, n. 3, and 440, n. 6.

433. LETTER OF THEODOSIUS II AND VALENTINIAN III ON SUCCESSIONS TO CLERICAL ESTATES, 439

(*LNV* 3)

This ordinance forbids curials to enter the clerical profession, but, foreseeing its inevitable violation, it makes certain concessions for those who in the past have been and in the future shall become clergymen. It also debars persons possessed of more than three hundred solidi, again with exceptions, from choosing an ecclesiastical career and it specifies the penalty for disobedience.

Emperors Theodosius and Valentinian Augusti to Maximus, praetorian prefect [1] for the second time.

In enhancing the condition of each and every city, while conserving respect for the Catholic religion, we renew the previous statutes of the ancients and of our fathers as well as decree by our laws that these should be observed, lest everywhere by the decrease of municipal senators,[2] when the multitude of clergymen is increased copiously, public losses may be engendered. For there is no doubt that when a curial, after his public duties have not been fulfilled, is admitted to the service of the venerable ministry, the burden of public service, diverted to a few persons, cannot be borne at all, and again, when curials' patrimonies pass to persons who are not held to municipal services, the community's own substance totters.

Therefore by the present law we decree that whoever ere the day of this sanction, without having fulfilled public duties and public services for his own city, has undertaken the post of clerical office should remain, indeed, in that service of religion which he has obtained, but should be compelled to acknowledge by a substitute all burdens—both personal and of his patrimony. He should divide his property in

433. SUCCESSIONS TO CLERICAL ESTATES, 439

an equal proportion to each and every child, after a similar share has been kept for himself; but if he shall not have had children, he should transfer two-thirds of his property—apart from any deceit of alienation—to relatives belonging to the municipal senate; and if they shall have been lacking, we ordain that the said eight-twelfths ought to benefit his own order,[3] since affection for one's native municipality is not less than that for one's kinsmen—but keeping, of course, one-third of his own substance.

But whoever, after his public duties have been performed for his native municipality, previously has come to the post of clerical office should not delay to deliver an equal portion of his property (just as we already have said) to each and every child, whom the municipal senate without doubt should demand for itself. But if he shall not have had children, he shall be compelled to observe those rules which previously have been established concerning the distribution of such a person's patrimony. For it is fitting for a person who desires to engage in the sacrosanct mysteries [4] to be approved rich by his faith rather than by his means.

For the future, moreover, by the present law we forbid a curial to be taken for ecclesiastical services, that the fiscal needs may be fulfilled more easily by a multitude of municipal senators. If, to be sure, anyone through devotion of spirit shall have hastened to the service of clerical office even against the laws' prohibitions, if he shall not have fulfilled the burden of his own community, he is compelled to perform all these by a substitute, dividing by similar observance of the law his property (just as has been written above) either with his children or with his relatives or with his native municipality.

But if, after his public duties have been fulfilled, he shall have been associated with the sacrosanct religion's ministry, he shall be compelled immediately by the governor to distribute his property equally to his children, keeping for himself an equal share among his children. But if he shall not have had children, he should know that straightway (just as has been said above) two-thirds of his patrimony must be conferred upon his relatives, who, however, are subject to the burdens of municipal senatorship,[5] without any contrivance of decrease, with all resources, which he shall have believed ought to be alienated for fraud of the law after the honour of the clerical office, brought to public notice, but distributing to whom he shall have desired one-third at his own free will.

And these rules testify that our Serenity by regard for humanity has modified the laws' old regulations,[6] by which a curial has been ordered to surrender all his patrimony to his own order,[3] as often as one is chosen for the ministry of the clerical office.

Also our regulation does not pass over the following part: that whatever citizen or, finally, sojourner shall have been found subject in no obligation, whose substance, however, did not exceed the amount of three hundred solidi,[7] should have the free power of obtaining the clerical office. But it should be permitted to him, whose patrimony shall be rated by a valuation greater than we have defined, to be associated with his municipal senate—pursuant to the old statutes—with the exception of those who serve in our sacred secretarial bureau [8] and in the corps of secret service agents [9] and others who labour in the maintenance of continued governmental service,[10] in order that by many kinds of precautions the number of the orders [3] may be supplied and still may not be lacking ministers for the venerable religion's services, Maximus, dearest and fondest cousin.

Your illustrious and exalted Grandeur shall cause this law's very salutary regulations—under the promulgation of edicts—to come to all persons' notice, that the guilt of sacrilege [11] may overwhelm and a fine of twenty pounds of gold may overthrow him who shall have shown clearly that he has disobeyed the edictal regulations.

Given on 28 August at Ravenna, Theodosius Augustus for the seventeenth time and the most distinguished Festus being consuls.

1. Of Italy.
2. That is, those who financially were able to perform compulsory public services but who sought an ecclesiastical career to exempt themselves from these duties.
3. The senatorial class (*ordo*), whence he came. See no. 325, n. 6.
4. See no. 75, n. 42.
5. This word (*curialitas*) is reported only in this law.
6. As in nos. 109, 114, 130, 188, 193, 210, 224, 233, 280, 322.
7. When (*c.* 312) Constantine I reduced the weight of the gold aureus (on which see no. 515, n. 18) from sixty to 72 in the pound, this lighter coin was called the *solidus* or the νόμισμα. Although the solidus is supposed to have continued for some eleven centuries as the standard gold coin with little appreciable variation, yet scholars have achieved no consensus about its value. Bury in 1923 sets its worth at "about twelve shillings and sixpence" (1. 54), while Pharr in 1952 says that it was "worth about $6, U.S.A., 1950" (op. cit., 594), thus practically doubling the British value. Neither apparently takes into account the oft-repeated statement that ancient currency—weight for weight, that is, an equivalent weight of gold, as in this instance—had ten times the purchasing power of modern money. But this statement, if ever true, is of no value after two world wars with their intervening world-wide depression and the present post-war inflation which have played havoc with national and international economies.
8. The *scrinia*, on which see no. 256, n. 2, and Bury, 1. 29–30.

9. The *schola* of *agentes in rebus*, on which see no. 256, n. 3, and Bury, I. 30–1.
10. See no. 186, n. 4.
11. See no. 168, n. 1.

434. MANDATE OF THEODOSIUS II AND VALENTINIAN III ON ECCLESIASTICAL LEVIES FOR IMPERIAL TOURS, 440–1
(*CI* 12. 50. 21)

Transportational assistance for the imperial court on tour through the provinces was a burden on the provincials so honoured by the sovereign's presence. This mandate does not exempt the Church from contribution to such service.

Emperors Theodosius and Valentinian Augusti to Cyrus, praetorian prefect.[1]

Absolutely none of any rank or dignity whatever or the sacrosanct Church or the imperial household should have at the time of a progress an excuse from transport animals [2] or from extra transport provisions.[3]

1. Of the East.
2. Transliterated from ἀγγαρεία. Sometimes the word is extended to include vehicles. See no. 530, n. 3.
3. See no. 32, n. 7, where immunity is granted on this part, and no. 107, n. 13, where apparently it is removed some eighty years before the present law, and no. 438, n. 4, where the present inclusion is confirmed. This was one of the extraordinary public services, on which see no. 226, n. 3.

435. LETTER OF THEODOSIUS II AND VALENTINIAN III ON CANCELLATION OF CLERICAL EXEMPTION FROM PUBLIC DUTIES, 441
(*LNV* 10)

It remained for Valentinian III to end all exemptions of clergymen from public burdens in an effort to bolster the moribund economy of the Western Empire, where increasing aversion from performance of public services accelerated the decline of public revenues, which were needed so markedly for maintenance of the military establishment against the barbarian invasions. Only so much of this long law as pertains to the Church is translated.

See nos. 106-8, 186, 226, 262, 265, 327, 377.

Emperors Theodosius and Valentinian Augusti to Maximus, praetorian prefect [1] for the second time.

... In this law's second section [2] we provide that whosoever of the illustrious ranks, whether an ecclesiastic either in the most sacred city [3] or in any provinces whatever, when assessed for taxes, according to the example of our household,[4] by any command whatsoever had made for himself a status different from others of that assessment for taxes which he appeared to pay, should bear his accustomed burden without any exception of privilege,[5] not only in taxes due to the State's treasury,[6] but also in these which ancient usage has assigned to the shares of the sacred or privy treasury, so that we, having sought a sacred regulation for the difficulty of expenses and for the harassment of poor persons, thus at last may offer the twin remedies of a salutary constitution.[7]

... By our Clemency's renewed command we ordain that by the abolition of all privileges, which either had been conferred upon dignitaries or guilds of varied governmental service [8] have earned or have been obtained in the name of the venerable religion, every assessment for taxes everywhere, which is not on persons but on lands, should be applied without any discrimination (as we have determined above) to all public services from at least the ninth indiction.[9] And in this share, as anyone is more distinguished or more wealthy, so he owes a more eager spirit for the public necessities, the management of which he understands will benefit him, Maximus, dearest and fondest cousin.

Therefore your illustrious and exalted Grandeur by the vigour of your wonted foresight shall bring this law to all provinces'and peoples' notice and shall order all persons speedily to obtain the salutariness of a long-awaited remedy, that, late at least, the loyalty alike of the rich and of the poor, when equalized by just shares, more willingly may cope with the hardship of affairs.

Given on 20 February at Ravenna. Accepted on 14 March, where above,[10] after the consulate of Valentinian Augustus for the fifth time and of the most distinguished Anatolius.

1. Of Italy.
2. Literally "step" or "rank" (*gradus*).
3. Probably Rome, since this law was enacted in the West.

435. CANCELLATION OF EXEMPTION FROM DUTIES, 441

4. In Valentinian III's immediate family at this time were his mother Galla Placidia, his wife Licinia Eudoxia, his daughters Eudocia and Placidia, and his sister Honoria, of whom the last, however, lived in Constantinople under the care of Theodosius II, her father's cousin. Since these were all females, of whom his mother was a widow and the rest—apart from his wife—were unmarried then, it is doubtful that they maintained separate establishments, if they adhered to the ancient Roman tradition of domestic economy whereby female dependants dwelt with their paterfamilias, who was Valentinian. Not even they are exempted—it appears from the omitted first section—from taxation.

5. In the first section (omitted) the emperor, to broaden the incidence of taxation, includes all persons who have acquired in any way any property from himself or his relatives or who have a usufruct on such property, for apparently such acquisition or possession previously was pleaded as an excuse for exemption from public service.

6. This phrase *due . . . treasury* is represented by the adjective *arcalis*, which is reported only here.

7. Wealthier owners assumed their share of public services easily in prosperous times past and consequently there was less financial hardship for the other and poorer proprietors, but now in a period of economic exhaustion some of the upper class have shunned such service successfully and the others, who ill can afford it, must bear the burden. This condition Valentinian hopes to correct by excluding all exemptions.

8. See no. 186, n. 4.

9. This period of time ran from 1 September 440 to 31 August 441. After 1 September 312 the indictional cycle became regularly a term of fifteen years. *The ninth indiction* is a loose, but standard, way of indicating the ninth year in any indiction, in this case that of the indiction which began in 432.

That the indictional cycle began in 312 (the commonly considered year of origin) and not in 297 (as strongly supported by O. Seeck in *Deutsche Zeitschrift für Geschichtswissenschaft*, 12. 2 [1894–5] 279–96) was reaffirmed convincingly by E. H. Kase, Jr, *A Papyrus Roll in the Princeton Collection* (Baltimore, 1933), 25–31.

10. This apparently means Ravenna. The words *ubi supra* occur nowhere else in *CT* or in the *Leges Novellae* usually printed with it, and in better English may be translated "at the aforesaid place" (Pharr).

436. MANDATE OF THEODOSIUS II AND VALENTINIAN III ON PRIVILEGE FOR THE NOBILITY, 442

(*CI* 1. 3. 21)

This statute affects the Church only indirectly, though evidently regarded by the compilers of Justinian's Code as pertaining to the Church from their inclusion of it in the title "On Bishops and Clergymen" as well as from Justinian's later reference to it in one of his constitutions concerning the clergy (no. 629). It extends to laymen of illustrious rank [1] the privilege which clerics enjoyed in providing substitutes for public service owed by them to the State.

The same Augusti to Thomas, praetorian prefect.[2]

According to the analogy of bishops of the orthodox faith as well as of a priest and a deacon, those who have attained illustrious rank [1] by an honorary title [3] should not be forbidden to satisfy a municipal senate in respect to public services by substitutes at the risk of their own property.

Given on 25 February at Constantinople, Eudoxius and Dioscore being consuls.

1. The title of *illustris*, conferred by imperial patent and sometimes simply *honoris causa*, entitled its holder to special consideration. See no. 586, n. 2.
2. Of the East.
3. The phrase is *honorarius titulus*. See no. 495, n. 9.

437. MANDATE OF THEODOSIUS II AND VALENTINIAN III ON ECCLESIASTICAL PRIVILEGES, 445

(*CI* 1. 3. 22)

Three subjects are treated in this statute: (1) malicious prosecution of a bishop on criminal charges; (2) confirmation of previous privileges conferred upon the ecclesiastical establishment; (3) episcopal authorization for clergymen and monks to travel from their residence to Constantinople.

The same Augusti to Florentius, praetorian prefect.[1]

If through malicious charge any claim on criminal cases shall have been laid before a competent judge for the purpose of bringing into court a bishop of the sacrosanct religion, we command that it should be overthrown by the condemnation of thirty pounds of gold payable to the public accounts.

Indeed also all privileges which have been given by the laws to the sacrosanct churches on account of refugees or clergymen or corpse-carriers or other ecclesiastics should be preserved intact and unimpaired.[2]

Moreover we order that all clergymen and monks who depart from their own communities for this genial city [3] for the purpose of business or of religion should come fortified with letters of the bishop [4] to whom each individual making the journey owes obedience, for they should know that if they shall have arrived without this assurance, they shall impute to themselves that they shall not be thought to be clergymen or monks.

Given on 11 February at Constantinople, Valentinian Augustus for the sixth time and Nomus being consuls.

1. Of the East.
2. This sentence, printed independently, lacks a principal verb and appears to be dependent upon the main verb of the preceding sentence.
3. Constantinople.
4. See no. 270, n. 3.

438. MANDATE OF THEODOSIUS II AND VALENTINIAN III ON ECCLESIASTICAL LEVIES FOR IMPERIAL TOURS, 445

(*CI* 10. 49. 2)

This order (abbreviated earlier in *CI* 1. 2. 11) prohibits exemption of persons attached to the Church from contribution to facilitate the imperial progress through the provinces.

Emperors Theodosius and Valentinian Augusti to Taurus, praetorian prefect.[1]

Since services must be tendered to us for our Divinity's most felicitous expedition through all provinces' districts, where we take our tour,[2] we command that none should be excused absolutely [3] from transport animals [4] or extra transport provisions [5] or wagons or any public service [6] whatever,[7] but we decree that all persons, whether they belong to our divine house or to that of the venerable Augusta [8] or to the sacrosanct churches or to any illustrious [9] houses whatever, excused neither by a pragmatic law nor by a divine annotation [10] nor by a sacred response,[11] should obey your magnificent office's [12] impositions during the time of our expedition.

Given on 17 February at Constantinople, Valentinian Augustus for the sixth time and Nomus being consuls.

1. Of the East.
2. In *CI* 1. 2. 11 these clauses succeed the principal clause.
3. Omitted in the earlier version.
4. See nos. 434, n. 2, and 530, n. 3.
5. See nos. 32, n. 7; 102, n. 7; 107, n. 13; 226, n. 3; 434, n. 3.
6. Probably related to transportation and entertainment of public officials.
7. *CI* 1. 2. 11 omits what follows, but from it salvages the clause "although estates belong to sacrosanct churches".
8. The empress.
9. See no. 436, n. 1.
10. See no. 317, n. 2.
11. See no. 218, n. 5.
12. See no. 311, n. 5.

439. RESCRIPT OF THEODOSIUS II AND VALENTINIAN III ON RECALL OF ROMAN GUILDSMEN FROM THE CLERICATE, 445

(*LNV* 20)

By this constitution the emperors order the recall of guildsmen in Rome to their organizations, when they have entered the ranks of the clergy before the expiration of their service.

Emperors Theodosius and Valentinian Augusti to Auxentius, urban prefect [1] for the second time.

Our Clemency ought to ordain salutarily whatever things have regard for the most sacred city's [2] advantage.

Accordingly, since we have followed, Auxentius, dearest and fondest cousin, your Honour's prudent report, which has been approved by the double fasces,[3] your illustrious Grandeur, after our pragmatic sanction's tenor has been learned, should know that a guildsman of the city of Rome who, when the order of the service which he has begun has not been completed, shall have believed that he ought to be transferred to an office [4] of any governmental service [5] whatever, before he shall have come to the first place among his fellows upon his retirement,[6] ought to be recalled to the guild to which he previously had dedicated his name. Even if he is found in the number of clergymen, the condition of the same command should be maintained, even to the rank of subdeacon, in order that by this salutary constitution provision may be made for the venerable city's [2] needs by restored services.

Given on 14 April at Rome, Valentinian Augustus for the sixth time and the most distinguished Nomus being consuls.

1. Of Rome.
2. Rome.
3. By *CT* 1. 6. 7 (dated 376) urban prefects—whether in Rome or Constantinople—took precedence over all other magistrates within those cities and, as such, doubtless were entitled to be escorted by at least, if not more than, twelve lictors, which quota (*c.* 300 B.C.) was allocated to the consuls, the highest magistrates of the Republic. Each lictor carried on his left shoulder the *fasces* (a bundle of birch rods, which were tied by a red thong and whence protruded the blade of an axe), symbolizing corporal (rods) and capital (axe) punishment. Both lictors and fasces probably were of Etruscan provenience, for they appeared in the Kingdom (*ante* 509 B.C.).

By metonymy and chiefly in poetry *fasces* stands for a high office: so *double fasces* indicates occupancy of an office for the second time.

4. Literally "belt" (*cingulum*), by metonymy for the office of which his official belt is a symbol (see no. 476, n. 39).
5. See no. 186, n. 4.
6. From his service due as a member of his guild. Retirement probably was controlled by a guildsman's age rather than by his years of service or by his rank attained, but doubtless exceptions were made. In the present instance retirement is regarded as occurring before attainment of the highest possible rank.

440. LETTER OF THEODOSIUS II AND VALENTINIAN III ON PENALTIES FOR MANICHAEANS, 445

(*LNV* 18)

This constitution, which confirms all previous laws against Manichaeans,[1] reaffirms that Manichaeism is a heresy,[2] permits anyone freely to accuse Manichaeans in court, forbids the concealment of these heretics, ousts them from governmental service, bans them from cities, inflicts various legal disabilities upon them, and fines officials who fail to discharge them from governmental posts.

Our Lords the Emperors Theodosius and Valentinian Augusti to Albinus, praetorian prefect [3] for the second time.

A superstition, condemned also in pagan times,[4] inimical to public discipline and hostile to the Christian faith, not undeservedly has provoked our Clemency to its own destruction.

We speak of the Manichaeans, whom the statutes of all previous emperors [1] have judged execrable and worthy to be expelled from the whole world. And their lately detected crimes do not permit neglect. For what things and how obscene to tell and to hear have been disclosed by their very open confession in most blessed Pope Leo's court in the presence of the most honourable Senate! So much so that even he who was said to be their bishop both betrayed with his own voice and wrote in full all secrets of their crimes.[5] And this could not be concealed from our notice, since for us it is not safe to overlook so detestable an outrage to the Divinity and to leave unpunished a crime by which not only the bodies but also the souls of deceived persons are polluted inexpiably.

Wherefore Albinus, dearest and fondest cousin, your illustrious and exalted Eminence should know that we have ordained by this law, which shall live for eternity and which you shall cause by posted edicts to come to the notice of all the provinces, that wherever in the world anyone of the Manichaeans shall have been arrested, he should receive by the authority of public severity the punishments which the laws have sanctioned against sacrilegious persons.

And let it be a public crime and for everyone who wishes let there be an opportunity to accuse such persons without hazard of an accusation.[6]

And let it not be lawful and safe for anyone either to conceal such persons or to connive at such persons, since all the constitutions of previous emperors [1] concerning these persons have been confirmed by us, in order that all persons may know by this published edictal law that the Manichaeans must be deprived of the dignity of governmental service [7] and of dwelling in cities, lest any innocent person should be caught by such persons' intercourse and association.

They neither should take nor should leave inheritances, but these should be added to our fisc's resources.

And by any fraud should not be sought what we openly prohibit to these persons.

They should lack the action for injuries; they absolutely should not have free contracts.[8]

441. PRIVILEGE OF CLERGY FOR TENANT FARMERS, 445

The chief men of every government service [7] or of every office staff then should be smitten by a fine of ten pounds of gold to be exacted by your apparitors,[9] if they allow anyone polluted by this superstition to be in governmental service.[7] For nothing seems too much to be able to be decreed against those persons whose unholy perversity in the name of religion commits deeds unknown or shameful even to brothels.

Given on 19 June at Rome, our Lord Valentinian for the sixth time and the most distinguished Nomus being consuls.

This law does not need interpretation.

1. Notably nos. 156, 185, 219, 275, 292, 301, 380.
2. See no. 156, n. 1 *ad init.*
3. Of Italy.
4. See no. 156, n. 1 *ad fin.*
5. In 444 Pope St Leo I, alarmed by the increase of Manichaeism in Rome, had the leaders of the sect arrested and presided over a mixed tribunal which investigated those haled before it and to which oral and written confessions were presented. Leo's encyclical on the investigation to the Italian episcopate (*PL* 54. 620–2) also fails to identify the Manichaean bishop.
6. So in no. 372 an accuser of a rapist of a nun may make his accusation without fear of being charged with delation, which ordinarily was considered a criminal act (*CT* 10. 10. 1, 2, 4, 10).
7. See no. 186, n. 4.
8. That is, they should not have freedom to make contracts.
9. Abstract for concrete in Latin.

441. RESCRIPT OF THEODOSIUS II AND VALENTINIAN III ON PRIVILEGE OF CLERGY FOR TENANT FARMERS, 445

(*LNV* 13)

In reply to a delegation of Numidians and of Moors, who have come to Rome, Valentinian issues a lengthy law to correct various complaints preferred by the petitioners. The only part (§ 8) translated as being of ecclesiastical interest, apart from brief prefatory and enabling sentences, is the prohibition of tenant farmers' pleading the privilege of clergy to win immunity, it seems, from public services.

Emperors Theodosius and Valentinian Augusti to Albinus, praetorian prefect [1] for the second time.

A recently conducted delegation of Numidians and of Sitifensian Moors,[2] which Palladius, the admirable count, and . . .[3] the most distinguished tribune, and Maximin, the laudable civil priest,[4] have performed approvedly, has earned from our Perpetuity this law's command . . .

Moreover, lest anyone from this very fewness of tenant farmers should think that he must be exempted by the privilege of the clericate or of governmental service,[5] you shall command the regulation of the former law,[6] which prohibits this, to be maintained . . .

Your illustrious and exalted Magnificence by posted edicts shall publish to each province's [2] delegation the present law's benefits, that relieved persons may know the things conceded, the governors may maintain the things established, the prohibited persons may not circumvent the things interdicted.

Issued on 21 June at Rome, Valentinian Augustus for the sixth time and the most distinguished Nomus being consuls.

1. Of Italy.

2. Numidia and Mauretania Sitifensis, on which see no. 19, n. 22, were contiguous provinces.

3. Editors indicate a hiatus here, for the combination of the titles of count and tribune in one person seems unknown.

4. See no. 337, n. 3.

5. See no. 186, n. 4.

6. The reference is uncertain, but an edict to the Moors of Sitifis (the same community which sent the commission to Valentinian), dated between 368 and 373 (*CT* 12. 1. 64), prohibits persons from claiming immunity from public duties because of the privilege of their fathers' governmental service.

Seven years later (no. 478) Valentinian forbids tenant farmers to become clerics.

442. RESCRIPT OF THEODOSIUS II AND VALENTINIAN III ON PAPAL JURISDICTION, 445
(*LNV* 17)

When St Hilary, archbishop of Arles, came into collision with the Roman see over the case of Celidon, bishop of Besançon, who was not subject ecclesiastically to him, but whom he deposed through a local council for irregularities of conduct,[1] Pope St Leo I restored Celidon to his bishopric, rebuked Hilary for exercising jurisdiction outside his province, deprived him of his metropolitan powers,² and procured from Valentinian III the following celebrated rescript to support his decision and to rivet another link in the chain of papalism.

This rescript, which increased considerably the large powers already granted by Gratian (no. 164) to the papal see,³ conferred on the popes a practically imperial jurisdiction and made them—so far as the West was concerned—sovereigns in the spiritual sphere, for by it western bishops became their subjects and exercised such authority as they had in the same way as in the temporal sphere the emperors' civil officers wielded their delegated authority.

Our Lords the Emperors Theodosius and Valentinian Augusti to the illustrious Aetius,⁴ count and master of each soldiery ⁵ and patrician.

It is certain that both for us and for our Empire the sole defence is in the Supernal Divinity's favour, to deserve which especially the Christian faith and the venerable religion must be supported by us.

Therefore, although the merit of the holy Peter, who is the prince of the episcopal crown,⁶ and the rank of the Roman city, and also the authority of a sacred synod had confirmed the primacy of the apostolic see,⁷ lest illicit presumption should try to attempt anything against that see's authority (for then the churches' peace everywhere will be preserved, if the whole body acknowledges its ruler), and although these matters have been observed hitherto inviolably, Hilary of Arles—as we have learned by a trustworthy report of the venerable Leo, the Roman pope—with a contumacious attempt has ventured upon certain illicit presumptions and therefore an abominable disorder has invaded the transalpine churches—to which fact a recent example particularly testifies. For Hilary, who is called the bishop of the Arletan Church, without having consulted the pontiff of the Roman city but with the temerity only of a usurper, has entered upon bishops' ordinations not incumbent upon himself. For wrongfully he has removed some, unbecomingly he has ordained others, although the citizens were unwilling and resisted. And indeed this man, since they were not readily received by those who had not chosen them, collected an armed troop for himself and the gates of the walls in a hostile manner by siege he surrounded and by attack he unlocked and to an abode of quiet he led his men for the purpose of proclaiming peace by means of war.

Since such deeds had been committed both against the majesty of the Empire and against the respect for the apostolic see, after in turn had been completed an investigation by the religious pope of the city,⁸ a definite judgement has been passed against him and concerning those whom he wrongfully had ordained. And indeed that very judgement was to be valid throughout the Gauls ⁹ even without imperial sanction. For what could not be permitted to so great a pontiff's authority over the churches? But this reasoning has evoked also our injunction:

that it may be allowed no longer either to Hilary, whom only the kindness of a mild director [10] permits still to be called a bishop, or to any other to interweave armed might with ecclesiastical matters or to oppose the Roman bishop's orders. For by such attempts loyalty toward and respect for our Empire are outraged.

Not only we remove this, which is a very great crime, but, lest even a trifling disturbance may arise among the churches or the discipline of religion may appear to be diminished in any degree, we decree by this perpetual ordinance: that it should be not lawful for Gallican bishops as well as for those of other provinces to attempt anything contrary to the old custom without the authority of the venerable pope of the eternal [11] city [8]; but whatever the authority of the apostolic see has ordained or shall have ordained, this should be as the law for those persons and for all persons, so that whosoever of the bishops summoned to the Roman bishop's tribunal shall have neglected to attend, he should be compelled by the governor for the same province to appear, in all respects being observed the privileges which our deified [12] parents have conferred upon the Roman Church,[13] dearest and fondest cousin Aetius.[4]

Wherefore your illustrious and exalted Magnificence, pursuant to the authority of the present edictal law, shall cause what has been enacted above to be observed, a fine of ten pounds of gold being exacted straightway from each and every governor who shall have allowed our commands to be violated.

And by the divine hand: May the Divinity preserve you for many years, dearest and fondest cousin.

Given on 8 July at Rome, Valentinian Augustus for the sixth time and the most distinguished Nomus being consuls.

1. Celidon, while a layman, had married a widow and, as a magistrate, had issued sentences in capital cases.

2. In 450, however, after Hilary's death Leo restored to Arles its former rank.

3. Valentinian clothes with the force of law the papal enactments (whether of the past or in the future), declares that what he grants is to the bishop of Rome (irrespective of who is the incumbent of the see), commands the civil authorities to compel the attendance of bishops cited for trial before the pope, and prohibits any bishop (wherever in the West the imperial rule was effective) from doing aught without papal authority.

The prudence of an episcopal (here papal) petition for imperial intervention to enforce ecclesiastical discipline may be questioned in various cases, but the resort to that right for secular support was exercised and was entertained ever after Constantine I's conversion (in 312) had made it possible.

4. The last great Roman general and the saviour of western Europe from Attila the Hun near Châlons-sur-Marne (451), which perhaps was the locale of

the Western Empire's last important victory over invaders and may have been one of history's decisive battles—on the site and the significance see Bury, 1. 293-4, who later confirmed his censure in his lectures on *The Invasion of Europe by the Barbarians* (London, 1928), 149-51, and J. F. C. Fuller, *A Military History of the Western World* (New York, 1954), 204-97, 299, who takes the traditional view. Jealous of his power and freed from fear of the Huns by Attila's death (453), Valentinian is said to have stabbed Aetius to death with his own hand (454), when Aetius was treating with Valentinian about the marriage of the latter's daughter to the former's son.

5. The *magister utriusque militiae*, on whom see no. 106, n. 4.

6. The word is *corona*, which by metonymy means with its adjective here "the circle of bishops" ruling the Church.

7. If by this statement is suggested the universal primacy of the pope, it seems that Leo, who probably provided Valentinian with the material for his rescript, misrepresented history. The First Ecumenical Council of Nicaea in 325 by its canon 6 indeed recognized the Roman bishop's authority, but only over the places immediately subject to the pope, just as in the same canon it authorized Alexandria's authority over Egypt and Libya and Pentapolis and Antioch's (and other churches') privileges. Nothing about primacy elsewhere for Rome was enacted at Nicaea. So far as canon 3 of the Second Ecumenical Council at Constantinople in 381 is concerned: that secured a primacy of honour for the bishop of Constantinople next after the bishop of [Old] Rome, because Constantinople was New Rome (see nos. 375, n. 7, and 470, n. 70). This honorific primacy was designed perhaps not only to degrade Alexandria's and Antioch's position, which had been confirmed at Nicaea, but also to exalt the position of Constantinople, where now the eastern emperor lived, on the eastern claim that an episcopal city's ecclesiastical rank should equal that city's civil rank. But even that canon failed to find that Rome exercised a *de iure* primacy over all Christendom. None of the canons of the Third Ecumenical Council at Ephesus in 431 mentions Rome at all, although inferences have been inspired by the fathers' silence in the face of Roman claims to a *de iure divino* primacy of jurisdiction advanced there (see S. H. Scott, *The Eastern Churches and the Papacy* [London, 1928], 150-4). And, of course, no particular (as opposed to a general) synod's canons, which could not pretend to express the universal mind of the Church, could promote authoritatively any such pretension as advanced here by Valentinian, whose words must mean no more than that in the West the bishop of Rome must be regarded as the highest bishop with primatial or patriarchal power over the other prelates in that part of the Empire. For the so-called canonical evidence to which the emperor alluded consult H. Burn-Murdoch, *The Development of the Papacy* (London, 1954), 258-63, where are assembled also the modern arguments *pro* and *con*.

On the patristic interpretation of Matt. 16. 18—the famous Petrine text on St Peter, who captured a place in history with his keys of heaven and hell because of Jesus' paronomastic utterance—Jean de Launoy (1603-78) published an exhaustive examination (*Opera Omnia* [Genève, 1731], 5. 2. 101-14). For the period of this sylloge's survey this French savant found fourteen theologians who taught that the Church was constructed on St Peter, five who held that it was built upon either the apostles or their successors, seventeen who claimed that it was founded upon the faith which St Peter confessed, three who interpreted the rock as Christ himself. It is interesting to note that SS. Jerome, Ambrose, and Augustine, the three Doctors of Western Christendom who lived within this sylloge's scope (the fourth—Pope St Gregory I—came after it), appear respectively in two, three, and four of these classes. And in a notable passage the last—St Augustine—presents two interpretations and says that his readers should select that which is the more likely to be correct (*Retract.* 1. 20 [21]. 2 [= *CSEL* 36. 98]). And see also Denny, 29-36, and Burn-Murdoch, op. cit., 49-51, respectively for a résumé of patristic opinion and for the main arguments for the Roman and the non-Roman interpretations. Add now another patristic survey by Jalland, 96-8, who earlier examines in 47-64 all references to St Peter in the New Testament, and a similar summary by E. J. Bicknell, *A Theological Introduction to the Thirty-nine Articles of the Church of England*[3] (London, 1955), 340-50, as well as by S. H. Hooke, "The Corner-Stone of Scripture" in his collected papers entitled *The Siege Perilous* (London, 1956), 235-49, esp. 248-9 for his interpretation of Dan. 2. 34-6, which may foreshadow Matt. 16. 18.

8. Rome.
9. See no. 203, n. 4.
10. That is, the pope (*praesul*).
11. See no. 140, n. 1.
12. See no. 127, n. 7.
13. See no. 164, beyond which this constitution far proceeds.

443. LETTER OF THEODOSIUS II AND VALENTINIAN III ON CLERICAL VIOLATORS OF SEPULCHRES, 447

(*LNV* 23)

After a long preamble the emperors inveigh particularly against those clergymen who ransack tombs,[1] set severer penalties for those than for laymen who violate sepulchres,[1] and establish punishments for venal judges and careless governors who permit the continuance of this sacrilege.

Our Lords the Emperors Theodosius and Valentinian Augusti to Albinus, praetorian prefect [2] for the second time and patrician.

The framers of the old laws, indeed, have provided diligently for wretched mortals even after death [3] by executing capital punishment on those who had violated sepulchres.[4] But since noxious minds always are drawn by blind madness into crime and think that they are not held to penalties previously ordained, it is necessary to renew their severity, which we see has been despised with impunity hitherto.

For who is ignorant that the resting shades of the dead [5] are disturbed by deadly attempts and that horrible violence is inflicted upon the ashes [6] of the dead? In daylight and openly sepulchres are cut to pieces and sacrilegious presumption has drawn into the usage of licence whatever religion prohibits. And an end of ills no longer is given to the dead, for whose sufferings the construction of their pitiable abode is torn away. For we know—and not vain is our faith—that souls released from members [7] have sensation and that the celestial spirit returns to its own origin. This is declared by the old books of wisdom, this by the mysteries [8] of religion, which we venerate and worship.[9] And though the divine spirit does not experience the necessity of death, yet the souls love the abode of the bodies, whence they have departed, and by some manner of secret reason rejoice in the honour of their sepulchre, for which so great concern continues through all times that we see mountains' precious minerals transferred at excessive expense to these uses and elaborate masses constructed, though one's estate suffers.[10] And certainly prudent persons' intelligence would reject this, if it should believe that nothing is after death. It is a too barbarous and insane cruelty to grudge a last service to persons deprived of light and in demolishment of sepulchres by an inexpiable crime to reveal the remains of buried bodies to the sky.

Among all other persons guilty of this unspeakable crime a rather vehement complaint pursues clergymen, whom a rather sad day often has beheld tarrying amid such monsters.[11] Girt with iron,[12] they harass the buried and, forgetful of the Divinity presiding over the sky and the stars,[13] they bring to sacred altars hands polluted by contagion of ashes, since they have been sunk by so great insensibility of their conscience into profound darkness that they dare to be present at reverend mysteries [8] and after destruction of tombs they believe that God can be placated, whom the guilty beseech vainly, but whom a better life persuades by entreaty.

The foulness of such deeds, lest longer our times should be polluted, by this edictal law we condemn. Therefore whoever as a violator of profound rest and as an enemy of the very light [14] shall have excavated sepulchres or from these shall have removed any marbles or stones whatsoever should be held forthwith subject to punishment.

It shall be proper that slaves and tenant farmers caught in this crime should be led straightway to tortures. If they shall have confessed only about their own temerity, by their own blood they should atone for the deeds; but if amid their sufferings and with none interrogating them they shall have involved their masters and landlords,[15] they [16] should be punished together.

Also free-born persons whom similar presumption shall have made guilty, if perchance they shall be plebeians and of no property, should pay the penalty by death; but nobler persons or persons noted for their dignities, when fined by half of their goods, should be branded with perpetual infamy.

But clergymen who, it shall have been established, are authors of so dreadful a deed we believe are deserving of greater punishment; for more vehemently must be repressed he at whom you would wonder that he has sinned: celebrity of person makes his every crime more serious. It is intolerable, it is too execrable, it is not endurable for a person to assume the name and the title of holiness and to abound in crimes. Therefore whoever of this number shall have been a violator of sepulchres should lose instantly the name of clergymen and, adjudged by a verdict of proscription, should be punished by perpetual deportation. And this we decide ought to be observed in such a way that we ordain that neither ministers nor bishops of the sacred religion must be spared in such a case. Let complaints cease: we wound none's innocence; our law pursues only the guilty.

But because very often effect is denied to salutary statutes by venal judges' dissimulation, by the present edict we order that the province's governor, sustained by the municipal senators' support, should exercise our law's censure. And although no guilty person can resist the fasces and the axes,[17] yet if anyone shall have been so proud, so violent, so rebellious that he [18] cannot proceed to his punishment, by a direct report he should inform immediately the most honourable powers,[19] lest just severity should be delayed. But if he [18] shall have neglected to punish pursuant to this sanction's regulation violators of sepulchres whom he could or shall have delayed to report to his superiors,[20] he should be deprived of his property and his post.

And whoever—whether still placed in power or private citizens—shall have wished to emerge as an accuser of him,[18] because punishment of a violator of a sepulchre has been omitted, he should have a free opportunity. And he should not dread the odium of an informer,[21] since worthier of reward is he who shall have shown that he constantly hates wicked persons, Albinus, dearest and fondest cousin.

Your illustrious and exalted Magnificence by posted edicts shall order the law, which by love of piety and of religion we have conceived, to be made known speedily to the provinces and to the provinces' governors, that there may be rendered punishment to the criminals, joy to those living innocently, peace to the buried.

443. CLERICAL VIOLATORS OF SEPULCHRES, 447

Given on 13 March at Rome. Accepted on 27 March at Rome, the most distinguished Calepius being consul. Posted in Trajan's Forum on 6 April. Prefixed to the edict of the illustrious Albinus, praetorian prefect [2] for the second time and patrician.

This law does not need interpretation.

1. Search for relics of saints would be the most charitable excuse for such sacrilege, but traffic in these and recovery of valuables buried with the dead could have been the motives for both clergy and laity. See no. 206, n. 6.
2. Of Italy.
3. Literally "fates", a euphemism.
4. Such legislation exists in *ILCV* 1. 14 (= no. 139); *CT* 3. 16. 1; 9. 17; 9. 38. 3, 7, 8; *CI* 9. 19. 1-6; of which the oldest is dated 240. For later legislation see *CI* 9. 19. 7 and *D* 47. 12. But in the praetorian *edictum perpetuum* (consolidated c. 129) are preserved earlier regulations (possibly of republican date) against this practice (*FIRA* 1. 353, 376-7). Two fragmentary laws on this subject are assigned to the third century B.C. (*FIRA* 3. 223-4). From the presence of the clause in the Twelve Tables (promulgated in 449 B.C.) to the effect that the vestibule of a sepulchre may not be acquired by usucapion (*FIRA* 1. 69; *TT* 10. 10), it may be conjectured that this celebrated code contained other provisions pertaining to the integrity of interment.
5. The phrase is *manes*, but it may mean merely "corpses" in late Latin.
6. This must be understood figuratively, for orthodox Christianity ever has opposed cremation as a general mode of disposition of the dead.
7. A case of synecdoche, where the part stands for the whole.
8. See no. 75, n. 42.
9. So far as is concerned the philosophical concept (*the old books of wisdom*) of the soul's immortality among pagans, the first and the classic presentation occurs in Plato's Dialogues, where three main demonstrations (physical, ideal, metaphysical) are found respectively in the *Phaedrus* (245C foll.), the *Politeia* (608D foll.), the *Phaedo* (*passim*). The Christian doctrine perhaps is too well known to need documentation, but reference may be made to the Judaeo-Christian belief expressed in Wisd. 3. 1-4, Luke 23. 46, John 11. 25-6, 1 Cor. 15. 53, 2 Tim. 1. 10.
10. Another evidence of the antiquity of the present and the modernity of the past!
11. The word is *portentum*, which from "portent" by transfer may mean tropically in a moral sense a "monster of depravity".
12. That is, equipped with iron implements to wreck the tombs.
13. Perhaps a hendiadys: "the stars in the sky".
14. For the thought cf. John 3. 19-21.
15. The Latin *dominus* means "master" in respect to a slave and "landlord" in respect to a tenant. Coupling of slaves and tenant farmers should cause no surprise, for long ere this time the latter, though free-born, had become slaves

of the soil (*servi terrae*) and had degenerated into a status hardly distinguishable from serfdom, according to an undated (but *c.* 394) constitution of Theodosius I, Honorius, and Arcadius (*CI* 11. 52). See also *CT* 5. 17. 1 (dated 332) and no. 528, n. 5.

16. Both superiors and inferiors.
17. On these symbols of magisterial authority see no. 439, n. 3.
18. The governor is meant.
19. These were vicars of dioceses wherein provinces were grouped. Beyond vicars were praetorian prefects, whose superior was the emperor.
20. An editorial conjecture is translated.
21. See no. 440, n. 6.

444. LETTER OF THEODOSIUS II AND VALENTINIAN III ON EXCLUSION OF PALATINES FROM THE CLERICATE, 447

(*LNV* 7. 3)

This law prohibits palatines [1] from deserting the imperial bureaux of finance with a view to entering the service of the Church.

The same Augusti to Florian, count of the sacred largesses.

It is fair for our Serenity to sanction by a prudent constitution of our response [2] that it should not be permitted that anyone with reckless contempt and by desertion of the governmental service [3] of his office should choose the inactivity of sluggish leisure and to caution for the future by a published threat that no one should dare to lay aside the oaths of the governmental service [3] without having consulted his own judge's [4] attestation, Florian, fondest brother.

Wherefore your illustrious Authority, having complied with our pragmatic sanction's precept, should know that according to its report all palatines [1] of the sacred largesses who, when their terms of service had not been completed, without the attestation or the authority of their chief [5] have passed to ecclesiastical duties or to another governmental service,[3] after they have been deprived of the name of clergymen and the privilege of their former belt,[6] must be returned straightway to the palatine office and to the governmental service,[3] which they contumaciously have left; and that this ought to be maintained regarding all persons whom this sanction's pragmatic regulation shall have found within a triennium after their change of governmental service,[3] but that absolutely no suit must be undertaken against all

445. PORPHYRY, NESTORIUS, AND IRENAEUS, 448

others who are protected by more extended periods of time—with this precept maintained for the future: that to none it may be permitted either to abandon or to change one's governmental service [3] without his chief's [7] order and attestation; that the provinces' governors must be compelled that they should dispatch to your Honour's office [8] the recorders of the accounts of the largesses along with their ledgers and instructions [9] and that they should know that they are bound by the laws in procuring taxes. For it is not doubtful that whoever shall have retarded our Majesty's precepts will be obligated both to us and to our laws.

Given on 25 April at Rome, the most distinguished Calepius being consul.

1. See no. 186, n. 3.
2. See no. 218, n. 5.
3. See no. 186, n. 4.
4. See no. 134, n. 2.
5. The *comes* (count) usually, but here *praesul*.
6. See no. 476, n. 39.
7. Here *praesidens*, the same as *praesul* (cf. *supra* n. 5).
8. See no. 311, n. 5.
9. The meaning of this word (*instructio*) is not too clear. There would be little point in producing the recorders' instructions, unless to demonstrate to them their disobedience of these; but doubtless some sort of document is meant.

445. MANDATE OF THEODOSIUS II ON CONDEMNATION OF PORPHYRY, NESTORIUS, AND IRENAEUS, 448

(M 5. 417–20)

This constitution, preserved by Justinian in shorter form (*CI* 1. 1. 3), consigns to fire the writings of Porphyry, the anti-Christian Neoplatonist,[1] expels from the churches the followers of Nestorius, sometime patriarch of Constantinople, orders the teaching of only the faith as propounded at the Nicene (325) and Ephesian (431) councils, and deposes Irenaeus, bishop of Tyre, who as a Nestorian protagonist had been exiled (no. 426), but returned from exile to become the ordinary of Tyre.

The Greek original is translated.

Copy of the sacred constitution of the most pious Emperor Theodosius against Porphyry and the Nestorians and against Irenaeus, bishop of the Tyrians.[2]

We consider that it becomes our Majesty to remind our subjects about piety. For thus we think that it is possible to acquire also more favour from God and our Saviour Jesus Christ, whenever we ourselves are zealous to please him to the best of our powers and we exhort persons subject to us toward this end.

Therefore we[3] ordain that all writings, as many as Porphyry, impelled by his madness,[4] has composed against the Christians' pious religion, when found in anyone's possession, should be surrendered to fire, for we desire that all compositions inciting God toward wrath and harming souls should not come to men's ears.

We also ordain that persons affecting Nestorius' impious opinion[5] or following his nefarious doctrine should be expelled from the holy churches, if they are bishops or clergymen, but anathematized, if they are laymen, according to the ordinances already made by our Divinity[6]—the orthodox, who so wish and who follow our pious admonition,[7] having licence without fear and hurt to denounce[8] and to accuse them.

But since it has come to our pious and most divine[9] ears that certain persons have composed certain doctrines and have exhibited ambiguities not accurately consonant with the orthodox faith exhibited by the holy synod of the holy fathers, who assembled in Nicaea and in Ephesus, and by Cyril of pious memory,[10] who was bishop of the Alexandrians' megalopolis, we command that such compositions[11] (whether produced previously or now) should be burned and should be surrendered to complete disappearance, so that these may not come to anyone's reading—persons who continue to have and to read such compositions or books being suspect for the last[12] punishment—and that henceforth it should be allowed to none to say or to teach anything contrary to the faith exhibited (as we have said) in Nicaea and in Ephesus[13]—persons transgressing this our divine constitution obviously being subject to the punishment contained in the law issued concerning Nestorius' impious faith.

But so that all persons may learn by experience, as our Divinity abhors persons affecting Nestorius' impious faith, we ordain that Irenaeus, who formerly for this reason has been subject to displeasure from us and afterward (we know not how), after two marriages (as we have learned), contrary to the apostolic canons became bishop of the Tyrians' city,[14] should be expelled from the holy Church in Tyre, but should live quietly in his native community alone, deprived entirely of the priest's character and title.

Therefore your Magnificence, having followed our Piety's objective, shall be eager to observe it and to carry it to completion.

1. See nos. 382, n. 1, and 459, n. 26.
2. Justinian's superscription is "Emperors Theodosius and Valentinian Augusti to Hormisdas, praetorian prefect" (see caption of no. 446, which implements this constitution).
3. Here begins *CI*.
4. *CI* inserts "or any other person".
5. *CI* reads "faith".
6. *CI* omits *according . . . Divinity*.
7. *CI* has "legislation".
8. Literally "to make public".
9. *CI* omits *and most divine*.
10. His death occurred in 444, not long before this law's date.
11. *CI* inserts "and especially those of Nestorius".
12. That is, capital.
13. Here *CI* ends, appending the following subscription: "Given on 16 February at Constantinople, Zeno and Postumian being consuls".
14. St Paul permitted to a bishop one marriage (1 Tim. 3. 2; Titus 1. 6). *CA* (2. 2, 6. 17, 8. 47. 17) also enjoins this condition.

446. EDICT OF HORMISDAS AND ALBINUS ON CONDEMNATION OF PORPHYRY, NESTORIUS, AND IRENAEUS, 448

(M 5. 420)

This implements an imperial constitution (no. 445), which condemns the writings of Porphyry and of Nestorius, patriarch of Constantinople, and commands the deposition of Irenaeus, bishop of Tyre, a notorious fautor of Nestorius.

The Greek archetype is translated.

Edict promulgated by the prefects [1] in co-operation with the divine pragmatic sanction against Porphyry and Nestorius and Irenaeus.

Our most divine emperor,[2] since he has proved well that the structure of the laws and of the State itself is the orthodox religion, by his own constitution has removed every seed of impiety, when he heals by measured castigation those persons who distress it and shows the road of well-living to all persons.

Therefore he has legislated against [3] both the books of Porphyry composed against the Christians' holy religion and those describing Nestorius' nefarious doctrines; and that no dogma concerning religion ought to prevail, except that which has been proved by the assembled most pious bishops formerly in Nicaea [4] and afterward with Cyril [5] of pious [6] memory in the Ephesians' city.[7]

Moreover concerning the deposition of Irenaeus, who has been the bishop of the Tyrians' city, you all shall know from the preceding divine constitution made known in the Greek language,[8] so that none should pretend ignorance of these matters.[9]

Therefore it is fitting that all persons with all strictness should observe these regulations by having before their eyes the displeasure contained in the divine script.

Read in the church of the monks in the deserts,[10] Pharmouthi 23,[11] Indiction 1,[12] Year of Diocletian 164.[13]

1. Besides Hormisdas (see no. 445, n. 2), praetorian prefect of the East, his only other colleague known for this year was Albinus, praetorian prefect of Italy for the second time (*LNV* 26).
2. Theodosius II.
3. A variant preposition is "about".
4. At the First General Council in 325.
5. Patriarch of Alexandria.
6. A variant adjective is "devout".
7. At the Third General Council in 431.
8. Literally "voice".
9. This explanation shows that, as may be expected from the persons and the beliefs involved, the law and its implementing instrument were designed for the Greek-speaking East. The style of the date shows that the edict was read in Egypt, where Greek was commoner than Latin.
10. The *locus classicus* for monachism in the Egyptian deserts is the *Historia Lausiaca*, written by Palladius *c*. 420.
11. See no. 400, n. 78.
12. See no. 435, n. 9.
13. Since Diocletian's reign began in 284, the addition of 164 brings the edict's date to 448.

447. MANDATE OF THEODOSIUS II ON TRIAL OF THREE BISHOPS BY AN EPISCOPAL COMMISSION, 448

(M 7. 209–10)

Four presbyters with influence at the imperial court persuaded Theodosius to issue a mandate creating an episcopal commission to hear the cases of Ibas (Yihȋbâ), bishop of Edessa and leader of the Nestorian party there, Daniel, bishop of Carrhae, and John, bishop of Theodosiopolis. While the course of

447. TRIAL OF BISHOPS BY EPISCOPAL COMMISSION, 448

events is obscure, it seems that early in 449 the commissioners met first at Beirut and then at Tyre, where they acquitted Ibas. However, Ibas was deposed by an imperial mandate in June 449 as well as by the so-called Robber Council of Ephesus in August 449, but survived many places of incarceration for the next biennium until after due recantation he was reinstated at the Fourth General Council of Chalcedon (451). Daniel apparently avoided trial by resignation of his bishopric. No record about John's case is extant.

Memorandum to the admirable Damascius, praetorian tribune and notary.

Knowing your Excellency's purpose and realizing how much zeal you have that you commend yourself to God and to our Piety, we have sanctioned that you depart with Uranius,[1] the most devout bishop of the Himerians' city, to the districts of the East and, with the magistrates in each place co-operating, you provide that Ibas, the most devout bishop of the Edessans' city, and Daniel, the most reverend bishop of the Carrhaeans' city, and John, the most reverend bishop of Theodosiopolis,[2] should depart for the Phoenicians' province and that there should be investigated the matters charged by the most devout clergymen [3] of the aforesaid cities, in the presence of the aforesaid most godly Uranius and Photius, the most devout bishop of the Tyrians' city, and Eustathius, the most devout bishop of the Beirutians' city, against the said most godly bishop.

Hasten, therefore, according to what has commended itself to our Divinity, to depart for the districts of the East and to provide that the aforesaid most devout bishops should come to the Phoenicians' province and that there all the chief points [4] charged by the most devout clergymen of the Edessans' city [5] should be examined accurately in the presence of the said most godly bishops and that the things by them decided should be brought to a conclusion.

Given on 26 October [6] at Constantinople.

1. He seems to have prompted the presbyters to accuse Ibas.
2. The Latin version is followed for the last two bishops, who were co-defendants with Ibas (M 7. 211–12). The Greek version names Daniel as bishop of Theodosiopolis and is silent about John.
3. These are the four presbyters, known as Cyrus, Eulogius, Maras, Samuel, who also presented a petition about Ibas to the commissioners (M 7. 219–28).
4. Eighteen charges are listed (M 7. 221–8), of which twelve treat mostly Ibas' episcopal administration, especially of ecclesiastical moneys and properties, and six describe Daniel's episcopal acts of somewhat similar character; nothing is said about John, the third defendant.
5. The Latin version adds "and of Carrhae and of Theodosiopolis".
6. The Latin version dates the document one day later.

448. MANDATE OF THEODOSIUS II ON ADMISSION OF A LAYMAN TO A SYNOD, 448
(M 6. 731-4)

When at a synod in Constantinople (448), where the archimandrite Eutyches had been accused before St Flavian, patriarch of Constantinople (under whose jurisdiction he was), on the charge that by confusing the notions of person and nature he was teaching that Christ had a single composite nature, Theodosius sent written instructions to its 55 members,[1] who were sitting in its seventh session, by one Magnus, an imperial officer,[2] that the emperor had appointed the patrician [3] Florentius to assist at the assembly and that he should be admitted to the discussions.[4]

Although one might suppose that the participation of a layman, who apparently was not even invested with arbitral authority,[5] would not have been welcomed by the clergymen, yet the record reveals that this instance of imperial interference in ecclesiastical affairs was accepted with acclaim.[6]

We take thought for peace and for the holy churches and for the orthodox faith and we desire that the faith which was pronounced rightly and by God's inspiration by our fathers (those 318 gathered in Nicaea [7] and those in Ephesus [8] for the deposition of Nestorius [9]) should be guarded.

Therefore we desire this: do not let a scandal be cast upon the aforesaid orthodoxy.

And since we know that the most magnificent patrician Florentius is faithful and has borne an attested character for rectitude,[10] we desire him to be engaged with the synod's hearing, since the discussion is concerning faith.

1. Of these 32 were bishops and 23 were archimandrites.
2. He was a silentiary and, as such, one of thirty armed usher-sentries maintaining order in the imperial palace under the command of the provost of the sacred bedchamber (*praepositus sacri cubiculi*), who, though usually a eunuch, exercised enormous power when his emperor was a weakling. See no. 246, n. 1.
3. Florentius is described also as an ex-prefect and an ex-consul.
4. Since he was a layman, Florentius had no vote. The synodal *acta* record brief statements and questions from him, after he was acquainted officially with the previous proceedings, and it appears that he had a guiding role in the process.
5. Imperial commissioners, empowered to maintain order and to keep councillors to the agenda, were, of course, known ere 448 (see e.g. no. 73, n. 17), but Florentius' powers seem to have fallen short of such authority.
6. Such were the acclamations: "Many years to the emperor! Great is the

emperor's faith! Many years to the faith's guardians! Many years to the orthodox emperors! To the pious, the orthodox, the pious emperor! To the high priest-emperor! We are thankful to the orthodox emperor!"

7. In 325 at the First General Council.

8. In 431 at the Third General Council, attended by about 160 bishops, to whom should be added some forty later subscribers to the canons enacted there.

9. Late patriarch of Constantinople and author of the heresy called after him.

10. Perhaps from the context "orthodoxy" is the better translation, for ὀρθότης sometimes stands for ὀρθοδοξία.

449. LETTER OF THEODOSIUS II AND VALENTINIAN III ON CONVOCATION OF THE EPHESIAN COUNCIL, 449

(M 6. 587–90)

After the heresiarch Eutyches had been condemned by a synod at Constantinople in 448, his interest at the imperial court influenced Theodosius II to call a council to convene at Ephesus on 1 August 449 for reviewing the situation with a view to revoking the sentence against Eutyches and to deposing St Flavian, the patriarch of Constantinople, before whom the heresiarch had been heard.

The present document is addressed to Dioscore, patriarch of Alexandria, who appears only too eager to entrap his Constantinopolitan colleague in the sad story of the strife between these sees,[1] and is a sample of the summons sent to convoke the council, which has become notorious as the Robber Council (*Latrocinium*) and whose decision was destined to be revoked in 451 by the Fourth General Council of the Church at Chalcedon.

The document exists also in two Syriac versions, which describe it as an ordinance (P 3–7, 402–4).

Letter of Emperor Theodosius of divine lot[2] to the most pious Dioscore, bishop of Alexandria.

Emperors Caesars Theodosius and Valentinian, Victors, Triumphers, Greatest, Ever-August, Augusti to Dioscore.

It has become clear to all persons that our Empire's state and all human affairs are controlled and are consolidated by piety toward God. And when the Almighty is propitious, matters are wont to advance and to be administered rightly and pursuant to our purpose. Therefore, having been assigned by Divine Providence to rule, we make as much provision as possible necessarily for our subjects' piety and welfare, so that both the true religion and our government, by being consolidated both by pure worship toward the Almighty and by piety, may be resplendent.

At present, therefore, since some sudden doubt has emerged in respect to the safeguarding of the Catholic and apostolic teaching of our orthodox faith, which (as is the case), when distracted by different opinions, both disturbs and confuses men's minds and souls, we, having deemed it not tolerable to disregard such an offence, lest this, when disregarded, should seem to mount to an outrage against the Almighty himself, have ordained that when most holy and most God-beloved men, in whom exists a very great consideration of piety and of the orthodox and true faith, have assembled into one place, all such foolish controversy, after accurate examination has been displayed, should be dissolved and that the true and God-pleasing, that is, the orthodox, faith should be confirmed.

Therefore your Sanctity, having taken with you ten most pious bishops, metropolitans in your diocese, and ten other most holy bishops, who have been distinguished for their reasoning and life and who are resplendent among all persons for correctness and knowledge and teaching of the constant [3] and true faith, shall hasten forthwith to go to the metropolis of the Ephesians of Asia by next 1 August—no other person, to be sure, beyond the aforesaid persons causing annoyance to the most sacred synod, so that, when all the most holy and most God-beloved bishops (whom we have ordained through our sacred letters to assemble) have gathered at the aforesaid city and have displayed the most accurate investigation and inquiry, all crooked error may be expelled and the doctrine of the orthodox and true faith, which is most pleasing to our Saviour Christ,[4] may be confirmed and customarily may be resplendent: and this all persons shall guard, with the Almighty's favour, unbroken and unshaken for the future time.

But if anyone should have chosen to disregard the synod, so necessary and pleasing to God, and with all ability should not have come at the aforesaid time to the determined place, he shall have no excuse before the Almighty or before our Piety, but a person who demands exemption from a sacerdotal assembly will be smitten necessarily in his soul by a bad conscience.[5] However, Theodoret, bishop of the city of Cyrus, whom already we have ordered to have to do [6] with only his own church,[7] we order not to come to the holy synod, when assembled, that he should come and should be a participant in the said holy synod. But if any discord about him should emerge, we order the holy synod to convene without him and to decree the matters which have been ordered.[8]

Given on 30 March at Constantinople, after the consulate of the most distinguished Zeno and the most distinguished Postumian.

1. See no. 284, n. 4.
2. The Greek phrase τῆς θείας λέξεως is usually Latinized as *divae memoriae*, whence our familiar "of divine memory" comes. See also no. 127, n. 7.
3. The Latin version reads for this adjective "alien from every error", which, if we omit "every", is a closer translation of the Greek ἀπλανής.
4. This clause represents an adjectival phrase "and most dear to our Saviour Christ" in the same attributive position as the other two adjectives attached to *faith*.
5. Perhaps the emperor means more than he says: that many persons with bad consciences—"bad" from the imperial viewpoint—will seek imperial permission to be absent.
6. This expression (σχολάζειν) is said of a bishop without a diocese. It means literally "to be at leisure", "to have spare time" and from its noun (σχολή) is derived the Latin *schola* and the English *school*.
7. The distinguished ecclesiastical historian, whose episcopate began in 423, was deposed in 449 (the year of this council), but was recalled in 450 and was reinstated in 451 (at the Council of Chalcedon) and remained in possession of his see till his death in 458. His exclusion from Ephesus was doubtless due to the knowledge that he would oppose any Monophysite opinion.
8. This command shows the conclusion which the imperial will wants.

450. LETTER OF THEODOSIUS II ON CONCILIAR ATTENDANCE, 449

(M 6. 593–4)

This directive is important, because in it is expressed the exercise of the imperial prerogative in summoning a fanatical anti-Nestorian abbot Barsumas (*al.* Bar-Saumâ) to represent eastern abbots at the Council of Ephesus. So far as is known, such monastic representation is the first in conciliar history.[1]

The letter is extant also in Syriac and is akin to no. 452.

Sacred letter sent to Barsumas, the most devout archimandrite.

It has not escaped our Piety in what kind of conflict the godliest and the holiest archimandrites in districts of the East have been placed, when fighting for the orthodox faith and when repulsing certain bishops [2] in eastern cities ailing with Nestorius' [3] impiety and when the orthodox laics share the contest with the said godliest archimandrites.

Therefore, since also your Holiness both has sustained such great toil on account of the orthodox faith and has come to our Piety's notice,[4] we consider it to be just for your Sanctity, approved for purity of life and for orthodox faith, to go to the Ephesians' city and, occupying the place of all the godliest archimandrites in the East, to sit with the holy synod ordered to convene thither and with the other holy fathers and bishops to decree matters pleasing to God.

Given on 14 May among the Alexandrians.[5]

1. Perhaps in this imperial summons may be seen the initial attempt on a small scale to have abbots at synodal sessions supply bishops with brains, since the former seem to have had sufficient leisure in the contemplative life (both as monks first and later as leaders of monasteries) to ponder theological problems, whereas the latter—at the least the ordinary ones of their order—from their "daily ... care of ... the churches" (2 Cor. 11. 28) often could save too little time for such study.

2. Such as Ibas, bishop of Edessa.

3. Late patriarch of Constantinople and in exile at the letter's date for his heretical doctrine.

4. The Latin version's interpretation is accepted for the idea of attention.

5. One Latin MS. substitutes "at Alexandria", but in any event it appears to be an error that Theodosius was at Alexandria in Egypt at this time.

451. LETTER OF THEODOSIUS II ON CONCILIAR ATTENDANCE, 449

(M 6. 593-4)

This letter informs Dioscore, patriarch of Alexandria, who was to preside at the notorious Robber Council of Ephesus (as it became known), that the emperor has ordered the archimandrite Barsumas to assist at and to vote in the council (no. 440).[1]

This letter, described as an ordinance, is extant in Syriac (P 405).

Sacred letter written to Dioscore, the most devout bishop of Alexandria.

It has come to our Serenity's ears that many of the most devout archimandrites throughout the East with the orthodox laics both are annoyed at certain bishops,[2] who in certain parts of the East are said to be ailing with Nestorius' impiety,[3] and are struggling for the orthodox faith.

On account of this, therefore, it has seemed best to our Divinity [4] for the most godly priest and archimandrite Barsumas, approved for purity of life and for orthodox faith, to come to the Ephesians' city and, occupying the place of all the most godly archimandrites in the East, to sit with your Sanctity and with all the most holy fathers assembling thither and thus to decree matters pleasing to God on all affairs.

Therefore your Godliness, comprehending that every care for the orthodox faith exists in us, shall deign both to receive favourably the aforesaid most pious archimandrite and to provide that he should participate in your holy synod.[5]

Given on 15 May [6] at Therallum,[7] in the consulate of the most distinguished Protogenes and of him who shall be announced.

1. The conciliar *acta* of this synod record that Theodosius wrote in the same tenor to Juvenal, bishop of Jerusalem.
2. See no. 450, n. 2.
3. Late patriarch of Constantinople and author of the heresy named after him.
4. The old Latin version reads "Serenity" for this title.
5. Such instruction seems necessary, because no abbot is known to have participated officially in synodal debate.
6. The Syriac version dates this on 2 April.
7. The site is uncertain and the name possibly may be Intherallum, which also is unknown.

452. LETTER OF THEODOSIUS II AND VALENTINIAN III ON CONCILIAR ATTENDANCE, 449

(P 39-40)

This letter, extant only in Syriac and akin to no. 450, summons to the Council of Ephesus in 449 an eastern archimandrite to assist in the extirpation of Nestorianism. Copies were sent to eleven other archimandrites.[1]

Emperors [2] Caesars Theodosius and Valentinian, Victors, Ever-August,[3] Augusti to James.[4]

It has not been concealed from your Clemency in how great a contest God-fearing presbyters and archimandrites have been engaged in contending for the true faith in the land of the East against certain bishops [5] of that land, who, infected with the impious tenets of Nestorius,[6] have rendered themselves retrograde (infamous),[7] while the God-loving archimandrites have been sustained by the faithful laity.

Since, then, we will that in every way the orthodox faith should shine forth, for this reason it has seemed to us just and right that your Piety, distinguished for purity of life and integrity of faith, should repair to Ephesus, a city of Asia, on 1 August and should take a seat in the holy synod which is appointed to meet there, and in concert with the rest of the holy fathers, the bishops, should accomplish that which is well-pleasing to God.

This ordinance was issued on 13 June at Constantinople during the consulate of the illustrious Protogenes and of him who is (yet) [7] to be notified.

1. According to the synodal *acta* (P 40–1).
2. See no. 456, n. 1.
3. See no. 456, n. 2.
4. Unidentified.
5. See no. 450, n. 2.
6. Late patriarch of Constantinople and originator of Nestorianism.
7. Parenthesized by Perry.

453. MANDATE OF THEODOSIUS II ON CONCILIAR DISCIPLINE, 449

(M 6. 595–6)

This constitution names Elpidius, count of the sacred consistory, imperial representative at the Council of Ephesus. The conciliar *acta* record that a directive of the same tenor was written to Eulogius, a tribune and notary, who apparently was appointed to assist Elpidius in maintenance of discipline at the discussions.

This is extant also in Syriac (P 407-9).

Memorandum [1] given to the admirable Elpidius, count of the sacred consistory.

The impious Nestorius'[2] blasphemous case against God has been produced at the synod already previously held in Ephesus [3] and, therefore, from the holy fathers convened thither has received its just decision.

But since even now again another controversy against the divine faith has awakened, we have ordained this second synod to be held in

453. CONCILIAR DISCIPLINE, 449

Ephesus, for we are eager in every way that the evil's root should be excised, that in ejecting from all quarters the dogma's confusion we may preserve prayer's pure righteousness by reasoning powers, and that this may be a security for the State and for human blessings.

On this account, therefore, we have chosen both your Excellency and the admirable Eulogius, praetorian tribune and notary, for the service of the faith (as both accepted rightly in other respects and observing religiously and truly the things pertaining to the Almighty) and being able both to serve genuinely by our commands in respect to the transactions in Ephesus by the holy synod and to permit no uproar to occur from any quarter,[4] but also, if you should see someone employing disturbances and uproars to the harm of the most holy faith, to put this person in custody [5] and to notify us; and to advance in order the circumstances of the proposed action and to be present for decision; and to provide that swift and considered scrutiny should occur by the holy synod and should be notified to us—the persons who previously judged Eutyches,[6] the most devout archimandrite, being present and silent and not keeping the role of judges, but awaiting the common decision of all the other holy fathers, since the things decided by them now are being scrutinized; and not to permit anyone to set in motion another principal business [7] before the matters of the orthodox faith have been executed.

For also on this account, through a letter to the admirable proconsul,[8] we have dispatched both civilian and military aid to you in the remaining matters, so that you, also strengthened by these auxiliaries besides your own zealous efforts, can be strong enough for the completion of what has been ordered (which is better for all other blessings by as much as divine things are better than human things) and that the transactions in this case should become known to us.

1. The *acta* of the synod call it a memorandum (ὑπομνηστικόν; *commonitorium*).
2. Late patriarch of Constantinople.
3. The Third General Council there in 431 condemned Nestorianism.
4. See no. 73, n. 17.
5. Literally "in safety", but the idea is punitive confinement rather than protection from other persons.
6. This founder of Eutychianism was condemned in 448 at a synod in Constantinople. The object of the present council was to exonerate him.
7. The translator has emended χρηματικόν (pecuniary) to χρηματισμόν (business) to give the translation in the text.
8. Proclus, to whom the emperor also wrote a letter (no. 454), whose first half is an almost exact copy of this memorandum.

454. MANDATE OF THEODOSIUS II ON CONCILIAR DISCIPLINE, 449

(M 6. 597-8)

The emperor orders Proclus, proconsul of Asia, to send aid for Elpidius and Eulogius, imperial commissioners at the Council of Ephesus in 449, to use in maintaining order thereat.

The first half of this directive copies the same part of the order appointing the commissioners (no. 453).[1]

Letter of the emperor to Proclus, proconsul of Asia.

The impious Nestorius'[2] blasphemous case against God has been produced at the synod already previously held in Ephesus[3] and, therefore, from the holy fathers convened thither has received its just decision.

But since even now again another controversy against the divine faith has awakened, we have ordained this second synod to be held in Ephesus, for we are eager in every way that the evil's root should be excised, that in ejecting from all quarters the dogma's confusion we may preserve prayer's pure righteousness by reasoning powers, and that this may be a security for the State and for human blessings.

On this account we have chosen both the admirable Elpidius, count of our sacred consistory, and the admirable Eulogius, tribune and notary, for the purpose, as fitting to serve piety and suitably attested in respect to this.[4]

And to them we desire that for their use aid should be contributed[5] by you, for they have been committed to expel disturbance from the transactions and by our Serenity have been ordered to permit no uproar to occur from any quarter.[6]

And if we should have learned from them that you have neglected the orders[7] and have not ministered to what they desire, we shall command your carelessness to be your harm.

---

1. Only two slight changes appear: (1) substitution of one preposition for another (εἰς for πρός [*against*] in first line of second paragraph), but both governing the same case; (2) reversal of the same adverb (νῦν [*now*] in first line of third paragraph after *even* instead of before *even*).
2. See no. 453, n. 2.
3. See no. 453, n. 3.
4. The Latin version reads "as worthy to administer this business and approved as suitable by many persons' testimony"—obviously an alternative version.
5. The verb (συνεισφέρειν) means literally "to join in payment" or "to

administer at the same time" or "to bring into the common stock" as to a marriage.

6. See nos. 73, n. 17, and 453, n. 4.
7. The Latin version appends "of our Gentleness".

455. LETTER OF THEODOSIUS II ON CONCILIAR MAINTENANCE OF ORTHODOXY, 449

(M 6. 597–600)

In this constitution, addressed to about 130 bishops of the so-called Robber Council of Ephesus in 449, is seen another instance of Caesaropapism, when the emperor ordered the prelates, in effect, to rescind the acts of the Synod of Constantinople in 448, when Eutyches, the heretical archimandrite, had been condemned, by reinstating Eutyches and by deposing St Flavian, patriarch of Constantinople, who had presided at the synod which anathematized Eutychianism.

The letter exists also in Syriac (P 409–11).

Letter of the emperor to the second synod in Ephesus.
To the most holy synod in Ephesus.[1]
We desired[2] that apart from every disturbance God's holy churches should exist and that you, adhering firmly to your most holy churches, customarily should perform the sacred rites pertaining to the Almighty's service and that so much toil and affliction should not happen to you.

But since Flavian, the most God-beloved bishop, desired to rouse certain matters concerning the holy faith against Eutyches, the most devout archimandrite, and, having collected a tribunal, began to do certain things, we, having dispatched frequently word to the said most God-beloved bishop, desired to check the aroused disturbance, since we have been persuaded that the orthodox faith, transmitted by the holy fathers in Nicaea[3] and which the holy synod in Ephesus[4] confirmed, suffices for us.

But since, though we frequently importuned the said most God-beloved bishop to desist from such inquiry, so that this cause of uproar may not exist throughout the whole world, he did not cease, we, having thought that it is not safe without your holy synod and the primates of the holy churches everywhere for such inquiry about faith to be roused, have considered it necessary to convene your Holinesses, so that you, when you have learned the transactions there and the

756   456. CONCILIAR ACTION ABOUT IBAS, 449

aroused inquiry, should excise every diabolical root and should eject from the holy churches the persons admiring or assisting the impious Nestorius' [5] blasphemy and should decree that the orthodox faith should be guarded firmly and unmovedly, since indeed all our hope and our Empire's strength has depended [2] on the orthodox faith in God and on your holy prayers.

Issued in the month of June at the city of Constantinople during the consulate of Protogenes.[6]

1. Mansi notes that only this part of the superscription is found in all the ancient copies, which have only "To the holy Ephesian synod".
2. This and other verbs in this letter appear to have been cast into the epistolary imperfect or perfect tenses, as if the letter is dated at the time when it is supposed to be received.
3. In 325 at the First Ecumenical Council.
4. In 431 at the Third Ecumenical Council.
5. Formerly patriarch of Constantinople and author of a heresy named after him.
6. Supplied from Syriac.

456. MANDATE OF THEODOSIUS II AND VALENTINIAN III ON CONCILIAR ACTION ABOUT IBAS, 449

(P 10–13)

This mandate in Syriac, discovered c. 1851 in Egypt, described as an ordinance, and translated by the author of the book whence the English translation (adapted stylistically for this sylloge) is taken, consigns to the Synod of Ephesus (later characterized as the *Latrocinium*) in 449 the case of Ibas, bishop of Edessa and leader of the Nestorian party there, about whose impiety and blasphemy the Edessans have complained to the imperial court at Constantinople. The synod deposed Ibas, who had been tried earlier in that year by an episcopal commission imperially appointed (no. 447). The Fourth General Council of Chalcedon in 451 restored Ibas to Edessa.

Emperors [1] Caesars Theodosius and Valentinian, Victors and Illustrious by Victory, Ever-August,[2] Augusti to the holy synod assembled at Ephesus, the metropolis.

Numerous reports from people at Edessa, a city in the province of Osrhoëne, with acts drawn up there, have been dispatched hither,[3] which contain the depositions of many venerable clergy and God-fearing archimandrites and civic dignitaries and (so to speak) of the whole population of the same city, who witness against Ibas, bishop of the city of Edessa, to a great deal of impiety and blasphemy.

Since, then, it appertains to (the office of) [4] your Holiness to correct such profanity—for that the evidence of all these persons, clerics and monks and civic magistrates and laics, should be false, your Holiness fairly cannot admit on reading the (formal) [4] account of these matters with the (accompanying) [4] affidavits—you will free that city from such blasphemy (scandal) [4] and will appoint over it a man honoured for integrity of life and renowned in the true faith—one who is master of himself.[5]

And if anything else of a similar (scandalous) [4] character occur in those parts,[6] let it be suppressed; for if those who preside over metropolitan cities [7] are orthodox, the others (bishops suffragan),[4] as a matter of necessity, will follow their teaching.

In reference to this same cause we have enjoined already that adjudicators of it should be the God-fearing Photius, bishop of the holy Church of Tyre, the metropolis, and Eustathius,[8] bishop of Beirut, and Uranius,[9] bishop of the city of Himeria,[10] whom also we now command to proceed to your holy synod in order to convey in person all these instructions to your Holiness.

This ordinance was issued on 27 June at Constantinople.

1. The usual style in imperial constitutions (Αὐτοκράτορες or *Imperatores*), not "autocratic" as the translator has.

2. Perry translates "the ever-Worshipful", but the present editor has altered this to *Ever-August* in conformity with his usual translation of ἀεὶ σεβαστοί and of *semper Augusti*.

3. Constantinople.

4. Parenthesized by Perry.

5. A certain Nonnus occupied Ibas' see for a biennium during Ibas' suspension.

6. The conditional clause has been rearranged to read more smoothly.

7. Edessa was of metropolitan rank over two hundred years before this time, as coins minted there show.

8. He was suffragan to Photius.

9. He was suffragan to Ibas.

10. On their activity see no. 447.

457. MANDATE OF ELPIDIUS ON CONCILIAR PROCEDURE, 449

(M 6. 619–20)

Elpidius, count of the sacred consistory and imperial representative at the Council of Ephesus in 449, issued the following directive, as an expression of the emperor's will, to the prelates to annul the proceedings of the Synod of Constantinople in 448, when Eutychianism had been condemned.

These instructions exist also in Syriac (P 406–7).

Elpidius, the admirable count, said:

For the Devil, the source of evil, must never be relaxation of the war against the holy churches, and the most pious emperor ever opposes him [1] who does not fight fairly, for he [2] has thought correctly that he will have a champion for his Majesty, if he himself should be armed fully with piety for the contests. And let him not find fault with this thought in being so minded, for many things are accomplished successfully by him [3] from above rather than by weapons.

Therefore also with you he has condemned Nestorius' [4] madness, because, though ordained for the Almighty's service, he became the father and the teacher of impious instructions, just as if accepting the priesthood of devils, but not of piety. But that person,[4] indeed, meanwhile has been condemned to a fitting place,[5] since he is being kept for inevitable punishment in the future life, because he has poured himself out into such great impiety and has swept many persons with him by changing their beliefs.

And the dispute [6] which now has arisen the most sacred emperor brings to you, as fathers and judges, and from you desires to find the solution of the excited matter, namely, security both for himself and for his subjects.

But what are the things which the most sacred emperor has enjoined upon us [7] he has written to you and now immediately I shall make clear, saying by way of preface only so much as one of those who are initiated correctly in piety by you.

Today the Lord of all and God the Word, the Saviour, surrenders himself to judgement and submits to judges and honours you with the powers of decisions, that, finding you judging justly in his case, he may honour you therein and again confess before the Father.[8] But if he should find any persons ejecting from their thought the sincerity of piety and by art of words bringing matters of faith into dispute contrary to the holy fathers' exposition,[9] alas for them from each judgement! [10] It would be good for them, if they had not been born,[11] because after the robber [12] and the publican [13] and the harlot [14] and the Canaanite woman [15] they do not confess sincerely in the glory [16] of God him on whom they believed, while he was in humility assumed for us.[17]

And I shall read aloud the duties enjoined upon us [7] by our most sacred king [18]-emperor.[19]

1. Satan.
2. The emperor, Theodosius II.
3. God.
4. Late patriarch of Constantinople, from whom was named his heresy.
5. Nestorius was in Egyptian exile and had only two years of life left to live.
6. Nestorianism.
7. Either the editorial plural or standing for Elpidius and Eulogius, his fellow-commissioner.
8. For the thought see Matt. 10. 32. The Greek version continues here, but the old Latin version begins a new sentence—an arrangement which is adopted in the translation.
9. Probably an allusion to previous conciliar decisions on faith.
10. The Latin version explains the last phrase by adding "of God and of the emperor".
11. The Latin version inserts "as says the Scripture"; the sentence is adapted from Matt. 26. 24 and Mark 14. 21.
12. The word is λῃστής (incorrectly translated "thief"—which is κλέπτης—in the King James Version). For the variant versions cf. Matt. 27. 38, 44 and Mark 15. 27, 32 with Luke 27. 39–43, where λῃσταί are called κακοῦργοι (malefactors).
13. Since Jesus was stigmatized as "a friend of publicans [tax farmers] and sinners" (Matt. 11. 19; Luke 7. 34) and since not a few must have believed in him, it is difficult to decide which allusion is meant. Perhaps Luke 7. 27–9 will suffice.
14. Possibly Matt. 21. 31 or John 4. 7–30 (the woman of Samaria, commonly —but not necessarily—thought to have been a harlot) is meant.
15. Matt. 15. 22–8 (Mark 7. 25–30 calls the same woman a Greek Syrophoenician).
16. The rest of this sentence follows the Latin version and the conjecture thereto, for it seems superior to the Greek version hitherto translated.
17. Probably a reminiscence of Phil. 2. 8.
18. The Latin version for *king* reads "and most pious".
19. The *acta* note that then Elpidius read the memorandum sent to him and to Eulogius by the emperor (no. 453).

458. LETTER OF THEODOSIUS II ON PRESIDENCY OF THE EPHESIAN COUNCIL, 449
(M 6. 599–600)

In this constitution Theodosius commits the presidency of the Robber Council of Ephesus in 449 to Dioscore, patriarch of Alexandria, whom he reminds that Theodoret, bishop of Cyrus, has been excluded from the synod (no. 449).

Two Syriac versions, describing this epistle as an ordinance, are known (P 8–10, and 8, n. † *ad fin.*).

Letter of the emperor to Dioscore of Alexandria.
To Dioscore, the most devout bishop of Alexandria.

Previously we have ordained that Theodoret, bishop of the city of Cyrus, should not go to the holy synod, until the holy synod should decree what seems best in his case, since we abhor him for having tried to offer doctrines opposite to what Cyril of holy memory, the late bishop of the megalopolis of Alexandria, has composed about the faith.

But since it is admitted that certain of the persons holding Nestorius'[1] opinions have tried to bring their zeal to bear for him, to the end that by all means he should go to the holy synod, for this reason we have considered it necessary to employ this sacred letter to your Godliness and to the whole holy synod, that indeed we, following the holy fathers' canons (not only on account of Theodoret, but also on account of all other persons who are involved in the now-congregated holy synod), offer to your Godliness the authority and the presidency,[2] since we know precisely that the most godly Juvenal, archbishop of Jerusalem, and the most godly Archbishop Thalassius[3] and every similar fervent lover and fautor of orthodoxy will be likeminded with your Holiness, who are resplendent, by God's grace, for both holiness of life and orthodox faith.

And also those persons who have tried to say anything by way of addition to or subtraction from the expositions about the faith by the holy fathers in Nicaea[4] and later in Ephesus[5] we permit absolutely to have no freedom of speech in the holy synod, but also we desire them to be under your judgement, since also for this reason and now we have ordained that the holy synod should be convened.[6]

1. Late patriarch of Constantinople.
2. Literally "first-rate things".
3. Exarch of Caesarea in Cappadocia.
4. In 325 at the First General Council.
5. In 431 at the Third General Council.
6. One Syriac version has the subscription: "This ordinance was issued on 6 August at Constantinople."

459. EDICT OF THEODOSIUS II ON CONFIRMATION OF THE EPHESIAN COUNCIL, 449 or 450

(P 364–70; M 7. 495–8, 9. 250–1)

The eunuch Chrysaphius, the last (441–50) and the worst of the imperial favourites to influence the feeble Theodosius II, in espousal of the cause of his monastic godfather Eutyches, the Constantinopolitan heresiarch, and in offence at St Flavian, patriarch of Constantinople, whose synod at Constantinople had condemned Eutyches in 448, prevailed upon Theodosius to convoke at Ephesus in 449 what later was called the Robber Council (*Latrocinium*)[1] both to rehabilitate Eutyches and to depose Flavian. After this council had secured for Chrysaphius each of his objects, the emperor approved the conciliar acts by the following edict, which also concerns consecration of heretical bishops, possession of heretical writings, association with heretics.

The edict is extant in Syriac and has two Latin interpretations. The law was rescinded by Marcian in 452 (no. 479).

Translation.[2]

We cannot allow by any means that the laws proclaimed for the benefit of the community be consigned to oblivion or, again, that the salutary ordinances of our (imperial)[3] government be depraved by the presumption of others. On the contrary, with that philanthropy which is constantly exercised by us, we apply ourselves to correct acts of presumption: that is, however, without (having recourse to)[3] capital punishment and only by a tempering of menace we reach those who are the originators (of crime)[3] as well as prevent others from offending in the same manner.

As to wit: when Nestorius[4] attacked the adorable religion, which the fathers transmitted (to us)[3] and for the purpose of confirming and of consolidating[5] which holy priests assembled of old at the city of Nicaea[6] from every quarter (of the world),[3] when (afterward, I say)[3] this Nestorius[4] publicly proclaimed positions (of doctrine calculated to conduce)[3] to the prejudice and the injury of the simple (the faithful),[3] immediately our Clemency, in case the evil, creeping in by a licence of speech, should render obdurate the minds of the simple-minded, rather (if it be proper to speak the truth)[3] lest it should destroy them completely, gave orders that the bishops should assemble not inconsiderately and suddenly—for it was no little or trifling subject on which there was deliberation, but one relating to our adorable religion (the principles of)[3] which uphold and consolidate our Kingdom—that, for this purpose, expounders and doctors of the divine religion, selected from the whole Empire (as is right and just to say) of the Romans, should proceed to and assemble together at Ephesus,[7] in order to search into and to investigate, with a judgement prompted by religion and by justice, certain hitherto insoluble (unsolved) [3] questions which we brought to their remembrance, who not only consolidated and confirmed for us the faith, which was from the beginning transmitted to us, but also, having proved the controversy of the aforesaid Nestorius [4] to be groundless, deposed him from the throne of the episcopate and divested him of (its) [3] dignity.

After (the report of) [3] all these transactions, therefore, had been dispatched and read over to our Clemency, we remitted to them their judicial sentence, so pleasing to God, and by a salutary law,[8] which necessarily has been promulgated, we enjoined that the aforementioned Nestorius [4] and his participators in impiety should be deprived of the company of Christians and the name of (Christian).[3]

We further decreed that they should be designated Simonians,[9] because, according to the investigation of the holy priests, they followed the practices of that person (Simon),[3] and by just punishment, which is placed clearly in our injunctions, we determined that they should be so designated.

Although, then, these results had been accomplished on principles of religion and justice, Flavian and Eusebius [10] resolved to resuscitate what had been set at rest by our Clemency and presumed to renew the depraved error of Nestorius [11] in opposition to our Clemency's injunction and threw into the churches the divisions and the scandals of heretics, when silenced and at rest. Consequently our Clemency, bound by necessity, commanded that holy bishops should go from various and distant cities and should assemble at Ephesus, the city aforenamed, in order that, on the eradication (by vigour and God-loving deliberation) of the pernicious seed from the (very) [3] roots, the faith alone might grow (flourish).[3]

Nor have we been disappointed in our expectation. For after the whole of the investigation which they undertook had become less and less and (finally) [3] closed and after the holy religion, which from the beginning had been transmitted to us, had become truly and powerfully strengthened, those persons (so often named above) together with their coadjutors, (viz.) [3] Domnus,[12] who is said to preside over the Church of Antioch, and Theodoret [13] and certain other persons,[14] beguiled by the same ignorance, were deposed from the throne of the episcopate, because they showed themselves unworthy of so great a dignity by corrupting the word of truth.

Moreover it was resolved by a God-fearing decree to determine that none should dare by any means—not even partially—to deprave the decision (definition) [3] of the 318 bishops who assembled at Nicaea [6] nor to presume to add to or to subtract anything from it . . .[15]

459. CONFIRMATION OF EPHESIAN COUNCIL, 449 OR 450

... and considering your work as our own, seeing we honour you as a father, we pray your Piety (Dioscorus)[16] to compose circular letters, in which to insert this our God-loving law, the creed of our holy faith, and the definition of the two synods aforementioned as well as this—that "nobody shall add to it, even one word, or shall subtract from it, and nobody shall presume to interpret it, seeing that it is its own expositor and obvious to everybody".

Your Piety, having taken then copies of it, will dispatch it to the venerable bishops of the royal city of Constantinople and Jerusalem and to the other metropolitans, in order that all those bishops, suffragan to them, may sign it also and may forward it to us with those letters, notifying the same to us and (in order that)[3] everyone of the bishops who has a copy may read it in church before all the people. But before anything else, your Piety with all your suffragan bishops will append your signatures and will forward the same to the auditory of our serene Highness.

Finally, as often as your Piety receives information of any author's books written in antagonism to the orthodox faith heretofore or at the present time or containing to the injury of mankind the polluted doctrine of Nestorius[4] (seeing we know nothing of these, these could not be inserted in our statute), your Piety will order that, on being claimed and surrendered, they must be committed to the flames by the hands of the God-fearing bishops, according to our law,[8] which was enacted on purpose to destroy everything that is in antagonism to our holy faith from the (very)[3] root.

Interpretation of the law by Theodosius the Younger, when he had been seduced by Chrysaphius, promulgated on behalf of Eutyches against Flavian and his associates and which the following[17] law of Marcian, the most religious prince, has destroyed.

Quite some time ago Nestorius, who was the Constantinopolitan bishop, attempting to introduce novel and pestiferous beliefs, contrary to those which have been transmitted and opposed to the pure and orthodox faith of Christian dogmas, was ejected by the holy synod which at Ephesus assembled from the entire world by imperial sanction.[7] And this holy synod likewise confirmed also the[18] Catholic faith, transmitted by the bishops who gathered at Nicaea.[6]

We, also confirming what salutarily[19] was defined by the said holy council which gathered at Ephesus,[7] have promulgated a general law,[20] which condemns the aforesaid Nestorius[4] as well as those who hold views similar to his, commanding that they at least should not be known by the name of Christians,[21] but that rather they should be called Simonians,[9] since they have loved Simon's blasphemy. We also have determined that we must subject them to certain punishments, which the aforesaid[22] command contains.[23]

But since at the present time, while afterward for a long time the churches had been quiet, Flavian, the Constantinopolitan bishop, and Eusebius, another bishop, by following Nestorius' pernicious seductions, have injected schisms into the churches, we have commanded that again a council should assemble from every side in the most holy Church of the said city of Ephesus, in order that, when the true faith has been supported with all exactness, the heresy injected by them may be removed from the holy churches.

Therefore this holy synod itself has defined that the faith which at Nicaea has been transmitted by the 318 fathers [6] should prevail, but that from the episcopate should be excluded not only Flavian and Eusebius [10] but also Domnus, who was the Antiochene bishop, and Theodoret [13] and certain others, who participate in the same blindness of the aforesaid heresy and on this account are unworthy of episcopal sees.

And therefore we praise and support the said holy synod's decrees, since we think and call this the orthodox faith, which has been expounded by the 318 fathers [6] and has been supported in the holy councils which have assembled at Ephesus.[24]

But also that for the rest of time the solution of the entire question may be made most complete, we order that in all the world everywhere all bishops through their metropolitans of each and every district should subscribe to this very faith which has been published in Nicaea [6] and that this very act should be notified to us by their own letters. Moreover absolutely none should be ordained in any way bishop who is held fast by the opinion of Nestorius [4] and of Flavian and of those persons of the said heresy. But even if anyone has been ordained already by wicked anticipation or if anyone in the future shall have been advanced by tumult and deceit, he should be rejected by decree of orthodox pontiffs.

And also nothing even word for word should be added to or subtracted from the said holy faith.[25]

But none should have or should read or should transcribe or should produce Nestorius [4] or his definitions or noxious books and especially those which Porphyry [26] has published against Christian literature alone or Theodoret's [27] writings,[28] but whosoever has books of this sort should produce those publicly and the books should be consigned to the fire in the sight of all persons.

And none should permit [29] those persons who cultivate this religion or their teachers to be either in a city or in the country or in a suburb or to have an assembly with themselves—otherwise, when his estate has been confiscated, he himself shall be relegated by perpetual exile.

If anyone at all—of whatever quality he shall have been [30]—shall have acted thus or if anyone shall have had books containing Nestorius'[4] and Theodoret's[13] interdicted[31] belief or their interpretations (whether these are called allocutory sermons or teachings[32] or if the matter which has been composed by them shall have been prefaced by another's name), he should be subject to the same torments.

1. So Pope St Leo I in *Ep.* 95. 2 (= *PL* 54. 943).
2. Perry explains this Syriac note as due to the transcriber who copied the law from a Greek version of the Latin original.
3. Parenthesized by Perry.
4. Late patriarch of Constantinople and founder of Nestorianism.
5. Perry's English has been rearranged here to read more smoothly.
6. The First General Council in 325.
7. The Third General Council in 431.
8. No. 422.
9. See no. 422, n. 7.
10. Bishop of Dorylaeum, a former friend of Eutyches and his later foe at the Synod of Constantinople in 448.
11. That either Flavian or Eusebius was Nestorian is simply the opinion of Theodosius, who himself had protected Nestorius. In fact, Eusebius, while still a layman, was among the earliest to protest against Nestorianism. And Flavian's sainthood should clear him from such a charge.
12. He was condemned partly because of Alexandrian rivalry against the Antiochene patriarch and principally because he had protected Ibas, bishop of Edessa, and Theodoret, bishop of Cyrus, both enemies of Eutyches.
13. Ecclesiastical historian and bishop (n. 12).
14. These included Ibas (n. 12), Irenaeus, bishop of Tyre, and Aquilinus, whom Irenaeus of Tyre consecrated as suffragan bishop of Byblus and who later was restored.
15. Perry indicates a loss of several folios here, but the lacuna may be filled partially by the following extract, which according to Dioscore's encyclical (ordered at n. 16 *infra*) was in the law (P 374):
"Nobody who is a follower of Nestorius or who holds such opinions as his shall be admitted to the priesthood: and, further, that he who may have been (so admitted) by surprise shall be removed from the grade of the priesthood and shall not be reckoned among the number of priests, but that such persons rather must be driven from every place and not be allowed to be received by anybody into houses or into public company, so that they may be apprehensive of (incurring) the punishments prescribed by the law, who act in violation of the law."
16. Perry supplies this parenthesis. Dioscore, patriarch of Alexandria, was president of the Robber Council in 449.
17. Mansi's caption in 7. 495-6 so characterizes Marcian's letter (no. 479), which he prints after the interpretation of the Theodosian law. In 9. 250-1,

however, Mansi calls the interpretation a law of Theodosius [II] and Valentinian [III] and adds that it was directed against Nestorius [patriarch of Constantinople] and Theodore [bishop of Mopsuestia] and those who held opinions similar to theirs.

The notable variations of Mansi's second Latin version, which is shorter than the first translation, will be noted.

18. M's second version reads from here to the sentence's end "orthodox faith explained by the 318 Nicene bishops".

19. M gives "piously" in his second version.

20. M has "constitution" in his second version.

21. M substitutes "that they should not deserve the name of Christians" in his second version.

22. M reads "present" in his second version.

23. Here M's second version suspends for some space.

24. Particularly the Third General Council and the *Latrocinium*.

25. After this point M's second version resumes.

26. This Neoplatonist's anti-Christian writings already had been condemned by an earlier emperor (no. 66, n. 3; see nos. 382, n. 1, and 445, n. 1).

27. It is true that Theodoret's theology was not unexceptionable.

28. For *and especially ... writings* M's second version has "either of Nestorius himself or of another and especially Nestorius' writings against the Christians alone or Diodore's and Theodore's and Theodoret's writings".

The Diodore mentioned here is probably the brilliant head of the theological school at Antioch, where he taught Theodore, bishop of Mopsuestia, whose unorthodoxy was charged to Diodore, who later became bishop of Tarsus.

29. M's second version reads "receive".

30. M's second version joins this conditional clause, with omission of the qualification, to the preceding sentence, where also is omitted the temporal clause concerning confiscation.

31. In M's second version "renounced" is substituted.

32. After this M's second version reads "they shall be subject to the same punishments, although what have been composed by them appear to be others' light". M suggests that *in nomine* (in the name) should be read for *lumen* (light).

460. LETTER OF THEODOSIUS II ON ORTHODOXY, 449 or 450

(P 370)

This fragmentary letter to Juvenal, bishop of Jerusalem, announces the issuance of an imperial edict enforcing adherence to orthodox creeds. It seems to exist only in Syriac.

Correspondence between our faithful and God-loving Emperor Theodosius and Juvenal, bishop of Jerusalem.

Seeing that our Clemency has exercised great solicitude on behalf of the holy faith in the matter of those scandals which have arisen concerning it and have disturbed the peace of the holy churches of God, I now likewise command by a God-loving edict all venerable bishops to subscribe to the holy faith of Nicaea [1] and to the definition concerning it communicated by these two holy and ecumenical synods,[2] established in compliance with our Clemency's will, and that nothing is to be added to it, not even a word, or subtracted from it, because it is final (perfect),[3] as that which has been accomplished by the co-operation of the Holy Spirit. . . .

1. The First General Council in 325.
2. The Ephesian synods of 431 and 449, the one being the Third General Council and the other, which the emperor considers ecumenical also, being the lately ended Robber Council.
3. Parenthesized by Perry.

461. LETTER OF VALENTINIAN III AND MARCIAN ON CONVOCATION OF A COUNCIL, 450

(PL 54. 899–900)

This letter, emanating really from Marcian, announces to Pope St Leo I his election as emperor of the East and suggests that the pope convoke a council of the Church to ensure the Church's peace. Since Leo was more concerned about the invasion of the Huns and since he realized that there was little prospect of convening a council in Italy, where he could control it, because he had to deal with a more energetic emperor in Marcian than was Theodosius II, his weak predecessor, the pope was averse from summoning a general synod at that time. But Marcian persisted in his purpose and on his own authority called (no. 464) a general council to meet at Nicaea (later transferred to Chalcedon), which became, as the event proved, the Fourth Ecumenical Council of the Church (451).

The letter exists both in Greek and in Latin, but the editors believe that both are original expressions of the imperial will and hold that neither has been translated from the other. The Latin text is translated.

Letter of Valentinian and Marcian to Leo, archbishop of Rome.

Victors Valentinian and Marcian, Glorious Triumphers, Ever-

August to Leo, the most reverend archbishop of the glorious city of Rome.

To this very great sovereignty we have come by God's providence and by the choice of the most excellent Senate and of the entire soldiery.[1] Wherefore, in view of the reverend and Catholic religion of the Christians' faith, by the aid of which we trust that the vigour of our power will be piloted, we believe that it is proper that your Sanctity, possessing the pre-eminence in the episcopate from the divine faith, ought to be addressed first by our sacred letter, urging and asking that your Sanctity should entreat the Eternal Divinity on behalf of the stable state [2] of our Sovereignty and that we should have such a purpose and a desire that, by the removal of all impious error through the summoning of a synod by you as originator, the greatest peace, existing pure and inviolate from all wickedness, may be made among all the Catholic faith's bishops.

Done at Constantinople, in the consulate of the Lord Valentinian Perpetual-Augustus for the seventh time and of the most distinguished Avienus.

1. Marcian succeeded Theodosius II, who had died on 28 July 450, by marrying the late emperor's sister, Pulcheria, who invested her husband with the imperial insignia on 25 August 450.
2. Literally "stability and state", a hendiadys.

462. LETTER OF MARCIAN ON CONVOCATION OF A COUNCIL, 450

(PL 54. 903–6)

This letter to Pope St Leo I follows by a few weeks a previous epistle on the same subject (no. 461) and enters more into detail about the proposed general council.

Letter of Marcian, emperor, to Leo, archbishop of Rome.
Marcian to Leo, the most reverend bishop of the Church of the most glorious city of Rome.

Your Sanctity does not doubt about our eagerness and plea, since we desire the true religion of the Christians and the apostolic faith to continue firm and to be maintained by all people with pious mind. Accordingly we are not undecided that the security of our power depends upon the right religion and the propitiation of our Saviour.

Wherefore the most reverend men,[1] whom your Sanctity has sent to our Piety, we have received gladly and, as was fitting, with grateful heart.

It remains that if it shall have pleased your Beatitude to journey into these parts and to hold a synod, you should deign to do this through love of religion: in that case your Sanctity will satisfy our desires and will decide what matters are useful for the sacred religion. But if this is burdensome that you journey to these parts, let your Sanctity make this very point clear to us in your own letter, that our sacred letter may be sent to all the East and to Thrace and to Illyricum, that all the most holy bishops ought to assemble at a certain specified place, where it shall have pleased us, and may declare by their own direction what may advantage the Christians' religion and the Catholic faith, according as your Sanctity has defined pursuant to ecclesiastical regulations.

1. Probably ecclesiastical bearers of a congratulatory message on Marcian's accession.

463. RESCRIPT OF PULCHERIA ON CONVOCATION OF A COUNCIL, 450

(PL 54. 905-8)

St Pulcheria, daughter of Arcadius, regent (414–16) for her younger brother Theodosius II, whom she succeeded on his death (450), virgin-wife (450–3) of Marcian, whom she elevated to the purple, seems to have been the first female to reign over the Roman Empire. This letter from her is the third addressed to Pope St Leo I about convocation of a council to work for the peace of the Church (see nos. 461 and 462).

Letter of Pulcheria Augusta to the most holy Leo, archbishop of Rome.

Pulcheria, the most venerable Augusta, to Leo, the most reverend bishop of the glorious city of Rome.

Your Beatitude's letter we have received with the respect due to every bishop and by it we have perceived that your faith is pure and of such a quality as ought to be rendered to the sacred temple with sanctity. In truth I likewise and my lord, the most tranquil emperor, my consort, in the same faith always have remained and now remain, avoiding all depravity and pollution and wickedness.

Therefore Anatolius, the most holy bishop of glorious Constantinople, has remained in the same faith and religion and embraces your letter's apostolic confession, after the removal of that error, which now has arisen from some persons,[1] just as your Sanctity will be able to perceive rather clearly also from his letter, for he also without any delay has subscribed likewise to the letter about the Catholic faith which your Beatitude has sent to Bishop Flavian [2] of holy memory.

And moreover let your Reverence deign to signify, in whatever way you shall have perceived, that also all bishops of the entire East, of Thrace, and of Illyricum—as it has pleased also our lord, the most pious emperor, my consort—may have the power to convene in one city speedily from eastern parts and that, when a council has been held therein with you as originator, they may decide concerning the Catholic confession and about those bishops who previously have been deposed,[3] according as faith and Christian piety demand.

Moreover, besides these matters, let your Sanctity know that since by the command of our lord and most tranquil prince, my consort, the body of Bishop Flavian of holy memory has been brought to the glorious city of Constantinople,[4] it has been placed suitably in the Basilica of the Apostles,[5] wherein his episcopal predecessors have been wont to be buried.

And similarly those bishops who for the same reason, because with the most holy Flavian they had concurred in the concord of the Catholic faith, have been deported by exile, he has commanded by the force of his ordinance to return, that by the synod's approval and by the decision of all the convening bishops they may be voted to recover their episcopate and churches.

1. Eutychianism is meant.

2. The patriarch of Constantinople who was deposed by the Robber Council (*Latrocinium*) of Ephesus in 449 for his deposition of the archimandrite Eutyches, who wielded great influence among the easte n monks and through his godson, the eunuch Chrysaphius, the chief minister of Theodosius II, had the eastern court on his side in his teaching of the heresy named after him.

3. The *Latrocinium* deposed not a few prelates, among whom the most eminent was the ecclesiastical historian, Theodoret, bishop of Cyrus.

4. Flavian had not survived the brutal blows inflicted by monks on him in his prison at Hypepe in Lydia.

5. This seems to have been the Church of the Holy Twelve Apostles, which was completed by Constantine I, repaired under Constantius II, rebuilt by Justinian I, razed by Mohammed II. On it consult G. Downey, *Nikolaos Mesarites: Description of the Church of the Holy Apostles at Constantinople* (Philadelphia, 1957).

464. LETTER OF VALENTINIAN III AND MARCIAN ON CONVOCATION OF THE CHALCEDONIAN COUNCIL, 451

(M 6. 553-4)

This letter, addressed to Anatolius, patriarch of Constantinople, sets the time and the place for what was to become the Fourth General Council of the Church, designed to deal with Eutychianism, which, confusing the notions of person and nature, taught that Christ had a single composite nature. The original site was Nicaea, as the document shows, but Marcian later shifted the sessions to Chalcedon, nearer to Constantinople.[1]

Mansi preserves (6. 551-4) a similar letter, sent to all bishops throughout the Empire, which is an exact copy of that to Anatolius, except for the necessary shifts from the singular to the plural number and for the subscription, which is lacking.

In English the latest study on this synod is R. V. Sellers' *The Council of Chalcedon* (London, 1953).

Victors Valentinian and Marcian, Renowned, Triumphers, Ever-August to Anatolius.

Before all affairs must be set divine matters, for we are confident that, when Almighty God is propitious, the common polity both is preserved and is improved.

Therefore, because certain doubts appear to have existed about our orthodox religion (as also a letter of Leo, the most God-beloved bishop of the renowned city of Rome, testifies), this especially has pleased our Clemency that a holy synod should be collected in the city of the Nicenes of the province of the Bithynians, in order that when intellects are agreed and after all truth has been examined and also when are removed factional spirits, by using which hitherto certain persons have confounded the holy and orthodox religion, our true faith may become more clearly known, so that henceforth no doubt or discord can exist.

Wherefore your Holiness should hasten to the aforesaid city of the Nicenes by 1 September with what most God-beloved bishops it has pleased you and whom from the churches, established under your Holiness' supervision, you have proved to be trustworthy and ready for the teaching of the orthodox religion.

Moreover your Godliness should know also that our Divinity will attend the venerable synod, unless perchance certain public needs for expeditions should engross us.[1]

May God guard you for many years, most holy and most saintly father.

Given on 17 May at Constantinople, in the consulate of our Lord Marcian Perpetual-Augustus and of him who shall be announced.

1. The probability of proceeding against the Huns, whose imminent reappearance south of the Danube River was dreaded, because Marcian had cancelled the annual tribute paid to them by Theodosius II since 424, induced the emperor to transfer the council from Nicaea to Chalcedon, which in the emergency was easier of access to him, for he was anxious to attend it.

The triple economic relation of the transfer of this tribute from the Empire's landowners to the Empire's merchants through the Huns, who were paid from the taxes of the former and who with these purchased manufactured luxuries from the latter, is treated by E. A. Thompson, *A History of Attila and the Huns* (Oxford, 1948), 184-97.

It is interesting to note that apparently in the East was more gold than in the West. If the East under Theodosius II could afford to avert the capture of Constantinople by paying potential captors large amounts of gold, the West was too poor to purchase such protection: hence the West experienced the invasions which the East escaped. We know also that after he had cancelled the Theodosian tribute "Marcian . . . was able in a reign of less than seven years to save the huge sum of seven million *solidi* [for the solidus see no. 433, n. 7]; and . . . Anastasius I, at his death in 518, left a treasure more than three times as large"—W. C. Bark, *Origins of the Medieval World* (Stanford, Calif., 1958), 34.

465. EDICT OF MARCIAN ON DECORUM IN CHURCHES, 451

(*CI* 1. 12. 5)

With the view to ensuring a peaceful discussion at the forthcoming Council of Chalcedon the emperor in this edict prohibits disturbances in churches and in other venerable places [1] and announces capital punishment for violators of this constitution.

Emperor Marcian Augustus to the people.

We announce to you all that in the sacrosanct churches and indeed in other venerable places, wherein with peace and quiet it is appropriate for prayers to be made,[2] you should abstain from all disturbance.

None should employ shouts,[3] none should instigate a tumult or should commit an assault or by collecting a multitude should attempt to convene or to hold meetings in any part whatsoever of a city or of a village or of any place whatsoever.

For if anyone should think that anything contrary to the laws is being perpetrated against himself by any persons, it should be permissible for the said person to approach a judge and to demand legitimate protection.

All persons should know, of course, that if anyone shall have tried to do anything contrary to this edict's rule or to instigate a disturbance, he shall be subject to the last punishment.[4]

Given on 13 July at Constantinople, Marcian Augustus being consul.

1. Councils usually convened in churches.
2. This qualifying clause looks especially to oratories.
3. Perhaps this admonition arose from St Paul's preachment in inconcinnity on congregational conduct that "all things be done decently and in order" (1 Cor. 14. 40). St Ambrose admired also the very great virtue of silence, especially in church, and confirmed his counsel by reference to Prov. 10. 19 (*De Virg.* 3. 3. 11 = PL 16. 234–5). But it is interesting to compare Marcian's edict with the adulatory acclaim which his address to the Chalcedonian fathers, assembled in church, later achieved (see no. 472, n. 4).
4. That is, death.

466. LETTER OF PULCHERIA ON CONCILIAR ATTENDANCE, 451

(M 6. 555–6)

To supplement her husband's edict (no. 465), which in preparation for peaceful discussion at the Council of Chalcedon forbids disturbances in churches and in other venerable places, St Pulcheria, who shared the sovereignty of the Eastern Empire with Marcian, orders the consular of Bithynia, in whose district lay Nicaea (where the forthcoming synod was to meet before its removal to Chalcedon nearer the capital), to expel from the conciliar precincts all persons except those whose presence has been permitted by imperial instructions or is necessary for attendance upon their bishops.

Copy of the royal letter sent by the most pious and Christ-loving Empress Pulcheria to the consular governor of Bithynia concerning provision for discipline in the synod, before it was resolved to transfer the synod from the Nicenes' city to the Chalcedonians' city.

It is the objective for our Serenity before civil matters that God's holy churches and the persons ordained to the priesthood in these should continue in peace and that the orthodox faith, which we have believed our Majesty should maintain, should be guarded undisturbed and unmoved by every kind of persons.

Wherefore formerly, when any slight discord had emerged, we devoted much care that the multitude [1] of the most holy bishops from everywhere should be gathered together in the Nicenes' city and that by the agreement of all every disturbance should be removed and that for the future the pure faith should prevail firm and unmoved.

Therefore, because pursuant to our ordinance all the most godly bishops have arrived, awaiting the presence of our Mightiness (which after not much time with God's co-operation will be present), certain persons—as we have learned—of those wont to disturb and to confound God's dear discipline, having needlessly introduced themselves into the Nicenes' city, both clergymen and monks and laymen, are trying to create an uproar by disputing earnestly against the matters approved by us, necessarily we have sent this pious letter to your Splendour, so that with all constancy you should expel in every way both from the city and from the places there those clergymen dwelling there without our citation or decision of their bishops—whether they happen to be in that rank or even certain ones of them removed by their bishops—or monks or laymen, whom no reason calls to the council, so that with all discipline, when the holy synod has sat in consultation, without any commotion and controversy the matters proceeding from Christ the Lord may be confirmed by all in common.

For know that if anyone henceforth should have been detected in creating an uproar while dwelling in the places there, either before our Serenity's presence or even after our presence, no fortuitous peril shall encompass you.[2]

1. This council surpassed all previous synods in numbers: some 630 bishops attended it.

2. The Latin version has an alternative reading in "him" referring to the subject of the conditional clause.

467. LETTER OF VALENTINIAN III AND MARCIAN ON CONCILIAR PROCEDURE, 451

(M 6. 553-4)

Emperor Marcian in this letter, addressed to the bishops gathered in council at Nicaea before their later resort to Chalcedon, excuses his promised presence at their sessions and orders them to proceed with their deliberations to procure peace for the Church distracted by dissensions emerging from Eutychianism.

468. TRANSFER FROM NICAEA TO CHALCEDON, 451

Divine letter sent to the synod in Nicaea by Emperors Valentinian and Marcian.

It is our desire that there should be decided fittingly those matters which belong to the holy and orthodox religion, in order that all ambiguity may be destroyed and becoming peace may be restored to the most holy and Catholic churches. For we think that this must be preferred to all things.

Therefore, because we have wished to be present at the holy council, but public and necessary needs detain us on an expedition,[1] your Worships should deign not to think it serious to endure our Tranquillity's absence,[2] but to pray that we, discharging well with God's help the matters which we have in hand, can come thither, that in our Piety's presence may be decided matters which may remove all discord and questioning and may confirm the true and venerable faith of orthodox persons.

1. It is believed that the invasion of Huns into Illyricum prevented Marcian from going so far from Constantinople as Nicaea and led eventually to the transfer of the council to Chalcedon (see no. 464, n. 1). While Chalcedon is only a little more than 1.6 miles distant from Constantinople across the Bosporus, Nicaea is almost sixty miles distant by direct line from the capital.
2. An editorial suggestion is "to wait for our Tranquillity's presence".

468. RESCRIPT OF VALENTINIAN III AND MARCIAN ON TRANSFER OF THE COUNCIL FROM NICAEA TO CHALCEDON, 451

(M 6. 557–8)

Although the council convoked by Marcian to discuss Eutychianism had not been ordered to convene before 1 September 451 at Nicaea, many of the fathers assembled well ere that date and expressed dissatisfaction, it seems, with their quarters in Nicaea as well as with the postponed presence of the emperor, who was detained in Constantinople to direct counter-measures against the Huns about to invade Illyricum. In this answer to a communication sent by them to him Marcian suggests that the fathers should shift their sessions from Nicaea to Chalcedon, where attendance would be easier for him.

Copy of the second[1] royal letter sent to the same holy synod, convened in Nicaea, concerning the necessity of transference to Chalcedon.

Victors Valentinian and Marcian, Renowned, Triumphers, Ever-August to the God-beloved synod.

The occasion of public and exceedingly necessary affairs has detained us, though eager to come to the holy synod.

But we know from the things written by your Godlinesses [2] that rather many of you are weary both because of weakness of body and because of other and different reasons.

Wherefore, although very many public affairs compel us to remain here,[3] nevertheless we consider that care for the holy and orthodox faith is preferable above all things. For the most devout bishops and priests,[4] who, have come on behalf of the most holy and most God-beloved Leo, the archbishop of all-blessed Rome, have begged our Serenity that by every means we should be present at the holy synod, since they have maintained strongly that they do not choose to be there in our Piety's absence.

Pursuant to your Godlinesses' petition, we ourselves, seeking exceedingly that your most holy synod should be convened speedily, are eager to come to you rather swiftly. Wherefore, if it should please your Godlinesses, deign to come to the Chalcedonians' city.[5] For we shall run out thither, although public needs detain us here,[3] since we consider that the matters which are profitable for the true and orthodox faith and for the most holy and Catholic churches' peace and discipline are preferable above all things, and we do not doubt that this pleases also your Holinesses, lest also the city's crampedness [6] should make you endure greater hardship and the affairs of the holy synod should seem to be protracted further by our Serenity's absence.

But deign to pray for our Majesty, that both the enemies [7] may be mastered by us and the peace of the world may be confirmed and Roman affairs may exist in security—and this also we have believed that you now do.

May God guard you, most holy ones, for many years.

1. For the first letter see no. 467.
Mansi gives a fragmentary Latin version of the present letter in 7. 757.
2. This communication has not survived.
3. Constantinople.
4. Three bishops and two priests were the papal legates, but only two bishops and one priest appear to have attended.
5. See no. 467, n. 1.
6. While no statistics on area and population seem procurable, all ancient accounts save this agree in considering Nicaea a more important community than Chalcedon. Since Strabo (*Geog.* 12. 4. 7) calls Nicaea the metropolis of Bithynia, it seems difficult to account for Marcian's disparagement of it. See no. 48, n. 12.

7. The Huns (see no. 464, n. 1), who may have seemed to Marcian the "evil and great destruction that appeareth out of the north" (Jer. 6. 1), if he thought of the prophet's word to "behold them that come from the north" (Jer. 13. 20).

469. LETTER OF VALENTINIAN III AND MARCIAN ON TRANSFER OF THE COUNCIL FROM NICAEA TO CHALCEDON, 451

(M 6. 559–62)

This directive is the third letter[1] sent by Marcian to the fathers assembled at Nicaea to settle the Eutychian controversy, but this communication, instead of suggesting that they shift their sessions from Nicaea to Chalcedon, where the emperor more easily could assist at the assembly, orders them to effect such a transfer without delay.

Likewise a copy of the third[1] royal letter sent to the holy synod in Nicaea, while the most pious emperor was detained in Thrace, concerning the necessity of transference forthwith to the Chalcedonians' city.

Emperors Caesars Valentinian and Marcian, Victors, Triumphers, Greatest, Ever-August, Augusti to the holy synod assembled in Nicaea pursuant to God's will and our ordinance.

Already, indeed, and by our other sacred letters[1] we have indicated to your Godlinesses that you should come to the Chalcedonians' city, that the matters, determined previously by our holy fathers,[2] concerning the holy and orthodox faith may be confirmed, that the divergently wandering multitude of orthodox persons no longer may be deceived, but that all persons may confess our Lord and Saviour Christ, as is proper and as our most holy fathers have decreed.[2] For because of fervent zeal for the faith we have deferred for the present the necessary needs of public affairs, since we esteem it of importance that the matters of the orthodox and true faith should be confirmed in our Serenity's presence. For the events which have befallen throughout Illyricum we believe also have come to your ears and, although by God's will these events have obtained a suitable vengeance, yet the advantage for public affairs demanded our Serenity's departure into Illyricum.[3] But since (as has been said) we consider nothing preferable to the orthodox faith and that it should be confirmed, on this account for a time we have deferred an expedition into farther places.

And now especially your Godlinesses we command by this our sacred letter that without any deferment you come to the Chalcedonians' city.

Since from Atticus,[4] archdeacon [5] of the most holy and Catholic Church in the royal city, reporting to our Serenity, we have learned that your Sanctities suspect that perchance certain ones of the persons holding Eutyches'—or some other one's—opinions will attempt to prepare strife or some tumult, on this account we declare to you that you, fearing not at all the aforesaid reason, should come to the Chalcedonians' city, for we hope in God's benevolence that apart from any disturbance and tumult, after all matters have been regulated according to the orthodox and true faith justly and as is pleasing to God, each one of you will return rather quickly to his own affairs.

Therefore hasten to come and interpose no deferment to the business, lest through your delay the search for truth may have deferment. For in us has been established the desire with the Almighty's favour, after the business has received an opportune conclusion, to return again speedily to the most successful expedition.[6]

May God guard you for many years, most holy and most God-beloved fathers.

Given on 22 September at Heraclea.[7]

1. For the two imperial letters sent previously see nos. 467 and 468. Mansi gives a fragmentary Latin version of the present letter in 7. 758-9.

2. Especially in the ecumenical councils at Nicaea (325) and Constantinople (381) and Ephesus (431).

3. See no. 464, n. 1.

4. An editorial conjecture for this man's name is Aetius, borrowed from this council's *acta*, where he is recorded as one of the secretaries.

5. A variant Latin reading degrades him to an ordinary deacon.

6. It is not known how long Marcian attended the sessions, which did not start until sixteen days after the dispatch of this letter and then continued for 24 days, but he seems to have addressed the fathers in proper person at least once (no. 472).

7. This subscription appears only in the Latin version.

470. DECREES OF IMPERIAL COMMISSIONERS ON CONCILIAR PROCEDURE, 451

(M 6. 935-8, 951-5; 7. 47-50, 59-62, 89-94, 179-84, 189-90, 289-300, 313-14, 355-8, 451-4)

In the absence of Valentinian III and Marcian, of whom the former had remained in the West and the latter had convoked the Fourth General Council of the Church at Chalcedon (though originally called to Nicaea) in 451, the procedure at the Chalcedonian Council was controlled by Marcian's representatives, whom, numbering eighteen, the emperor had selected from Constantinopolitan senators and high imperial officials (past and present).[1]

Since the proceedings appear to have been conducted primarily in Greek, though provision for translation from Greek into Latin was made,[2] the Greek version, whenever available, is translated.

For translation have been chosen only the important and lengthier decisions, not the shorter and interlocutory rulings.[3]

I[4]

The most distinguished officials and the excellent Senate said:

We see that it is necessary that more fully, when the synod has met, on the next day should be a preciser examination concerning the orthodox and Catholic faith.

But since Flavian[5] of devout memory and the most devout bishop Eusebius[6]—from the scrutiny of the acts and the decisions and the very voice of certain leaders of the synod then present, confessing that they have erred and that they have deposed them[7] without reason, because they[7] have erred in no respect concerning the faith—are shown to have been deposed unjustly, it appears to us (according to what pleases God) to be just (if it should be commanded by our most sacred and most pious lord)[8] that Dioscore, the most devout bishop of Alexandria, and Juvenal, the most devout bishop of Jerusalem, and Thalassius, the most devout bishop of Caesarea of Cappadocia, and Eusebius, the most devout bishop of Ancyra,[9] and Eustathius, the most devout bishop of Beirut, and Basil, the most devout bishop of Seleucia of Isauria, who had control and leadership of the synod then, should fall under the same penalty[10] and by the holy synod should be deprived[11] of the episcopal rank according to the canons—all consequences being reported to the sacred head[8]. . .[12]

Each of the most devout bishops of the present holy synod, writing, in such manner as he believes, without any fear, placing the fear of God before his eyes, should hasten to profess, knowing, since our most sacred and most pious lord[8] believes according to the profession of the 318 holy fathers in Nicaea[13] and according to the profession of the 150 afterward[14] and the canonical epistles and professions of the holy fathers, Gregory,[15] Basil,[16] Athanasius,[17] Hilary,[18] Ambrose,[19] and Cyril's[17] two canonical epistles,[20] which were confirmed and published in the first synod in Ephesus,[21] because he in no way departs from their faith. And also Leo, the most devout archbishop of Elder Rome,[22] seems to have sent to Flavian[5] of devout memory an epistle[23] against the doubt emerging from Eutyches[4] beyond belief and opposed to the Catholic Church.

II [24]

The most magnificent and most distinguished officials and the excellent Senate said:

At the previous session[25] occurred the inquiry about the deposition relative to Flavian[5] of devout memory and the most devout bishop Eusebius.[6] And to you all it has become clear that the examination's procedure progressed both justly and according to regular sequence.[26] And they have been shown then to have been deposed cruelly and not fittingly. Therefore what seemed best to us to be necessary to be done on this point then was made clear by you from your interlocution.

But now it must be examined and decided and pursued, so that there may be established the true faith, on account of which particularly also the synod has been held. Therefore, knowing that each of you will give account to God both about your own soul and about us all, who desire that what pertains to religion should be taught rightly and that all controversy should be removed as a result of all the holy fathers' concord and agreement and harmonious exposition and teaching, hasten without fear or favour or enmity to expound purely the faith, so that also persons who seem not to have held the same opinions with all may be restored to concord by full knowledge of the truth. For we desire you to know that the most sacred and most pious lord of the world[8] and we guard the orthodox faith transmitted by the 318[13] and by the 150[14] and also by the rest of the holy and glorious fathers and that we believe according to it.

III [27]

The most magnificent and most distinguished officials[28] said:

Our most pious emperor,[8] having learned your requests, has granted to your judgement to determine what matters would please you about Juvenal and Thalassius and Eusebius and Basil and Eustathius, the most devout bishops.[29]

Therefore it is proper for your Godlinesses, knowing that you will give to God account for what will occur, to debate what ought to be done about them.[30]

IV [31]

The most magnificent and most distinguished officials[28] said:

Yesterday[32] certain bishops of the Egyptian diocese, having given petitions to our most sacred and most pious lord,[8] explained their faith. And it has pleased his Piety that these should be read before your holy synod. Therefore, yielding to what has been commanded by the sacred and triumphant head,[8] we order both them to enter and the petitions to be read in their presence and your Devoutnesses to show what would please you about them . . .

Since the most devout bishops of the Egyptians [33] postponed for the present to subscribe to the most sacred archbishop Leo's letter,[34] not as opposing the Catholic faith, but saying that it is customary in the Egyptian diocese not to do such a thing contrary to their archbishop's judgement and order, and beg that concession be granted to them until the ordination of the future bishop of the Alexandrians' megalopolis,[35] it has appeared to us reasonable and humane that to them, staying in their own character [36] in the royal city,[37] should be offered alleviation, until an archbishop of the Alexandrians' megalopolis should be ordained . . . The judgement of the most holy bishop Paschasinus shall be confirmed.[38] Wherefore, staying in their own character,[36] the most devout bishops of the Egyptians either shall offer sureties, if this is possible for them, or shall be believed on oath that they await the ordination of the future bishop of the Alexandrians' megalopolis.

V [39]

The most distinguished officials said:

It has pleased the most sacred lord of the world [8] that the affairs of the most holy bishops should proceed not according to sacred letters or pragmatic sanctions,[40] but according to what has been ordained by the holy fathers . . .

According to the canons of the 318 holy fathers [13] and according to the vote and right judgement of the whole holy synod,[41] Photius, the most devout bishop of the Tyrians' metropolis, shall have the entire authority of ordination in all the cities of the province of Phoenicia Prima; but Eustathius, the most devout bishop, from the sacred pragmatic sanction [40] shall claim for himself nothing more than the remaining [42] bishops of the said province.[43]

VI [44]

The most magnificent and most distinguished officials said:

Our most sacred and most pious lord,[8] having been asked by Maximus and Juvenal, the most holy bishops, has asked us to decide about the principal points at issue between them.[44] And the aforesaid most holy men, having met together, have formulated matters mutually clear to each other, but not in writing,[45] and these matters, which they have established clearly to us,[46] seem to have been arranged justly in accordance with their agreement.[47] Therefore we have considered it necessary also that each man should explain these matters in the holy synod's presence, so that both from our decision and from your vote may be confirmed what things are acceptable . . .

o

This has been the work of the Holy Trinity and of our most sacred emperor's [8] proposition, so that the matters disputed by those who seemed to be contentious should be decided by concordant statement. Therefore the agreement made according to the approval of Maximus, the most holy bishop of the Antiochenes' city, and of Juvenal, the most holy bishop of the Jerusalemites' city, which the statement of each has declared, confirmed both by our decision and by the holy synod's vote, shall endure for all time: that is, that Maximus, the most holy bishop, that is to say the most holy Church of the Antiochenes, should have the two Phoenicias [48] and Arabia under its own control, but that Juvenal, the most holy bishop of the Jerusalemites' city, that is to say the most holy church under him, should have the three Palestines [49] under its own control—all pragmatic sanctions [40] and matters procured in another way by parts of sacred letters and penalties contained in these being voided for the sake of this action according to our most sacred and most pious emperor's [8] command.

VII [50]

The most devout officials said:

All doubt about the most God-beloved Theodoret now has been dissolved. For in our presence he has anathematized Nestorius [51] and he has been received by the most God-beloved and most holy Leo, archbishop of Old Rome,[22] and readily has accepted the definition of faith [52] given by your Godlinesses, and also besides this has subscribed to the letter of Leo,[34] the said most holy archbishop.

It remains, therefore, that a decision should be produced by your Godlinesses that he should receive his church, just as Leo, the most holy archbishop, has judged.

VIII [53]

The most distinguished officials said:

It indeed appears to us that neither Bassian, the most devout bishop, is worthy of being bishop of the Ephesians' city, since indeed from his violent assault he claimed it [54] for himself, nor the most devout Stephen, who as a result of conspiracies and such fraud procured the bishopric for himself; but that it is just that another should be chosen, one who both knows the faith accurately and has been adorned in his life, as a bishop ought to be.

But we leave the whole problem to the most holy synod, so that it may give a ruling acceptable to it for the matter . . .

Solicitude for public affairs, which happens to be necessary for the State, is neglected, when we have been brought by the sacred head [8] to meet thus continually with the holy synod on account of the faith.⁵⁵ But since it is not possible for us to be dragged away for a long time from matters necessary for the State, we, eager to apply a speedy solution to the investigations, demand that the holy synod should say in the first place, if it has deliberated anything more about the most holy Church in Ephesus, whether it is necessary that another bishop should be ordained for it or the most devout Bassian should regain his bishopric or the most devout Stephen should be the bishop, for all things pertaining to them—as the said holy synod knows—have been investigated sufficiently yesterday . . .⁵⁶

Since, though frequently we have intervened in the discussions and have demanded that a vote should be produced about the bishopric of the most holy Church in Ephesus, a complete response has not been given by all, let the Revered and Immaculate Gospel be brought into the midst . . . We bring a similar demand to the holy synod, since the Venerable Gospels are set before us, urging this: that you neither should harm anyone of the two men, if indeed anyone of them is worthy to obtain the bishopric, nor the said church, if indeed each is unworthy, but that, according to God and according to what is worthy and fitting and advantageous for the most holy church, you should decide what seems best . . .⁵⁷

Since the discussion of Anatolius, the most God-beloved archbishop of royal Constantinople, and of Paschasinus, the most devout bishop holding the place of the most God-beloved Leo, archbishop of Elder Rome,²² pleases all in that it recommends that, because both ⁵⁸ have been created uncanonically, neither of them should bear the title or have authority over the most holy Church in Ephesus, and since the whole holy synod has shown that these men had been ordained uncanonically and has concurred with the most devout bishops' discussions, Bassian and Stephen, most devout men, shall be removed indeed from the holy Church in Ephesus, but let them have the rank of bishop and from the revenues of the said most holy church, for the sake of sustenance and of consolation, let them each receive in each year two hundred gold coins.⁵⁹

And another man shall be ordained according to the canons bishop for the said most holy church . . .⁶⁰

If Bassian, the most devout bishop, has been deprived of anything of what belongs to him, whether by Stephen, the most devout bishop, or by any other persons whomsoever, this shall be restored to him, after judicial proofs, by those who have taken it or who have been responsible for the damage.

IX ⁶¹

The most distinguished officials said:
The most devout bishop of Nicomedia shall have the authority of

metropolitan in the churches throughout Bithynia, the bishop of Nicaea having only the honour of metropolitan and being subject to the bishop of Nicomedia after the example of the province's other bishops. For this disposition has appeared best also to the holy synod.

X [62]

The most magnificent and most distinguished officials said:

Sabinian, the most devout bishop, since after the most devout Athanasius' deposition he was ordained by the synod in the province, ought to remain in the bishopric of the Perrhenes' city (as we ourselves perceive), for if he should be removed, on the one hand, it is not just for him to suffer prejudgement, since he neither had been summoned nor had kept for himself a defence.[63] But the deposed Athanasius, since he did not obey the summons,[64] on the other hand, ordered later by Dioscore to cling to the bishopric, meanwhile ought to be quiet (as we perceive).

We judge that the case concerning the charges brought against him [65] should be considered by Maximus, the most holy bishop of the Antiochenes' city and by the synod with him;[66] in such manner, however, that within eight months counted from the present day should occur the examination of the persons who previously had made the accusation against him or also of any other who has been engaged in the affair; and that if he should have been convicted of having been bold to do all the things imputed to him on criminal and financial charges and contained in the memorials or even one of them worthy of deposition,[67] not only he should be deprived [11] of the said bishopric, but also he should fall under the public laws; but that if within this set period there should not have been an accusation or, if accused, he should not have been convicted (as aforesaid), Athanasius indeed should receive the bishopric and the church of the said city at the hands of Maximus, the most holy bishop of the Antiochenes' megalopolis, but the most devout Sabinian also should have the rank of the episcopate and should be replaced [68] and supported, just as Maximus, the most holy bishop of the Antiochenes' city, should arrange in regard to the ability of the most holy Church in Perrha.

When it has heard these decisions, the most holy synod shall say if it confirms the decrees or decrees something else.[69]

XI [70]

The most distinguished officials said:

From the acts and from each one's statement we perceive that the first place before all and the special honour according to the canons is preserved for the most God-beloved archbishop of Old Rome;[22] but

470. CONCILIAR PROCEDURE, 451

that the most holy archbishop of royal Constantinople, the New Rome, ought to enjoy the same privileges of honour and to have authoritative power to ordain metropolitans in the Asian and the Pontic and the Thracian dioceses [71] according to this manner: it should be voted by each metropolis' clergymen and rentiers and most splendid men and also by all or several most devout bishops in the province [72] and there should be selected whomever the aforesaid persons shall approve to be worthy of the church in the metropolis; but by all the selectors it should be referred to the most holy archbishop of royal Constantinople, in whose power it should be if he wishes the selected man to appear here and to be ordained or pursuant to his decision by decree [73] to obtain the episcopate in the province; and that, however, the most holy bishops in any city should be ordained by all or several most devout bishops of the province—the metropolitan having the power according to the fathers' established canon [74] and the most holy archbishop of royal Constantinople not sharing in the ordinations of these men.

These matters have been considered thus by us. This holy and ecumenical synod shall deign to teach what has been stated.[75]

1. Their names and dignities are listed in 6. 563–6. The chief commissioner seems to have been Anatolius, most magnificent and most distinguished master of the soldiers, ex-consul ordinary, patrician.

2. E.g. the papal delegates spoke in Latin, which was turned into Greek by one of the clerks.

Of the (estimated) 630 prelates in attendance—never before had been registered so many bishops at a council and seldom later this number was exceeded or even equalled—all except four of the five papal legates and two African bishops, who came rather as fugitives from the Vandals than as delegates from their provinces, were from the Greek-speaking eastern districts of the Empire.

3. Some examples: "The petition shall be read" (6. 584); "Meanwhile it is proper for you to answer the accusation. Wherefore endure that the reading of the acts should occur—a procedure which you yourself asked to occur" (6. 585); "The most devout Theodoret shall enter for participation in the synod, since both the most holy archbishop Leo has restored to him his episcopate and the most sacred and pious emperor has decreed that he should be present at the holy synod" (6. 589).

4. At the first session (8 October) the first business was the case of Dioscore, patriarch of Alexandria, who had presided two years earlier over the Robber Council of Ephesus, at which the heresiarch Eutyches was rehabilitated and St Flavian, patriarch of Constantinople, and other prelates were deposed. At the end of the session the commissioners pronounced their verdict, whereby Dioscore and five other prelates associated with him in the misdeeds at Ephesus

in 449 were condemned. The assembled fathers hailed the judgement as just and united—for the first time, so far as is known—in the celebrated *Trisagion* ("Holy God, holy [and] strong, holy [and] immortal, have mercy upon us"), an anthem appearing chiefly in all the Greek liturgies, but sung in the Roman liturgy only on Good Friday.

This decree is repeated as a recapitulation at the beginning of the fourth session (7. 5-8).

5. Patriarch of Constantinople.

6. Bishop of Dorylaeum in Phrygia Salutaris and the accuser of Eutyches at the Synod of Constantinople in 448.

7. Flavian and Eusebius.

8. Emperor Marcian.

9. Later Angora, now Ankara.

10. As that suffered by Flavian and Eusebius in 449.

11. Literally "to become alien from".

12. At this point the fathers acclaimed the commissioners' sentence with such ejaculations as "This is a just judgement! . . . Many years for the Senate! . . . Many years also for the emperors! . . . Christ has deposed Dioscore! . . . This is a just decree!"

13. The First General Council in 325.

14. The Second General Council in 381 at Constantinople.

15. Both St Gregory of Nazianzus, bishop of Constantinople, and St Gregory, bishop of Nyssa, are represented, though this decree suggests only only one Gregory, in the documents mentioned *intra* in n. 21.

16. Archbishop of Caesarea in Cappadocia.

17. Patriarch of Alexandria.

18. Bishop of Poitiers.

19. Bishop of Milan.

20. By *canonical epistles* (here and two lines *supra*) is meant the letters of the fathers (listed at nn. 15-19) accepted both as authentic and as authoritative, particularly in the latter sense as providing principles which serve as a criterion or a canon in interpreting doctrine and in enunciating ecclesiastical rules.

21. The Third General Council in 431. These documents are in M 4. 888-92, 1068-84, 1183-96, but nothing of St Hilary (n. 18) appears therein.

22. In comparison with New Rome, i.e. Constantinople, as characterized by the Second General Council there in 381 (canon 3). See no. 375, n. 7.

23. In M 5. 1265-90. Cf. *infra* n. 34.

24. The second session (10 October) was directed toward the establishment of the true faith in consonance with earlier ecumenical councils' canons and in accordance with orthodox theologians' doctrines.

25. Literally "at the synod on the day before"; but one day (9 October) intervened between the two sessions.

26. The inconcinnity occurs also in the Greek and the Latin versions.

27. Midway through the fourth session (17 October) the commissioners reported the emperor's acquiescence in the council's petition that it should deliberate about five bishops who had joined Dioscore, patriarch of Alexandria, in rehabilitating the heretical Eutyches at the Robber Council of Ephesus in 449 and they ordered the council to proceed to such deliberation.

28. The Latin version adds "and the most honoured Senate".

29. These prelates are mentioned in the text between nn. 8 and 10 *supra*.

30. Their retraction was accepted by the council (7. 47–50).

31. Thirteen Egyptian bishops (names in 7. 49–50) declared to the council in substance at the fourth session (17 October) that, while willing to sacrifice Eutyches, to repudiate their metropolitan Dioscore by such action (since he had led in rehabilitation of Eutyches at Ephesus) would ensure certain death for them on their return to Egypt (7. 51–60). The commissioners gave the following decision.

32. 16 October.

33. Cf. *supra* n. 31.

34. This is usually known as the *Tome* of Pope St Leo I, who published on 13 June 449 the papal repudiation of Nestorianism and Eutychianism in consonance with the faith as defined at the Church's three ecumenical councils held thus far (Nicaea, 325; Constantinople, 381; Ephesus, 431). Cf. *supra* n. 23.

35. Proterius succeeded Dioscore.

36. That is, with status unchanged.

37. Constantinople.

38. The papal legate Paschasinus proposed that the Egyptians should give sureties that they would not leave Constantinople before the installation of a patriarch for Alexandria. With this amendment the commissioners concurred.

39. At the fourth session (17 October) also was raised a jurisdictional problem, when Eustathius, bishop of Beirut, who had secured from Theodosius II the erection of his city, the seat of an eminent school of law, into a titular metropolis (*CI* 11. 22. 1; dated 448–50), then proceeded to oppose the jurisdictional rights of Photius, bishop of Tyre and metropolitan of Phoenicia Prima, to whom Eustathius was a suffragan. After having heard the evidence, the commissioners gave the following decision.

40. Such an ordinance ordinarily concerned some public matter ($\pi\rho\tilde{\alpha}\gamma\mu\alpha$); hence *pragmatic*.

41. Reference is to canon 4 of Nicaea and its interpretation on consecration of bishops.

42. That is, other.

43. Eustathius had attempted to annex six of the provincial bishoprics for his metropolitanate, which seems to have been conferred on Beirut *honoris causa* for civil, but not for ecclesiastical, purposes (*CI* 11. 22. 1; dated 448–50).

44. The seventh session (26 October) effected the elevation of Jerusalem into the fifth (and last and smallest) patriarchate of the ancient Church (see nos. 53. n. 3, and 375, n. 7)—at the territorial expense of the patriarchate of Antioch,

then occupied by Maximus. Thus ended a long dispute between the two rival sees, for the titular rank accorded to the Church of Jerusalem by the First General Council of Nicaea in 325 (canon 7) was unsupported by any territorial jurisdiction beyond Jerusalem, until this cession secured at Chalcedon by the astute Juvenal, bishop of Jerusalem, who twenty years earlier at the Third General Council of Ephesus vainly had attempted to attain patriarchal dignity.

The commissioners presented the business according to imperial instructions and by their decree confirmed the agreement achieved by the bishops concerned.

45. A Greek variant reading is "in copies" for *but . . . writing*.

46. The Latin version's *us* is translated.

47. The Latin version is translated here, because the Greek version seems corrupt.

48. Phoenice and Phoenice Libanensis.

49. The civil provinces were called Palaestina Prima, Palaestina Secunda, Palaestina Tertia. Subject to the new patriarch were three metropolitans: (1) Caesarea in Palestine with 29 suffragans, (2) Scythopolis with fourteen suffragans, (3) Petra with thirteen suffragans. Each metropolitan presided over a provincial metropolis.

50. At the synod's eighth session (26 October) the ecclesiastical historian Theodoret, bishop of Cyrus, who had been deposed by the Robber Council of Ephesus in 449, was restored to his bishopric after the commissioners had made the following ruling.

51. The heretical patriarch of Constantinople, whom Theodoret had defended.

52. The so-called Definition of Chalcedon, proposed and accepted at the fifth session (22 October).

53. The rival claims of Bassian and Stephen, who, it seems, had been consecrated successively bishop of Ephesus in 444 and 449, were left by imperial order (no. 473) to the council for settlement. After hearing the evidence at the eleventh session of the synod (29 October), the commissioners made the following decision, which was accepted with acclamation. But when the bishops of the Asian province, while admitting the justice of the decision, professed alarm at its probable effect on the Ephesian populace, whose record in rioting ascended into the apostolic age (cf. Acts 19. 23–41), the commissioners postponed until the next day further deliberation about the succession to Bassian and Stephen.

54. The reference is to the episcopal dignity.

55. The commissioners, of whom most were high officials on active duty, had presided at the synod's sessions since 8 October and now were present at the twelfth session on 30 October.

56. After four bishops had spoken briefly, the commissioners prodded the prelates into action by the following order.

57. Fourteen bishops then gave brief opinions, after which the commissioners ruled as follows.

58. Bassian and Stephen.

59. The value is not known.

60. When the synod had accepted this decision and after Bassian had asked restoration of what property had been taken from him, the commissioners ruled in his favour.

61. At the thirteenth session (30 October) Eunomius, bishop of Nicomedia, and Anastasius, bishop of Nicaea, presented their claims to metropolitical rights over the province of Bithynia. It appeared that, though Nicaea had been raised by Constantine I to the rank of a metropolis in honour of the First General Council held there in 325 and this grade had been confirmed by Valentinian I and Valens (M 7. 309–10), yet such status was only honorary, for Nicomedia, once the capital of the Eastern Empire (284–330), antedated Nicaea in metropolitanship and was so recognized by Valentinian I (M 7. 311–12). The commissioners, relying on canon 4 of the Nicene Council, decided that the ecclesiastical establishment was not affected by these evidences of the emperor's esteem and that Nicaea, retaining its honorary rank, should remain subject to Nicomedia in ecclesiastical matters.

62. At the fourteenth session (31 October) were discussed the rival claims of Athanasius and Sabinian to the see of Perrha in Syria. It appears that Athanasius *c.* 444 refused to reply to serious (but now unknown) charges against him and resigned his bishopric voluntarily; that then he influenced the Alexandrian and Constantinopolitan patriarchs to persuade the patriarch of Antioch to consider his case; that, when cited to come to a council convened at Antioch, Athanasius declined to appear and was deposed by default; that Sabinian was consecrated to the vacant see *c.* 445; that the Robber Council of Ephesus, under the leadership of Dioscore, patriarch of Alexandria, in 449 deposed Sabinian and restored Athanasius.

63. Sabinian apparently did not attend the *Latrocinium* at Ephesus.

64. This refers to his refusal to appear at the Council of Antioch.

65. Athanasius.

66. The metropolitan in a civil province constructed his suffragan bishops in that province into a kind of domestic synod, which met on call to consider matters affecting the ecclesiastical establishment in the province. Patriarchs also had their synods. If the four so-called apostolic councils (Acts 1. 15–26, 6. 1–7, 15. 6–29, 21. 17–25), though showing the seeds of synodical character, are excluded as not satisfying the above-stated situation, then the recorded practice ascends to at least the middle of the second century, when in 152 Theodotus, bishop of Pergamum, convened seven of his bishops (M 1. 669–70), for the provincial council at which a dozen bishops assisted, attributed to Pope St Telesphorus (125–36) seems to have been called by Pope St Victor I (189–99), according to Mansi's *marginalia* (1. 662). See also Eusebius, *HE* 5. 23. 2–4.

67. The Latin version substitutes "condemnation".

68. Literally "substituted" (ὑποκατάστατος and *substitutus*: the Greek is

reported apparently here for the first time), but such a significance is senseless here.

69. After three bishops had concurred with the commissioners, the synod approved the verdict and ordered it to be effected, because the officials had judged "with God".

The result of the investigation at Antioch, if it ever was held, is unknown.

70. At the sixteenth session (1 November) was created or recognized the patriarchate of Constantinople—like that of Jerusalem also at the expense of the patriarchate of Antioch (cf. *supra* VI and nn. 44–9)—over the opposition of the papal legates.

The Second Ecumenical Council at Constantinople in 381—just seventy years earlier—by its canon 3 had raised Constantinople to the second rank in Christendom after the see of Rome—a precedence of honour, however, not of jurisdiction (see no. 375, n. 7). At the fifteenth session of Chalcedon (31 October) the archbishop of Constantinople in effect was elevated to be a patriarch by canon 28 (see M 7. 369–70, 427–8 for four versions—two Greek and two Latin), which conferred on the Constantinopolitan prelate the right to consecrate the metropolitans of three civil dioceses: Asia, Pontus, Thrace.

On the next day the Roman legates protested against this canon on various counts, but in vain, for the commissioners, after hearing evidence from both sides, gave the following decision, which repeated in substance the canon already adopted. Pope St Leo I later refused to accept canon 28 on the pretext that it was both contrary to the Nicene canons and inimical to the prerogatives of the Roman and the Antiochene and the Alexandrian patriarchates, but Emperor Marcian confirmed it and the council's other 29 canons (see nos. 475–7, 479, 480) and Justinian I also conferred civil sanction upon it (N 131. 1 in 545) and still later the Fourth Lateran Council (1215), which Roman Catholics reckon as the Twelfth General Council, recognized that the patriarchate of Constantinople should rank after that of Rome and before those of Alexandria and Antioch.

For a detailed discussion see Denny, 192–210; Kidd, 3. 332–8; S. H. Scott, *The Eastern Churches and the Papacy* (London, 1928), 193–201; H. Burn-Murdoch, *The Development of the Papacy* (London, 1954), 250–4.

71. That is, the civil dioceses, which comprised several civil provinces.

72. Cf. *supra* n. 71.

73. That is, the patriarch has the power to authorize the consecration to occur outside Constantinople in the province wherein the selection has been made.

74. Either canon 4 or canon 6 of the Nicene Council in 325 is meant.

75. Or "to declare what has been its opinions".

471. MANDATE OF MARCIAN ON CONCILIAR PROCEDURE, 451

(M 7. 103-6)

When the Council of Chalcedon at its fifth session (22 October 451) was ready to adopt a doctrinal formulary, which had been drafted by a committee headed by Anatolius, patriarch of Constantinople, and appointed at its second session (10 October) by the imperial commissioners, the papal legates and a few eastern prelates opposed its adoption on the ground that it was not in complete accord with Pope St Leo I's *Tome*.[1] When the Roman delegates threatened, therefore, to secede from the synod, the imperial commissioners, who controlled the procedure (no. 470), proposed another committee to report. But when the majority of the bishops still insisted that they were ready to subscribe to the first committee's draft, which they professed to believe was not at all deficient in respect to the papal interpretation of the faith, and that there was no need for a second committee, the commissioners ruled that it was necessary to refer the situation to Emperor Marcian for instructions.

So Beronician, the secretary of the sacred consistory, who also attended the synod in an official capacity, crossed from Chalcedon to Constantinople, consulted the emperor, and reported the following imperial ruling, which (an excellent example of Byzantinism) was obeyed after further discussion. Of the three possible choices of procedure proposed by Marcian in his mandate the first—to amend the committee's draft—was accepted, with the result that what has become known as the Definition of the Council of Chalcedon[2] was adopted with acclamation[3] and has procured for itself a secure place among the standards of Christian doctrine.

Our most sacred and most pious lord[4] has ordered either that, pursuant to what has seemed best to the most magnificent and most distinguished officials,[5] six most devout bishops from the Eastern diocese and three from the Pontic diocese[6] and three from the Asian diocese[6] and three from Thrace and three from Illyricum,[7] being present also with the most holy Archbishop Anatolius[8] and the most devout persons from Rome,[9] should assemble in the most holy martyr's oratory[10] and should formulate rightly and unassailably matters about the faith for the concurrence of all and nothing ambiguous should be left remaining, or that, if this does not seem best, each one should make clear his faith through his metropolitan, so that no ambiguity or disagreement similarly should be left remaining; but that if your Holinesses should not have desired this,[11] you should know that in the western districts a synod must be held, because your Godlinesses here are not willing to formulate unambiguously matters about the true and orthodox faith.

1. The committee's report did not contain the phrase "in two natures" (ἐπὶ or ἐκ δύο φύσεων) in respect to the person of Christ, against which Eutychianism (to condemn which heresy the council had been convoked) had taught in its insistence on a single composite nature for Christ. On the *Tome* see no. 470, n. 34.
2. In M 7. 107–10.
3. "The most devout bishops shouted: 'This is the faith of the fathers! Let the metropolitans now subscribe! In the presence of the officials [commissioners] themselves let them now subscribe! Let what has been defined well not receive postponement! This is the faith of the apostles! With this we all agree! Thus we all think!' " (M 7. 117–18).
4. Marcian.
5. The imperial commissioners (ἄρχοντες).
6. This noun is understood with the proper adjective.
7. The first four divisions were civil dioceses in the prefecture of the East, while Illyricum represents the prefecture of Illyricum itself, divided into the civil dioceses of Macedonia and of Dacia.
8. Patriarch of Constantinople.
9. These were the papal legates.
10. A chapel in St Euphemia's Church.
11. Either alternative already announced.

472. ORATION AND DECREES OF MARCIAN ON CONCILIAR PROCEDURE, 451

(M 7. 129–30, 169–78)

Pursuant to the precedent set by Constantine the Great at the First General Council of the Church at Nicaea in 325 (no. 49), Marcian addressed the assembled prelates at the Fourth Ecumenical Council at Chalcedon in 451 and thus at the same time fulfilled his promise to appear before the council (nos. 464, 467, 468), although he deferred his appearance till its sixth session (25 October), when he was accompanied by Empress Pulcheria and was escorted by numerous nobles.

Marcian is said to have spoken in Latin [1] first and then in Greek.[2] Of these orations that in Latin is translated. In *PL* 130. 303–4 is a shorter version of his speech with minor variations, perhaps translated from Greek by Isidorus Mercator, who included it in his *Collectio Decretalium* (commonly called the *False Decretals*, because many documents therein are forgeries), which he published *c.* 850. Zacharias Rhetor *sive* Mytilenaeus gives what professes to be the exordium of Marcian's allocution in his Syriac *Chronicon* (3. 1 *ad fin.*), but Zacharias' account appears to cover more than the opening part.[3]

Since after his address, which gained great acclamation with subservient shouts,[4] Marcian stayed to preside over the session, the emperor's rulings on procedure are suppended to his speech (7. 169-78).

I

Allocution of Emperor Marcian.

As soon as we were elected by divine judgement to the sovereignty, amid the State's so many needs no cause constrained us more than that the orthodox and true Christian faith, which is holy and pure, indubitably might occupy the hearts of all. But it is known that by certain persons' greed or factional spirits, since in the meantime several are having contrary thoughts and pursuant to their own wish—not as truth and the fathers' teaching demand—are seducing the people, as many persons as possible have been diverted into error.[5]

Wherefore, because this condition obviously has been revealed, we have desired a holy synod to be held and we appear to have imposed upon you a task, that after all error and obscurity have been removed, just as the Divinity has desired to manifest itself to mankind and as the fathers' teaching shows, our religion, which is pure and holy, when it has been introduced into the minds of all persons, may shine by the light of its own virtue [6] and that hereafter none may dare to discuss about our Lord and Saviour Jesus Christ's nativity otherwise than the apostolic preaching and the 318 holy fathers' principles [7] agreeing with it are known to have transmitted to posterity, just as also testify the writings of the holy Leo, pope of the city of Rome, who governs the apostolic see, sent to Flavian of holy memory, bishop of the Constantinopolitan city.

Accordingly, by removal of factional spirits, by withdrawal of special pleadings, by cessation of greed, let truth become known to all persons. For to confirm the faith, not to wield [8] any power, by the example of Constantine, a religious emperor, we have wished to be present at the synod, lest the people even any longer may be divided by wicked persuasions. For certain persons' simplicity has been deceived easily hitherto by several persons' cleverness and superfluous wordiness and it is known that by contrary-minded persons' wicked ingratiations are born dissensions and heresies.[9]

Moreover it is our desire that all people, perceiving unity through true and holy doctrine, should return to the same religion and should cherish the true Catholic faith, which according to the fathers' principles [7] you will have expounded.

Therefore with concordant minds let your Worships hasten,[10] that, just as from the Nicene Synod [11] until the most recent time, after errors had been abolished, the true faith has been known to all persons, so even now by this holy synod, after have been removed the obscurities which in these few years—as has been said above—seem to have emerged because of certain persons' wickedness and greed, may be preserved forever what principles shall have been ordained. Moreover it shall be the duty of Divine Majesty [12] to guard firmly forever that which we with holy mind desire to be done.

II

Our most sacred and most pious lord [12] said to the holy synod:[13]

Let the holy synod say if according to the assent of all the most holy fathers the definition now read has been pronounced.[14]

Although we have imposed on your Devoutnesses toil and trouble, we acknowledge very great gratitude to Christ the Saviour of all, because, after the discord of many in error about the faith has been destroyed, we all have come together unanimously into one and the same religion, hoping that by your supplications to the Almighty a very speedy [15] peace in respect to all matters will be granted to us by God.[16]

Since our pious and Catholic faith has been manifested by the holy and universal synod according to the fathers' exposition, our Serenity has approved it to be just and likewise expedient that for the future every occasion for contention about the holy religion should be destroyed. Therefore, if any private person or governmental official or one belonging to the clergy, having discoursed or having collected an assemblage publicly about the faith, creates an uproar in pretext of discourse, he shall know that, if he is registered in the rank of a private person, he shall be expelled from the royal city;[17] but, if he is in governmental service,[18] he shall run a risk in respect to his governmental service [18] and, if a clergyman, he shall run a risk in respect to his rank, and both shall be subjected to other penalties.[19]

III

There are certain chief points which we have maintained for you for the honour of your Devoutnesses, having considered it proper that these should be formulated canonically by you in synod rather than should be legislated by our laws . . .[20]

We deem worthy of due honour the men who truly and sincerely pursue the solitary life. But since certain persons, having used monasticism as a pretext, confuse both the churches and public affairs, it has seemed best that none should build a monastery contrary to the judgement of the bishop of a city or on properties contrary to the judgement of the owner of the property;[21] but that the monks throughout each city and district should be subordinated to the bishop and should cleave to quiet and should be intent on only fasting and prayer and should not cause annoyance to [22] ecclesiastical and public affairs, unless perchance indeed by the bishop of a city they should have been commanded because of necessary need; and that the monks should not have the power to receive in their monasteries slaves or serfs [23] contrary to their masters' judgement.

Since certain persons of those enrolled in the clergy and of the monks, when suffering with love of money, subject themselves to cares of business affairs as leaseholders of properties,[24] either established as managers or overseeing in houses as stewards, it has seemed best to this holy and great synod that no clergyman should lease properties or should undertake managership, unless perchance indeed by his own bishop he should have been commanded to have the care of ecclesiastical properties; but that if anyone after this definition either himself should dare to be a leaseholder or to undertake such care on any other's behalf, this person should be subjected to ecclesiastical penalty and, if he should persist in being obstinate, he should be stripped of his rank.

Clergymen enrolled in a church should not be allowed to be appointed to the church of another city, but should be content with that wherein from the beginning they have been thought fit to minister, except for those who, when they have lost their native communities,[25] of necessity have migrated to another church. But if anyone after this definition should have received a clergyman belonging to another bishop, it has seemed best that both he who has been received and he who receives should be outside communion, until the clergyman who has withdrawn should have returned to his own church.[26]

For the honour of the holy martyr Euphemia [27] and of your Sanctities [28] we have ordained that the Chalcedonians' city, wherein the synod of the holy faith has been conducted,[29] should have the prerogatives of a metropolis, honouring this in name only and with its own rank obviously preserved for the Nicomedians' metropolis.[30]

IV

You [31] have been wearied by sustaining fatigue because of a fair [32] interval. Remain three or four days longer [33] and in the presence of our most magnificent officials promote what individual points you wish, thus being about to merit suitable assistance.[34] None of you [35] shall depart from the holy synod before perfect formulas on all matters have been given.

1. While the Empire's official language still was Latin, yet it was an imperial courtesy to address also in Greek the assembly, which was overwhelmingly Greek-speaking.

Mansi has another Latin version with minor variants in 7. 746-7.

2. Mansi's Greek version with a Latin translation of it is in 7. 131-4.

3. F. J. Hamilton and E. W. Brooks, *The Syriac Chronicle Known as that of Zachariah of Mitylene* (London, 1899), 47, give the following translation of it:

" 'From the first time that we were chosen and accounted worthy of the kingdom by God, amidst all the care of public business, no concern whatever in which we might be involved was allowed to hinder us, but we made it our choice to honour the true faith of the Christians, and to accustom the minds of men to it, with purity; all novelty of false doctrines and preachings that do not agree with the well proved doctrine of the Fathers being taken out of our midst. Therefore we summoned this holy synod that it might cleanse away all darkness, and put away filth of thoughts: that so, in pure mind, the doctrine of the faith which is in our Lord Jesus Christ might be established', and so on, to the same effect."

4. "Many years for the emperor! Many years for the Augusta! Many years for the orthodox! The only son of Constantine! To Marcian, the new Constantine! May the rule of Marcian, lover of Christ, worthy lover of the orthodox faith, endure for the ages! May envy be far distant from them [Marcian and Pulcheria]!" (7. 131-2).

Here, as elsewhere at conciliar sessions (see e.g. nos. 470, n. 12, and 471, n. 3), the scribes preserved only the prevailing party's shouts. It would be interesting to read the minority's ejaculations.

Although acclamations were not unknown in republican Rome, especially at triumphs (e.g. Suetonius, *Iul.* 49. 4; Dio Cassius, *Hist. Rom.* 43. 20) and at public appearances of certain personages (usually magistrates or even ex-magistrates) occasionally at spectacles of various sorts (Cicero, *Ad Att.* 1. 16. 11, 2. 19. 3, 14. 2. 1), yet in imperial Rome developed the custom of acclaiming the emperor by cries and shouts both on his election and in his presence at public spectacles. Early examples of each type of tribute occurred in the first century, when Nero was saluted emperor on the steps of the palace (Suetonius, *Nero*, 8) and when the audience in the theatre applauded him with prescribed forms chanted in rhythm (Suetonius, *Nero*, 20. 3; Tacitus, *Ann.* 16. 4. 4; Dio Cassius, *Hist. Rom.* 62 [61]. 20. 5, 62 [63]. 20. 5; cf. Suetonius, *Aug.* 56. 2 and see M. P. Charlesworth, "*Pietas* and *Victoria*: The Emperor and the Citizen" in *JRS* 33 [1943] 4-7). In the second century the Senate started to acclaim the emperors on various occasions: thus Aurelius was greeted for an act of mercy (Scriptores Historiae Augustae, *Avid. Cass.* 13. 1-5). The third century shows many instances: Severus Alexander was saluted by the senators with shouts probably drafted previously and shouted in chorus (id., *Sev. Alex,* 6. 1, 3-5; 7; 8. 2-3; 9. 1, 3, 5-6; 10. 1, 3, 6-8; 11. 2; 12. 1; 56. 9-10), Gordian I and II won senatorial approval at their election (id., *Maxim.* 16. 3-7; *Gord.* 11. 9-10) and at the death of Maximin I (id., *Maxim.* 26. 1-4), Pupienus Maximus and Balbinus were acclaimed at their election the Senate by (id., *Max. et Balb.* 2. 9-12), Claudius II was saluted with carefully enumerated senators' outcries at his election (id., *Claud*. 4. 3-4; cf. 18. 1-3), Tacitus was so greeted (id., *Tac*. 4. 1-4; 5. 1-2; cf. 7. 1, 4) and Probus achieved similar acclaim (id., *Prob*. 11. 6-9; 12. 8). Indeed, such electoral acclamations were not unlike the modern artillery salvoes of a salute to a chief of state. Such practices were the prototypes of the imperial and royal and papal acclamations widespread in Europe at coronational ceremonies, of which one of the most recent was observed at the inthronization of Queen Elizabeth II in 1953, for which the official ceremonial thus directed the audience in Westminster Abbey: "When the Homage of the Lords Spiritual and Lords Temporal is ended, the Drums shall beat, and the Trumpets sound, and all the people shout, crying out: 'God Save Queen Elizabeth. Long Live Queen Elizabeth. May The Queen Live Forever!' " (L. E. Tanner, *The History of the Coronation* [New York, 1953], 38).

For Christians the custom also ascended into Hebrew antiquity, where popular acclaim was accorded to Saul (1 Sam. 10. 24) and to Solomon (1 Kings 1. 34, 39) at their coronations. Jesus' entry into Jerusalem also was the occasion of salutation (Matt. 21. 9; Mark 11. 10; Luke 19. 37-8; John 12. 12-13). Cf. also the acclamations addressed to God in the Apocalypse (4. 11, 5. 9-14, 7. 9-12, 11. 15-17, 15. 3-4, 19. 1-4, 6-7).

For the senatorial acclamations on the occasion of the publication of the Theodosian Code in 438 see the *Gesta Senatus Romani de* <*Codice*> *Theodosiano Publicando*, 5 (usually prefixed to editions of *CT*), where of 43 acclamations fifteen are addressed to Emperors Theodosius II and Valentinian III and of these fifteen all save three are shouted either above twenty times in concert or by twenty or more different senators.

5. He hits at Eutychianism here.

6. An alternative reading is "truth".

7. The canons of the Nicene Council in 325, attended by that number.

8. An alternative lection is "display".

9. Here ends Isidore's version.

10. For *you* [previous paragraph] . . . *hasten* the text gives "your Worships should hasten to expound with equally concordant minds". But the Greek version supports the translated alternative reading.

11. In 325.

12. The emperor is meant.

13. This formula, though repeated before each imperial utterance, will be omitted from the translation.

14. After Marcian's oration Aetius, archdeacon of Constantinople, who served as chief of the conciliar notaries, read the Definition of the Council of Chalcedon (see no. 471, n. 2), adopted at its fifth session, and the names of the subscribing prelates. Thereupon the emperor made this ruling, which elicited a chorus of consent six times longer and with more variations (7. 169-72) than that with which his allocution had been acclaimed. Cf. *supra* n. 4.

15. A variant Latin translation substitutes for *by* . . . *speedy*: "as soon as possible all things are converted for the better by your prayers and".

16. This statement followed immediately upon the shouts which greeted Marcian's previous pronouncement (at n. 14 in text), and itself was succeeded by another series of acclamations, about thrice as prolonged as that which his speech had provoked (7. 171-4). Cf. *supra* nn. 4 and 14.

17. Constantinople.

18. See no. 186, n. 4.

19. This decree, commonly called the *Si quis igitur*, gives civil sanction to the Definition. Hailed with acclamations by the assembly (7. 173-4), it was incorporated later in Marcian's edict (no. 476).

20. Next Marcian proposed three drafts of canons for the council's consideration (7. 173-6). At the emperor's order these were read by Beronician, the secretary of the sacred consistory, and with modification became respectively the council's canons, 4, 3, 5.

The first concerned the restraint of monks, whose fanaticism in ecclesiastical affairs had been notorious since the previous century and then had been made the subject of imperial legislation (no. 272).

The second discouraged clerical secularity by forbidding clergymen from engaging in business pursuits for gain.

The third, with a view to decreasing clerical ambition, prohibited a clergyman from leaving the church of his ordination and from migrating to another church.

21. The contrast seems to be between urban and rural sites.

22. A variant Latin translation is "should not insert themselves into".

23. The expression is ἐναπόγραφοι or *inscripticii* (usually *adscripticii*), applied in the Dominate to persons bound to the soil as tenants and transferred with such real property from owner to owner. See no. 528, n. 2.

24. The word is κτήματα or *possessiones*, specifically connoting vineyards or orchards, but used generally for estates, farms, fields, possessions.

25. That is, when their community has been destroyed through hostile invasion or by natural catastrophe or from act of God.

26. The customary approval of varied complimentary acclamations attended the reading of these proposals.

27. In her church the council sat.

28. To signalize the synod's significance.

29. A variant Greek version reads "wherein the matters of the holy faith have been conducted by the holy synod". The meaning of the verb διακροτεῖν (reported only in Euripides and in Plutarch) is not too clear, unless the alternative Greek version is preferred. Literally it is "to resolve into components", as words into their elements.

30. That is, the elevation of the see of Chalcedon into a titular metropolitanate would not impair the Nicomedian see's metropolitical position, for Chalcedon in other respects would remain suffragan to Nicomedia. Thus in 1951 on the Roman Catholic bishop of Brooklyn, N.Y. (whose diocese is the largest in population in the United States and in 1961 was exceeded by only

four of the 26 archdioceses in the United States), was conferred the personal dignity of archbishop, which was not inherited by his successor and which did not remove him from the jurisdiction of the Roman Catholic archbishop of New York City.

31. The bishops, after having saluted with shouts the emperor's decision to elevate the status of the Chalcedonian see, asked dismissal. Marcian replied in this paragraph, which Mansi also gives isolatedly in Latin as an appendix to his address (6. 1225).

32. The word is καλός and seems to be used in the sense of "goodly" as applied to a space of time.

33. Ten more sessions were needed, the sixteenth and last being on 1 November.

34. That is, either present defence from disturbers of their sessions or future escort to their sees.

35. A marginal emendation for "of us" is translated. Both Latin versions (6. 1225 and 7. 178) agree with the emendation.

473. MANDATE OF VALENTINIAN III AND MARCIAN ON CONCILIAR PROCEDURE, 451

(M 7. 273-4)

Bassian, irregularly elected bishop of Ephesus in 444, was seized by a mob in 448 and was imprisoned. When he had been removed by Theodosius II and his election had been declared invalid by Pope St Leo I and by the patriarchs of Alexandria, Antioch, and Constantinople, a certain Stephen was chosen to succeed Bassian in 449. After Theodosius' death in 450 Bassian presented a petition [1] for reinstatement to Valentinian III and Marcian, of whom the latter in the present directive orders the Council of Chalcedon to hear Bassian's case.

The rivals' claims occupied the eleventh and the twelfth sessions of this synod (29-30 October 451), which, seeing such complex irregularities in the situation, ruled that the see should be vacant, retired both Bassian and Stephen on pensions, while allowing them retention of their episcopal rank, and decided that a new bishop for Ephesus should be selected.[2]

Emperors Caesars Valentinian and Marcian, Victors, Triumphers [3] to the holy synod assembled in Chalcedon according to our sacred ordinance.

The most devout Bassian, who has suffered many unwonted things, which are contained in his entreaties suppended to this our sacred letter, has petitioned that these should be discussed by your Holinesses.

Therefore let your Devoutnesses be disposed, on receipt of this our sacred letter, to examine the case and to give a ruling acceptable to you.

1. Printed in M 7. 273-6.
2. See no. 470, VIII.
3. The Latin version adds "Greatest, Ever-Worshipful Augusti".

474. MANDATE OF VALENTINIAN III AND MARCIAN ON CONFIRMATION OF ECCLESIASTICAL PRIVILEGES, 451

(CI 1. 2. 12)

In this ordinance Emperor Marcian both confirms whatever privileges orthodox emperors have conferred upon the Church and cancels whatever pragmatic sanctions are contrary to ecclesiastical canons.

Pitra prints (2. 469) a late Greek version of the second and the third paragraphs.

Emperors Valentinian and Marcian Augusti to Palladius, praetorian prefect.[1]

We decree that the privileges which previously princes of the orthodox religion have granted by general constitutions to all sacrosanct churches should be guarded firm and unimpaired in perpetuity.

We also command that all pragmatic sanctions which have been elicited against ecclesiastical canons by the intervention of partiality and of flattery, when voided of their strength and stability, should be invalid.

And because it is part of our Humanity to provide for the needy and to bestow care that to the poor may be not lacking aliments, also pensions,[2] which hitherto by the sacrosanct churches have been administered in various kinds at public cost, we order now also that these, undisturbed and not at all lessened by anyone, should be given and we confer stability upon this very prompt liberality.

Given on 12 November at Constantinople, Marcian Augustus being consul.

1. Of the East.
2. In view of the preceding *alimenta*, which generally means "food" and sometimes means "financial doles", *salaria* may mean "salt rations", though it originally means "salt-money", i.e. money given to soldiers for purchase of salt, and later means "allowances", "salaries", "stipends", "pensions".

It seems that the State started a systematic alimentation of financial aid for pauper children as early as 97 in Nerva's reign, although occasional public and private largess of money to citizens was not unknown both earlier and later. Thus, besides bonuses to soldiers, purchase of lands for veterans, donations to the military treasury (which he established), Augustus, the first emperor, gave to the Roman populace—either directly or by paying into the public treasury—about $33,000,000 (U.S.A. 1914), according to his own account (*Res Gestae Divi Augusti*, 3. 15, 17).

Nerva's system, supervised by a prefect of aliments (*praefectus alimentorum*), was continued by his successors until Commodus suspended it, but it was revived by Septimius Severus, who extended it from Italy into the provinces, and it still existed under Constantine I, who maintained it at least until 323 in Italy and in Africa (*CT* 11. 27. 1-2). In the State's supply of free grain to the Roman and the Constantinopolitan proletariat (on which see no. 141, n. 3), as well as in the State's system of financial and material assistance for poor children, were the precedents for imperial concern about governmental aid for the State's poorer classes, to whose support the Church also contributed (no. 515, n. 3).

475. LETTER OF VALENTINIAN III AND MARCIAN ON CONFIRMATION OF THE CHALCEDONIAN COUNCIL, 451

(*PL* 54. 970–4)

This letter to Pope St Leo I, extant in both Greek and Latin (of which the editors think that the latter, translated here, is the original), announces the successful conclusion of the Fourth General Council at Chalcedon in 451 and asks that Constantinople should be given the place of honour next to Rome in ecclesiastical administration.[1]

It supplements a conciliar letter to the pope (*PL* 54. 951–60), in which masterpiece of appeasement the council informs the pope that for the electoral peace of metropolitical cities in the civil dioceses of Asia and Pontus and Thrace the council has voted to transform the eastern precedence of the Constantinopolitan patriarchate from one of honour into one of jurisdiction with reference to the aforesaid dioceses.

See nos. 470, XI, n. 70, and 482.

Letter of Emperor Marcian to Pope Leo.

Victors Valentinian and Marcian, Renowned, Triumphers, Ever-August to the holy father, the deservedly venerable Bishop Leo.

Divine and human writings agree that the Divinity is especially worthy of worship and there the Almighty God is well disposed where religion is practised duly. Therefore we have found that which we were seeking and our prayers have earned their accomplishment. Religious love has found religious faith and it is not doubtful that with God as the originator there has been defined what was being sought about his majesty. Therefore, when the strife and the discord, which malice, inimical to faith, had presented, have been dissipated, all with one mind recognize God. No longer we accuse the perfidious nor are we ungrateful. Religion's enemies have enabled us to seek God more earnestly and to find him more clearly. For there appears a greater light, which has shone after the darkness;[2] drink is sweeter for the thirsty, rest for the weary.[3] Therefore let your Holiness rejoice at the victory of faith,[4] of which the triumph must be referred to the Omnipotent Christ, who caused the conquest over the perfidious. And so we ourselves hastened to attend the holy synod, although expeditions and public needs were trying to detain us in our places.[5]

And so, with God as the originator, all matters which become the faith have been ordained in respect to your Worship's prayers and plea. When the most reverend bishops of the whole world, which is under our Sovereignty, had been called to Chalcedon, after discussion had been held, after many conflicts the true faith has prevailed and in consequence of your Sanctity's letter [6] all have assembled to your exposition, just as truth has demanded. Nor do we doubt that thankfulness on this circumstance is common to us and to your Sanctity and that those who equally, it is clear, desired truth are equally glad. It remains that, since all matters have been arranged in accord with Catholic faith and truth and since peace has been restored to the churches, your Sanctity should appeal to the Divine Majesty with all prayers for the enemies' destruction—a thing which even before our letter it has been determined that you should do.

But since also it has been ordained that there should be kept constant those matters which 150 most holy bishops [7] under the deified [8] Theodosius the Elder [9] have ordained concerning the honour of the venerable Constantinopolitan Church and which now concerning the same matter have been ordained by the holy synod, namely that after the apostolic see the bishop of the Constantinopolitan city should possess second place, inasmuch as also the said most splendid city is called the Younger Rome,[10] your Sanctity should deign to give your own consent to this point, although the most reverend bishops, who came to the holy synod representing your Worship, spoke in opposition, for they were trying vehemently to prevent anything concerning this venerable church [11] from being ordained by the synod.[12]

Moreover we hope that, since the bishops throughout the whole world are in agreement, divine favour will deign to vouchsafe those things which will advantage the Roman State. Wherefore through Lucian, the religious bishop, and Basil, the deacon, the bearers of this letter, we have decided that all these matters ought to be made known to you in their true relation. And we ask that your Worship should order that the rules which the holy synod has ordained should be observed forever.

And by another hand: May the Divinity guard you, holy and most religious father, for many years.

Given on 18 December at Constantinople, our Lord Marcian Perpetual-Augustus and he [13] who shall be named being consuls.

1. Leo's reasons for refusal are well summarized by Kidd, 3. 336.
2. Cf. Isa. 9. 2 and Matt. 4. 16.
3. Cf. Job 3. 17; Isa. 28. 12.
4. Cf. 1 John 5. 4.
5. Marcian refers to the incursions of the Huns into Illyricum, which was the chief cause of the council's change of site from Nicaea to Chalcedon, nearer to Constantinople (see no. 464, n. 1).
6. The pope sent to the council his celebrated *Tome* (on which see no. 470, n. 34) defining the orthodox position on Eutychianism. When read, it evoked the acclamation: "Peter has spoken thus through Leo" (Πέτρος διὰ Λέοντος ταῦτα ἐξεφώνησεν or *Petrus per Leonem ita locutus est*), meaning that either Leo had explained the true import of St Peter's confession (Matt. 16. 16), on which see no. 442, n. 7 *ad fin.*, or that Leo's theological insight had led them to acknowledge the justice of his claim to be the successor of St Peter. See also no. 472, n. 4 *ad fin.*
7. The traditional number present at the Second General Council of the Church held at Constantinople in 381.
8. See no. 127, n. 7.
9. The grandfather of Marcian's wife and the last ruler of the undivided Empire, in whose reign the Council of Constantinople met.
10. So canon 3 of Constantinople and canon 28 of Chalcedon. See no. 375, n. 7.
11. I.e. Constantinople.
12. The council's letter to the pope also admits that the papal legates opposed the plan to confirm the Chalcedonian canon (28) conferring second place on Constantinople after Rome and suggests that this opposition stemmed from the legates' wish that the pope himself might have the honour of proposing it (*PL* 54. 957).
13. The other consul, if the year is correct, was Adelphius.

476. EDICT OF VALENTINIAN III AND MARCIAN ON CONFIRMATION OF THE CHALCEDONIAN COUNCIL, 452

(PL 56. 547-9)

Of the several imperial constitutions concerning the definitions decided by the Fourth Ecumenical Council at Chalcedon in 451 this edict is the most important because of its lasting influence.

Justinian I incorporates most of it into his Code (1. 1. 4) in 534 and supplements it in his Novels (131. 1) in 545, when he uses it to erect the first four general councils [1] as the civilian standard of orthodoxy, to which subsequent generations have repaired and which still confirms the Anglican Church's doctrinal continuity and Catholicity.[2]

This edict also sets the administrative seal on open opposition to Monophysitism as advanced by Eutyches, the Constantinopolitan archimandrite, who was condemned at Chalcedon. In political history the synod's decisions, which the State had directed (no. 470) and which the State supported (nos. 475-7, 479-89—to record only the constitutions during the reign of the council's convocator), served to estrange especially Syrians and Egyptians, who overwhelmingly opposed either conformity with or compromise on the conciliar canons and whose racial intransigence and national indifference toward the Eastern Empire were fanned into flame from this theological tinder. Sanguinary suppression of religious riots failed to solve the fundamental issues, which seemed incapable of settlement short of separation. It is not a matter for marvel, then, that thus were created conditions which led to the loss of these lands (see Introd., n. 43), despite the desperate efforts of such subsequent emperors as Zeno (see no. 527) and Anastasius (see no. 542) to save these by making theirs the Monophysite cause, for heterodoxy among these peoples had taken too deep a root as an emblem of nationality to be eradicated and orthodoxy, long identified with overseas overlordship, had become inimical to Catholicity.

The text selected for translation is preserved in the *Codex Canonum Ecclesiasticorum et Constitutorum Sanctae Sedis Apostolicae*, 26, printed as an appendix to the writings of Pope St Leo I (440-61), and is believed to be the original form. Both St Isidore of Seville in his *Collectio Canonum* (PL 84. 173-4) and Isidorus Mercator in his *Collectio Decretalium* (PL 130. 314-15) also have in Latin the edict, from which in Latin Facundus quotes twice in his *Defensio Trium Capitulorum*, 12. 2 (PL 67. 837). Mansi gives both a Greek and a Latin text in 7. 475-8).

Here begins the constitution of Marcian of divine memory concerning the Chalcedonian Synod.[3]

Emperors Valentinian and Marcian Augusti to all peoples.[4]

476. CHALCEDONIAN COUNCIL, 452

At long last has happened what we were wishing with highest longings and prayers.[5] Controversy concerning the Christians' orthodox [6] law has been removed. At last remedies for culpable error have been found and the peoples' discordant opinion has united into one consent and concord. For from different provinces most religious [7] bishops have come to Chalcedon [8] pursuant to our orders [9] and by clear [10] definition have taught what ought to be observed in religion. Therefore now let profane contention cease.[11] For [12] truly he is impious and sacrilegious, who after so many bishops' decision reserves [13] for his own opinion anything to be investigated. Surely it is a sign of utmost madness [14] to search for [15] counterfeit light in full and clear daylight,[16] for whoever after the truth has been found discusses anything further, seeks [15] falsehood.

Accordingly none,[17] either clergyman or [18] governmental official or [19] of any other condition,[20] henceforth should [21] try to treat [22] publicly about the Christian [23] faith by collecting crowds and auditors,[24] seeking from this tumults and an occasion [25] of disbelief, for he does an injury to the most religious [26] synod's judgement, if anyone strives to retraverse [27] and to dispute publicly matters once decided and rightly disposed,[28] since those points, which now have been ordained about the Christian [23] faith,[29] according to the apostolic [30] expositions and the ordinances of the 318 and the 150 holy [30] fathers [31] are recognized [32] to have been determined.

For punishment against the despisers of this law shall not be lacking, because not only they attack the well-ordered [33] faith, but also by strife of this character they profane the venerable mysteries [34] before Jews and pagans.[35] Therefore, if there shall be a clergyman who shall have dared to treat [36] publicly about religion, he shall be removed from the society [37] of clergymen; moreover, if he has been provided with a governmental office,[38] he shall be deprived of his belt;[39] also all others guilty of this [40] crime shall be expelled from this most holy [41] city,[42] after they have been made liable to appropriate punishments by judicial activity.[43] For it is known that hence are furnished [44] the tinder [45] and the sources of heretical insanity,[46] while certain persons dispute and strive publicly.

All[47] therefore shall be [48] bound to maintain the matters which have been determined by the holy Chalcedonian [49] Synod, doubting [50] nothing henceforth. Accordingly, reminded by our Serenity's [51] edict, abstain from profane words and cease further to dispute [52] about divine matters—which is wrong, because this sin not only shall be punished by divine judgement, as we believe, but also shall be restrained by the authority of laws and of judges.

Given [53] on 27 January [54] at Constantinople, Sporatius being consul.[55]

1. Nicaea (325), Constantinople (381), Ephesus (431), Chalcedon (451).
2. So Kidd, 3. 339.
3. Isidore's caption is "The emperors' edict in confirmation of the Chalcedonian Council", while Isidorus Mercator has "Emperor Martian's [sic] edict in confirmation of the Chalcedonian Council". Mansi gives "Edict of Emperors Valentinian and Marcian, whereby are prohibited disputations about the faith in the presence of the people".
4. Both Isidores agree with the *Codex*, but Justinian reads "Emperor Marcian Augustus to Palladius, praetorian prefect".

Mansi has three variant superscriptions: 1 (in Greek, 7. 476) "Emperors Flavius Valentinian and Flavius Marcian, Ever-August, about prohibiting debates about Christian matters: edict to our Constantinopolitan citizens"; 2 (in Latin, 7. 475) "Emperors Caesars Flavius Valentinian and Flavius Marcian: edict about matters of the Christian faith to our Constantinopolitan citizens"; 3 (in Latin, 7. 721) "Emperors Caesars Flavius Valentinian, Renowned Pontifex, Renowned Germanicus, Renowned Alamannicus, Renowned Sarmaticus, with the Tribunician Power for the twenty-seventh time, with the Imperium for the twenty-seventh time, Consul for the seventh time, and Flavius Marcian, Renowned Pontifex, Renowned Germanicus, Renowned Sarmaticus, Renowned Alamannicus, Renowned Francicus, with the Tribunician Power for the twenty-seventh time, Imperator, Consul for the first time: edict about prohibited disputations by Christians to our Constantinopolitan citizens".

While Marcian was a senator ere his coronation on 25 August 450 by St Pulcheria, his virginal empress-consort and the late Theodosius II's sister, there is no evidence that he had held the tribunician power 27 times other than the statement here, which seems repeated from what is recorded about Valentinian III and which should be reduced from 27 to two. On the other hand, the epithetical proper adjectives need not be questioned, for he had distinguished himself in several campaigns as an aide to Aspar, master of the soldiers.

5. M's Greek gives "At long last has happened what is our concern with greatest prayer and zeal".
6. M transfers this adjective to the proper noun.
7. M substitutes "devout" for the superlative adjective.
8. M has "the Chalcedonians' city".
9. M has "ordinance".
10. M converts the adjective into an adverb.
11. M adds "henceforth".
12. Facundus starts his first excerpt here.
13. Isidorus Mercator and Facundus have the perfect tense.
14. The Latin versions have *dementia* (dementia) and the Greek version has παράνοια (paranoia), which psychiatrically are not mutually synonymous.
15. Isidorus Mercator and M's Greek use the same verb ("seek") in each case.
16. M has "in midday".
17. Here begins Justinian's excerpt.

476. CHALCEDONIAN COUNCIL, 452

18. M inserts "indeed" and Isidorus Mercator omits the conjunction.
19. M inserts "indeed" again and both Isidores read "and" for *or*.
20. M's Greek substitutes αἵρεσις (sect), which in astrological terminology equals *conditio* (condition *or* status *or* rank) found in all the Latin versions.
21. Facundus has "presume".
22. M has "to make disputations".
23. M has "of the Christians".
24. The Isidores read "faith as defined and by collecting auditors". St Paul condemns such convocations (1 Tim. 6. 3–5).
25. Plural in M.
26. *CI* reads "most reverend" and M has "holy".
27. M inserts "as a result of disputation".
28. Here Facundus ends his first excerpt.
29. Justinian inserts "through our commands by bishops who have convened at Chalcedon".
30. M omits this word.
31. The traditional numbers present at Nicaea in 325 and at Constantinople in 381 respectively.
32. M omits the rest of the sentence.
33. M and *CI* read "truly-ordered".
34. See no. 75, n. 42.
35. Isidorus Mercator alone makes *Jews and pagans* the verb's subject. M's Greek gives "Hellenes", of course, for *pagans* (as usual), on which see no. 121, n. 3.
36. M has "strive".
37. M has "catalogue".
38. See no. 186, n. 4.
39. After Septimius Severus (193–211) had reorganized the imperial bureaucracy on military lines (see nos. 186, n. 4, and 320, n. 3), belts or sashes adapted from military personnel and habit became part of the regalia of civilian officials, who were considered as soldiers of the emperor and who, it is said, were required to wear belts in the imperial presence. To be deprived of one's belt (*cingulum* or ζώνη) was to be dismissed from the governmental service (*militia* or στρατεία).

It may be noted that a modern survival of such bureaucratic belts exists in several European countries, notably France, wherein a municipal mayor wears—at least on official occasions—a coloured sash suspended from one shoulder and diagonally across the body, as a baldric to support a sword used to be arranged. Sashes symbolizing knightly orders also are worn in this way and may have come from this ancient custom.

40. *CI* reads "such".
41. *CI* reads "most sacred", but M has "royal".
42. Constantinople. *CI* adds "if they are freemen".

43. M reads "by the courts' activity"; Justinian concludes his excerpt here, but by reading "but if slaves, they shall be smitten with severest punishments".
44. Isidorus Mercator has "nourished".
45. M reads "the issues" and with the Latin versions has *the sources* in first position, thus avoiding the text's hysteron proteron.
46. M has "for the heretics' insanity".
47. Facundus resumes here and with Isidorus Mercator has "They" as subject and with him joins *All* with *matters*.
48. Present tense in Greek.
49. M and Facundus read "at Chalcedon".
50. Facundus converts the participle into an infinitive.
51. "Tranquillity's" in Facundus.
52. M has "seek".
53. Omitted by Isidore of Seville and by M's Latin version, but Isidorus Mercator reads "Published".
54. Both Isidores and M's Greek and Latin and *CI* have 26 January.
55. Sporacius in Isidore of Seville and *CI*; Patrick in Isidorus Mercator; omitted by M's Greek, but M's Latin has "the most distinguished Sporatius and he who shall be announced being consuls".

477. CONSTITUTION OF MARCIAN ON CONFIRMATION OF THE CHALCEDONIAN COUNCIL, 452

(M 7. 477–80)

Since scant attention apparently had been paid to an earlier edict on confirmation of the Council of Chalcedon (no. 476), Marcian issued the following ordinance in another attempt to achieve adherence to the conciliar canons.

What appears to be the original text in Greek is translated, but a Latin version is preserved in the *Codex Canonum Ecclesiasticorum et Constitutorum Sanctae Sedis Apostolicae,* 27 (PL 56. 549–51).

Constitution of the most pious and Christ-loving Emperor Marcian, published in Constantinople after the synod, confirming the acts done by it.[1]

Desiring to establish the [2] sanctity of the Catholic faith of the orthodox as evident to and undoubted by all people, our Serenity has ordered so great and so excellent a synod to be gathered in the Chalcedonians'[3] city, from bishops collected from almost every province, that greater piety for the Divinity [4] may be transmitted to men, and there, after discussion held for very many days, it [5] has found what was true and genuine in respect to the Christians' [3] faith. For by very many prayers and pleas they have prevailed upon the Divinity that the holy and fullest [6] truth may not lie hid from them and they have followed the holy [2] fathers' ordinances, namely those which have been declared by the 318 most holy [6] bishops [7] at Nicaea [8] and likewise those which the 150, assembled in this royal [9] city,[10] have defined and those which have been defined already [11] at Ephesus,[12] when of blessed [13] memory Celestine, bishop of the Romans' [3] city, and Cyril, bishop of the Alexandrians' [3] city, took the lead in [14] the truth. And at that time also Nestorius' [3] error was excluded, when its author was condemned.[15]

And when these matters had been investigated duly and reverently at Chalcedon, Eutyches,[16] who was asserting rather many unlawful principles, has been rejected along with his assertion, lest for him may be provided an opportunity for deceiving men any longer.

Accordingly, since religiously and faithfully had been ordained those principles, which are known to lay [17] the foundation of the venerable faith of the orthodox, so that no doubt might remain for the future even to those who are wont to calumniate the Divinity, we, having confirmed by our Serenity's sacred edict the holy [2] synod, have admonished all persons that they should cease disputes [18] about religion, since one or another could not discover such a great mystery,[19] especially since with greatest industry and great pleas [20] so many holy [2] bishops, unless with God—as it must be believed—as the originator, could not have been able to attain to a capture of the truth.[21] But, as we have learned by clear reasoning, certain persons cease not to persist in the insanity of the said [22] perversity and to contend publicly, when people have been collected, about religion and in the sight of Jews and of pagans,[23] so as to make public and profane the divine mysteries,[24] which it is more proper to respect than to investigate.

Accordingly it was necessary for persons steadfast in the said stubbornness to be curbed by an already determined chastisement, that punishment might correct those whom reverence for matters [25] has not been able to amend. But following our custom in this matter and knowing before all things that the Divinity delights in a pious person, we have believed that the punishment of the guilty must be postponed, ordaining through our repeated command [26] that for the future all persons should desist from prohibited matters and should not convoke a meeting [19] when contending about religion, because, when detected in perversity and deception of such character, they shall receive the punishments already determined and, as befits pious times, shall be punished by the courts' activity.[27] For it is necessary to follow the synod in Chalcedon,[2] wherein, when all matters had been investigated diligently, have been defined these principles which already the three aforesaid synods, having followed the apostles'[2] faith, have transmitted[28] to be observed by all.

Given on 13 March[29] at Constantinople, in the consulate of Sphoracius[30] and of him who shall be announced.[31]

It was written to Palladius, praetorian prefect in the East, to Valentinian, praetorian prefect in Illyricum, to Tatian, urban prefect,[32] to Bencomalus,[33] master of the divine offices[34] and consul-designate.[35]

1. In the *Codex* is read "Here begins another constitution of Marcian of divine memory to Christian Catholics meeting in synod. The same Augusti to Palladius, praetorian prefect." Three variants for the superscription are reported: (1) "The same Augusti to Palladius, praetorian prefect"; (2) "Emperor Marcian Augustus to Palladius, praetorian prefect"; (3) "The same Augusti to our Constantinopolitan citizens".

In M's Latin version is "Edict of the most pious and most Christian Emperor Marcian, published at Constantinople, about confirmation of the Chalcedonian Synod's acts and their observance." To this caption in the margin M notes a variant: "The same Augustus to our Constantinopolitan citizens."

2. The *Codex*, which follows M's Latin version closely, substitutes "venerable".

3. Proper adjective agreeing with noun in Latin.

4. The Latin reads "for the Divinity's services".

5. The understood subject is either emperor or synod.

6. Positive degree in Latin.

7. The Latin inserts "decision" and turns *bishops* into a possessive genitive.

8. In 325.

9. The Latin substitutes "most renowned".

10. Constantinople. The date is 381.

11. For the adverb, retained by M's Latin version, the *Codex* substitutes "about the faith".

12. In 431.

13. Superlative degree in Latin.

14. The *Codex* reads "found" for *took the lead in*, but M's Latin supports the Greek and reads "were leaders of the truth".

15. Nestorius, patriarch of Constantinople, was deposed at Ephesus in 431.

16. The Constantinopolitan archimandrite and founder of Eutychianism.

17. The Latin more correctly uses the perfect tense of the infinitive.

18. The Latin converts the noun into an infinitive.

19. Plural in Latin. See no. 75, n. 42.

20. M's Latin has "with highest industry and great pleas", which the *Codex* also has except for the second adjective which is superlative. The *pleas* pre-

sumably are those addressed by orthodox bishops to their heretical colleagues in the council.
21. See no. 476.
22. The Latin transfers this word into the previous phrase.
23. "Hellenes" in Greek, as usual. See no. 121, n. 3.
24. See no. 75, n. 42.
25. The Latin reads "ordinances", taking the Greek πραγμάτων as πραγματικῶν.
26. The *Codex* reads "we do not punish the guilty, but our Clemency repeats the order" for *and . . . command*, but M's Latin adheres to the Greek.
27. The Latin reads "by judicial activity".
28. The *Codex* substitutes "proclaimed".
29. Variant dates to the version of the *Codex* are 9 and 10 March.
30. Sporatius is the better spelling in the Latin versions.
31. The Latin versions read "the most distinguished Sporatius and he who shall be announced being consuls".
32. Of Constantinople.
33. Probably Vincomalus is meant (as M translates it).
34. Transliterated into Greek from Latin *officia*.
35. The *Codex* omits this paragraph.

478. LETTER OF VALENTINIAN III ON EPISCOPAL JUDGEMENT AND ON VARIOUS MATTERS, 452

(*LNV* 35)

Of this exceedingly lengthy law only so much is translated as touches the Church.[1] The editors' Latin title is translated, but "on various matters" includes matters of ecclesiastical interest besides "episcopal judgement". In the sections concerning the Church the emperor establishes rules about resort to bishops as judges in lawsuits, about certain classes of persons who attempt to avoid their compulsory municipal duties by entering into ecclesiastical service, about clergy engaged in commercial pursuits, and about the clerical claims that on the Church should be conferred abandoned public sites (probably of pagan temples).

Emperor Valentinian Augustus to Firminus, praetorian prefect [2] and patrician.

Concerning episcopal judgement there frequently is complaint of various persons; lest the complaining should proceed farther, it is necessary for an ordinance to be made by the present law.

Accordingly, when altercation is agitated between clergymen and there is agreement on the part of the litigants themselves, let a bishop have the liberty of judging, nevertheless with the preceding bond of mutual promise to abide by the arbiter's award.[3]

And this also our Authority allows in the case of laymen, if they should consent; otherwise we do not permit them to be judges, unless the willingness of the disputants precedes in the matter of the interposed condition (as has been said),[4] since it is established that bishops and priests[5] have no forum[6] for the laws and cannot investigate judicially—apart from religion—concerning other cases, pursuant to Arcadius' and Honorius' divine ordinances,[7] which the Theodosian *Corpus*[8] exhibits.

If each or either litigant of the said office objects,[9] they should litigate by public laws and common law; but if indeed the claimant is a layman, whether in a civil or in a criminal case, he should compel the clergyman of whatever rank, his adversary, to answer,[10] if he rather chooses this, by lawful authority in a public court.

And we decree that this regulation ought to be observed in the case of the person of bishops: that if it shall have been necessary for an action of forcible entry and of atrocious injuries to be directed against men of this order,[11] they should contend legally and rightly[12] in a public judge's presence through an agent appointed in the customary way, the result of the matter judged being returnable without doubt to the mandators.[13] And this we allow to these persons because of respect for religion and for the episcopate.[14] For it is known that in criminal matters agency cannot be conceded. But that there may be some discrimination of merits, only this much ought to be applied to bishops and to priests;[15] in remaining criminal cases they should be compelled to undergo trial in their own persons according to the laws' regular procedure. If they, summoned by the prosecutor, should refuse to attend, a verdict, when the law's regular procedure has been maintained, should hold them contumacious.

In the case of a clergyman as claimant it shall be suitable that pursuant to the laws he should follow the forum[6] of the accused person,[16] if (as has been said) his adversary does not give assent to a hearing by a bishop or by a priest:[15] the punishment for such a case's defenders,[17] who shall have been present and shall have pleaded in the said extraordinary court, having been established to the effect that loss of office should strike a barrister and losses of reputation and of citizenship, which has been interdicted, should strike a solicitor.[18]

No registered cultivator,[19] tenant,[19] slave, or tenant farmer,[19] not a guildsman of the city of Rome or of any other city at all, not a

478. EPISCOPAL JUDGEMENT, 452

municipal senator, not a leading municipal senator,[20] not a receiver of the gold tax,[21] a citizen who is a sevir of a guild,[22] or a public slave should attain to the clerical service nor should attach himself to monks or to monasteries, that he may evade the bond of his obligated status.

We order that clergymen absolutely should not engage in trade.[23] If they should wish to be in trade, they should know that they, when subjected to judges, are not protected by privilege of the clergy.

It should not be lawful for defenders of the Church to be appointed from the cities' mentioned ministries;[24] loss of their property, which we command to be added to their municipal senate or guild, should attend persons assenting to this post.

If the competent judges shall have neglected to maintain and to execute these regulations, they should be deprived of their property and the privileges of their status—capital punishment having been ordained for the chief men of their office staff and they themselves [25] of necessity being nonetheless expelled from such an office, that they may not withdraw from their city's proper services.

Moreover those persons who within a decade passed from the day of this law's enactment have been ordained deacons shall be obligated to give substitutes for themselves; if they do not have the means whereby they may provide for themselves in this way, they themselves should be returned to their own status—all others of inferior rank [26] being necessarily restored to their lawful services (bishops and priests excepted), but there being retained, however, the rules which the statutes of previous laws have sanctioned concerning such persons' patrimony.[27]

Moreover registered cultivators [19] or slaves, who, avoiding the bond of birth, have transferred themselves to an ecclesiastical order,[11] should return to their masters' legal controls (bishops and priests excepted), if they have not completed the thirtieth year in the said office; likewise a deacon of this status should give to his master a substitute for himself, all his peculium [28] also having been restored. And in his case, if the means of giving a substitute should not exist, what has been determined above about their cities' ministries,[24] nevertheless, should be maintained.

For all clergymen it is seemly that there should be nothing at all in common, save for ecclesiastical actions, with other law cases or with places of public ownership,[29] which they often raze on the plea that they have been abandoned and are not necessary, by elicited supplications, as if for some use of religion: a penalty of twenty pounds of gold should be imposed on the chief men of the secretarial bureaus, if the right of admittance to this supplication shall have been bestowed . . .[30]

Wherefore your illustrious and exalted Grandeur [31] shall publish by posted edicts this very salutary edictal law, which will be advantageous for matters pending in the forum,[6] that how great is our care in arranging for the public peace may become known to all persons.

Given on 15 April at Rome, the most distinguished Herculan being consul.

Interpretation: This law ordains many things about various matters, but principally what has been said about clergymen, that, unless by the bond of mutual promise to abide by the arbiter's award,[32] they should not go to an episcopal court, has been abrogated by Majorian's later law.[33]

Concerning the rest it commands that if any layman shall have called through a judge's authority to public account a clergyman, whether in a civil or in a criminal matter, the accused should answer without delay; bishops also shall be called to court, whether for forcible entry of anyone's property or for any grave injuries. Although in criminal cases it should be permitted to none to answer by another, yet it is granted to bishops and to priests by this law that in such cases they may reply by an agent sent by them, but that without doubt the verdict of the matter judged should be brought to them.[13] But in remaining criminal cases, where a person must be convicted of crime, they should take care to show their own presence in court. But if, when summoned by the prosecutor for the third time, they shall have been unwilling to come to court, they should receive a sentence of contumacy. If a clergyman shall have accused anyone by lawsuit, he should be heard in the forum [6] of that person whom he calls to court, if, however, the accused shall not have assented to come to a bishop's or a priest's [5] court. But if he who accuses shall have done otherwise, it orders the defenders[17] of the case to be stigmatized in such a way that they may be considered removed [34] from every post and prosecution of cases.

It orders also no registered cultivator,[19] tenant,[19] slave, or tenant farmer [19] to attain to the clerical office nor to be received in monasteries, lest by this opportunity he can evade his obligated status. For neither a guildsman of any community, who owes public service, nor a municipal senator or a guildsman should presume to be a clergyman.

It orders also clergymen that they by no means should presume to engage in businesses; but if they shall have done this, they should be punished by the judges, just as other tradesmen.[35]

And indeed this law ordains that no defender of the Church should be created from public guilds. But if anyone from a municipal senate shall have consented that he should be created a defender of the Church, he shall know that all his property must be added to the municipal senate or to that guild whence he had departed and that he himself must be recalled in his own person [36] to the community's service. Both the governor and the office staff of that province, if they shall not have recalled these persons, must be smitten by a severe penalty, just as the law itself declares.[37]

It orders that deacons who have been created from municipal senators or from any public guild at all should be obligated to give for themselves substitutes for performing what things are due to the public interest. But if they shall not have given this, they themselves should be recalled to their obligated status. For it does not order bishops and priests to be bound by this law, except only that they should observe clearly about their patrimonies what rules have been established by Majorian's Law.[38]

Moreover registered cultivators [19] or slaves who shall have aspired to the ecclesiastical office are bound to be recalled within thirty years by their masters, in such a way, nevertheless, that a deacon may provide for himself a substitute, if he shall have had such, and his master may seize all his peculium.[39] But if he shall not have had the means whereby he may provide a substitute, he himself should be recalled to his own status.

For it orders all clergymen that they should plead no other cases save only ecclesiastical actions and that they should not destroy public places with a view of repair of churches . . .[40]

1. Cf. *infra* n. 30 for omitted topics.
2. Of Italy.
3. The brevity of Latin is well illustrated by the four words represented by *nevertheless . . . award* (*praeeunte tamen vinculo compromissi*).
4. That is, they too must agree to abide by the award, as in the case of the clergy.
5. Editors suspect this addition and bracket it here and twice later, for nowhere else in Roman law apparently is episcopal audience extended to priests to judge without delegation.
6. See no. 334, n. 5.
7. Nos. 271, 278, 309.
8. That is, the *Codex Theodosianus* of 438, as it now is known. It is interesting to see that only fourteen years after its publication it was called a *corpus* ("body" or collection of laws).
9. That is, either clergy or laity.
10. That is, to defend himself.
11. On *order* see no. 325, n. 6; on *injuries* and its action see no. 334, n. 25.

The action of forcible entry (*actio pervasionis*) appears to be unknown elsewhere under this phrase, but it probably was associated with actions for trespass upon another's land (*ingressus in alienum fundum*) and entry into someone's home by violence (*introitus in domum alicuius vi*).

The former was actionable by a restitutory interdict (issued by a magistrate), the interdict on violence (*interdictum de vi*), whereby a person deprived of possession by force could regain possession. When armed persons had aided the aggressor, a special interdict on armed violence (*interdictum de vi armata*) was issued (*GI* 4. 154-5; *II* 4. 15. 6). These interdicts are illustrated in *D* 43. 16.

The latter was punishable under the Cornelian Law on Injuries (*Lex Cornelia de iniuriis*) of 81 B.C. (*II* 4. 4. 8).

12. Literally "amid laws and rights". Perhaps a periphrasis gives a better meaning: "they should fight the legal rights of the case", "they should contest their case according to the laws and the rights about it".

13. That is, a bishop who has given a mandate to an agent that the latter should appear for the former in court should receive the verdict as applicable to himself and not to his representative.

14. See no. 158, n. 1.

15. Cf. *supra* n. 5.

16. It was an old rule of Roman law that a claimant must press his claim in the place where the person from whom he sought satisfaction was subject to jurisdiction through either origin or domicile (*CI* 3. 13. 2; 3. 13. 5; 3. 19. 3). See no. 582, n. 5.

17. Not the defendants, as it will appear immediately, but the lawyers of the accusers.

18. The text shows many variations toward the sentence's end. The extraordinary court is not the secular court, but is the episcopal court. The jurisconsult and the pleader are penalized because the former advises the cleric to plead and the latter pleads for the cleric in an episcopal court, when the laic defendant is unwilling to submit his case to episcopal judgement and nevertheless is cited to appear therein. Cf. also n. 5 *supra*.

19. The distinction between *originarius* (registered cultivator) and *inquilinus* (tenant) may be no more than that between persons who are descended from farmers originally settled in a community and persons who moved thither to become tenants. See no. 528, n. 5. At any rate, Valentinian casts his net widely to include the farming class.

20. This word (*exprimario*, found only here) causes difficulty, for it is interpreted in the lexica as one of the chief *curiales* or *decuriones* who comprised municipal senates (*curiae*). But there is no point in excluding first *any* municipal senator (*curialis*) and then a leading municipal senator (*exprimario*). Probably the solution is in reading *curialis ex primario* < *ordine* > "a curial from the first class" for *curialis . . . exprimario*.

21. Other meanings for *aurarius* are "goldsmith" and "patron".

22. A sevir or sexvir is any one of six members of a group, here of an administrative board of a guild.

23. The prohibition probably proceeds from Ecclus. 26. 29.

24. The guilds which served the cities in compulsory services.

25. The defenders of the Church.

26. That is, the minor clergy.

27. Perhaps are meant *CT* 5. 18. 1 (dated 419) and *LNV* 27 (dated 449) and *LNV* 31 (dated 451).
28. See nos. 337, n. 6, and 624, n. 3.
29. These are probably pagan temples now deserted and no longer fulfilling their original need in the Christianized Empire. Apparently Valentinian wanted these preserved for the sake of art.

It seems that hitherto clerics—as the next line of the text shows—successfully petitioned (*by elicited supplications*) the emperors for permission to demolish such buildings.

30. At this point the law turns to other topics not specifically touching the Church, among which are rules about succession to estates, betrothal gifts, dowries, divorce, statute of limitations, procedure in court, appeal of cases, migration of tenant farmers.
31. Firminus, the emperor's "dearest and fondest cousin", who is addressed in the last sentence of the omitted sections, is meant.
32. Cf. *supra* n. 3.
33. No. 500.
34. Literally "strangers".
35. When convicted in suits emanating from their trafficking.
36. Or "in his own guild".
37. This sentence is in *oratio obliqua* and depends on some such understood construction as "The law provides that".
38. No. 497.
39. Cf. *supra* nn. 28 and 37.
40. Apparently, as often, older buildings served as quarries for restoration of buildings.

Translation of the Interpretation ends here (cf. *supra* n. 30).

479. MANDATE OF VALENTINIAN III AND MARCIAN ON CONFIRMATION OF THE CHALCEDONIAN COUNCIL, 452

(M 7. 497–500)

This is the third in the series of imperial constitutions ratifying the acts of the Fourth General Council of Chalcedon in 451. It also annuls Theodosius II's law confirming the decisions of the Robber Council of Ephesus in 449 (no. 459) and vindicates the memory of St Flavian, patriarch of Constantinople, and acquits Theodoret, bishop of Cyrus, and Eusebius, bishop of Dorylaeum, who were deposed at Ephesus.

Justinian adapts a short section of this law (*CI* 1. 3. 23).

Concerning overthrowing the things against Flavian of holy memory, bishop of the royal Church in Constantinople,[1] and confirming the things afterward decided about him by the holy synod.

The emperors to Palladius, the most magnificent prefect of the praetorians,[2] Valentinian, prefect of Illyricum, Tatian, prefect of the city,[3] Vincomalus, master of the sacred offices and consul-designate.

Glory never perishes by the death of glorious persons, nor do virtues die together with dying persons; rather the estimation of good persons is enhanced by death, because all envy against dead persons disappears.[4] Hence with such great zeal and praises the ancestors' right actions win good words;[5] hence by us the memory of the best persons is celebrated with greatest adoration;[5] hence the souls of the best men often have chosen renowned deaths.[6] For it has been agreed mutually that those alone die perpetually whose life and death have been kept silent.[7] That this is so at the present time both divine and human judgement demonstrates.

For since through false envy and by a licentiously contrived and dishonest prosecution Flavian of holy and worshipful memory, the bishop of this glorious city, had been ejected from its archiepiscopate and since in reality to hold the bishopric with rather absolute authority was not otherwise than to maintain the faith which he had received (for he alone was worthy of being bishop), nevertheless this most royal city has sought and has received his relics,[8] as these have appeared more blessed than all living beings, so that that death, which was considered bitter, should be believed to have happened because of prayer, through which he has purchased for himself that immortal renown. And to these matters has succeeded the following: that God has granted to his honours that a worshipful synod of almost countless bishops should convene at the Chalcedonians' city, which, while it has inquired [9] carefully concerning the faith through the authority of the most blessed Leo, bishop of eternally glorious [10] Rome, and has fixed [9] religion's foundations, has attributed to Flavian the prize of past life and of glorious death.

Therefore, since Flavian of worshipful memory has been adorned with so great a testimony [11] that Eutyches,[12] who has held contrary opinions, with his abominable sayings has been condemned by all with one mouth, there shall be expunged the provisions of that ordinance which is known to have been ordained against him by the rapacity of abominable persons after the death of Flavian of holy memory. And there shall be vacated entirely the provisions which had their origin from injustice.[13]

And the unjust sentence shall not harm either Eusebius or Theodoret, the most God-beloved bishops, whom the same decree includes, since indeed by an ordinance cannot be condemned bishops whom a synodical sentence has adorned because of maintenance of the faith.[14]

Therefore, since that legislation has been annulled, Flavian shall retain the eternal praise of his life and of his glory, whereof indeed he is worthy—his constancy concerning the faith being a future example for all others.

Therefore your super-splendid and noble-natured Authority shall cause this present salutary law by posted edicts to come to all persons' knowledge.

Given on 6 July at Constantinople, in the consulate of the most splendid Sporacius and of him who shall be announced.[15]

1. The Latin version characterizes Flavian as "bishop of the Constantinopolitan city".
2. In the Latin version, which begins "Valentinian and Marcian Augusti", Palladius is called simply "prefect of the praetorians of the East". *CI*'s superscription reads "Emperors Valentinian and Marcian Augusti to Palladius, praetorian prefect".
3. Of Constantinople.
4. Literally "becomes away from the feet", i.e. "out of the way".
5. Cf. Tacitus, *Agr.* 1. 1-2, 46. 4.
6. Among the best-known examples of men "choosing renowned deaths" in Roman antiquity are those of the three Decii, grandfather, son, grandson, who all had the same name, Publius Decius Mus, and who "devoted" themselves to death by charging into the enemy's ranks and thus ensured victory for the Romans. These heroes' traditional deaths occurred in their consulates: 340, 295, 279 B.C. See Cicero, *Tusc. Disp.* 1. 37. 89.
7. Cf. Ecclus. 44. 9; Horace, *Carm.* 4. 9. 25-8; Tacitus, *Agr.* 46. 4.
8. Flavian died in a Lydian prison from blows and kicks administered by monks. His relics were translated to Constantinople on 18 February 451.
9. Historical present form.
10. Literally "eternal in respect to glory"; see no. 140, n. 1.
11. Flavian's memory was rehabilitated at Chalcedon's first session (see no. 470, I).
12. The Constantinopolitan heresiarch, condemned by a local synod over which Flavian presided in 448.
13. This paragraph only is used by Justinian, who reads: "Since Flavian of venerable remembrance, bishop of this genial city, with the venerable synod of almost countless bishops, who convened in Chalcedon, has been adorned with so great and such testimony, that Eutyches, who had thought contrariwise, with his abominable sayings was condemned by all with one mouth, there should be abolished indeed Eutyches' damned memory, but Flavian's laudable remembrance should be revealed."

Pitra prints (2. 546) a late Greek paraphrase of Justinian's excerpt: "Since the famous Flavian, bishop of this splendid city, with the most august synod having almost a countlessness [conjecturing τὸ ἀνάριθμον σχεδόν for Pitra's seemingly senseless τὸν ἀριθμὸν σχεδόν] of bishops, who had convened in Chalcedon, has been adorned with so great and such testimony, that Eutyches, having agreed [sc. with contrary opinions], with his most abominable teachings has been condemned by all with one mouth, Eutyches of condemned memory should be abolished, but the laudable Flavian should be restored."

The Greek paraphrast certainly has garbled at the end, at least, Justinian's Latin.

14. Eusebius and Theodoret were cleared at Chalcedon's first and eighth sessions respectively (see no. 470, I and VII).

15. *CI*'s subscription after date and place simply has "Sporacius being consul".

480. LETTER OF VALENTINIAN III AND MARCIAN ON CONFIRMATION OF THE CHALCEDONIAN COUNCIL AND ON PENALTIES FOR EUTYCHIANS, 452

(M 7. 501–6)

This document is the last in the series of constitutions confirming the Council of Chalcedon (451). It also condemns Eutychians to various penalties.

Isidorus Mercator in his *Collectio Decretalium* (PL 130. 315–17) and St Isidore of Seville in his *Collectio Canonum* (PL 84. 174–6) have the ordinance in Latin.

About confirming these things which have been determined by the holy synod in Chalcedon against Eutyches [1] and his monks.[2]

The same Augusti to the same magistrates.[3]

One ought to have and to confess great thanks to the Omnipotent God,[4] because he allows abominations neither to lie hidden absolutely nor to remain unpunished.[5] And of these [6] he has the most [7] opportunity of afflicting [8] the one and provides for all other persons the example of avoiding [9] the other.

Therefore it evidently has been shown that men's acts and especially reverence for religion are a care for God [10] in that recently the Catholic faith was confirmed, when he has not allowed Eutyches, who follows abominable dogmas, to lie hidden,[11] as he had lain hidden for a long time, and has not permitted him, when [12] detected, to escape the punishment of his abomination. And so, when condemned by God's and men's [13] verdicts, he received the synodal decision as he deserved, a defendant against God,[10] to whom he was doing injury, and a defendant against men,[14] whom he was trying to deceive. For [15] very

480. THE COUNCIL AND EUTYCHIANS, 452

many most holy [16] bishops from —so to speak [17]—the whole world, when they had assembled at Chalcedon, have rejected the aforesaid Eutyches' most impious [18] inventions along with the error of the Synod of Ephesus held for this purpose,[19] having followed [20] the holy fathers' dogmas [21] which have been established in Nicaea [22] by the 318 and by the 150 in this city [23] and in Ephesus,[24] when they excluded Nestorius' [25] error, bishops Celestine of the Romans' [26] city and Cyril of the Alexandrians' [26] city presiding.[27]

Therefore those matters, which according to the most ancient teaching have been defined by the venerable synod in the Chalcedonians' city,[28] we have ordained and we ordain ought to be observed in all respects according to that faith with which we worship God, for it is exceedingly reasonable to observe with supreme [29] veneration the [30] bishops', who worship God with a pure mind, definitions, which for the most holy and orthodox [31] faith were issued pursuant to the fathers' canons.

Since it belongs to the imperial foresight to check every evil in the beginning and by the medicine of the laws to excise a creeping disease, by this law we ordain that those persons who by Eutyches' [1] error are deceived after the example of the Apollinarians, whom Eutyches [1] has followed and [29] whom the fathers' venerable rules, that is, the Church's [32] canons and the previous [33] emperors' sacred [34] ordinances, condemn, should have no priest and should not have or should not name any clergymen,[35] and Eutyches [1] himself entirely should be deprived of the name of priest, of which he has been despoiled as unworthy.[36] However, if any persons contrary to our rulings should have dared to ordain bishops or priests or other clergymen, both so ordained and so ordaining or appropriating for themselves by anticipation the rank of clergymen,[37] we command that they, after having been smitten with the loss of their goods, should be repressed by perpetual exile.[38] We order that they should have no [39] opportunity to gather or to collect or to convene monks or to build a monastery;[40] that the very places, wherein perhaps in their boldness they should have tried at any time to assemble, should be confiscated, if indeed they should have assembled with the knowledge of the owner of the place; but, if he does not know about it, we ordain that the manager or the leaseholder of the place,[41] when beaten with rods, after confiscation should undergo deportation.

Moreover we allow these persons to take nothing in accordance with anyone's will, to leave by will nothing to those who are of the said error, to seek no governmental service,[42] except perhaps cohortaline [43] or on the frontiers.

Also, if any should have been found to be serving in another governmental service [42] than the aforesaid,[44] either because his perversity in religion was not known or because he has deviated to this error after he had acquired the belt,[45] let him, after he has been discharged from the governmental service,[42] have this fruit of his infidelity—that he should be deprived of association with good [34] men and with the palace and they [46] should not dwell elsewhere than in the village or the city wherein they [46] were born; but if any of these have begun from [47] this all-blessed [48] city (which it is abominable to believe),[49] they should be excluded both from this royal [50] city and from the sacred [34] court and from every metropolitan city. And these [51] things [51] generally we decree concerning all persons who are overpowered or will be caught in this pollution of disease.[52]

Moreover those persons who hitherto indeed had been clergymen and monks of the orthodox faith,[53] who have dwelt in the same inn as Eutyches [54] (for it is not proper to call it a monastery, because it has harboured [55] enemies of piety), who have advanced [56] to this point of madness so that they,[57] by having abandoned the piously [58] venerable religion and [59] the synodal [59] decree (which bishops, gathered from almost the whole world, have determined in Chalcedon), follow [60] Eutyches' [1] impious teachings,[61] because,[62] when they had deserted the true light, they have believed that shadows should be selected—those persons we order to be restrained by all penalties which have been determined against heretics either by this law or [63] by previous laws,[64] just as previous pious [34] ordinances have regulated concerning Manichaeans,[65] lest by their poisonous deceits and most cursed [18] sophisms the minds of innocent and weaker [18] persons should be beguiled.

Moreover we have learned that these persons make certain false declarations to the affront of piety and to the odium of the holy synod's definitions [66] and, by having composed books and tomes in very many pages, fashion [67] these things which expose very clearly [18] their madness against the true faith. And so we command that wheresoever such writings [51] should have been found, they should be burned by fire;[40] but those who either have written these or through zeal for teaching or for learning have delivered these to others for perusal we ordain should be punished by deportation after confiscation.[68] For just as already it is included in our Divinity's [69] edicts, we deprive all persons of the opportunity to teach this impious heresy,[70] because he [71] who tries to teach illicit things shall be punished by the last penalty.[72]

Moreover those who are eager to hear persons [73] using abominable discourse we check by a fine of ten pounds of gold, for thus will be removed material for error, if both a hearer and a teacher of sinful things shall have been lacking.[74]

Therefore your super-splendid and noble-natured [75] Authority by posted edicts shall make known to all persons what we have ordered, with the governors in provinces [76] and their office staffs and the persons defending the cities [77] knowing that if either they should value indifference [78] or should allow to be transgressed those matters, which we have decreed by pure [79] faith and by holy resolution must be guarded by you[80], each,[81] when smitten by a fine of ten pounds of gold, as betrayers of piety and of the laws, also shall be in peril of their own reputation.

Given on 28 July [82] in Constantinople, in the consulate of the most splendid Sphoracius and of him who shall be announced.[83]

And similarly it was written to Valentinian, prefect of Illyricum, and to Tatian, urban prefect,[84] and to Bencomalus,[85] master [86] and consul-designate.[87]

1. The archimandrite who had ruled a monastery of over three hundred monks outside Constantinople for more than thirty years and who founded the heresy named after him.

2. For this caption Isidorus Hispalensis reads "Letter of Valentinian and Marcian Augusti published after the Chalcedonian Council for affirmation of the said council and damnation of heretics" and Isidorus Mercator has "Here begins the sacred sanction of Valentinian and Marcian Augusti after the Chalcedonian Council in confirmation of the said council and damnation of heretics".

3. Both Isidores give for this "Emperors Valentinian and Marcian Augusti to Palladius, praetorian prefect" and M's Latin version has "The same Augusti to Palladius, praetorian prefect".

The *same magistrates* are those named after the subscription, where doubtless should be added "Palladius, praetorian prefect in the East" on the analogy of no. 477 *ad fin*.

4. Both Isidores read "Thanks always ought to be paid and brought to the Divine Power".

5. Isidore of Seville has "because he neither allows the authors of heresy and secret things to lie hidden nor permits these to remain unpunished", but the other Isidore reads "which neither allows the authors of heresy, which is secret, to lie hidden nor permits these to remain unpunished".

6. Both Isidores insert "evils".

7. Isidorus Mercator substitutes "full".

8. Isidorus Mercator reads "choosing".

9. M's Latin substitutes "sinning in".

10. Both Isidores substitute "the Divinity".

11. Isidorus Mercator reads "when he has not known how to neglect Eutyches, who follows abominable dogmas".

12. Both Isidores insert "his wickedness"; thus the reading would be "when his wickedness had been detected".

13. Both Isidores have "divine and human".
14. The Isidores substitute "all persons".
15. The Isidores insert "most recently".
16. The Isidores read "most blessed".
17. Isidore of Seville reads "almost" and the other Isidore omits the parenthesis.
18. The Isidores use the positive degree.
19. Both Isidores read "along with the synod held for this purpose". The reference is to the Robber Council of 449.
20. Isidorus Mercator reads *sicut* (just as) for the other Isidore's *secuti* (having followed), which faithfully translates the Greek participle ἀκολουθήσαντες.
21. The Isidores read "the holy elders' decisions".
22. In 325.
23. The Isidores read "afterward by the 150 bishops in this genial city", the place and the date being Constantinople in 381.
24. In 431.
25. Patriarch of Constantinople and founder of Nestorianism. The Isidores turn the clause into a passive construction.
26. The Isidores have the singular proper adjective for the plural proper noun.
27. Pope St Celestine I presided at Ephesus only in a strained sense, for in his absence at Rome he was represented by three legates (two bishops and one priest), and St Cyril actually presided.
28. For *in . . . city* Isidore of Seville has "at Chalcedon" and Isidorus Mercator omits the phrase, but reads "Chalcedonian" before *synod*.
29. Isidorus Mercator omits the word.
30. Isidore of Seville inserts "630", one of the traditional estimates (the highest) of prelates present.
31. The Isidores read "the sacrosanct faith of the orthodox".
32. The Isidores substitute "ecclesiastical".
33. The Isidores substitute "deified".
34. The Isidores have the superlative degree.
35. The Isidores after *condemn* read "should create or should name no bishop, no priest, no clergymen".
36. Isidorus Mercator adds "in using", but the other Isidore reads "of which he is unworthy and has been despoiled".
37. Isidorus Mercator omits *the . . . clergymen*.
38. Isidorus Mercator reads "they should be subject to the loss of all their goods and to the danger of perpetual exile".
39. Isidorus Mercator has "that none of them should have an" and then omits *to gather or to collect or*.
40. Plural in both Isidores.
41. Both Isidores place the manager in the conditional clause and St Isidore adds there also the leaseholder. The other Isidore pluralizes *leaseholder*.
42. See no. 186, n. 4.

43. See no. 320, n. 5.
44. Both Isidores for *in . . . aforesaid* read "outside the aforesaid governmental service".
45. On this phrase see no. 476, n. 39.
46. Singular in both Isidores.
47. Both Isidores read "been born in".
48. Both Isidores substitute "genial".
49. St Isidore adds "and have been condemned".
50. Both Isidores substitute "venerable".
51. Singular in Isidorus Mercator.
52. St Isidore reads "who have been polluted or will be polluted by this stain" and the other Isidore reads "who have been polluted or are polluted by this disaster of pollution".
53. Both Isidores read "of the faith of the orthodox".
54. Both Isidores "in Eutyches' inn".
55. Isidorus Mercator inserts "in itself".
56. Isidorus Mercator reads "retreated" and both Isidores insert "so far".
57. St Isidore omits *so that they*.
58. Both Isidores read "the cult of the" for the adverb.
59. Isidorus Mercator substitutes "in" and transfers after *decree* the phrase *in Chalcedon* as a proper adjective from the parenthesis.
60. Perfect tense in Isidorus Mercator.
61. Both Isidores read "assertion".
62. Isidorus Mercator turns the causal clause into a relative clause.
63. Isidorus Mercator omits *either . . . or*.
64. The Isidores and M's Latin insert "rather to be expelled outside Roman soil".
65. Such as nos. 156, 176, 185, 190, 192, 219, 382, 387, 388, 395, 440.
66. Both Isidores read "venerable synodal definition".
67. Perfect tense in both Isidores.
68. The Isidores omit the phrase and add "for this impious heresy must be deleted".
69. "Serenity's" in the Isidores.
70. The Isidores omit *to . . . heresy*.
71. Plural in Isidorus Mercator.
72. That is, death.
73. The Isidores read "who through zeal of following shall have heard a person".
74. The Isidores add "Palladius, dearest and fondest cousin".
After *fire* Isidorus Mercator rearranges what follows to this point. First comes *Moreover . . . gold*, then *but . . . deportation* with the material in n. 68, next *just . . . penalty*, finally *for thus . . . lacking*.
75. For these epithets St Isidore has "illustrious and magnificent" and the other Isidore has only the latter.

76. The Isidores convert the prepositional phrase into an objective genitive.
77. The Isidores read "defenders of cities".
78. The Isidores for *value indifference* read "should have neglected".
79. St Isidore reads "true".
80. Isidorus Mercator reads for *that . . . you* "that we decrease that the holy and true faith must be guarded by holy resolution. And if they should have neglected this [the faith] or should have allowed it [the faith] to be transgressed".
81. Both Isidores omit these three words.
82. The Isidores' date is 18 July.
83. The Isidores read "Sporacius [Mercator has "Aspiratus"] and he who shall be announced being consuls". See no. 477, n. 31.
84. Of Constantinople.
85. Vincomalus is in M's Latin (as in no. 477, n. 33).
86. M's Latin supplies "of the offices".
87. The Isidores omit the paragraph.

481. LETTER OF MARCIAN ON CONFORMITY WITH ORTHODOXY, 452
(M 7. 481-4)

In Egypt the Monophysite formula persisted in firm opposition to the Definition of Chalcedon (451) and led eventually to the creation of the national Coptic Church of Egypt. This imperial letter attempts to win the monks of Alexandria, where feeling about doctrines proverbially ran high, to accept the orthodox position, as professed by the Fourth Ecumenical Council of Chalcedon, by threat of legal penalties.

Copy of the sacred letter of the most pious Emperor Marcian sent to the monks in Alexandria.[1]

It is not the property of the God and Lord of all to err in any way at all, but it is the duty of wise men (since it is impossible for them, being human beings, not to make mistakes), when they have erred, to repent straightway and by repentance to correct their faults. To remain in mistakes and to contend for these and to be eager to heap evil upon evil is the part of a wicked and very insane person.

And because we have learned that certain of the devout monks living in and around Alexandria have experienced this and because we have thought that they not through simplicity of character have persisted in this, we have employed a sacred letter which manifests our orthodox faith, also because the holy and Catholic synod, held in Chalcedon, has made absolutely no innovation about the apostolic faith, but in all respects having followed the teaching of Athanasius and Theophilus and Cyril,[2] who of devout memory were bishops of the Alexandrians' megalopolis, has condemned Eutyches'[3] blasphemy, which expresses no other thought than the unholy instructions of Apollinaris,[4] and also has excised Nestorius'[5] impiety,[6] and has guarded in all respects intact and not disturbed either by subtraction[7] or by addition the venerable creed of the 318 holy fathers who had assembled in Nicaea.[8]

And indeed our Tranquillity believes that our sacred letters and likewise commands, published long ago in the Alexandrians' megalopolis,[9] suffice for the persuasion of those who somehow still doubt; for this reason, because no innovation has been made by the holy and Catholic council. And thanks to this circumstance it should remain that none might doubt concerning anything else.[10] For we do not believe that anyonesoever is so rather simple that, when reading such important doctrines, so clearly pronouncing the orthodox faith, he should persist thus far in error itself. But if perchance there are some persons— which we do not believe—not following the clemency innate in us,[11] we desire again that they most certainly should be satisfied by this our most sacred letter, because the most holy and Catholic synod, following the holy and venerable fathers' doctrines, has arranged all matters and indeed has destroyed the impiety of Eutyches,[3] who has been followed by Dioscore[12] and by certain other persons, who have not hesitated to scatter Apollinaris'[4] books among the people by entitling these with the names of holy fathers, that they by their own falsity may deceive the minds of completely simple persons.

Moreover it has confirmed the venerable creed of the 318 holy fathers meeting in Nicaea,[8] neither subtracting nor adding anything, according to which our Tranquillity has been baptized and has been discreet from the age of adolescence and wishes to stand fast, believing that our Lord and Saviour Christ, the Only-Begotten Son of God, co-eternal and consubstantial with the Father, for us and for our salvation became man, born from the Holy Spirit and the Virgin Mary, the Mother of God, the same is truly both God and man, not one and another (may this not be!), but one and the same, in no way divided or separated or convertible.[13]

Moreover we abominate and anathematize even as enemies of God those persons who say that there ever were either two Sons or two persons.

Recognizing, therefore and now, these things, if any of you perchance hitherto have been deceived by falsehood, hasten to recur to truth, keeping your own selves also from unspeakable canons and contrary assemblies, lest in addition to the loss of your souls you should be subjected to legal punishment; but do you all join the most holy and Catholic Church of the orthodox, which is one, just as also the fathers' venerable definitions teach us. For in doing this you indeed shall give your soul to salvation; moreover you shall do things which are pleasing to the God of all;[14] but also in commending yourselves to our Tranquillity you shall enjoy its protection.

Furthermore, therefore, we have selected and sent John, the most distinguished [15] decurion,[1] who most certainly should be capable to explain the matters which concern the faith. For he also has been present at the holy bishops' universal council and knows clearly what matters have been done, so that, when satisfaction has been received in all respects, those persons—which we do not believe—who still doubt at last somehow or other may hasten to return to the true and immaculate faith.

1. The title to the Latin version adds "by John, the decurion". While *decurio* in late Latin usually means a municipal senator as opposed to a senator in either Rome or Constantinople, it also may be applied to an officer of the imperial court (see no. 353, n. 6). Perhaps the latter is meant here, unless the emperor chose to send his letter by a municipal senator either returning to Alexandria or passing by it to his own municipality.

2. Of these three patriarchs only the second never achieved official sainthood despite eastern and western honours paid to his memory. His theological orthodoxy was offset by his lithomania and by his lawless persecution of St John Chrysostom, patriarch of Constantinople (see nos. 284, n. 4, and 295, n. 8).

3. The heresiarch, whose name has been given to his heresy.

4. Bishop of Laodicea in Syria and originator of the Christological heresy called after him.

5. Patriarch of Constantinople and founder of Nestorianism.

6. Here the Greek original ends. What follows is from the Latin version.

7. A variant is "alteration".

8. In 325 at the First General Council.

9. The Latin *magna civitas* must represent the Greek μεγαλόπολις, which here is translated.

10. If *de cetero* stands for τοῦ λοιποῦ, as it probably does, then the phrase is simply "hereafter".

11. That is, not obedient to the imperial intention.

12. Patriarch of Alexandria, deposed at Chalcedon and in exile.

13. The resemblance to various credal phrases is clear.

14. Cf. 1 John 3. 22.

15. This seems to be the true lection: *v* (*irum*). *c* (*larissimum*). was corrupted into *v.d.*, which then became *vid* for *videlicet* (printed in the text by Mansi, who conjectured *virum devotum* and noted in the apparatus an ancient testimony to *virum clarissimum*).

482. LETTER OF VALENTINIAN III AND MARCIAN ON CONFIRMATION OF THE CHALCEDONIAN COUNCIL, 453

(PL 54. 1017–20)

When Pope St Leo I was reluctant to approve the administrative canons of the Council of Chalcedon in 451 for personal, political, and ecclesiastical reasons [1] and when Emperor Marcian had to employ troops to secure adherence to the council's doctrinal ordinances, with which the pope agreed, it was obvious that some accommodation must be made. So in this letter the emperor requests again the pope to confirm what was enacted at Chalcedon.[2] But, when Leo still refused to approve the council's administrative canon (28) conferring on the Constantinopolitan patriarchate an eastern precedence in jurisdiction next after Rome, the need for papal assent to this action was ignored and thereby were sown the seeds of future schism.

Letter of Marcian to Pope Leo.
Epistle of the most pious Emperor Marcian to Leo, archbishop of Rome.
Victors Valentinian and Marcian, Glorious, Triumphers, Ever-August to the most holy and truly venerable Leo, archbishop.
That your Beatitude is in good health we most earnestly pray by the words of our Serenity, asking that you bestow on us Almighty God's favour by the intercession of your prayers, in order that his merciful and pacific magnanimity may deign to grant all things favourable and desirable to our reign.
We wonder beyond measure that after the Chalcedonian Council and the venerable bishops' letter sent to your Sanctity, wherein they made known all things done in the synod itself, in absolutely no way by your Clemency was returned a letter of such kind as, when read in the most holy churches, ought to come to the attention of all persons.[3] And this has injected much uncertainty in the minds of several persons, who even now follow Eutyches'[4] base fancy and perversity, whether your Beatitude has confirmed what has been decreed in the holy synod. And on this account your Piety shall deign to send a letter, by which it may become clear to all churches and peoples that what has been transacted by the holy synod is held valid by your Beatitude. Surely your Sanctity excellently has proved—as became the apostolic see's bishop—the following point: that by guarding the ecclesiastical canons you have allowed no innovation to be made upon ancient custom and order once ordained and even to this day observed inviolably.
Moreover because of your Beatitude's letter as to what and how

many things have been done by some persons [5] your Sanctity will be able to learn most clearly from others,[6] to whom we have not wished to be opposed, that although not yet your Charity in God confirms it, the Chalcedonian Synod of the Catholic and true orthodox faith, with all the bishops in agreement, has been obeyed.

Wherefore let your venerable Dignity as speedily as possible dispatch a decree, whereby it most clearly shows that it confirms the Chalcedonian Synod itself, that those who greatly desire pathless detours [7] can have no suspicion about your Sanctity's judgement.

Given on 15 February at Constantinople.

1. Well summarized by Kidd, 3. 336.
2. See no. 475 for Marcian's previous letter and no. 470, XI, n. 70 for the conciliar action.
3. This sentence points to the necessary custom of papal confirmation of conciliar acts.

According to Socrates (*HE* 2. 17), Sazomen (*HE* 3. 10), Cassiodorus (*HE* 4. 19. 4) Pope St Julius I maintained that by ecclesiastical law no conciliar canons could be valid without the pope's approval. However, since no such ecclesiastical law is extant, perhaps the historians refer to a principle then acknowledged as existing prior to later enactment on this subject.

4. Eutychianism was condemned at Chalcedon in 451.
5. Probably Marcian indicates Leo's letter to Anatolius, patriarch of Constantinople, wherein, while he confirms the doctrinal points passed at Chalcedon, he objects to the canon (28) affecting the Constantinopolitan see (*PL* 54. 1001-10).
6. Such a one would be the papal legate, Julian, bishop of Cos, from whom the pope had heard about the imperial attempt to secure adherence to the synod's decrees.
7. That is, those who long to lurk along the bypaths of faith and thus fall off the straight and narrow way (cf. Matt. 7. 14) into the pits of heresy.

483. LETTER OF MARCIAN ON LAWLESSNESS OF THEODOSIUS, 453

(M 7. 483-8)

This letter not only reasserts Marcian's concurrence with the faith as enunciated by the Fourth General Council of Chalcedon in 451, but also exhorts the monks on Mount Sinai to surrender for justice the heretical and lawless monk Theodosius, who, opposed to the conciliar definition, seized and held for twenty months the patriarchate of Jerusalem against Juvenal its rightful incumbent, removed and murdered occupants of its suffragan sees, and, after the emperor had been informed about the reign of terror in Palestine and had initiated counter-measures, fled for refuge to the monastic establishments on the holy hill, where for a time he eluded capture by moving from place to place among the monks.

Titleless [1] letter of Marcian Augustus for Juvenal against Theodosius to Bishop Macarius [2] and the Sinaitic monks.

When he [3] had been sent by him [4] to war on the holy and orthodox faith, he thought that he would accomplish nothing evil, if he should imitate Eutyches' [5] impiety. And he [3] rose in revolt against the pious religion of the orthodox, in emulating Photinus [6] (estranged from truth), in desiring to be an imitator of the God-fighting opinion of Apollinaris [7] and Valentine [8] and Nestorius,[9] and in being openly revealed as a denouncer of the most holy synod, which (recently collected in the Chalcedonians' city [10] at our command because of ardour for the faith) has confirmed the 318 holy fathers' [11] creed for support of the faith, by making no change in respect to addition or subtraction in the said holy fathers' teaching, when it judged Eutyches,[5] as fighting against truth and as having wished to undermine the faith, to be alien from the name of the orthodox.

And Theodosius, following his [12] rascally and reckless daring, comes [13] into the region of the Palestines [14] and deceives [13] the ignorant by fabricating that some things instead of other things have been decreed as ordinances by the holy synod. For he asserted that the said most holy synod has decreed as ordinances that two Sons and two Christs and two persons should be worshipped and that it has interpreted the faith contrary to the holy fathers' [11] creed. And when he gathered for himself a multitude of deceived persons and acquired as an ally—so to speak—the ignorance of the simple-minded persons, thence he assaults [13] the Aelians' city,[15] undertaking burnings of houses, killings of devout men, loosings of persons convicted on capital charges, and by these deeds in hunting for the reputation of some devout person he riskily assumed power by breaking open the prisons, that when those who were accountable to justice had been freed as far as was in his power, he might provide for all—so to speak— the unaccountable readiness to offend. And with a view to treason itself and transgressing our Divinity's laws, he closed the city's gates and contrary to all canons he firmly laid hands on the title of the episcopate for himself, though the most holy Juvenal both was alive and was living in the city—thus defiling and confounding [16] at the same time both divine and human rights.

Thence proceeding on the road to worse deeds, he encompasses [13] all the most holy churches and cities throughout Palestine with greater evils by preparing to kill the most devout bishops and by ordaining persons whom he wished in these.[17] For, possessed of mad audacity, he ordered—as it occurred to him—the bishops of the cities, formerly created by just vote according to the sacred canons, to be reckoned as deprived of the priesthood [18] and to be expelled from the sees to which they had been assigned. And he wars [13] against Juvenal, the most holy bishop, by undertaking his destruction through a multitude dispatched from every side, for thus he supposed that he firmly would occupy the bishopric, which did not at all belong to him, and that the details of his own attempt would succeed at last. But indeed the Holy Trinity and (as the circumstance showed) courage in the faith saved Juvenal, the most holy bishop. But instead of him Severian of devout memory, bishop of the Scythopolitans' city,[19] nefariously removed along with others, became a secondary product of Theodosius' insanity.

Theodosius, having dared these things and things more terrible than these, after, when all things about him had been made known to our Mightiness, it had been ordered that from every side he should be hunted with his satellites and associates of crimes, flees [13] from the region of the Palestines [14] which he thus had mistreated, showing by these very matters that he had been the servant and the precursor [20] of Antichrist. Exchanging place for place, disturbing the most holy churches, contriving that persons who are rather simple in respect to the faith should think things contrary to the truth and should worship the Divinity impiously, thus (as we learned) he came to Mount Sinai, the dwelling of devoutness and the approach for holy men, where monasteries, dear to the Almighty and worthy of all honour from us, have been founded by you.[21] And lying hid there, he still makes plans against orthodoxy and expects that an occasion will come for him. But now there is not a single report about him, inasmuch as none can find a measure worthy of punishment of the wrongs done by him and his satellites.

But our Mightiness, although it has had very much confidence that in no way Theodosius' evil and God-fighting doctrine really will be able to undermine even the steadfast faith firmly set in you, nevertheless, lest the work of the Demon (whom he serves) should be able to prevail contrary to both your and our Mightiness' purpose, by this sacred letter urges your Devoutnesses to surrender him—so profane and alien from the orthodox faith and an enemy of the most holy churches, who with his accomplices has been hunted from all sides— to the one who rules the province for future conveyance to the supreme court of the most distinguished master of the soldiers of the East,[22] ex-consul and patrician, not that he may undergo punishment for so many things, but that for the future at least he may cease—as a result of his roving for the destruction of the districts to which he could come—to ensnare devout souls and souls disposed with rather simple thoughts about the Divinity.²³

For your Devoutnesses should know that we, born from ancestors of the orthodox faith and by the Sacred Scriptures taught to worship the Holy Trinity, embrace the creed of the 318 fathers of holy memory,²⁴ thus walking and according to it believing and rejecting the impiety of Photinus ⁶ and of Apollinaris ⁷ and of Valentine ⁸ and of Nestorius ⁹ and of Eutyches ⁵ and of all others whosoever have determined to think in opposition to the creed, and believing that our Lord and Saviour Jesus Christ has been born from the Holy Spirit and the Virgin Mary, the Mother of God; and confessing one and the same Son Jesus, the same perfect God and perfect man, the same truly God and truly man, in no way divided or separated or converted, we continually worship the Saviour Christ, praying to continue steadfastly in this faith, openly anathematizing those who say or have said or have written or even have dared to say that there are two Sons or two Christs or two persons.

And this aforesaid most holy faith, which is true and orthodox, the most holy synod, convened lately in the Chalcedonians' city,¹⁰ has confirmed by having proclaimed with concordant thought about the holy and orthodox religion and by having condemned the heretical opinion of Eutyches ⁵ alone by a vote of one mind with the holy fathers.

1. Since the letter lacks a head (ἀκέφαλος is Mansi's adjective), Mansi supplies it.
2. Bishop of Pharan or Mount Sinai.
3. Although the letter begins abruptly, it seems that Theodosius, the machinating and militant monk, is meant.
4. The allusion is not known, but it may refer to Satan for want of a better possibility.
5. The Constantinopolitan heresiarch, whose name has been given to his heresy.
6. Bishop of Sirmium, who held heretical views on Christ's nature. Photinianism takes its name from him.
7. Bishop of Laodicea in Syria, founder of the Christological heresy named after him.
8. The Gnostic, who flourished 135–60 and became one of Gnosticism's great exponents.
9. Patriarch of Constantinople and inaugurator of Nestorianism.
10. The Fourth General Council (451).
11. The First General Council at Nicaea (325).

12. Eutyches'.
13. Historical present tense in Greek.
14. The three provinces of Palestine are meant.
15. Jerusalem, for which Marcian used the Roman name of the inhabitants as derived from Emperor Hadrian's name for his re-foundation of the city in 130, Aelia Capitolina—Aelia having been chosen from Hadrian's gentile name Aelius.

Even if Jews and Christians had not associated the Roman capture of Jerusalem and the destruction of the Jewish Temple in 70 with the word of the Lord to Jeremiah about Jerusalem's fate (Jer. 22. 1–9), yet the callous circumstances of Hadrian's creation of temples to Jupiter and to Venus on the respective sites of the Temple and the Holy Sepulchre (see no. 54, n. 6) and of his construction of these shrines from the Temple's ruins might have recalled two generations later the question "Wherefore hath the Lord done thus unto this great city?" (Jer. 22. 8).

16. The metaphor perhaps is in hysteron proteron: to mix by pouring and then to produce a polluted concoction from such a mixture.
17. The cities.
18. See no. 158, n. 1. For *deprived* a more literal rendering is "estranged from".
19. The metropolitical see of Palaestina Secunda. St Severian was murdered in 452.
20. Both *servant* and *precursor* have a military significance in Greek: the one a soldier's attendant (later a general's aide), the other a mounted skirmisher who reconnoitres before an advancing army.
21. Persecutions during the third century caused the flight of many Christian anchorites to Sinai. Evidences of a monastery built in the next century have been found. At St Catharine's Convent (founded by Justinian I *c.* 556) Tischendorf discovered the famous *Codex Sinaiticus* in 1844.
22. There is a variance in the title with that given in no. 487 at n. 26. Each is possible and which is correct is unknown. Here it is στρατηλάτης τῆς ἕω = *magister militum per Orientem*, on which see no. 106, n. 4 *ad fin*.
23. It was not until later that Theodosius was betrayed to the imperial constabulary, who apprehended him near Sidon after he had left Mount Sinai. He died in a Constantinopolitan monastery in 457.
24. At the First General Council of Nicaea in 325.

484. RESCRIPT OF MARCIAN ON LAWLESSNESS OF PALESTINIAN MONKS, 453

(M 7. 487–96)

The emperor excoriates the monks living near Jerusalem not only for their outrages, inspired by the monk Theodosius (no. 483), who had usurped that city's see for twenty months, but also for their opposition to the definition of the faith as decreed by the Fourth Ecumenical Council of Chalcedon in 451 (which the emperor defends in this rescript), and commands reparations for their lawlessness and orders punishment for those found guilty of rapine.

Copy of the sacred letter sent to the archimandrites and the rest in Aelia [1] and to the monks dwelling around it by our most sacred and most pious Lord Marcian Perpetual-Augustus.

Our Mightiness, after it had become acquainted with the petitions which you sent to the most pious and the most sacred lady, our Serenity's consort,[2] had been persuaded by the circumstances that you have not sent a supplication, but in the guise of a petition you have shown your objective to be set contrary both to God's laws and to the Romans' State. For when it is proper for you to live in quiet and to be rated under priests and to be conversant with the lessons taught by them, you have contrived for yourselves by excessive presumption the rank of teachers, since you have not permitted yourselves to learn lessons from persons teaching rightly, but you have persuaded yourselves foolishly that it is proper in regard to knowledge of the faith for all to follow you rather than the holy apostles' and prophets' books and the commands of the fathers of sacred memory. And just as if you are erring less than in previous matters, if you wished by false teachings to overshadow your emboldened deeds, you have demonstrated that no truth is in your supplications,[3] since you allege that you or the monasteries have been guilty neither of conflagrations nor of murders nor of other offences, but that the mentioned terrible deeds have been the work of persons inhabiting the city and of some strangers.

And none of the emboldened deeds, by actions of memorials and by reports of what has become known in each case, has escaped our Piety's notice: that the Aelians' city [1] has been captured by you (as if by enemies), who ought to inhabit monasteries and to be engaged only in such places, and that the slaying of a deacon of devout memory has been undertaken boldly and impiously and that his body after the murder, when common funeral rites were defiled, was insulted by being dragged, though it was insensible, and that houses have been burned and the city's gates have been shut (as if in independence) and the city's walls were guarded and, when the prison had been opened forcibly, remission of punishments and occasion of dangerous [4] flight were provided for persons who had been emboldened to do terrible deeds.

But since the evil has progressed for the worse, in that you show that the former cruelties are small in comparison with later ones, you wished to kill Juvenal,[5] the most holy bishop, and other devout priests by a person sent for this. But since the person sent had been balked of his hope, he made Severian,[6] the bishop of holy memory, a secondary work of his madness and of that of those who had sent him by slaying him with a sword and by not sparing those with him.

And these and more terrible offences than these and how they have been undertaken boldly and who have been the doers are known, because they properly have been demonstrated variously in the courts and have been revealed to our sacred hearing [7] and provide an accurate proof of your will, on account of which you have turned readily to offending very greatly, not wishing to vindicate or at any rate to assist God's faith, but eager to procure for yourselves—for the defilement of the cities—the episcopal offices and the priesthoods, to which you have appeared to be altogether foreign.

It is permitted to our Piety to wonder for what reason you, doing at least this well, anathematize Eutyches,[8] but have delivered yourselves to Theodosius, who dares boldly all things and holds Eutyches'[8] opinions, who, having emulated the madness of Valentine [9] and of Apollinaris [10] against the orthodox faith, has become the patron of uproars for the most holy churches, of upset and of unbearable damage for the cities, and for you has been established as the chief of such unbearable and lawless actions.

And therefore to the Lord of all and to the Saviour Christ you shall pay proper penalties for the impiety and for all the offences of which you have given the cause. For the Divine Power will not permit to progress unpunished the emboldened deeds done blasphemously against the pure faith and against the holy churches and nefariously against the holy men pitiably destroyed.

Our Serenity has ordered nothing such to be done against the monks, but that only the Aelians' city [1] should be controlled in such a way that for the future at least it will be guarded for the inhabitants' peace. But your presumption, arranging affairs contrary to the monks' precepts, has raised war against the common good order and, having collected a mob of bandits and of persons wont to transgress in other ways and having moved armed forces against persons living orderly, has become the cause of slaughter and of conquest and of other cruelties for persons inhabiting the district, so that our Mightiness when moved has been indignant at the offenders, but when conquered [11] by innate kindliness has ordered those guilty of the murders and of the

484. LAWLESSNESS OF PALESTINIAN MONKS, 453

conflagrations, when found guilty, to pay the penalties, although it was proper for the effects of our indignation to proceed against you, who have left the monasteries, wherein your profession prescribes you to reside constantly, and have been emboldened to do such deeds as have become deserving of extreme punishments. And since you endeavour to teach instead of to learn, not knowing the divine declarations clearly saying that "A disciple is not above his teacher nor a servant above his lord",[12] what teachings of the Saviour of our souls or of the most holy apostles and fathers have you followed? For, following your own impieties, you will not be bold to say that the saints' instructions progress to murders and other offences, which you have committed. But because, when you hear of two natures, you have shown that your souls are amazed, as if some novelty has been brought to your hearing,[7] know that it is not fitting for you to meddle with an inquiry of these matters, since you are not able to understand the nicety in regard to these matters.

But we, having accepted the fathers' teachings, perceive nature to be truth. For this is what we think and say: that our Lord and Saviour Jesus Christ, truly God and truly man, is the same, just as also the most holy Apostle Paul, perceiving nature to be truth, in the Epistle to the Galatians teaches, saying wisely: "Howbeit at that time, not knowing God, you were in bondage to them who by nature are not gods."[13] From these words he clearly signifies that nature is truth, although you say that nothing about natures is contained in the creed of faith exhibited by the 318 holy fathers,[14] for neither any inquiry about this was aroused nor now any novelty against this faith has been contrived, but the announcements of the saints who shone in orthodoxy have been confirmed.

But you who say that one ought not to investigate nature are caught in doing this very thing, when mentioning expressly nature in the petitions sent by you and saying: "How does a virgin give birth and still remain a virgin? And how does she according to nature bear him who is above nature?" (And so forth in these.) For the Word became flesh.[15] But how did it become? How can it be separated? But it so became, not changed in respect to nature and not altered in respect to divinity. You see, therefore, how you mention nature everywhere, when you are in disorder in respect to the very name of nature, and from every side you acquire for yourselves occasions of slandering the doctrines about the faith truly ratified by the holy synod,[16] when you sin also in this, because, lying, you say that it has ordained that we say that these are two Sons and two Christs—which, indeed, is not so. For we, renouncing this, anathematize those who say this or have written it or have said it or even dare to say it. For our Mightiness previously has followed the creed of the 318 holy fathers [14] and complies with that which succeeded it,[16] believing that our Lord and Saviour Jesus Christ has been born from the Holy Spirit and the Virgin Mary. For the orthodox faith—as we have received—we are eager to maintain from beginning to end, as also the holy synod, which recently in the Chalcedonians' city was assembled, believing teaches, confirming the creed [14] and thinking things consonant with the said holy fathers and the synod at Ephesus,[17] at which Celestine [18] and Cyril,[19] both of devout memory, had been prominent in rejecting Nestorius' [20] error.

And indeed our Serenity has ordered that on none at all should be imposed compulsion that he either should subscribe or should concur, if he should not be willing. For not by threats or by force do we wish to draw anyone to the road of truth. But on the contrary, besides your already emboldened deeds committed by swords and other cruelties and even outrages and tortures upon illustrious and noble women, you have not hesitated to impose compulsion upon many persons to believe in your perverted teachings and by clamours and by subscriptions to anathematize the said most holy synod [16] and the most holy Leo, patriarch of the apostolic see of Great Rome, and the other holy fathers, for which audacity necessarily you shall render account to God, the Lord of all, to whose injury—if it is right to say so—you have been emboldened to do these things in having become justly reproachful and ridiculous to both the abominable pagans [21] and heretics, to whom you have become an example of dishonour.

But also because you have accused the Samaritans, as if they had committed terrible and lawless deeds against the most holy churches and murders or some other unnatural sins, know that we have ordained that after an accurate inquiry has been conducted studiously by Dorotheus,[22] the admirable count, the stolen things must be restored to the most holy churches and to those who have lost these and that the persons found guilty of these things must undergo punishment according to the laws, since vengeance in these matters does not befit you, who, when taught that our Mightiness believes and when invited by our Piety, ought not to stray from [23] the holy and orthodox faith, but to be engaged in the monasteries and to devote time to prayers to the Almighty, by accomplishing things consonant with your profession and by altogether not participating in a disturbance, neither by simply believing in the things said for the destruction of souls by persons teaching base doctrines nor by being separated from the orthodox faith and from God's churches by those persons' impious assemblies. Do not dare at all to have clandestine assemblies, since you know what long ago has been legislated by the emperors of sacred lot who lived in former times, who, welding together the holy and Catholic religion, commanded that persons daring to assemble clandestinely should be subjected to the greatest penalties.[24]

484. LAWLESSNESS OF PALESTINIAN MONKS, 453

But we, believing that you will repent of your previous acts, have not renounced benevolence, since Juvenal, the most holy bishop, has employed many exhortations through which he has entreated us to inscribe this sacred letter to you. Taught by these petitions that your oratories are disturbed by the soldiers ordered to guard the Aelians' city [1] and by the throngs of both horses and men, and vexed at this, we have commanded Dorotheus, the admirable count, to free you from the annoyance, although we had not ordered previously that your monasteries should be outraged or that your lodgings should be crowded.[25]

1. On the use of Aelia and Aelians for Jerusalem and Jerusalemites see no. 483, n. 15.
2. Pulcheria, sister of and successor to Theodosius II.
3. The idea in *And . . . supplications,* more fully expanded, seems to be that if the monks had been wishing by their teachings, which the emperor considers false, to camouflage their audacious acts, just as if they had erred less in their opposition to the recent definition of faith (but in fact they err as much now as previously), so they have failed in their object, since they have shown that no truth is in their supplications.
  In the last line of the paragraph *the city* is Jerusalem.
4. A causative use to indicate that such criminals' escape from jail would endanger other persons' security.
5. Patriarch of Jerusalem.
6. Bishop of Scythopolis, the metropolitical see of Palaestina Secunda, murdered in 452.
7. Literally "ears".
8. The heresiarch, whose name has been given to his heresy.
9. The Gnostic, who flourished 135–60 and became one of Gnosticism's great exponents.
10. Bishop of Laodicea in Syria, founder of the Christological heresy called after him.
11. Mansi's clever marginal conjecture νικηθέν, with which the Latin version agrees, for κινηθέν (moved) has been translated.
12. Matt. 10. 24. Mansi noted that the second half of this quotation is not in the old codices and editions, for the argument concerns not a master's authority over a slave, but is about a learner's obedience, and that later editions have added the additional words which, of course, follow in the Matthaean verse.
13. Gal. 4. 8.
14. At the First General Council of Nicaea in 325.
15. John 1. 14.
16. Probably the Second General Council at Constantinople in 381 is meant.
17. The Third General Council in 431.

18. The pope, who earlier had authorized St Cyril, patriarch of Alexandria, to act as his proxy in reclaiming Nestorius (n. 20 *infra*), and then sent his personal legates *a latere* to co-operate with Cyril at the council.

19. Patriarch of Alexandria, who dominated the council.

20. Patriarch of Constantinople and author of a heresy named after him.

21. See no. 121, n. 3.

22. He was governor of Palaestina Prima. Theodosius had debarred him and his army from Jerusalem, when Dorotheus returned from a war with barbarians, and then escaped into Mount Sinai, when the emperor had ordered the governor to capture the monk.

23. The Latin infinitive (*deviare*) is translated for what in Greek appears to be a misprint (χειρίζεσθαι, "to handle", for χωρίζεσθαι, "to deviate").

24. As early as 322 (or 332) Constantine I proscribed heretical assemblies (no. 40). Succeeding sovereigns similarly legislated again and again on this subject.

25. Apparently the guest-houses providing accommodation for travellers and for pilgrims to the sacred sites had been requisitioned by the soldiers sent to restrain the monks from further depredations.

Of the several *Itineraria* in *CSEL* 39 the *Peregrinatio ad Loca Sancta* is for historians and linguists perhaps the most interesting account of an early pilgrimage to Palestine and adjacent regions. The author, long supposed to be Silvia (Sylvia) Aquitana of Gaul, is now generally believed to be Aetheria (Etheria), a Spanish abbess, who made this journey *c*. 380—about two generations before this rescript's date.

485. LETTER OF PULCHERIA ON ANATHEMATIZATION OF HERETICS, 453

(M 7. 505-8)

In this letter, addressed to Bassa, abbess of a convent in Jerusalem, Empress St Pulcheria, Marcian's consort, not only defends the canons of the Fourth General Council of Chalcedon in 451 against the calumnies of Theodosius, a monk, who caused much violence and commotion throughout Palestine in his attack upon the conciliar acts (nos. 483, 484, 486, 487), but also anathematizes those who hold inadequate opinions about Christ's person.

Copy of the royal letter written to Bassa, abbess of a monastery in Aelia,[1] by the most pious and Christ-loving Pulcheria Augusta.

We think that to none is ambiguous our Serenity's zeal and eagerness concerning the pure and orthodox faith and that we are zealous both

485. ANATHEMATIZATION OF HERETICS, 453

to increase and to assist it in all ways; but above all we have been confident that your Devoutness understands this accurately.

But since in these times has appeared plainly Theodosius, the precursor of Simon's [2] error, rather of Antichrist, and it has not escaped your Devoutness' notice how he has treated the Aelians' city [3] and has disturbed the most holy churches in Palestine, by having committed countless [4] terrible deeds against divine and human rights and by calumniating the holy and ecumenical synod convened in Chalcedon, as if it had sapped the creed of the 318 holy fathers [5] and had decreed that two Sons and two Christs and two persons should be worshipped, our Piety has considered it necessary to expose through our previously dispatched sacred letters the aforesaid abominable man's falsehoods and to manifest our faith transmitted from our ancestors to us and that we believe according to the creed of the 318,[5] which also the holy synod in Chalcedon, adding nothing to it nor lessening it, has confirmed. And since through the benevolence of our Lord and Saviour Christ those inhabiting the Aelians' city [1] know the true and orthodox faith of my Serenity and of the most devout lord of the world and my Divinity's consort, to this they have run and with various praises have celebrated our Lord and Saviour Jesus Christ and our Majesty and have requested pardon for their past errors. And concerning them the most sacred and most devout lord and my Serenity's consort, having employed his habitual benevolence, has given an ordinance befitting his Piety.

But our Serenity, considering the calumnies of the aforesaid abominable and unholy Theodosius, lest he should deceive the more simple of some most devout women and by his trickeries and falsehoods should be able to lead these persons from the truth, and desiring to obliterate from every side the aforesaid abominable person's exposed impiety, on this account we dispatch to you this our sacred letter, wherein we manifest the faith transmitted from our fathers to us, and we desire this to be made clear by you to all the women dedicated to God: that we maintain the faith according to the creed exhibited by the 318 holy fathers,[5] but we detest Photinus' [6] and Apollinaris' [7] and Valentine's [8] and Nestorius' [9] impiety and besides Eutyches' [10] recent heretical opinion; and we believe that our Lord and Saviour Jesus Christ has been born from the Holy Spirit and the Virgin Mary, the Mother of God, confessing one and the same Son Jesus, perfect God and perfect man the same, truly God and truly man the same; we worship continually the Saviour Christ, in no way divided or separated or converted, praying to continue in this faith unshakenly and anathematizing persons saying or having said or having written or even daring to say that there are two Sons or two Christs or two persons. And the ecumenical synod lately convened in

Chalcedon has confirmed this holy and orthodox faith, by having made no increase or decrease in the holy creed exhibited by the 318 holy fathers [5] and by having condemned by a verdict agreeable to the holy fathers the heretical opinion of Eutyches alone.

Therefore let your Devoutness, after it has learned our Serenity's true and orthodox faith, be eager to pray for us and our Empire rather assiduously.

1. On this synonym for Jerusalem see no. 483, n. 15.
2. The reference is to Simon Magus, on whom see no. 422, n. 7.
3. For twenty months he had usurped its see.
4. Literally "10,000"—used for a very high and indefinite number.
5. At the First General Council of Nicaea in 325.
6. Bishop of Sirmium and contriver of Photinianism.
7. Bishop of Laodicea in Syria and author of Apollinarianism.
8. One of the principal proponents of Gnosticism. His *floruit* is 135-60.
9. Patriarch of Constantinople and founder of Nestorianism.
10. Constantinopolitan heresiarch, whose name has been given to his heresy.

486. RESCRIPT OF PULCHERIA ON ANATHEMATIZATION OF HERETICS, 453
(M 7. 509–12)

Empress St Pulcheria, Marcian's consort, explains her husband's measures (nos. 483 and 484) about the ecclesiastical tumult in Palestine, caused by the monk Theodosius' rejection of the acts of the Fourth General Council of Chalcedon in 451, explains her and Marcian's adherence to orthodoxy, denounces heretics, and exhorts the monks in and near Jerusalem to return to the true religion.

Copy of the sacred letter written to the archimandrites and the rest of the monks living in Aelia [1] and around it by our most sacred Lady Pulcheria Perpetual-Augusta.

Indeed the petitions which you have sent to our Piety carry proof of your error.

We, the most sacred and most clement emperor, my Serenity's consort, and our Divinity, have determined to prefer piety above all things and we embrace benevolence, which is innate in us. And his Divinity's letters, which his Serenity, when importuned by many supplications of Juvenal,[2] the most holy bishop, wrote in reply to you, show what things his Serenity, after having read the supplications,[3] wrote to you.

486. ANATHEMATIZATION OF HERETICS, 453

Our Mightiness finds fault with the emboldened deeds against the holy religion and the common discipline done by you in past time contrary to the profession of monks, and by sacred letters advises you, though late, to have regard for repentance, to repel all error of your souls, to discover the truth of the faith which our Piety maintains for all time, just as the 318 holy fathers [4] of holy memory have taught, having received it from our ancestors, having believed it without contradiction, having justly turned from Nestorius' [5] impiety (as fighting against God), which has been repelled by the holy synod in Ephesus,[6] over which Celestine and Cyril, men of devout memory, presided,[7] and having hated necessarily Eutyches' [8] insurrection against orthodoxy, since he, having been guided by the teachings of Valentine [9] and of Apollinaris [10] against the orthodox faith, has been eager to disturb the true religion. Following the holy synod recently assembled in the Chalcedonians' city,[11] because by harmonious interpretation it has confirmed the creed of the 318 holy fathers,[4] our Mightiness [12] believes that our Lord and Saviour Christ has been born from the Holy Spirit and the Virgin Mary, the Mother of God, having been taught to perceive nature to be truth and that our Lord and Master Jesus Christ, truly God and truly man, is the same. For thus also the most holy Apostle Paul in the Epistle to the Galatians teaches by these words: "Howbeit at that time, not knowing God, you were in bondage to them who by nature are not gods";[13] that is, not knowing God truly, they were in bondage to them who are truly not gods. For by these words he clearly teaches us to perceive that nature is truth. In vain has false opinion smitten your souls, as if the most holy synod assembled in Chalcedon [11] has taught or our Serenity has believed that two Sons or two Christs through two natures are perceived. But the truth is not so. For we, renouncing this, anathematize the persons who have written or have said or even have dared to say this. Our Mightiness, praying to continue unshakenly in this faith, always confesses that the Saviour Christ is one and the same Jesus Christ, perfect God and perfect man, the same God truly and the same man truly, in no way divided or converted. Therefore, having been taught the simplicity and the truth of our faith, this we are eager to maintain according to the fathers' truest tradition.

And knowing the orthodox faith and the benevolent objective of the most serene lord of the world and my Piety's consort and believing in these matters, because of which he with only pious regard toward the Almighty has delayed to subject to worthy punishments the persons who have dared to do impious and lawless deeds, and expecting to make trial of honour and favour from us for future time, henceforth cast from your souls indeed every doubt, persevering in your monasteries and devoutly following the solitary life, being separated not at all from the right faith and the churches' unity, lest anyone—which our Mightiness does not hope—may inscribe you with the name of heresy which wars against truth.

Know also that his Serenity by a letter to Dorotheus,[14] the admirable count, has ordered an accurate search to be made about the looting of property, which is said to have been done boldly by Samaritans. And he has decreed that as many things as should have been shown to have been seized should be restored by them both to the most holy churches and to those who have lost these and that the persons found guilty should undergo correction from the laws.

And he has ordered your monasteries and dwellings, by the care of the said man,[14] to be maintained free from molestation by the soldiers. For his Mightiness believes with us that through such provision and exhortation you will repent of the deeds previously done by you and the affairs of the Catholic Church will be unified by harmonious faith, when the orthodox religion is maintained in peace and unanimity.

And by another hand: May God guard you, most reverend men, for many years.[15]

1. On this synonym for Jerusalem see no. 483, n. 15.
2. Patriarch of Jerusalem, dispossessed for twenty months by the monk Theodosius, who conducted an ecclesiastical reign of terror in Palestine.
3. Originally this word meant the olive branch held in a suppliant's hand.
4. At the First General Council of Nicaea in 325.
5. Patriarch of Constantinople and author of Nestorianism.
6. The Third General Council in 431.
7. Pope St Celestine I was not present, but he sent legates *a latere* to co-operate with St Cyril, patriarch of Alexandria, who presided.
8. The Constantinopolitan heresiarch and founder of Eutychianism.
9. The Gnostic, whose *floruit* is 135–60 and who is ranked as one of Gnosticism's principal prophets.
10. Bishop of Laodicea in Syria and founder of Apollinarianism.
11. The Fourth General Council in 451.
12. The subject is supplied from the previous sentence. The English paragraph through the lower Biblical quotation is one sentence in Greek.
13. Gal. 4. 8.
14. Governor of Palaestina Prima.
15. This conclusion appears only in the Latin version, whence it is taken for this translation from the Greek original.

www.ingramcontent.com/pod-product-compliance
Lightning Source LLC
Chambersburg PA
CBHW052047290426
44111CB00011B/1655